MARVEL MASTERWORKS

PRESENTS

THE Fantastic Four

VOLUME 6

COLLECTING

THE FANTASTIC FOUR NOS. 51 - 60
& ANNUAL No. 4

STAN LEE • JACK KIRBY

MARVEL ENTERPRISES, INC.

MARVEL MASTERWORKS
CREDITS

THE
FANTASTIC FOUR
NOS. 51 - 60 & ANNUAL NO. 4

Writer: Stan Lee
Penciler: Jack Kirby

Inker: Joe Sinnott

Letterers: Art Simek (Nos. 51, 53, 56-59)
Sam Rosen (Nos. 52, 54, 55, 60, Annual No. 4)

Color Reconstruction: VLM

Special Thanks: Tom Brevoort & Ralph Macchio

MARVEL MASTERWORKS: THE FANTASTIC FOUR VOL. 6. Contains material originally published in magazine form as FANTASTIC FOUR (Vol. 1) #51-60 and ANNUAL #4. Second edition. First printing 2004. ISBN# 0-7851-1266-9. Published by MARVEL COMICS, a division of MARVEL ENTERTAINMENT GROUP, INC. OFFICE OF PUBLICATION: 10 East 40th Street, New York, NY 10016. Copyright © 1966, 1967 and 2000 Marvel Characters, Inc. All rights reserved. $49.99 per copy in the U.S. and $80.00 in Canada (GST #R127032852); Canadian Agreement #40668537. All characters featured in this issue and the distinctive names and likenesses thereof, and all related indicia are trademarks of Marvel Characters, Inc. No similarity between any of the names, characters, persons, and/or institutions in this magazine with those of any living or dead person or institution is intended, and any such similarity which may exist is purely coincidental. **Printed in Italy.** STAN LEE, Chairman Emeritus. For information regarding advertising in Marvel Comics or on Marvel.com, please contact Russell Brown, Executive Vice President, Consumer Products, Promotions and Media Sales at 212-576-8561 or rbrown@marvel.com

10 9 8 7 6 5 4 3 2 1

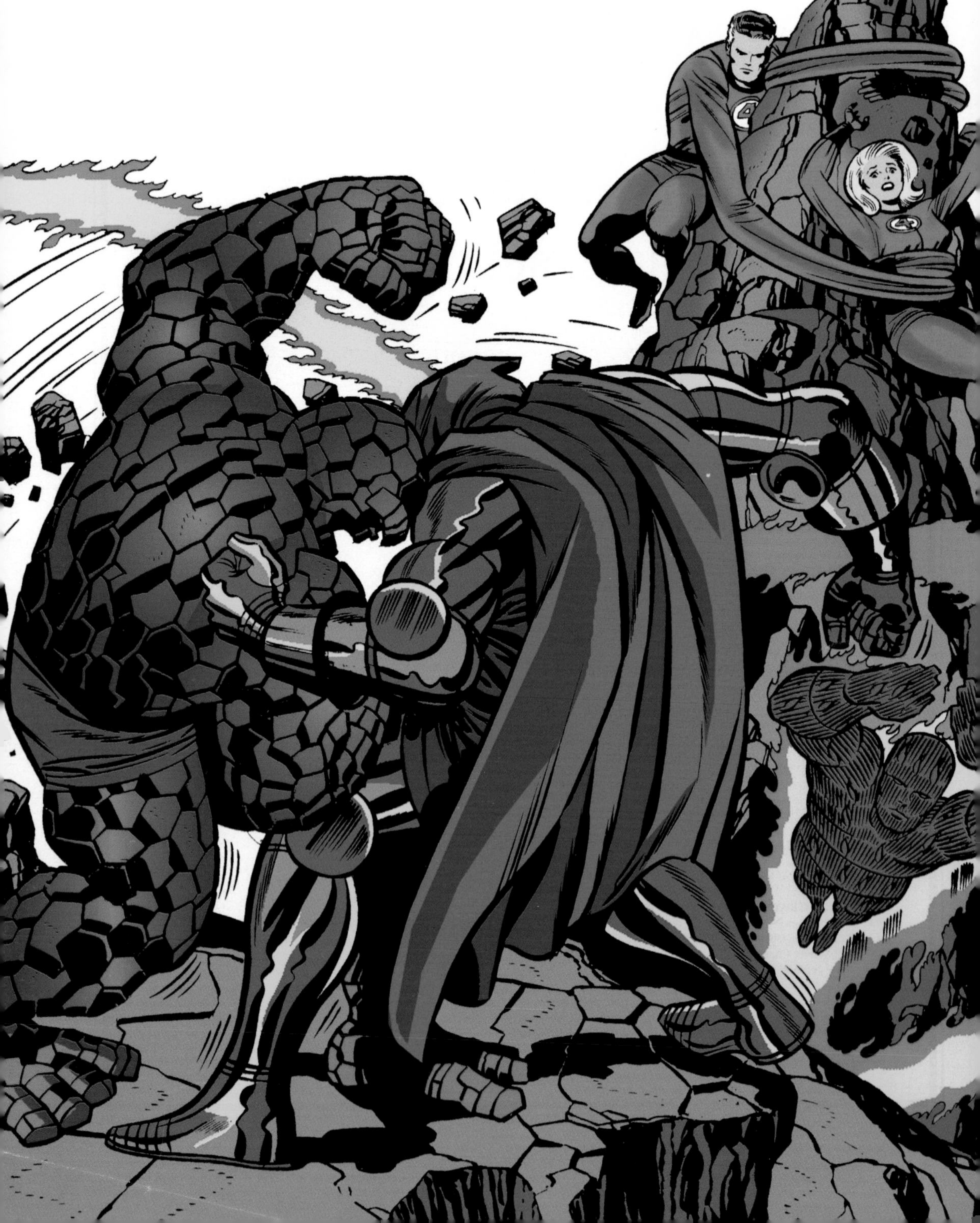

MARVEL MASTERWORKS
Contents

INTRODUCTION
BY STAN LEE

First of all, I have a confession to make. I'm not the one who should be writing this intro!

It should be written by somebody who's impartial, who can look at the incredible episodes in this book with objectivity. Personally, I can't. I love every illustration, every panel, every caption and word balloon much too much. I'm too big a fan of Jack "King" Kirby's indescribable artwork and storytelling magic, too great an admirer of Joe Sinnott's inking, and, to tell the truth, I'm just too big a fan of the comic book itself which years ago, I dared to dub "The World's Greatest Comic Magazine." I meant it then and I mean it now.

If you've never read these stories before, I can unhesitatingly say you're in for the treat of a lifetime. As for me, I did read them before. Matter of fact, I wrote them, in collaboration with the most imaginative illustrator and co-plotter I've ever known. However, having the world's worst memory, I decided to reread each yarn to reacquaint myself with them before writing this introduction. And y'know something? I enjoyed them as much as if I'd never read them before!

Let's start with "This Man...This Monster!" I've always been particularly proud of this one, in which a deadly super-villain makes the supreme sacrifice in order to—aw, this isn't fair. I've no right to give the plot twists away; but I'll bet you too will find it hard to finish the last page without a lump in your throat. I'm particularly partial to it because it involves heavy characterization and emotion as much as action and suspense. As for the title itself, it's been paraphrased and imitated in more stories than any other that I know of.

Another favorite of mine is "The Way It Began...!" featuring the mysterious and charismatic Black Panther, the first African super hero in comics. I've always strongly believed he has all the qualities necessary to become one of the most popular, best-selling heroes in all of comicdom. When you combine his unique and glamorous panther power with the strange gripping legend of the Wakanda nation and add the fact that T'Challa is guardian of the world's only priceless store of vibranium, you've got a combo that's hard to beat. After reading this yarn, I suspect you'll agree.

But how can I talk about my favorites when, as I read each separate story, I realize that they're all my favorites! It's been so long since I've written about them that I had almost forgotten the Inhumans. But as I turned each page of the story you'll soon be reading, I couldn't help but relive again the wonder and excitement of the regal Black Bolt and his strange and colorful family. From the gigantic dog Lockjaw to Gorgon, Medusa, Karnak and Crystal, I defy you to find a more unique group of heroes anywhere in comicdom.

Incidentally, I hope you'll be aware of the way we tried to intertwine and link the various heroes and villains through all our tales. You'll notice how Dr. Doom interfaces with both the Fantastic Four and the Silver Surfer, and how we even managed to add the seemingly invulnerable Sandman into the mix.

Speaking of Dr. Doom, who has always been my favorite super-villain, I particularly enjoyed pitting him against the Silver Surfer who is definitely one of my all-time favorite heroes. The thing that grabs me about the silver spanner of the spaceways is his unshakable nobility. I always tried to have him say the things that I myself feel deeply about and would like to say about the human condition and the state of the world. To me, he has ever been the visual depiction of our own conscience, an eloquent sounding board for Marvel—and me.

But the character that totally grabbed me each and every time I wrote these yarns was inevitably the ever-lovin' blue-eyed Thing. There is something about his rough, tough, always-looking-for-a-fight attitude that conceals his true soft-hearted, generous and loyal nature, which I find totally irresistible. In fact, I'm sure that almost any Marvel reader, if asked which of our characters he would prefer for his best friend, would be tempted to say none other than Aunt Petunia's favorite nephew, Benjamin J. Grimm.

But how could I fail to mention the other members of the Fantastic Four? You may not know it, but I got a big kick out of modeling Reed Richards after myself in one special way. No, my body doesn't stretch and I'm not the world's greatest scientist. But I do sometimes tend to talk too much and to use a few big words when some little ones would do the trick just as well. Oh, how I used to enjoy writing the Thing's dialogue when he tried to deflate Mr. Fantastic's pomposity by telling him to stifle it and start speaking plain English.

I also invariably got a kick out of the Human Torch. You see, I never liked the idea of heroes hangin' around with teenaged sidekicks. It always seemed too corny to me for some kid to follow the hero around and try to help him during a fight. But, I figured if I had to have a teenager, I'd make him old enough to do his own thing, his own way, instead of being a carbon copy of the hero. Besides, I love writing expressions like "Flame On!" (And leave us not forget my arguable masterpiece, "It's Clobberin' Time!")

Well, I could go on and on—and you're probably groaning, "I hope he doesn't mean it!"—but we have to stop somewhere, and this is as good a place as any. Jack Kirby and I had done our very best for you; we tried to give you imaginative, cutting-edge stories with action, fantasy and suspense, and above all, stories that stress drama and characterization and which would never insult your intelligence.

How well we succeeded is for you to decide. But let me say, in a brash display of overconfidence, I've a hunch that once you start reading the pages ahead, you won't be able to put the book down! I know that I couldn't and hey, I even wrote the stuff!

EXCELSIOR

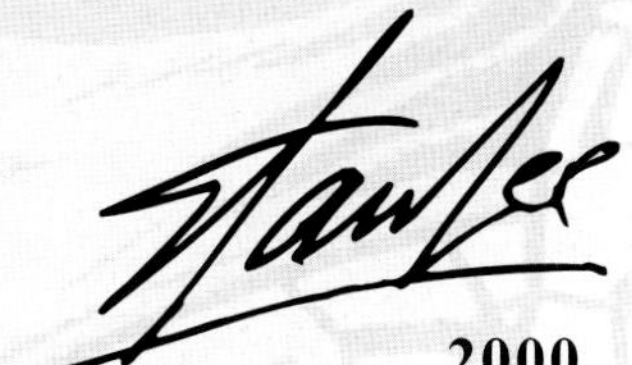

2000

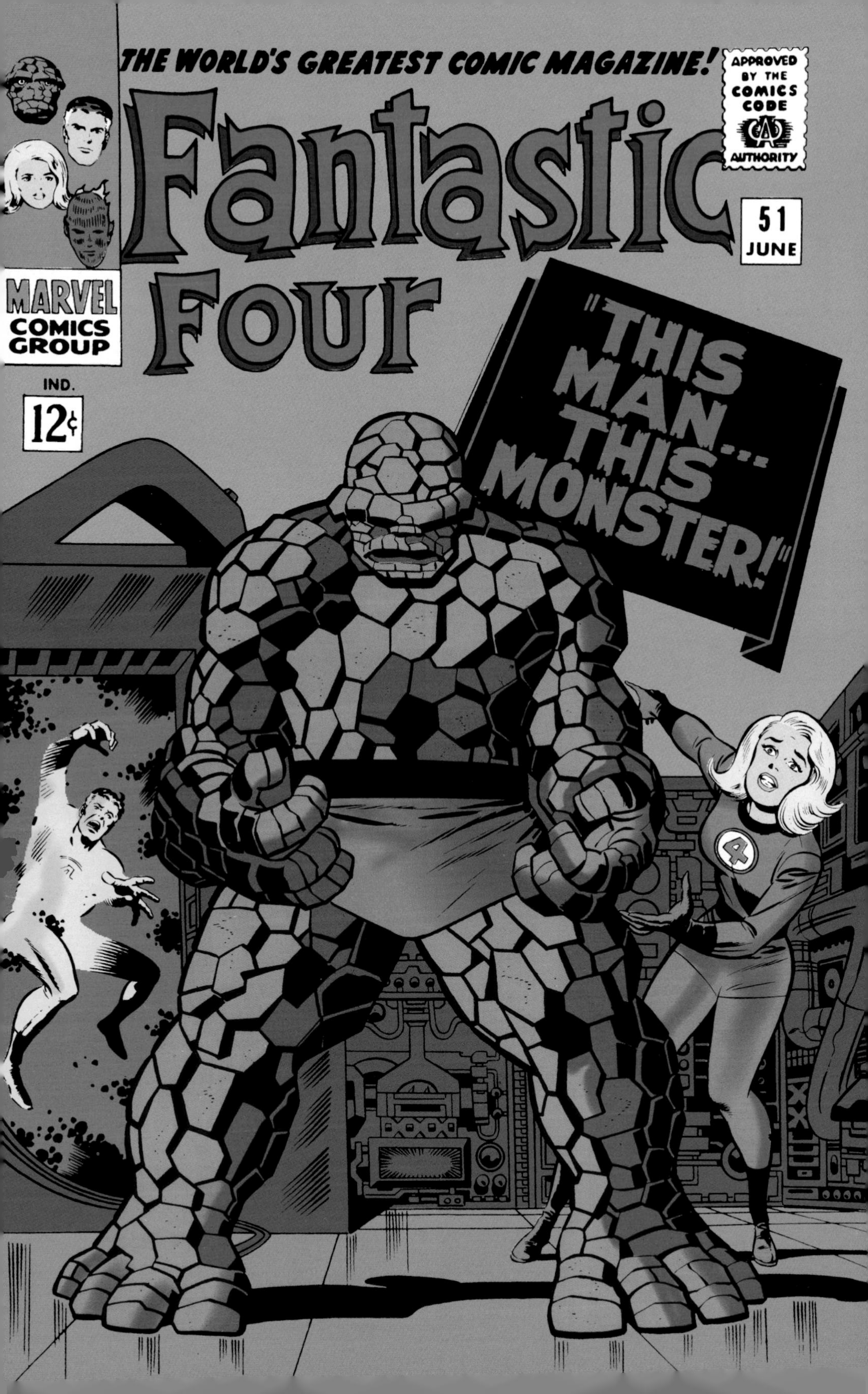

THE WORLD'S GREATEST COMIC MAGAZINE!
APPROVED BY THE COMICS CODE AUTHORITY
Fantastic Four
MARVEL COMICS GROUP
51
JUNE
IND.
12¢
"THIS MAN... THIS MONSTER!"
4

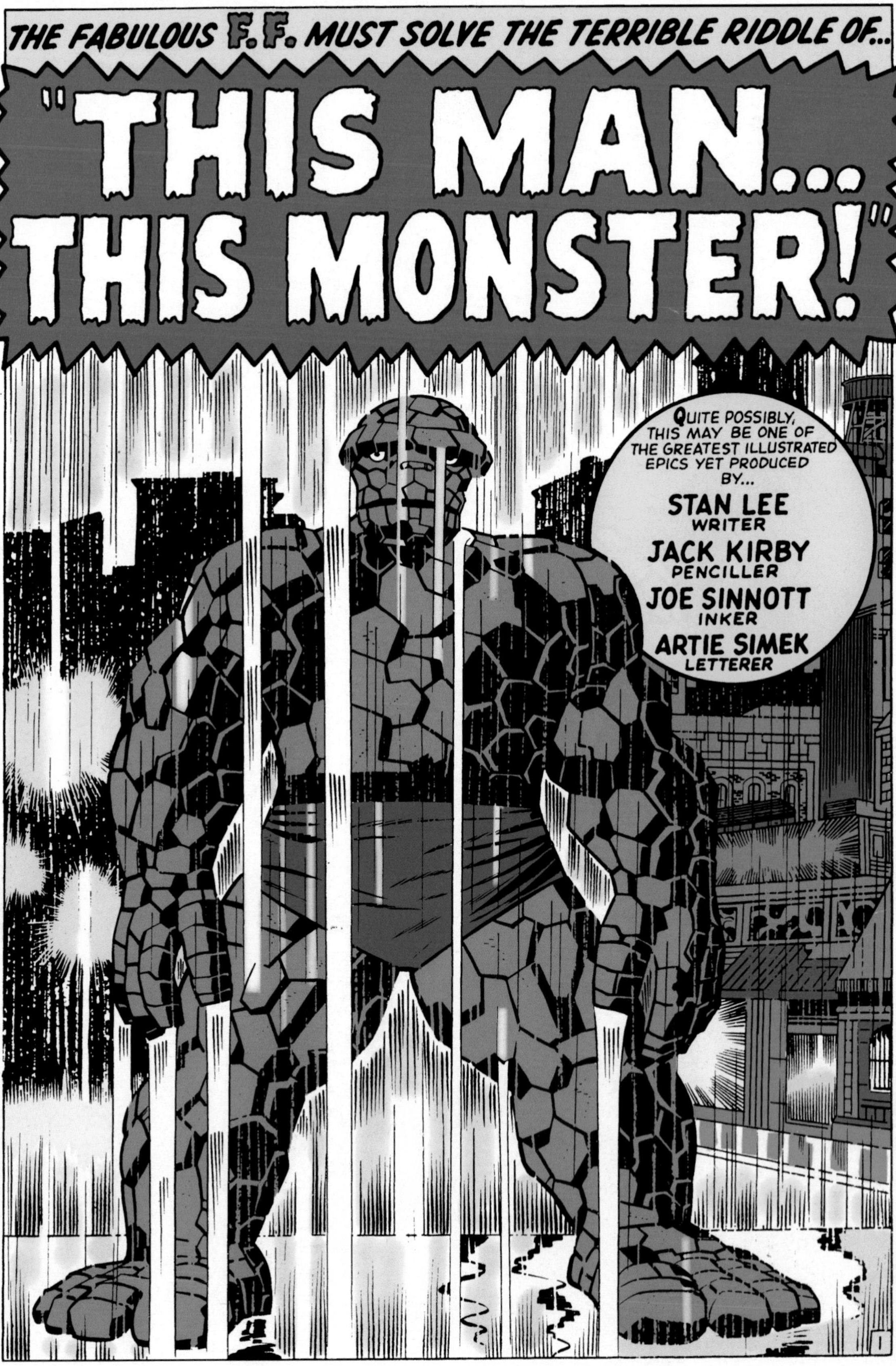
THE FABULOUS F.F. MUST SOLVE THE TERRIBLE RIDDLE OF...
"THIS MAN... THIS MONSTER!"
QUITE POSSIBLY, THIS MAY BE ONE OF THE GREATEST ILLUSTRATED EPICS YET PRODUCED BY...
STAN LEE WRITER
JACK KIRBY PENCILLER
JOE SINNOTT INKER
ARTIE SIMEK LETTERER
1

OCCASIONALLY, A TALE NEEDS NO INTRODUCTION! THIS IS SUCH A TALE! A RAINY NIGHT--A STRANGELY FORLORN FIGURE--AND RARE WONDERMENT AWAITS US--!

I'LL NEVER BE HUMAN AGAIN! I'LL LIVE--AND DIE--JUST THE WAY I *AM!*

LOOK, DAVE! ISN'T THAT --THE *THING?*

HE *MUST* BE! TODAY ISN'T HALLOWEEN!

WANT A *LIFT*, BIG FELLA? A GUY CAN CATCH A *COLD* THAT WAY!

A *NORMAL* GUY, Y'MEAN! WEATHER DON'T BOTHER *ME!*

IS ANYTHING *WRONG?* YOU LOOK KINDA *BEAT!*

SO WOULD *YOU*, IF YA HAD A FACE LIKE *MINE!*

AWW, DON'T MIND *ME!* I'M OKAY! EVERYTHIN'S COMIN' UP ROSES! SEE YA AROUND!

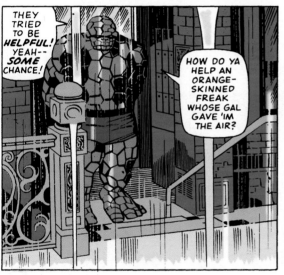

THEY TRIED TO BE *HELPFUL!* YEAH-- *SOME* CHANCE!

HOW DO YA HELP AN ORANGE-SKINNED FREAK WHOSE GAL GAVE 'IM THE AIR?

I WONDER WHAT MADE ME WALK TA *THIS* NEIGHBORHOOD? ALMOST LIKE SOMETHIN' WAS PULLIN'-- *HEY!*

I *SAW* YOU OUT THERE IN THE RAIN! WHY NOT COME IN WHERE IT'S WARM AND DRY?

WHAT *IS* THIS-- "BE NICE TO GARGOYLES" WEEK, OR SOMETHIN'?

I CAN UNDERSTAND YOUR BITTERNESS-- AND SYMPATHIZE WITH IT! I, TOO, KNOW HOW IT FEELS TO BE LONELY-- AND SAD OF HEART!

HE STILL SUSPECTS *NOTHING!* I MUST BE CAREFUL--SO VERY CAREFUL--!

I'LL JUST SIT HERE FER A MINUTE! I'M TIRED'A WALKIN'--TIRED'A THINKIN'--!

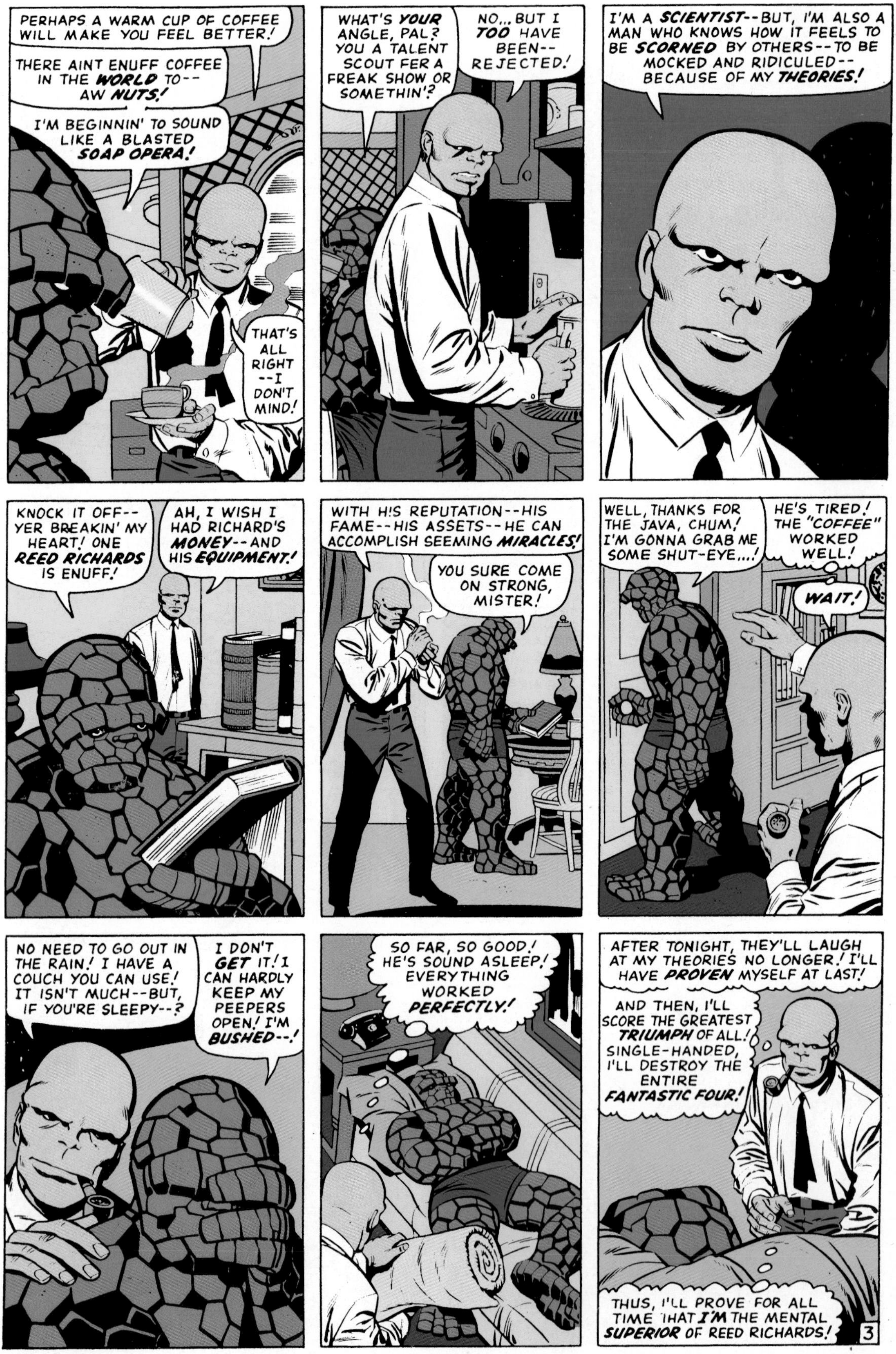
PERHAPS A WARM CUP OF COFFEE WILL MAKE YOU FEEL BETTER!
THERE AINT ENUFF COFFEE IN THE WORLD TO-- AW NUTS!
I'M BEGINNIN' TO SOUND LIKE A BLASTED SOAP OPERA!
THAT'S ALL RIGHT --I DON'T MIND!
WHAT'S YOUR ANGLE, PAL? YOU A TALENT SCOUT FER A FREAK SHOW OR SOMETHIN'?
NO... BUT I TOO HAVE BEEN-- REJECTED!
I'M A SCIENTIST--BUT, I'M ALSO A MAN WHO KNOWS HOW IT FEELS TO BE SCORNED BY OTHERS--TO BE MOCKED AND RIDICULED-- BECAUSE OF MY THEORIES!
KNOCK IT OFF-- YER BREAKIN' MY HEART! ONE REED RICHARDS IS ENUFF!
AH, I WISH I HAD RICHARD'S MONEY--AND HIS EQUIPMENT!
WITH HIS REPUTATION--HIS FAME--HIS ASSETS--HE CAN ACCOMPLISH SEEMING MIRACLES!
YOU SURE COME ON STRONG, MISTER!
WELL, THANKS FOR THE JAVA, CHUM! I'M GONNA GRAB ME SOME SHUT-EYE...!
HE'S TIRED! THE "COFFEE" WORKED WELL!
WAIT!
NO NEED TO GO OUT IN THE RAIN! I HAVE A COUCH YOU CAN USE! IT ISN'T MUCH--BUT, IF YOU'RE SLEEPY--?
I DON'T GET IT! I CAN HARDLY KEEP MY PEEPERS OPEN! I'M BUSHED--!
SO FAR, SO GOOD! HE'S SOUND ASLEEP! EVERYTHING WORKED PERFECTLY!
AFTER TONIGHT, THEY'LL LAUGH AT MY THEORIES NO LONGER! I'LL HAVE PROVEN MYSELF AT LAST!
AND THEN, I'LL SCORE THE GREATEST TRIUMPH OF ALL! SINGLE-HANDED, I'LL DESTROY THE ENTIRE FANTASTIC FOUR!
THUS, I'LL PROVE FOR ALL TIME THAT I'M THE MENTAL SUPERIOR OF REED RICHARDS!
3

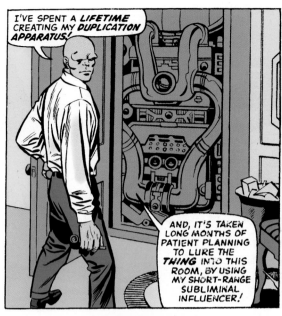

I'VE SPENT A *LIFETIME* CREATING MY *DUPLICATION APPARATUS!*

AND, IT'S TAKEN LONG MONTHS OF PATIENT PLANNING TO LURE THE *THING* INTO THIS ROOM, BY USING MY SHORT-RANGE SUBLIMINAL INFLUENCER!

BUT NOW, ALL THE LABOR, ALL THE WAITING, ALL THE SCHEMING, WILL PAY OFF AT *LAST!* I'M *THRU* BEING A *LOSER*-- *THIS* TIME I'VE GOT THE *WINNING HAND!*

AS FOR THE *THING*--- THERE'S *NO WAY* HE CAN EVER *STOP* ME!

HE WAS THE PERFECT CHOICE FOR MY EXPERIMENT, BECAUSE OF OUR SLIGHT SKELETAL RESEMBLANCE...

THAT FACT WILL MAKE THE *DUPLICATION PROCESS* ALL THE MORE EFFECTIVE!

AND NOW--LET IT *BEGIN!*

IT'S *WORKING*--AS I *KNEW* IT WOULD! I CAN SENSE IT--I CAN *FEEL* IT--!

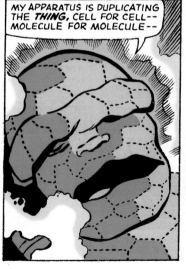

MY APPARATUS IS DUPLICATING THE *THING*, CELL FOR CELL-- MOLECULE FOR MOLECULE--

IT'S *OVER!* I'M AN EXACT *REPLICA* OF HIM!

NOW, ALL HIS FAME--AND HIS *POWER*--ARE *MINE!*

4

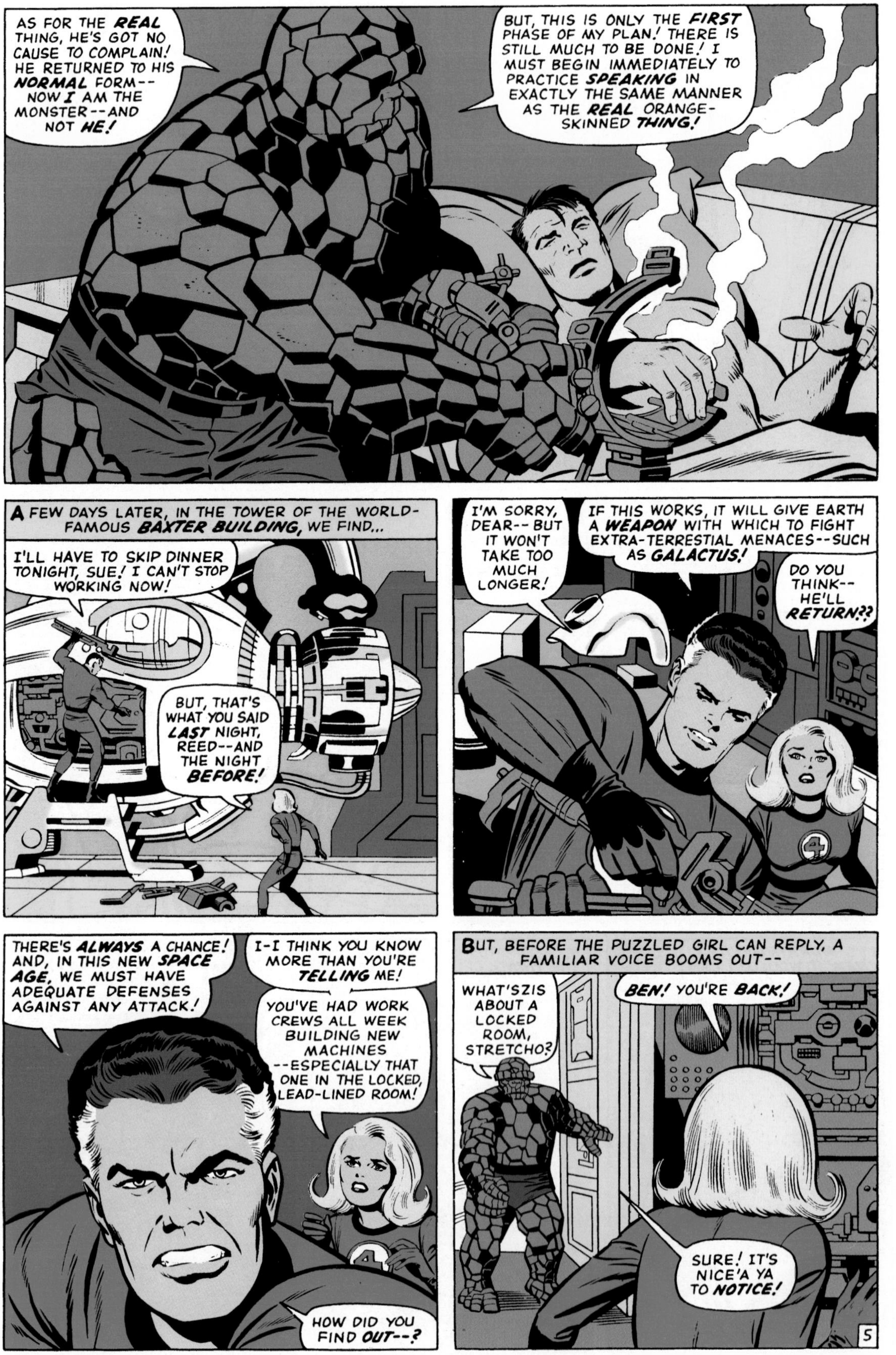
AS FOR THE REAL THING, HE'S GOT NO CAUSE TO COMPLAIN! HE RETURNED TO HIS NORMAL FORM-- NOW I AM THE MONSTER--AND NOT HE!
BUT, THIS IS ONLY THE FIRST PHASE OF MY PLAN! THERE IS STILL MUCH TO BE DONE! I MUST BEGIN IMMEDIATELY TO PRACTICE SPEAKING IN EXACTLY THE SAME MANNER AS THE REAL ORANGE-SKINNED THING!
A FEW DAYS LATER, IN THE TOWER OF THE WORLD-FAMOUS BAXTER BUILDING, WE FIND...
I'LL HAVE TO SKIP DINNER TONIGHT, SUE! I CAN'T STOP WORKING NOW!
BUT, THAT'S WHAT YOU SAID LAST NIGHT, REED--AND THE NIGHT BEFORE!
I'M SORRY, DEAR-- BUT IT WON'T TAKE TOO MUCH LONGER!
IF THIS WORKS, IT WILL GIVE EARTH A WEAPON WITH WHICH TO FIGHT EXTRA-TERRESTIAL MENACES--SUCH AS GALACTUS!
DO YOU THINK-- HE'LL RETURN??
THERE'S ALWAYS A CHANCE! AND, IN THIS NEW SPACE AGE, WE MUST HAVE ADEQUATE DEFENSES AGAINST ANY ATTACK!
I-I THINK YOU KNOW MORE THAN YOU'RE TELLING ME!
YOU'VE HAD WORK CREWS ALL WEEK BUILDING NEW MACHINES --ESPECIALLY THAT ONE IN THE LOCKED, LEAD-LINED ROOM!
HOW DID YOU FIND OUT--?
BUT, BEFORE THE PUZZLED GIRL CAN REPLY, A FAMILIAR VOICE BOOMS OUT--
WHAT'SZIS ABOUT A LOCKED ROOM, STRETCHO?
BEN! YOU'RE BACK!
SURE! IT'S NICE'A YA TO NOTICE!
5

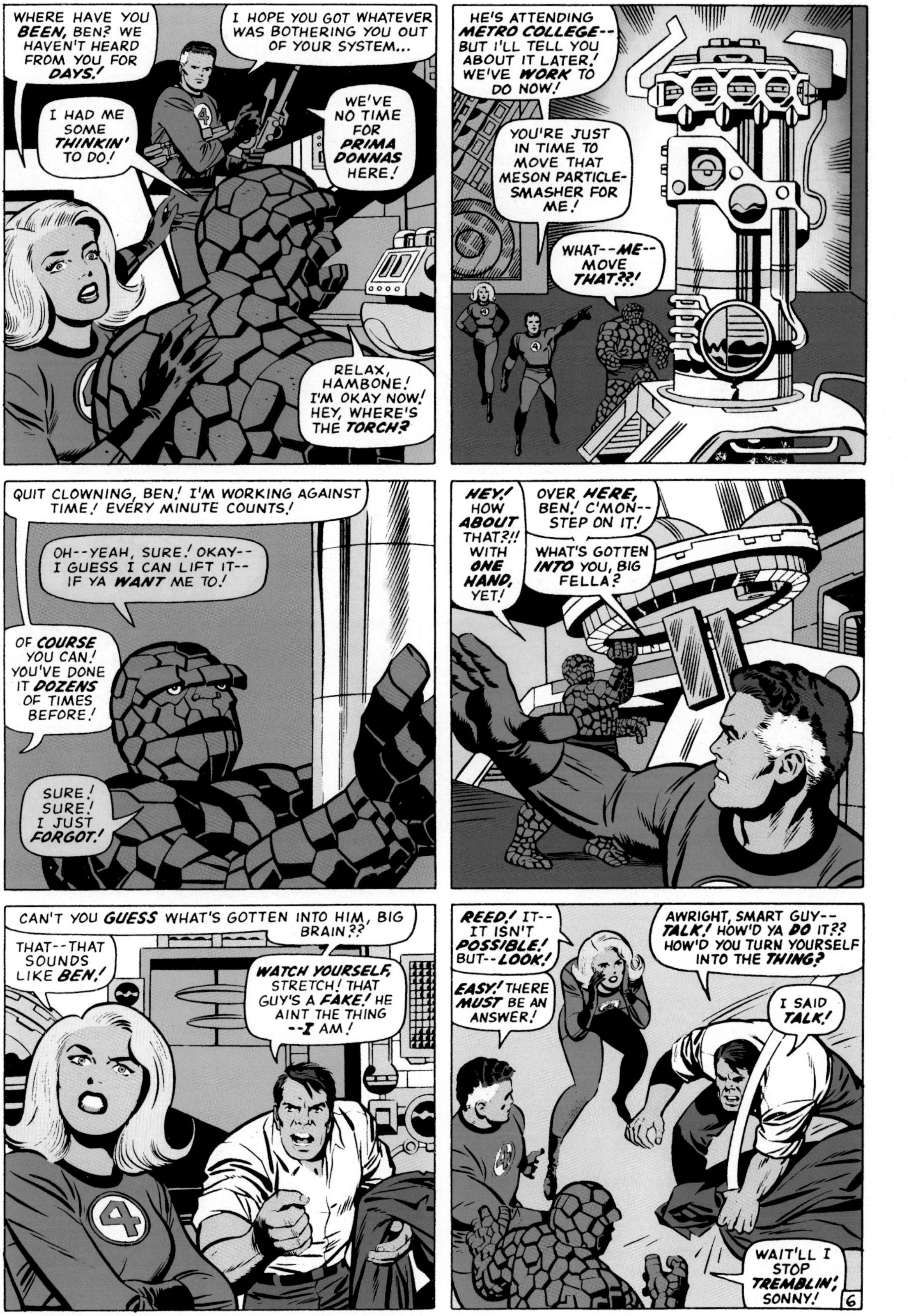
WHERE HAVE YOU BEEN, BEN? WE HAVEN'T HEARD FROM YOU FOR DAYS!
I HOPE YOU GOT WHATEVER WAS BOTHERING YOU OUT OF YOUR SYSTEM...
I HAD ME SOME THINKIN' TO DO!
WE'VE NO TIME FOR PRIMA DONNAS HERE!
RELAX, HAMBONE! I'M OKAY NOW! HEY, WHERE'S THE TORCH?
HE'S ATTENDING METRO COLLEGE-- BUT I'LL TELL YOU ABOUT IT LATER! WE'VE WORK TO DO NOW!
YOU'RE JUST IN TIME TO MOVE THAT MESON PARTICLE-SMASHER FOR ME!
WHAT--ME--MOVE THAT??!
QUIT CLOWNING, BEN! I'M WORKING AGAINST TIME! EVERY MINUTE COUNTS!
OH--YEAH, SURE! OKAY-- I GUESS I CAN LIFT IT-- IF YA WANT ME TO!
OF COURSE YOU CAN! YOU'VE DONE IT DOZENS OF TIMES BEFORE!
SURE! SURE! I JUST FORGOT!
HEY! HOW ABOUT THAT?!! WITH ONE HAND, YET!
OVER HERE, BEN! C'MON-- STEP ON IT!
WHAT'S GOTTEN INTO YOU, BIG FELLA?
CAN'T YOU GUESS WHAT'S GOTTEN INTO HIM, BIG BRAIN??
THAT--THAT SOUNDS LIKE BEN!
WATCH YOURSELF, STRETCH! THAT GUY'S A FAKE! HE AINT THE THING --I AM!
REED! IT-- IT ISN'T POSSIBLE! BUT--LOOK!
EASY! THERE MUST BE AN ANSWER!
AWRIGHT, SMART GUY-- TALK! HOW'D YA DO IT?? HOW'D YOU TURN YOURSELF INTO THE THING?
I SAID TALK!
WAIT'LL I STOP TREMBLIN', SONNY!
6

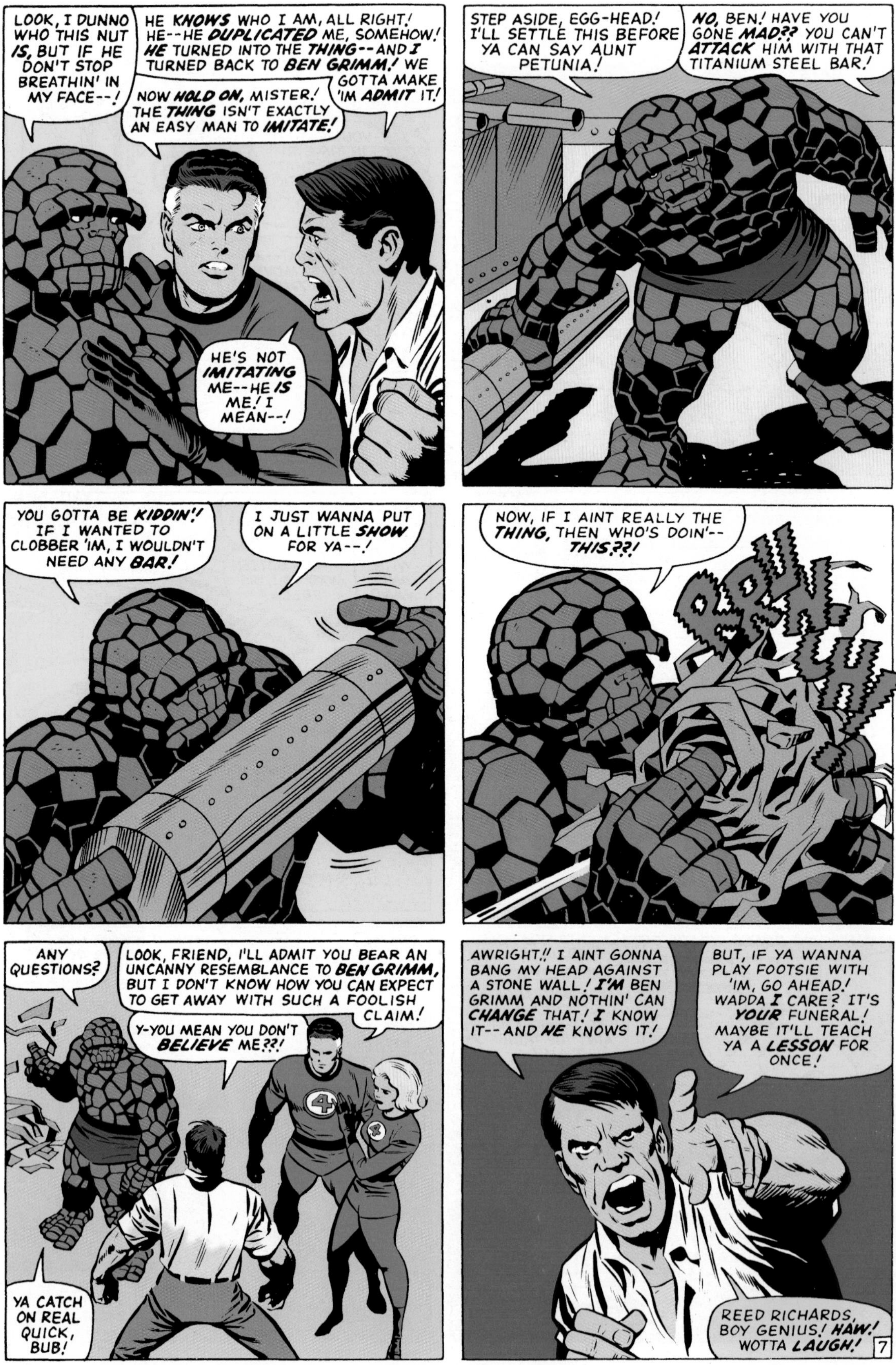
LOOK, I DUNNO WHO THIS NUT IS, BUT IF HE DON'T STOP BREATHIN' IN MY FACE--!
HE KNOWS WHO I AM, ALL RIGHT! HE--HE DUPLICATED ME, SOMEHOW! HE TURNED INTO THE THING--AND I TURNED BACK TO BEN GRIMM! WE GOTTA MAKE 'IM ADMIT IT!
NOW HOLD ON, MISTER! THE THING ISN'T EXACTLY AN EASY MAN TO IMITATE!
HE'S NOT IMITATING ME--HE IS ME! I MEAN--!
STEP ASIDE, EGG-HEAD! I'LL SETTLE THIS BEFORE YA CAN SAY AUNT PETUNIA!
NO, BEN! HAVE YOU GONE MAD?? YOU CAN'T ATTACK HIM WITH THAT TITANIUM STEEL BAR!
YOU GOTTA BE KIDDIN'! IF I WANTED TO CLOBBER 'IM, I WOULDN'T NEED ANY BAR!
I JUST WANNA PUT ON A LITTLE SHOW FOR YA--!
NOW, IF I AINT REALLY THE THING, THEN WHO'S DOIN'-- THIS??!
KRRUNNCHH
ANY QUESTIONS?
LOOK, FRIEND, I'LL ADMIT YOU BEAR AN UNCANNY RESEMBLANCE TO BEN GRIMM, BUT I DON'T KNOW HOW YOU CAN EXPECT TO GET AWAY WITH SUCH A FOOLISH CLAIM!
Y-YOU MEAN YOU DON'T BELIEVE ME??!
YA CATCH ON REAL QUICK, BUB!
AWRIGHT!! I AINT GONNA BANG MY HEAD AGAINST A STONE WALL! I'M BEN GRIMM AND NOTHIN' CAN CHANGE THAT! I KNOW IT-- AND HE KNOWS IT!
BUT, IF YA WANNA PLAY FOOTSIE WITH 'IM, GO AHEAD! WADDA I CARE? IT'S YOUR FUNERAL! MAYBE IT'LL TEACH YA A LESSON FOR ONCE!
REED RICHARDS, BOY GENIUS! HAW! WOTTA LAUGH!
7

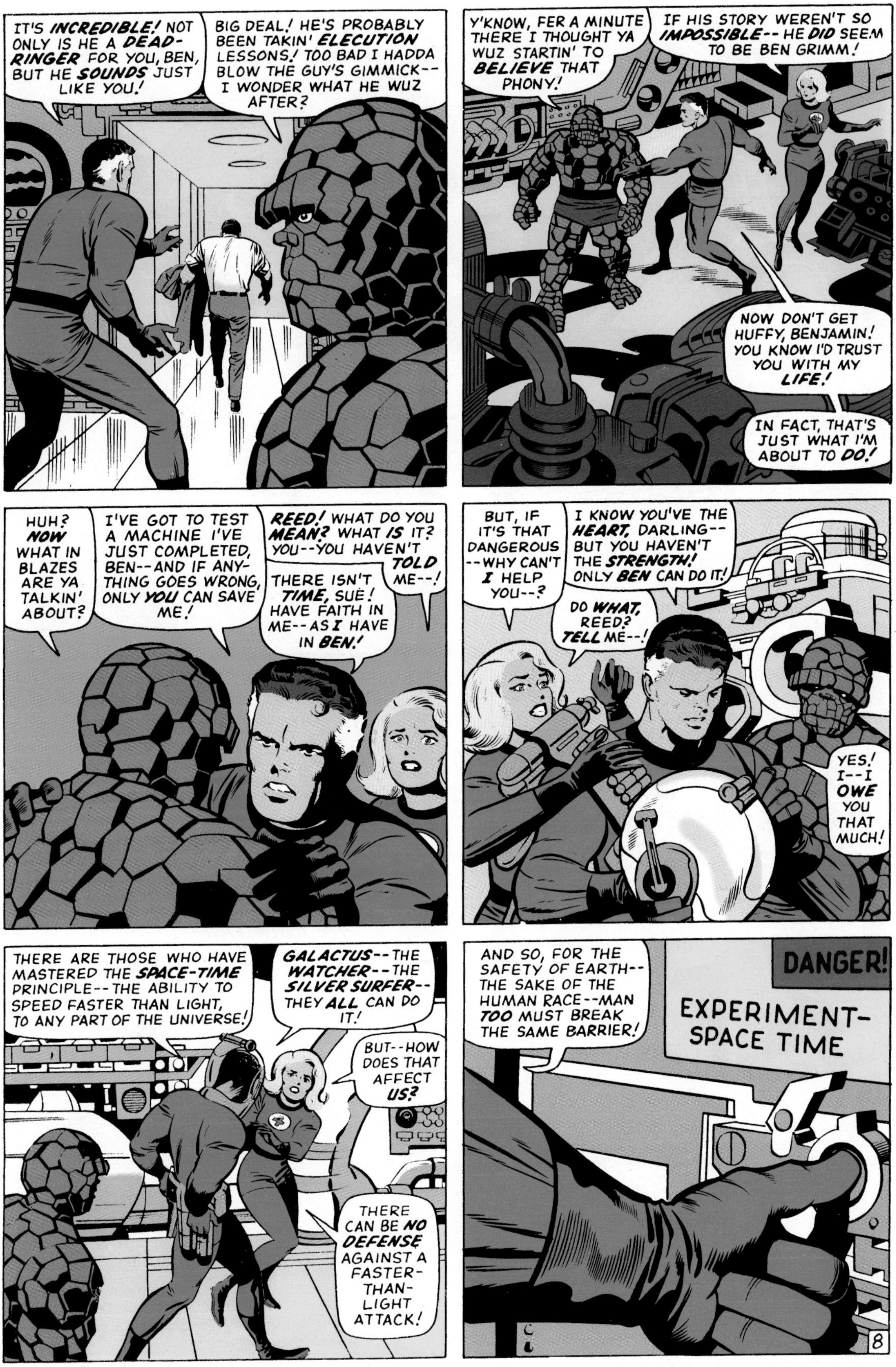

IT'S INCREDIBLE! NOT ONLY IS HE A DEAD-RINGER FOR YOU, BEN, BUT HE SOUNDS JUST LIKE YOU!
BIG DEAL! HE'S PROBABLY BEEN TAKIN' ELECUTION LESSONS! TOO BAD I HADDA BLOW THE GUY'S GIMMICK-- I WONDER WHAT HE WUZ AFTER?
Y'KNOW, FER A MINUTE THERE I THOUGHT YA WUZ STARTIN' TO BELIEVE THAT PHONY!
IF HIS STORY WEREN'T SO IMPOSSIBLE-- HE DID SEEM TO BE BEN GRIMM!
NOW DON'T GET HUFFY, BENJAMIN! YOU KNOW I'D TRUST YOU WITH MY LIFE!
IN FACT, THAT'S JUST WHAT I'M ABOUT TO DO!
HUH? NOW WHAT IN BLAZES ARE YA TALKIN' ABOUT?
I'VE GOT TO TEST A MACHINE I'VE JUST COMPLETED, BEN--AND IF ANY-THING GOES WRONG, ONLY YOU CAN SAVE ME!
REED! WHAT DO YOU MEAN? WHAT IS IT? YOU--YOU HAVEN'T TOLD ME--!
THERE ISN'T TIME, SUE! HAVE FAITH IN ME--AS I HAVE IN BEN!
BUT, IF IT'S THAT DANGEROUS --WHY CAN'T I HELP YOU--?
I KNOW YOU'VE THE HEART, DARLING-- BUT YOU HAVEN'T THE STRENGTH! ONLY BEN CAN DO IT!
DO WHAT, REED? TELL ME--!
YES! I--I OWE YOU THAT MUCH!
THERE ARE THOSE WHO HAVE MASTERED THE SPACE-TIME PRINCIPLE--THE ABILITY TO SPEED FASTER THAN LIGHT, TO ANY PART OF THE UNIVERSE!
GALACTUS--THE WATCHER--THE SILVER SURFER-- THEY ALL CAN DO IT!
BUT--HOW DOES THAT AFFECT US?
THERE CAN BE NO DEFENSE AGAINST A FASTER-THAN-LIGHT ATTACK!
AND SO, FOR THE SAFETY OF EARTH-- THE SAKE OF THE HUMAN RACE--MAN TOO MUST BREAK THE SAME BARRIER!
DANGER!
EXPERIMENT-SPACE TIME
8

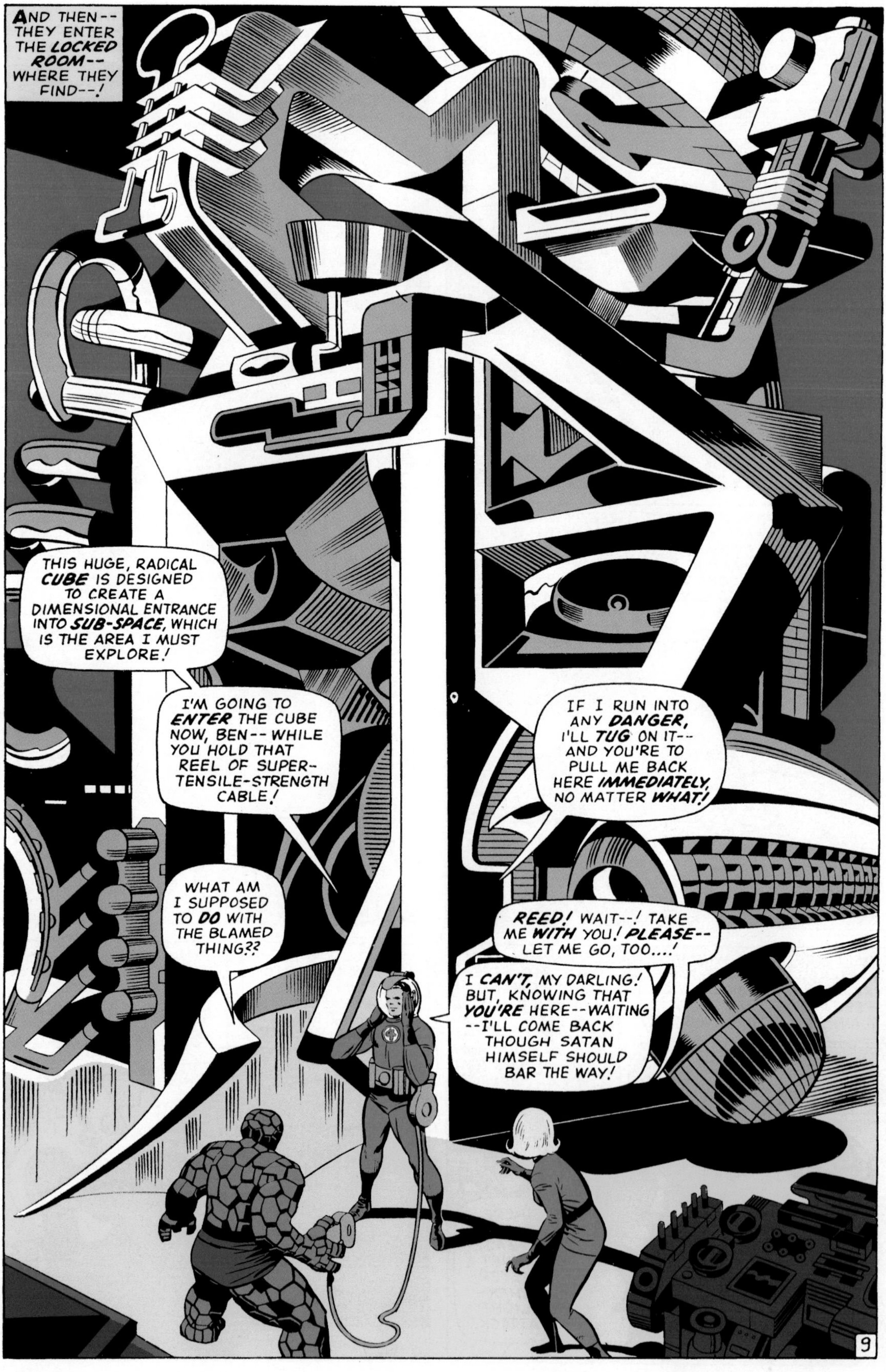
AND THEN-- THEY ENTER THE LOCKED ROOM-- WHERE THEY FIND--!
THIS HUGE, RADICAL CUBE IS DESIGNED TO CREATE A DIMENSIONAL ENTRANCE INTO SUB-SPACE, WHICH IS THE AREA I MUST EXPLORE!
I'M GOING TO ENTER THE CUBE NOW, BEN-- WHILE YOU HOLD THAT REEL OF SUPER-TENSILE-STRENGTH CABLE!
IF I RUN INTO ANY DANGER, I'LL TUG ON IT-- AND YOU'RE TO PULL ME BACK HERE IMMEDIATELY, NO MATTER WHAT!
WHAT AM I SUPPOSED TO DO WITH THE BLAMED THING??
REED! WAIT--! TAKE ME WITH YOU! PLEASE-- LET ME GO, TOO....!
I CAN'T, MY DARLING! BUT, KNOWING THAT YOU'RE HERE--WAITING --I'LL COME BACK THOUGH SATAN HIMSELF SHOULD BAR THE WAY!
9

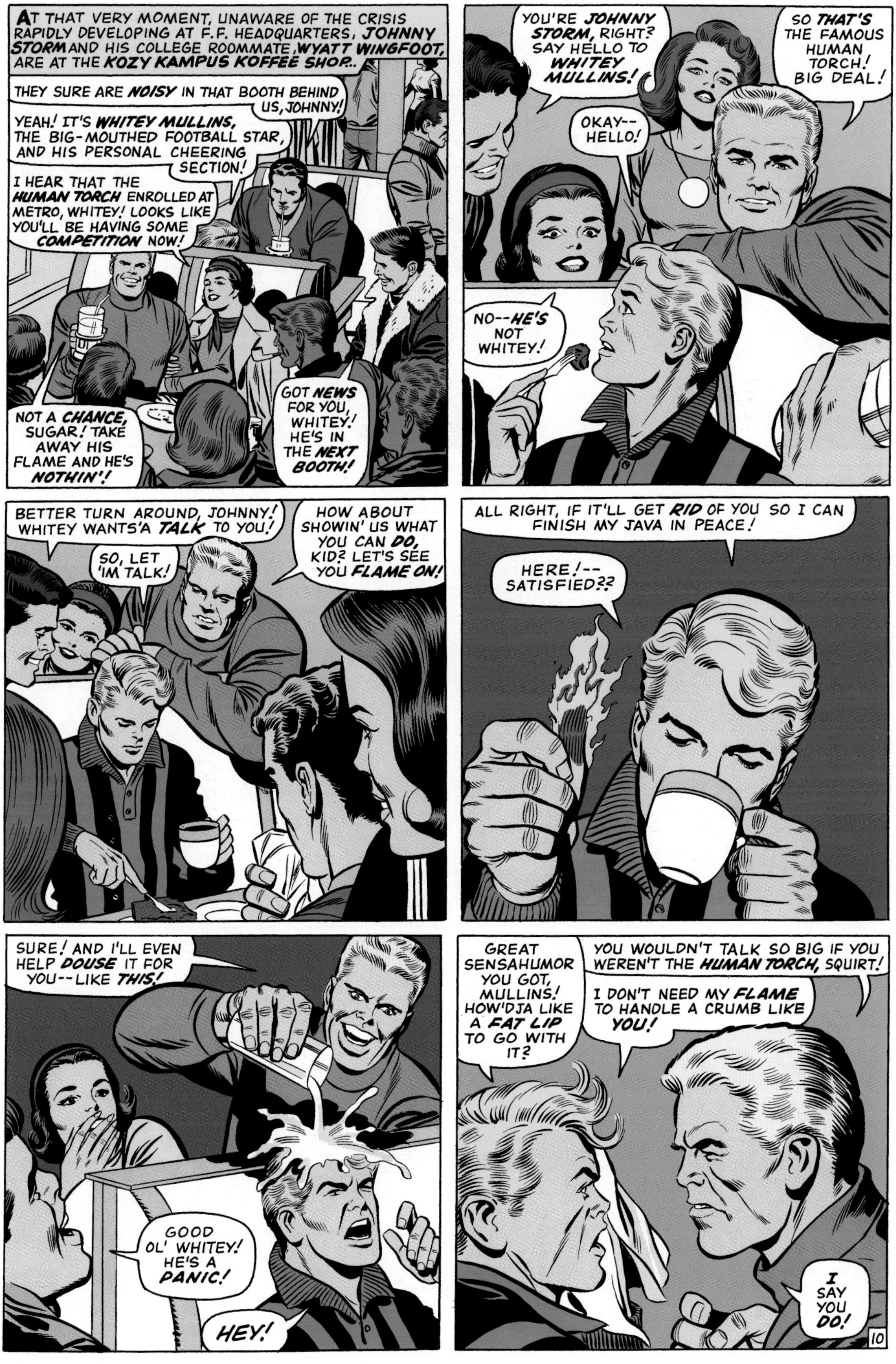
AT THAT VERY MOMENT, UNAWARE OF THE CRISIS RAPIDLY DEVELOPING AT F.F. HEADQUARTERS, JOHNNY STORM AND HIS COLLEGE ROOMMATE, WYATT WINGFOOT, ARE AT THE KOZY KAMPUS KOFFEE SHOP..
THEY SURE ARE NOISY IN THAT BOOTH BEHIND US, JOHNNY!
YEAH! IT'S WHITEY MULLINS, THE BIG-MOUTHED FOOTBALL STAR, AND HIS PERSONAL CHEERING SECTION!
I HEAR THAT THE HUMAN TORCH ENROLLED AT METRO, WHITEY! LOOKS LIKE YOU'LL BE HAVING SOME COMPETITION NOW!
NOT A CHANCE, SUGAR! TAKE AWAY HIS FLAME AND HE'S NOTHIN'!
GOT NEWS FOR YOU, WHITEY! HE'S IN THE NEXT BOOTH!
YOU'RE JOHNNY STORM, RIGHT? SAY HELLO TO WHITEY MULLINS!
SO THAT'S THE FAMOUS HUMAN TORCH! BIG DEAL!
OKAY-- HELLO!
NO--HE'S NOT WHITEY!
BETTER TURN AROUND, JOHNNY! WHITEY WANTS'A TALK TO YOU!
SO, LET 'IM TALK!
HOW ABOUT SHOWIN' US WHAT YOU CAN DO, KID? LET'S SEE YOU FLAME ON!
ALL RIGHT, IF IT'LL GET RID OF YOU SO I CAN FINISH MY JAVA IN PEACE!
HERE!-- SATISFIED??
SURE! AND I'LL EVEN HELP DOUSE IT FOR YOU--LIKE THIS!
GOOD OL' WHITEY! HE'S A PANIC!
HEY!
GREAT SENSAHUMOR YOU GOT, MULLINS! HOW'DJA LIKE A FAT LIP TO GO WITH IT?
YOU WOULDN'T TALK SO BIG IF YOU WEREN'T THE HUMAN TORCH, SQUIRT!
I DON'T NEED MY FLAME TO HANDLE A CRUMB LIKE YOU!
I SAY YOU DO!
10

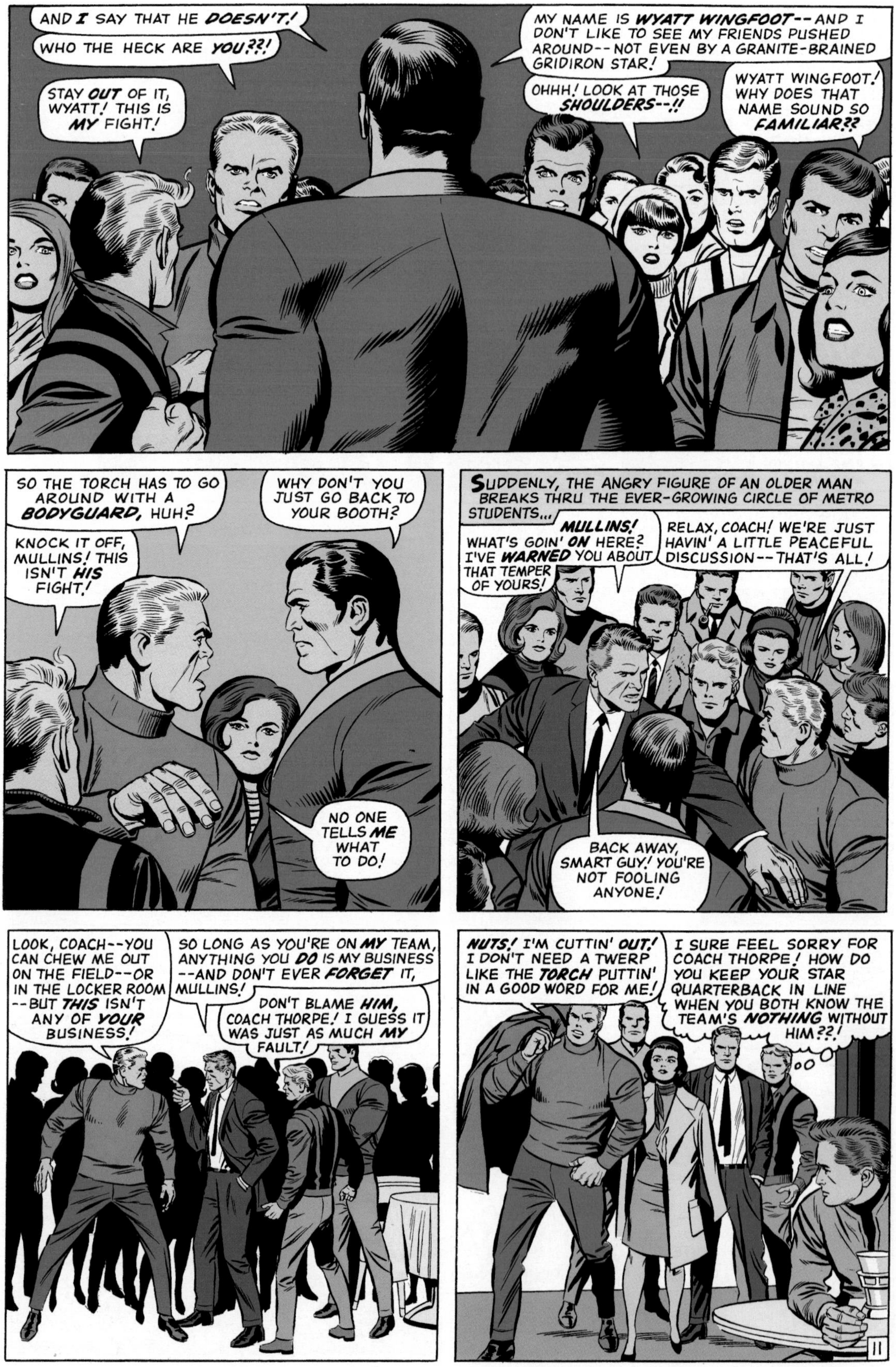
AND I SAY THAT HE DOESN'T!
WHO THE HECK ARE YOU??!
STAY OUT OF IT, WYATT! THIS IS MY FIGHT!
MY NAME IS WYATT WINGFOOT-- AND I DON'T LIKE TO SEE MY FRIENDS PUSHED AROUND-- NOT EVEN BY A GRANITE-BRAINED GRIDIRON STAR!
OHHH! LOOK AT THOSE SHOULDERS--!!
WYATT WINGFOOT! WHY DOES THAT NAME SOUND SO FAMILIAR??
SO THE TORCH HAS TO GO AROUND WITH A BODYGUARD, HUH?
KNOCK IT OFF, MULLINS! THIS ISN'T HIS FIGHT!
WHY DON'T YOU JUST GO BACK TO YOUR BOOTH?
NO ONE TELLS ME WHAT TO DO!
SUDDENLY, THE ANGRY FIGURE OF AN OLDER MAN BREAKS THRU THE EVER-GROWING CIRCLE OF METRO STUDENTS...
MULLINS! WHAT'S GOIN' ON HERE? I'VE WARNED YOU ABOUT THAT TEMPER OF YOURS!
RELAX, COACH! WE'RE JUST HAVIN' A LITTLE PEACEFUL DISCUSSION-- THAT'S ALL!
BACK AWAY, SMART GUY! YOU'RE NOT FOOLING ANYONE!
LOOK, COACH-- YOU CAN CHEW ME OUT ON THE FIELD-- OR IN THE LOCKER ROOM-- BUT THIS ISN'T ANY OF YOUR BUSINESS!
SO LONG AS YOU'RE ON MY TEAM, ANYTHING YOU DO IS MY BUSINESS-- AND DON'T EVER FORGET IT, MULLINS!
DON'T BLAME HIM, COACH THORPE! I GUESS IT WAS JUST AS MUCH MY FAULT!
NUTS! I'M CUTTIN' OUT! I DON'T NEED A TWERP LIKE THE TORCH PUTTIN' IN A GOOD WORD FOR ME!
I SURE FEEL SORRY FOR COACH THORPE! HOW DO YOU KEEP YOUR STAR QUARTERBACK IN LINE WHEN YOU BOTH KNOW THE TEAM'S NOTHING WITHOUT HIM??!
11

SORRY IF I'VE CAUSED ANY TROUBLE, COACH--!

FORGET IT, SON! SAY, WHAT'S *YOUR* NAME, BIG FELLA? I HAVEN'T SEEN YOU HERE BEFORE!

I AM--WYATT WINGFOOT, SIR--!

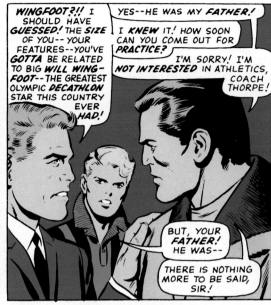

WINGFOOT?!! I SHOULD HAVE *GUESSED!* THE *SIZE* OF YOU-- YOUR FEATURES--YOU'VE *GOTTA* BE RELATED TO BIG *WILL WINGFOOT*--THE GREATEST OLYMPIC *DECATHLON* STAR THIS COUNTRY EVER *HAD!*

YES--HE WAS MY *FATHER!*

I *KNEW* IT! HOW SOON CAN YOU COME OUT FOR *PRACTICE?*

I'M SORRY! I'M *NOT INTERESTED* IN ATHLETICS, COACH THORPE!

BUT, YOUR *FATHER!* HE WAS--

THERE IS NOTHING MORE TO BE SAID, SIR!

WHAT'S *WRONG,* DEAR? YOU LOOK AS THOUGH YOU'VE SEEN A *GHOST!*

I ALMOST *HAVE!* THAT BOY IS WILL WINGFOOT'S *SON!* IF HE'S INHERITED EVEN A *FRACTION* OF HIS FATHER'S PROWESS--!

BUT, WHAT AM I *SAYING?* WHAT *DIFFERENCE* DOES IT MAKE?

HE DOESN'T *WANT* TO TRY OUT FOR THE TEAM! HE WON'T EVEN *DISCUSS* ATHLETICS!

DON'T WORRY, JIM-- THERE'LL BE *OTHER* PLAYERS--!

NO! NOT LIKE *HIM!* DON'T YOU *SEE,* BELLE? HIS *FATHER* AND I--WE WERE *TEAM MATES!* WE WERE *GREAT* TOGETHER! AND NOW--FATE HAS SENT *WYATT* TO ME! IT'S MY BIG CHANCE-- TO COACH THE GREATEST TEAM OF ALL, BEFORE I RETIRE!

I'VE *GOT* TO MAKE HIM PLAY!

BUT NOW, IT'S TIME TO RETURN TO THE *BAXTER BUILDING,* WHERE REED RICHARDS IS ABOUT TO UNDERTAKE ONE OF THE MOST DANGEROUS FEATS OF HIS CAREER--

REED--MY DARLING--DON'T *DO* IT! I-I HAVE A *PREMONITION*-- OF DISASTER! OR, AT LEAST--LET ME COME *WITH* YOU--!

IT'S *IMPOSSIBLE,* SUE! BUT, I CAN'T TURN BACK NOW! SUB-SPACE *MUST* BE EXPLORED-- AND CONQUERED-- FOR THE GOOD OF MANKIND!

I ALWAYS THOUGHT HE WAS JUST A *GLAMOR-PANTS*--OUT FOR ALL THE DOUGH AND GLORY HE COULD GET! BUT HE'S TACKLIN' A JOB THAT WON'T NET HIM A PLUGGED NICKEL--

AND HE'S DOING IT WITHOUT ANY FANFARE-- OR ANY PUBLICITY!

12

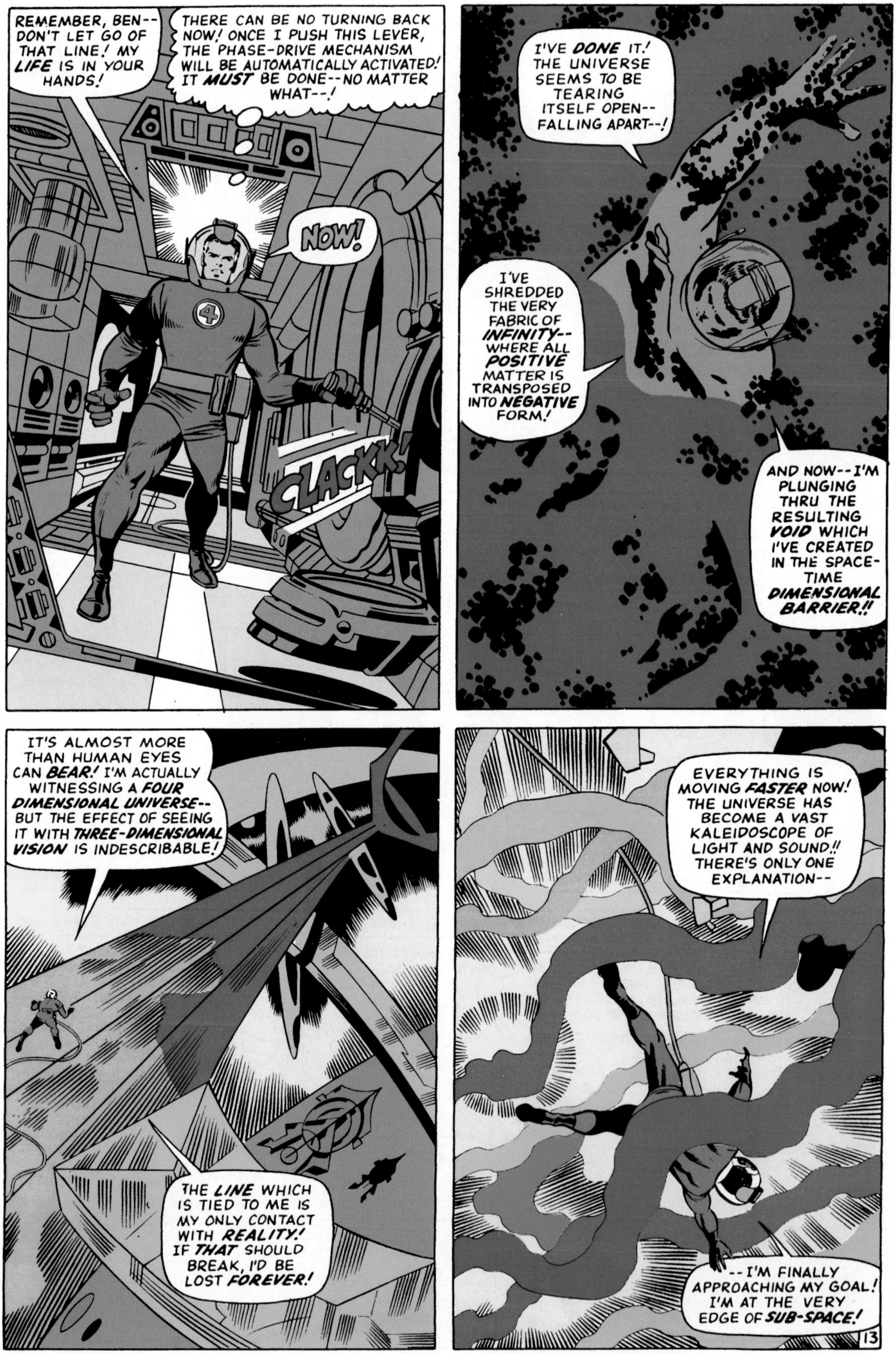
REMEMBER, BEN-- DON'T LET GO OF THAT LINE! MY LIFE IS IN YOUR HANDS!
THERE CAN BE NO TURNING BACK NOW! ONCE I PUSH THIS LEVER, THE PHASE-DRIVE MECHANISM WILL BE AUTOMATICALLY ACTIVATED! IT MUST BE DONE--NO MATTER WHAT--!
NOW!
CLACKK!
I'VE DONE IT! THE UNIVERSE SEEMS TO BE TEARING ITSELF OPEN-- FALLING APART--!
I'VE SHREDDED THE VERY FABRIC OF INFINITY-- WHERE ALL POSITIVE MATTER IS TRANSPOSED INTO NEGATIVE FORM!
AND NOW--I'M PLUNGING THRU THE RESULTING VOID WHICH I'VE CREATED IN THE SPACE-TIME DIMENSIONAL BARRIER!!
IT'S ALMOST MORE THAN HUMAN EYES CAN BEAR! I'M ACTUALLY WITNESSING A FOUR DIMENSIONAL UNIVERSE-- BUT THE EFFECT OF SEEING IT WITH THREE-DIMENSIONAL VISION IS INDESCRIBABLE!
THE LINE WHICH IS TIED TO ME IS MY ONLY CONTACT WITH REALITY! IF THAT SHOULD BREAK, I'D BE LOST FOREVER!
EVERYTHING IS MOVING FASTER NOW! THE UNIVERSE HAS BECOME A VAST KALEIDOSCOPE OF LIGHT AND SOUND!! THERE'S ONLY ONE EXPLANATION--
--I'M FINALLY APPROACHING MY GOAL! I'M AT THE VERY EDGE OF SUB-SPACE!
13

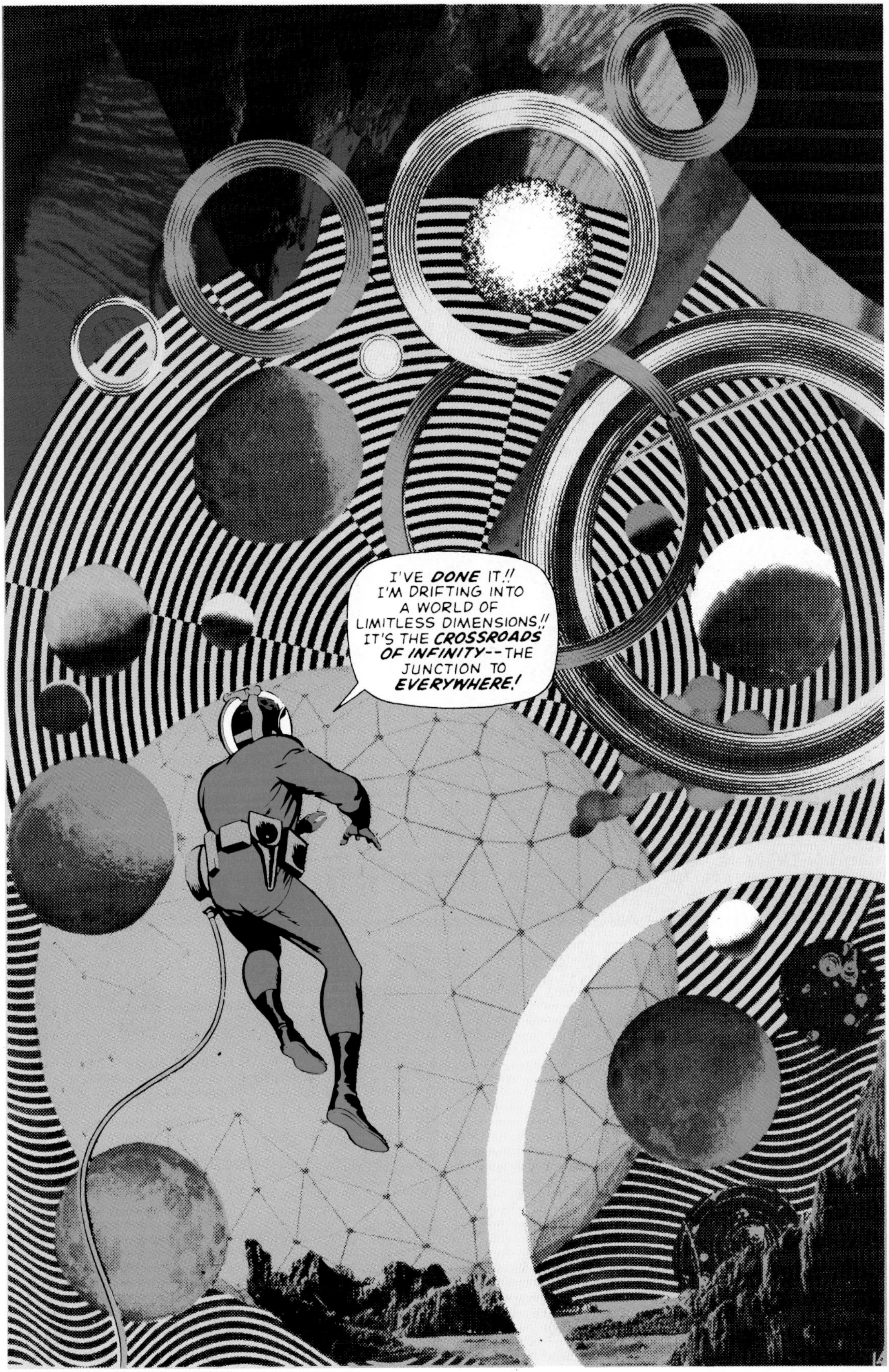
I'VE DONE IT!! I'M DRIFTING INTO A WORLD OF LIMITLESS DIMENSIONS!! IT'S THE CROSSROADS OF INFINITY--THE JUNCTION TO EVERYWHERE!

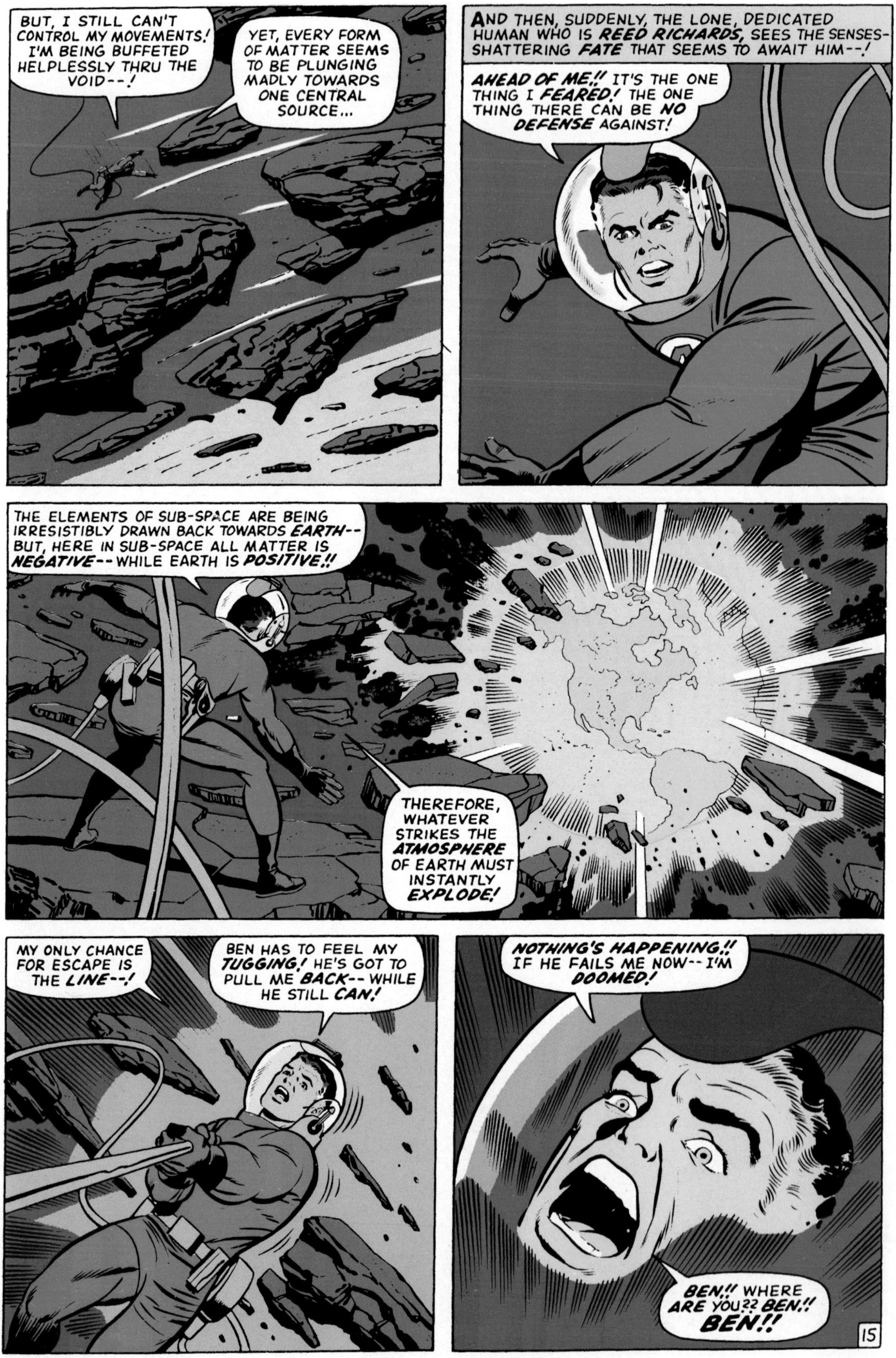
BUT, I STILL CAN'T CONTROL MY MOVEMENTS! I'M BEING BUFFETED HELPLESSLY THRU THE VOID--!
YET, EVERY FORM OF MATTER SEEMS TO BE PLUNGING MADLY TOWARDS ONE CENTRAL SOURCE...
AND THEN, SUDDENLY, THE LONE, DEDICATED HUMAN WHO IS REED RICHARDS, SEES THE SENSES-SHATTERING FATE THAT SEEMS TO AWAIT HIM--!
AHEAD OF ME!! IT'S THE ONE THING I FEARED! THE ONE THING THERE CAN BE NO DEFENSE AGAINST!
THE ELEMENTS OF SUB-SPACE ARE BEING IRRESISTIBLY DRAWN BACK TOWARDS EARTH-- BUT, HERE IN SUB-SPACE ALL MATTER IS NEGATIVE-- WHILE EARTH IS POSITIVE!!
THEREFORE, WHATEVER STRIKES THE ATMOSPHERE OF EARTH MUST INSTANTLY EXPLODE!
MY ONLY CHANCE FOR ESCAPE IS THE LINE--!
BEN HAS TO FEEL MY TUGGING! HE'S GOT TO PULL ME BACK-- WHILE HE STILL CAN!
NOTHING'S HAPPENING!! IF HE FAILS ME NOW-- I'M DOOMED!
BEN!! WHERE ARE YOU?? BEN!! BEN!!
15

AND, AT THE OTHER END OF THE FATEFUL LINE, WE FIND--

HE'S *TUGGING!* ALL I GOTTA DO IS *IGNORE* HIM, AND I'LL HAVE BEATEN THE ONE MAN I'VE ALWAYS ENVIED--THE ONE MAN NO ONE *ELSE* COULD EVER DEFEAT!

BUT--ALL OF A SUDDEN, I *DON'T* ENVY HIM ANY MORE! I-I NEVER KNEW HOW *BRAVE* HE WAS --HOW UNSELFISH--!

BEN! THE LINE IS GROWING *TAUT!* IT'S *REED!* IT'S HIS *SIGNAL!*

ALL THESE YEARS-- WHEN I THOUGHT I NEVER GOT THE BREAKS--NOW I KNOW THE *TRUTH!* IT WAS *MY* FAULT--NOBODY *ELSE'S!* I WOULDN'T WORK *HARD* ENOUGH--I WOULDN'T MAKE THE SACRIFICES THAT A *REED RICHARDS* WOULD--!

PULL HIM IN, BEN! QUICKLY-- *BEN!*

I NEVER *SAW* THINGS SO *CLEAR* BEFORE! IT--IT'S ALMOST LIKE I'VE *REALLY* BECOME THE *THING*--NOT JUST AN IMITATION!

BEN!! FOR THE *LOVE* OF *HEAVEN*--!

I NEVER DID A WORTHWHILE THING IN MY WHOLE LIFE!! BUT NOW--I'VE FINALLY GOT THE *CHANCE!* I CAN REALLY *BE* BEN GRIMM!!

I'VE GOTTA *DO* IT! I'LL *SAVE* RICHARDS!!

DON'T WORRY, LADY!! I'LL GET 'IM-- *NOW!*

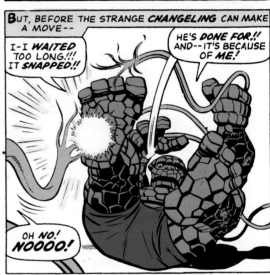

BUT, BEFORE THE STRANGE *CHANGELING* CAN MAKE A MOVE--

I-I *WAITED* TOO LONG!!! IT *SNAPPED!!*

HE'S *DONE FOR!!* AND--IT'S BECAUSE OF *ME!*

OH *NO!* NOOOO!

I'VE GOT TO *GO* TO HIM!! HE CAN'T BE LEFT *ALONE* IN THERE!! HE *NEEDS* ME! HE *NEEDS* ME!!

STAY BACK, DO Y'HEAR?? *STAY BACK!!* THERE'S NOTHIN' *YOU* CAN DO! WHATEVER'S HAPPENIN' TO 'IM IN THERE--ONLY A MASS OF *MUSCLE* CAN HELP!

YOU WAIT OUT *THERE* BABY! I'LL *WHISTLE* IF I NEED YA!

MEBBE, IF I'M *LUCKY,* I CAN STILL GRAB THAT BUSTED HUNK'A LINE--BEFORE IT'S TOO LATE!

16

I GOT IT!

BUT, IN MAKING HIS LAST-DITCH, DESPERATE LEAP AFTER THE THIN STRAND OF CABLE, THE MAN WITH THE *THING'S* BODY IS *HIMSELF* INSTANTLY DRAWN INTO THE INCREDIBLE BARRIER BETWEEN THE DIMENSIONS--

NOW I'VE DONE IT! WHATEVER HAPPENED TO *RICHARDS* WILL HAPPEN TO *ME*, TOO! I CAN'T TURN *BACK*!

LUCKY THE BODY OF THE *THING* IS STRONG ENOUGH TO STAND EXTREME CONDITIONS WITHOUT A PROTECTIVE HELMET, OR I'D BE DONE FOR *ALREADY*!

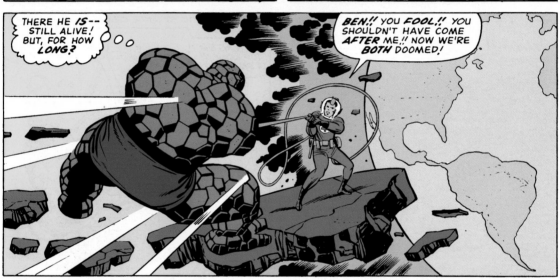

THERE HE *IS*-- STILL ALIVE! BUT, FOR HOW *LONG*?

BEN!! YOU *FOOL*!! YOU SHOULDN'T HAVE COME *AFTER* ME!! NOW WE'RE *BOTH* DOOMED!

YOU WERE JUST SUPPOSED TO PULL THE *LINE* IN WHEN I *TUGGED*!! BEN--OLD FRIEND--I-I DIDN'T WANT THIS TO HAPPEN TO *YOU*!!

IN A FEW SECONDS-- WE'LL REACH THE ATMOSPHERE BELOW US, AND IT'LL MEAN INSTANT *DEATH*!! IF ONLY *YOU* HADN'T COME--!

SO *THIS* IS HOW IT'S GONNA END! AND EVEN *NOW*-- HE'S WORRIED MORE ABOUT *ME* THAN HIMSELF!!

BRACE YOURSELF, BEN! WE DID THE BEST WE COULD-- ONE CAN DO NO MORE! YOU--YOU WERE THE GREATEST PARTNER A MAN EVER HAD--!

THAT'S THE GUY I SPENT YEARS *HATING*-- BEING *JEALOUS* OF!! I-I AINT EVEN WORTH HIS LITTLE *PINKY*!

17

18

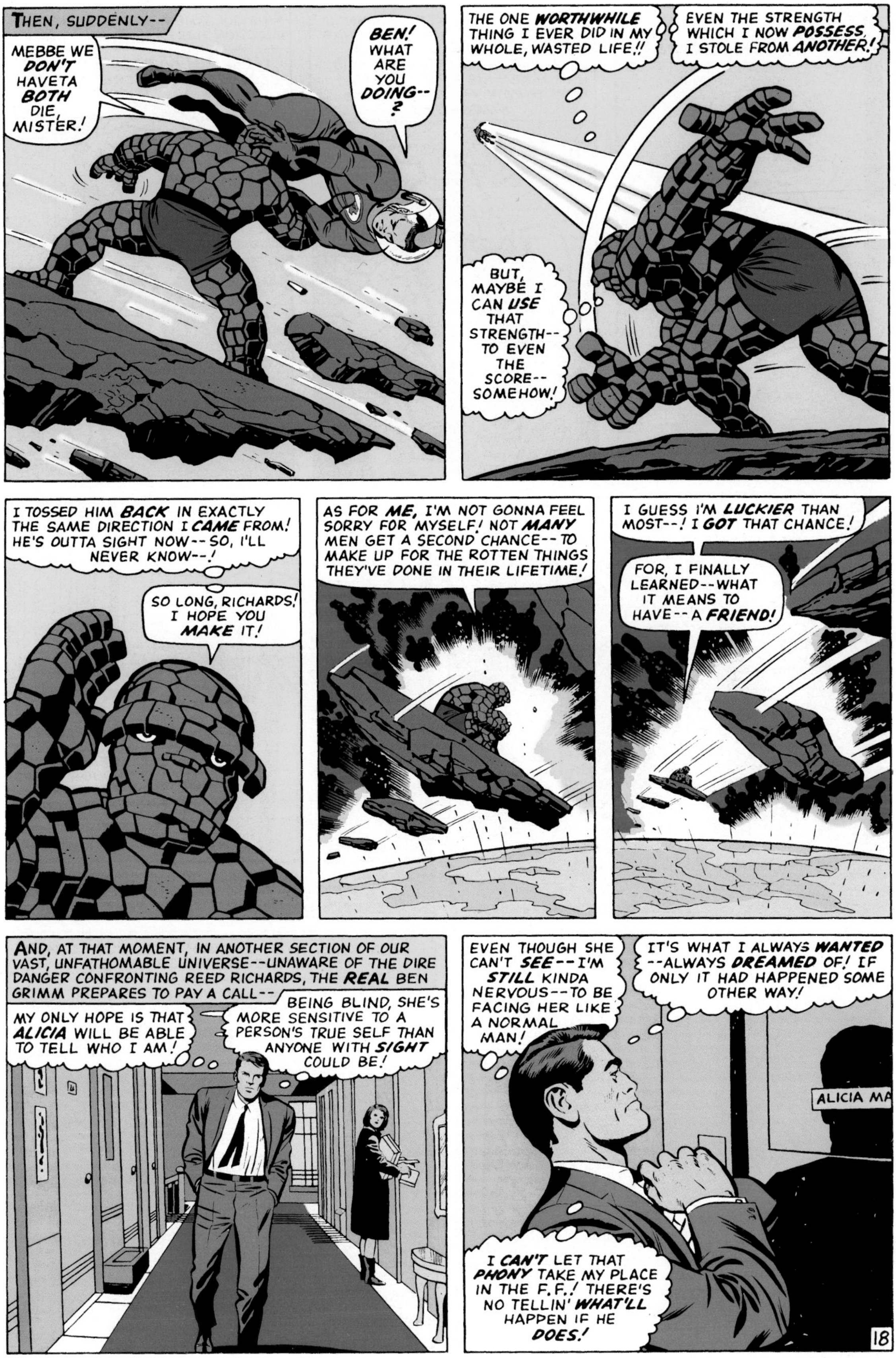
THEN, SUDDENLY--
MEBBE WE DON'T HAVETA BOTH DIE, MISTER!
BEN! WHAT ARE YOU DOING--?
THE ONE WORTHWHILE THING I EVER DID IN MY WHOLE, WASTED LIFE!!
EVEN THE STRENGTH WHICH I NOW POSSESS, I STOLE FROM ANOTHER!
BUT, MAYBE I CAN USE THAT STRENGTH--TO EVEN THE SCORE--SOMEHOW!
I TOSSED HIM BACK IN EXACTLY THE SAME DIRECTION I CAME FROM! HE'S OUTTA SIGHT NOW--SO, I'LL NEVER KNOW--!
SO LONG, RICHARDS! I HOPE YOU MAKE IT!
AS FOR ME, I'M NOT GONNA FEEL SORRY FOR MYSELF! NOT MANY MEN GET A SECOND CHANCE--TO MAKE UP FOR THE ROTTEN THINGS THEY'VE DONE IN THEIR LIFETIME!
I GUESS I'M LUCKIER THAN MOST--! I GOT THAT CHANCE!
FOR, I FINALLY LEARNED--WHAT IT MEANS TO HAVE--A FRIEND!
AND, AT THAT MOMENT, IN ANOTHER SECTION OF OUR VAST, UNFATHOMABLE UNIVERSE--UNAWARE OF THE DIRE DANGER CONFRONTING REED RICHARDS, THE REAL BEN GRIMM PREPARES TO PAY A CALL--
MY ONLY HOPE IS THAT ALICIA WILL BE ABLE TO TELL WHO I AM!
BEING BLIND, SHE'S MORE SENSITIVE TO A PERSON'S TRUE SELF THAN ANYONE WITH SIGHT COULD BE!
EVEN THOUGH SHE CAN'T SEE--I'M STILL KINDA NERVOUS--TO BE FACING HER LIKE A NORMAL MAN!
IT'S WHAT I ALWAYS WANTED--ALWAYS DREAMED OF! IF ONLY IT HAD HAPPENED SOME OTHER WAY!
ALICIA MA
I CAN'T LET THAT PHONY TAKE MY PLACE IN THE F.F.! THERE'S NO TELLIN' WHAT'LL HAPPEN IF HE DOES!
18

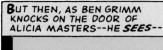

BUT THEN, AS BEN GRIMM KNOCKS ON THE DOOR OF ALICIA MASTERS--HE SEES--

MY--MY HAND!!!

STARTLED--SHOCKED--STUNNED INTO SPEECHLESSNESS--HE HAS NO WAY OF KNOWING THAT, A UNIVERSE AWAY, THE MAN WHO HAD TAKEN HIS IDENTITY HAS NOW *GIVEN IT UP* AGAIN--FOREVER!

FINALLY, WHEN THE INITIAL NUMBED REACTION HAS PASSED...

I--I'VE BECOME THE THING AGAIN!

NOW I CAN GO BACK 'N CLOBBER THAT CREEP WHO'S POSIN' AS ME!

BESIDES, BY TURNIN' INTO BEN GRIMM AGAIN, I MIGHTA HAD A CHANCE WITH ALICIA--EVEN AGAINST THE SILVER SURFER!

BUT NOW--IT'S TOO LATE! I'M A WALKIN', LIVIN' MONSTER AGAIN!

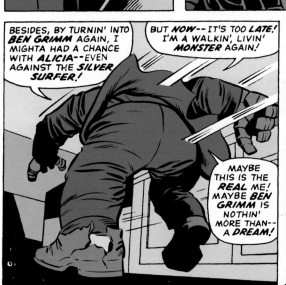

MAYBE THIS IS THE REAL ME! MAYBE BEN GRIMM IS NOTHIN' MORE THAN--A DREAM!

AND, A SCANT FEW SECONDS LATER...

I--I THOUGHT I HEARD SOMEONE--AT THE DOOR--?

BUT--NO ONE IS HERE NOW!

YET, I HAD THE STRANGEST FEELING--IN MY HEART--AS THOUGH IT WAS SOMEONE--WHOM I LOVE!

BUT NOW, LET'S RUSH BACK TO THE BAXTER BUILDING BEFORE THE THING GETS THERE, BECAUSE WE DON'T WANT TO MISS THIS NEXT EVENT--

REED! REED, MY DARLING--IT'S YOU--YOU'RE ALIVE!

HE DID IT! I'M BACK!

THWOOSH

BEN SAVED YOU! I KNEW HE WOULD--I KNEW IT! HE'S NEVER FAILED US YET!

BUT--REED! WHERE IS HE? HE DIDN'T RETURN WITH YOU! WHAT HAPPENED TO HIM??

SUE--I DON'T KNOW--HOW TO SAY IT--! IT HAPPENED SO QUICKLY! ONE MINUTE WE WERE TOGETHER--AND THEN--IT WAS OVER!

I OWE HIM MY LIFE--!

19

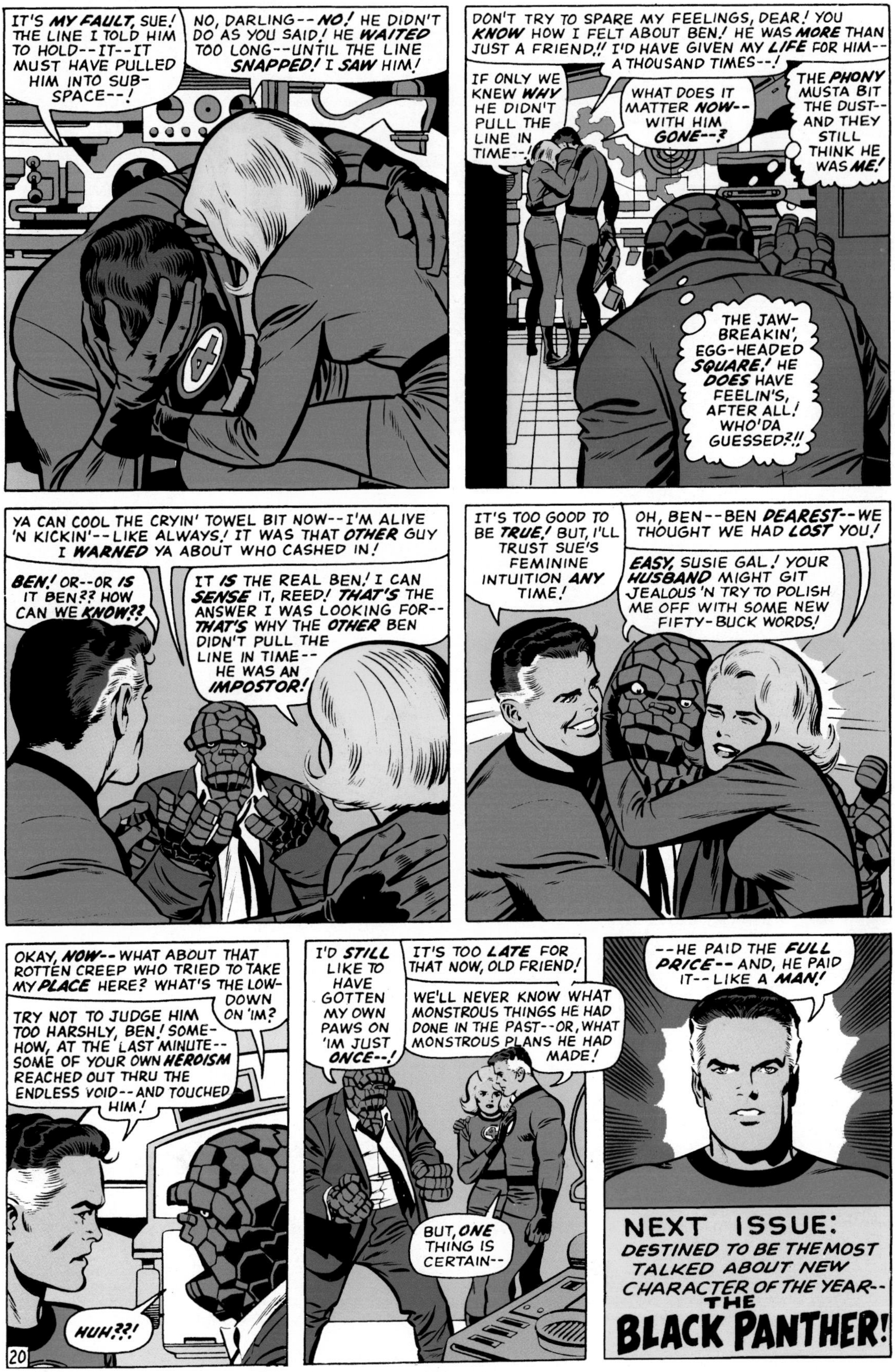
IT'S MY FAULT, SUE! THE LINE I TOLD HIM TO HOLD--IT--IT MUST HAVE PULLED HIM INTO SUB-SPACE--!
NO, DARLING--NO! HE DIDN'T DO AS YOU SAID! HE WAITED TOO LONG--UNTIL THE LINE SNAPPED! I SAW HIM!
DON'T TRY TO SPARE MY FEELINGS, DEAR! YOU KNOW HOW I FELT ABOUT BEN! HE WAS MORE THAN JUST A FRIEND!! I'D HAVE GIVEN MY LIFE FOR HIM--A THOUSAND TIMES--!
IF ONLY WE KNEW WHY HE DIDN'T PULL THE LINE IN TIME--!
WHAT DOES IT MATTER NOW--WITH HIM GONE--?
THE PHONY MUSTA BIT THE DUST--AND THEY STILL THINK HE WAS ME!
THE JAW-BREAKIN', EGG-HEADED SQUARE! HE DOES HAVE FEELIN'S, AFTER ALL! WHO'DA GUESSED?!!
YA CAN COOL THE CRYIN' TOWEL BIT NOW--I'M ALIVE 'N KICKIN'--LIKE ALWAYS! IT WAS THAT OTHER GUY I WARNED YA ABOUT WHO CASHED IN!
BEN! OR--OR IS IT BEN?? HOW CAN WE KNOW??
IT IS THE REAL BEN! I CAN SENSE IT, REED! THAT'S THE ANSWER I WAS LOOKING FOR--THAT'S WHY THE OTHER BEN DIDN'T PULL THE LINE IN TIME--HE WAS AN IMPOSTOR!
IT'S TOO GOOD TO BE TRUE! BUT, I'LL TRUST SUE'S FEMININE INTUITION ANY TIME!
OH, BEN--BEN DEAREST--WE THOUGHT WE HAD LOST YOU!
EASY, SUSIE GAL! YOUR HUSBAND MIGHT GIT JEALOUS 'N TRY TO POLISH ME OFF WITH SOME NEW FIFTY-BUCK WORDS!
OKAY, NOW--WHAT ABOUT THAT ROTTEN CREEP WHO TRIED TO TAKE MY PLACE HERE? WHAT'S THE LOW-DOWN ON 'IM?
TRY NOT TO JUDGE HIM TOO HARSHLY, BEN! SOMEHOW, AT THE LAST MINUTE--SOME OF YOUR OWN HEROISM REACHED OUT THRU THE ENDLESS VOID--AND TOUCHED HIM!
HUH??!
20
I'D STILL LIKE TO HAVE GOTTEN MY OWN PAWS ON 'IM JUST ONCE--!
IT'S TOO LATE FOR THAT NOW, OLD FRIEND!
WE'LL NEVER KNOW WHAT MONSTROUS THINGS HE HAD DONE IN THE PAST--OR, WHAT MONSTROUS PLANS HE HAD MADE!
BUT, ONE THING IS CERTAIN--
--HE PAID THE FULL PRICE--AND, HE PAID IT--LIKE A MAN!
NEXT ISSUE:
DESTINED TO BE THE MOST TALKED ABOUT NEW CHARACTER OF THE YEAR--THE BLACK PANTHER!

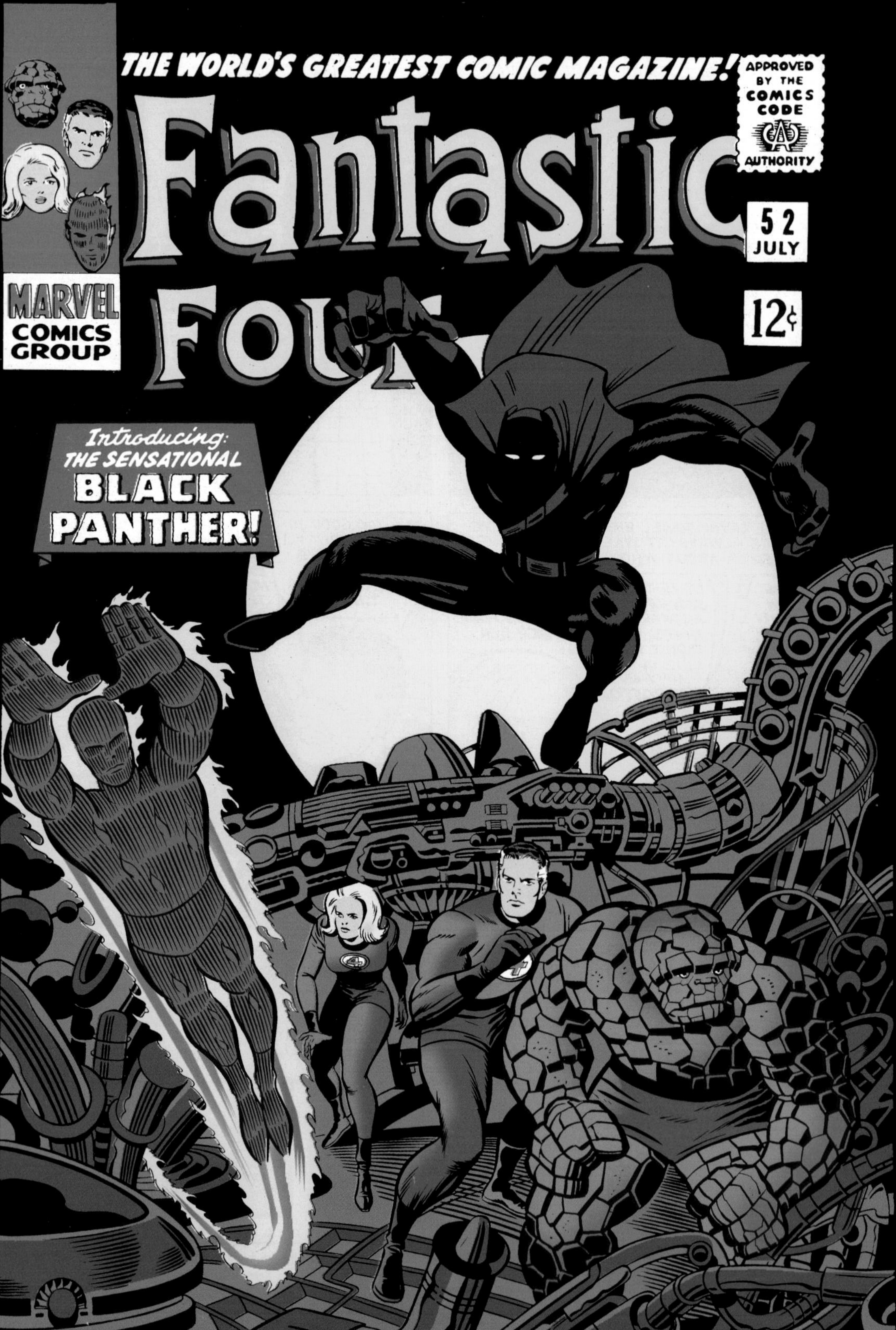
THE WORLD'S GREATEST COMIC MAGAZINE!
APPROVED BY THE COMICS CODE AUTHORITY
Fantastic Four
52 JULY
MARVEL COMICS GROUP
12¢
Introducing: THE SENSATIONAL BLACK PANTHER!

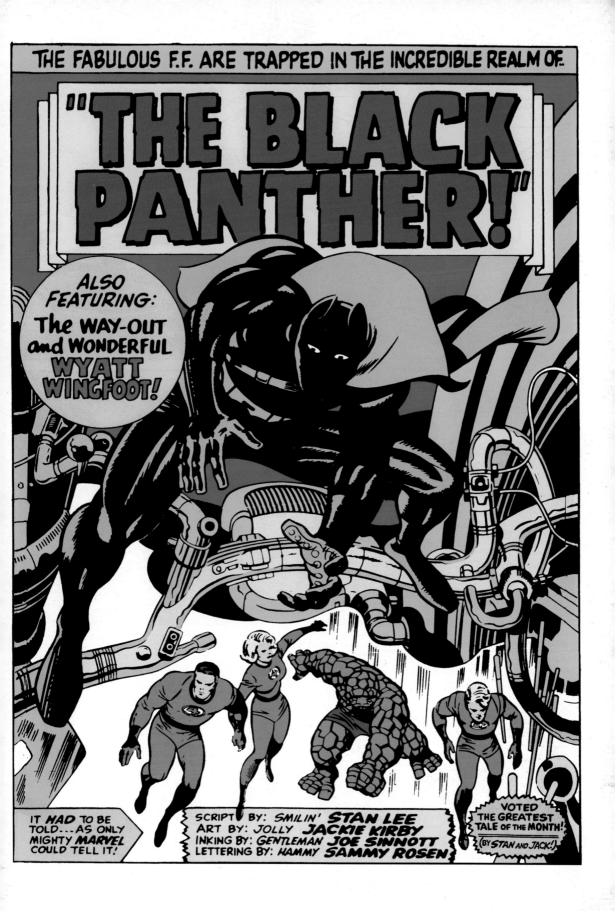

THE FABULOUS F.F. ARE TRAPPED IN THE INCREDIBLE REALM OF...

"THE BLACK PANTHER!"

ALSO FEATURING: The WAY-OUT and WONDERFUL WYATT WINGFOOT!

IT *HAD* TO BE TOLD...AS ONLY MIGHTY *MARVEL* COULD TELL IT!

SCRIPT BY: SMILIN' **STAN LEE**
ART BY: JOLLY **JACKIE KIRBY**
INKING BY: GENTLEMAN **JOE SINNOTT**
LETTERING BY: HAMMY **SAMMY ROSEN**

VOTED THE GREATEST TALE OF THE MONTH! (BY *STAN* AND *JACK!*)

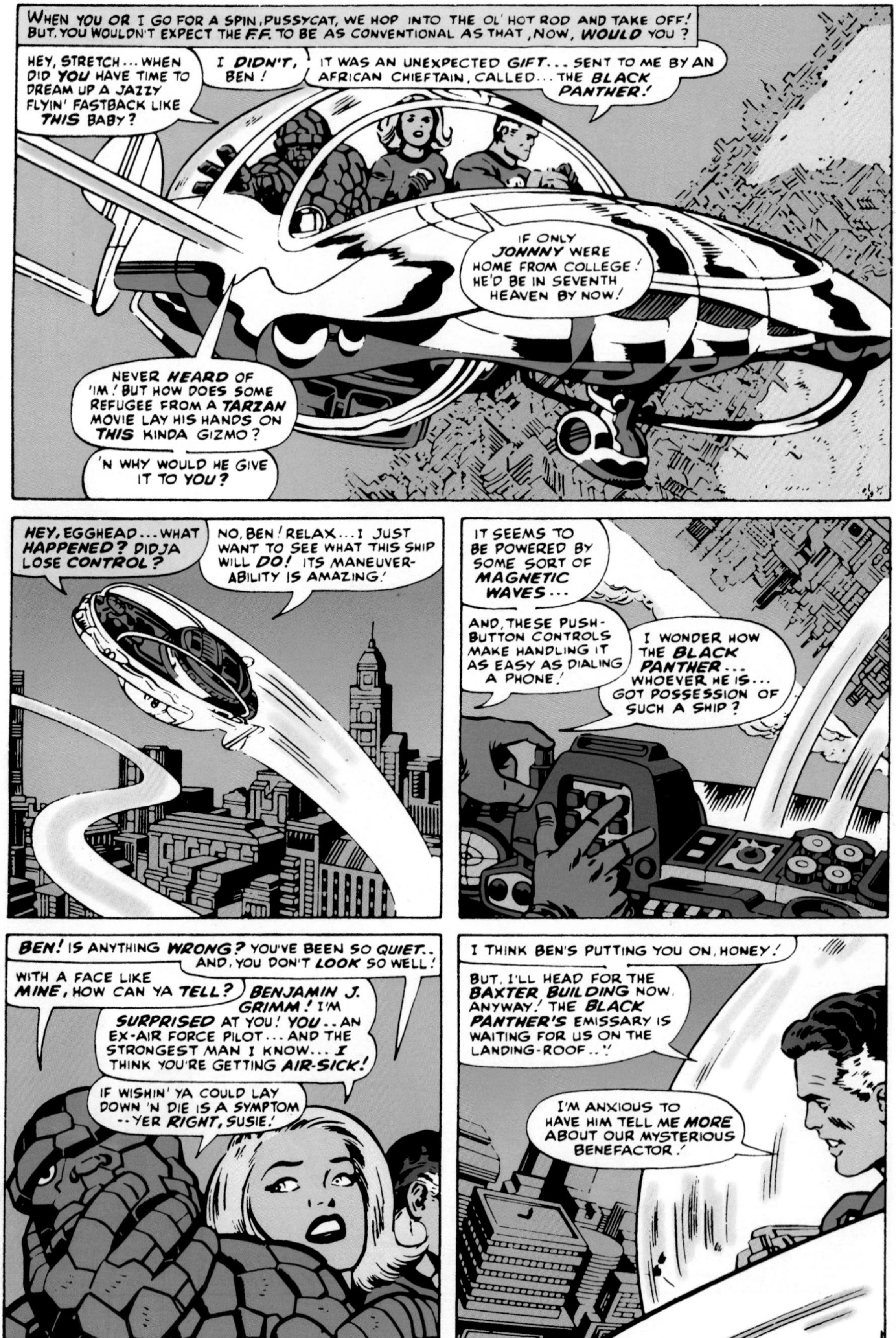
WHEN YOU OR I GO FOR A SPIN, PUSSYCAT, WE HOP INTO THE OL' HOT ROD AND TAKE OFF! BUT, YOU WOULDN'T EXPECT THE F.F. TO BE AS CONVENTIONAL AS THAT, NOW, WOULD YOU?
HEY, STRETCH... WHEN DID YOU HAVE TIME TO DREAM UP A JAZZY FLYIN' FASTBACK LIKE THIS BABY?
I DIDN'T, BEN!
IT WAS AN UNEXPECTED GIFT... SENT TO ME BY AN AFRICAN CHIEFTAIN, CALLED... THE BLACK PANTHER!
IF ONLY JOHNNY WERE HOME FROM COLLEGE! HE'D BE IN SEVENTH HEAVEN BY NOW!
NEVER HEARD OF 'IM! BUT HOW DOES SOME REFUGEE FROM A TARZAN MOVIE LAY HIS HANDS ON THIS KINDA GIZMO?
'N WHY WOULD HE GIVE IT TO YOU?
HEY, EGGHEAD... WHAT HAPPENED? DIDJA LOSE CONTROL?
NO, BEN! RELAX... I JUST WANT TO SEE WHAT THIS SHIP WILL DO! ITS MANEUVER-ABILITY IS AMAZING!
IT SEEMS TO BE POWERED BY SOME SORT OF MAGNETIC WAVES...
AND, THESE PUSH-BUTTON CONTROLS MAKE HANDLING IT AS EASY AS DIALING A PHONE!
I WONDER HOW THE BLACK PANTHER... WHOEVER HE IS... GOT POSSESSION OF SUCH A SHIP?
BEN! IS ANYTHING WRONG? YOU'VE BEEN SO QUIET.. AND, YOU DON'T LOOK SO WELL!
WITH A FACE LIKE MINE, HOW CAN YA TELL?
BENJAMIN J. GRIMM! I'M SURPRISED AT YOU! YOU.. AN EX-AIR FORCE PILOT... AND THE STRONGEST MAN I KNOW... I THINK YOU'RE GETTING AIR-SICK!
IF WISHIN' YA COULD LAY DOWN 'N DIE IS A SYMPTOM --YER RIGHT, SUSIE!
I THINK BEN'S PUTTING YOU ON, HONEY!
BUT, I'LL HEAD FOR THE BAXTER BUILDING NOW, ANYWAY! THE BLACK PANTHER'S EMISSARY IS WAITING FOR US ON THE LANDING-ROOF..!
I'M ANXIOUS TO HAVE HIM TELL ME MORE ABOUT OUR MYSTERIOUS BENEFACTOR!

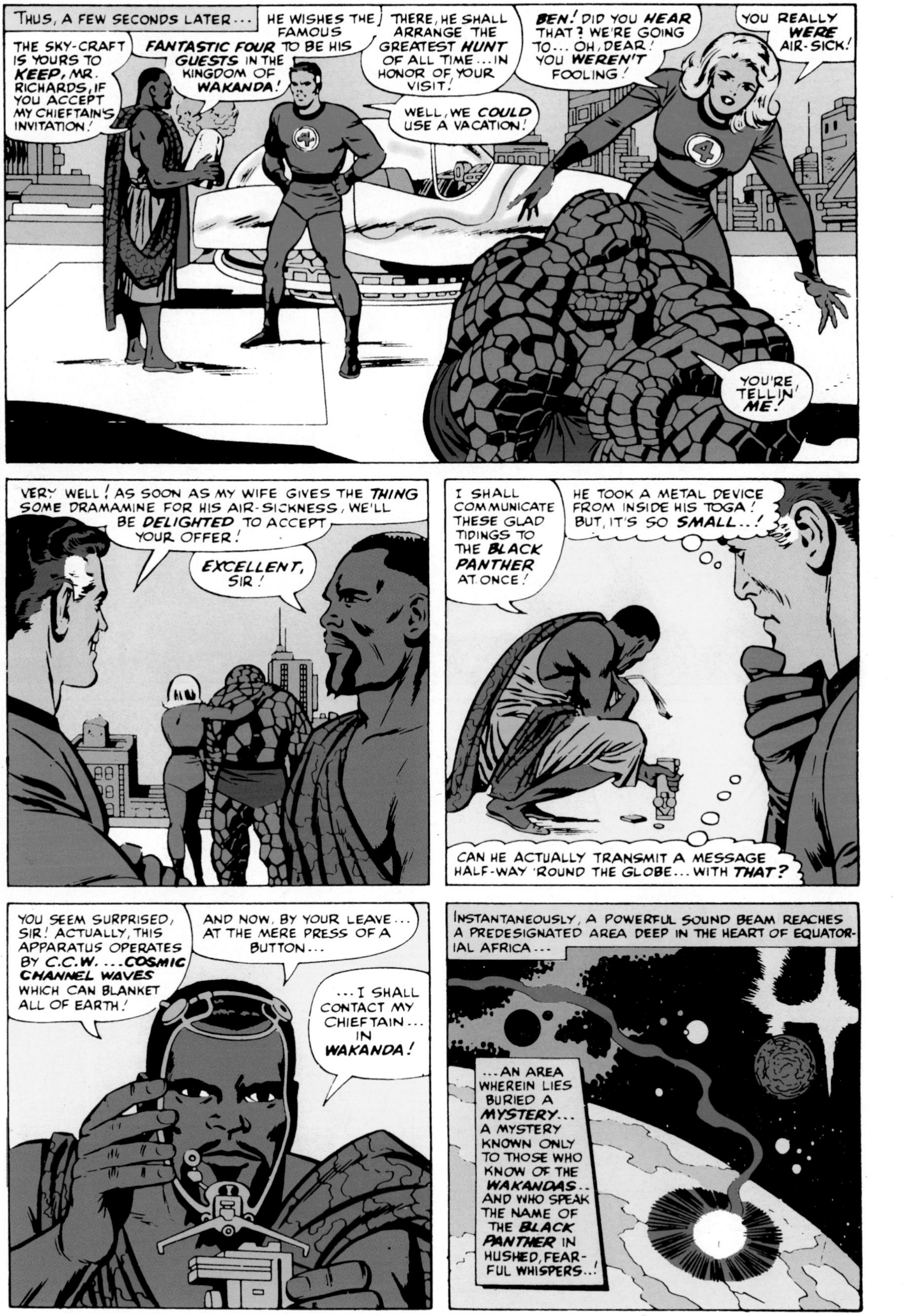
THUS, A FEW SECONDS LATER...
THE SKY-CRAFT IS YOURS TO KEEP, MR. RICHARDS, IF YOU ACCEPT MY CHIEFTAIN'S INVITATION!
HE WISHES THE FAMOUS FANTASTIC FOUR TO BE HIS GUESTS IN THE KINGDOM OF WAKANDA!
THERE, HE SHALL ARRANGE THE GREATEST HUNT OF ALL TIME... IN HONOR OF YOUR VISIT!
WELL, WE COULD USE A VACATION!
BEN! DID YOU HEAR THAT? WE'RE GOING TO... OH, DEAR! YOU WEREN'T FOOLING!
YOU REALLY WERE AIR-SICK!
YOU'RE TELLIN' ME!
VERY WELL! AS SOON AS MY WIFE GIVES THE THING SOME DRAMAMINE FOR HIS AIR-SICKNESS, WE'LL BE DELIGHTED TO ACCEPT YOUR OFFER!
EXCELLENT, SIR!
I SHALL COMMUNICATE THESE GLAD TIDINGS TO THE BLACK PANTHER AT ONCE!
HE TOOK A METAL DEVICE FROM INSIDE HIS TOGA! BUT, IT'S SO SMALL..!
CAN HE ACTUALLY TRANSMIT A MESSAGE HALF-WAY 'ROUND THE GLOBE... WITH THAT?
YOU SEEM SURPRISED, SIR! ACTUALLY, THIS APPARATUS OPERATES BY C.C.W. ... COSMIC CHANNEL WAVES WHICH CAN BLANKET ALL OF EARTH!
AND NOW, BY YOUR LEAVE... AT THE MERE PRESS OF A BUTTON...
...I SHALL CONTACT MY CHIEFTAIN... IN WAKANDA!
INSTANTANEOUSLY, A POWERFUL SOUND BEAM REACHES A PREDESIGNATED AREA DEEP IN THE HEART OF EQUATORIAL AFRICA...
...AN AREA WHEREIN LIES BURIED A MYSTERY... A MYSTERY KNOWN ONLY TO THOSE WHO KNOW OF THE WAKANDAS.. AND WHO SPEAK THE NAME OF THE BLACK PANTHER IN HUSHED, FEARFUL WHISPERS..!

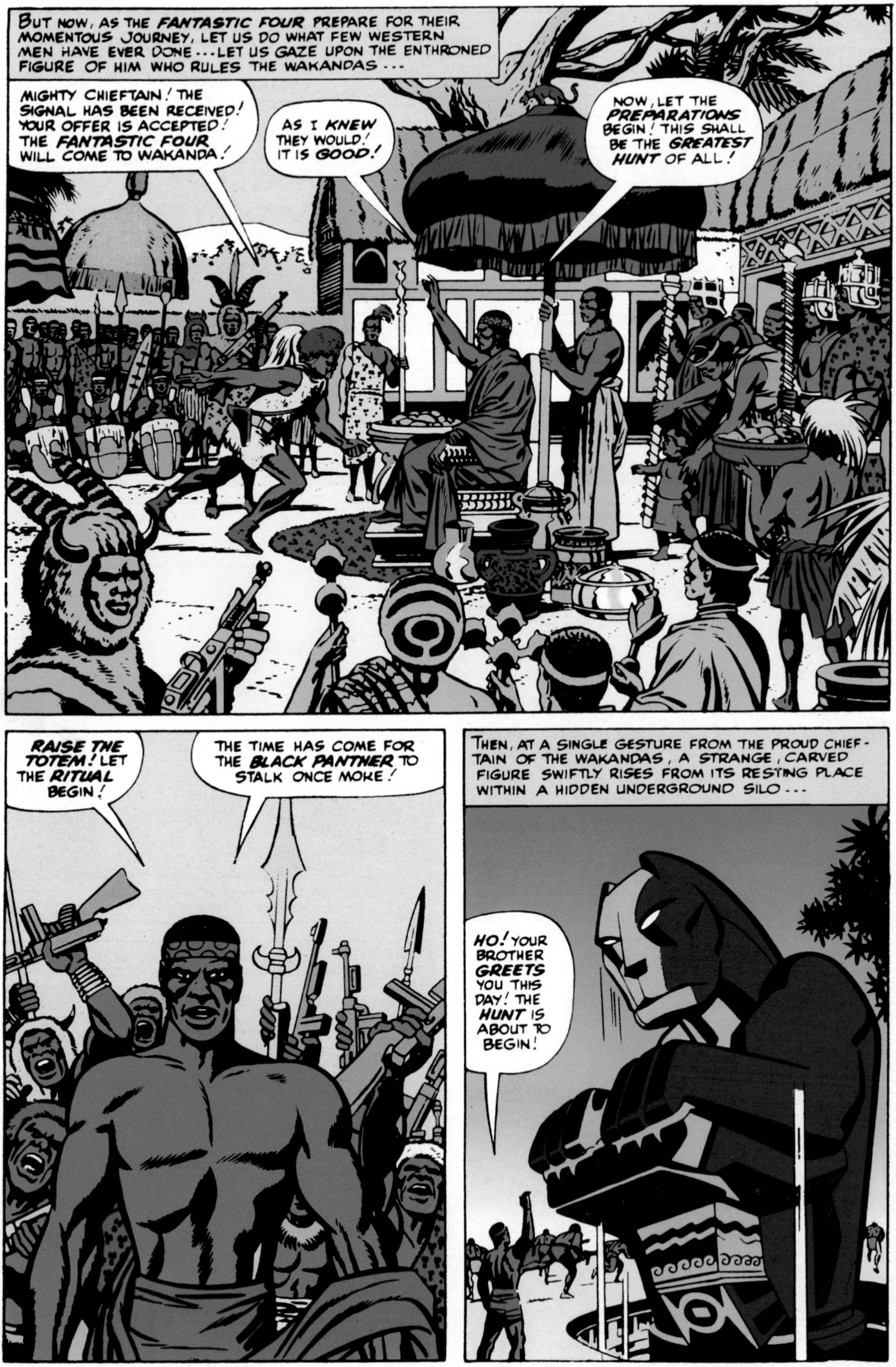

BUT NOW, AS THE FANTASTIC FOUR PREPARE FOR THEIR MOMENTOUS JOURNEY, LET US DO WHAT FEW WESTERN MEN HAVE EVER DONE... LET US GAZE UPON THE ENTHRONED FIGURE OF HIM WHO RULES THE WAKANDAS...
MIGHTY CHIEFTAIN! THE SIGNAL HAS BEEN RECEIVED! YOUR OFFER IS ACCEPTED! THE FANTASTIC FOUR WILL COME TO WAKANDA!
AS I KNEW THEY WOULD! IT IS GOOD!
NOW, LET THE PREPARATIONS BEGIN! THIS SHALL BE THE GREATEST HUNT OF ALL!
RAISE THE TOTEM! LET THE RITUAL BEGIN!
THE TIME HAS COME FOR THE BLACK PANTHER TO STALK ONCE MORE!
THEN, AT A SINGLE GESTURE FROM THE PROUD CHIEFTAIN OF THE WAKANDAS, A STRANGE, CARVED FIGURE SWIFTLY RISES FROM ITS RESTING PLACE WITHIN A HIDDEN UNDERGROUND SILO...
HO! YOUR BROTHER GREETS YOU THIS DAY! THE HUNT IS ABOUT TO BEGIN!

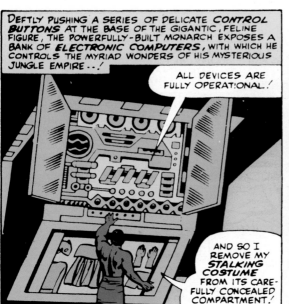

DEFTLY PUSHING A SERIES OF DELICATE *CONTROL BUTTONS* AT THE BASE OF THE GIGANTIC, FELINE FIGURE, THE POWERFULLY-BUILT MONARCH EXPOSES A BANK OF *ELECTRONIC COMPUTERS*, WITH WHICH HE CONTROLS THE MYRIAD WONDERS OF HIS MYSTERIOUS JUNGLE EMPIRE...!

ALL DEVICES ARE FULLY OPERATIONAL!

AND SO I REMOVE MY *STALKING COSTUME* FROM ITS CAREFULLY CONCEALED COMPARTMENT!

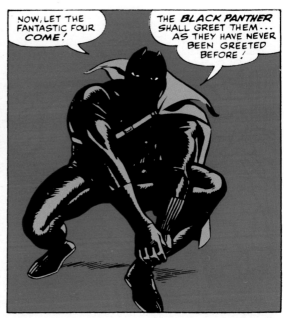

NOW, LET THE FANTASTIC FOUR *COME!*

THE *BLACK PANTHER* SHALL GREET THEM... AS THEY HAVE NEVER BEEN GREETED BEFORE!

WHILE, IN A QUIET ROOM IN NORTHFIELD DORMITORY, ON THE CAMPUS OF *METRO COLLEGE*, WE FIND...

I WONDER IF I PASSED TODAY'S EXAM?

I SURE DON'T WANT REED, SUE AND BEN TO BE *ASHAMED* OF ME!

NOTHING BOTHERS OL' WYATT! I'M SURPRISED HE EVEN MANAGED TO STAY AWAKE *DURING* THE TEST!

I CAN'T WAIT TILL *MORNING*... TO HEAD BACK HOME FOR *VACATION!*

IT'S HARD...HARDER THAN I *THOUGHT* IT WOULD BE...TO CONCENTRATE ON MY COURSES... WHEN I CAN'T GET *CRYSTAL* OUT OF MY MIND!

BUT, I'VE GOT TO KEEP *TRYING!* UNTIL REED CAN FIND SOME WAY TO BREAK THE *BARRIER* THAT HOLDS HER PRISONER,* THERE'S NOTHING I CAN DO!

NOTHING BUT HOPE...AND DREAM... AND PRAY!

I'VE GOT TO SNAP *OUT* OF IT...AND I *WILL!* IF ONLY THE *EVENINGS* WEREN'T SO LONG..!

* IF YOU MISSED F.F. #46, DON'T TELL US! YOU KNOW HOW UPSET WE GET! ... SHAKY STAN.

HEY!! HOLY HANNAH!! WHAT THE...?!!

SURPRISE!

HIYA, JOE COLLEGE! WHAT'S THE GOOD WORD, LITTLE ITTY BITTY BUDDY?

I'LL ITTY BITTY BUDDY *YOU,* YOU BLUE-EYED BIRDBRAIN!!

I *KNOWED* YA'D BE AS GOOD-NATURED AS EVER, JUNIOR!

LEGGO, BEFORE I GIVE YOU A HOTFOOT BETWEEN WHERE YOUR *EARS* OUGHTTA BE!

WHAT KINDA CRUMMY COLLEGE *IS* THIS? YA DON'T LOOK ANY MORE *EJJICATED* TO *ME!*

OH, JOHNNY... JOHNNY! IT'S SO GOOD TO SEE MY LITTLE KID BROTHER AGAIN!

SAME HERE, SIS! BUT YOU DON'T HAVETA BREAK MY RIBS TO *PROVE* IT!

GIMME *FIVE*, NEW BROTHER-IN-LAW! BUT TELL ME...HOW'D YOU ALL *GET* HERE SO FAST?

IT WAS A *BREEZE*, JOHNNY! WE FLEW IN BY LIGHTNING-FAST *MAGNETIC WAVES!*

GOSH, REED... YOU'VE TURNED INTO A GREAT *KIDDER* WHILE I WAS GONE, HUH?

I'M NOT KIDDING, LAD!

IT'S A NEW SHIP...OPERATES ON A BRAND NEW PRINCIPLE! IT WAS THE GIFT OF AN AFRICAN CHIEFTAIN!

NOW I *KNOW* YOU'RE CONNIN' ME! HOW DOES AN AFRICAN CHIEFTAIN LATCH ONTO A PLANE THAT FLIES BY MAGNETIC WAVES?

THAT, LITTLE PARTNER, IS JUST WHAT WE'RE GOING TO *FIND OUT!*

WE'RE LEAVING FOR *WAKANDA*... RIGHT AWAY! AND *YOU'RE* GOING WITH US!

LIKE *WOW*, BROTHER-IN-LAW! THAT'S THE *GEAREST!*

BUT LOOK... CAN I BRING MY BUDDY, *WYATT WINGFOOT*? HE'LL *FLIP!*

SURE, JOHNNY!

ANY BUDDY OF *YOURS* IS A BUDDY OF *OURS*, JOHNNY BOY!

ONE THING GOOD ABOUT 'IM...ANY GUY WHO CAN SLEEP LIKE *THAT* AIN'T GONNA BE KEEPIN' US AWAKE BY *JAWIN'* ALL NIGHT!

HEY, KID... HE'S *ALIVE*, AIN'T HE?

IT'S HARD TO TELL, BEN! WYATT DOESN'T *MOVE* VERY FAST... UNLESS HE *WANTS* TO! BUT WHEN HE *DOES*... WATCH OUT!

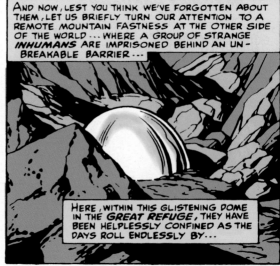

AND NOW, LEST YOU THINK WE'VE FORGOTTEN ABOUT THEM, LET US BRIEFLY TURN OUR ATTENTION TO A REMOTE MOUNTAIN FASTNESS AT THE OTHER SIDE OF THE WORLD...WHERE A GROUP OF STRANGE *INHUMANS* ARE IMPRISONED BEHIND AN UN-BREAKABLE BARRIER...

HERE, WITHIN THIS GLISTENING DOME IN THE *GREAT REFUGE*, THEY HAVE BEEN HELPLESSLY CONFINED AS THE DAYS ROLL ENDLESSLY BY...

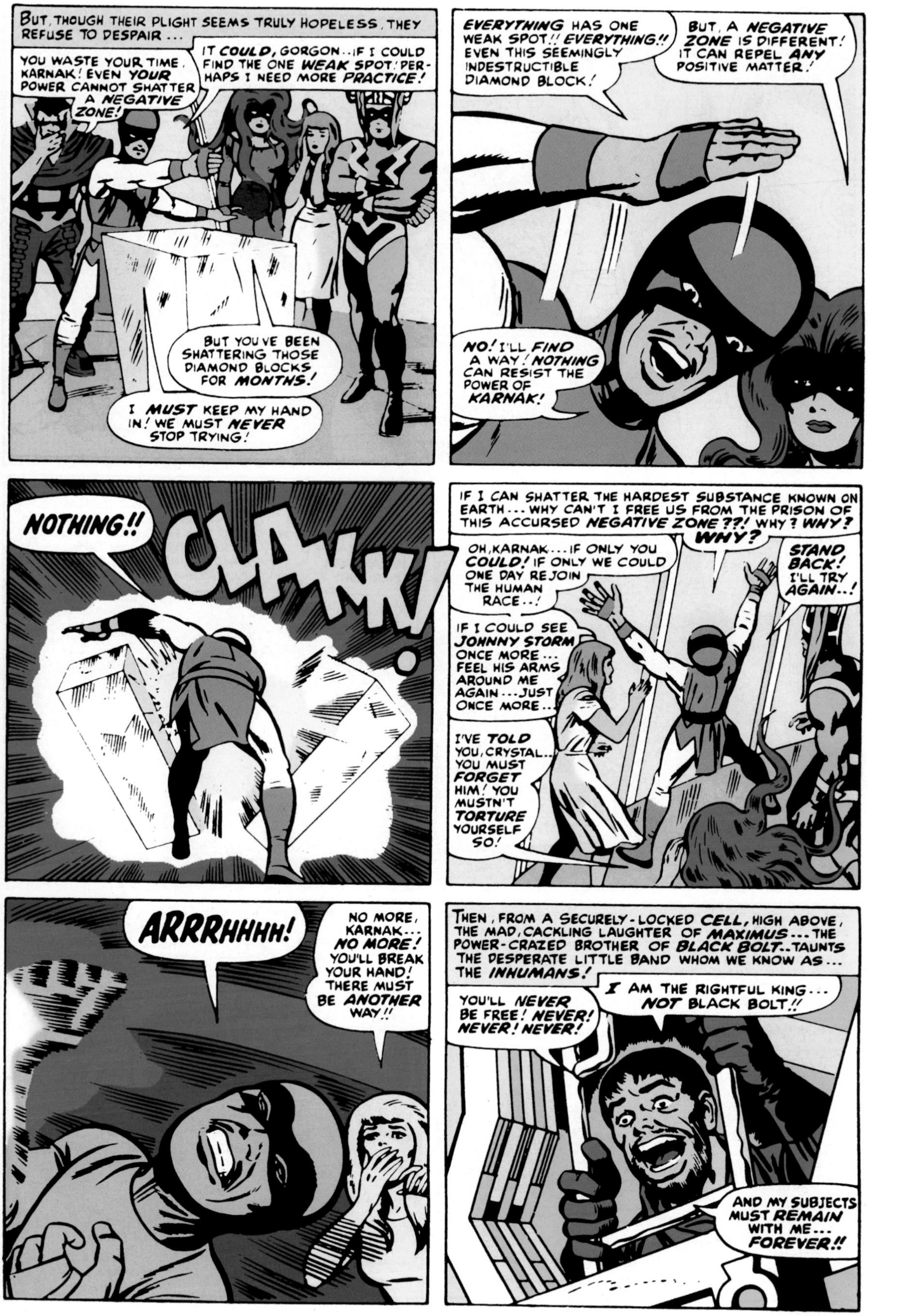

BUT, THOUGH THEIR PLIGHT SEEMS TRULY HOPELESS, THEY REFUSE TO DESPAIR...
YOU WASTE YOUR TIME, KARNAK! EVEN YOUR POWER CANNOT SHATTER A NEGATIVE ZONE!
IT COULD, GORGON.. IF I COULD FIND THE ONE WEAK SPOT! PERHAPS I NEED MORE PRACTICE!
BUT YOU'VE BEEN SHATTERING THOSE DIAMOND BLOCKS FOR MONTHS!
I MUST KEEP MY HAND IN! WE MUST NEVER STOP TRYING!
EVERYTHING HAS ONE WEAK SPOT!! EVERYTHING!! EVEN THIS SEEMINGLY INDESTRUCTIBLE DIAMOND BLOCK!
BUT, A NEGATIVE ZONE IS DIFFERENT! IT CAN REPEL ANY POSITIVE MATTER!
NO! I'LL FIND A WAY! NOTHING CAN RESIST THE POWER OF KARNAK!
NOTHING!!
CLAKK!
IF I CAN SHATTER THE HARDEST SUBSTANCE KNOWN ON EARTH... WHY CAN'T I FREE US FROM THE PRISON OF THIS ACCURSED NEGATIVE ZONE??! WHY? WHY? WHY?
OH, KARNAK... IF ONLY YOU COULD! IF ONLY WE COULD ONE DAY REJOIN THE HUMAN RACE..!
STAND BACK! I'LL TRY AGAIN..!
IF I COULD SEE JOHNNY STORM ONCE MORE... FEEL HIS ARMS AROUND ME AGAIN... JUST ONCE MORE...
I'VE TOLD YOU, CRYSTAL... YOU MUST FORGET HIM! YOU MUSTN'T TORTURE YOURSELF SO!
ARRRHHHH!
NO MORE, KARNAK... NO MORE! YOU'LL BREAK YOUR HAND! THERE MUST BE ANOTHER WAY!!
THEN, FROM A SECURELY-LOCKED CELL, HIGH ABOVE, THE MAD, CACKLING LAUGHTER OF MAXIMUS... THE POWER-CRAZED BROTHER OF BLACK BOLT.. TAUNTS THE DESPERATE LITTLE BAND WHOM WE KNOW AS... THE INHUMANS!
YOU'LL NEVER BE FREE! NEVER! NEVER! NEVER!
I AM THE RIGHTFUL KING... NOT BLACK BOLT!!
AND MY SUBJECTS MUST REMAIN WITH ME... FOREVER!!

WHAT MONUMENTAL *IRONY!* ONLY *MAXIMUS* KNOWS THE SECRET OF ESCAPING FROM THE NEGATIVE ZONE!! THUS, THE KEY WILL BE ETERNALLY LOCKED IN A *MADMAN'S BRAIN!*

BUT, FOR *ME,* IT MAY BE... TOO LATE! WHAT IF *JOHNNY STORM* HAS FOUND ANOTHER?

AHH, *BLACK BOLT*.. IT IS *YOU* WHO ARE THE MIGHTIEST AMONG US... AND EVEN *YOU* STAND HELPLESS!

WE MUST *NEVER* ABANDON HOPE! I KNOW THE MAN I LOVE WILL NOT FAIL US! SOME DAY.. SOMEHOW..*BLACK BOLT* WILL FIND THE WAY TO FREE US ALL!

I'LL NEVER STOP TRYING! NEVER! NEVER...

'TIS ALMOST *GOOD* THAT YOU HAVE LOST THE POWER OF SPEECH... FOR, OF WHAT USE ARE *WORDS* TO US..NOW?

AND *THAT,* FRANTIC ONE, IS ALL WE'LL SEE OF THE INHUMANS THIS ISH.! WE JUST WANTED TO WHET YOUR APPETITE A BIT! BESIDES, IT'S TIME TO VISIT *WAKANDA*...SO C'MON..THE SAFARI'S JUST LEAVING...

SHIP APPROACHES! ALL GOES AS PLANNED!

AS THE CHIEFTAIN HAS PROMISED... THIS WILL BE HIS GREATEST HUNT!

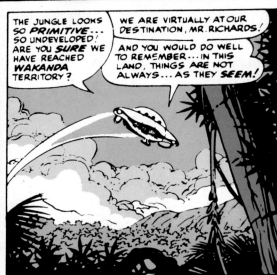

THE JUNGLE LOOKS SO *PRIMITIVE*... SO UNDEVELOPED! ARE YOU *SURE* WE HAVE REACHED *WAKANDA* TERRITORY?

WE ARE VIRTUALLY AT OUR DESTINATION, MR. RICHARDS!

AND YOU WOULD DO WELL TO REMEMBER....IN THIS LAND, THINGS ARE NOT ALWAYS... AS THEY *SEEM!*

IT'S SO HARD TO BELIEVE THAT A SHIP SUCH AS *THIS* ONE COULD HAVE COME FROM A LAND WITH NO SIGN OF TECHNOLOGY ...OF INDUSTRIAL DEVELOPMENT...!

BEFORE YOUR VISIT IS ENDED, MRS. RICHARDS, YOU WILL FIND MANY *MORE* SURPRISING FACETS OF OUR·LITTLE KINGDOM!

I DON'T *LIKE* IT! THERE'S SOMETHING *OMINOUS* IN THE AIR... AND YET, I DON'T WANT TO ALARM *SUE!*

IT'S TOO LATE TO TURN BACK NOW! I'LL JUST HAVE TO REMAIN *ON GUARD!*

GOOD OL' *WYATT!* I GUESS HE'S JUST NOT MUCH FOR SIGHT-SEEING!

IF THEY HAD A *KENTUCKY DERBY* FOR SLEEPERS....I'D PUT MY WHOLE WAD ON *HIM!*

I'LL BET HE COULDA SNORED HIS WAY THROUGH THE BATTLE OF THE BULGE!

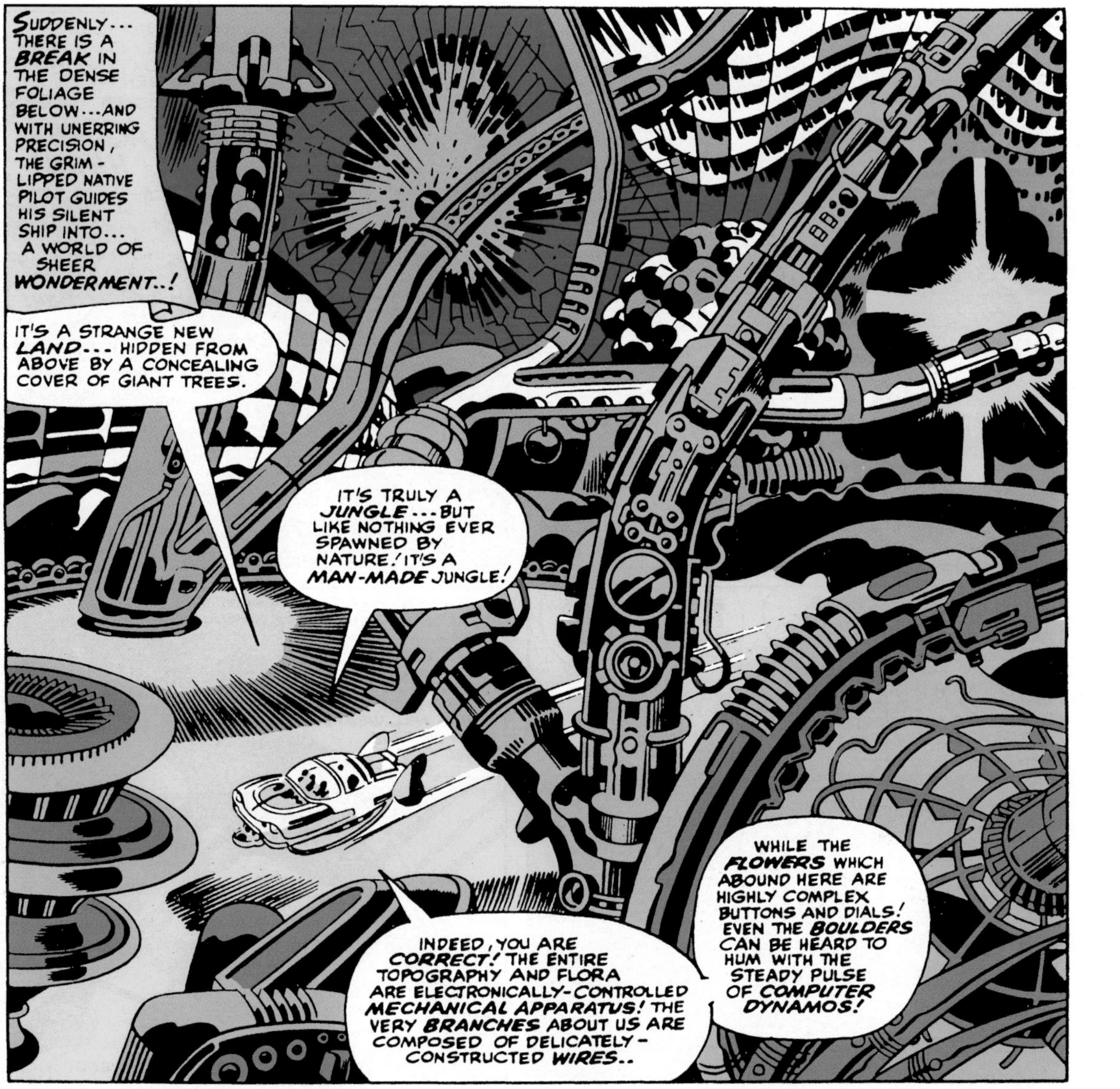
SUDDENLY... THERE IS A BREAK IN THE DENSE FOLIAGE BELOW...AND WITH UNERRING PRECISION, THE GRIM-LIPPED NATIVE PILOT GUIDES HIS SILENT SHIP INTO... A WORLD OF SHEER WONDERMENT..!
IT'S A STRANGE NEW LAND... HIDDEN FROM ABOVE BY A CONCEALING COVER OF GIANT TREES.
IT'S TRULY A JUNGLE... BUT LIKE NOTHING EVER SPAWNED BY NATURE! IT'S A MAN-MADE JUNGLE!
INDEED, YOU ARE CORRECT! THE ENTIRE TOPOGRAPHY AND FLORA ARE ELECTRONICALLY-CONTROLLED MECHANICAL APPARATUS! THE VERY BRANCHES ABOUT US ARE COMPOSED OF DELICATELY-CONSTRUCTED WIRES..
WHILE THE FLOWERS WHICH ABOUND HERE ARE HIGHLY COMPLEX BUTTONS AND DIALS! EVEN THE BOULDERS CAN BE HEARD TO HUM WITH THE STEADY PULSE OF COMPUTER DYNAMOS!

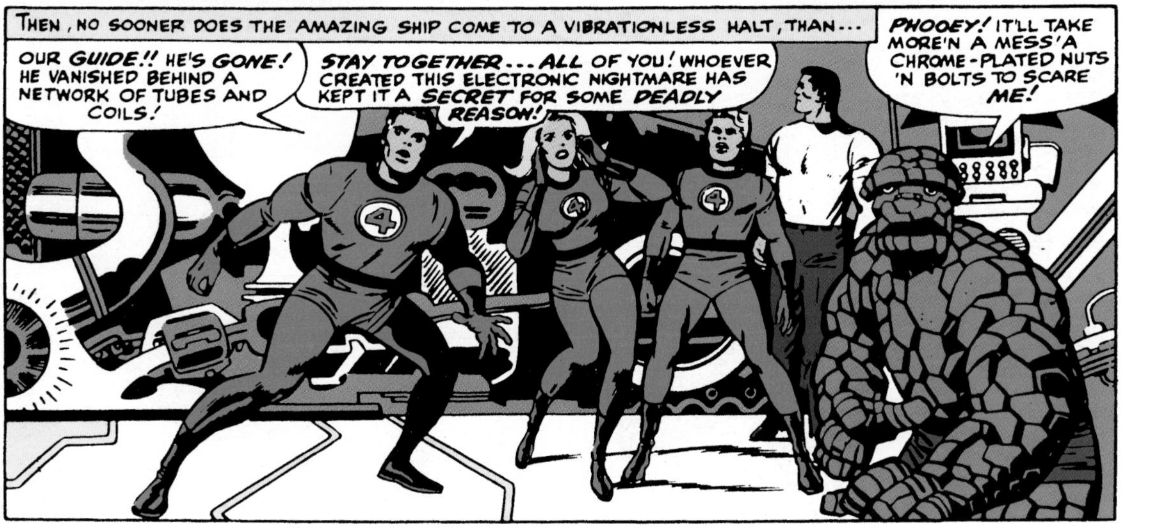
THEN, NO SOONER DOES THE AMAZING SHIP COME TO A VIBRATIONLESS HALT, THAN...
OUR GUIDE!! HE'S GONE! HE VANISHED BEHIND A NETWORK OF TUBES AND COILS!
STAY TOGETHER... ALL OF YOU! WHOEVER CREATED THIS ELECTRONIC NIGHTMARE HAS KEPT IT A SECRET FOR SOME DEADLY REASON!
PHOOEY! IT'LL TAKE MORE'N A MESS'A CHROME-PLATED NUTS 'N BOLTS TO SCARE ME!

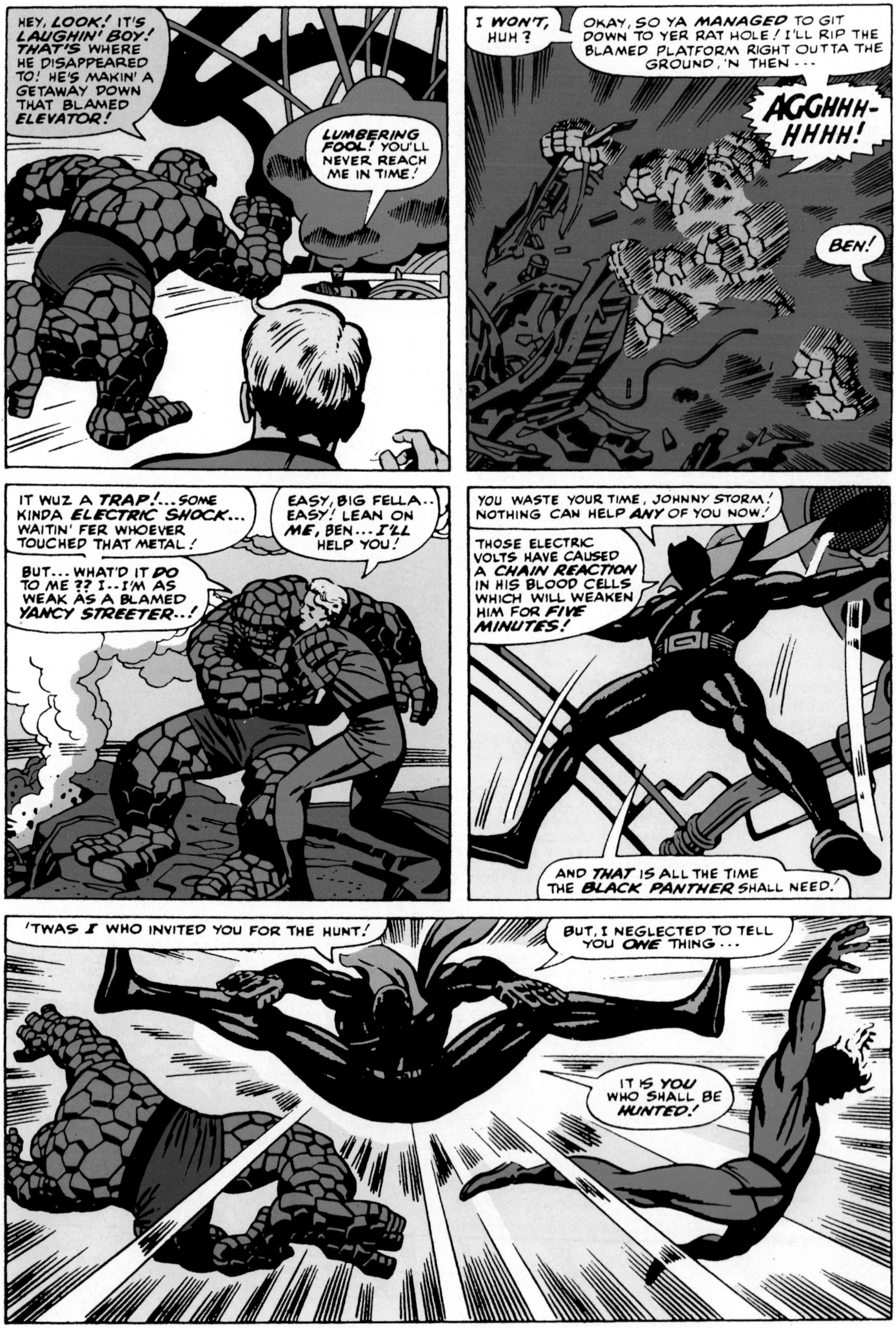

HEY, LOOK! IT'S LAUGHIN' BOY! THAT'S WHERE HE DISAPPEARED TO! HE'S MAKIN' A GETAWAY DOWN THAT BLAMED ELEVATOR!
LUMBERING FOOL! YOU'LL NEVER REACH ME IN TIME!
I WON'T, HUH?
OKAY, SO YA MANAGED TO GIT DOWN TO YER RAT HOLE! I'LL RIP THE BLAMED PLATFORM RIGHT OUTTA THE GROUND, 'N THEN ---
AGGHHH-HHHH!
BEN!
IT WUZ A TRAP!...SOME KINDA ELECTRIC SHOCK... WAITIN' FER WHOEVER TOUCHED THAT METAL!
EASY, BIG FELLA.. EASY! LEAN ON ME, BEN... I'LL HELP YOU!
BUT... WHAT'D IT DO TO ME?? I--I'M AS WEAK AS A BLAMED YANCY STREETER--!
YOU WASTE YOUR TIME, JOHNNY STORM! NOTHING CAN HELP ANY OF YOU NOW!
THOSE ELECTRIC VOLTS HAVE CAUSED A CHAIN REACTION IN HIS BLOOD CELLS WHICH WILL WEAKEN HIM FOR FIVE MINUTES!
AND THAT IS ALL THE TIME THE BLACK PANTHER SHALL NEED!
'TWAS I WHO INVITED YOU FOR THE HUNT!
BUT, I NEGLECTED TO TELL YOU ONE THING ...
IT IS YOU WHO SHALL BE HUNTED!

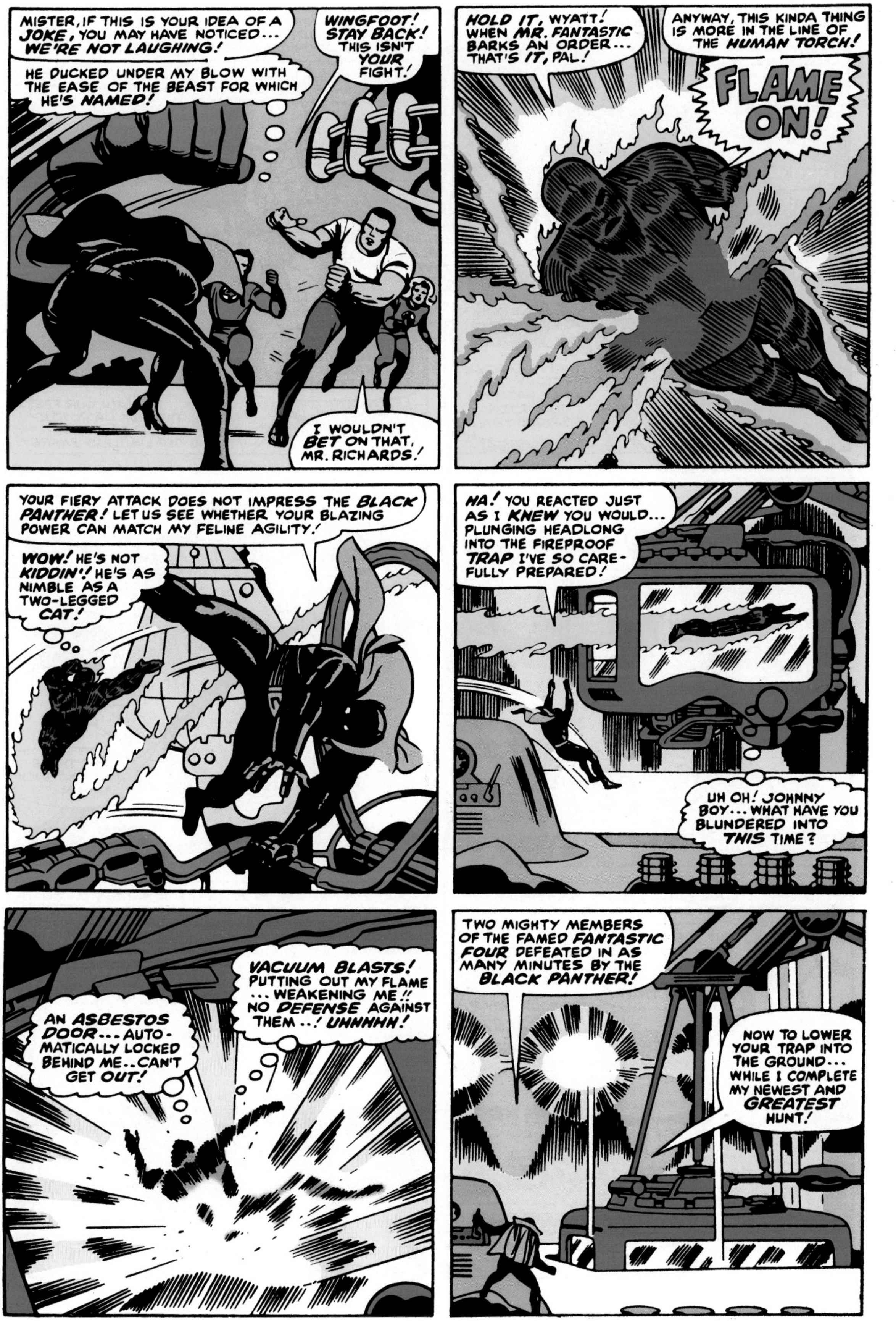
MISTER, IF THIS IS YOUR IDEA OF A JOKE, YOU MAY HAVE NOTICED... WE'RE NOT LAUGHING!
HE DUCKED UNDER MY BLOW WITH THE EASE OF THE BEAST FOR WHICH HE'S NAMED!
WINGFOOT! STAY BACK! THIS ISN'T YOUR FIGHT!
I WOULDN'T BET ON THAT, MR. RICHARDS!
HOLD IT, WYATT! WHEN MR. FANTASTIC BARKS AN ORDER... THAT'S IT, PAL!
ANYWAY, THIS KINDA THING IS MORE IN THE LINE OF THE HUMAN TORCH!
FLAME ON!
YOUR FIERY ATTACK DOES NOT IMPRESS THE BLACK PANTHER! LET US SEE WHETHER YOUR BLAZING POWER CAN MATCH MY FELINE AGILITY!
WOW! HE'S NOT KIDDIN'! HE'S AS NIMBLE AS A TWO-LEGGED CAT!
HA! YOU REACTED JUST AS I KNEW YOU WOULD... PLUNGING HEADLONG INTO THE FIREPROOF TRAP I'VE SO CAREFULLY PREPARED!
UH OH! JOHNNY BOY... WHAT HAVE YOU BLUNDERED INTO THIS TIME?
AN ASBESTOS DOOR... AUTOMATICALLY LOCKED BEHIND ME.. CAN'T GET OUT!
VACUUM BLASTS! PUTTING OUT MY FLAME ... WEAKENING ME!! NO DEFENSE AGAINST THEM..! UHNHHH!
TWO MIGHTY MEMBERS OF THE FAMED FANTASTIC FOUR DEFEATED IN AS MANY MINUTES BY THE BLACK PANTHER!
NOW TO LOWER YOUR TRAP INTO THE GROUND... WHILE I COMPLETE MY NEWEST AND GREATEST HUNT!

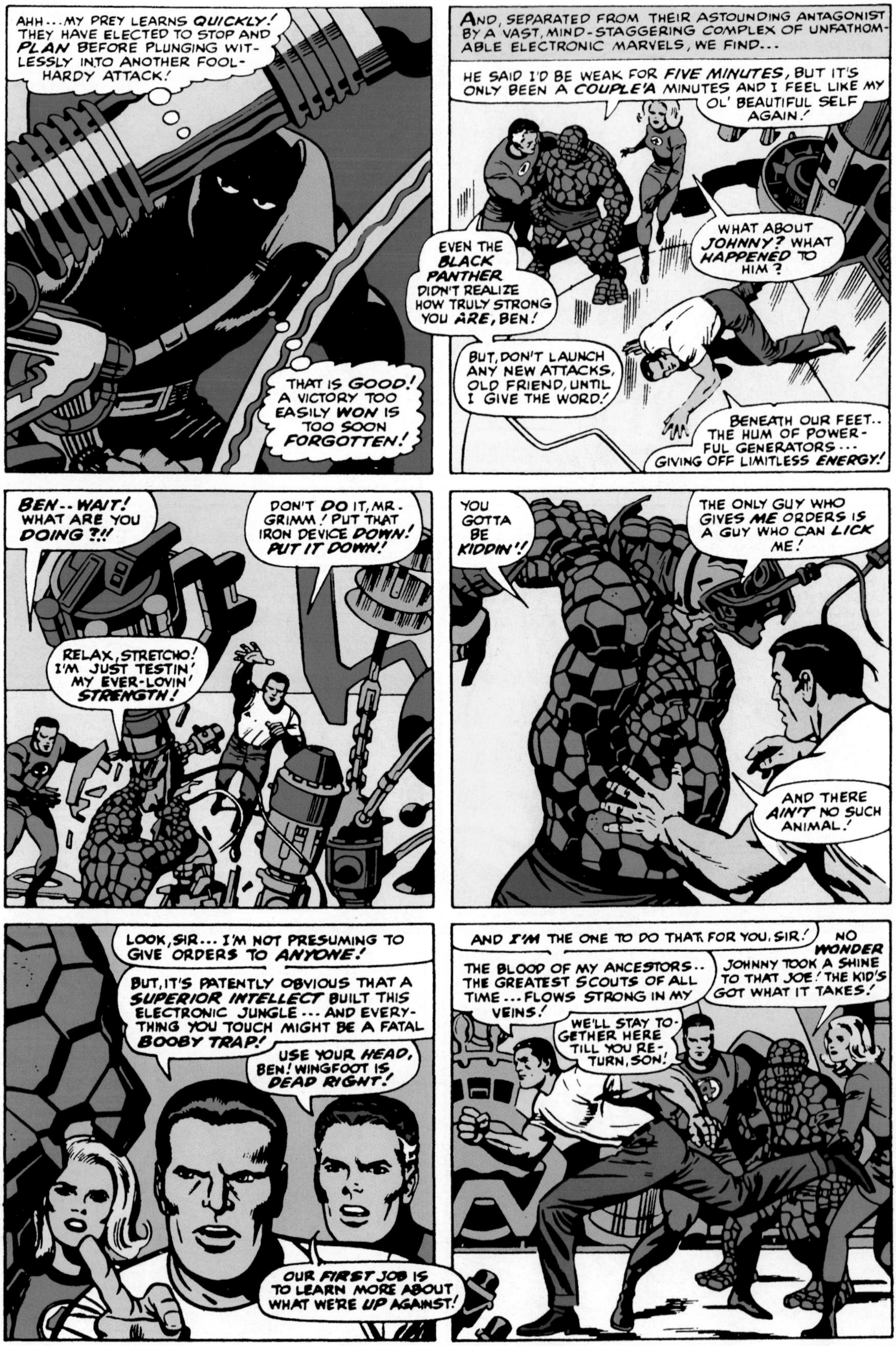
AHH... MY PREY LEARNS QUICKLY! THEY HAVE ELECTED TO STOP AND PLAN BEFORE PLUNGING WITLESSLY INTO ANOTHER FOOLHARDY ATTACK!
THAT IS GOOD! A VICTORY TOO EASILY WON IS TOO SOON FORGOTTEN!
AND, SEPARATED FROM THEIR ASTOUNDING ANTAGONIST BY A VAST, MIND-STAGGERING COMPLEX OF UNFATHOMABLE ELECTRONIC MARVELS, WE FIND...
HE SAID I'D BE WEAK FOR FIVE MINUTES, BUT IT'S ONLY BEEN A COUPLE'A MINUTES AND I FEEL LIKE MY OL' BEAUTIFUL SELF AGAIN!
WHAT ABOUT JOHNNY? WHAT HAPPENED TO HIM?
EVEN THE BLACK PANTHER DIDN'T REALIZE HOW TRULY STRONG YOU ARE, BEN!
BUT, DON'T LAUNCH ANY NEW ATTACKS, OLD FRIEND, UNTIL I GIVE THE WORD!
BENEATH OUR FEET.. THE HUM OF POWERFUL GENERATORS... GIVING OFF LIMITLESS ENERGY!
BEN--WAIT! WHAT ARE YOU DOING?!!
DON'T DO IT, MR. GRIMM! PUT THAT IRON DEVICE DOWN! PUT IT DOWN!
RELAX, STRETCHO! I'M JUST TESTIN' MY EVER-LOVIN' STRENGTH!
YOU GOTTA BE KIDDIN'!!
THE ONLY GUY WHO GIVES ME ORDERS IS A GUY WHO CAN LICK ME!
AND THERE AIN'T NO SUCH ANIMAL!
LOOK, SIR... I'M NOT PRESUMING TO GIVE ORDERS TO ANYONE!
BUT, IT'S PATENTLY OBVIOUS THAT A SUPERIOR INTELLECT BUILT THIS ELECTRONIC JUNGLE... AND EVERYTHING YOU TOUCH MIGHT BE A FATAL BOOBY TRAP!
USE YOUR HEAD, BEN! WINGFOOT IS DEAD RIGHT!
OUR FIRST JOB IS TO LEARN MORE ABOUT WHAT WE'RE UP AGAINST!
AND I'M THE ONE TO DO THAT FOR YOU, SIR!
THE BLOOD OF MY ANCESTORS.. THE GREATEST SCOUTS OF ALL TIME... FLOWS STRONG IN MY VEINS!
NO WONDER JOHNNY TOOK A SHINE TO THAT JOE! THE KID'S GOT WHAT IT TAKES!
WE'LL STAY TOGETHER HERE TILL YOU RETURN, SON!

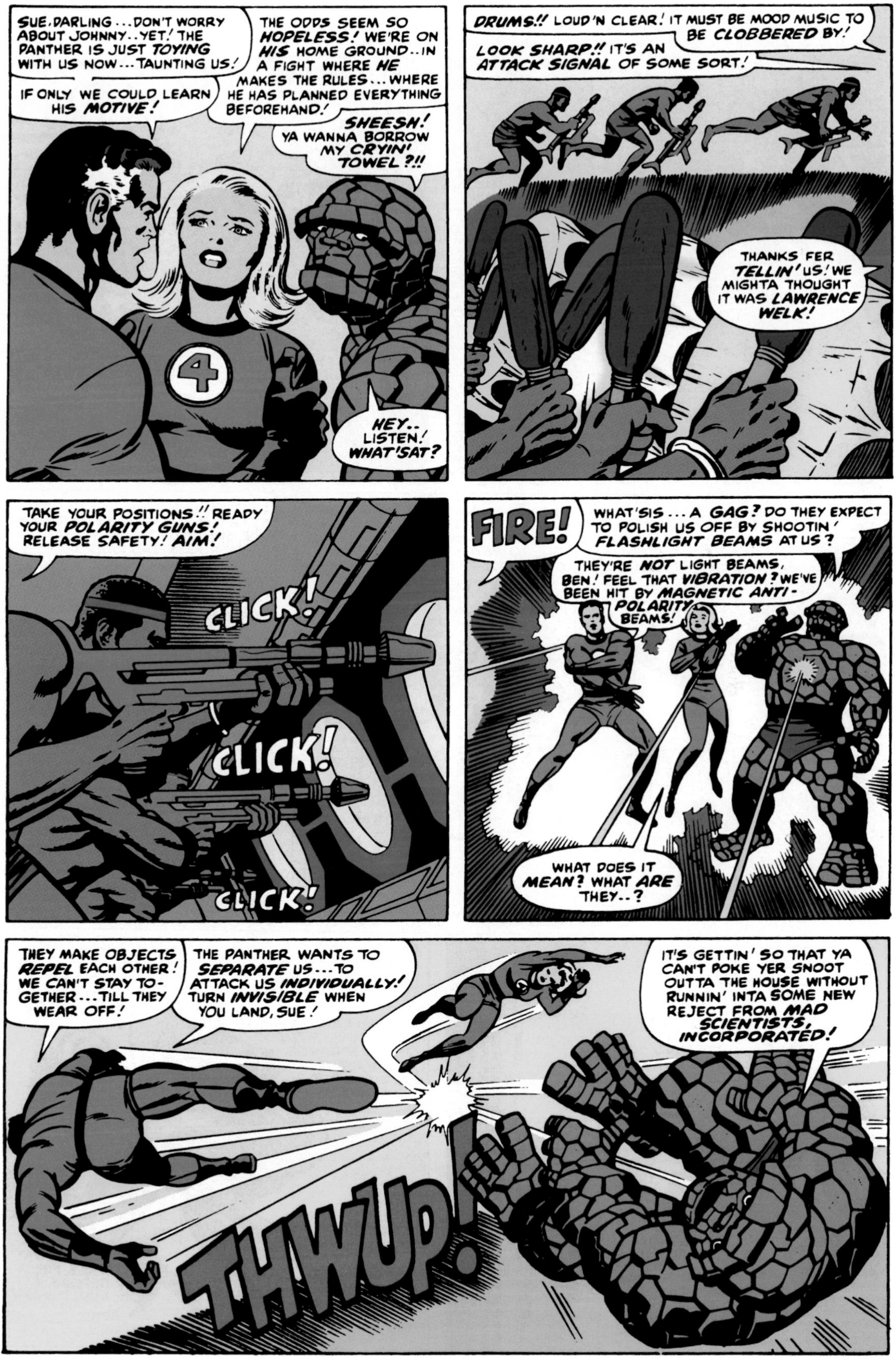
SUE, DARLING... DON'T WORRY ABOUT JOHNNY.. YET! THE PANTHER IS JUST TOYING WITH US NOW... TAUNTING US!
IF ONLY WE COULD LEARN HIS MOTIVE!
THE ODDS SEEM SO HOPELESS! WE'RE ON HIS HOME GROUND.. IN A FIGHT WHERE HE MAKES THE RULES... WHERE HE HAS PLANNED EVERYTHING BEFOREHAND!
SHEESH! YA WANNA BORROW MY CRYIN' TOWEL ?!!
HEY.. LISTEN! WHAT'SAT?
DRUMS!! LOUD 'N CLEAR! IT MUST BE MOOD MUSIC TO BE CLOBBERED BY!
LOOK SHARP!! IT'S AN ATTACK SIGNAL OF SOME SORT!
THANKS FER TELLIN' US! WE MIGHTA THOUGHT IT WAS LAWRENCE WELK!
TAKE YOUR POSITIONS!! READY YOUR POLARITY GUNS! RELEASE SAFETY! AIM!
CLICK!
CLICK!
CLICK!
FIRE!
WHAT'SIS... A GAG? DO THEY EXPECT TO POLISH US OFF BY SHOOTIN' FLASHLIGHT BEAMS AT US?
THEY'RE NOT LIGHT BEAMS, BEN! FEEL THAT VIBRATION? WE'VE BEEN HIT BY MAGNETIC ANTI-POLARITY BEAMS!
WHAT DOES IT MEAN? WHAT ARE THEY..?
THEY MAKE OBJECTS REPEL EACH OTHER! WE CAN'T STAY TO-GETHER... TILL THEY WEAR OFF!
THE PANTHER WANTS TO SEPARATE US... TO ATTACK US INDIVIDUALLY! TURN INVISIBLE WHEN YOU LAND, SUE!
IT'S GETTIN' SO THAT YA CAN'T POKE YER SNOOT OUTTA THE HOUSE WITHOUT RUNNIN' INTA SOME NEW REJECT FROM MAD SCIENTISTS, INCORPORATED!
THWUP!

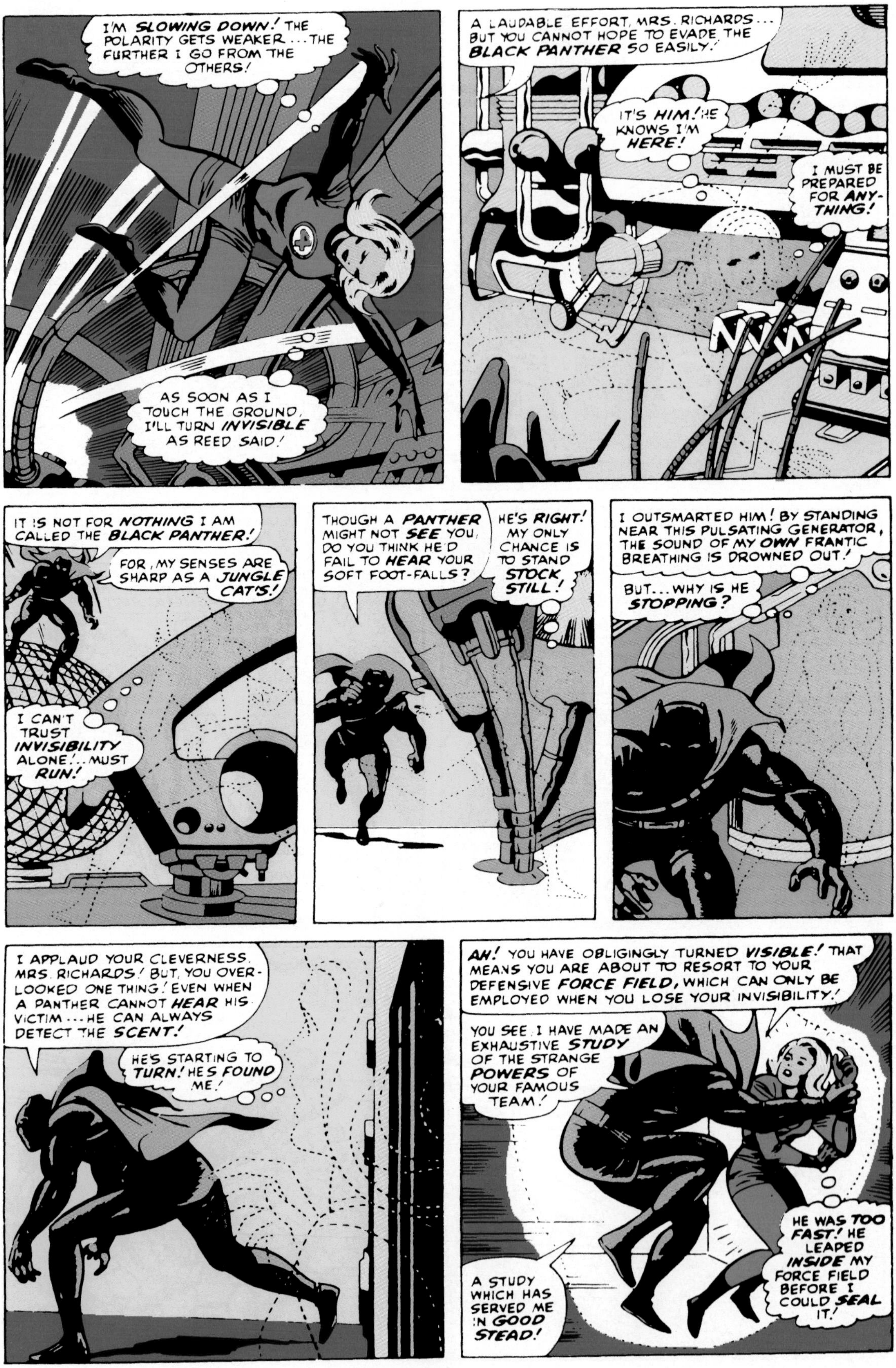

I'M SLOWING DOWN! THE POLARITY GETS WEAKER ... THE FURTHER I GO FROM THE OTHERS!
AS SOON AS I TOUCH THE GROUND, I'LL TURN INVISIBLE AS REED SAID!
A LAUDABLE EFFORT, MRS. RICHARDS... BUT YOU CANNOT HOPE TO EVADE THE BLACK PANTHER SO EASILY!
IT'S HIM! HE KNOWS I'M HERE!
I MUST BE PREPARED FOR ANYTHING!
IT IS NOT FOR NOTHING I AM CALLED THE BLACK PANTHER!
FOR, MY SENSES ARE SHARP AS A JUNGLE CAT'S!
I CAN'T TRUST INVISIBILITY ALONE!.. MUST RUN!
THOUGH A PANTHER MIGHT NOT SEE YOU, DO YOU THINK HE'D FAIL TO HEAR YOUR SOFT FOOT-FALLS?
HE'S RIGHT! MY ONLY CHANCE IS TO STAND STOCK STILL!
I OUTSMARTED HIM! BY STANDING NEAR THIS PULSATING GENERATOR, THE SOUND OF MY OWN FRANTIC BREATHING IS DROWNED OUT!
BUT... WHY IS HE STOPPING?
I APPLAUD YOUR CLEVERNESS, MRS. RICHARDS! BUT, YOU OVERLOOKED ONE THING! EVEN WHEN A PANTHER CANNOT HEAR HIS VICTIM --- HE CAN ALWAYS DETECT THE SCENT!
HE'S STARTING TO TURN! HE'S FOUND ME!
AH! YOU HAVE OBLIGINGLY TURNED VISIBLE! THAT MEANS YOU ARE ABOUT TO RESORT TO YOUR DEFENSIVE FORCE FIELD, WHICH CAN ONLY BE EMPLOYED WHEN YOU LOSE YOUR INVISIBILITY!
YOU SEE, I HAVE MADE AN EXHAUSTIVE STUDY OF THE STRANGE POWERS OF YOUR FAMOUS TEAM!
A STUDY WHICH HAS SERVED ME IN GOOD STEAD!
HE WAS TOO FAST! HE LEAPED INSIDE MY FORCE FIELD BEFORE I COULD SEAL IT!

YOU ARE FORTUNATE IN *ONE* RESPECT, YOUNG LADY! UNLIKE THE CLAWS OF MY NAMESAKE, *MINE* HAVE THE POWER TO EMIT A HARMLESS *SLEEP GAS!*

OHHHH...!

BY THE TIME YOU AWAKEN, THE HUNT WILL BE *OVER* AND THE *BLACK PANTHER* SHALL HAVE WON HIS GREATEST VICTORY!

BY NOW, THE *BLUNDERING THING* SHOULD HAVE STUMBLED INTO THE *SECOND* TRAP I'VE PREPARED FOR HIM!

THE TIMING IS *PERFECT!*

THERE HE *IS*--- REFRESHING HIMSELF BY WASHING HIS FACE AT WHAT *SEEMS* TO BE A FOUNTAIN OF CRYSTAL-CLEAR WATER--!

I TRUST YOU'VE *ENJOYED* SPLASHING A DANGEROUS AMOUNT OF *DEVITALIZING FLUID* UPON YOURSELF!

GLURRGLE! ...NUH..??

THAT LIQUID IS BUT ONE OF *MANY* TRAPS I'VE PREPARED TO SAP YOUR STRENGTH..!

...SAP IT JUST ENOUGH SO THAT WE TWO CAN BATTLE, *HAND-TO-HAND!*

FOR, IN *ANY* EQUAL MATCH, THE *BLACK PANTHER* IS CERTAIN TO *WIN!*

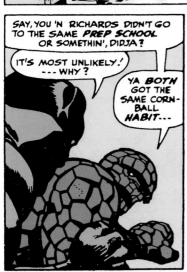

SAY, YOU 'N RICHARDS DIDN'T GO TO THE SAME *PREP SCHOOL* OR SOMETHIN', DIDJA?

IT'S MOST UNLIKELY! --- WHY?

YA *BOTH* GOT THE SAME *CORN-BALL HABIT*...

...YA CAN *TALK* A GUY TO DEATH WHILE YER *FIGHTIN'* 'IM!

PERHAPS, BUT I CAN DO FAR *MORE* THAN TALK..

..AS YOU SHALL SEE..!

AMONG OTHER THINGS, I HAVE LONG BEEN THE *BOXING CHAMPION* OF THIS ENTIRE CONTINENT!

WOK!

WELL GOODY FER *YOU!*...*URPPP!*

JUST *STAY* THERE WISE GUY...TILL I GIT TO MY FEET! THAT'S *ALL* I ASK!

I SHALL BE *HAPPY* TO OBLIGE YOU!

FOR, AFTER ALL... *UNTIL* YOU STAND, I'LL BE DENIED THE EXQUISITE PLEASURE OF *FLOORING* YOU AGAIN!

GOTTA *STEADY* MYSELF! CAN'T FALL APART JUST 'CAUSE HE *WEAKENED* ME WITH THAT *PHONY* WATER!

THEN SUDDENLY...WITH FEROCIOUS SPEED TOTALLY BELYING HIS MAMMOTH BULK, THE *THING* STRIKES BACK...!

POW!

MEBBE *THIS'LL* SHUT YER YAP FER A WHILE!

NUTS! IF NOT FER DRINKIN' THAT BLASTED *WATER*, I'DA *DEMOLISHED* 'IM WITH THAT WHAP! BUT, I'LL BEAT 'IM *ANYHOW!*

YOUR *COURAGE* IS TRULY A MATCH FOR YOUR *FAME!*

BUT YOUR *SKILL*, ALAS, CANNOT NEARLY COMPARE WITH *MINE!*

YEAH? WE'LL *SEE* ABOUT THAT!

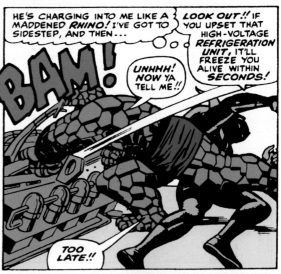

HE'S CHARGING INTO ME LIKE A MADDENED *RHINO!* I'VE GOT TO SIDESTEP, AND THEN...

BAM!

UNHHH! NOW YA TELL ME!!

LOOK OUT!! IF YOU UPSET THAT HIGH-VOLTAGE *REFRIGERATION* UNIT, IT'LL *FREEZE* YOU ALIVE WITHIN *SECONDS!*

TOO LATE!!

YOU ARE INDEED *FORTUNATE*, THING!

YOUR OWN MASSIVE *STRENGTH* WAS BEGINNING TO *RETURN* AGAIN AT THE EXACT MOMENT OF IMPACT!

THUS, YOU WILL *SURVIVE* THE DEEP FREEZE...THOUGH IT WILL TAKE YOU A WHILE TO *THAW OUT!*

AND NOW FOR YOUR *LEADER*...THE ONE WHOM I CONSIDER THE MOST *DANGEROUS* FOE OF ALL!

BUT, EVEN THE FABULOUS *MR. FANTASTIC* WILL BE NO MATCH FOR *ME!*

16

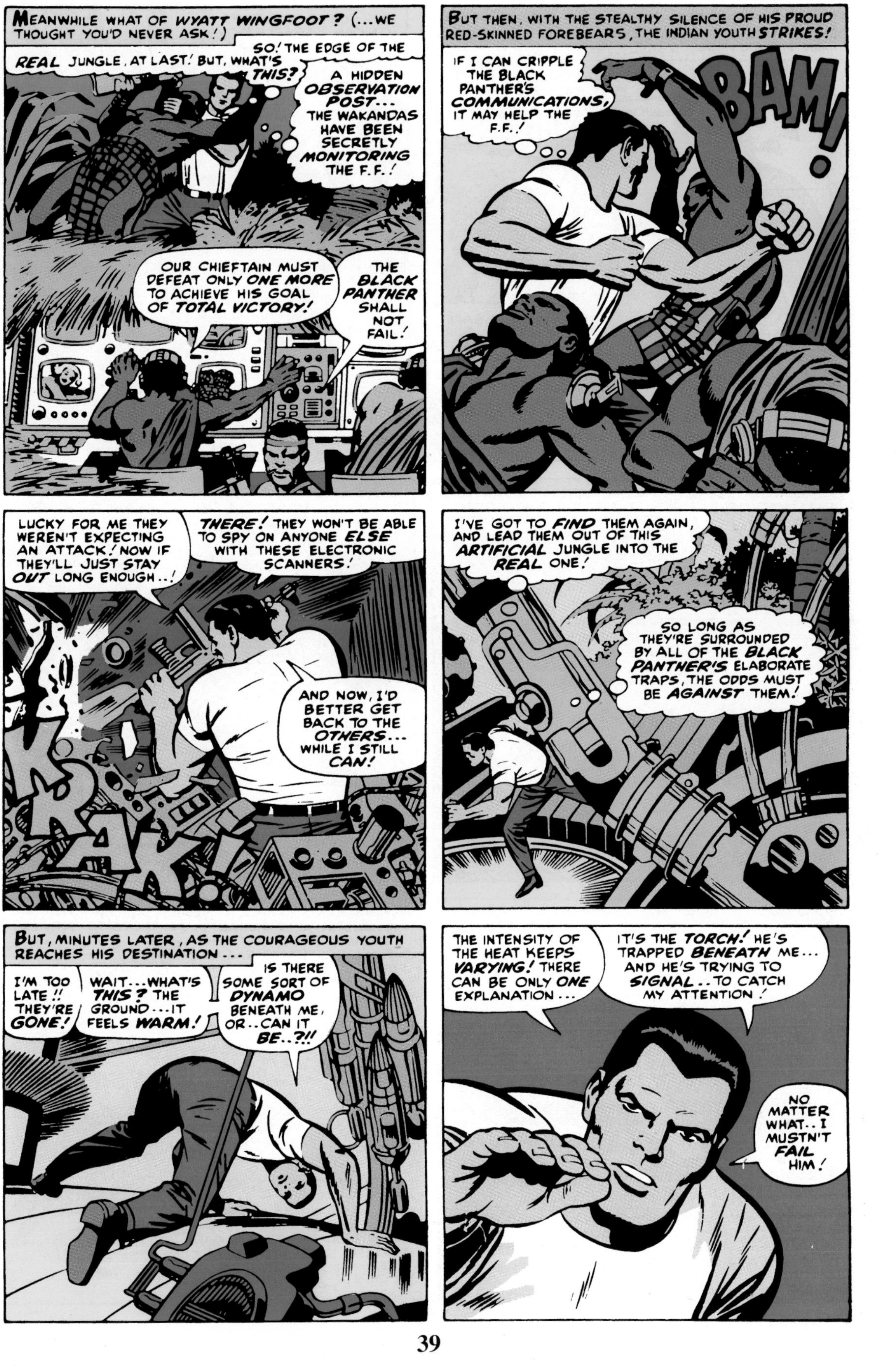
MEANWHILE WHAT OF WYATT WINGFOOT? (...WE THOUGHT YOU'D NEVER ASK!)
SO! THE EDGE OF THE REAL JUNGLE, AT LAST! BUT, WHAT'S THIS?
A HIDDEN OBSERVATION POST... THE WAKANDAS HAVE BEEN SECRETLY MONITORING THE F.F.!
OUR CHIEFTAIN MUST DEFEAT ONLY ONE MORE TO ACHIEVE HIS GOAL OF TOTAL VICTORY!
THE BLACK PANTHER SHALL NOT FAIL!
BUT THEN, WITH THE STEALTHY SILENCE OF HIS PROUD RED-SKINNED FOREBEARS, THE INDIAN YOUTH STRIKES!
IF I CAN CRIPPLE THE BLACK PANTHER'S COMMUNICATIONS, IT MAY HELP THE F.F.!
BAM!
LUCKY FOR ME THEY WEREN'T EXPECTING AN ATTACK! NOW IF THEY'LL JUST STAY OUT LONG ENOUGH..!
THERE! THEY WON'T BE ABLE TO SPY ON ANYONE ELSE WITH THESE ELECTRONIC SCANNERS!
AND NOW, I'D BETTER GET BACK TO THE OTHERS... WHILE I STILL CAN!
KRAK!
I'VE GOT TO FIND THEM AGAIN, AND LEAD THEM OUT OF THIS ARTIFICIAL JUNGLE INTO THE REAL ONE!
SO LONG AS THEY'RE SURROUNDED BY ALL OF THE BLACK PANTHER'S ELABORATE TRAPS, THE ODDS MUST BE AGAINST THEM!
BUT, MINUTES LATER, AS THE COURAGEOUS YOUTH REACHES HIS DESTINATION...
I'M TOO LATE!! THEY'RE GONE!
WAIT...WHAT'S THIS? THE GROUND...IT FEELS WARM!
IS THERE SOME SORT OF DYNAMO BENEATH ME, OR..CAN IT BE..?!!
THE INTENSITY OF THE HEAT KEEPS VARYING! THERE CAN BE ONLY ONE EXPLANATION...
IT'S THE TORCH! HE'S TRAPPED BENEATH ME... AND HE'S TRYING TO SIGNAL..TO CATCH MY ATTENTION!
NO MATTER WHAT..I MUSTN'T FAIL HIM!

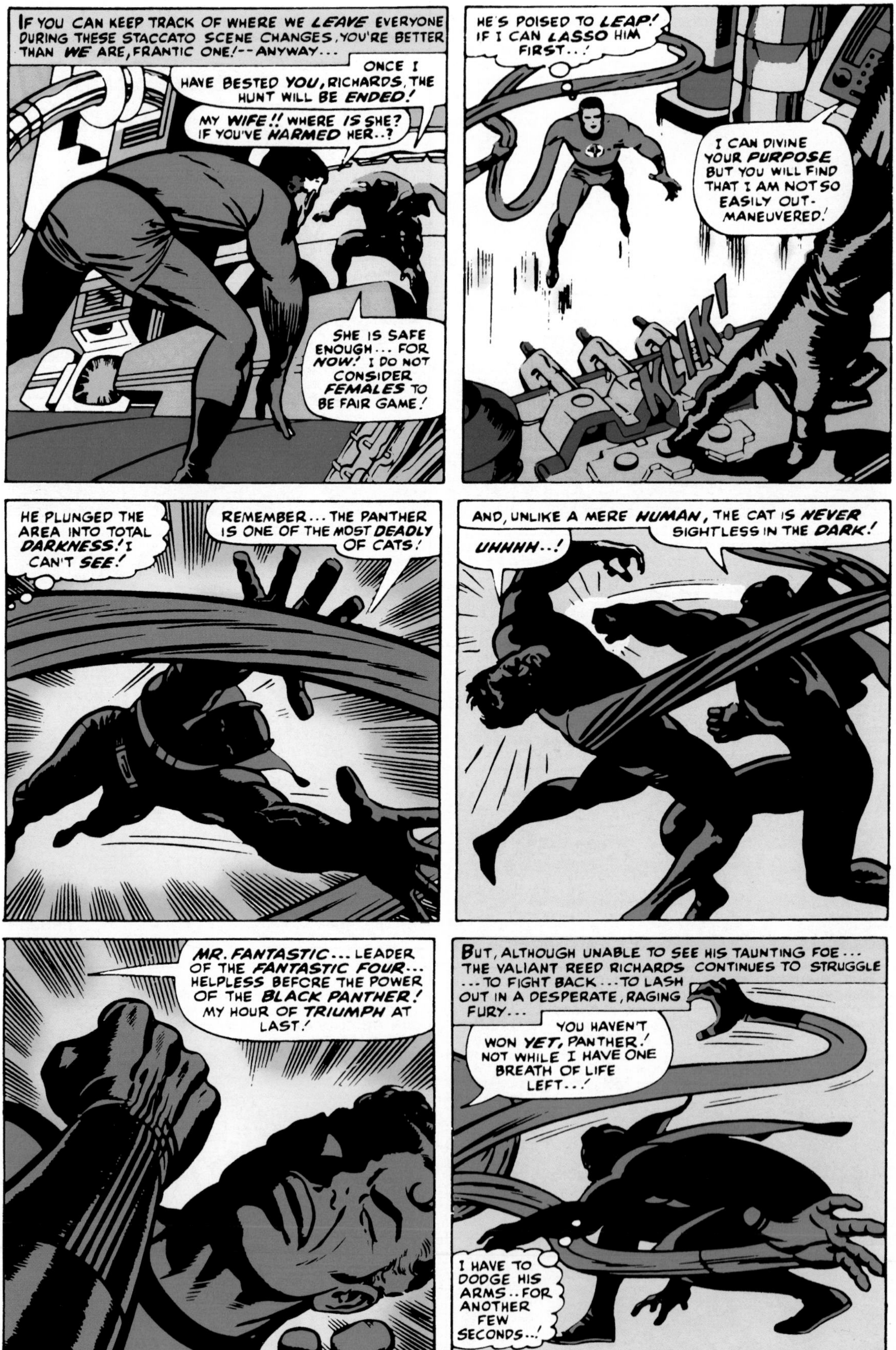

IF YOU CAN KEEP TRACK OF WHERE WE LEAVE EVERYONE DURING THESE STACCATO SCENE CHANGES, YOU'RE BETTER THAN WE ARE, FRANTIC ONE!-- ANYWAY...
ONCE I HAVE BESTED YOU, RICHARDS, THE HUNT WILL BE ENDED!
MY WIFE!! WHERE IS SHE? IF YOU'VE HARMED HER..?
SHE IS SAFE ENOUGH... FOR NOW! I DO NOT CONSIDER FEMALES TO BE FAIR GAME!
HE'S POISED TO LEAP! IF I CAN LASSO HIM FIRST...!
I CAN DIVINE YOUR PURPOSE BUT YOU WILL FIND THAT I AM NOT SO EASILY OUT-MANEUVERED!
KLIK!
HE PLUNGED THE AREA INTO TOTAL DARKNESS! I CAN'T SEE!
REMEMBER... THE PANTHER IS ONE OF THE MOST DEADLY OF CATS!
AND, UNLIKE A MERE HUMAN, THE CAT IS NEVER SIGHTLESS IN THE DARK!
UHHHH..!
MR. FANTASTIC... LEADER OF THE FANTASTIC FOUR... HELPLESS BEFORE THE POWER OF THE BLACK PANTHER! MY HOUR OF TRIUMPH AT LAST!
BUT, ALTHOUGH UNABLE TO SEE HIS TAUNTING FOE... THE VALIANT REED RICHARDS CONTINUES TO STRUGGLE ...TO FIGHT BACK...TO LASH OUT IN A DESPERATE, RAGING FURY...
YOU HAVEN'T WON YET, PANTHER! NOT WHILE I HAVE ONE BREATH OF LIFE LEFT...!
I HAVE TO DODGE HIS ARMS.. FOR ANOTHER FEW SECONDS..!

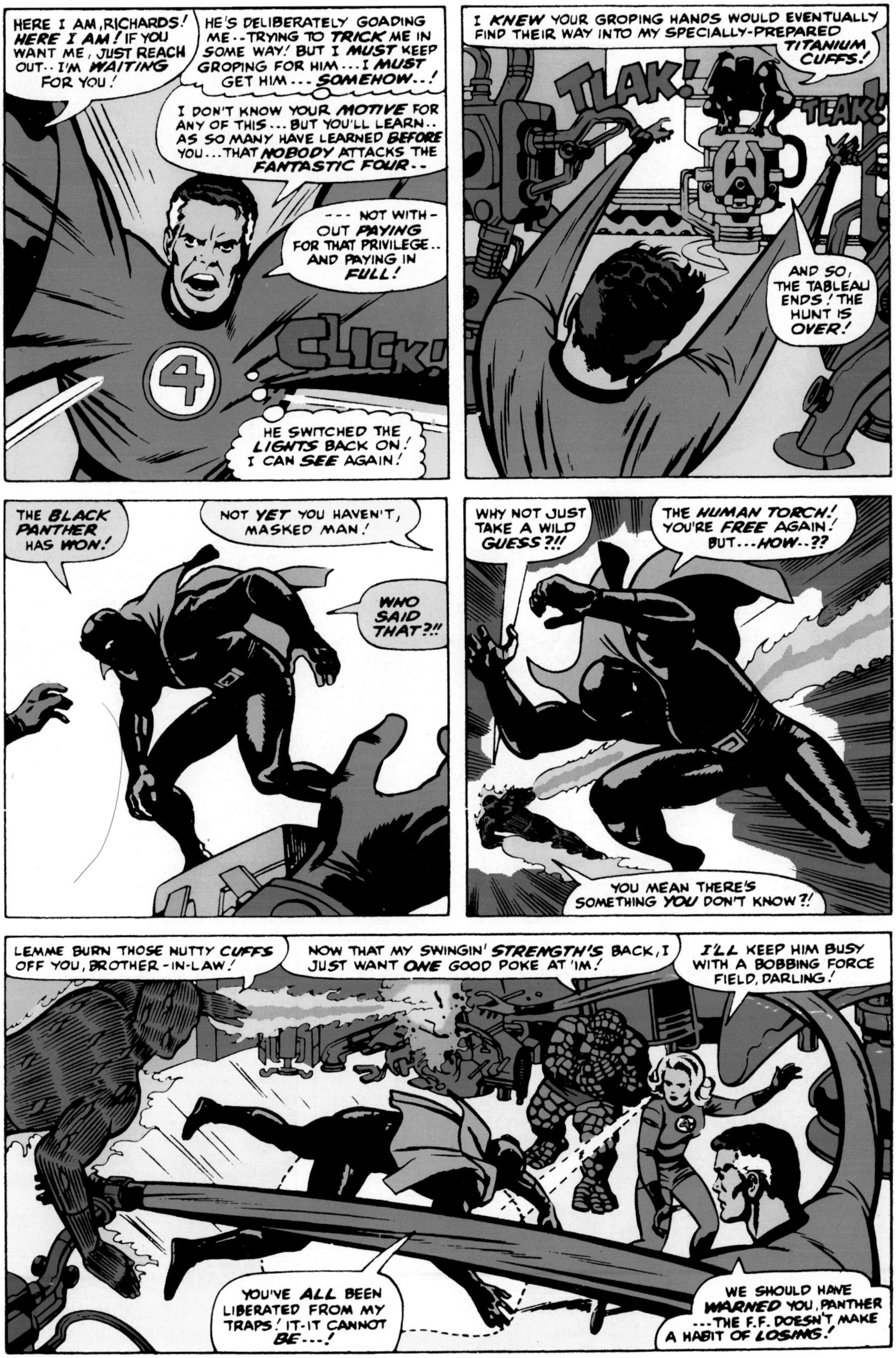
HERE I AM, RICHARDS! HERE I AM! IF YOU WANT ME, JUST REACH OUT.. I'M WAITING FOR YOU!
HE'S DELIBERATELY GOADING ME..TRYING TO TRICK ME IN SOME WAY! BUT I MUST KEEP GROPING FOR HIM... I MUST GET HIM... SOMEHOW..!
I DON'T KNOW YOUR MOTIVE FOR ANY OF THIS... BUT YOU'LL LEARN.. AS SO MANY HAVE LEARNED BEFORE YOU... THAT NOBODY ATTACKS THE FANTASTIC FOUR--
--- NOT WITH-OUT PAYING FOR THAT PRIVILEGE.. AND PAYING IN FULL!
CLICK!
HE SWITCHED THE LIGHTS BACK ON! I CAN SEE AGAIN!
I KNEW YOUR GROPING HANDS WOULD EVENTUALLY FIND THEIR WAY INTO MY SPECIALLY-PREPARED TITANIUM CUFFS!
TLAK!
TLAK!
AND SO, THE TABLEAU ENDS! THE HUNT IS OVER!
THE BLACK PANTHER HAS WON!
NOT YET YOU HAVEN'T, MASKED MAN!
WHO SAID THAT?!!
WHY NOT JUST TAKE A WILD GUESS?!!
THE HUMAN TORCH! YOU'RE FREE AGAIN! BUT...HOW..??
YOU MEAN THERE'S SOMETHING YOU DON'T KNOW?!
LEMME BURN THOSE NUTTY CUFFS OFF YOU, BROTHER-IN-LAW!
NOW THAT MY SWINGIN' STRENGTH'S BACK, I JUST WANT ONE GOOD POKE AT 'IM!
I'LL KEEP HIM BUSY WITH A BOBBING FORCE FIELD, DARLING!
YOU'VE ALL BEEN LIBERATED FROM MY TRAPS! IT-IT CANNOT BE---!
WE SHOULD HAVE WARNED YOU, PANTHER ---THE F.F. DOESN'T MAKE A HABIT OF LOSING!

YOU CAN *RELEASE* YOUR FORCE FIELD NOW, SUE! HE'S LOST THE ELEMENT OF *SURPRISE*... AND, WITHOUT *THAT*, HE'S NO MATCH FOR US!

C'MON..TAKE A SWING AT ME! YA WANT ME TO GIT *FRUSTRATED*?!!

SURRENDER, PANTHER! IT'S THE ONLY CHOICE *LEFT* TO YOU!

HOW? HOW DID YOU *DO* IT? I *MUST* KNOW!

IT WAS OL' *WYATT*! HE FREED *ME*, AND I FREED THE *OTHERS*!

YOU TOOK EVERY PRECAUTION AGAINST THE GREATEST SUPER-POWERED TEAM IN THE WORLD...

...BUT, YOU OVER-LOOKED ONE FACTOR! SOMETIMES A MAN WITH *NO* SUPER POWERS CAN TIP THE SCALES FOR, OR *AGAINST* YOU!

ORDER YOUR MEN *BACK*, PANTHER! I DON'T WANT TO *HURT* ANY OF THEM...!

THEN, MINUTES LATER, AFTER THE MIGHTY, MASKED JUNGLE MYSTERY MAN HAS ACCEPTED THE STARTLING TURN OF FATE...!

WHAT HAPPENS TO HIM *NOW?*

HE PROMISED NOT TO LAUNCH ANY NEW ATTACK AGAINST US!

WE CAN ALL STAND BACK NOW...

A MAN SUCH AS THE *BLACK PANTHER* DOES NOT GIVE HIS WORD LIGHTLY --- NOR DOES HE *DISHONOR* IT, ONCE GIVEN!

BUT, I THINK YOU MIGHT REMOVE YOUR *MASK* NOW...AND TELL US WHAT THIS IS ALL ABOUT!

I SHALL DO AS YOU SAY...!

MY MASK IS NOT FOR CONCEAL-MENT..BUT RATHER A SYMBOL OF MY *PANTHER POWER!*

NOW THAT THE HUNT IS OVER..THE GAME IS ENDED...I SHALL OFFER YOU THE EXPLANATION...FOR YOU HAVE *EARNED* IT INDEED!

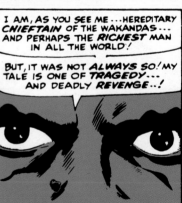

I AM, AS YOU *SEE* ME...HEREDITARY *CHIEFTAIN* OF THE WAKANDAS... AND PERHAPS THE *RICHEST* MAN IN ALL THE WORLD!

BUT, IT WAS NOT *ALWAYS* SO! MY TALE IS ONE OF *TRAGEDY*... AND DEADLY *REVENGE*...!

NEXT ISSUE: "THE REASON WHY!"

42

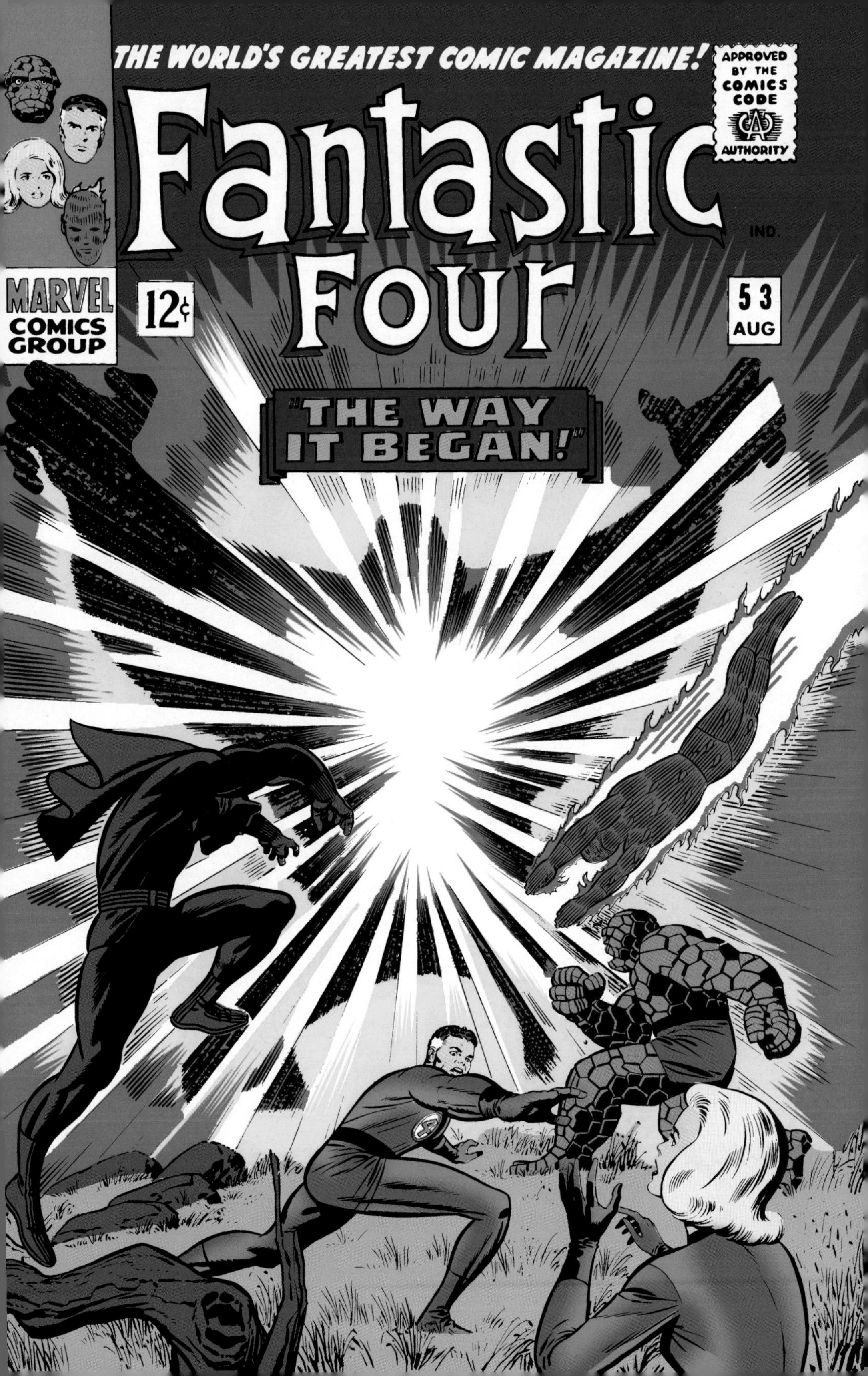
THE WORLD'S GREATEST COMIC MAGAZINE!
APPROVED BY THE COMICS CODE AUTHORITY
Fantastic Four
IND.
MARVEL COMICS GROUP
12¢
53 AUG
"THE WAY IT BEGAN!"

THE FABULOUS F.F. LEARN THE SECRET OF THE BLACK PANTHER

"THE WAY IT BEGAN!"...

HAVING SUCCESSFULLY EVADED ALL THE UNCANNY TRAPS OF THE *BLACK PANTHER*, THE TRIUMPHANT *FANTASTIC FOUR*, ACCOMPANIED BY *WYATT WINGFOOT*, ARE AWARDED A HEROES' CEREMONY---

LET THE *DANCE OF FRIENDSHIP* BEGIN!

SHEESH! A BUNCH'A FRED ASTAIRES THEY *AINT!*

THOUGH THE *WAKANDA TRIBE* LIVES IN THE TRADITION OF THEIR FOREFATHERS, THEY POSSESS MODERN, *SUPER-SCIENTIFIC WONDERS* WE CAN ONLY MARVEL AT! THERE'S AN INCREDIBLE *MYSTERY* HERE--AND ONLY THE *BLACK PANTHER* HIMSELF KNOWS ALL THE ANSWERS!

THEY ARE *NOT* THE ORDINARY NATIVE TRIBE THEY *SEEM* TO BE!

RELAX, BEN! IT'S BETTER'N BEING *SHOT* AT BY THEM!

SCRIPT: STAN LEE	ART: JACK KIRBY
INKS: JOE SINNOTT	LETTERING: ARTIE SIMEK
NATIVE DANCES:	THE BALLET FORBUSH TERPSICHOREAN TROUPE

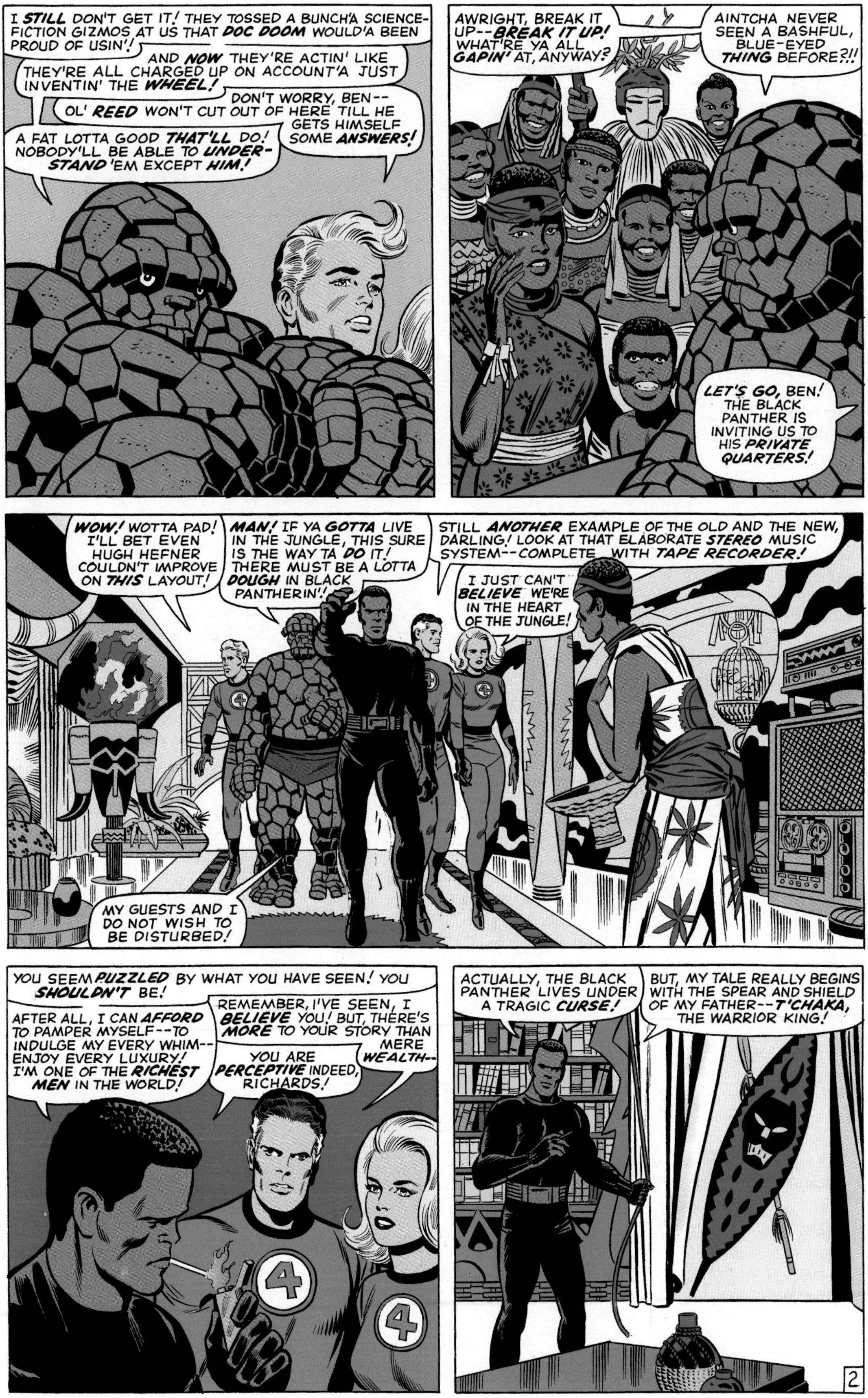
I STILL DON'T GET IT! THEY TOSSED A BUNCH'A SCIENCE-FICTION GIZMOS AT US THAT DOC DOOM WOULD'A BEEN PROUD OF USIN'!
AND NOW THEY'RE ACTIN' LIKE THEY'RE ALL CHARGED UP ON ACCOUNT'A JUST INVENTIN' THE WHEEL!
DON'T WORRY, BEN-- OL' REED WON'T CUT OUT OF HERE TILL HE GETS HIMSELF SOME ANSWERS!
A FAT LOTTA GOOD THAT'LL DO! NOBODY'LL BE ABLE TO UNDER-STAND 'EM EXCEPT HIM!
AWRIGHT, BREAK IT UP--BREAK IT UP! WHAT'RE YA ALL GAPIN' AT, ANYWAY?
AINTCHA NEVER SEEN A BASHFUL, BLUE-EYED THING BEFORE?!!
LET'S GO, BEN! THE BLACK PANTHER IS INVITING US TO HIS PRIVATE QUARTERS!
WOW! WOTTA PAD! I'LL BET EVEN HUGH HEFNER COULDN'T IMPROVE ON THIS LAYOUT!
MAN! IF YA GOTTA LIVE IN THE JUNGLE, THIS SURE IS THE WAY TA DO IT! THERE MUST BE A LOTTA DOUGH IN BLACK PANTHERIN'!
STILL ANOTHER EXAMPLE OF THE OLD AND THE NEW, DARLING! LOOK AT THAT ELABORATE STEREO MUSIC SYSTEM--COMPLETE WITH TAPE RECORDER!
I JUST CAN'T BELIEVE WE'RE IN THE HEART OF THE JUNGLE!
MY GUESTS AND I DO NOT WISH TO BE DISTURBED!
YOU SEEM PUZZLED BY WHAT YOU HAVE SEEN! YOU SHOULDN'T BE!
AFTER ALL, I CAN AFFORD TO PAMPER MYSELF--TO INDULGE MY EVERY WHIM--ENJOY EVERY LUXURY! I'M ONE OF THE RICHEST MEN IN THE WORLD!
REMEMBER, I'VE SEEN, I BELIEVE YOU! BUT, THERE'S MORE TO YOUR STORY THAN MERE WEALTH--
YOU ARE PERCEPTIVE INDEED, RICHARDS!
ACTUALLY, THE BLACK PANTHER LIVES UNDER A TRAGIC CURSE!
BUT, MY TALE REALLY BEGINS WITH THE SPEAR AND SHIELD OF MY FATHER--T'CHAKA, THE WARRIOR KING!
2

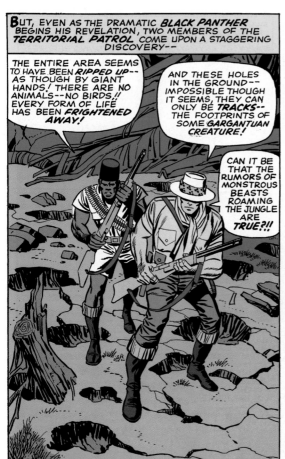

BUT, EVEN AS THE DRAMATIC **BLACK PANTHER** BEGINS HIS REVELATION, TWO MEMBERS OF THE **TERRITORIAL PATROL** COME UPON A STAGGERING DISCOVERY--

THE ENTIRE AREA SEEMS TO HAVE BEEN *RIPPED UP*-- AS THOUGH BY GIANT HANDS.! THERE ARE NO ANIMALS--NO BIRDS.!! EVERY FORM OF LIFE HAS BEEN *FRIGHTENED AWAY!*

AND THESE HOLES IN THE GROUND-- IMPOSSIBLE THOUGH IT SEEMS, THEY CAN ONLY BE *TRACKS*-- THE FOOTPRINTS OF SOME *GARGANTUAN CREATURE!*

CAN IT BE THAT THE RUMORS OF MONSTROUS BEASTS ROAMING THE JUNGLE ARE *TRUE?!!*

AT FIRST, I THOUGHT THEY WERE JUST SUPERSTITION--OLD WIVES' TALES TO FRIGHTEN LITTLE CHILDREN! BUT NOW--I CAN ALMOST *SENSE* THE DANGER UPON US!

HOLD IT! DID YOU JUST FEEL THE GROUND *TREMBLE*--AS THOUGH BENEATH THE PRESSURE OF SOME TITANTIC *WEIGHT?!!*

THERE! I FELT IT *AGAIN!!* THERE'S NO DOUBT ABOUT IT-- *SOMETHING IS BEHIND US!*

SWIFTLY TURNING, THE TWO MEN RECOIL IN MUTE *SHOCK* AT THE AWESOME SIGHT THAT GREETS THEIR EYES--AS THEY FIRE WILDLY--DESPERATELY, AT THAT WHICH CONFRONTS THEM--!

IT'S LIKE A GIGANTIC *GORILLA*--AN UNBELIEVABLE CRIMSON ANTHROPOID!!

GRAK!

CRAK!

KEEP FIRING! OUR ONLY CHANCE IS TO FRIGHTEN HIM AWAY WITH OUR GUNSHOTS!! IT'S *TOO LATE* TO RUN!

HOWEVER, THE GUNFIRE OF THE TWO COURAGEOUS PATROLMEN CAUSES A PHENOMENON FAR DIFFERENT THAN EITHER OF THEM EXPECTS--!

IT-IT SEEMED TO *EXPLODE*--RIGHT BEFORE OUR EYES.!!

IT'S *IMPOSSIBLE!* IT *CAN'T* BE--!

AND YET-- *I* SAW IT, TOO!

3

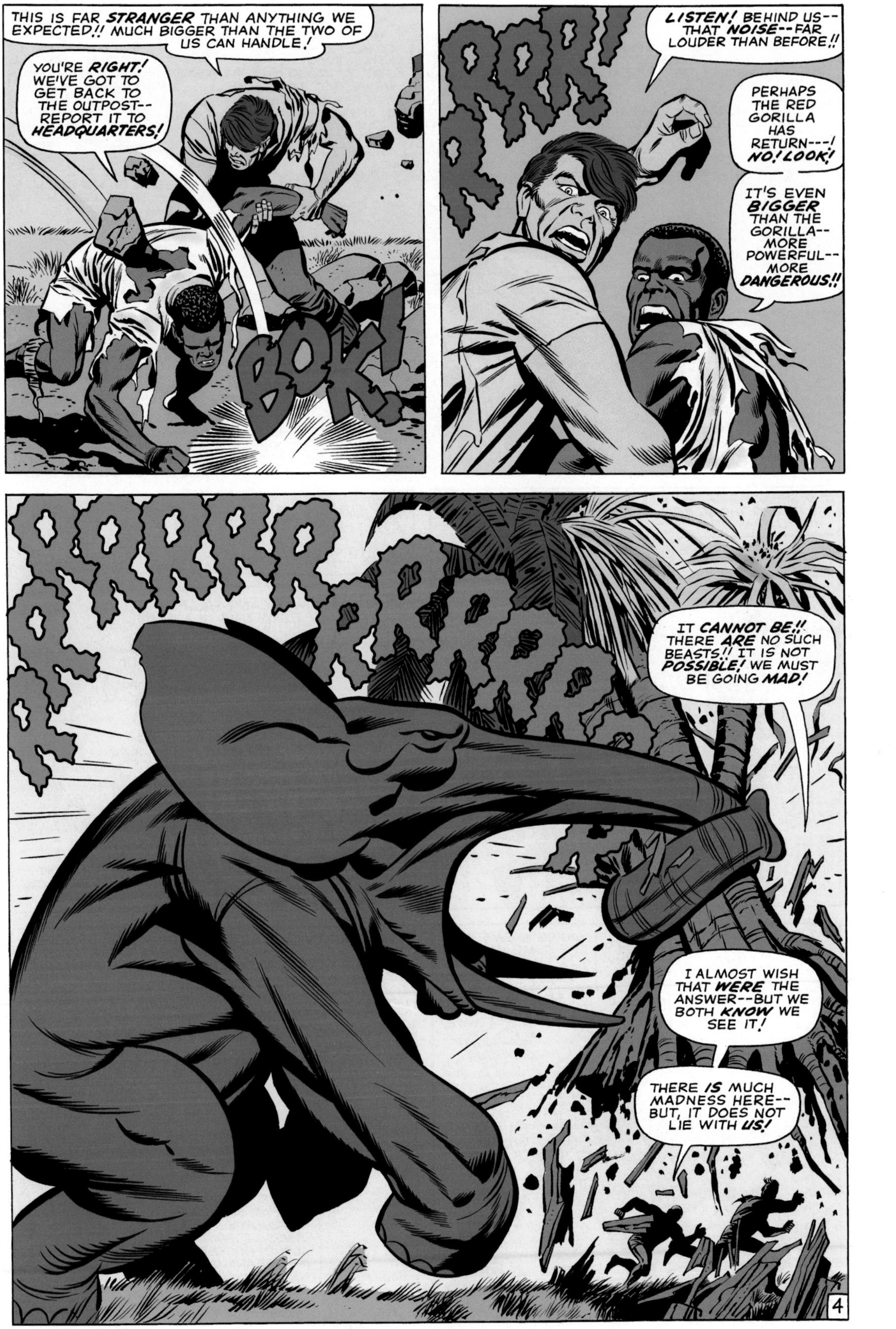
THIS IS FAR STRANGER THAN ANYTHING WE EXPECTED!! MUCH BIGGER THAN THE TWO OF US CAN HANDLE!
YOU'RE RIGHT! WE'VE GOT TO GET BACK TO THE OUTPOST-- REPORT IT TO HEADQUARTERS!
BOK!
RRR!
LISTEN! BEHIND US-- THAT NOISE--FAR LOUDER THAN BEFORE!!
PERHAPS THE RED GORILLA HAS RETURN---! NO! LOOK!
IT'S EVEN BIGGER THAN THE GORILLA-- MORE POWERFUL-- MORE DANGEROUS!!
RRRRR RRRRRRR
IT CANNOT BE!! THERE ARE NO SUCH BEASTS!! IT IS NOT POSSIBLE! WE MUST BE GOING MAD!
I ALMOST WISH THAT WERE THE ANSWER--BUT WE BOTH KNOW WE SEE IT!
THERE IS MUCH MADNESS HERE-- BUT, IT DOES NOT LIE WITH US!
4

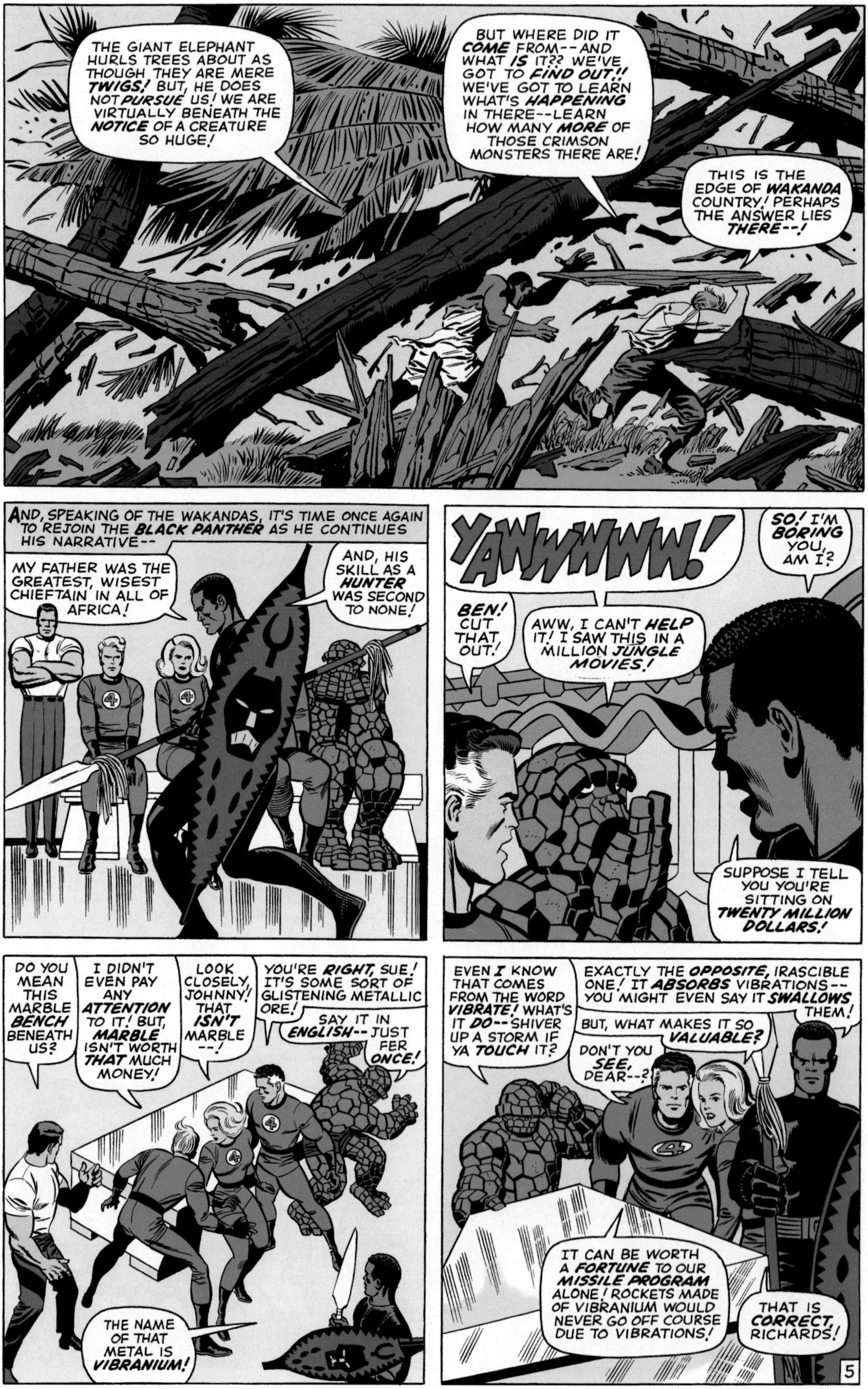
THE GIANT ELEPHANT HURLS TREES ABOUT AS THOUGH THEY ARE MERE TWIGS! BUT, HE DOES NOT PURSUE US! WE ARE VIRTUALLY BENEATH THE NOTICE OF A CREATURE SO HUGE!
BUT WHERE DID IT COME FROM--AND WHAT IS IT?? WE'VE GOT TO FIND OUT!! WE'VE GOT TO LEARN WHAT'S HAPPENING IN THERE--LEARN HOW MANY MORE OF THOSE CRIMSON MONSTERS THERE ARE!
THIS IS THE EDGE OF WAKANDA COUNTRY! PERHAPS THE ANSWER LIES THERE--!
AND, SPEAKING OF THE WAKANDAS, IT'S TIME ONCE AGAIN TO REJOIN THE BLACK PANTHER AS HE CONTINUES HIS NARRATIVE--
MY FATHER WAS THE GREATEST, WISEST CHIEFTAIN IN ALL OF AFRICA!
AND, HIS SKILL AS A HUNTER WAS SECOND TO NONE!
YAWWWWW!
SO! I'M BORING YOU, AM I?
BEN! CUT THAT OUT!
AWW, I CAN'T HELP IT! I SAW THIS IN A MILLION JUNGLE MOVIES!
SUPPOSE I TELL YOU YOU'RE SITTING ON TWENTY MILLION DOLLARS!
DO YOU MEAN THIS MARBLE BENCH BENEATH US?
I DIDN'T EVEN PAY ANY ATTENTION TO IT! BUT, MARBLE ISN'T WORTH THAT MUCH MONEY!
LOOK CLOSELY, JOHNNY! THAT ISN'T MARBLE--!
YOU'RE RIGHT, SUE! IT'S SOME SORT OF GLISTENING METALLIC ORE!
SAY IT IN ENGLISH--JUST FER ONCE!
THE NAME OF THAT METAL IS VIBRANIUM!
EVEN I KNOW THAT COMES FROM THE WORD VIBRATE! WHAT'S IT DO--SHIVER UP A STORM IF YA TOUCH IT?
EXACTLY THE OPPOSITE, IRASCIBLE ONE! IT ABSORBS VIBRATIONS--YOU MIGHT EVEN SAY IT SWALLOWS THEM!
BUT, WHAT MAKES IT SO VALUABLE?
DON'T YOU SEE, DEAR--?
IT CAN BE WORTH A FORTUNE TO OUR MISSILE PROGRAM ALONE! ROCKETS MADE OF VIBRANIUM WOULD NEVER GO OFF COURSE DUE TO VIBRATIONS!
THAT IS CORRECT, RICHARDS!
5

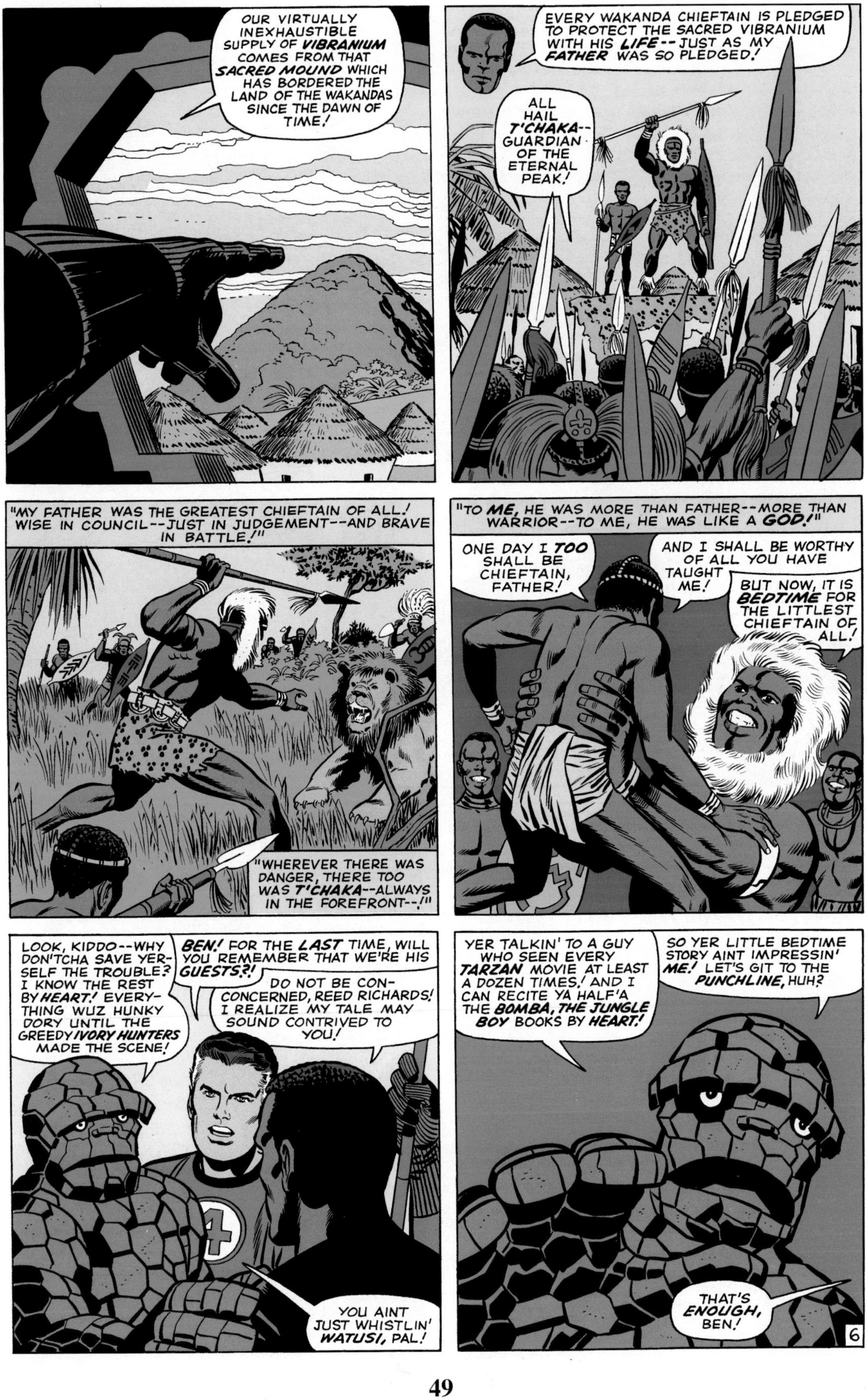

OUR VIRTUALLY INEXHAUSTIBLE SUPPLY OF VIBRANIUM COMES FROM THAT SACRED MOUND WHICH HAS BORDERED THE LAND OF THE WAKANDAS SINCE THE DAWN OF TIME!
EVERY WAKANDA CHIEFTAIN IS PLEDGED TO PROTECT THE SACRED VIBRANIUM WITH HIS LIFE--JUST AS MY FATHER WAS SO PLEDGED!
ALL HAIL T'CHAKA--GUARDIAN OF THE ETERNAL PEAK!
"MY FATHER WAS THE GREATEST CHIEFTAIN OF ALL! WISE IN COUNCIL--JUST IN JUDGEMENT--AND BRAVE IN BATTLE!"
"WHEREVER THERE WAS DANGER, THERE TOO WAS T'CHAKA--ALWAYS IN THE FOREFRONT--!"
"TO ME, HE WAS MORE THAN FATHER--MORE THAN WARRIOR--TO ME, HE WAS LIKE A GOD!"
ONE DAY I TOO SHALL BE CHIEFTAIN, FATHER!
AND I SHALL BE WORTHY OF ALL YOU HAVE TAUGHT ME!
BUT NOW, IT IS BEDTIME FOR THE LITTLEST CHIEFTAIN OF ALL!
LOOK, KIDDO--WHY DON'TCHA SAVE YERSELF THE TROUBLE? I KNOW THE REST BY HEART! EVERYTHING WUZ HUNKY DORY UNTIL THE GREEDY IVORY HUNTERS MADE THE SCENE!
BEN! FOR THE LAST TIME, WILL YOU REMEMBER THAT WE'RE HIS GUESTS?!
DO NOT BE CONCERNED, REED RICHARDS! I REALIZE MY TALE MAY SOUND CONTRIVED TO YOU!
YOU AINT JUST WHISTLIN' WATUSI, PAL!
YER TALKIN' TO A GUY WHO SEEN EVERY TARZAN MOVIE AT LEAST A DOZEN TIMES! AND I CAN RECITE YA HALF'A THE BOMBA, THE JUNGLE BOY BOOKS BY HEART!
SO YER LITTLE BEDTIME STORY AINT IMPRESSIN' ME! LET'S GIT TO THE PUNCHLINE, HUH?
THAT'S ENOUGH, BEN!
6

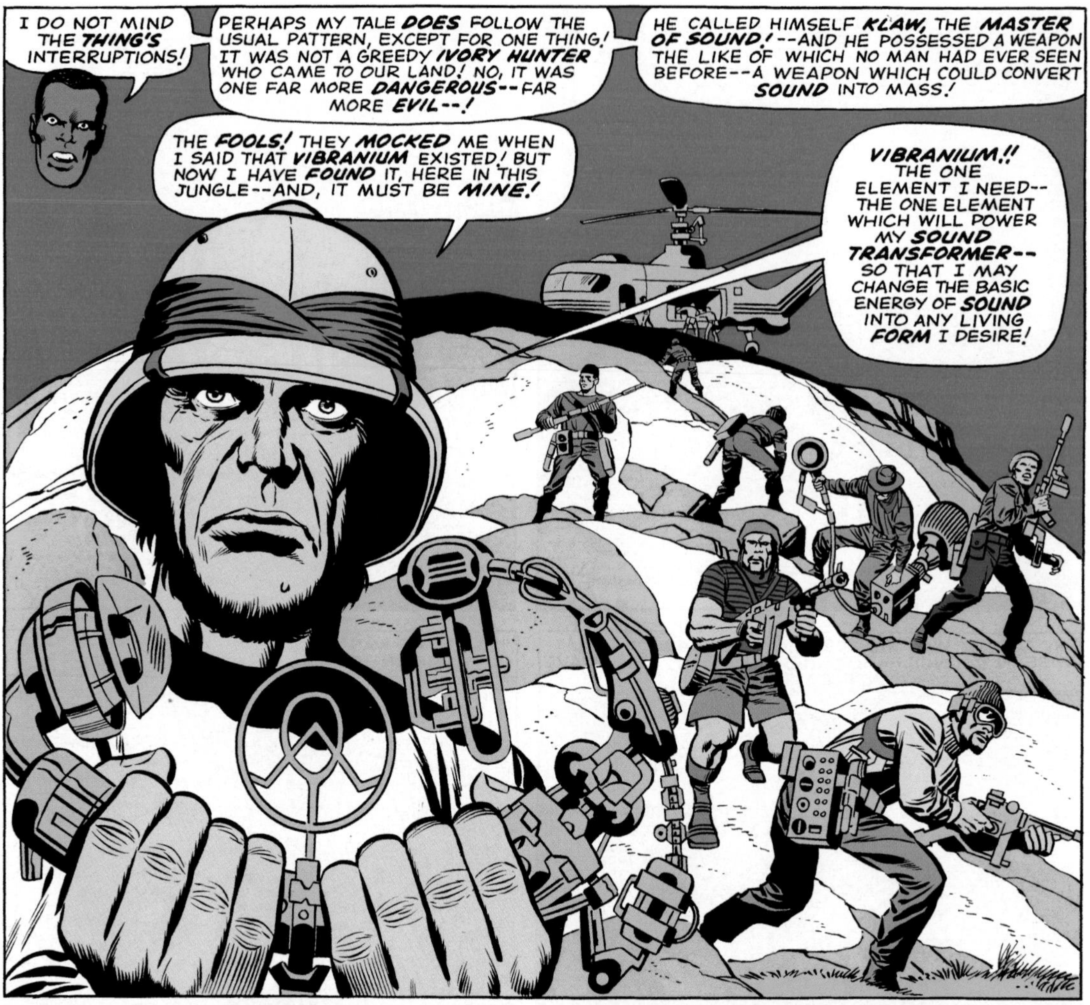
I DO NOT MIND THE THING'S INTERRUPTIONS!
PERHAPS MY TALE DOES FOLLOW THE USUAL PATTERN, EXCEPT FOR ONE THING! IT WAS NOT A GREEDY IVORY HUNTER WHO CAME TO OUR LAND! NO, IT WAS ONE FAR MORE DANGEROUS--FAR MORE EVIL--!
HE CALLED HIMSELF KLAW, THE MASTER OF SOUND! --AND HE POSSESSED A WEAPON THE LIKE OF WHICH NO MAN HAD EVER SEEN BEFORE--A WEAPON WHICH COULD CONVERT SOUND INTO MASS!
THE FOOLS! THEY MOCKED ME WHEN I SAID THAT VIBRANIUM EXISTED! BUT NOW I HAVE FOUND IT, HERE IN THIS JUNGLE--AND, IT MUST BE MINE!
VIBRANIUM!! THE ONE ELEMENT I NEED--THE ONE ELEMENT WHICH WILL POWER MY SOUND TRANSFORMER--SO THAT I MAY CHANGE THE BASIC ENERGY OF SOUND INTO ANY LIVING FORM I DESIRE!

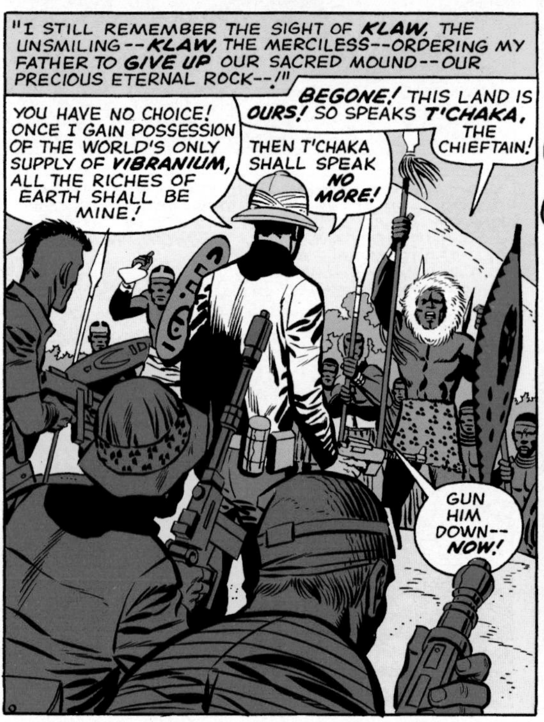
"I STILL REMEMBER THE SIGHT OF KLAW, THE UNSMILING--KLAW, THE MERCILESS--ORDERING MY FATHER TO GIVE UP OUR SACRED MOUND--OUR PRECIOUS ETERNAL ROCK--!"
BEGONE! THIS LAND IS OURS! SO SPEAKS T'CHAKA, THE CHIEFTAIN!
YOU HAVE NO CHOICE! ONCE I GAIN POSSESSION OF THE WORLD'S ONLY SUPPLY OF VIBRANIUM, ALL THE RICHES OF EARTH SHALL BE MINE!
THEN T'CHAKA SHALL SPEAK NO MORE!
GUN HIM DOWN--NOW!

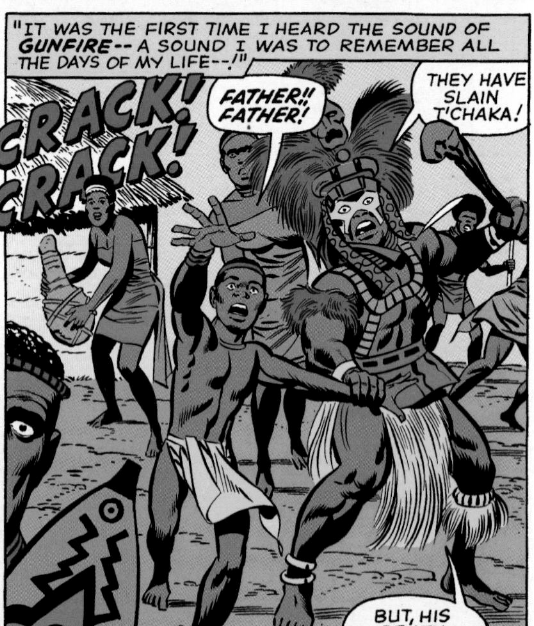
"IT WAS THE FIRST TIME I HEARD THE SOUND OF GUNFIRE--A SOUND I WAS TO REMEMBER ALL THE DAYS OF MY LIFE--!"
CRACK! CRACK!
FATHER!! FATHER!
THEY HAVE SLAIN T'CHAKA!
BUT, HIS DEATH SHALL BE AVENGED!
7

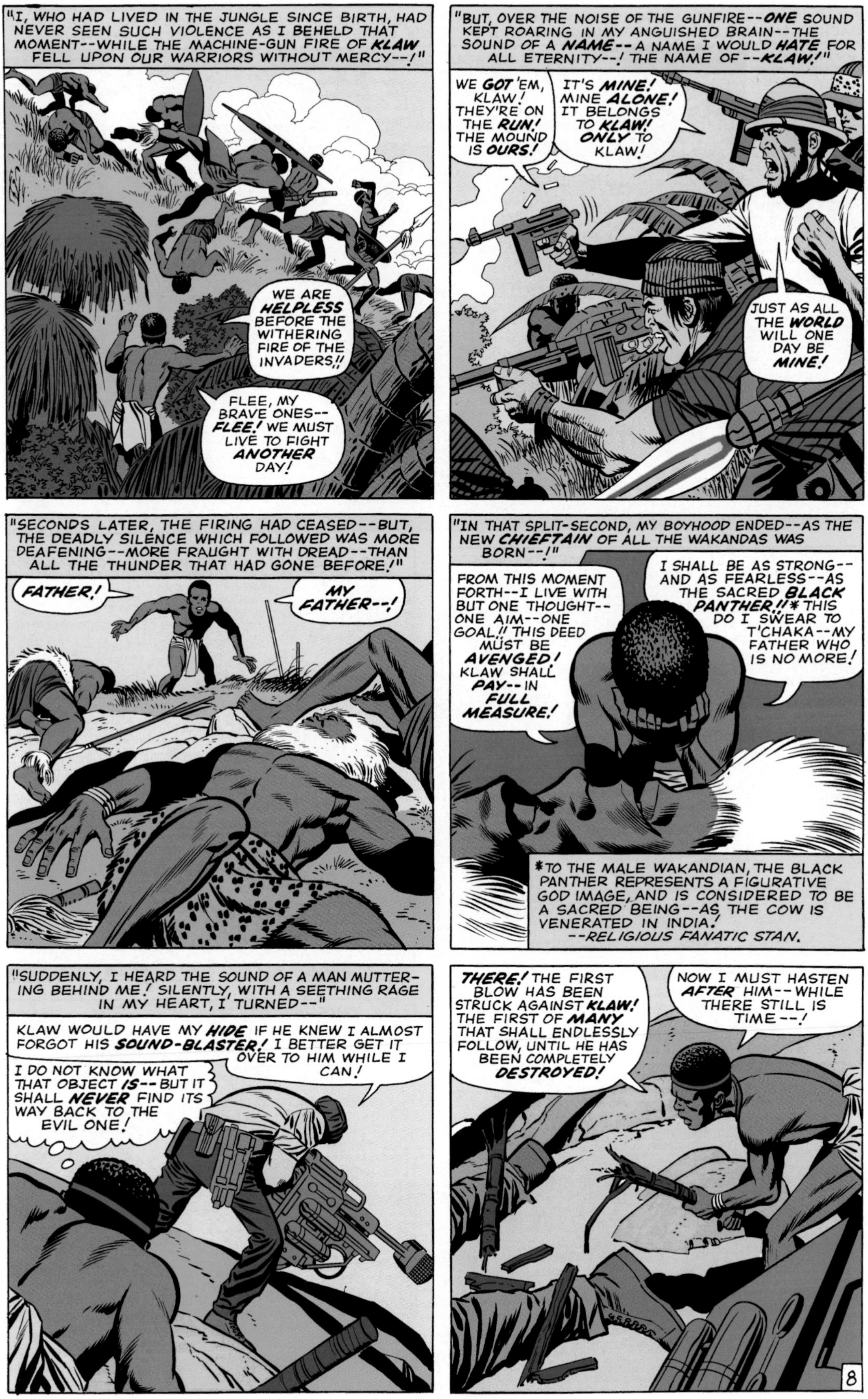
"I, WHO HAD LIVED IN THE JUNGLE SINCE BIRTH, HAD NEVER SEEN SUCH VIOLENCE AS I BEHELD THAT MOMENT--WHILE THE MACHINE-GUN FIRE OF KLAW FELL UPON OUR WARRIORS WITHOUT MERCY--!"
WE ARE HELPLESS BEFORE THE WITHERING FIRE OF THE INVADERS!!
FLEE, MY BRAVE ONES-- FLEE! WE MUST LIVE TO FIGHT ANOTHER DAY!
"BUT, OVER THE NOISE OF THE GUNFIRE--ONE SOUND KEPT ROARING IN MY ANGUISHED BRAIN--THE SOUND OF A NAME--A NAME I WOULD HATE FOR ALL ETERNITY--! THE NAME OF --KLAW!"
WE GOT 'EM, KLAW! THEY'RE ON THE RUN! THE MOUND IS OURS!
IT'S MINE! MINE ALONE! IT BELONGS TO KLAW! ONLY TO KLAW!
JUST AS ALL THE WORLD WILL ONE DAY BE MINE!
"SECONDS LATER, THE FIRING HAD CEASED--BUT, THE DEADLY SILENCE WHICH FOLLOWED WAS MORE DEAFENING--MORE FRAUGHT WITH DREAD--THAN ALL THE THUNDER THAT HAD GONE BEFORE!"
FATHER!
MY FATHER--!
"IN THAT SPLIT-SECOND, MY BOYHOOD ENDED--AS THE NEW CHIEFTAIN OF ALL THE WAKANDAS WAS BORN--!"
FROM THIS MOMENT FORTH--I LIVE WITH BUT ONE THOUGHT--ONE AIM--ONE GOAL!! THIS DEED MUST BE AVENGED! KLAW SHALL PAY--IN FULL MEASURE!
I SHALL BE AS STRONG--AND AS FEARLESS--AS THE SACRED BLACK PANTHER!!* THIS DO I SWEAR TO T'CHAKA--MY FATHER WHO IS NO MORE!
*TO THE MALE WAKANDIAN, THE BLACK PANTHER REPRESENTS A FIGURATIVE GOD IMAGE, AND IS CONSIDERED TO BE A SACRED BEING--AS THE COW IS VENERATED IN INDIA! --RELIGIOUS FANATIC STAN.
"SUDDENLY, I HEARD THE SOUND OF A MAN MUTTERING BEHIND ME! SILENTLY, WITH A SEETHING RAGE IN MY HEART, I TURNED--"
KLAW WOULD HAVE MY HIDE IF HE KNEW I ALMOST FORGOT HIS SOUND-BLASTER! I BETTER GET IT OVER TO HIM WHILE I CAN!
I DO NOT KNOW WHAT THAT OBJECT IS--BUT IT SHALL NEVER FIND ITS WAY BACK TO THE EVIL ONE!
THERE! THE FIRST BLOW HAS BEEN STRUCK AGAINST KLAW! THE FIRST OF MANY THAT SHALL ENDLESSLY FOLLOW, UNTIL HE HAS BEEN COMPLETELY DESTROYED!
NOW I MUST HASTEN AFTER HIM--WHILE THERE STILL IS TIME--!
8

"FINDING THE STRANGE WEAPON SURPRISINGLY LIGHT IN WEIGHT, I LIFTED IT, CARRYING IT WITH ME, UNTIL I REACHED THE GATES OF OUR VILLAGE, WHERE MY EYES BEHELD KLAW'S FINAL ACT OF VILLAINY--!"

MY *PEOPLE*-- FLEEING FOR THEIR LIVES,!! OUR VILLAGE IN *FLAMES*!!

THIS IS NO *MAN* I SEEK TO BATTLE.!! TRULY, HE IS *EVIL INCARNATE*!! HIS VERY PRESENCE BEFOULS THE EARTH UPON WHICH HE STANDS!

OUT! DRIVE THEM *OUT!* THE MOUND OF *VIBRANIUM* MUST BELONG TO *KLAW!* ONLY *I* AM DESTINED TO BE SUPREME! ONLY *I* AM *MASTER OF SOUND!*

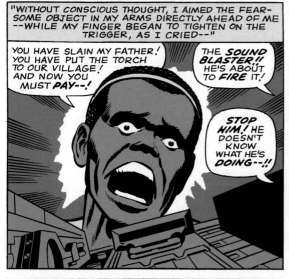

"WITHOUT CONSCIOUS THOUGHT, I AIMED THE FEARSOME OBJECT IN MY ARMS DIRECTLY AHEAD OF ME --WHILE MY FINGER BEGAN TO TIGHTEN ON THE TRIGGER, AS I CRIED--"

YOU HAVE SLAIN MY FATHER! YOU HAVE PUT THE TORCH TO OUR VILLAGE! AND NOW YOU MUST *PAY*--!

THE *SOUND BLASTER*!! HE'S ABOUT TO *FIRE* IT!

STOP HIM! HE DOESN'T KNOW WHAT HE'S *DOING*--!!

TOO LATE! HE *DETONATED* IT!

IT WAS AN *ACCIDENT!* HE DOESN'T EVEN KNOW HOW TO *AIM* IT! THE SHOT FELL *SHORT!*

I'LL MAKE SURE HE GETS *NO* SECOND CHANCE!

YOU LITTLE *FOOL!* YOU CANNOT REALIZE THE *FORCES* YOU ARE TAMPERING WITH! THE DEVICE YOU HOLD CONVERTS *SOUND* INTO PURE *ENERGY!* IN THE WRONG HANDS, IT CAN WREAK UNMENTIONABLE *HAVOC*!!

YOURS ARE THE HANDS THAT ARE WRONG, EVIL ONE--NOT *MINE!*

LOOK OUT! HE'S GONNA FIRE *AGAIN!*

THE LITTLE *SAVAGE* WOULDN'T *DARE!*

I *SEE* YOU STARTING TO SQUEEZE YOUR TRIGGER! BUT, YOU ARE *TOO LATE*--!

THIS IS FOR T'CHAKA-- THE WARRIOR KING!

MY *HAND!*

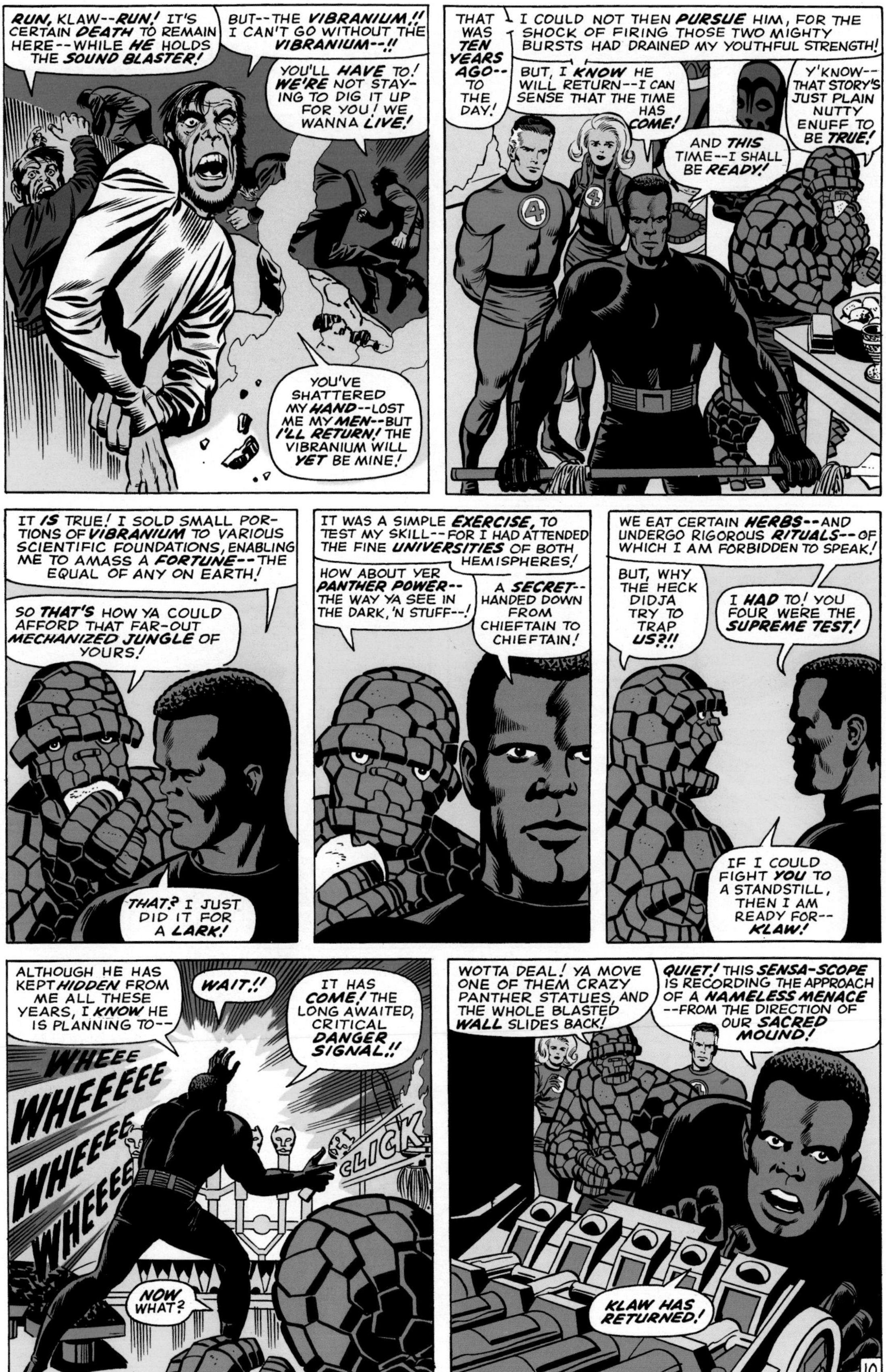
RUN, KLAW--RUN! IT'S CERTAIN DEATH TO REMAIN HERE--WHILE HE HOLDS THE SOUND BLASTER!
BUT--THE VIBRANIUM!! I CAN'T GO WITHOUT THE VIBRANIUM--!!
YOU'LL HAVE TO! WE'RE NOT STAYING TO DIG IT UP FOR YOU! WE WANNA LIVE!
YOU'VE SHATTERED MY HAND--LOST ME MY MEN--BUT I'LL RETURN! THE VIBRANIUM WILL YET BE MINE!
THAT WAS TEN YEARS AGO--TO THE DAY!
I COULD NOT THEN PURSUE HIM, FOR THE SHOCK OF FIRING THOSE TWO MIGHTY BURSTS HAD DRAINED MY YOUTHFUL STRENGTH!
BUT, I KNOW HE WILL RETURN--I CAN SENSE THAT THE TIME HAS COME!
AND THIS TIME--I SHALL BE READY!
Y'KNOW--THAT STORY'S JUST PLAIN NUTTY ENUFF TO BE TRUE!
IT IS TRUE! I SOLD SMALL PORTIONS OF VIBRANIUM TO VARIOUS SCIENTIFIC FOUNDATIONS, ENABLING ME TO AMASS A FORTUNE--THE EQUAL OF ANY ON EARTH!
SO THAT'S HOW YA COULD AFFORD THAT FAR-OUT MECHANIZED JUNGLE OF YOURS!
THAT? I JUST DID IT FOR A LARK!
IT WAS A SIMPLE EXERCISE, TO TEST MY SKILL--FOR I HAD ATTENDED THE FINE UNIVERSITIES OF BOTH HEMISPHERES!
HOW ABOUT YER PANTHER POWER--THE WAY YA SEE IN THE DARK, 'N STUFF--!
A SECRET--HANDED DOWN FROM CHIEFTAIN TO CHIEFTAIN!
WE EAT CERTAIN HERBS--AND UNDERGO RIGOROUS RITUALS--OF WHICH I AM FORBIDDEN TO SPEAK!
BUT, WHY THE HECK DIDJA TRY TO TRAP US?!!
I HAD TO! YOU FOUR WERE THE SUPREME TEST!
IF I COULD FIGHT YOU TO A STANDSTILL, THEN I AM READY FOR--KLAW!
ALTHOUGH HE HAS KEPT HIDDEN FROM ME ALL THESE YEARS, I KNOW HE IS PLANNING TO--
WAIT!!
IT HAS COME! THE LONG AWAITED, CRITICAL DANGER SIGNAL!!
WHEEEE
WHEEEEEE
WHEEEEE
WHEEEEE
CLICK
NOW WHAT?
WOTTA DEAL! YA MOVE ONE OF THEM CRAZY PANTHER STATUES, AND THE WHOLE BLASTED WALL SLIDES BACK!
QUIET! THIS SENSA-SCOPE IS RECORDING THE APPROACH OF A NAMELESS MENACE --FROM THE DIRECTION OF OUR SACRED MOUND!
KLAW HAS RETURNED!
10

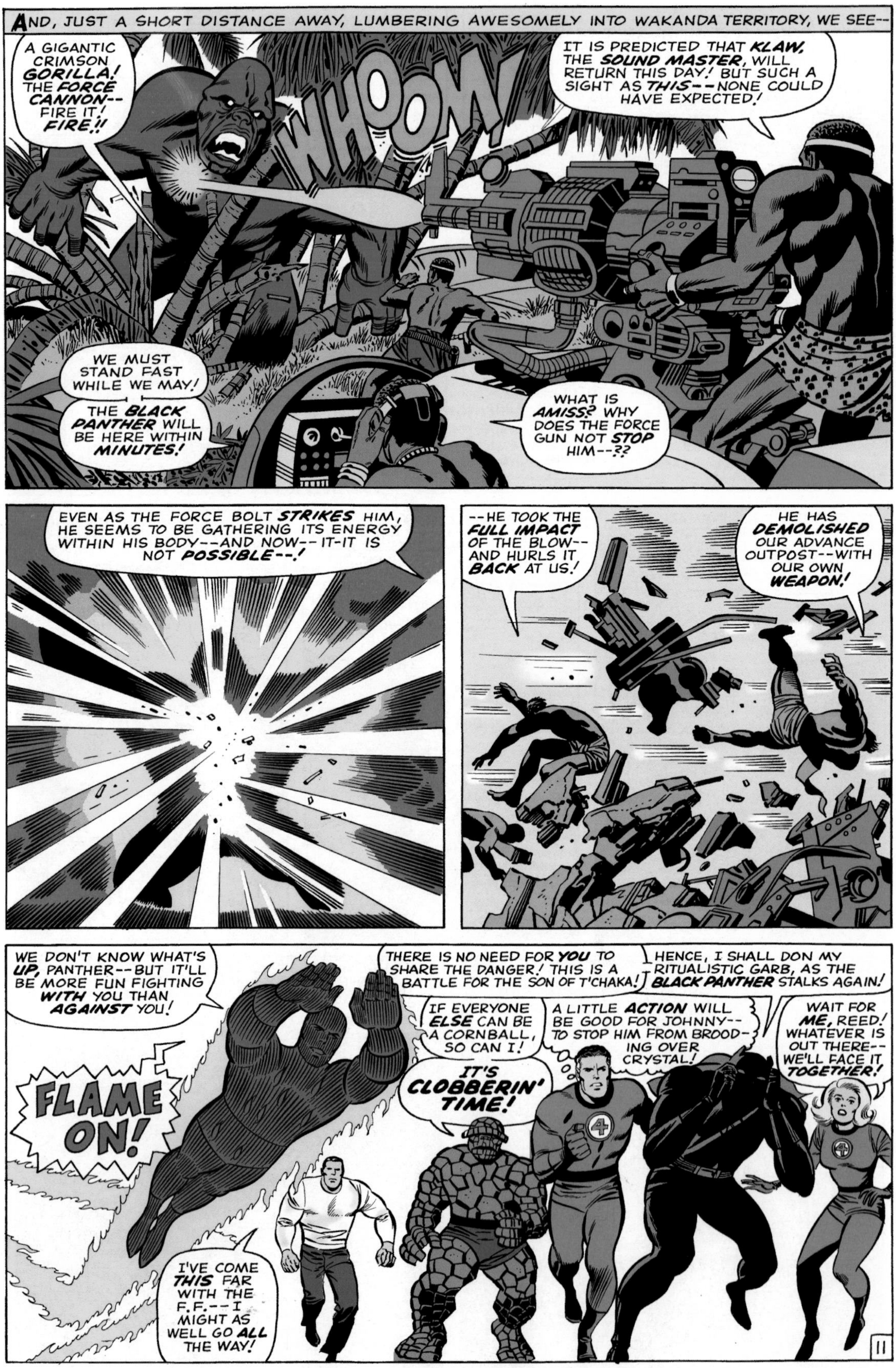

AND, JUST A SHORT DISTANCE AWAY, LUMBERING AWESOMELY INTO WAKANDA TERRITORY, WE SEE--
A GIGANTIC CRIMSON GORILLA! THE FORCE CANNON-- FIRE IT! FIRE!!
WHOOM!
IT IS PREDICTED THAT KLAW, THE SOUND MASTER, WILL RETURN THIS DAY! BUT SUCH A SIGHT AS THIS--NONE COULD HAVE EXPECTED!
WE MUST STAND FAST WHILE WE MAY!
THE BLACK PANTHER WILL BE HERE WITHIN MINUTES!
WHAT IS AMISS? WHY DOES THE FORCE GUN NOT STOP HIM--??
EVEN AS THE FORCE BOLT STRIKES HIM, HE SEEMS TO BE GATHERING ITS ENERGY WITHIN HIS BODY--AND NOW--IT-IT IS NOT POSSIBLE--!
--HE TOOK THE FULL IMPACT OF THE BLOW-- AND HURLS IT BACK AT US!
HE HAS DEMOLISHED OUR ADVANCE OUTPOST--WITH OUR OWN WEAPON!
WE DON'T KNOW WHAT'S UP, PANTHER--BUT IT'LL BE MORE FUN FIGHTING WITH YOU THAN AGAINST YOU!
THERE IS NO NEED FOR YOU TO SHARE THE DANGER! THIS IS A BATTLE FOR THE SON OF T'CHAKA!
HENCE, I SHALL DON MY RITUALISTIC GARB, AS THE BLACK PANTHER STALKS AGAIN!
IF EVERYONE ELSE CAN BE A CORNBALL, SO CAN I!
A LITTLE ACTION WILL BE GOOD FOR JOHNNY-- TO STOP HIM FROM BROODING OVER CRYSTAL!
WAIT FOR ME, REED! WHATEVER IS OUT THERE-- WE'LL FACE IT TOGETHER!
FLAME ON!
IT'S CLOBBERIN' TIME!
I'VE COME THIS FAR WITH THE F.F.--I MIGHT AS WELL GO ALL THE WAY!
11

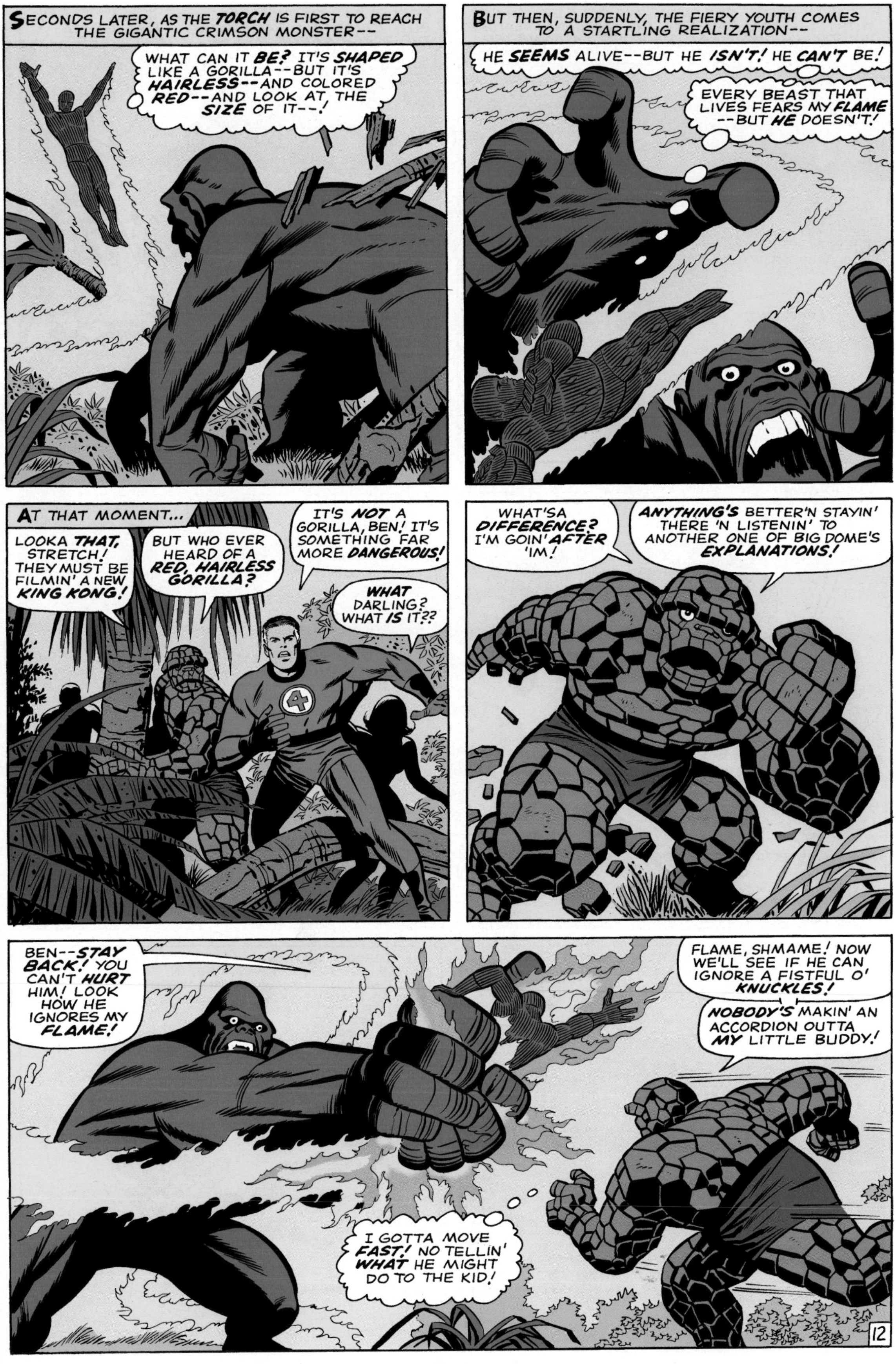
SECONDS LATER, AS THE TORCH IS FIRST TO REACH THE GIGANTIC CRIMSON MONSTER--
WHAT CAN IT BE? IT'S SHAPED LIKE A GORILLA--BUT IT'S HAIRLESS--AND COLORED RED--AND LOOK AT THE SIZE OF IT--!
BUT THEN, SUDDENLY, THE FIERY YOUTH COMES TO A STARTLING REALIZATION--
HE SEEMS ALIVE--BUT HE ISN'T! HE CAN'T BE!
EVERY BEAST THAT LIVES FEARS MY FLAME --BUT HE DOESN'T!
AT THAT MOMENT...
LOOKA THAT, STRETCH! THEY MUST BE FILMIN' A NEW KING KONG!
BUT WHO EVER HEARD OF A RED, HAIRLESS GORILLA?
IT'S NOT A GORILLA, BEN! IT'S SOMETHING FAR MORE DANGEROUS!
WHAT DARLING? WHAT IS IT??
WHAT'SA DIFFERENCE? I'M GOIN' AFTER 'IM!
ANYTHING'S BETTER'N STAYIN' THERE 'N LISTENIN' TO ANOTHER ONE OF BIG DOME'S EXPLANATIONS!
BEN--STAY BACK! YOU CAN'T HURT HIM! LOOK HOW HE IGNORES MY FLAME!
FLAME, SHMAME! NOW WE'LL SEE IF HE CAN IGNORE A FISTFUL O' KNUCKLES!
NOBODY'S MAKIN' AN ACCORDION OUTTA MY LITTLE BUDDY!
I GOTTA MOVE FAST! NO TELLIN' WHAT HE MIGHT DO TO THE KID!
12

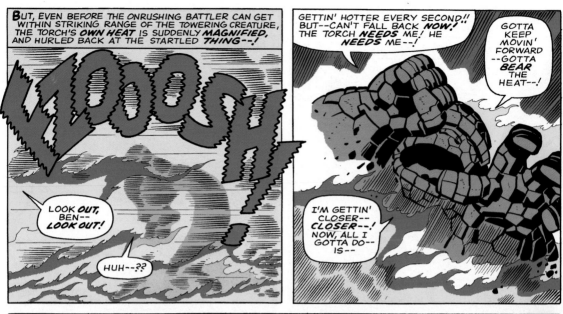

BUT, EVEN BEFORE THE ONRUSHING BATTLER CAN GET WITHIN STRIKING RANGE OF THE TOWERING CREATURE, THE TORCH'S *OWN HEAT* IS SUDDENLY *MAGNIFIED*, AND HURLED BACK AT THE STARTLED *THING*--!

WZOOOSH!

LOOK *OUT*, BEN-- *LOOK OUT!*

HUH--??

GETTIN' HOTTER EVERY SECOND!! BUT--CAN'T FALL BACK *NOW!* THE TORCH *NEEDS* ME! HE *NEEDS* ME--!

GOTTA KEEP MOVIN' FORWARD --GOTTA *BEAR* THE HEAT--!

I'M GETTIN' CLOSER-- *CLOSER*--! NOW, ALL I GOTTA DO-- IS--

--LAND *ONE* SOLID SOCK-- THAT'S ALL I-- *HEY!* I *DID* IT!

JUST IN *TIME*, BENJY! YOUR PUNCH MADE HIM LET ME *GO!*

BTOOSH!

BUT, BEFORE THE ORANGE-SKINNED CLOBBERER CAN *ENJOY* HIS VICTORY-- LOOK WHAT HAPPENS--

THAT *NOISE!!* IT ALMOST *DEAFENED* ME! WHA--WHAT *WAS* IT?

DON'TCHA KNOW A *SONIC BOOM* WHEN YA HEAR ONE, JUNIOR! BUT, I DON'T *GET* IT-- IT CAME FROM THAT OVER-SIZE *APE*--!

HOW IN THUNDERATION DID *HE* BREAK THE SOUND BARRIER!??

I'LL ANSWER YOU *LATER*, BIG BUDDY! RIGHT NOW, I WANNA ENJOY SINKING INTO SUSIE'S FRIENDLY LITTLE *FORCE FIELD!*

DIDJA EVER HAVE A FEELIN' YA GOT STUCK IN THE WRONG *NIGHTMARE?*

I *GOT* THEM, REED! JUST IN TIME!

13

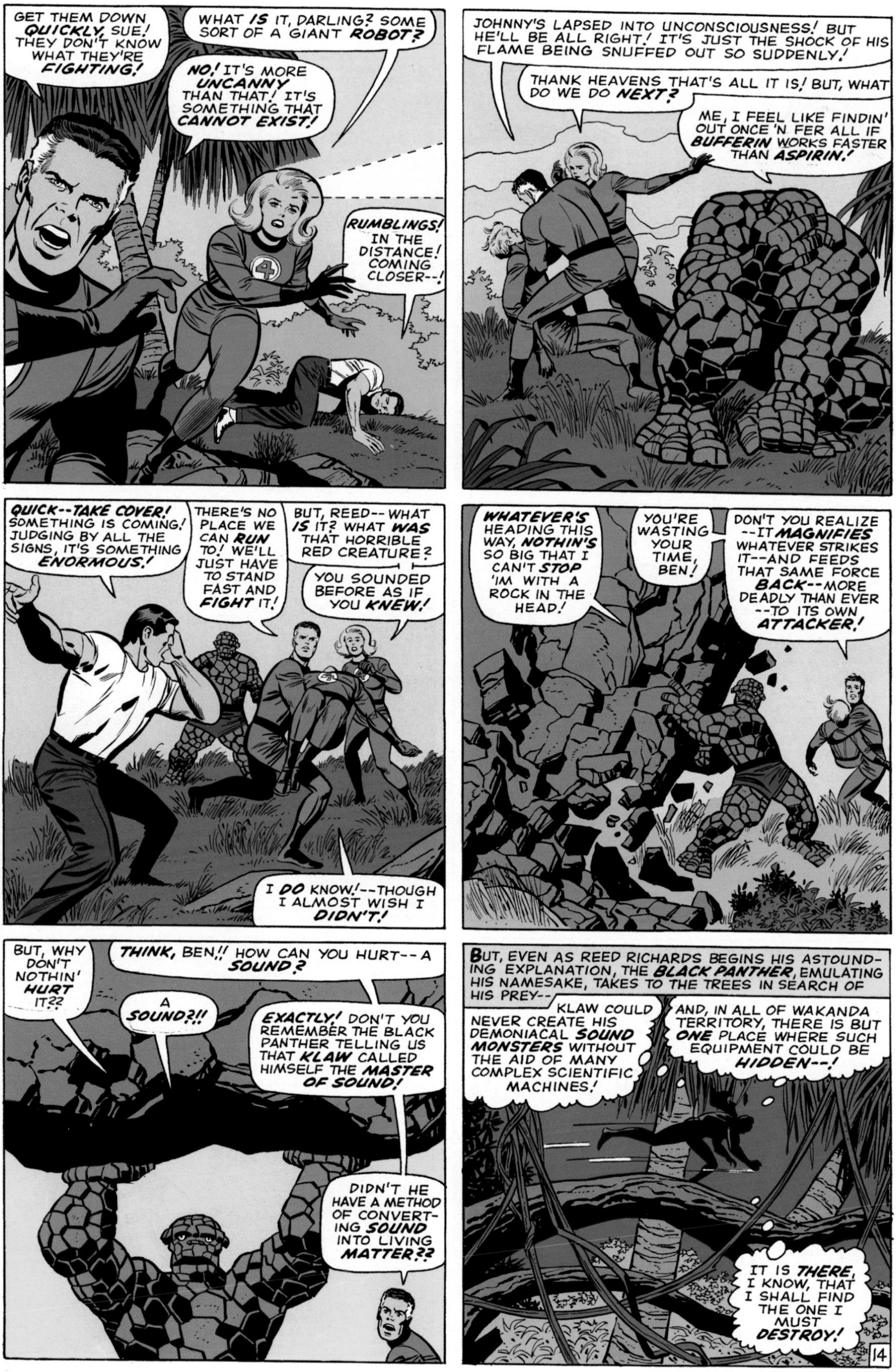
GET THEM DOWN QUICKLY, SUE! THEY DON'T KNOW WHAT THEY'RE FIGHTING!
WHAT IS IT, DARLING? SOME SORT OF A GIANT ROBOT?
NO! IT'S MORE UNCANNY THAN THAT! IT'S SOMETHING THAT CANNOT EXIST!
RUMBLINGS! IN THE DISTANCE! COMING CLOSER--!
JOHNNY'S LAPSED INTO UNCONSCIOUSNESS! BUT HE'LL BE ALL RIGHT! IT'S JUST THE SHOCK OF HIS FLAME BEING SNUFFED OUT SO SUDDENLY!
THANK HEAVENS THAT'S ALL IT IS! BUT, WHAT DO WE DO NEXT?
ME, I FEEL LIKE FINDIN' OUT ONCE 'N FER ALL IF BUFFERIN WORKS FASTER THAN ASPIRIN!
QUICK--TAKE COVER! SOMETHING IS COMING! JUDGING BY ALL THE SIGNS, IT'S SOMETHING ENORMOUS!
THERE'S NO PLACE WE CAN RUN TO! WE'LL JUST HAVE TO STAND FAST AND FIGHT IT!
BUT, REED-- WHAT IS IT? WHAT WAS THAT HORRIBLE RED CREATURE?
YOU SOUNDED BEFORE AS IF YOU KNEW!
I DO KNOW!--THOUGH I ALMOST WISH I DIDN'T!
WHATEVER'S HEADING THIS WAY, NOTHIN'S SO BIG THAT I CAN'T STOP 'IM WITH A ROCK IN THE HEAD!
YOU'RE WASTING YOUR TIME, BEN!
DON'T YOU REALIZE --IT MAGNIFIES WHATEVER STRIKES IT--AND FEEDS THAT SAME FORCE BACK--MORE DEADLY THAN EVER --TO ITS OWN ATTACKER!
BUT, WHY DON'T NOTHIN' HURT IT??
THINK, BEN!! HOW CAN YOU HURT-- A SOUND?
A SOUND?!!
EXACTLY! DON'T YOU REMEMBER THE BLACK PANTHER TELLING US THAT KLAW CALLED HIMSELF THE MASTER OF SOUND!
DIDN'T HE HAVE A METHOD OF CONVERTING SOUND INTO LIVING MATTER??
BUT, EVEN AS REED RICHARDS BEGINS HIS ASTOUNDING EXPLANATION, THE BLACK PANTHER, EMULATING HIS NAMESAKE, TAKES TO THE TREES IN SEARCH OF HIS PREY--
KLAW COULD NEVER CREATE HIS DEMONIACAL SOUND MONSTERS WITHOUT THE AID OF MANY COMPLEX SCIENTIFIC MACHINES!
AND, IN ALL OF WAKANDA TERRITORY, THERE IS BUT ONE PLACE WHERE SUCH EQUIPMENT COULD BE HIDDEN--!
IT IS THERE, I KNOW, THAT I SHALL FIND THE ONE I MUST DESTROY!
14

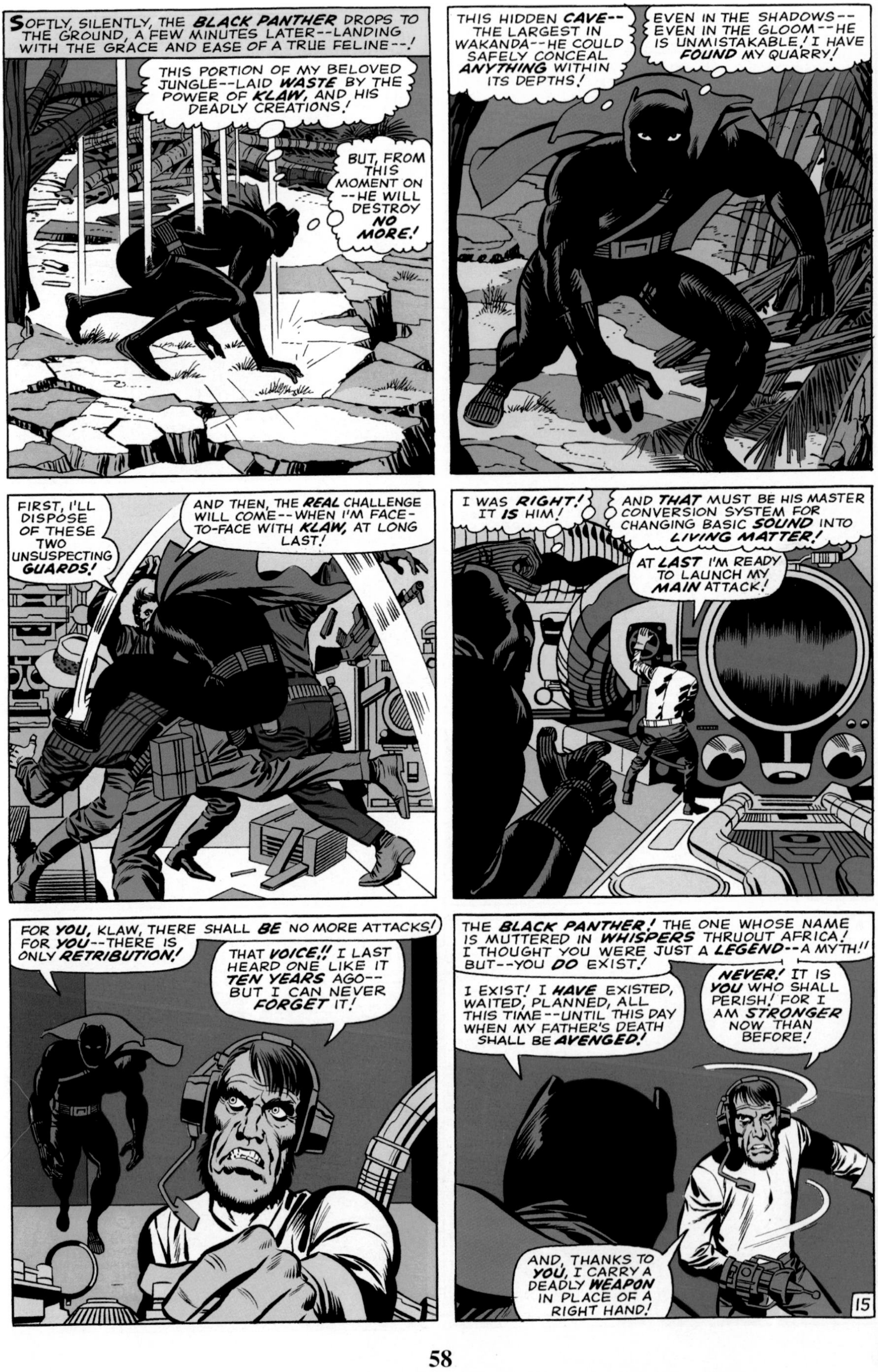
SOFTLY, SILENTLY, THE BLACK PANTHER DROPS TO THE GROUND, A FEW MINUTES LATER--LANDING WITH THE GRACE AND EASE OF A TRUE FELINE--!
THIS PORTION OF MY BELOVED JUNGLE--LAID WASTE BY THE POWER OF KLAW, AND HIS DEADLY CREATIONS!
BUT, FROM THIS MOMENT ON --HE WILL DESTROY NO MORE!
THIS HIDDEN CAVE-- THE LARGEST IN WAKANDA--HE COULD SAFELY CONCEAL ANYTHING WITHIN ITS DEPTHS!
EVEN IN THE SHADOWS-- EVEN IN THE GLOOM--HE IS UNMISTAKABLE! I HAVE FOUND MY QUARRY!
FIRST, I'LL DISPOSE OF THESE TWO UNSUSPECTING GUARDS!
AND THEN, THE REAL CHALLENGE WILL COME--WHEN I'M FACE-TO-FACE WITH KLAW, AT LONG LAST!
I WAS RIGHT! IT IS HIM!
AND THAT MUST BE HIS MASTER CONVERSION SYSTEM FOR CHANGING BASIC SOUND INTO LIVING MATTER!
AT LAST I'M READY TO LAUNCH MY MAIN ATTACK!
FOR YOU, KLAW, THERE SHALL BE NO MORE ATTACKS! FOR YOU--THERE IS ONLY RETRIBUTION!
THAT VOICE!! I LAST HEARD ONE LIKE IT TEN YEARS AGO-- BUT I CAN NEVER FORGET IT!
THE BLACK PANTHER! THE ONE WHOSE NAME IS MUTTERED IN WHISPERS THRUOUT AFRICA! I THOUGHT YOU WERE JUST A LEGEND--A MYTH!! BUT--YOU DO EXIST!
I EXIST! I HAVE EXISTED, WAITED, PLANNED, ALL THIS TIME--UNTIL THIS DAY WHEN MY FATHER'S DEATH SHALL BE AVENGED!
NEVER! IT IS YOU WHO SHALL PERISH! FOR I AM STRONGER NOW THAN BEFORE!
AND, THANKS TO YOU, I CARRY A DEADLY WEAPON IN PLACE OF A RIGHT HAND!
15

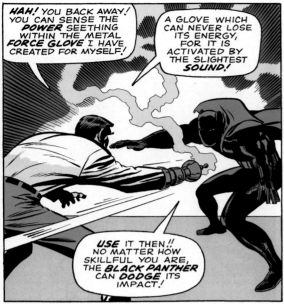

HAH! YOU BACK AWAY! YOU CAN SENSE THE **POWER** SEETHING WITHIN THE METAL **FORCE GLOVE** I HAVE CREATED FOR MYSELF!

A GLOVE WHICH CAN NEVER LOSE ITS ENERGY, FOR IT IS ACTIVATED BY THE SLIGHTEST **SOUND!**

USE IT THEN!! NO MATTER HOW SKILLFUL YOU ARE, THE **BLACK PANTHER** CAN **DODGE** ITS **IMPACT!**

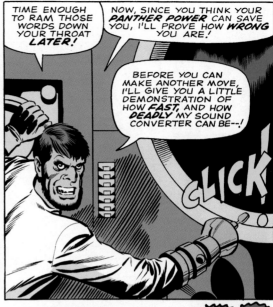

TIME ENOUGH TO RAM THOSE WORDS DOWN YOUR THROAT **LATER!**

NOW, SINCE YOU THINK YOUR **PANTHER POWER** CAN SAVE YOU, I'LL PROVE HOW **WRONG** YOU ARE!

BEFORE YOU CAN MAKE ANOTHER MOVE, I'LL GIVE YOU A LITTLE DEMONSTRATION OF HOW **FAST,** AND HOW **DEADLY** MY SOUND CONVERTER CAN BE--!

CLICK!

ONLY **KLAW** CAN INSTANTANEOUSLY CHANGE THE BASIC ENERGY OF **SOUND**--AND TRANSFORM IT INTO A SIMULATION OF ANY **LIVING CREATURE**--

AND, WHAT CAN BE MORE IRONIC-- MORE **JUST**--THAN HAVING YOU MEET YOUR FATE BENEATH THE TALONS OF **ANOTHER** BLACK PANTHER--A FAR **SUPERIOR** ONE!

THUS, DOES THE **MASTER OF SOUND** EXACT HIS FINAL **REVENGE!**

BUT, JUST IN CASE THE PRECEDING SEQUENCE WAS TOO NERVE-WRACKING IN ITS SHEER, STARK INTENSITY, WE'LL EXERCISE OUR EDITORIAL PEROGATIVE BY BRIEFLY **SWITCHING SCENES** ONCE MORE, AS WE REJOIN THE GIGANTIC RED **ELEPHANT** WHICH IS CHARGING MURDER-OUSLY TOWARDS THE INDOMITABLE **THING**--

CRASH!

YOU DON'T SCARE **ME,** DUMBO! IF YER FEELIN' **HUNGRY**--HERE'S A KING-SIZED **PEANUT** TO CHEW ON!

16

BUT, NO SOONER DOES THE MOUNTAINOUS BOULDER *STRIKE* THE CHARGING BEAST, THAN IT CRUMBLES INTO A THOUSAND SMALLER FRAGMENTS, RICOCHETTING *BACK* AT THE DUMBFOUNDED HUMAN POWERHOUSE--!

WHOOM

IF THERE'S ONE THING THAT REALLY BUGS ME, IT'S A *WISE-GUY* ELEPHANT!

IT'S THE ONES LIKE *YOU* THAT MAKE A JOKE OUTTA *"BE KIND TO DUMB ANIMALS WEEK"!*

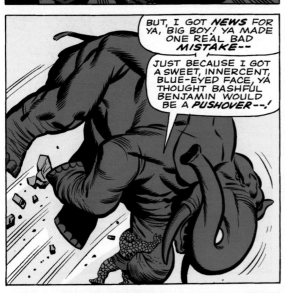

BUT, I GOT *NEWS* FOR YA, BIG BOY! YA MADE ONE REAL BAD *MISTAKE*--

JUST BECAUSE I GOT A SWEET, INNERCENT, BLUE-EYED FACE, YA THOUGHT BASHFUL BENJAMIN WOULD BE A *PUSHOVER*--!

BUT, NOW I'M GONNA--

HEY! WHAT'S GOIN' ON?? THIS IS *CRAZY!!* IT-IT DON'T MAKE *SENSE*--!

THE MORE *PRESSURE* I PUT ON 'IM, THE MORE IT HURTS *ME*--JUST LIKE HE'S REFLECTIN' IT ALL *BACK*-- LIKE A *MIRROR!*

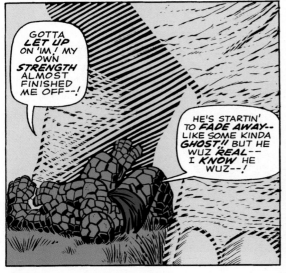

GOTTA *LET UP* ON 'IM! MY OWN *STRENGTH* ALMOST FINISHED ME OFF--!

HE'S STARTIN' TO *FADE AWAY*-- LIKE SOME KINDA *GHOST!!* BUT HE WUZ *REAL*-- I *KNOW* HE WUZ--!

WYATT! THE ELEPHANT'S *GONE!* SEE IF *BEN* NEEDS ANY HELP--WHILE I LOWER SUE AND JOHNNY TO THE GROUND!

HE *SEEMS* ALL RIGHT, MR. RICHARDS! HE'S STARTING TO GET UP!

'COURSE I'M AWRIGHT! I WUZ JUST TRYIN' TO FIND ME A FOUR-LEAF CLOVER!

17

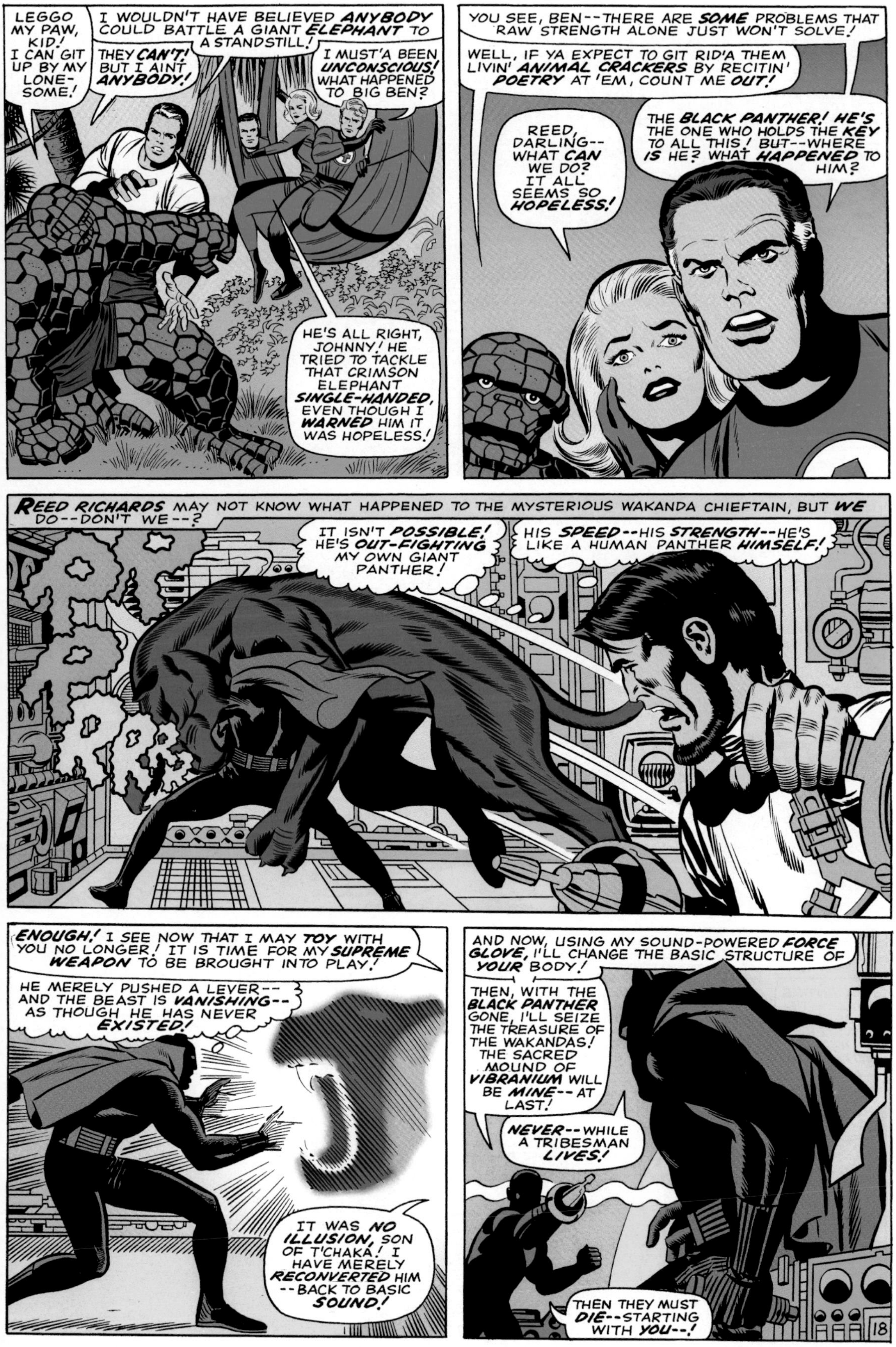
LEGGO MY PAW, KID! I CAN GIT UP BY MY LONE-SOME!
I WOULDN'T HAVE BELIEVED ANYBODY COULD BATTLE A GIANT ELEPHANT TO A STANDSTILL!
THEY CAN'T! BUT I AINT ANYBODY!
I MUST'A BEEN UNCONSCIOUS! WHAT HAPPENED TO BIG BEN?
HE'S ALL RIGHT, JOHNNY! HE TRIED TO TACKLE THAT CRIMSON ELEPHANT SINGLE-HANDED, EVEN THOUGH I WARNED HIM IT WAS HOPELESS!
YOU SEE, BEN--THERE ARE SOME PROBLEMS THAT RAW STRENGTH ALONE JUST WON'T SOLVE!
WELL, IF YA EXPECT TO GIT RID'A THEM LIVIN' ANIMAL CRACKERS BY RECITIN' POETRY AT 'EM, COUNT ME OUT!
REED, DARLING-- WHAT CAN WE DO? IT ALL SEEMS SO HOPELESS!
THE BLACK PANTHER! HE'S THE ONE WHO HOLDS THE KEY TO ALL THIS! BUT--WHERE IS HE? WHAT HAPPENED TO HIM?
REED RICHARDS MAY NOT KNOW WHAT HAPPENED TO THE MYSTERIOUS WAKANDA CHIEFTAIN, BUT WE DO--DON'T WE--?
IT ISN'T POSSIBLE! HE'S OUT-FIGHTING MY OWN GIANT PANTHER!
HIS SPEED--HIS STRENGTH--HE'S LIKE A HUMAN PANTHER HIMSELF!
RRRR
ENOUGH! I SEE NOW THAT I MAY TOY WITH YOU NO LONGER! IT IS TIME FOR MY SUPREME WEAPON TO BE BROUGHT INTO PLAY!
HE MERELY PUSHED A LEVER-- AND THE BEAST IS VANISHING-- AS THOUGH HE HAS NEVER EXISTED!
IT WAS NO ILLUSION, SON OF T'CHAKA! I HAVE MERELY RECONVERTED HIM --BACK TO BASIC SOUND!
AND NOW, USING MY SOUND-POWERED FORCE GLOVE, I'LL CHANGE THE BASIC STRUCTURE OF YOUR BODY!
THEN, WITH THE BLACK PANTHER GONE, I'LL SEIZE THE TREASURE OF THE WAKANDAS! THE SACRED MOUND OF VIBRANIUM WILL BE MINE--AT LAST!
NEVER--WHILE A TRIBESMAN LIVES!
THEN THEY MUST DIE--STARTING WITH YOU--!
18

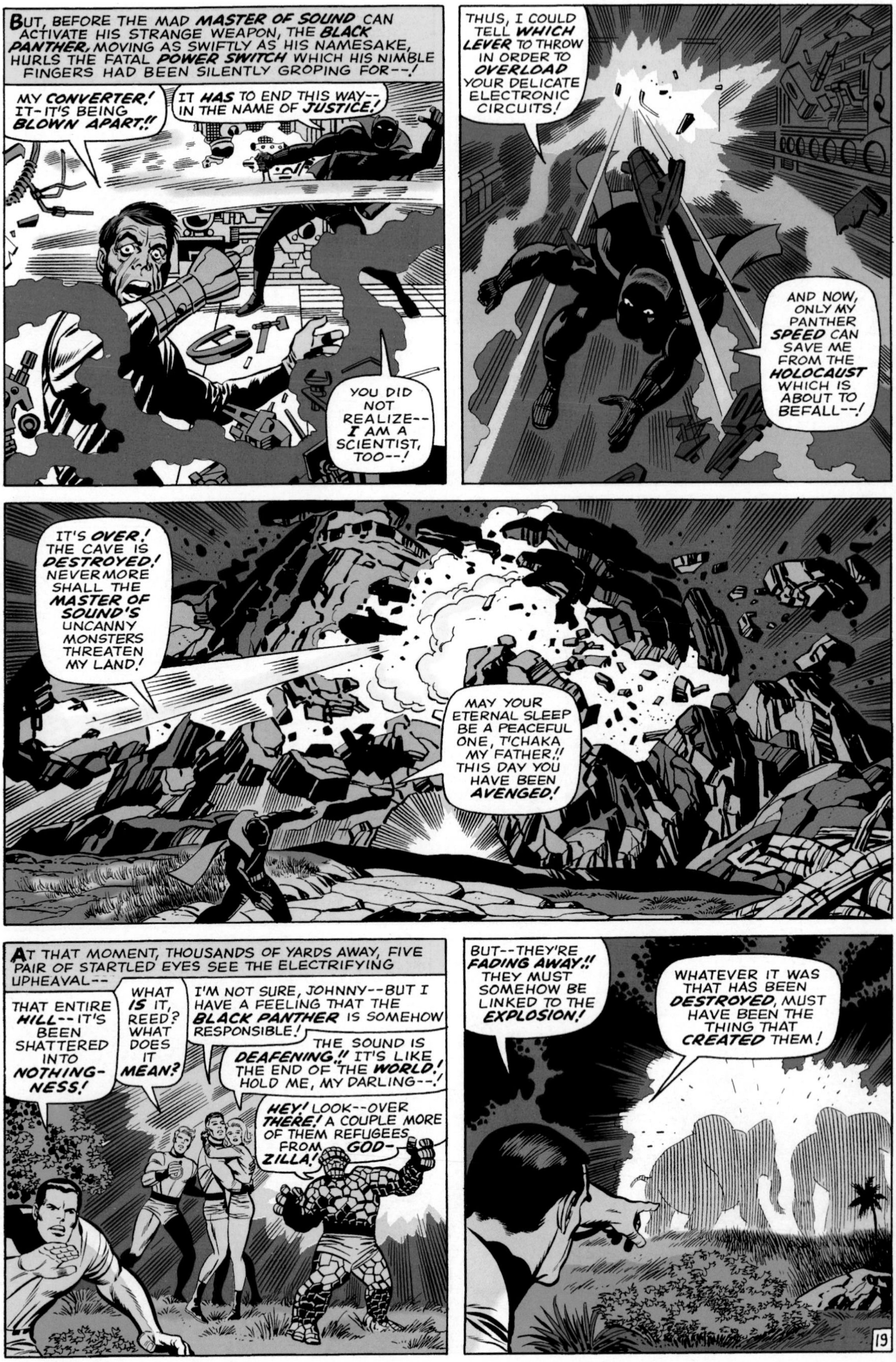
BUT, BEFORE THE MAD MASTER OF SOUND CAN ACTIVATE HIS STRANGE WEAPON, THE BLACK PANTHER, MOVING AS SWIFTLY AS HIS NAMESAKE, HURLS THE FATAL POWER SWITCH WHICH HIS NIMBLE FINGERS HAD BEEN SILENTLY GROPING FOR--!
MY CONVERTER! IT-IT'S BEING BLOWN APART!!
IT HAS TO END THIS WAY-- IN THE NAME OF JUSTICE!
YOU DID NOT REALIZE-- I AM A SCIENTIST, TOO--!
THUS, I COULD TELL WHICH LEVER TO THROW IN ORDER TO OVERLOAD YOUR DELICATE ELECTRONIC CIRCUITS!
AND NOW, ONLY MY PANTHER SPEED CAN SAVE ME FROM THE HOLOCAUST WHICH IS ABOUT TO BEFALL--!
IT'S OVER! THE CAVE IS DESTROYED! NEVERMORE SHALL THE MASTER OF SOUND'S UNCANNY MONSTERS THREATEN MY LAND!
MAY YOUR ETERNAL SLEEP BE A PEACEFUL ONE, T'CHAKA MY FATHER!! THIS DAY YOU HAVE BEEN AVENGED!
AT THAT MOMENT, THOUSANDS OF YARDS AWAY, FIVE PAIR OF STARTLED EYES SEE THE ELECTRIFYING UPHEAVAL--
THAT ENTIRE HILL-- IT'S BEEN SHATTERED INTO NOTHING-NESS!
WHAT IS IT, REED? WHAT DOES IT MEAN?
I'M NOT SURE, JOHNNY--BUT I HAVE A FEELING THAT THE BLACK PANTHER IS SOMEHOW RESPONSIBLE!
THE SOUND IS DEAFENING!! IT'S LIKE THE END OF THE WORLD! HOLD ME, MY DARLING--!
HEY! LOOK--OVER THERE! A COUPLE MORE OF THEM REFUGEES FROM GOD-ZILLA!
BUT--THEY'RE FADING AWAY!! THEY MUST SOMEHOW BE LINKED TO THE EXPLOSION!
WHATEVER IT WAS THAT HAS BEEN DESTROYED, MUST HAVE BEEN THE THING THAT CREATED THEM!
19

IT WAS **KLAW** WHO CREATED THEM--**KLAW**, WHO, IN HIS MADNESS, LEARNED THE INCREDIBLE SECRET OF TRANSFORMING **SOUND** INTO **MASS**!

BUT, I DESTROYED HIS ELECTRONIC EQUIPMENT! IT WOULD TAKE HIM A **LIFETIME** TO REPLACE IT--IF HE **SURVIVED**!

SO **THAT'S** WHY THEM **NUTTY** ANIMALS FADED AWAY!

THEN YOUR MISSION IS **ENDED**!

YES--THE **MASTER OF SOUND** HAS BEEN DEFEATED!

BUT, SOMEHOW, I CANNOT BELIEVE IT IS OVER! I CANNOT BELIEVE THAT THE **BLACK PANTHER** WILL STALK NO MORE!

DON'T GIT ALL SHOOK UP, PAL! MEBBE THE **YANCY STREET GANG** CAN USE YA!

BENJAMIN J. GRIMM! THAT WASN'T **FUNNY**!

WELL, YA CAN'T WIN EM **ALL**!

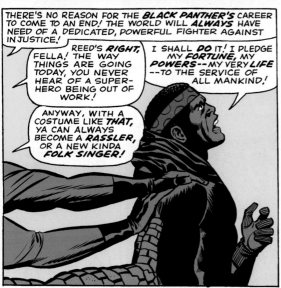

THERE'S NO REASON FOR THE **BLACK PANTHER'S** CAREER TO COME TO AN END! THE WORLD WILL **ALWAYS** HAVE NEED OF A DEDICATED, POWERFUL FIGHTER AGAINST INJUSTICE!

REED'S **RIGHT**, FELLA! THE WAY THINGS ARE GOING TODAY, YOU NEVER HEAR OF A SUPER-HERO BEING OUT OF WORK!

I SHALL **DO** IT! I PLEDGE MY **FORTUNE**, MY **POWERS**--MY VERY **LIFE** --TO THE SERVICE OF ALL MANKIND!

ANYWAY, WITH A COSTUME LIKE **THAT**, YA CAN ALWAYS BECOME A **RASSLER**, OR A NEW KINDA **FOLK SINGER**!

BUT, EVEN AS THE GALLANT **BLACK PANTHER** DEDICATES HIMSELF TO AIDING HUMANITY; AMIDST THE CARNAGE AND RUBBLE OF THE SHATTERED HILLOCK, **ANOTHER** TYPE OF DEDICATION IS ABOUT TO BE MADE--

MY LIFE'S WORK--SHATTERED-- RUINED--ALL BECAUSE OF T'CHAKA'S **SON** AGAIN!

BUT, BY SOME STRANGE QUIRK OF FATE --THE **MASTER OF SOUND** STILL **LIVES**!

AND, MY **CONVERTER** STILL POSSESSES A GLIMMER OF ENERGY--PERHAPS ENOUGH FOR **ONE** FINAL TRANS-FORMATION!!

THERE IS **ONE** EXPERIMENT I NEVER DARED TO MAKE--ONE **CHALLENGE** I NEVER DARED ACCEPT!

I NEVER LEARNED WHAT WOULD HAPPEN IF--A **HUMAN** ALTERED HIS OWN BASIC STRUCTURE VIA MY **SOUND TRANSFORMER**!!

IF I **SURVIVE**, I'LL EMERGE WITH POWERS FAR **DIFFERENT** THAN THOSE EVER POSSESSED BY MORTAL MAN--!

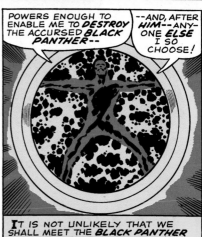

POWERS ENOUGH TO ENABLE ME TO **DESTROY** THE ACCURSED **BLACK PANTHER**--

--AND, AFTER **HIM**--ANY-ONE **ELSE** I SO CHOOSE!

IT IS NOT UNLIKELY THAT WE SHALL MEET THE **BLACK PANTHER** AND HIS ARCH-FOE, **KLAW**, ONCE AGAIN--BUT, TILL WE DO, DON'T MISS THE START OF A BRAND-NEW STORY LINE NEXT ISH! YOU KNOW HOW IT **UPSETS** US WHEN YOU'RE NOT IN AT THE **BEGINNING**!

20

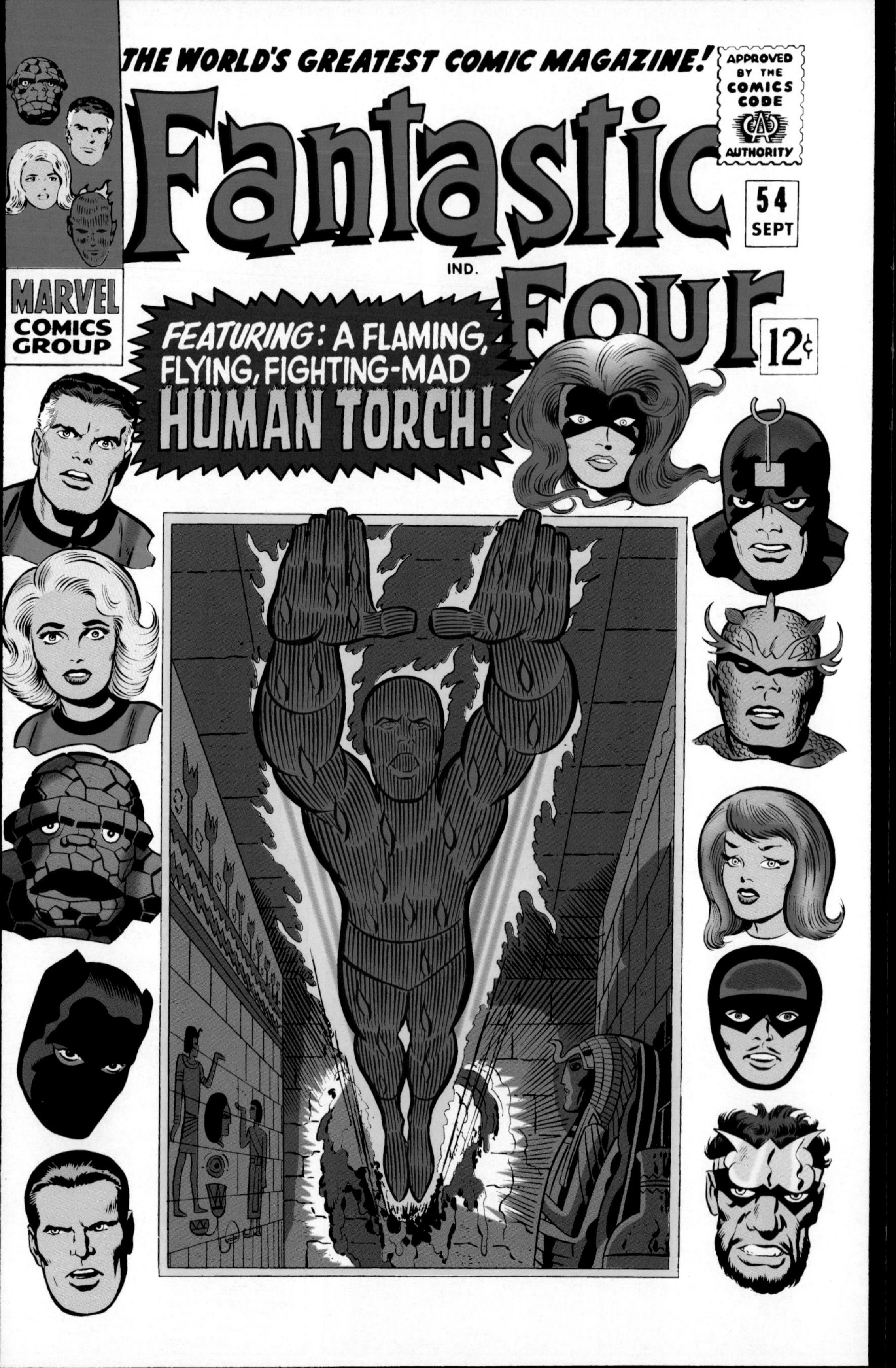
THE WORLD'S GREATEST COMIC MAGAZINE!
APPROVED BY THE COMICS CODE AUTHORITY
Fantastic Four
IND.
54 SEPT
12¢
MARVEL COMICS GROUP
FEATURING: A FLAMING, FLYING, FIGHTING-MAD HUMAN TORCH!

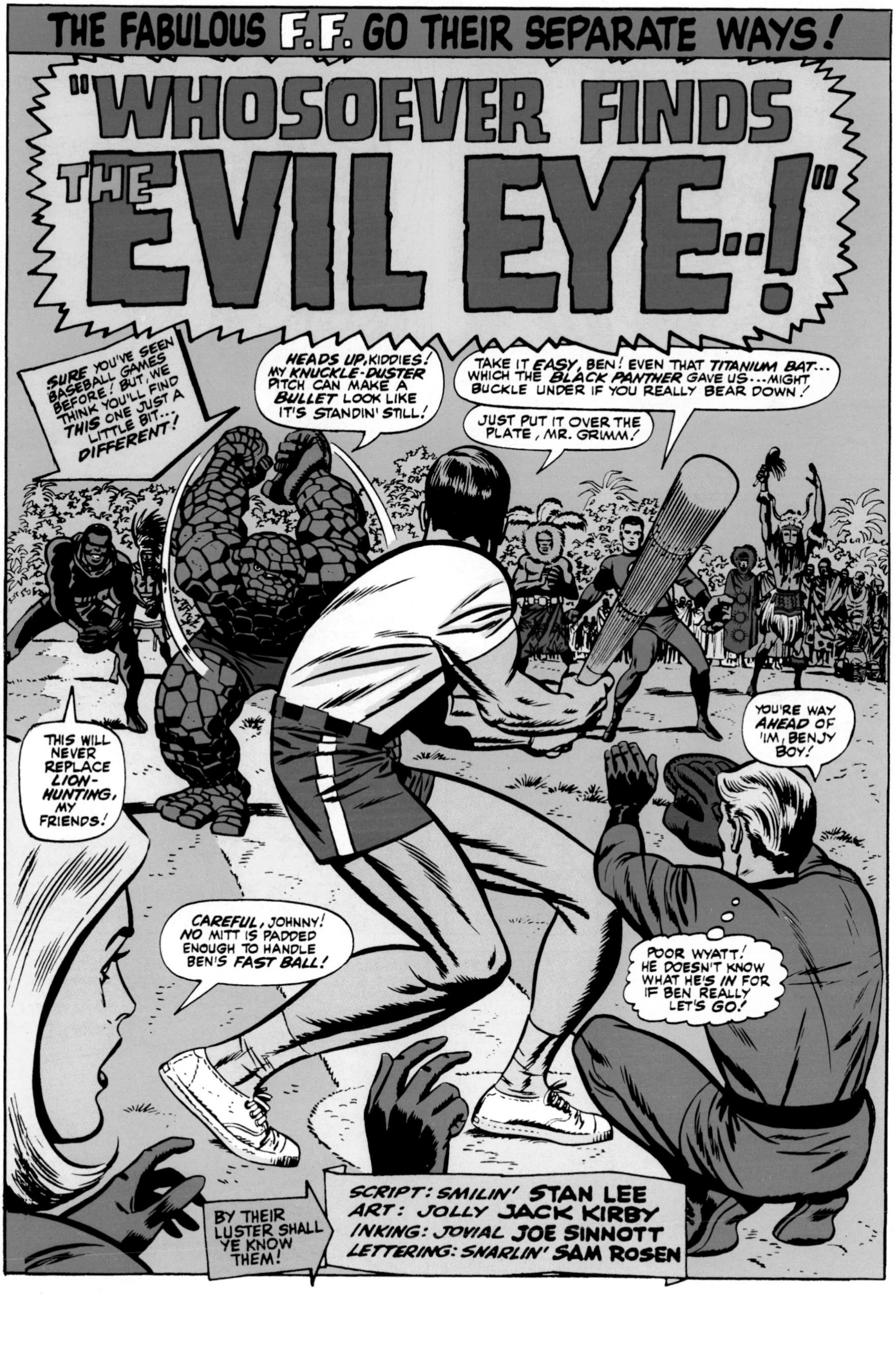
THE FABULOUS F.F. GO THEIR SEPARATE WAYS!
"WHOSOEVER FINDS THE EVIL EYE..!"
SURE YOU'VE SEEN BASEBALL GAMES BEFORE! BUT, WE THINK YOU'LL FIND THIS ONE JUST A LITTLE BIT... DIFFERENT!
HEADS UP, KIDDIES! MY KNUCKLE-DUSTER PITCH CAN MAKE A BULLET LOOK LIKE IT'S STANDIN' STILL!
TAKE IT EASY, BEN! EVEN THAT TITANIUM BAT... WHICH THE BLACK PANTHER GAVE US... MIGHT BUCKLE UNDER IF YOU REALLY BEAR DOWN!
JUST PUT IT OVER THE PLATE, MR. GRIMM!
THIS WILL NEVER REPLACE LION-HUNTING, MY FRIENDS!
YOU'RE WAY AHEAD OF 'IM, BENJY BOY!
CAREFUL, JOHNNY! NO MITT IS PADDED ENOUGH TO HANDLE BEN'S FAST BALL!
POOR WYATT! HE DOESN'T KNOW WHAT HE'S IN FOR IF BEN REALLY LET'S GO!
BY THEIR LUSTER SHALL YE KNOW THEM!
SCRIPT: SMILIN' STAN LEE
ART: JOLLY JACK KIRBY
INKING: JOVIAL JOE SINNOTT
LETTERING: SNARLIN' SAM ROSEN

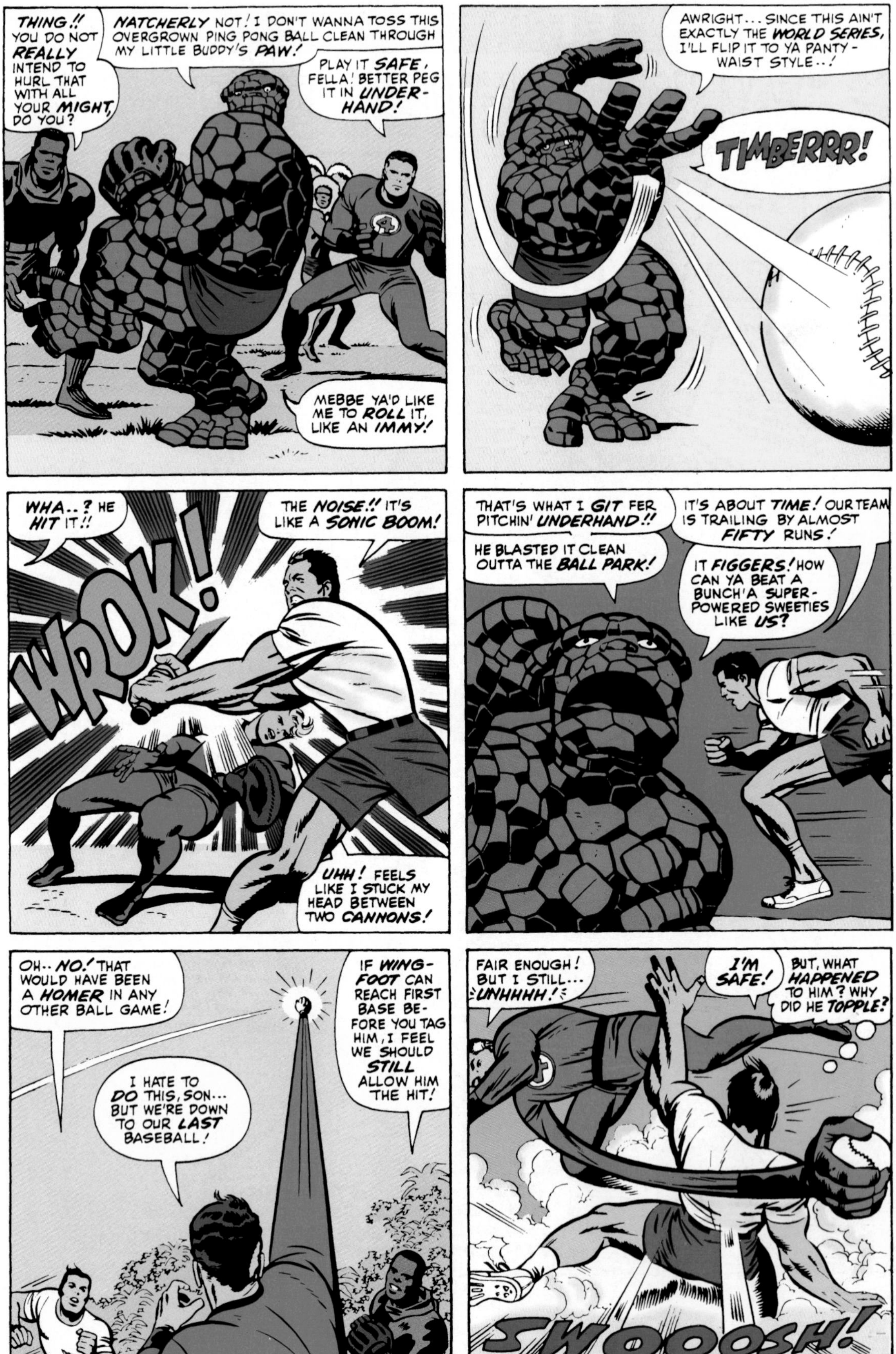

THING!! YOU DO NOT REALLY INTEND TO HURL THAT WITH ALL YOUR MIGHT, DO YOU?
NATCHERLY NOT! I DON'T WANNA TOSS THIS OVERGROWN PING PONG BALL CLEAN THROUGH MY LITTLE BUDDY'S PAW!
PLAY IT SAFE, FELLA! BETTER PEG IT IN UNDER-HAND!
MEBBE YA'D LIKE ME TO ROLL IT, LIKE AN IMMY!
AWRIGHT... SINCE THIS AIN'T EXACTLY THE WORLD SERIES, I'LL FLIP IT TO YA PANTY-WAIST STYLE..!
TIMBERRR!
WHA..? HE HIT IT!!
THE NOISE!! IT'S LIKE A SONIC BOOM!
WROK!
UHH! FEELS LIKE I STUCK MY HEAD BETWEEN TWO CANNONS!
THAT'S WHAT I GIT FER PITCHIN' UNDERHAND!!
HE BLASTED IT CLEAN OUTTA THE BALL PARK!
IT'S ABOUT TIME! OUR TEAM IS TRAILING BY ALMOST FIFTY RUNS!
IT FIGGERS! HOW CAN YA BEAT A BUNCH'A SUPER-POWERED SWEETIES LIKE US?
OH.. NO! THAT WOULD HAVE BEEN A HOMER IN ANY OTHER BALL GAME!
IF WING-FOOT CAN REACH FIRST BASE BE-FORE YOU TAG HIM, I FEEL WE SHOULD STILL ALLOW HIM THE HIT!
I HATE TO DO THIS, SON... BUT WE'RE DOWN TO OUR LAST BASEBALL!
FAIR ENOUGH! BUT I STILL... UNHHHH!
I'M SAFE!
BUT, WHAT HAPPENED TO HIM? WHY DID HE TOPPLE?
SWOOOSH!

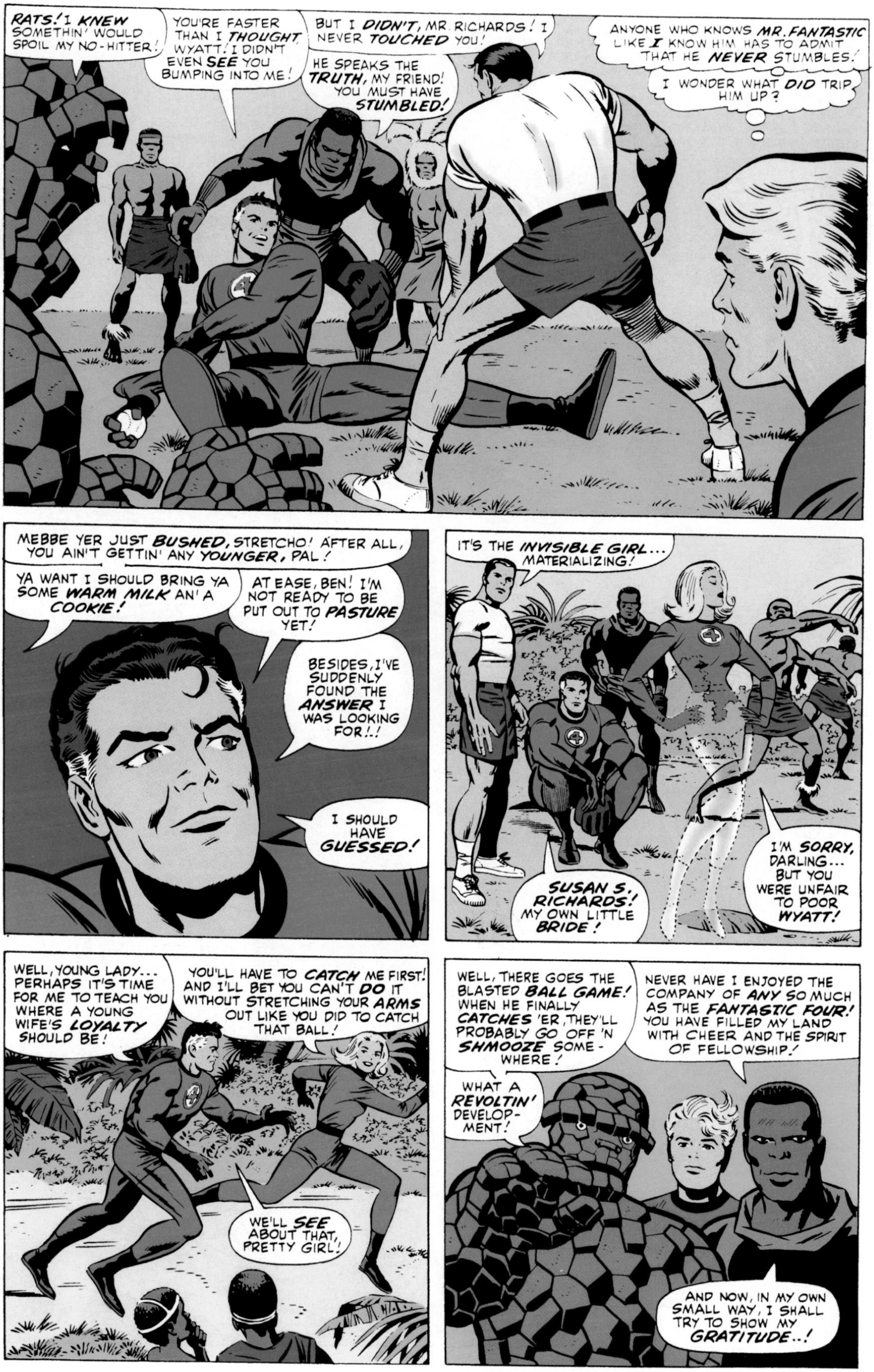
RATS! I KNEW SOMETHIN' WOULD SPOIL MY NO-HITTER!
YOU'RE FASTER THAN I THOUGHT, WYATT! I DIDN'T EVEN SEE YOU BUMPING INTO ME!
BUT I DIDN'T, MR. RICHARDS! I NEVER TOUCHED YOU!
HE SPEAKS THE TRUTH, MY FRIEND! YOU MUST HAVE STUMBLED!
ANYONE WHO KNOWS MR. FANTASTIC LIKE I KNOW HIM HAS TO ADMIT THAT HE NEVER STUMBLES!
I WONDER WHAT DID TRIP HIM UP?
MEBBE YER JUST BUSHED, STRETCHO! AFTER ALL, YOU AIN'T GETTIN' ANY YOUNGER, PAL!
YA WANT I SHOULD BRING YA SOME WARM MILK AN' A COOKIE!
AT EASE, BEN! I'M NOT READY TO BE PUT OUT TO PASTURE YET!
BESIDES, I'VE SUDDENLY FOUND THE ANSWER I WAS LOOKING FOR!!
I SHOULD HAVE GUESSED!
IT'S THE INVISIBLE GIRL... MATERIALIZING!
SUSAN S. RICHARDS! MY OWN LITTLE BRIDE!
I'M SORRY, DARLING... BUT YOU WERE UNFAIR TO POOR WYATT!
WELL, YOUNG LADY... PERHAPS IT'S TIME FOR ME TO TEACH YOU WHERE A YOUNG WIFE'S LOYALTY SHOULD BE!
YOU'LL HAVE TO CATCH ME FIRST! AND I'LL BET YOU CAN'T DO IT WITHOUT STRETCHING YOUR ARMS OUT LIKE YOU DID TO CATCH THAT BALL!
WE'LL SEE ABOUT THAT, PRETTY GIRL!
WELL, THERE GOES THE BLASTED BALL GAME! WHEN HE FINALLY CATCHES 'ER, THEY'LL PROBABLY GO OFF 'N SHMOOZE SOME-WHERE!
WHAT A REVOLTIN' DEVELOP-MENT!
NEVER HAVE I ENJOYED THE COMPANY OF ANY SO MUCH AS THE FANTASTIC FOUR! YOU HAVE FILLED MY LAND WITH CHEER AND THE SPIRIT OF FELLOWSHIP!
AND NOW, IN MY OWN SMALL WAY, I SHALL TRY TO SHOW MY GRATITUDE..!

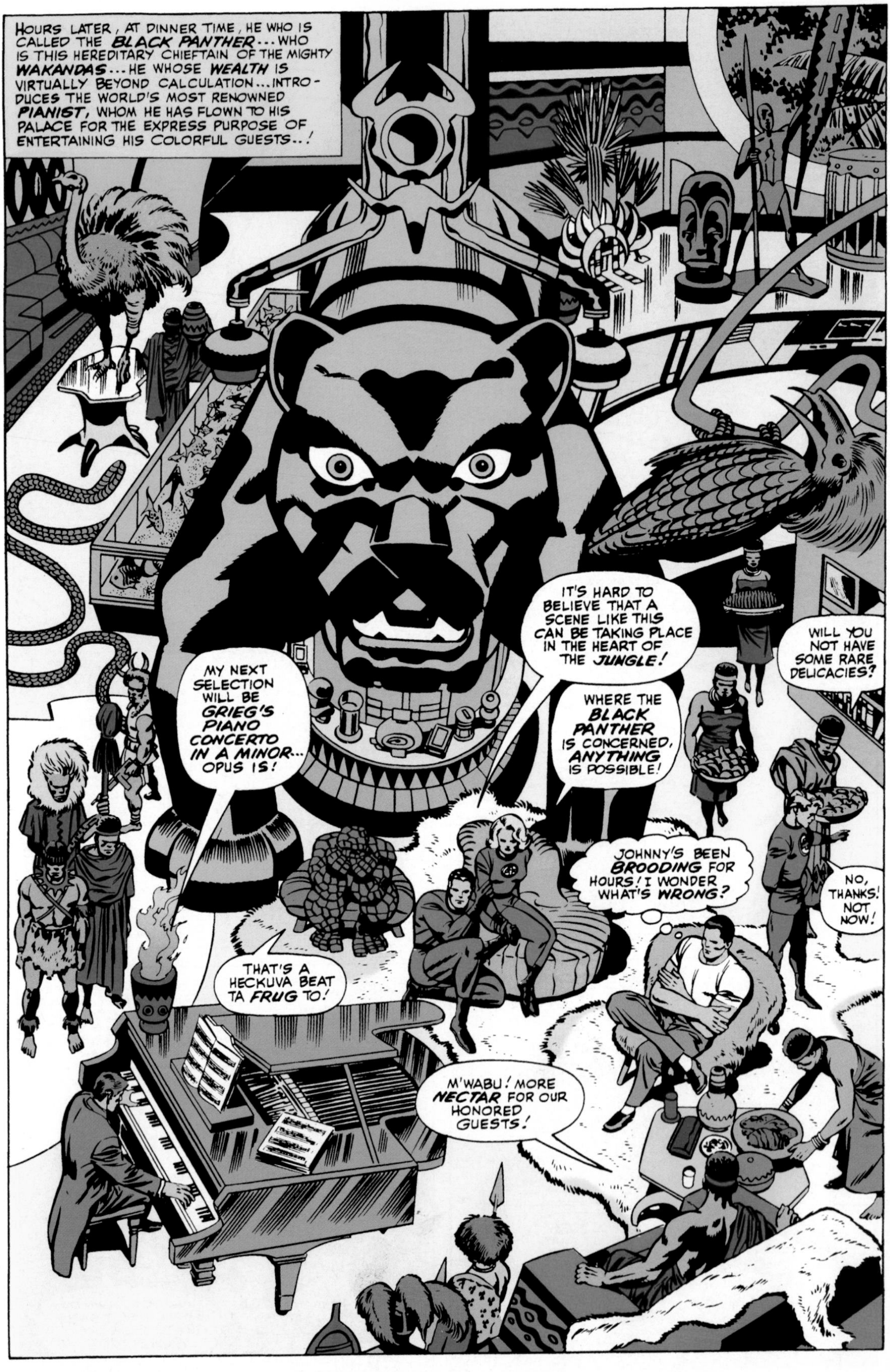
HOURS LATER, AT DINNER TIME, HE WHO IS CALLED THE BLACK PANTHER... WHO IS THIS HEREDITARY CHIEFTAIN OF THE MIGHTY WAKANDAS... HE WHOSE WEALTH IS VIRTUALLY BEYOND CALCULATION...INTRODUCES THE WORLD'S MOST RENOWNED PIANIST, WHOM HE HAS FLOWN TO HIS PALACE FOR THE EXPRESS PURPOSE OF ENTERTAINING HIS COLORFUL GUESTS..!
IT'S HARD TO BELIEVE THAT A SCENE LIKE THIS CAN BE TAKING PLACE IN THE HEART OF THE JUNGLE!
WILL YOU NOT HAVE SOME RARE DELICACIES?
MY NEXT SELECTION WILL BE GRIEG'S PIANO CONCERTO IN A MINOR... OPUS 16!
WHERE THE BLACK PANTHER IS CONCERNED, ANYTHING IS POSSIBLE!
JOHNNY'S BEEN BROODING FOR HOURS! I WONDER WHAT'S WRONG?
NO, THANKS! NOT NOW!
THAT'S A HECKUVA BEAT TA FRUG TO!
M'WABU! MORE NECTAR FOR OUR HONORED GUESTS!

BUT, ONE GUEST THERE IS WHO DOES NOT EVEN *HEAR* THE MAGNIFICENT MELODIES... FOR HIS THOUGHTS CONSTANTLY RETURN TO A SAD-EYED GIRL... A GIRL HE CAN NEVER FORGET!

THE *NIGHTS* ARE THE HARDEST! I KEEP HEARING HER *VOICE* IN MY BRAIN... WHISPERING... PLEADING... CALLING TO ME..!

JOHNNY! WHERE *ARE* YOU? I'LL NEVER STOP *WAITING* FOR YOU.. MY JOHNNY!

...A GIRL, UNLIKE ANY *OTHER* GIRL ON THE FACE OF THE EARTH! AND, IN A LAND WHERE FEW HAVE EVER TROD, SHE IS IMPRISONED BEHIND A BARRIER WHICH NO MAN CAN SHATTER... THE BARRIER BENEATH WHICH THE *INHUMANS* DWELL!

WE SHALL *NEVER* STOP TRYING TO FIND A MEANS OF *SMASHING* THIS ACCURSED BARRIER!

EVEN NOW, *BLACK BOLT* RETURNS... FROM HIS DAILY MISSION OF GLIDING AROUND THE CITY, SEEKING ANY POSSIBLE *WEAK SPOT* IN THE ETERNAL DOME!

'TIS ALL THE DOING OF *MAXIMUS*, THE NOW-MAD BROTHER OF BLACK BOLT!

BUT, THE LOOK ON HIS FACE IS ENOUGH TO TELL US HE HAS *FAILED* ONCE MORE! NO WEAK SPOT *EXISTS*! WE SHALL *NEVER* ESCAPE!

'TWAS *HE* WHO CREATED THE BARRIER.. AND ONLY *HE* KNOWS THE SECRET OF ITS *DESTRUCTION*!

BUT, THE SECRET IS *FOREVER LOCKED* WITHIN HIS MADDENED BRAIN!

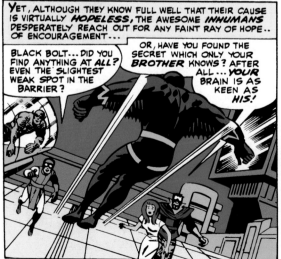

YET, ALTHOUGH THEY KNOW FULL WELL THAT THEIR CAUSE IS VIRTUALLY *HOPELESS*, THE AWESOME *INHUMANS* DESPERATELY REACH OUT FOR ANY FAINT RAY OF HOPE.. OF ENCOURAGEMENT...

BLACK BOLT... DID YOU FIND ANYTHING AT *ALL*? EVEN THE *SLIGHTEST* WEAK SPOT IN THE BARRIER?

OR, HAVE YOU FOUND THE SECRET WHICH ONLY YOUR *BROTHER* KNOWS? AFTER ALL... *YOUR* BRAIN IS AS KEEN AS *HIS*!

THOUGH YOU ARE DENIED THE POWER OF *SPEECH*, YOUR MEANING IS ABUNDANTLY *CLEAR*! WE ARE *STILL* DOOMED TO LIVE OUT OUR LIVES BENEATH THIS ACCURSED DOME!

OH, GORGON... IF I CANNOT SEE *JOHNNY STORM* AGAIN, THEN NOTHING ELSE MATTERS! IT IS AS THOUGH MY LIFE HAS *ALREADY* COME TO AN END!

DO NOT DESPAIR, MY CHILD! WE SHALL *YET* FIND A WAY!

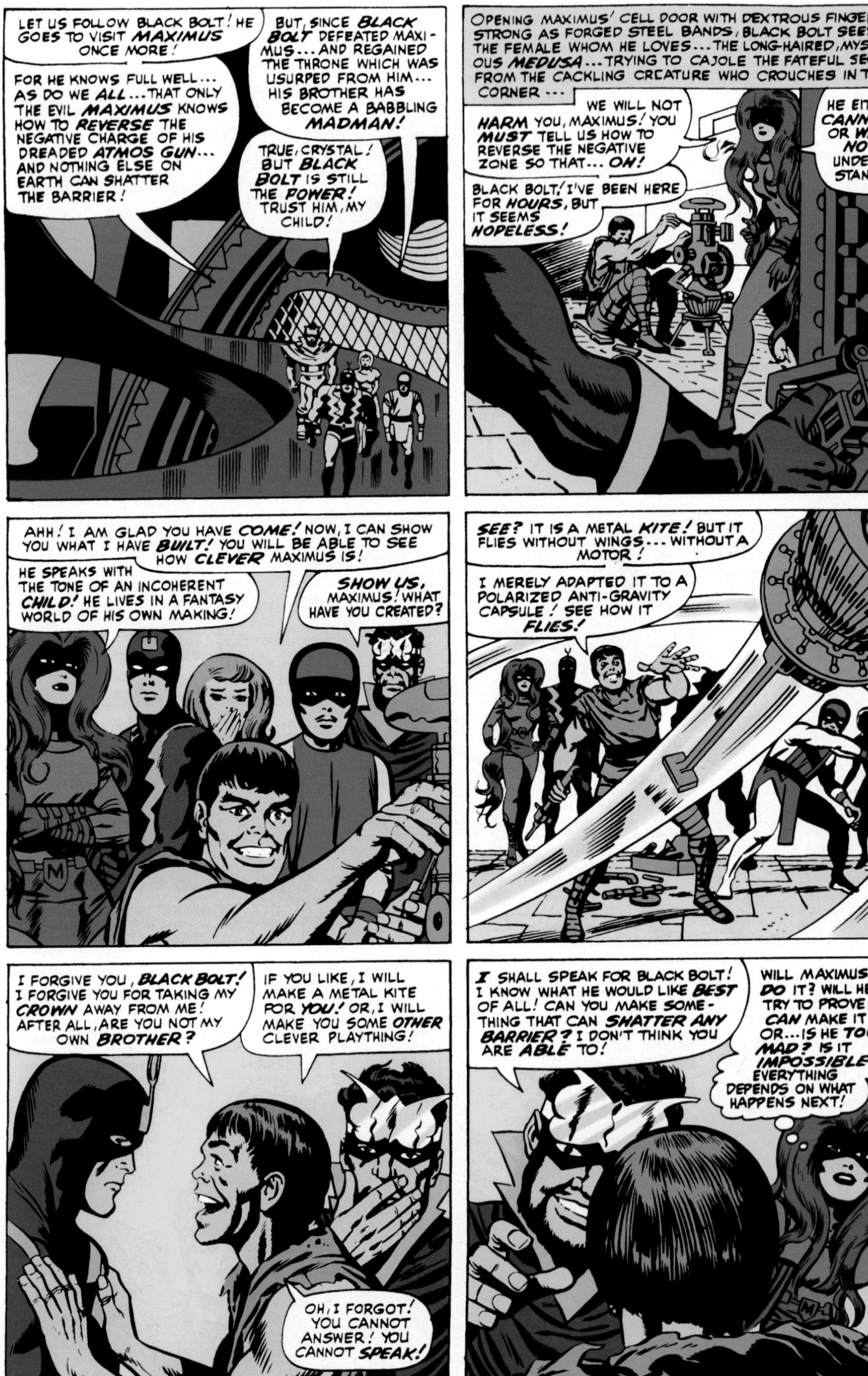
LET US FOLLOW BLACK BOLT! HE GOES TO VISIT MAXIMUS ONCE MORE!
FOR HE KNOWS FULL WELL... AS DO WE ALL... THAT ONLY THE EVIL MAXIMUS KNOWS HOW TO REVERSE THE NEGATIVE CHARGE OF HIS DREADED ATMOS GUN... AND NOTHING ELSE ON EARTH CAN SHATTER THE BARRIER!
BUT, SINCE BLACK BOLT DEFEATED MAXIMUS... AND REGAINED THE THRONE WHICH WAS USURPED FROM HIM... HIS BROTHER HAS BECOME A BABBLING MADMAN!
TRUE, CRYSTAL! BUT BLACK BOLT IS STILL THE POWER! TRUST HIM, MY CHILD!
OPENING MAXIMUS' CELL DOOR WITH DEXTROUS FINGERS STRONG AS FORGED STEEL BANDS, BLACK BOLT SEES THE FEMALE WHOM HE LOVES... THE LONG-HAIRED, MYSTERIOUS MEDUSA... TRYING TO CAJOLE THE FATEFUL SECRET FROM THE CACKLING CREATURE WHO CROUCHES IN THE CORNER ---
WE WILL NOT HARM YOU, MAXIMUS! YOU MUST TELL US HOW TO REVERSE THE NEGATIVE ZONE SO THAT... OH!
BLACK BOLT! I'VE BEEN HERE FOR HOURS, BUT IT SEEMS HOPELESS!
HE EITHER CANNOT.. OR WILL NOT UNDERSTAND!
AHH! I AM GLAD YOU HAVE COME! NOW, I CAN SHOW YOU WHAT I HAVE BUILT! YOU WILL BE ABLE TO SEE HOW CLEVER MAXIMUS IS!
HE SPEAKS WITH THE TONE OF AN INCOHERENT CHILD! HE LIVES IN A FANTASY WORLD OF HIS OWN MAKING!
SHOW US, MAXIMUS! WHAT HAVE YOU CREATED?
SEE? IT IS A METAL KITE! BUT IT FLIES WITHOUT WINGS--- WITHOUT A MOTOR!
I MERELY ADAPTED IT TO A POLARIZED ANTI-GRAVITY CAPSULE! SEE HOW IT FLIES!
I FORGIVE YOU, BLACK BOLT! I FORGIVE YOU FOR TAKING MY CROWN AWAY FROM ME! AFTER ALL, ARE YOU NOT MY OWN BROTHER?
IF YOU LIKE, I WILL MAKE A METAL KITE FOR YOU! OR, I WILL MAKE YOU SOME OTHER CLEVER PLAYTHING!
OH, I FORGOT! YOU CANNOT ANSWER! YOU CANNOT SPEAK!
I SHALL SPEAK FOR BLACK BOLT! I KNOW WHAT HE WOULD LIKE BEST OF ALL! CAN YOU MAKE SOMETHING THAT CAN SHATTER ANY BARRIER? I DON'T THINK YOU ARE ABLE TO!
WILL MAXIMUS DO IT? WILL HE TRY TO PROVE HE CAN MAKE IT? OR... IS HE TOO MAD? IS IT IMPOSSIBLE? EVERYTHING DEPENDS ON WHAT HAPPENS NEXT!

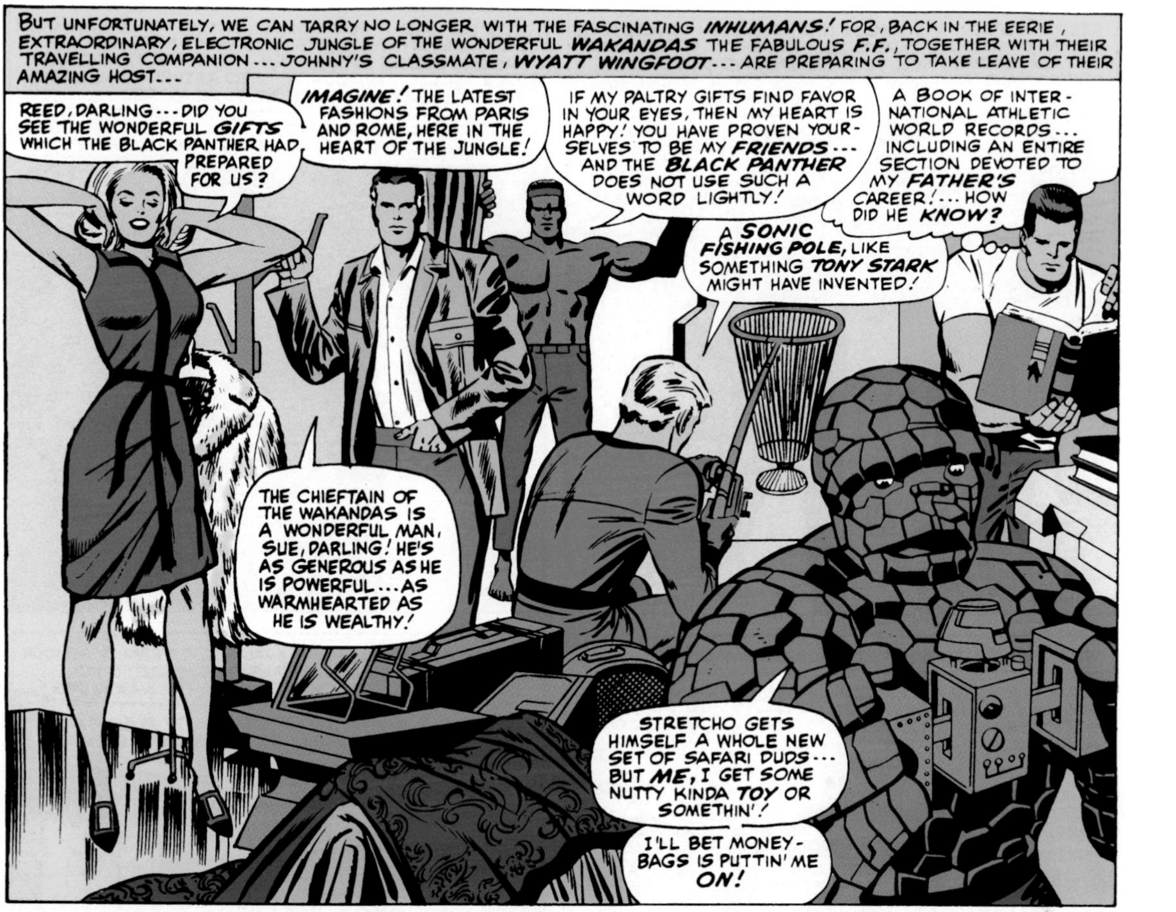
BUT UNFORTUNATELY, WE CAN TARRY NO LONGER WITH THE FASCINATING INHUMANS! FOR, BACK IN THE EERIE, EXTRAORDINARY, ELECTRONIC JUNGLE OF THE WONDERFUL WAKANDAS THE FABULOUS F.F., TOGETHER WITH THEIR TRAVELLING COMPANION... JOHNNY'S CLASSMATE, WYATT WINGFOOT... ARE PREPARING TO TAKE LEAVE OF THEIR AMAZING HOST...
REED, DARLING... DID YOU SEE THE WONDERFUL GIFTS WHICH THE BLACK PANTHER HAD PREPARED FOR US?
IMAGINE! THE LATEST FASHIONS FROM PARIS AND ROME, HERE IN THE HEART OF THE JUNGLE!
IF MY PALTRY GIFTS FIND FAVOR IN YOUR EYES, THEN MY HEART IS HAPPY! YOU HAVE PROVEN YOURSELVES TO BE MY FRIENDS... AND THE BLACK PANTHER DOES NOT USE SUCH A WORD LIGHTLY!
A BOOK OF INTERNATIONAL ATHLETIC WORLD RECORDS... INCLUDING AN ENTIRE SECTION DEVOTED TO MY FATHER'S CAREER!... HOW DID HE KNOW?
A SONIC FISHING POLE, LIKE SOMETHING TONY STARK MIGHT HAVE INVENTED!
THE CHIEFTAIN OF THE WAKANDAS IS A WONDERFUL MAN, SUE, DARLING! HE'S AS GENEROUS AS HE IS POWERFUL... AS WARMHEARTED AS HE IS WEALTHY!
STRETCHO GETS HIMSELF A WHOLE NEW SET OF SAFARI DUDS... BUT ME, I GET SOME NUTTY KINDA TOY OR SOMETHIN'!
I'LL BET MONEYBAGS IS PUTTIN' ME ON!

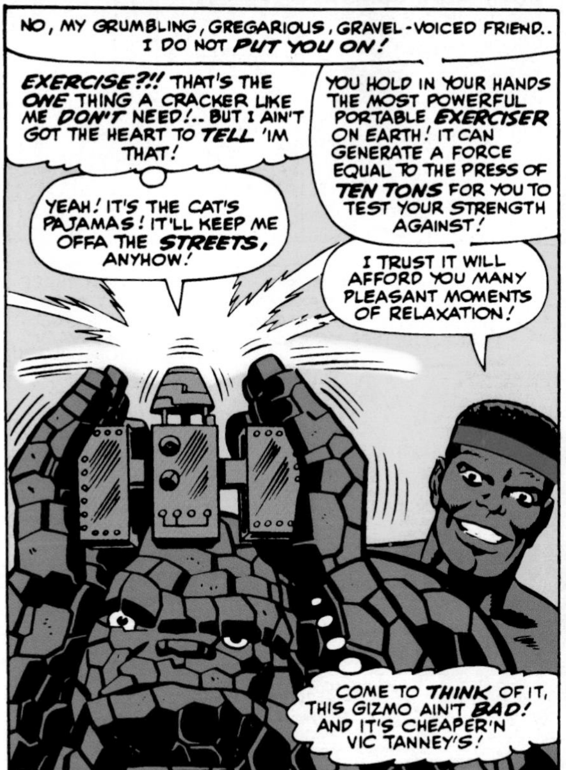
NO, MY GRUMBLING, GREGARIOUS, GRAVEL-VOICED FRIEND.. I DO NOT PUT YOU ON!
EXERCISE?!! THAT'S THE ONE THING A CRACKER LIKE ME DON'T NEED!.. BUT I AIN'T GOT THE HEART TO TELL 'IM THAT!
YOU HOLD IN YOUR HANDS THE MOST POWERFUL PORTABLE EXERCISER ON EARTH! IT CAN GENERATE A FORCE EQUAL TO THE PRESS OF TEN TONS FOR YOU TO TEST YOUR STRENGTH AGAINST!
YEAH! IT'S THE CAT'S PAJAMAS! IT'LL KEEP ME OFFA THE STREETS, ANYHOW!
I TRUST IT WILL AFFORD YOU MANY PLEASANT MOMENTS OF RELAXATION!
COME TO THINK OF IT, THIS GIZMO AIN'T BAD! AND IT'S CHEAPER'N VIC TANNEY'S!

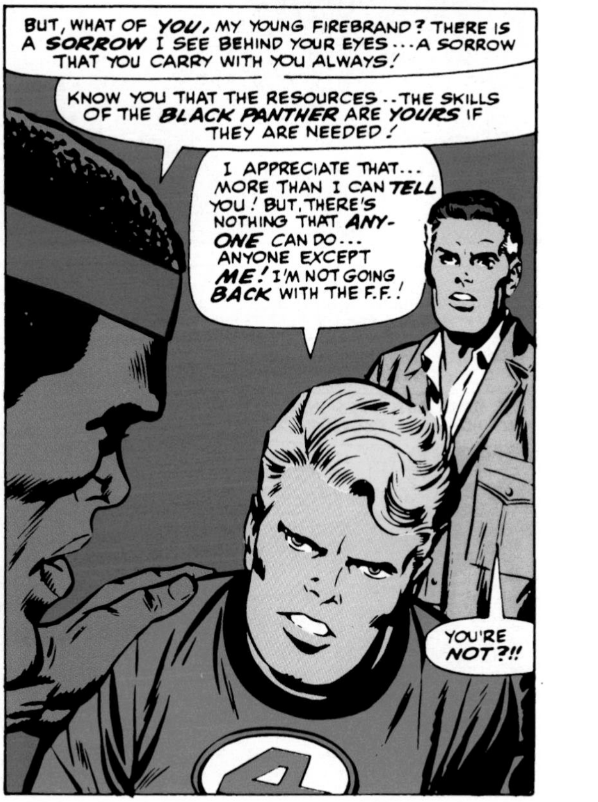
BUT, WHAT OF YOU, MY YOUNG FIREBRAND? THERE IS A SORROW I SEE BEHIND YOUR EYES... A SORROW THAT YOU CARRY WITH YOU ALWAYS!
KNOW YOU THAT THE RESOURCES.. THE SKILLS OF THE BLACK PANTHER ARE YOURS IF THEY ARE NEEDED!
I APPRECIATE THAT... MORE THAN I CAN TELL YOU! BUT, THERE'S NOTHING THAT ANYONE CAN DO... ANYONE EXCEPT ME! I'M NOT GOING BACK WITH THE F.F.!
YOU'RE NOT?!!

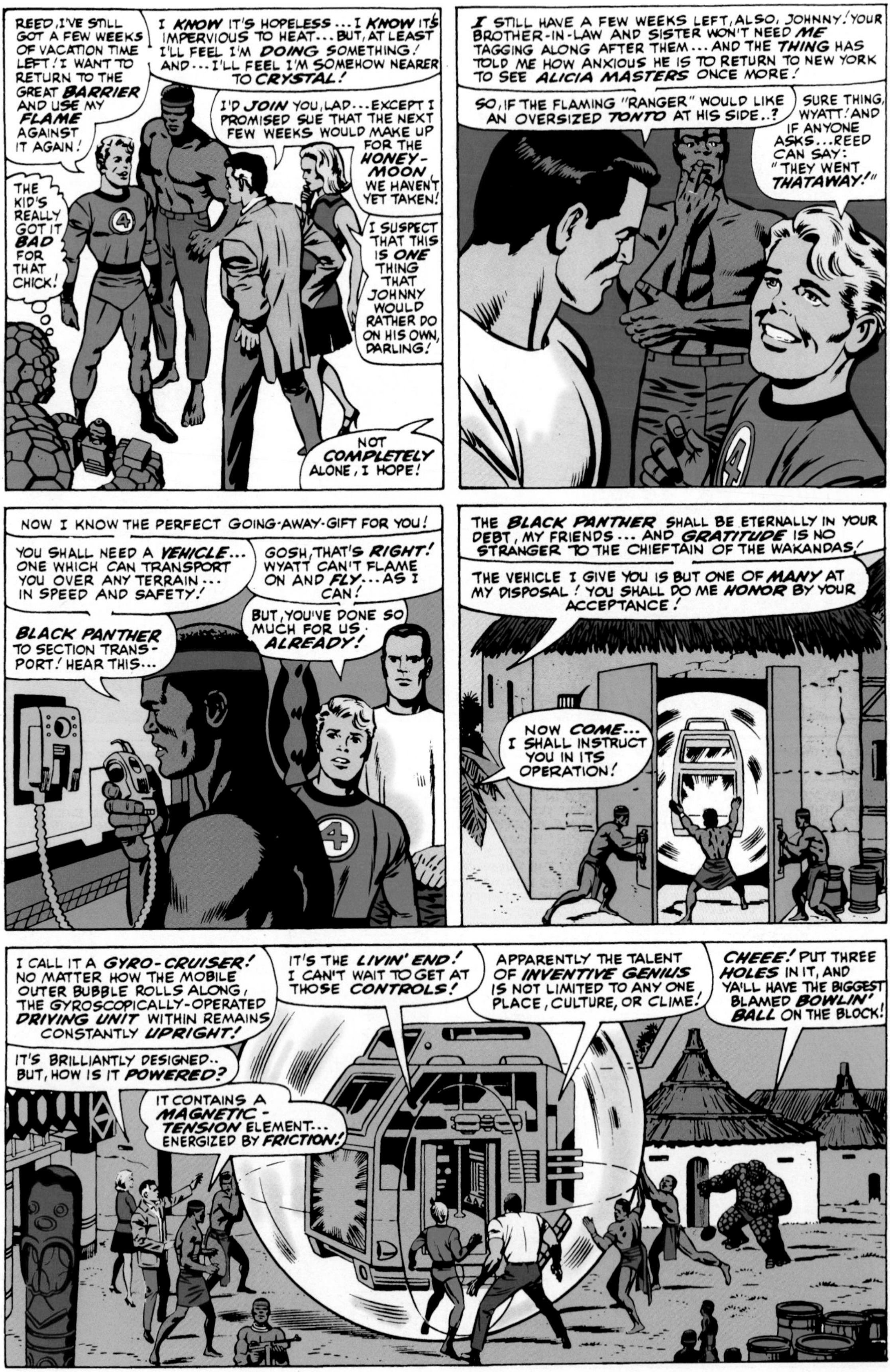
REED, I'VE STILL GOT A FEW WEEKS OF VACATION TIME LEFT! I WANT TO RETURN TO THE GREAT BARRIER AND USE MY FLAME AGAINST IT AGAIN!
I KNOW IT'S HOPELESS... I KNOW IT'S IMPERVIOUS TO HEAT... BUT, AT LEAST I'LL FEEL I'M DOING SOMETHING! AND... I'LL FEEL I'M SOMEHOW NEARER TO CRYSTAL!
I'D JOIN YOU, LAD... EXCEPT I PROMISED SUE THAT THE NEXT FEW WEEKS WOULD MAKE UP FOR THE HONEY-MOON WE HAVEN'T YET TAKEN!
THE KID'S REALLY GOT IT BAD FOR THAT CHICK!
I SUSPECT THAT THIS IS ONE THING THAT JOHNNY WOULD RATHER DO ON HIS OWN, DARLING!
NOT COMPLETELY ALONE, I HOPE!
I STILL HAVE A FEW WEEKS LEFT, ALSO, JOHNNY! YOUR BROTHER-IN-LAW AND SISTER WON'T NEED ME TAGGING ALONG AFTER THEM... AND THE THING HAS TOLD ME HOW ANXIOUS HE IS TO RETURN TO NEW YORK TO SEE ALICIA MASTERS ONCE MORE!
SO, IF THE FLAMING "RANGER" WOULD LIKE AN OVERSIZED TONTO AT HIS SIDE..?
SURE THING, WYATT! AND IF ANYONE ASKS... REED CAN SAY: "THEY WENT THATAWAY!"
NOW I KNOW THE PERFECT GOING-AWAY-GIFT FOR YOU!
YOU SHALL NEED A VEHICLE... ONE WHICH CAN TRANSPORT YOU OVER ANY TERRAIN... IN SPEED AND SAFETY!
GOSH, THAT'S RIGHT! WYATT CAN'T FLAME ON AND FLY... AS I CAN!
BUT, YOU'VE DONE SO MUCH FOR US ALREADY!
BLACK PANTHER TO SECTION TRANS-PORT! HEAR THIS...
THE BLACK PANTHER SHALL BE ETERNALLY IN YOUR DEBT, MY FRIENDS... AND GRATITUDE IS NO STRANGER TO THE CHIEFTAIN OF THE WAKANDAS!
THE VEHICLE I GIVE YOU IS BUT ONE OF MANY AT MY DISPOSAL! YOU SHALL DO ME HONOR BY YOUR ACCEPTANCE!
NOW COME... I SHALL INSTRUCT YOU IN ITS OPERATION!
I CALL IT A GYRO-CRUISER! NO MATTER HOW THE MOBILE OUTER BUBBLE ROLLS ALONG, THE GYROSCOPICALLY-OPERATED DRIVING UNIT WITHIN REMAINS CONSTANTLY UPRIGHT!
IT'S BRILLIANTLY DESIGNED.. BUT, HOW IS IT POWERED?
IT CONTAINS A MAGNETIC-TENSION ELEMENT... ENERGIZED BY FRICTION!
IT'S THE LIVIN' END! I CAN'T WAIT TO GET AT THOSE CONTROLS!
APPARENTLY THE TALENT OF INVENTIVE GENIUS IS NOT LIMITED TO ANY ONE PLACE, CULTURE, OR CLIME!
CHEEE! PUT THREE HOLES IN IT, AND YA'LL HAVE THE BIGGEST BLAMED BOWLIN' BALL ON THE BLOCK!

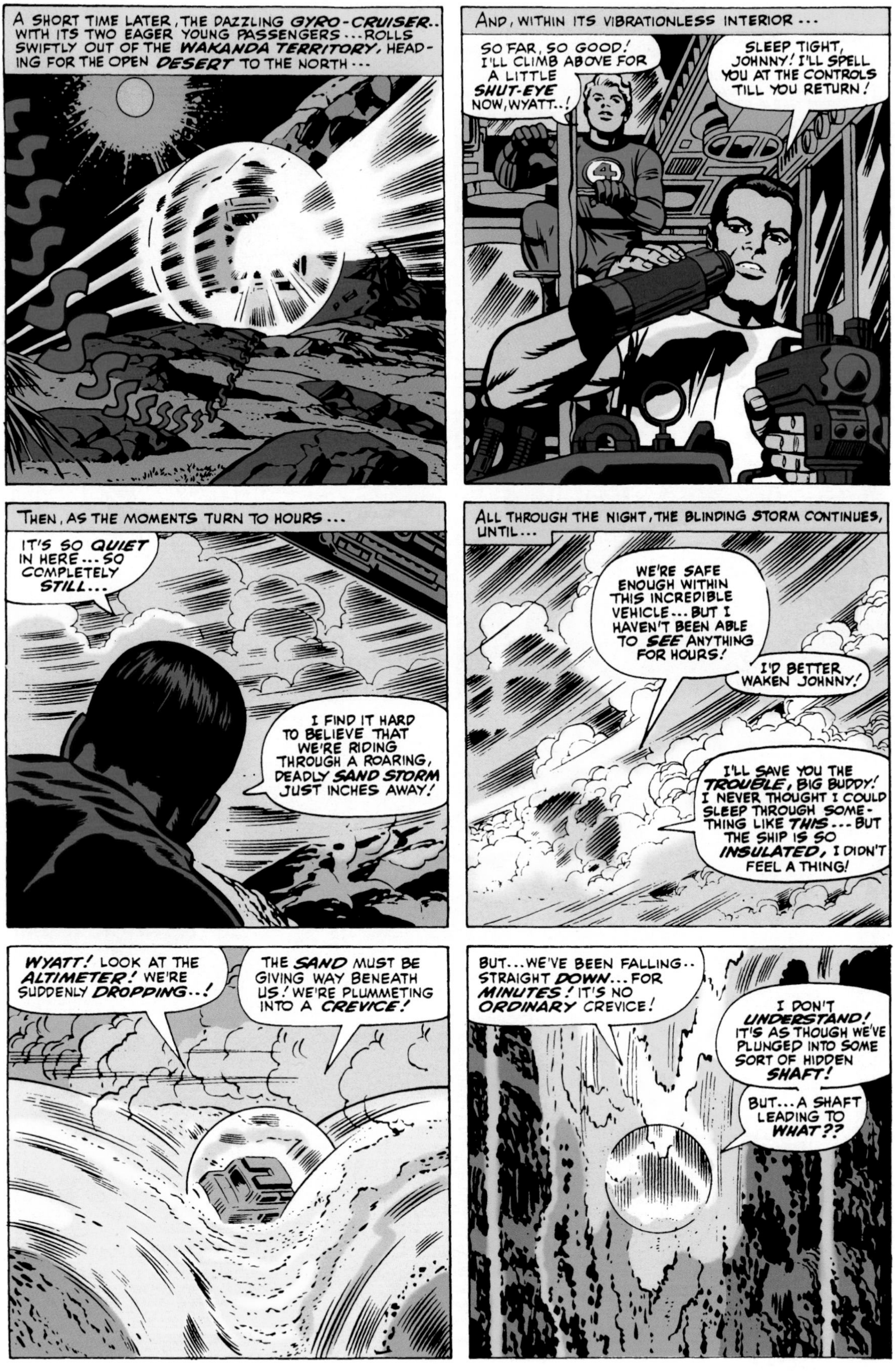

A SHORT TIME LATER, THE DAZZLING GYRO-CRUISER.. WITH ITS TWO EAGER YOUNG PASSENGERS...ROLLS SWIFTLY OUT OF THE WAKANDA TERRITORY, HEADING FOR THE OPEN DESERT TO THE NORTH...
AND, WITHIN ITS VIBRATIONLESS INTERIOR...
SO FAR, SO GOOD! I'LL CLIMB ABOVE FOR A LITTLE SHUT-EYE NOW, WYATT..!
SLEEP TIGHT, JOHNNY! I'LL SPELL YOU AT THE CONTROLS TILL YOU RETURN!
THEN, AS THE MOMENTS TURN TO HOURS...
IT'S SO QUIET IN HERE...SO COMPLETELY STILL...
I FIND IT HARD TO BELIEVE THAT WE'RE RIDING THROUGH A ROARING, DEADLY SAND STORM JUST INCHES AWAY!
ALL THROUGH THE NIGHT, THE BLINDING STORM CONTINUES, UNTIL...
WE'RE SAFE ENOUGH WITHIN THIS INCREDIBLE VEHICLE...BUT I HAVEN'T BEEN ABLE TO SEE ANYTHING FOR HOURS!
I'D BETTER WAKEN JOHNNY!
I'LL SAVE YOU THE TROUBLE, BIG BUDDY! I NEVER THOUGHT I COULD SLEEP THROUGH SOMETHING LIKE THIS...BUT THE SHIP IS SO INSULATED, I DIDN'T FEEL A THING!
WYATT! LOOK AT THE ALTIMETER! WE'RE SUDDENLY DROPPING..!
THE SAND MUST BE GIVING WAY BENEATH US! WE'RE PLUMMETING INTO A CREVICE!
BUT...WE'VE BEEN FALLING.. STRAIGHT DOWN...FOR MINUTES! IT'S NO ORDINARY CREVICE!
I DON'T UNDERSTAND! IT'S AS THOUGH WE'VE PLUNGED INTO SOME SORT OF HIDDEN SHAFT!
BUT...A SHAFT LEADING TO WHAT??

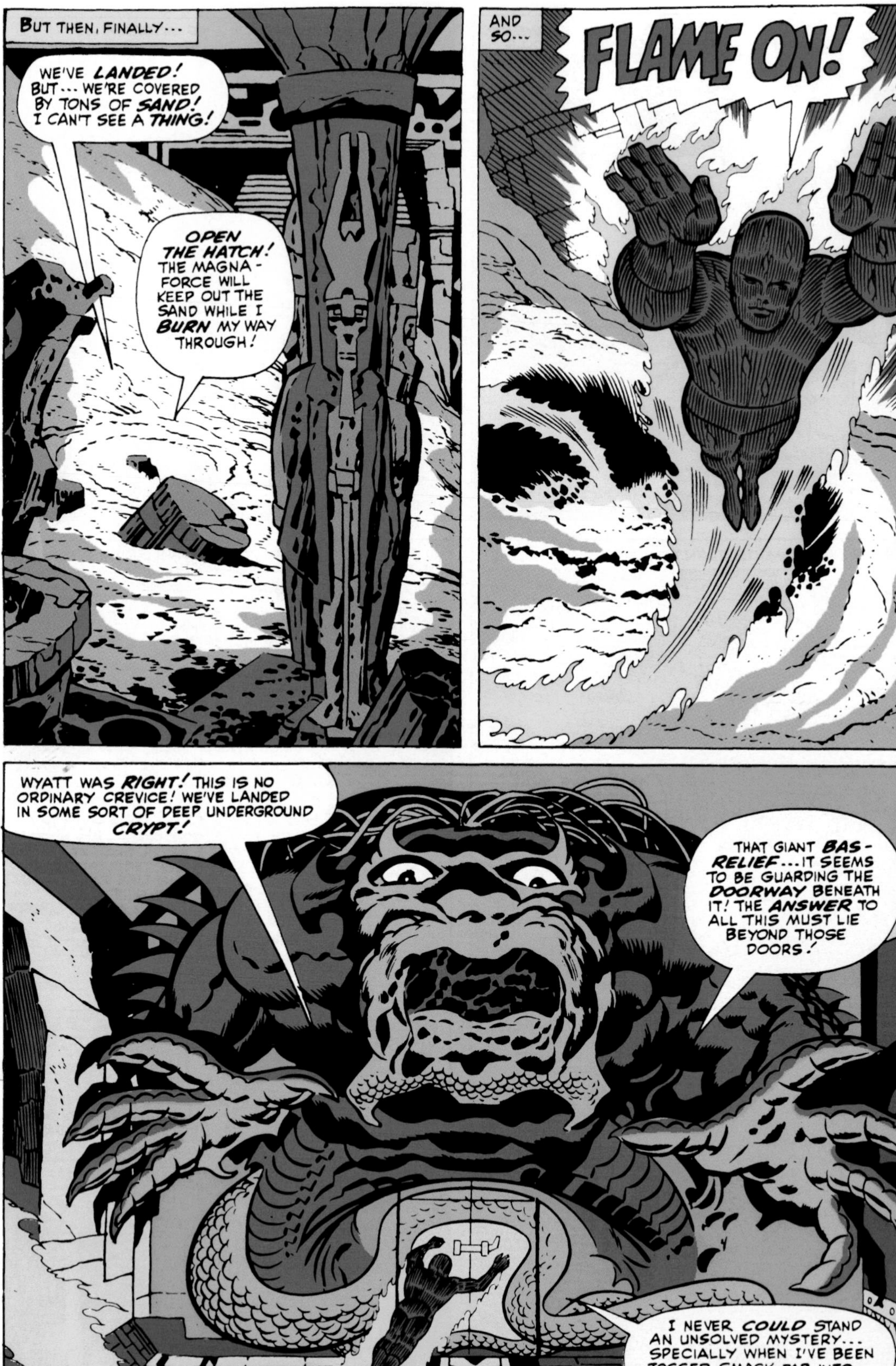
BUT THEN, FINALLY...
WE'VE LANDED! BUT... WE'RE COVERED BY TONS OF SAND! I CAN'T SEE A THING!
OPEN THE HATCH! THE MAGNA-FORCE WILL KEEP OUT THE SAND WHILE I BURN MY WAY THROUGH!
AND SO...
FLAME ON!
WYATT WAS RIGHT! THIS IS NO ORDINARY CREVICE! WE'VE LANDED IN SOME SORT OF DEEP UNDERGROUND CRYPT!
THAT GIANT BAS-RELIEF... IT SEEMS TO BE GUARDING THE DOORWAY BENEATH IT! THE ANSWER TO ALL THIS MUST LIE BEYOND THOSE DOORS!
I NEVER COULD STAND AN UNSOLVED MYSTERY... SPECIALLY WHEN I'VE BEEN TOSSED SMACK-DAB INTO THE MIDDLE OF IT! SO, HERE GOES..!

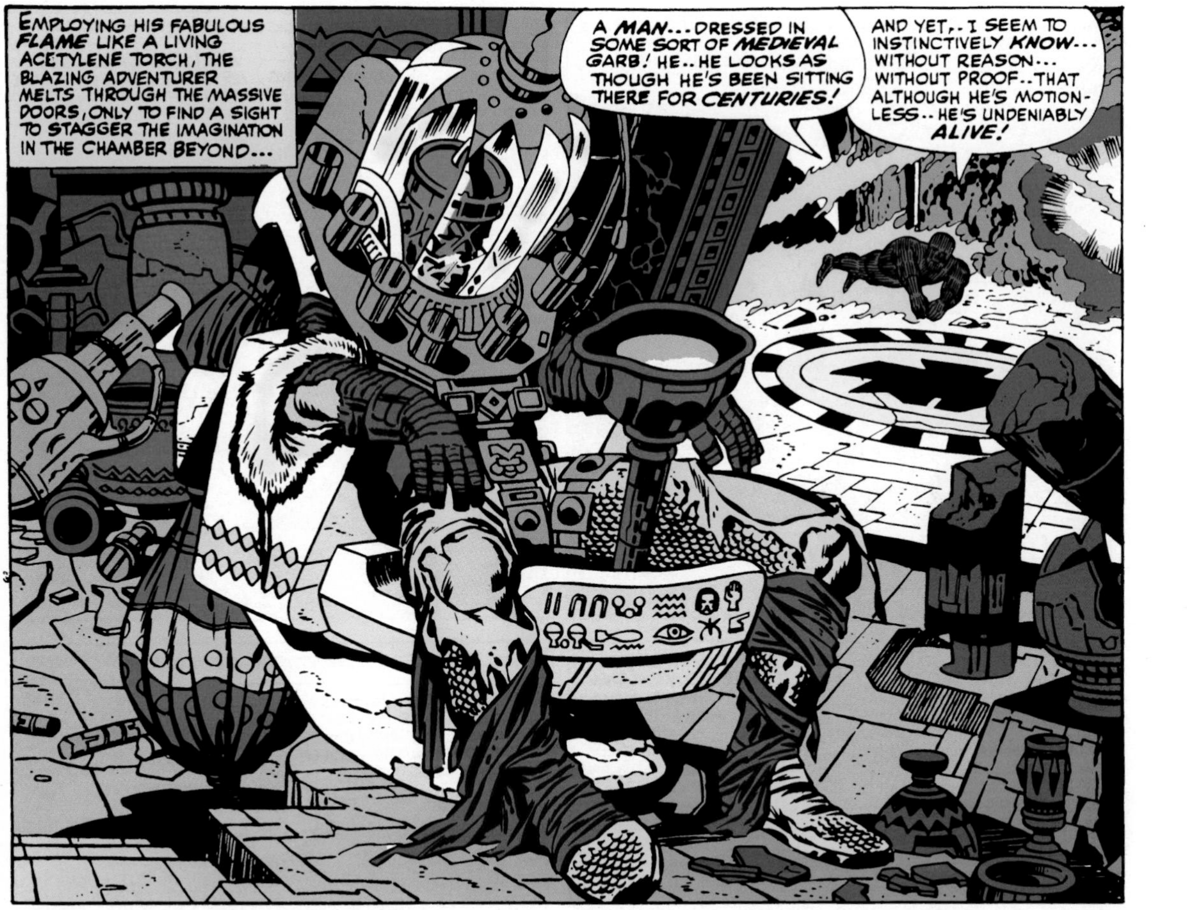
EMPLOYING HIS FABULOUS FLAME LIKE A LIVING ACETYLENE TORCH, THE BLAZING ADVENTURER MELTS THROUGH THE MASSIVE DOORS, ONLY TO FIND A SIGHT TO STAGGER THE IMAGINATION IN THE CHAMBER BEYOND...
A MAN...DRESSED IN SOME SORT OF MEDIEVAL GARB! HE..HE LOOKS AS THOUGH HE'S BEEN SITTING THERE FOR CENTURIES!
AND YET,-I SEEM TO INSTINCTIVELY KNOW... WITHOUT REASON... WITHOUT PROOF..THAT ALTHOUGH HE'S MOTIONLESS..HE'S UNDENIABLY ALIVE!

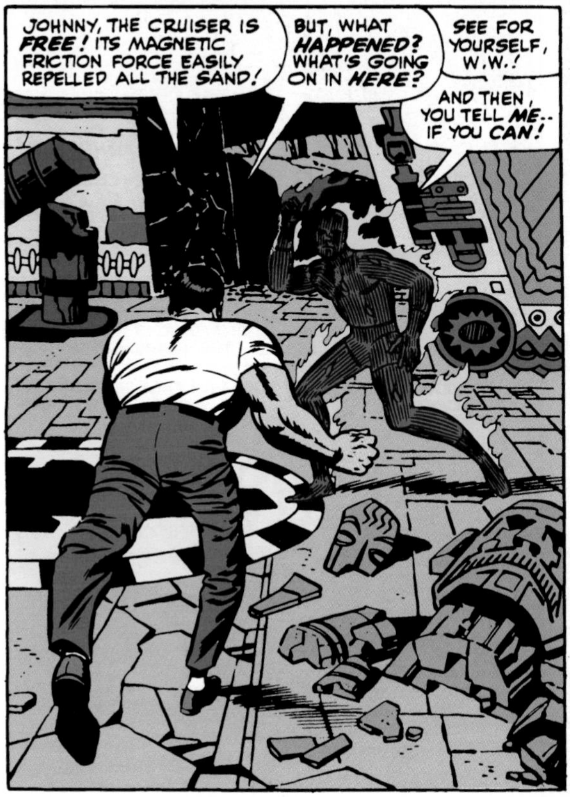
JOHNNY, THE CRUISER IS FREE! ITS MAGNETIC FRICTION FORCE EASILY REPELLED ALL THE SAND!
BUT, WHAT HAPPENED? WHAT'S GOING ON IN HERE?
SEE FOR YOURSELF, W.W.!
AND THEN, YOU TELL ME.. IF YOU CAN!

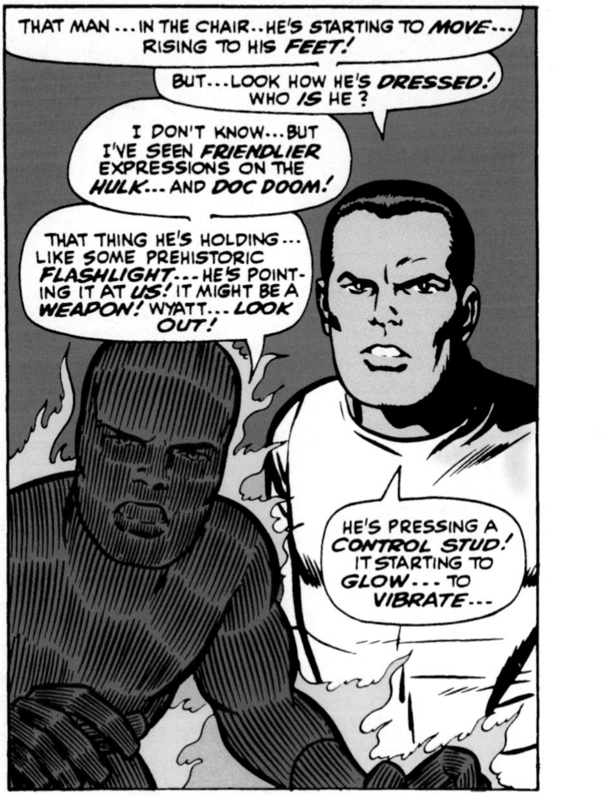
THAT MAN...IN THE CHAIR..HE'S STARTING TO MOVE... RISING TO HIS FEET!
BUT...LOOK HOW HE'S DRESSED! WHO IS HE?
I DON'T KNOW...BUT I'VE SEEN FRIENDLIER EXPRESSIONS ON THE HULK...AND DOC DOOM!
THAT THING HE'S HOLDING... LIKE SOME PREHISTORIC FLASHLIGHT...HE'S POINTING IT AT US! IT MIGHT BE A WEAPON! WYATT...LOOK OUT!
HE'S PRESSING A CONTROL STUD! IT STARTING TO GLOW...TO VIBRATE...

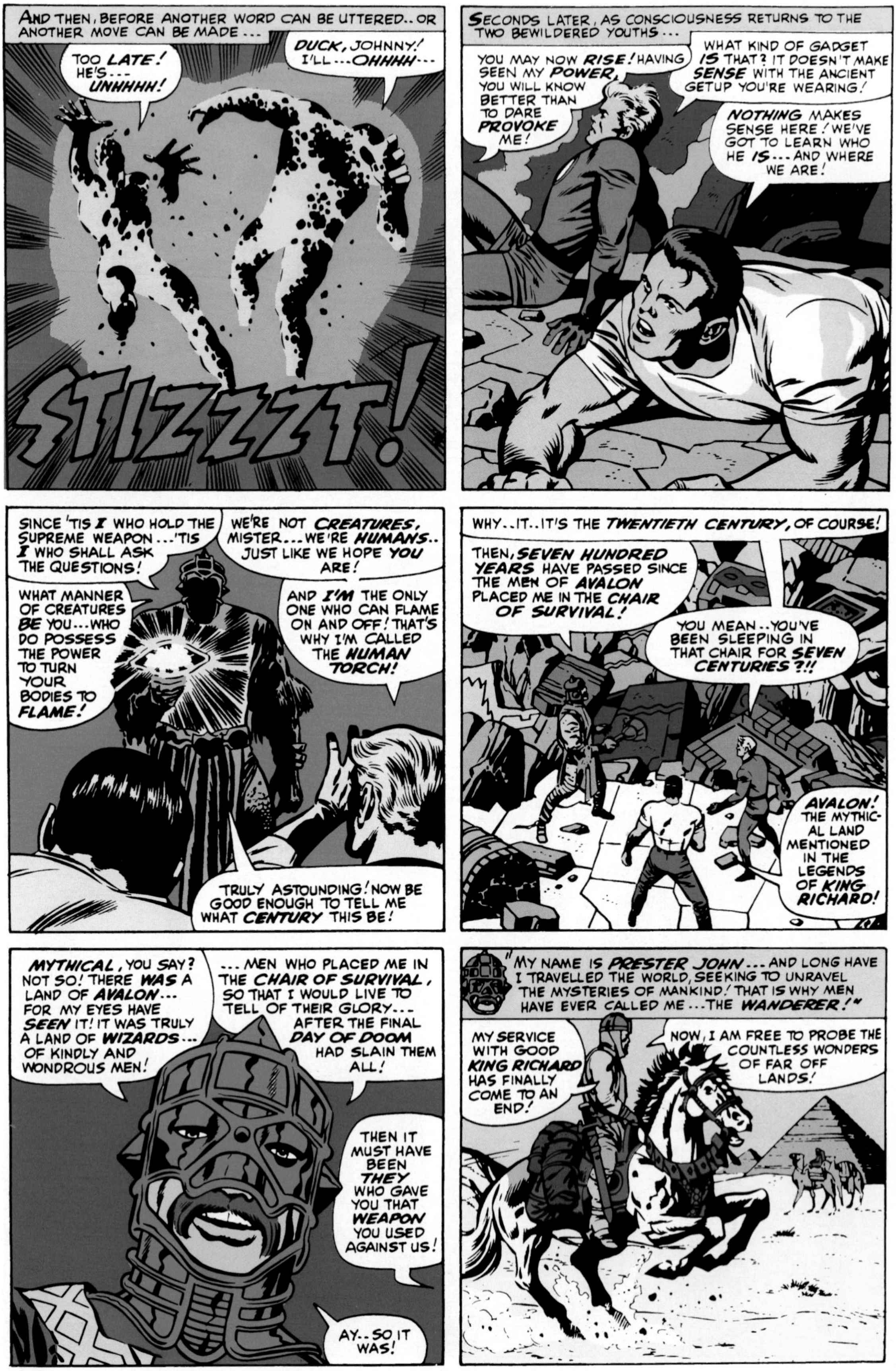
AND THEN, BEFORE ANOTHER WORD CAN BE UTTERED.. OR ANOTHER MOVE CAN BE MADE ...
TOO LATE! HE'S--- UNHHHH!
DUCK, JOHNNY! I'LL ---OHHHH---
STIZZZT!
SECONDS LATER, AS CONSCIOUSNESS RETURNS TO THE TWO BEWILDERED YOUTHS ...
YOU MAY NOW RISE! HAVING SEEN MY POWER, YOU WILL KNOW BETTER THAN TO DARE PROVOKE ME!
WHAT KIND OF GADGET IS THAT? IT DOESN'T MAKE SENSE WITH THE ANCIENT GETUP YOU'RE WEARING!
NOTHING MAKES SENSE HERE! WE'VE GOT TO LEARN WHO HE IS--- AND WHERE WE ARE!
SINCE 'TIS I WHO HOLD THE SUPREME WEAPON ...'TIS I WHO SHALL ASK THE QUESTIONS!
WHAT MANNER OF CREATURES BE YOU...WHO DO POSSESS THE POWER TO TURN YOUR BODIES TO FLAME!
WE'RE NOT CREATURES, MISTER... WE'RE HUMANS.. JUST LIKE WE HOPE YOU ARE!
AND I'M THE ONLY ONE WHO CAN FLAME ON AND OFF! THAT'S WHY I'M CALLED THE HUMAN TORCH!
TRULY ASTOUNDING! NOW BE GOOD ENOUGH TO TELL ME WHAT CENTURY THIS BE!
WHY..IT..IT'S THE TWENTIETH CENTURY, OF COURSE!
THEN, SEVEN HUNDRED YEARS HAVE PASSED SINCE THE MEN OF AVALON PLACED ME IN THE CHAIR OF SURVIVAL!
YOU MEAN..YOU'VE BEEN SLEEPING IN THAT CHAIR FOR SEVEN CENTURIES?!!
AVALON! THE MYTHIC-AL LAND MENTIONED IN THE LEGENDS OF KING RICHARD!
MYTHICAL, YOU SAY? NOT SO! THERE WAS A LAND OF AVALON--- FOR MY EYES HAVE SEEN IT! IT WAS TRULY A LAND OF WIZARDS... OF KINDLY AND WONDROUS MEN!
... MEN WHO PLACED ME IN THE CHAIR OF SURVIVAL, SO THAT I WOULD LIVE TO TELL OF THEIR GLORY... AFTER THE FINAL DAY OF DOOM HAD SLAIN THEM ALL!
THEN IT MUST HAVE BEEN THEY WHO GAVE YOU THAT WEAPON YOU USED AGAINST US!
AY.. SO IT WAS!
"MY NAME IS PRESTER JOHN... AND LONG HAVE I TRAVELLED THE WORLD, SEEKING TO UNRAVEL THE MYSTERIES OF MANKIND! THAT IS WHY MEN HAVE EVER CALLED ME ...THE WANDERER!"
MY SERVICE WITH GOOD KING RICHARD HAS FINALLY COME TO AN END!
NOW, I AM FREE TO PROBE THE COUNTLESS WONDERS OF FAR OFF LANDS!

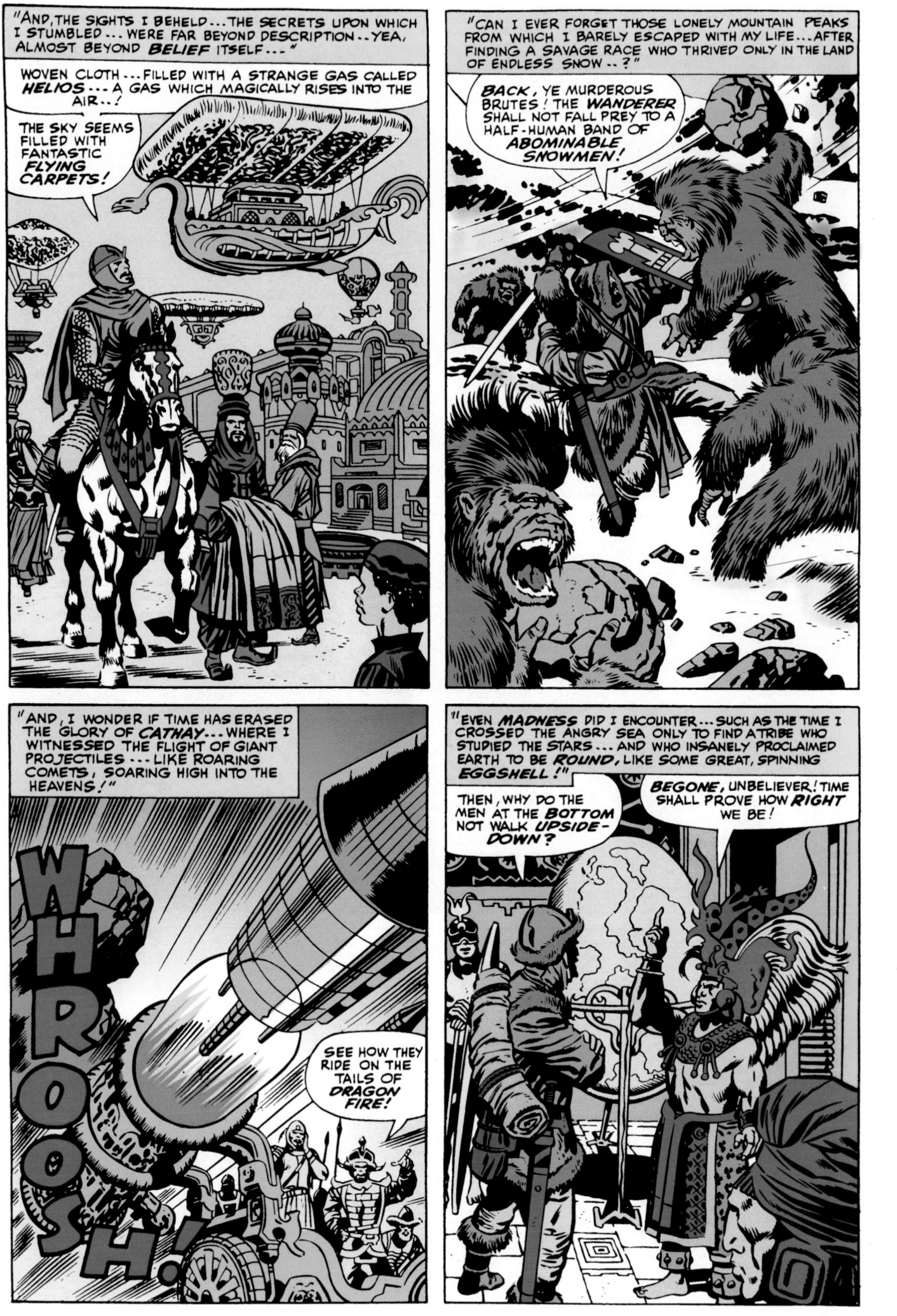
"AND, THE SIGHTS I BEHELD... THE SECRETS UPON WHICH I STUMBLED... WERE FAR BEYOND DESCRIPTION..YEA, ALMOST BEYOND BELIEF ITSELF..."
WOVEN CLOTH... FILLED WITH A STRANGE GAS CALLED HELIOS... A GAS WHICH MAGICALLY RISES INTO THE AIR..!
THE SKY SEEMS FILLED WITH FANTASTIC FLYING CARPETS!
"CAN I EVER FORGET THOSE LONELY MOUNTAIN PEAKS FROM WHICH I BARELY ESCAPED WITH MY LIFE... AFTER FINDING A SAVAGE RACE WHO THRIVED ONLY IN THE LAND OF ENDLESS SNOW..?"
BACK, YE MURDEROUS BRUTES! THE WANDERER SHALL NOT FALL PREY TO A HALF-HUMAN BAND OF ABOMINABLE SNOWMEN!
"AND, I WONDER IF TIME HAS ERASED THE GLORY OF CATHAY... WHERE I WITNESSED THE FLIGHT OF GIANT PROJECTILES ... LIKE ROARING COMETS, SOARING HIGH INTO THE HEAVENS!"
WHROOSH!
SEE HOW THEY RIDE ON THE TAILS OF DRAGON FIRE!
"EVEN MADNESS DID I ENCOUNTER... SUCH AS THE TIME I CROSSED THE ANGRY SEA ONLY TO FIND A TRIBE WHO STUDIED THE STARS... AND WHO INSANELY PROCLAIMED EARTH TO BE ROUND, LIKE SOME GREAT, SPINNING EGGSHELL!"
THEN, WHY DO THE MEN AT THE BOTTOM NOT WALK UPSIDE-DOWN?
BEGONE, UNBELIEVER! TIME SHALL PROVE HOW RIGHT WE BE!

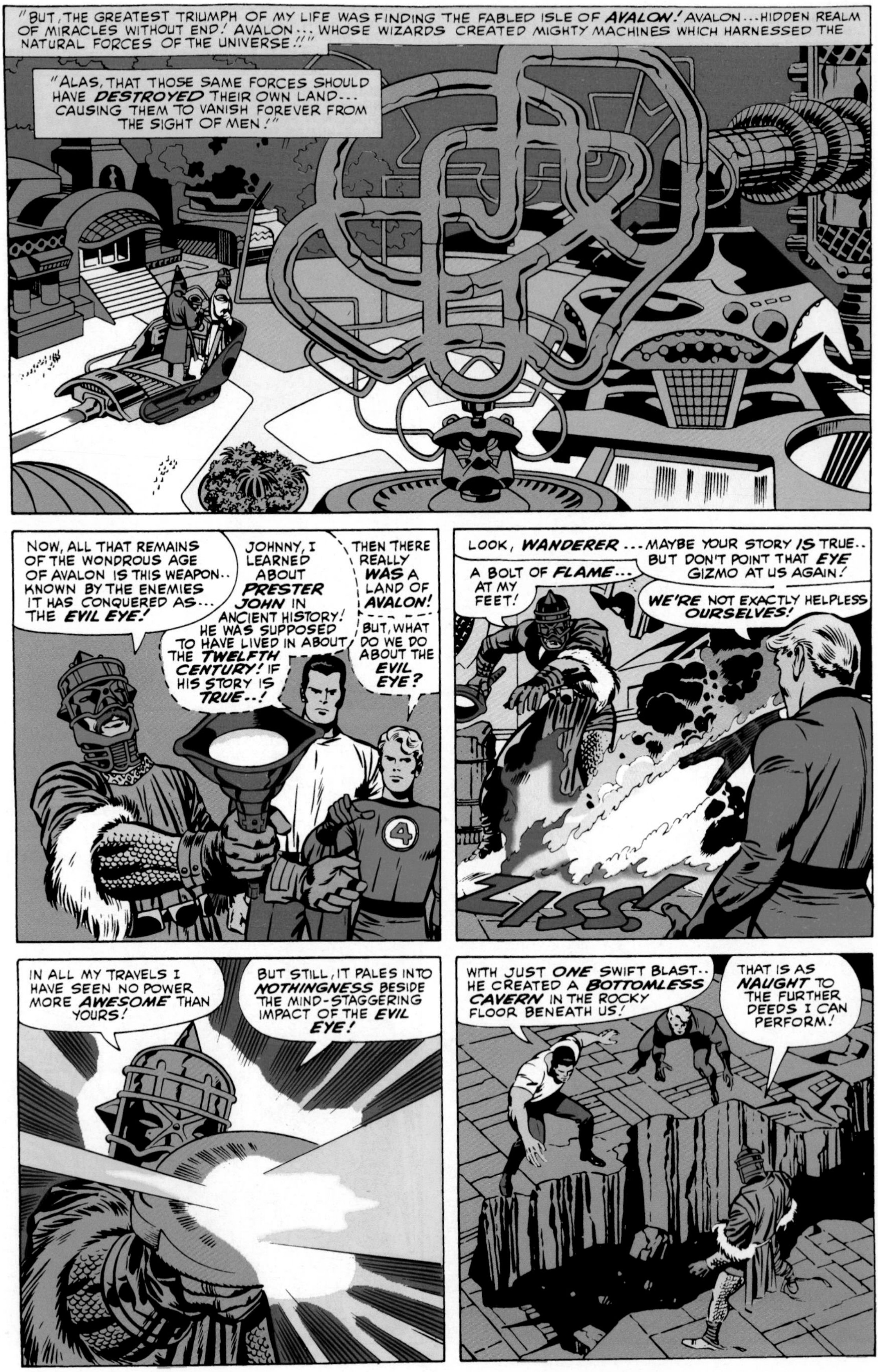

"BUT, THE GREATEST TRIUMPH OF MY LIFE WAS FINDING THE FABLED ISLE OF AVALON! AVALON... HIDDEN REALM OF MIRACLES WITHOUT END! AVALON... WHOSE WIZARDS CREATED MIGHTY MACHINES WHICH HARNESSED THE NATURAL FORCES OF THE UNIVERSE!!"
"ALAS, THAT THOSE SAME FORCES SHOULD HAVE DESTROYED THEIR OWN LAND... CAUSING THEM TO VANISH FOREVER FROM THE SIGHT OF MEN!"
NOW, ALL THAT REMAINS OF THE WONDROUS AGE OF AVALON IS THIS WEAPON.. KNOWN BY THE ENEMIES IT HAS CONQUERED AS... THE EVIL EYE!
JOHNNY, I LEARNED ABOUT PRESTER JOHN IN ANCIENT HISTORY! HE WAS SUPPOSED TO HAVE LIVED IN ABOUT THE TWELFTH CENTURY! IF HIS STORY IS TRUE..!
THEN THERE REALLY WAS A LAND OF AVALON!
BUT, WHAT DO WE DO ABOUT THE EVIL EYE?
LOOK, WANDERER ... MAYBE YOUR STORY IS TRUE.. BUT DON'T POINT THAT EYE GIZMO AT US AGAIN!
A BOLT OF FLAME... AT MY FEET!
WE'RE NOT EXACTLY HELPLESS OURSELVES!
ZISSS!
IN ALL MY TRAVELS I HAVE SEEN NO POWER MORE AWESOME THAN YOURS!
BUT STILL, IT PALES INTO NOTHINGNESS BESIDE THE MIND-STAGGERING IMPACT OF THE EVIL EYE!
WITH JUST ONE SWIFT BLAST.. HE CREATED A BOTTOMLESS CAVERN IN THE ROCKY FLOOR BENEATH US!
THAT IS AS NAUGHT TO THE FURTHER DEEDS I CAN PERFORM!

IT'S SMASHING THROUGH EVERY OBSTACLE LIKE A CANNONBALL PIERCING A PAPER BAG!

HE'S AIMING IT *UP* ...TOWARDS THE *SURFACE!*

SHABOWW!

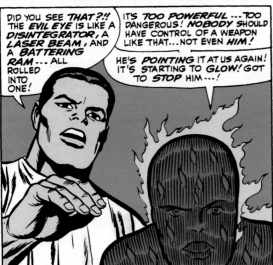

DID YOU SEE *THAT*?!! THE *EVIL EYE* IS LIKE A *DISINTEGRATOR,* A *LASER BEAM,* AND A *BATTERING RAM* ... ALL ROLLED INTO ONE!

IT'S *TOO POWERFUL* ...TOO *DANGEROUS! NOBODY* SHOULD HAVE CONTROL OF A WEAPON LIKE THAT...NOT EVEN *HIM!*

HE'S *POINTING* IT AT US AGAIN! IT'S STARTING TO *GLOW!* GOT TO *STOP* HIM ...!

YOU *CANNOT* STOP ME!

I CAN SEE YOU STILL DO NOT *TRUST* ME ... THEREFORE, UNTIL YOU *DO,* I MUST *PROTECT* MYSELF FROM YOU!

YOU DIDN'T REALIZE THE *EVIL EYE* POSSESSES *MANY* POWERS... SUCH AS THE POWER OF FORMING AN UN- BREAKABLE *SHIELD* ...WHICH GROWS *STRONGER* EVERY SECOND!

NOW.. *THERE* YOU SHALL REMAIN, UNTIL YOU REALIZE THAT THE *WANDERER* MAY NEVER BE CHALLENGED ...MAY NEVER BE *ATTACKED!*

WE'RE *TRAPPED!* THERE'S NO WAY *OUT!* THE DOME IS STRONGER THAN STEEL ...WITH *NO* OPENING ...ANY- WHERE!

WYATT! I JUST *REALIZED* ...!! IT'S EXACTLY LIKE THE TERRIBLE *BARRIER* BEHIND WHICH *CRYSTAL* ...AND THE *INHUMANS* ...ARE IMPRISONED!!

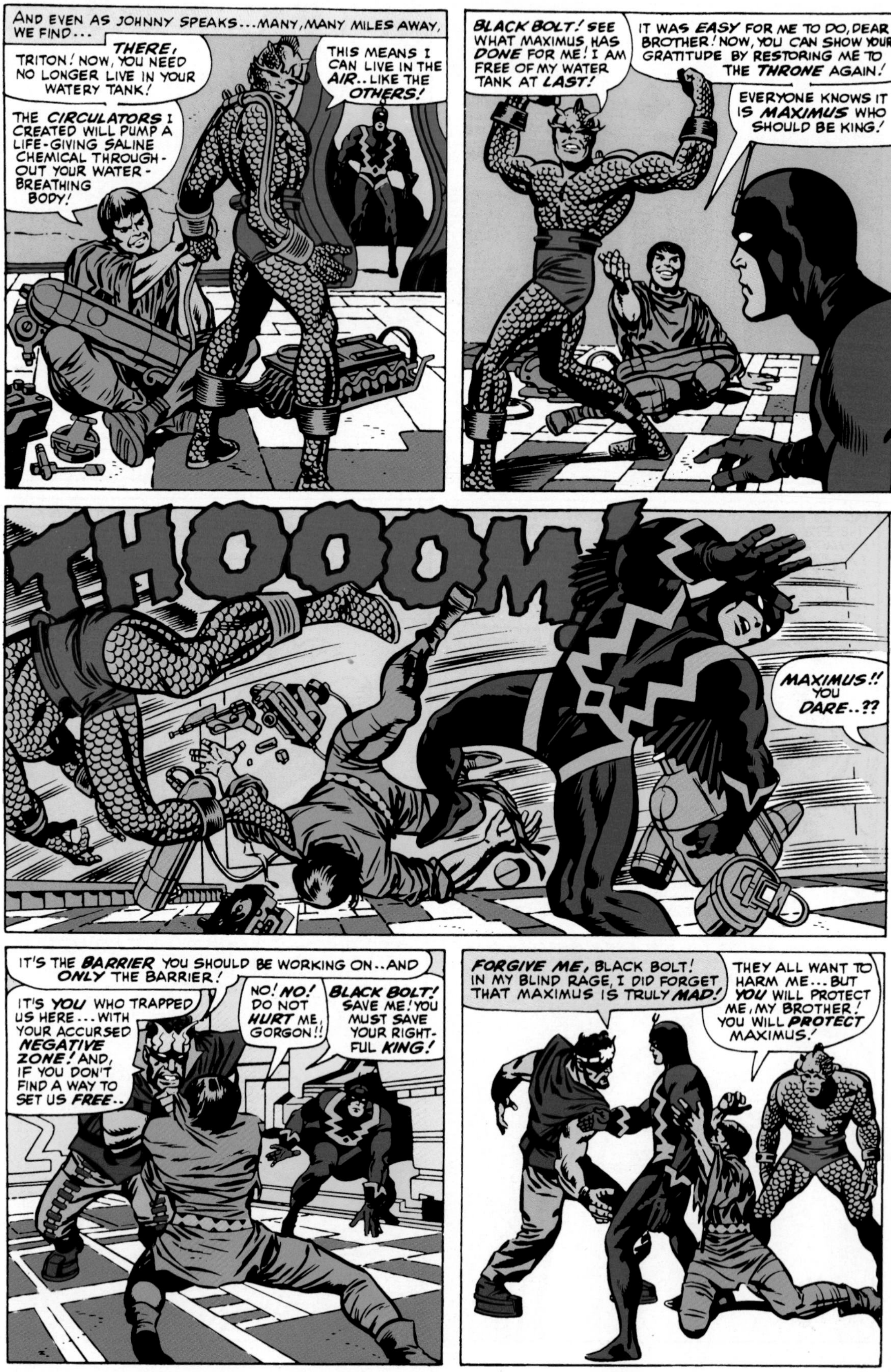
AND EVEN AS JOHNNY SPEAKS...MANY, MANY MILES AWAY, WE FIND...
THERE, TRITON! NOW, YOU NEED NO LONGER LIVE IN YOUR WATERY TANK!
THE CIRCULATORS I CREATED WILL PUMP A LIFE-GIVING SALINE CHEMICAL THROUGH-OUT YOUR WATER-BREATHING BODY!
THIS MEANS I CAN LIVE IN THE AIR.. LIKE THE OTHERS!
BLACK BOLT! SEE WHAT MAXIMUS HAS DONE FOR ME! I AM FREE OF MY WATER TANK AT LAST!
IT WAS EASY FOR ME TO DO, DEAR BROTHER! NOW, YOU CAN SHOW YOUR GRATITUDE BY RESTORING ME TO THE THRONE AGAIN!
EVERYONE KNOWS IT IS MAXIMUS WHO SHOULD BE KING!
THOOOM!
MAXIMUS!! YOU DARE..??
IT'S THE BARRIER YOU SHOULD BE WORKING ON..AND ONLY THE BARRIER!
IT'S YOU WHO TRAPPED US HERE...WITH YOUR ACCURSED NEGATIVE ZONE! AND, IF YOU DON'T FIND A WAY TO SET US FREE..
NO! NO! DO NOT HURT ME, GORGON!!
BLACK BOLT! SAVE ME! YOU MUST SAVE YOUR RIGHT-FUL KING!
FORGIVE ME, BLACK BOLT! IN MY BLIND RAGE, I DID FORGET THAT MAXIMUS IS TRULY MAD!
THEY ALL WANT TO HARM ME...BUT YOU WILL PROTECT ME, MY BROTHER! YOU WILL PROTECT MAXIMUS!

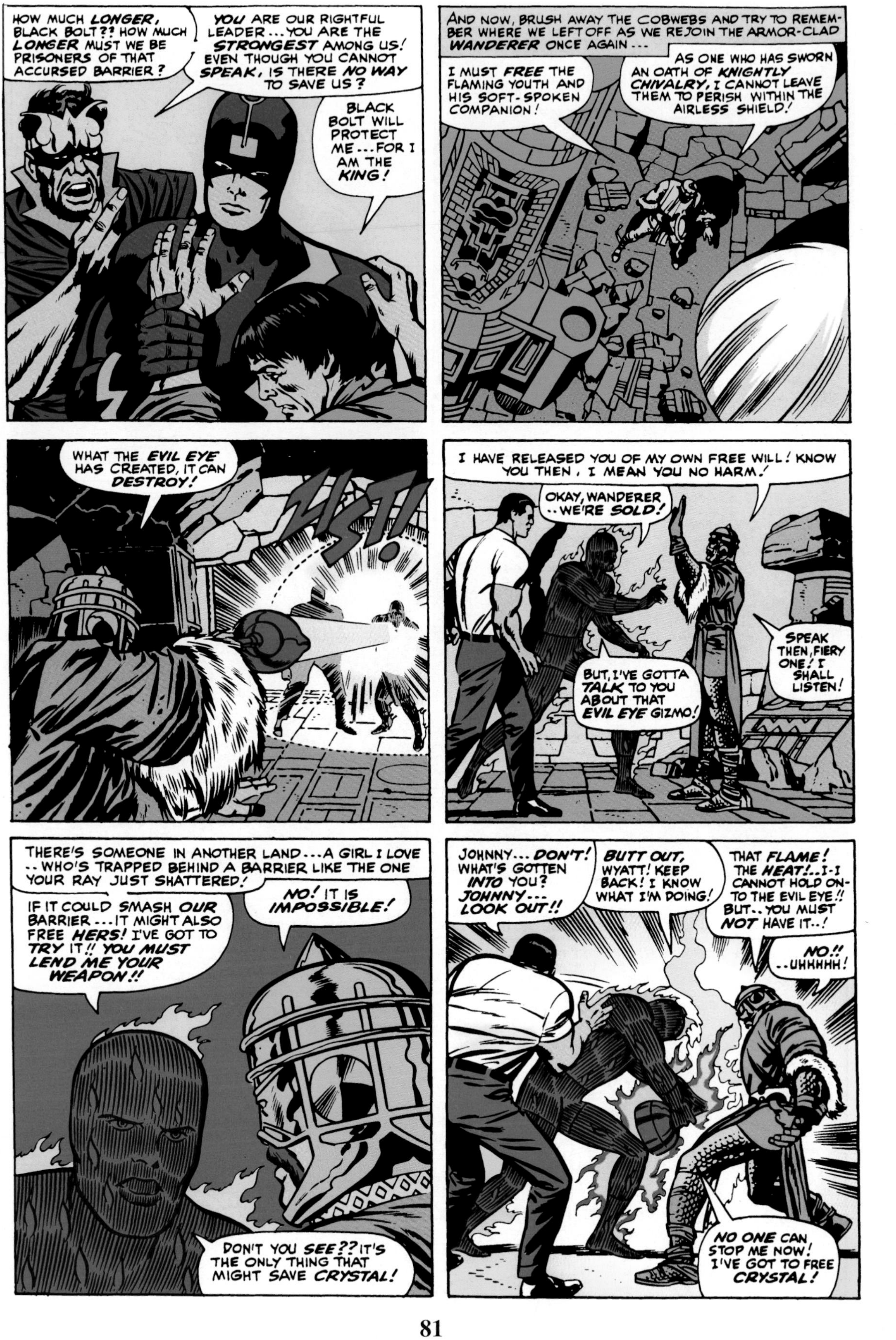
HOW MUCH LONGER, BLACK BOLT?? HOW MUCH LONGER MUST WE BE PRISONERS OF THAT ACCURSED BARRIER?
YOU ARE OUR RIGHTFUL LEADER... YOU ARE THE STRONGEST AMONG US! EVEN THOUGH YOU CANNOT SPEAK, IS THERE NO WAY TO SAVE US?
BLACK BOLT WILL PROTECT ME... FOR I AM THE KING!
AND NOW, BRUSH AWAY THE COBWEBS AND TRY TO REMEMBER WHERE WE LEFT OFF AS WE REJOIN THE ARMOR-CLAD WANDERER ONCE AGAIN...
I MUST FREE THE FLAMING YOUTH AND HIS SOFT-SPOKEN COMPANION!
AS ONE WHO HAS SWORN AN OATH OF KNIGHTLY CHIVALRY, I CANNOT LEAVE THEM TO PERISH WITHIN THE AIRLESS SHIELD!
WHAT THE EVIL EYE HAS CREATED, IT CAN DESTROY!
ZIST!
I HAVE RELEASED YOU OF MY OWN FREE WILL! KNOW YOU THEN, I MEAN YOU NO HARM!
OKAY, WANDERER.. WE'RE SOLD!
BUT, I'VE GOTTA TALK TO YOU ABOUT THAT EVIL EYE GIZMO!
SPEAK THEN, FIERY ONE! I SHALL LISTEN!
THERE'S SOMEONE IN ANOTHER LAND... A GIRL I LOVE.. WHO'S TRAPPED BEHIND A BARRIER LIKE THE ONE YOUR RAY JUST SHATTERED!
IF IT COULD SMASH OUR BARRIER... IT MIGHT ALSO FREE HERS! I'VE GOT TO TRY IT!! YOU MUST LEND ME YOUR WEAPON!!
NO! IT IS IMPOSSIBLE!
DON'T YOU SEE?? IT'S THE ONLY THING THAT MIGHT SAVE CRYSTAL!
JOHNNY... DON'T! WHAT'S GOTTEN INTO YOU? JOHNNY... LOOK OUT!!
BUTT OUT, WYATT! KEEP BACK! I KNOW WHAT I'M DOING!
THAT FLAME! THE HEAT!.. I-I CANNOT HOLD ON-TO THE EVIL EYE!! BUT.. YOU MUST NOT HAVE IT..!
NO!! ..UHHHHH!
NO ONE CAN STOP ME NOW! I'VE GOT TO FREE CRYSTAL!

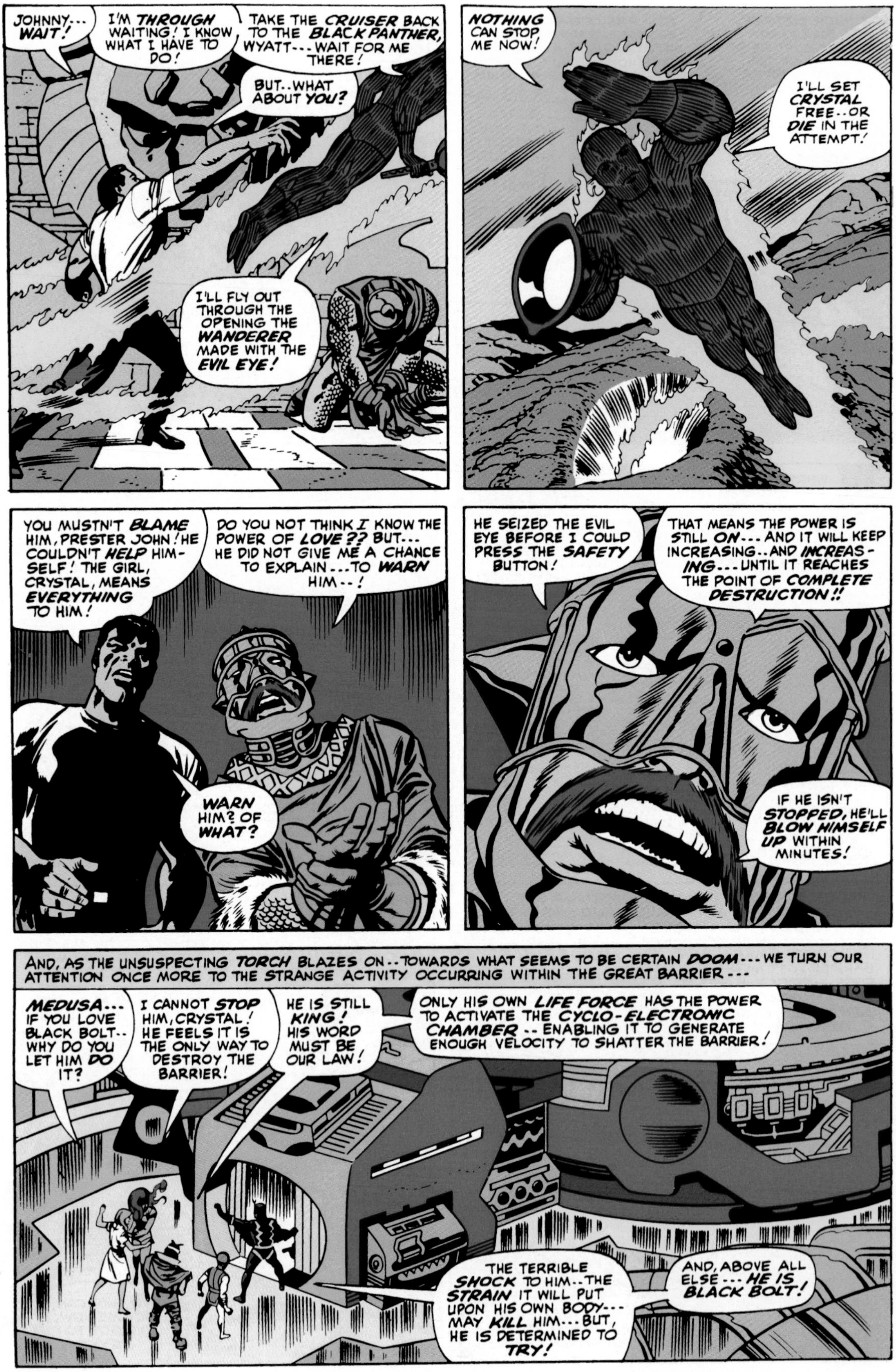
JOHNNY--- WAIT!
I'M THROUGH WAITING! I KNOW WHAT I HAVE TO DO!
TAKE THE CRUISER BACK TO THE BLACK PANTHER, WYATT--- WAIT FOR ME THERE!
BUT..WHAT ABOUT YOU?
I'LL FLY OUT THROUGH THE OPENING THE WANDERER MADE WITH THE EVIL EYE!
NOTHING CAN STOP ME NOW!
I'LL SET CRYSTAL FREE..OR DIE IN THE ATTEMPT!
YOU MUSTN'T BLAME HIM, PRESTER JOHN! HE COULDN'T HELP HIMSELF! THE GIRL, CRYSTAL, MEANS EVERYTHING TO HIM!
DO YOU NOT THINK I KNOW THE POWER OF LOVE?? BUT--- HE DID NOT GIVE ME A CHANCE TO EXPLAIN---TO WARN HIM--!
WARN HIM? OF WHAT?
HE SEIZED THE EVIL EYE BEFORE I COULD PRESS THE SAFETY BUTTON!
THAT MEANS THE POWER IS STILL ON--- AND IT WILL KEEP INCREASING..AND INCREASING--- UNTIL IT REACHES THE POINT OF COMPLETE DESTRUCTION!!
IF HE ISN'T STOPPED, HE'LL BLOW HIMSELF UP WITHIN MINUTES!
AND, AS THE UNSUSPECTING TORCH BLAZES ON..TOWARDS WHAT SEEMS TO BE CERTAIN DOOM--- WE TURN OUR ATTENTION ONCE MORE TO THE STRANGE ACTIVITY OCCURRING WITHIN THE GREAT BARRIER---
MEDUSA--- IF YOU LOVE BLACK BOLT-- WHY DO YOU LET HIM DO IT?
I CANNOT STOP HIM, CRYSTAL! HE FEELS IT IS THE ONLY WAY TO DESTROY THE BARRIER!
HE IS STILL KING! HIS WORD MUST BE OUR LAW!
ONLY HIS OWN LIFE FORCE HAS THE POWER TO ACTIVATE THE CYCLO-ELECTRONIC CHAMBER -- ENABLING IT TO GENERATE ENOUGH VELOCITY TO SHATTER THE BARRIER!
THE TERRIBLE SHOCK TO HIM..THE STRAIN IT WILL PUT UPON HIS OWN BODY--- MAY KILL HIM--- BUT, HE IS DETERMINED TO TRY!
AND, ABOVE ALL ELSE--- HE IS BLACK BOLT!

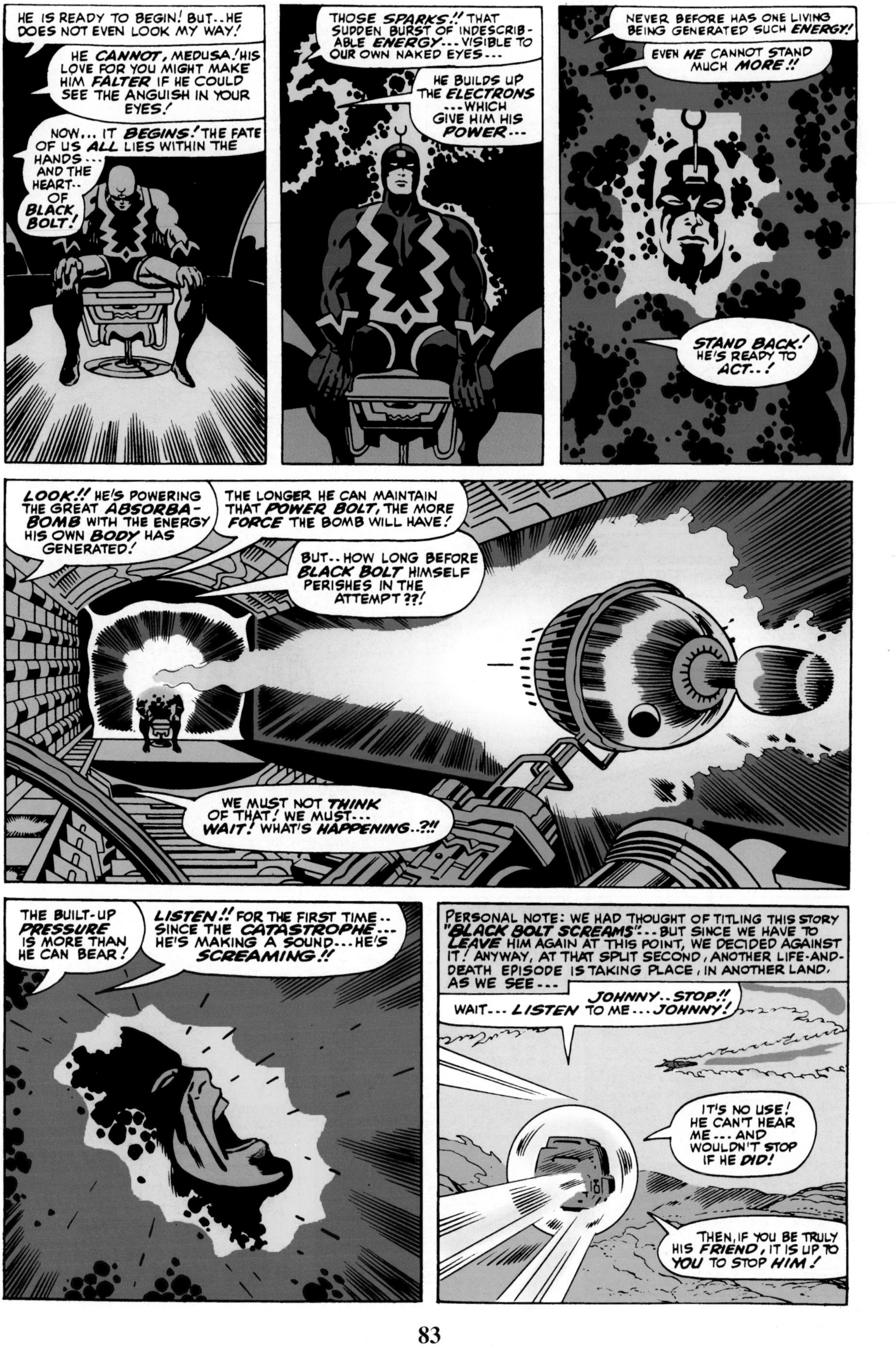
HE IS READY TO BEGIN! BUT..HE DOES NOT EVEN LOOK MY WAY!
HE CANNOT, MEDUSA! HIS LOVE FOR YOU MIGHT MAKE HIM FALTER IF HE COULD SEE THE ANGUISH IN YOUR EYES!
NOW... IT BEGINS! THE FATE OF US ALL LIES WITHIN THE HANDS... AND THE HEART.. OF BLACK BOLT!
THOSE SPARKS!! THAT SUDDEN BURST OF INDESCRIBABLE ENERGY... VISIBLE TO OUR OWN NAKED EYES...
HE BUILDS UP THE ELECTRONS ...WHICH GIVE HIM HIS POWER...
NEVER BEFORE HAS ONE LIVING BEING GENERATED SUCH ENERGY!
EVEN HE CANNOT STAND MUCH MORE!!
STAND BACK! HE'S READY TO ACT..!
LOOK!! HE'S POWERING THE GREAT ABSORBA-BOMB WITH THE ENERGY HIS OWN BODY HAS GENERATED!
THE LONGER HE CAN MAINTAIN THAT POWER BOLT, THE MORE FORCE THE BOMB WILL HAVE!
BUT.. HOW LONG BEFORE BLACK BOLT HIMSELF PERISHES IN THE ATTEMPT??!
WE MUST NOT THINK OF THAT! WE MUST-- WAIT! WHAT'S HAPPENING..?!!
THE BUILT-UP PRESSURE IS MORE THAN HE CAN BEAR!
LISTEN!! FOR THE FIRST TIME.. SINCE THE CATASTROPHE... HE'S MAKING A SOUND... HE'S SCREAMING!!
PERSONAL NOTE: WE HAD THOUGHT OF TITLING THIS STORY "BLACK BOLT SCREAMS"... BUT SINCE WE HAVE TO LEAVE HIM AGAIN AT THIS POINT, WE DECIDED AGAINST IT! ANYWAY, AT THAT SPLIT SECOND, ANOTHER LIFE-AND-DEATH EPISODE IS TAKING PLACE, IN ANOTHER LAND, AS WE SEE...
JOHNNY.. STOP!! WAIT... LISTEN TO ME... JOHNNY!
IT'S NO USE! HE CAN'T HEAR ME... AND WOULDN'T STOP IF HE DID!
THEN, IF YOU BE TRULY HIS FRIEND, IT IS UP TO YOU TO STOP HIM!

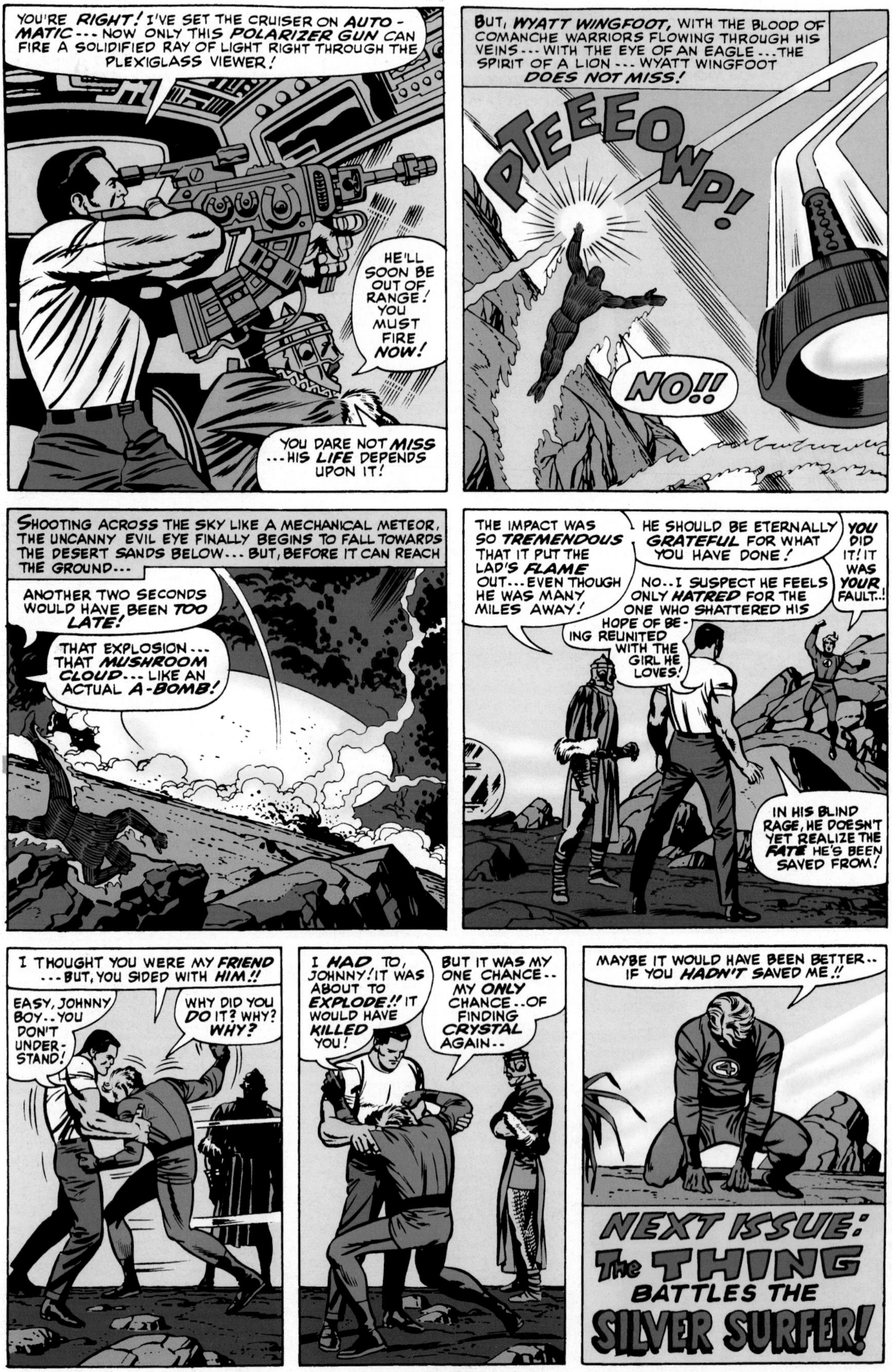
YOU'RE RIGHT! I'VE SET THE CRUISER ON AUTO-MATIC--- NOW ONLY THIS POLARIZER GUN CAN FIRE A SOLIDIFIED RAY OF LIGHT RIGHT THROUGH THE PLEXIGLASS VIEWER!
HE'LL SOON BE OUT OF RANGE! YOU MUST FIRE NOW!
YOU DARE NOT MISS ---HIS LIFE DEPENDS UPON IT!
BUT, WYATT WINGFOOT, WITH THE BLOOD OF COMANCHE WARRIORS FLOWING THROUGH HIS VEINS--- WITH THE EYE OF AN EAGLE---THE SPIRIT OF A LION--- WYATT WINGFOOT DOES NOT MISS!
PTEEEOWP!
NO!!
SHOOTING ACROSS THE SKY LIKE A MECHANICAL METEOR, THE UNCANNY EVIL EYE FINALLY BEGINS TO FALL TOWARDS THE DESERT SANDS BELOW--- BUT, BEFORE IT CAN REACH THE GROUND---
ANOTHER TWO SECONDS WOULD HAVE BEEN TOO LATE!
THAT EXPLOSION--- THAT MUSHROOM CLOUD--- LIKE AN ACTUAL A-BOMB!
THE IMPACT WAS SO TREMENDOUS THAT IT PUT THE LAD'S FLAME OUT--- EVEN THOUGH HE WAS MANY MILES AWAY!
HE SHOULD BE ETERNALLY GRATEFUL FOR WHAT YOU HAVE DONE!
YOU DID IT! IT WAS YOUR FAULT..!
NO--I SUSPECT HE FEELS ONLY HATRED FOR THE ONE WHO SHATTERED HIS HOPE OF BE-ING REUNITED WITH THE GIRL HE LOVES!
IN HIS BLIND RAGE, HE DOESN'T YET REALIZE THE FATE HE'S BEEN SAVED FROM!
I THOUGHT YOU WERE MY FRIEND ---BUT, YOU SIDED WITH HIM!!
EASY, JOHNNY BOY--YOU DON'T UNDER-STAND!
WHY DID YOU DO IT? WHY? WHY?
I HAD TO, JOHNNY! IT WAS ABOUT TO EXPLODE!! IT WOULD HAVE KILLED YOU!
BUT IT WAS MY ONE CHANCE-- MY ONLY CHANCE--OF FINDING CRYSTAL AGAIN--
MAYBE IT WOULD HAVE BEEN BETTER-- IF YOU HADN'T SAVED ME!!
NEXT ISSUE: The THING BATTLES THE SILVER SURFER!

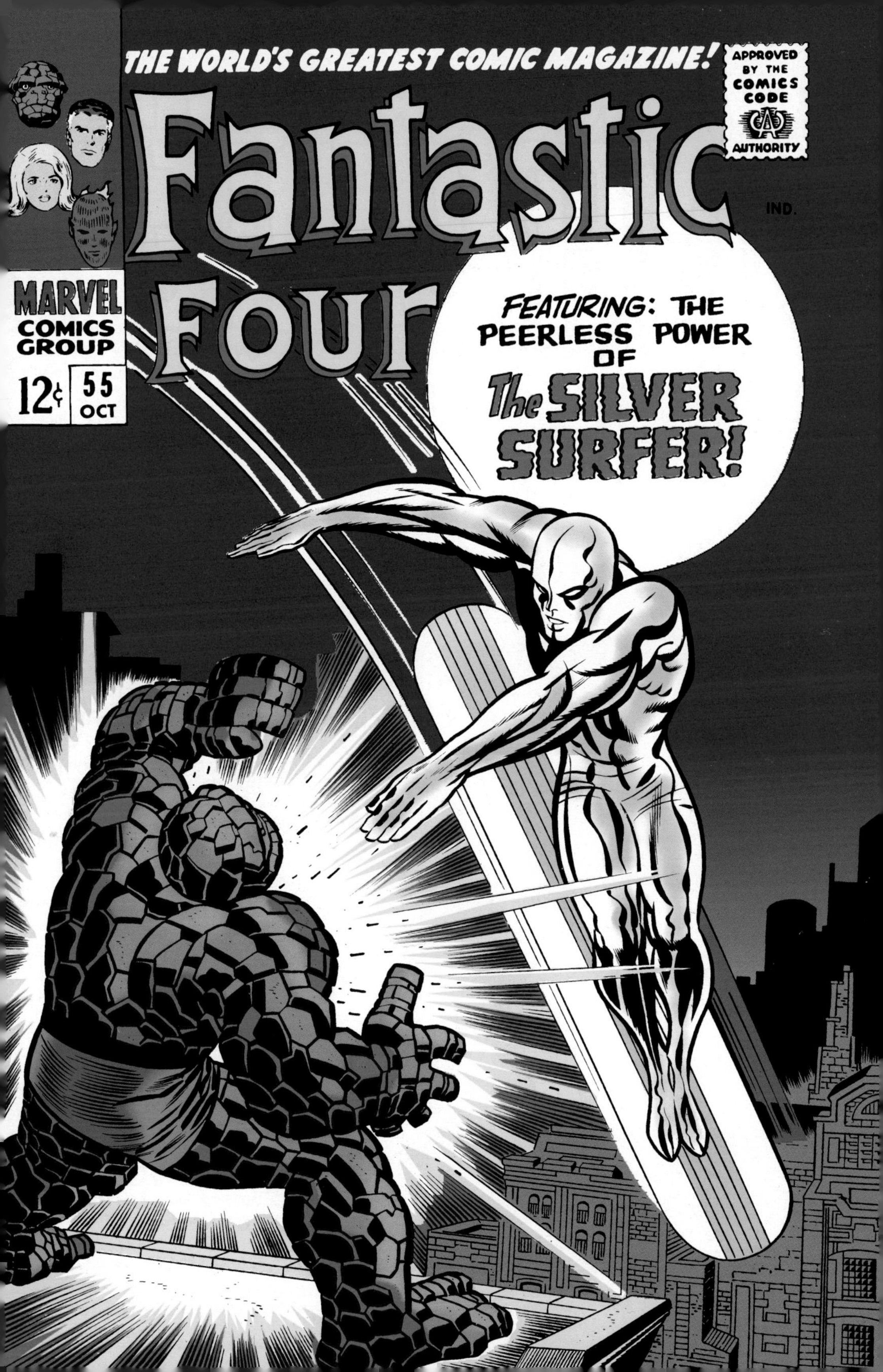
THE WORLD'S GREATEST COMIC MAGAZINE!
APPROVED BY THE COMICS CODE AUTHORITY
Fantastic Four
IND.
MARVEL COMICS GROUP
12¢
55 OCT
FEATURING: THE PEERLESS POWER OF The SILVER SURFER!

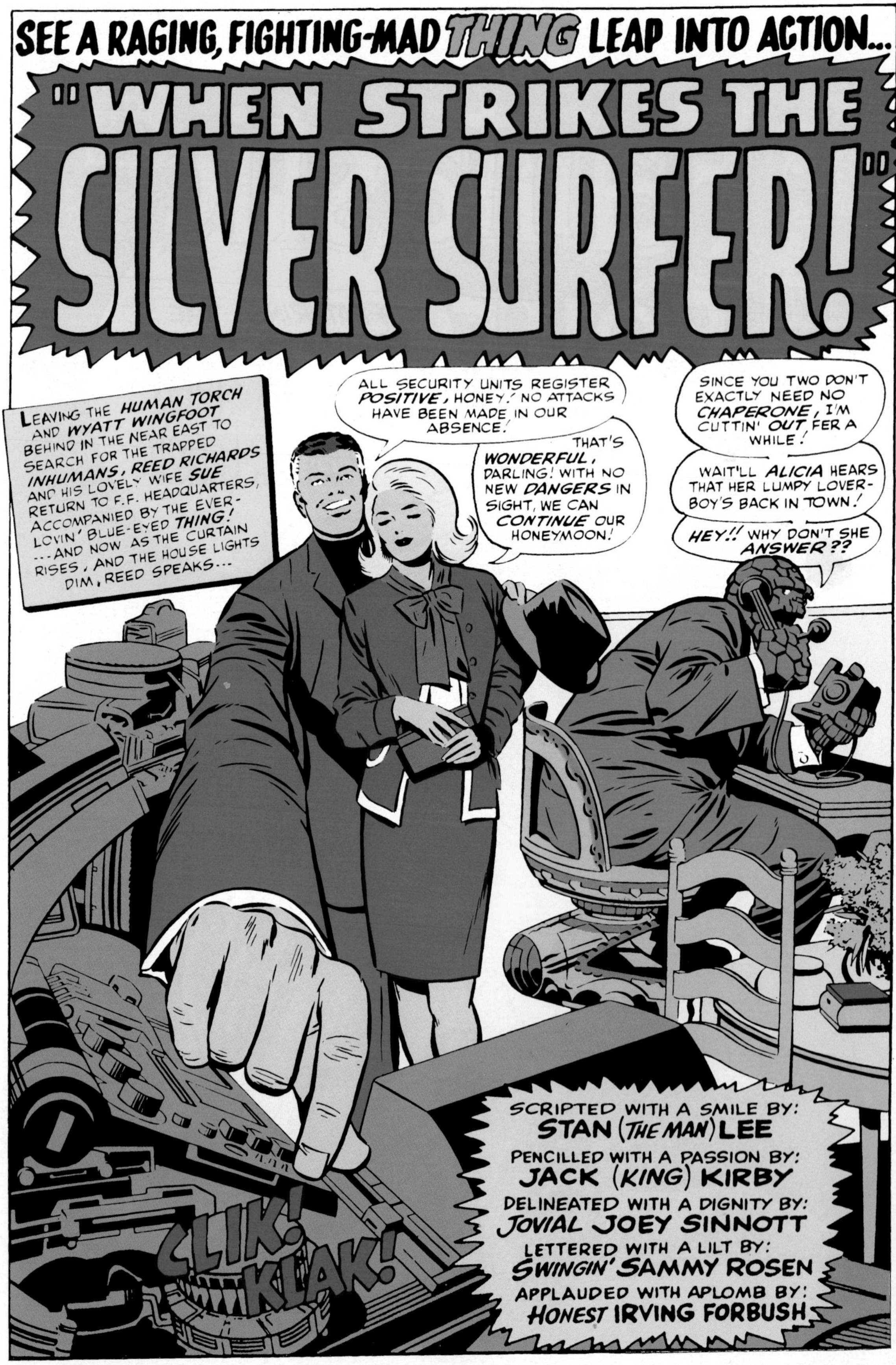

SEE A RAGING, FIGHTING-MAD THING LEAP INTO ACTION...
"WHEN STRIKES THE SILVER SURFER!"
LEAVING THE HUMAN TORCH AND WYATT WINGFOOT BEHIND IN THE NEAR EAST TO SEARCH FOR THE TRAPPED INHUMANS, REED RICHARDS AND HIS LOVELY WIFE SUE RETURN TO F.F. HEADQUARTERS, ACCOMPANIED BY THE EVER-LOVIN' BLUE-EYED THING! ...AND NOW AS THE CURTAIN RISES, AND THE HOUSE LIGHTS DIM, REED SPEAKS...
ALL SECURITY UNITS REGISTER POSITIVE, HONEY! NO ATTACKS HAVE BEEN MADE IN OUR ABSENCE!
THAT'S WONDERFUL, DARLING! WITH NO NEW DANGERS IN SIGHT, WE CAN CONTINUE OUR HONEYMOON!
SINCE YOU TWO DON'T EXACTLY NEED NO CHAPERONE, I'M CUTTIN' OUT FER A WHILE!
WAIT'LL ALICIA HEARS THAT HER LUMPY LOVER-BOY'S BACK IN TOWN!
HEY!! WHY DON'T SHE ANSWER??
CLIK! KLAK!
SCRIPTED WITH A SMILE BY: STAN (THE MAN) LEE
PENCILLED WITH A PASSION BY: JACK (KING) KIRBY
DELINEATED WITH A DIGNITY BY: JOVIAL JOEY SINNOTT
LETTERED WITH A LILT BY: SWINGIN' SAMMY ROSEN
APPLAUDED WITH APLOMB BY: HONEST IRVING FORBUSH

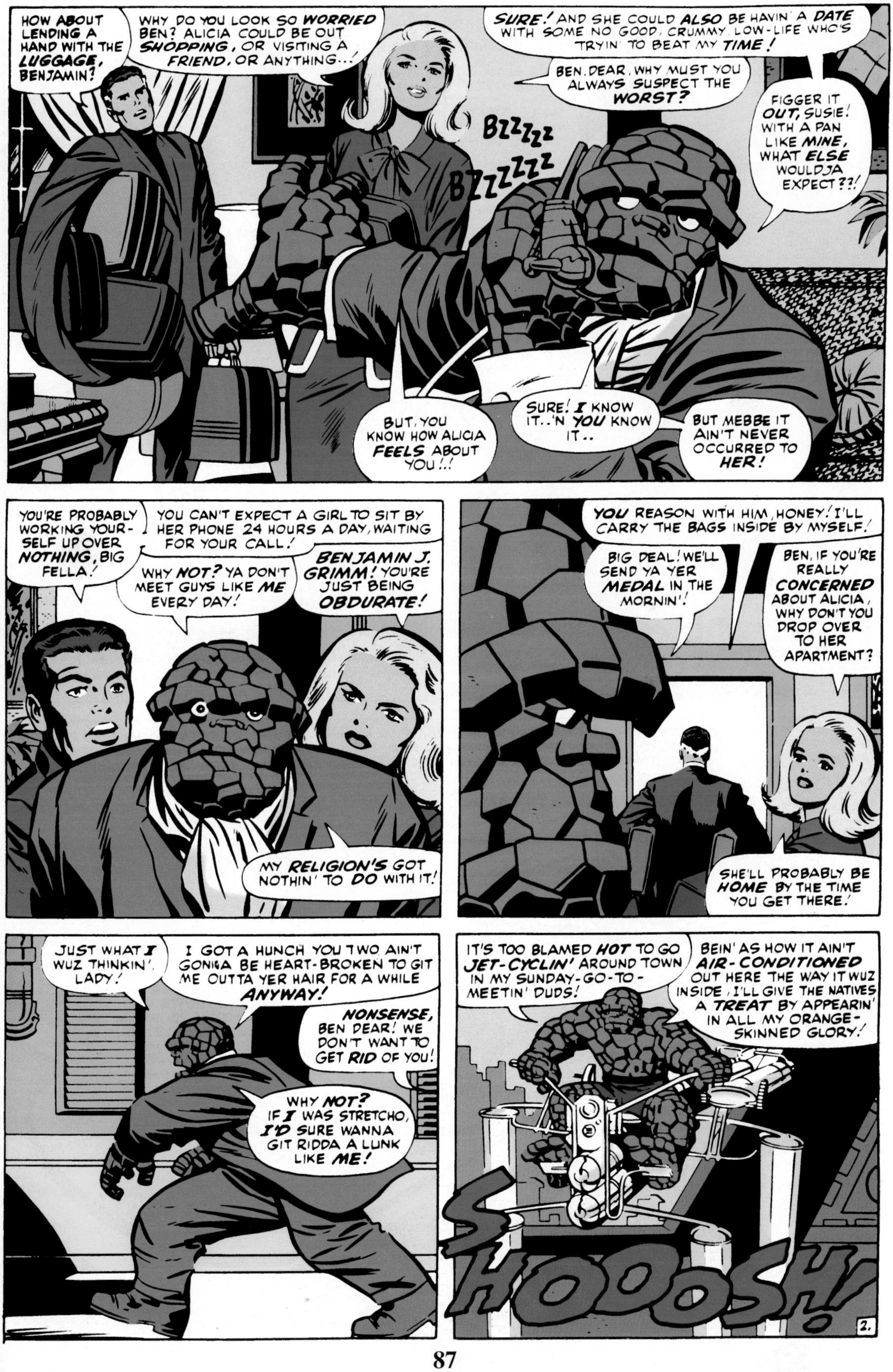

HOW ABOUT LENDING A HAND WITH THE LUGGAGE, BENJAMIN?
WHY DO YOU LOOK SO WORRIED BEN? ALICIA COULD BE OUT SHOPPING, OR VISITING A FRIEND, OR ANYTHING...!
SURE! AND SHE COULD ALSO BE HAVIN' A DATE WITH SOME NO GOOD, CRUMMY, LOW-LIFE WHO'S TRYIN' TO BEAT MY TIME!
BEN, DEAR, WHY MUST YOU ALWAYS SUSPECT THE WORST?
FIGGER IT OUT, SUSIE! WITH A PAN LIKE MINE, WHAT ELSE WOULDJA EXPECT??!
BZZZZZ
BZZZZZZ
BUT, YOU KNOW HOW ALICIA FEELS ABOUT YOU!!
SURE! I KNOW IT..'N YOU KNOW IT..
BUT MEBBE IT AIN'T NEVER OCCURRED TO HER!
YOU'RE PROBABLY WORKING YOURSELF UP OVER NOTHING, BIG FELLA!
YOU CAN'T EXPECT A GIRL TO SIT BY HER PHONE 24 HOURS A DAY, WAITING FOR YOUR CALL!
WHY NOT? YA DON'T MEET GUYS LIKE ME EVERY DAY!
BENJAMIN J. GRIMM! YOU'RE JUST BEING OBDURATE!
MY RELIGION'S GOT NOTHIN' TO DO WITH IT!
YOU REASON WITH HIM, HONEY! I'LL CARRY THE BAGS INSIDE BY MYSELF!
BIG DEAL! WE'LL SEND YA YER MEDAL IN THE MORNIN'!
BEN, IF YOU'RE REALLY CONCERNED ABOUT ALICIA, WHY DON'T YOU DROP OVER TO HER APARTMENT?
SHE'LL PROBABLY BE HOME BY THE TIME YOU GET THERE!
JUST WHAT I WUZ THINKIN', LADY!
I GOT A HUNCH YOU TWO AIN'T GONNA BE HEART-BROKEN TO GIT ME OUTTA YER HAIR FOR A WHILE ANYWAY!
NONSENSE, BEN DEAR! WE DON'T WANT TO GET RID OF YOU!
WHY NOT? IF I WAS STRETCHO, I'D SURE WANNA GIT RIDDA A LUNK LIKE ME!
IT'S TOO BLAMED HOT TO GO JET-CYCLIN' AROUND TOWN IN MY SUNDAY-GO-TO-MEETIN' DUDS!
BEIN' AS HOW IT AIN'T AIR-CONDITIONED OUT HERE THE WAY IT WUZ INSIDE, I'LL GIVE THE NATIVES A TREAT BY APPEARIN' IN ALL MY ORANGE-SKINNED GLORY!
SHOOOSH!
2.

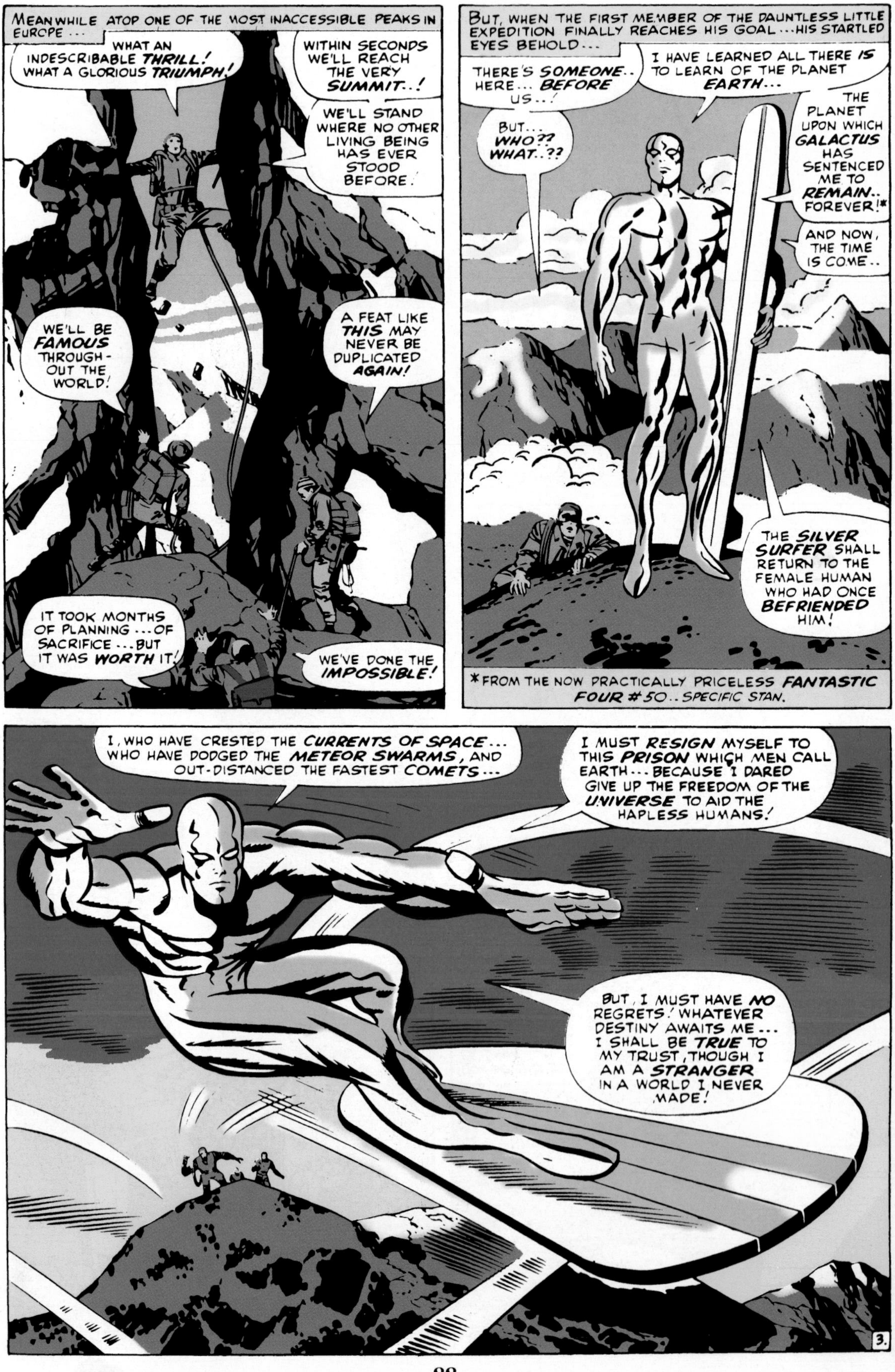
MEANWHILE ATOP ONE OF THE MOST INACCESSIBLE PEAKS IN EUROPE ...
WHAT AN INDESCRIBABLE THRILL! WHAT A GLORIOUS TRIUMPH!
WITHIN SECONDS WE'LL REACH THE VERY SUMMIT..!
WE'LL STAND WHERE NO OTHER LIVING BEING HAS EVER STOOD BEFORE!
WE'LL BE FAMOUS THROUGH-OUT THE WORLD!
A FEAT LIKE THIS MAY NEVER BE DUPLICATED AGAIN!
IT TOOK MONTHS OF PLANNING ... OF SACRIFICE ... BUT IT WAS WORTH IT!
WE'VE DONE THE IMPOSSIBLE!
BUT, WHEN THE FIRST MEMBER OF THE DAUNTLESS LITTLE EXPEDITION FINALLY REACHES HIS GOAL ... HIS STARTLED EYES BEHOLD ...
THERE'S SOMEONE.. HERE... BEFORE US..!
BUT... WHO?? WHAT..??
I HAVE LEARNED ALL THERE IS TO LEARN OF THE PLANET EARTH...
THE PLANET UPON WHICH GALACTUS HAS SENTENCED ME TO REMAIN.. FOREVER!*
AND NOW, THE TIME IS COME..
THE SILVER SURFER SHALL RETURN TO THE FEMALE HUMAN WHO HAD ONCE BEFRIENDED HIM!
*FROM THE NOW PRACTICALLY PRICELESS FANTASTIC FOUR #50.. SPECIFIC STAN.
I, WHO HAVE CRESTED THE CURRENTS OF SPACE... WHO HAVE DODGED THE METEOR SWARMS, AND OUT-DISTANCED THE FASTEST COMETS...
I MUST RESIGN MYSELF TO THIS PRISON WHICH MEN CALL EARTH... BECAUSE I DARED GIVE UP THE FREEDOM OF THE UNIVERSE TO AID THE HAPLESS HUMANS!
BUT, I MUST HAVE NO REGRETS! WHATEVER DESTINY AWAITS ME... I SHALL BE TRUE TO MY TRUST, THOUGH I AM A STRANGER IN A WORLD I NEVER MADE!
3.

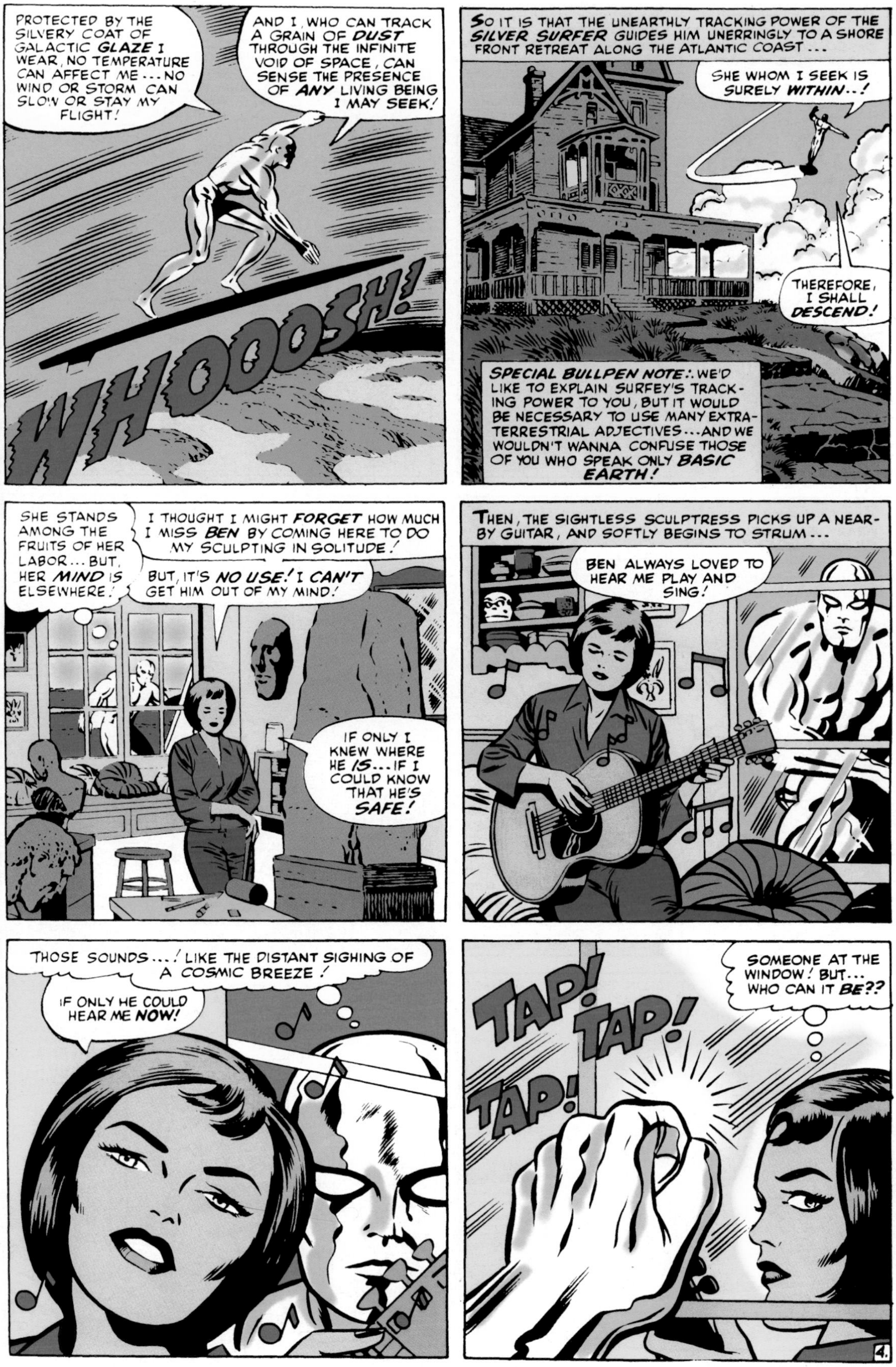
PROTECTED BY THE SILVERY COAT OF GALACTIC GLAZE I WEAR, NO TEMPERATURE CAN AFFECT ME...NO WIND OR STORM CAN SLOW OR STAY MY FLIGHT!
AND I, WHO CAN TRACK A GRAIN OF DUST THROUGH THE INFINITE VOID OF SPACE, CAN SENSE THE PRESENCE OF ANY LIVING BEING I MAY SEEK!
WHOOOSH!
SO IT IS THAT THE UNEARTHLY TRACKING POWER OF THE SILVER SURFER GUIDES HIM UNERRINGLY TO A SHORE FRONT RETREAT ALONG THE ATLANTIC COAST...
SHE WHOM I SEEK IS SURELY WITHIN..!
THEREFORE, I SHALL DESCEND!
SPECIAL BULLPEN NOTE: WE'D LIKE TO EXPLAIN SURFEY'S TRACKING POWER TO YOU, BUT IT WOULD BE NECESSARY TO USE MANY EXTRA-TERRESTRIAL ADJECTIVES...AND WE WOULDN'T WANNA CONFUSE THOSE OF YOU WHO SPEAK ONLY BASIC EARTH!
SHE STANDS AMONG THE FRUITS OF HER LABOR...BUT, HER MIND IS ELSEWHERE!
I THOUGHT I MIGHT FORGET HOW MUCH I MISS BEN BY COMING HERE TO DO MY SCULPTING IN SOLITUDE!
BUT, IT'S NO USE! I CAN'T GET HIM OUT OF MY MIND!
IF ONLY I KNEW WHERE HE IS...IF I COULD KNOW THAT HE'S SAFE!
THEN, THE SIGHTLESS SCULPTRESS PICKS UP A NEAR-BY GUITAR, AND SOFTLY BEGINS TO STRUM...
BEN ALWAYS LOVED TO HEAR ME PLAY AND SING!
THOSE SOUNDS...! LIKE THE DISTANT SIGHING OF A COSMIC BREEZE!
IF ONLY HE COULD HEAR ME NOW!
TAP! TAP! TAP!
SOMEONE AT THE WINDOW! BUT... WHO CAN IT BE??
4.

AT A SINGLE GESTURE, A LIGHTNING-LIKE BOLT OF SHEER *ENERGY* SURROUNDS THE SILVER-SURFER... INSTANTLY *DISSOLVING* THE WINDOW WHICH STANDS BETWEEN HIM AND THE BLIND ALICIA...: THEN...

DO NOT FEAR! IT IS *I*!

THAT *VOICE*! ONE WHICH I NEVER THOUGHT I WOULD HEAR AGAIN!

YOU'VE *RETURNED*... AS YOU SAID YOU WOULD!

YES! I HAVE FLOWN OVER THIS STRANGE PLANET UPON WHICH HUMANS DWELL!

I HAVE SEEN MEN BUILD...AND DESTROY! I HAVE SEEN THIS WORLD, WHICH COULD BE *PARADISE*, REDUCED TO A PLANET OF *GREED*, AND *FEAR*, AND *HATRED*! I HAVE SEEN *HUMANITY* WITH ITS HERITAGE BETRAYED!

I CAN STOMACH *NO MORE*!

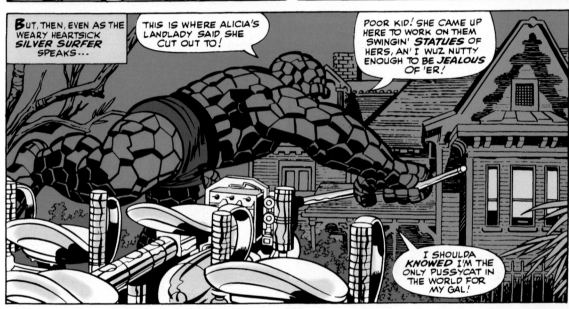

BUT, THEN, EVEN AS THE WEARY HEARTSICK *SILVER SURFER* SPEAKS...

THIS IS WHERE ALICIA'S LANDLADY SAID SHE CUT OUT TO!

POOR KID! SHE CAME UP HERE TO WORK ON THEM SWINGIN' *STATUES* OF HERS, AN' I WUZ NUTTY ENOUGH TO BE *JEALOUS* OF 'ER!

I SHOULDA *KNOWED* I'M THE ONLY PUSSYCAT IN THE WORLD FOR MY GAL!

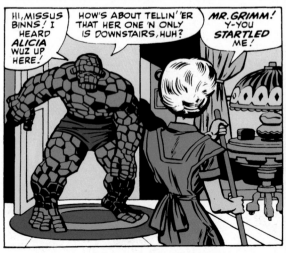

HI, MISSUS BINNS! I HEARD *ALICIA* WUZ UP HERE!

HOW'S ABOUT TELLIN' 'ER THAT HER ONE 'N ONLY IS DOWNSTAIRS, HUH?

MR. GRIMM! Y-YOU *STARTLED* ME!

YEAH! I GUESS IT AIN'T EVERY DAY THAT A *PRINCE CHARMIN'* COMES CHARGIN' INTA...

HEY! WAIT A MINNIT! WHAT'S A *MAN'S VOICE* DOIN' UP THERE?

A MAN'S VOICE..?

WELL, IT SURE AIN'T *MINNIE MOUSE*!

5.

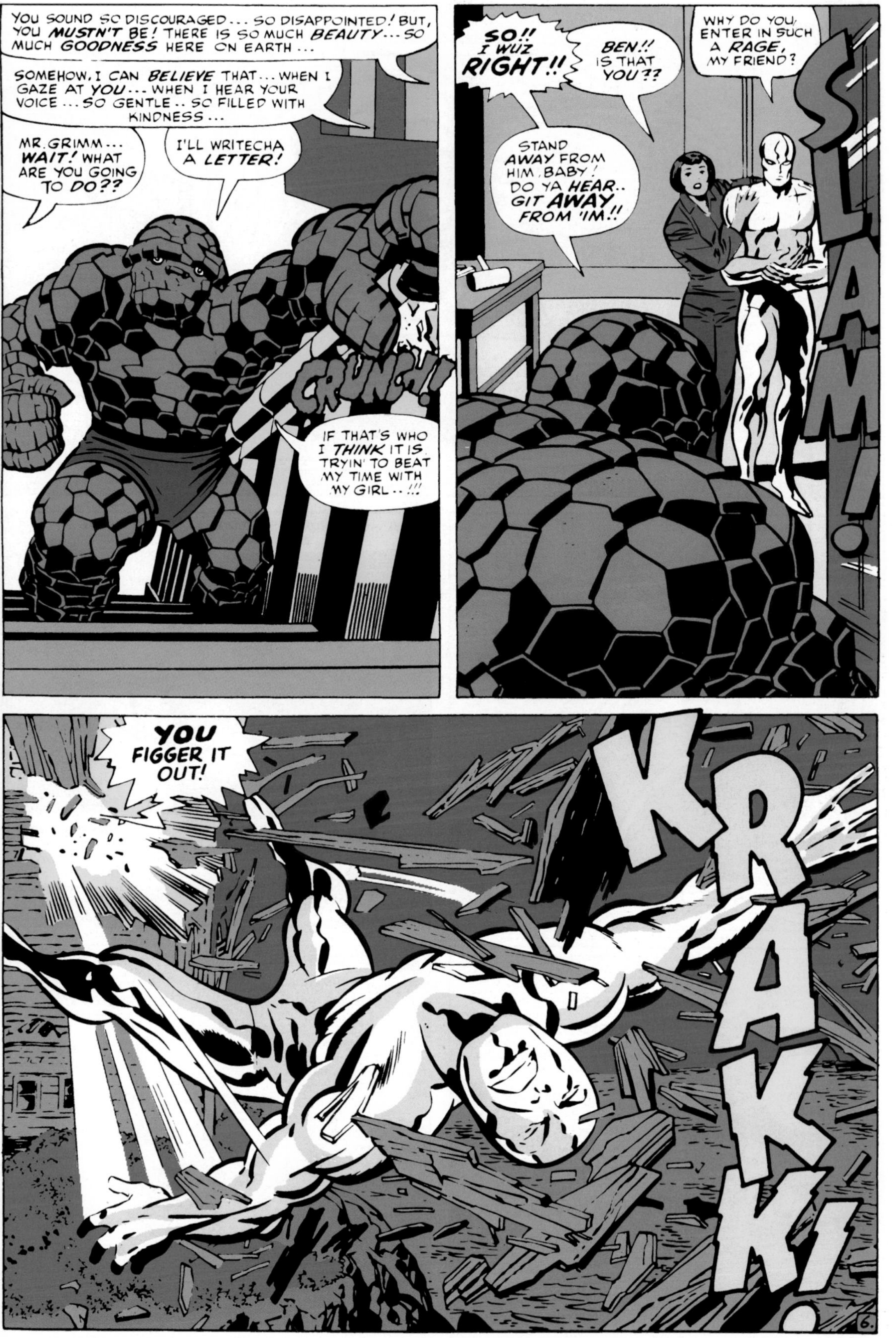
YOU SOUND SO DISCOURAGED... SO DISAPPOINTED! BUT, YOU MUSTN'T BE! THERE IS SO MUCH BEAUTY... SO MUCH GOODNESS HERE ON EARTH...
SOMEHOW, I CAN BELIEVE THAT... WHEN I GAZE AT YOU... WHEN I HEAR YOUR VOICE... SO GENTLE.. SO FILLED WITH KINDNESS...
MR. GRIMM... WAIT! WHAT ARE YOU GOING TO DO??
I'LL WRITECHA A LETTER!
CRUNCH!
IF THAT'S WHO I THINK IT IS TRYIN' TO BEAT MY TIME WITH MY GIRL..!!!
SO!! I WUZ RIGHT!!
BEN!! IS THAT YOU??
WHY DO YOU ENTER IN SUCH A RAGE, MY FRIEND?
STAND AWAY FROM HIM, BABY! DO YA HEAR.. GIT AWAY FROM 'IM!!
SLAM!
YOU FIGGER IT OUT!
KRAKK!
6.

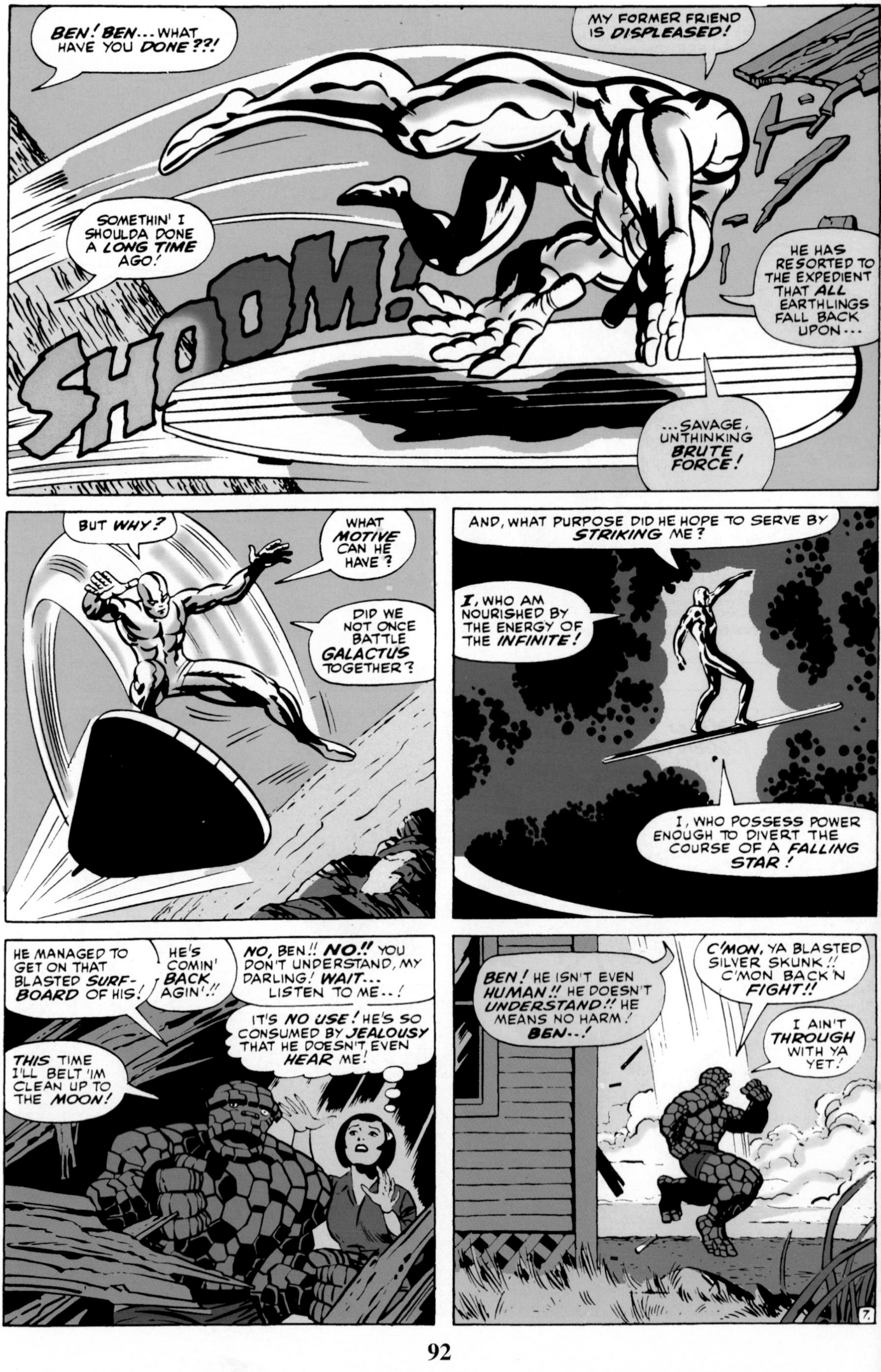
BEN! BEN... WHAT HAVE YOU DONE??!
MY FORMER FRIEND IS DISPLEASED!
SOMETHIN' I SHOULDA DONE A LONG TIME AGO!
SHOOM!
HE HAS RESORTED TO THE EXPEDIENT THAT ALL EARTHLINGS FALL BACK UPON...
...SAVAGE, UNTHINKING BRUTE FORCE!
BUT WHY?
WHAT MOTIVE CAN HE HAVE?
DID WE NOT ONCE BATTLE GALACTUS TOGETHER?
AND, WHAT PURPOSE DID HE HOPE TO SERVE BY STRIKING ME?
I, WHO AM NOURISHED BY THE ENERGY OF THE INFINITE!
I, WHO POSSESS POWER ENOUGH TO DIVERT THE COURSE OF A FALLING STAR!
HE MANAGED TO GET ON THAT BLASTED SURF-BOARD OF HIS!
HE'S COMIN' BACK AGIN'!!
NO, BEN!! NO!! YOU DON'T UNDERSTAND, MY DARLING! WAIT... LISTEN TO ME--!
IT'S NO USE! HE'S SO CONSUMED BY JEALOUSY THAT HE DOESN'T EVEN HEAR ME!
THIS TIME I'LL BELT 'IM CLEAN UP TO THE MOON!
BEN! HE ISN'T EVEN HUMAN!! HE DOESN'T UNDERSTAND!! HE MEANS NO HARM! BEN--!
C'MON, YA BLASTED SILVER SKUNK!! C'MON BACK'N FIGHT!!
I AIN'T THROUGH WITH YA YET!
7.

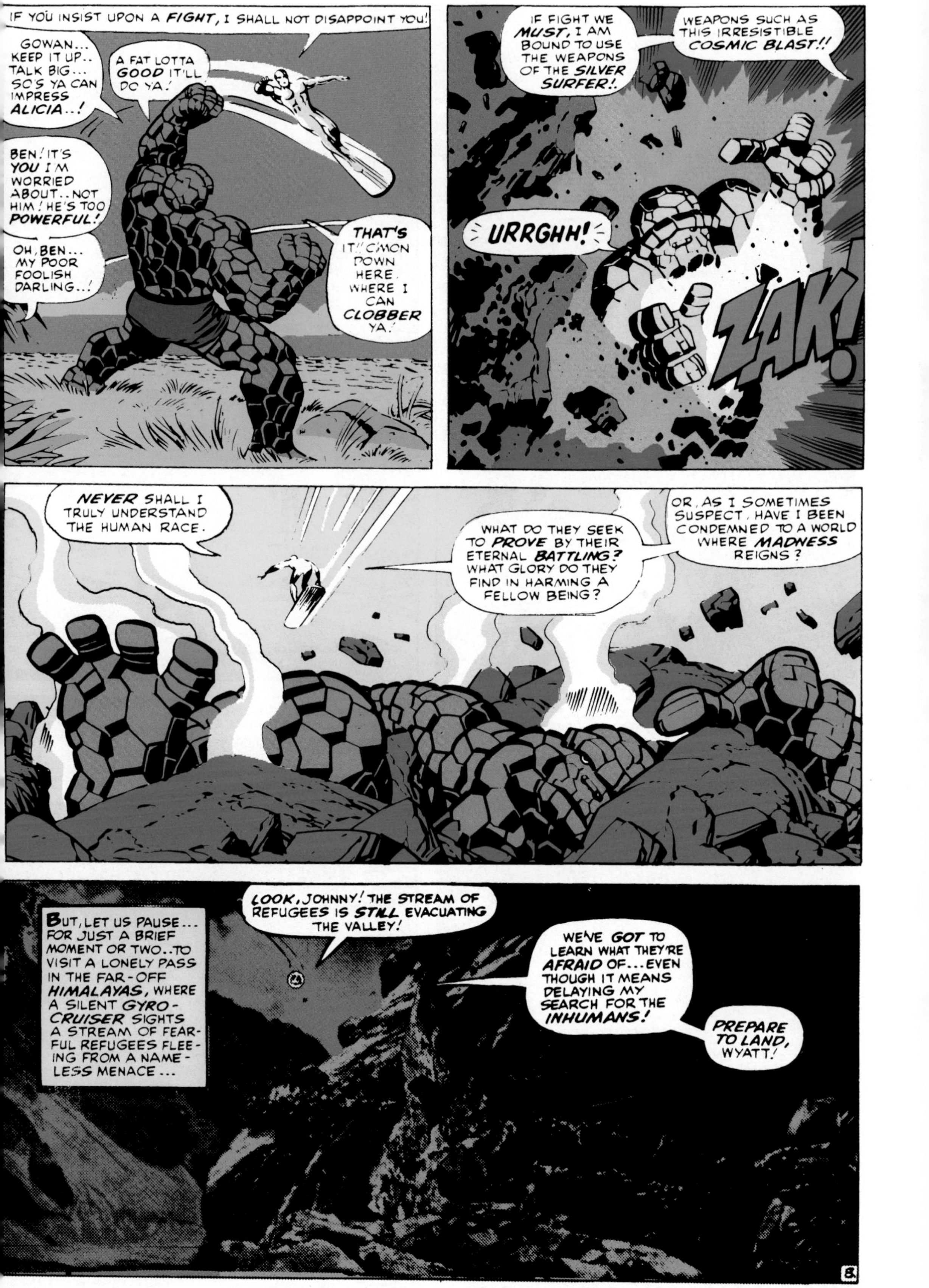
IF YOU INSIST UPON A FIGHT, I SHALL NOT DISAPPOINT YOU!
GOWAN... KEEP IT UP.. TALK BIG... SO'S YA CAN IMPRESS ALICIA..!
A FAT LOTTA GOOD IT'LL DO YA!
BEN! IT'S YOU I'M WORRIED ABOUT..NOT HIM! HE'S TOO POWERFUL!
OH, BEN... MY POOR FOOLISH DARLING..!
THAT'S IT!! C'MON DOWN HERE, WHERE I CAN CLOBBER YA!
IF FIGHT WE MUST, I AM BOUND TO USE THE WEAPONS OF THE SILVER SURFER!.
WEAPONS SUCH AS THIS IRRESISTIBLE COSMIC BLAST!!
URRGHH!
ZAK!
NEVER SHALL I TRULY UNDERSTAND THE HUMAN RACE.
WHAT DO THEY SEEK TO PROVE BY THEIR ETERNAL BATTLING? WHAT GLORY DO THEY FIND IN HARMING A FELLOW BEING?
OR, AS I SOMETIMES SUSPECT, HAVE I BEEN CONDEMNED TO A WORLD WHERE MADNESS REIGNS?
BUT, LET US PAUSE... FOR JUST A BRIEF MOMENT OR TWO..TO VISIT A LONELY PASS IN THE FAR-OFF HIMALAYAS, WHERE A SILENT GYRO-CRUISER SIGHTS A STREAM OF FEARFUL REFUGEES FLEEING FROM A NAMELESS MENACE...
LOOK, JOHNNY! THE STREAM OF REFUGEES IS STILL EVACUATING THE VALLEY!
WE'VE GOT TO LEARN WHAT THEY'RE AFRAID OF... EVEN THOUGH IT MEANS DELAYING MY SEARCH FOR THE INHUMANS!
PREPARE TO LAND, WYATT!
8

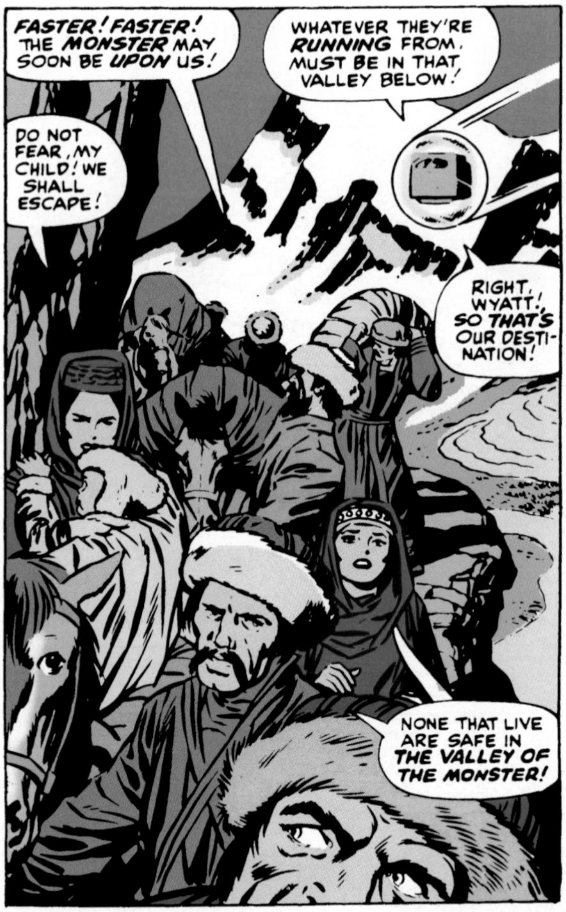
FASTER! FASTER! THE MONSTER MAY SOON BE UPON US!
WHATEVER THEY'RE RUNNING FROM, MUST BE IN THAT VALLEY BELOW!
DO NOT FEAR, MY CHILD! WE SHALL ESCAPE!
RIGHT, WYATT! SO THAT'S OUR DESTINATION!
NONE THAT LIVE ARE SAFE IN THE VALLEY OF THE MONSTER!

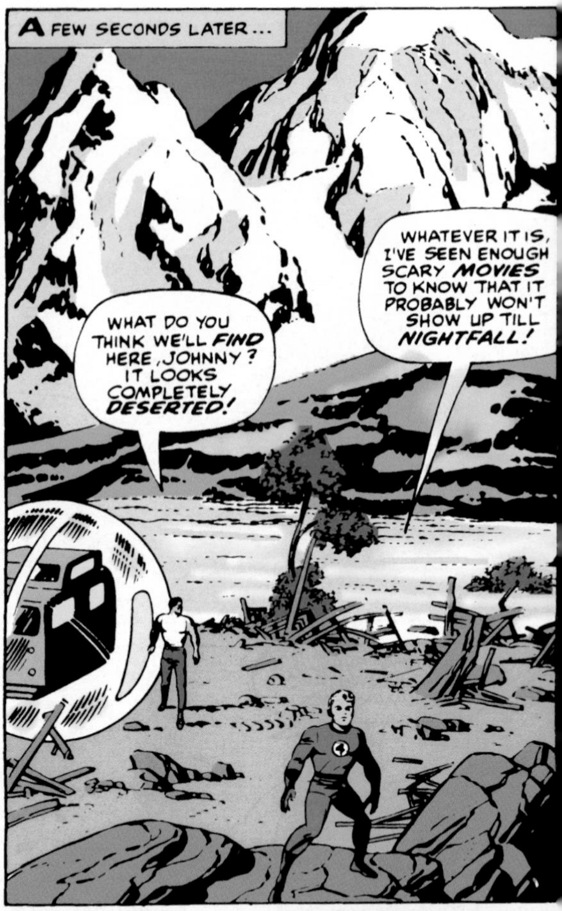
A FEW SECONDS LATER...
WHAT DO YOU THINK WE'LL FIND HERE, JOHNNY? IT LOOKS COMPLETELY DESERTED!
WHATEVER IT IS, I'VE SEEN ENOUGH SCARY MOVIES TO KNOW THAT IT PROBABLY WON'T SHOW UP TILL NIGHTFALL!

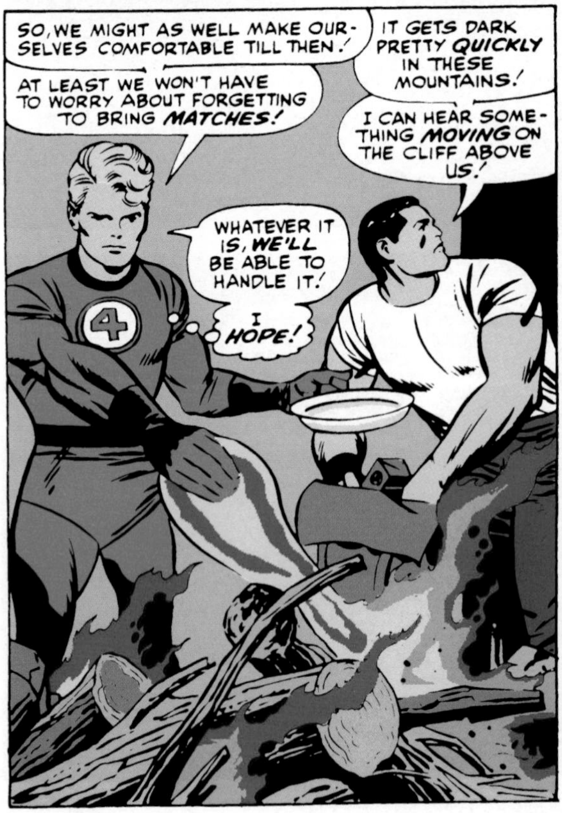
SO, WE MIGHT AS WELL MAKE OURSELVES COMFORTABLE TILL THEN!
AT LEAST WE WON'T HAVE TO WORRY ABOUT FORGETTING TO BRING MATCHES!
IT GETS DARK PRETTY QUICKLY IN THESE MOUNTAINS!
I CAN HEAR SOMETHING MOVING ON THE CLIFF ABOVE US!
WHATEVER IT IS, WE'LL BE ABLE TO HANDLE IT!
I HOPE!

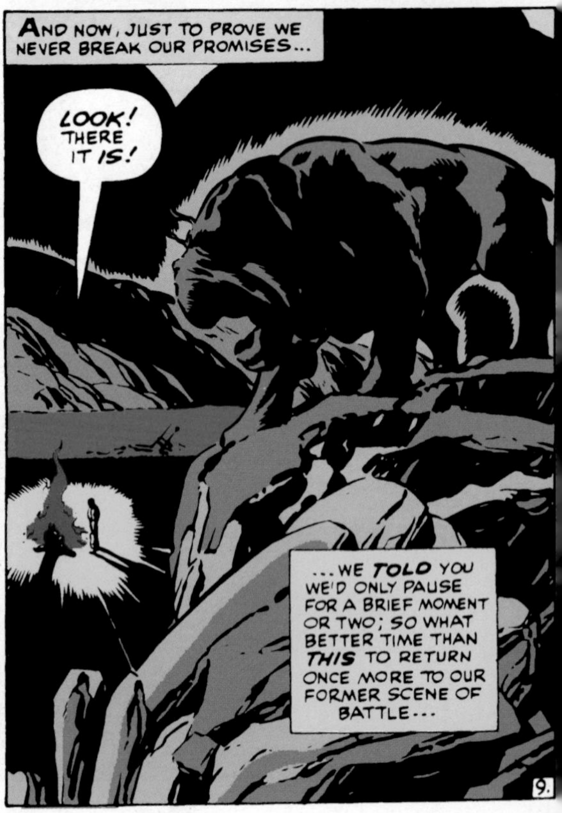
AND NOW, JUST TO PROVE WE NEVER BREAK OUR PROMISES...
LOOK! THERE IT IS!
...WE TOLD YOU WE'D ONLY PAUSE FOR A BRIEF MOMENT OR TWO; SO WHAT BETTER TIME THAN THIS TO RETURN ONCE MORE TO OUR FORMER SCENE OF BATTLE...
9.

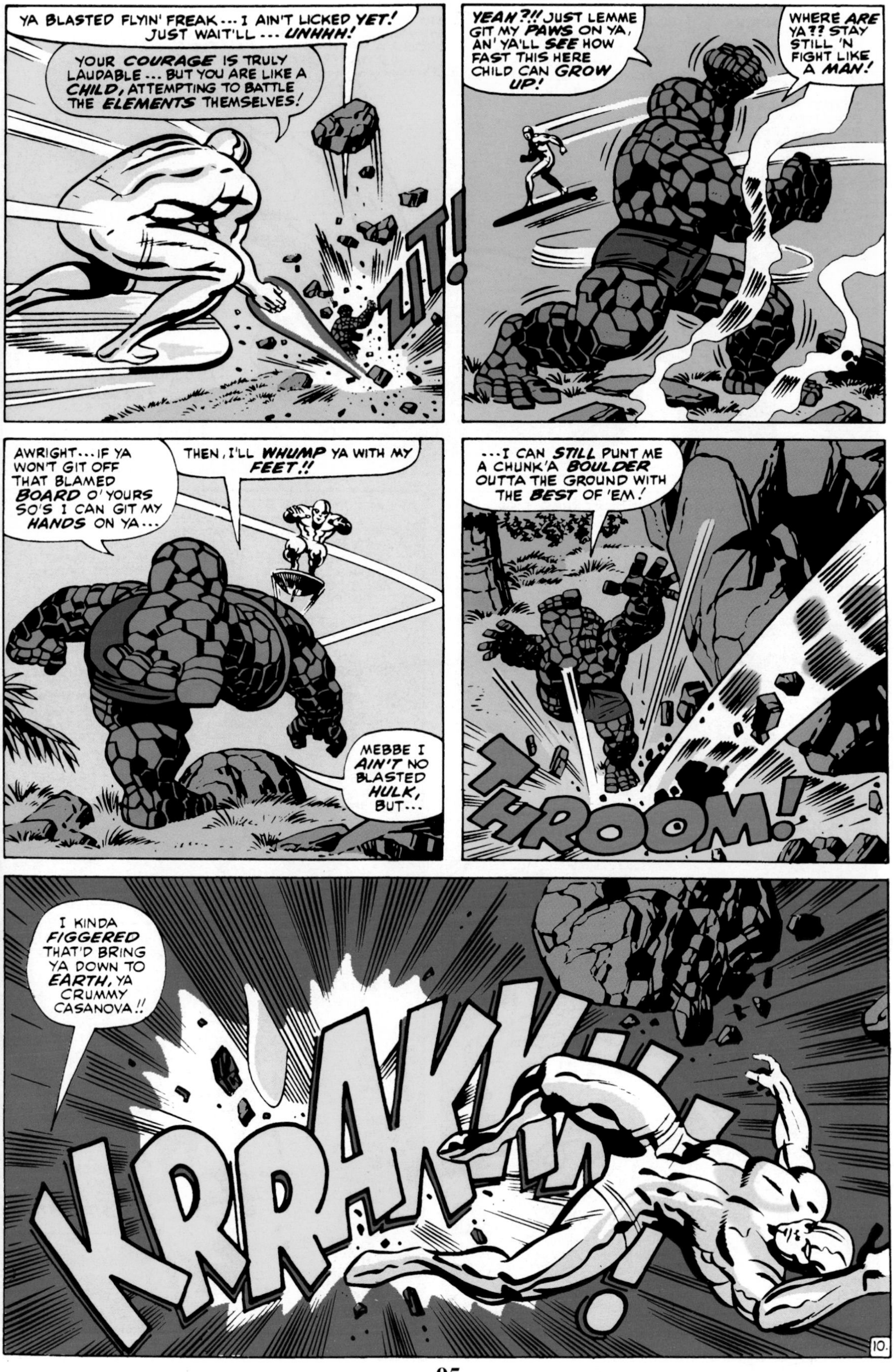
YA BLASTED FLYIN' FREAK... I AIN'T LICKED YET! JUST WAIT'LL... UNHHH!
YOUR COURAGE IS TRULY LAUDABLE... BUT YOU ARE LIKE A CHILD, ATTEMPTING TO BATTLE THE ELEMENTS THEMSELVES!
ZIT!
YEAH?!! JUST LEMME GIT MY PAWS ON YA, AN' YA'LL SEE HOW FAST THIS HERE CHILD CAN GROW UP!
WHERE ARE YA?? STAY STILL 'N FIGHT LIKE A MAN!
AWRIGHT... IF YA WON'T GIT OFF THAT BLAMED BOARD O' YOURS SO'S I CAN GIT MY HANDS ON YA...
THEN, I'LL WHUMP YA WITH MY FEET!!
MEBBE I AIN'T NO BLASTED HULK, BUT...
...I CAN STILL PUNT ME A CHUNK'A BOULDER OUTTA THE GROUND WITH THE BEST OF 'EM!
THROOM!
I KINDA FIGGERED THAT'D BRING YA DOWN TO EARTH, YA CRUMMY CASANOVA!!
KRRAKK!!
10.

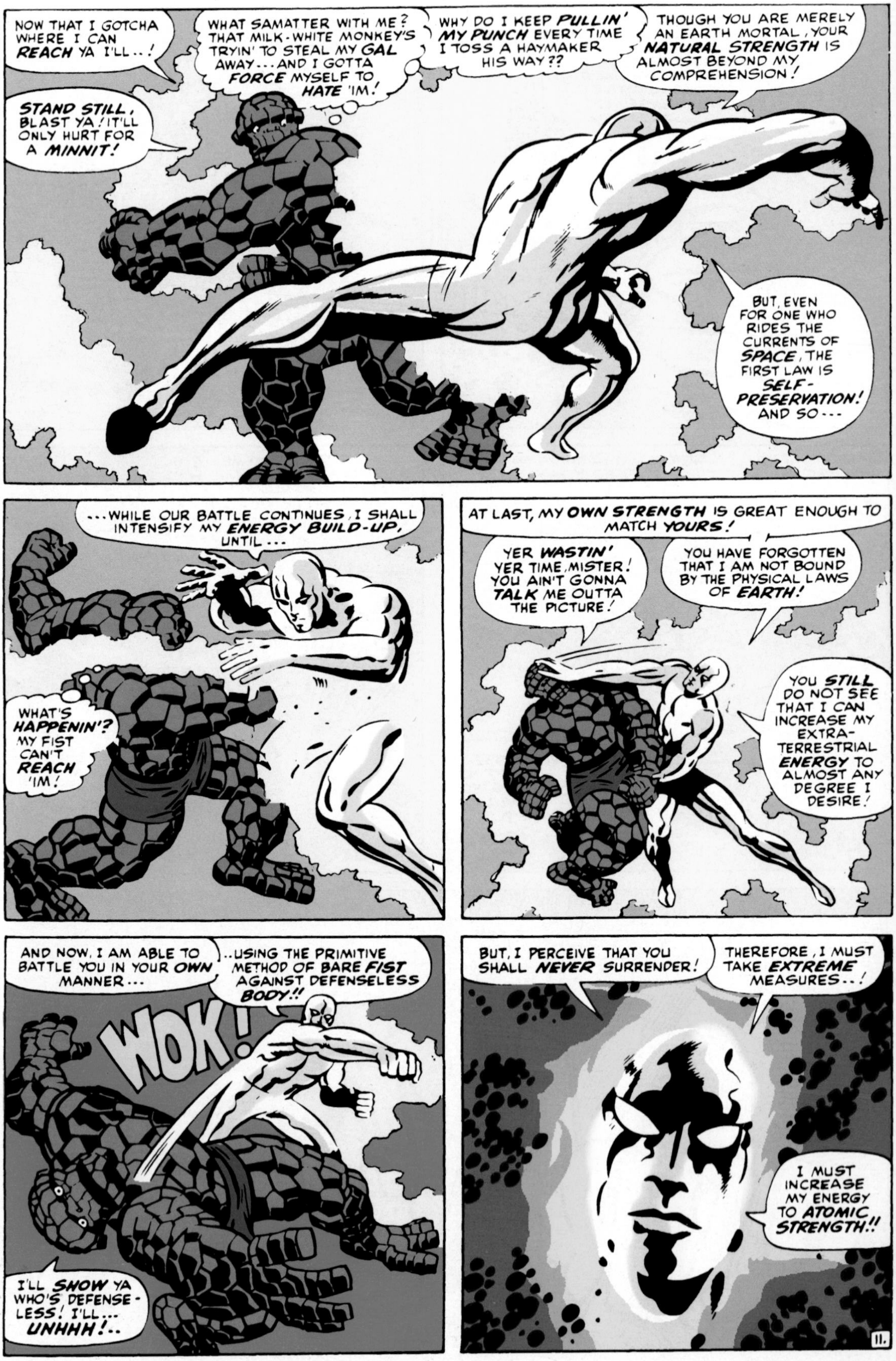
NOW THAT I GOTCHA WHERE I CAN REACH YA I'LL..!
STAND STILL, BLAST YA! IT'LL ONLY HURT FOR A MINNIT!
WHAT SAMATTER WITH ME? THAT MILK-WHITE MONKEY'S TRYIN' TO STEAL MY GAL AWAY... AND I GOTTA FORCE MYSELF TO HATE 'IM!
WHY DO I KEEP PULLIN' MY PUNCH EVERY TIME I TOSS A HAYMAKER HIS WAY??
THOUGH YOU ARE MERELY AN EARTH MORTAL, YOUR NATURAL STRENGTH IS ALMOST BEYOND MY COMPREHENSION!
BUT, EVEN FOR ONE WHO RIDES THE CURRENTS OF SPACE, THE FIRST LAW IS SELF-PRESERVATION! AND SO---
...WHILE OUR BATTLE CONTINUES, I SHALL INTENSIFY MY ENERGY BUILD-UP, UNTIL...
WHAT'S HAPPENIN'? MY FIST CAN'T REACH 'IM!
AT LAST, MY OWN STRENGTH IS GREAT ENOUGH TO MATCH YOURS!
YER WASTIN' YER TIME, MISTER! YOU AIN'T GONNA TALK ME OUTTA THE PICTURE!
YOU HAVE FORGOTTEN THAT I AM NOT BOUND BY THE PHYSICAL LAWS OF EARTH!
YOU STILL DO NOT SEE THAT I CAN INCREASE MY EXTRA-TERRESTRIAL ENERGY TO ALMOST ANY DEGREE I DESIRE!
AND NOW, I AM ABLE TO BATTLE YOU IN YOUR OWN MANNER...
..USING THE PRIMITIVE METHOD OF BARE FIST AGAINST DEFENSELESS BODY!!
WOK!
I'LL SHOW YA WHO'S DEFENSE-LESS! I'LL... UNHHH!..
BUT, I PERCEIVE THAT YOU SHALL NEVER SURRENDER!
THEREFORE, I MUST TAKE EXTREME MEASURES..!
I MUST INCREASE MY ENERGY TO ATOMIC STRENGTH!!
11.

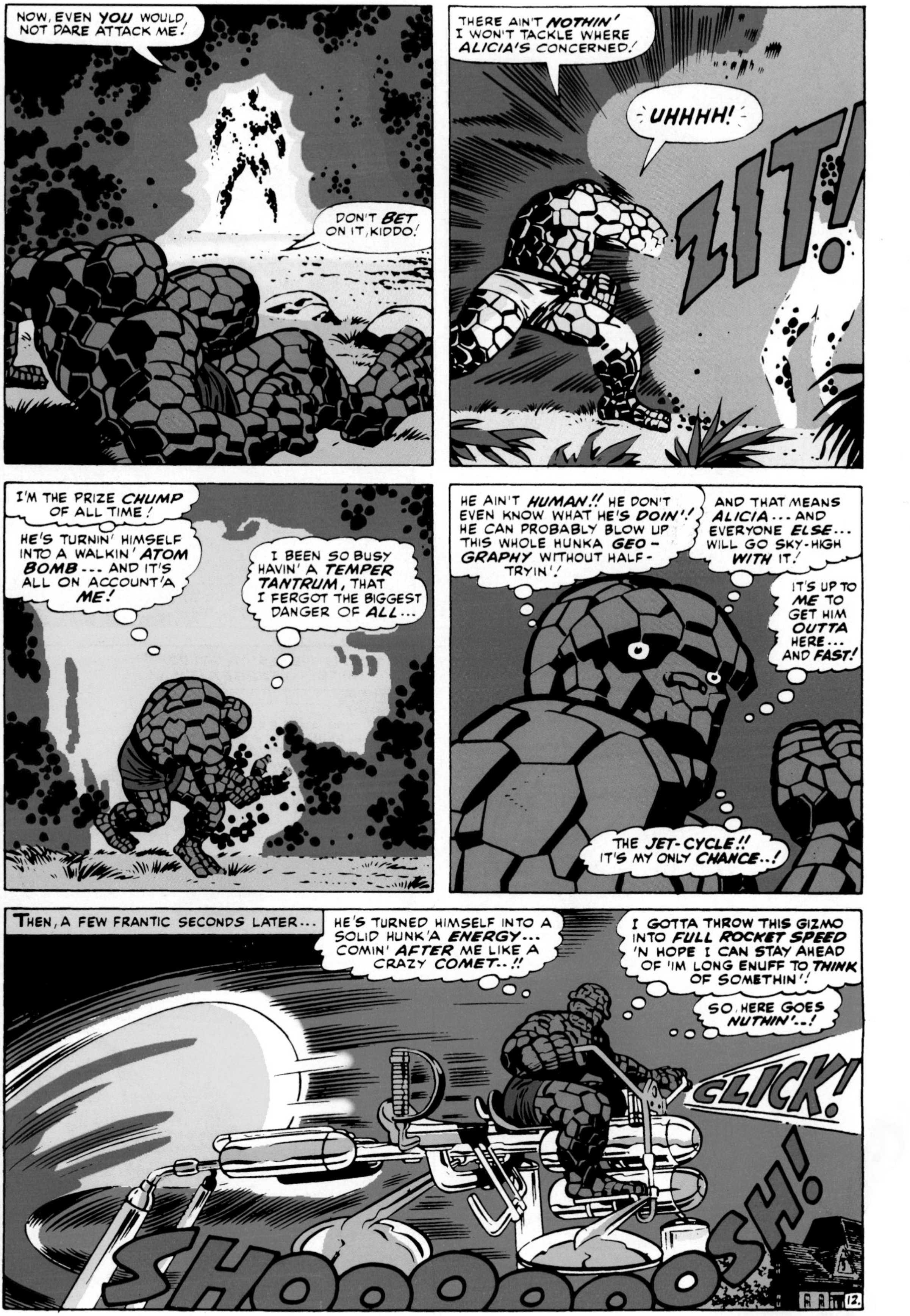
NOW, EVEN YOU WOULD NOT DARE ATTACK ME!
DON'T BET ON IT, KIDDO!
THERE AIN'T NOTHIN' I WON'T TACKLE WHERE ALICIA'S CONCERNED!
UHHHH!
ZIT!
I'M THE PRIZE CHUMP OF ALL TIME!
HE'S TURNIN' HIMSELF INTO A WALKIN' ATOM BOMB--- AND IT'S ALL ON ACCOUNT'A ME!
I BEEN SO BUSY HAVIN' A TEMPER TANTRUM, THAT I FERGOT THE BIGGEST DANGER OF ALL...
HE AIN'T HUMAN!! HE DON'T EVEN KNOW WHAT HE'S DOIN'! HE CAN PROBABLY BLOW UP THIS WHOLE HUNKA GEO-GRAPHY WITHOUT HALF-TRYIN'!
AND THAT MEANS ALICIA... AND EVERYONE ELSE... WILL GO SKY-HIGH WITH IT!
IT'S UP TO ME TO GET HIM OUTTA HERE... AND FAST!
THE JET-CYCLE!! IT'S MY ONLY CHANCE..!
THEN, A FEW FRANTIC SECONDS LATER...
HE'S TURNED HIMSELF INTO A SOLID HUNK'A ENERGY... COMIN' AFTER ME LIKE A CRAZY COMET..!!
I GOTTA THROW THIS GIZMO INTO FULL ROCKET SPEED 'N HOPE I CAN STAY AHEAD OF 'IM LONG ENUFF TO THINK OF SOMETHIN'!
SO, HERE GOES NUTHIN'..!
CLICK!
SHOOOOOOSH!
12.

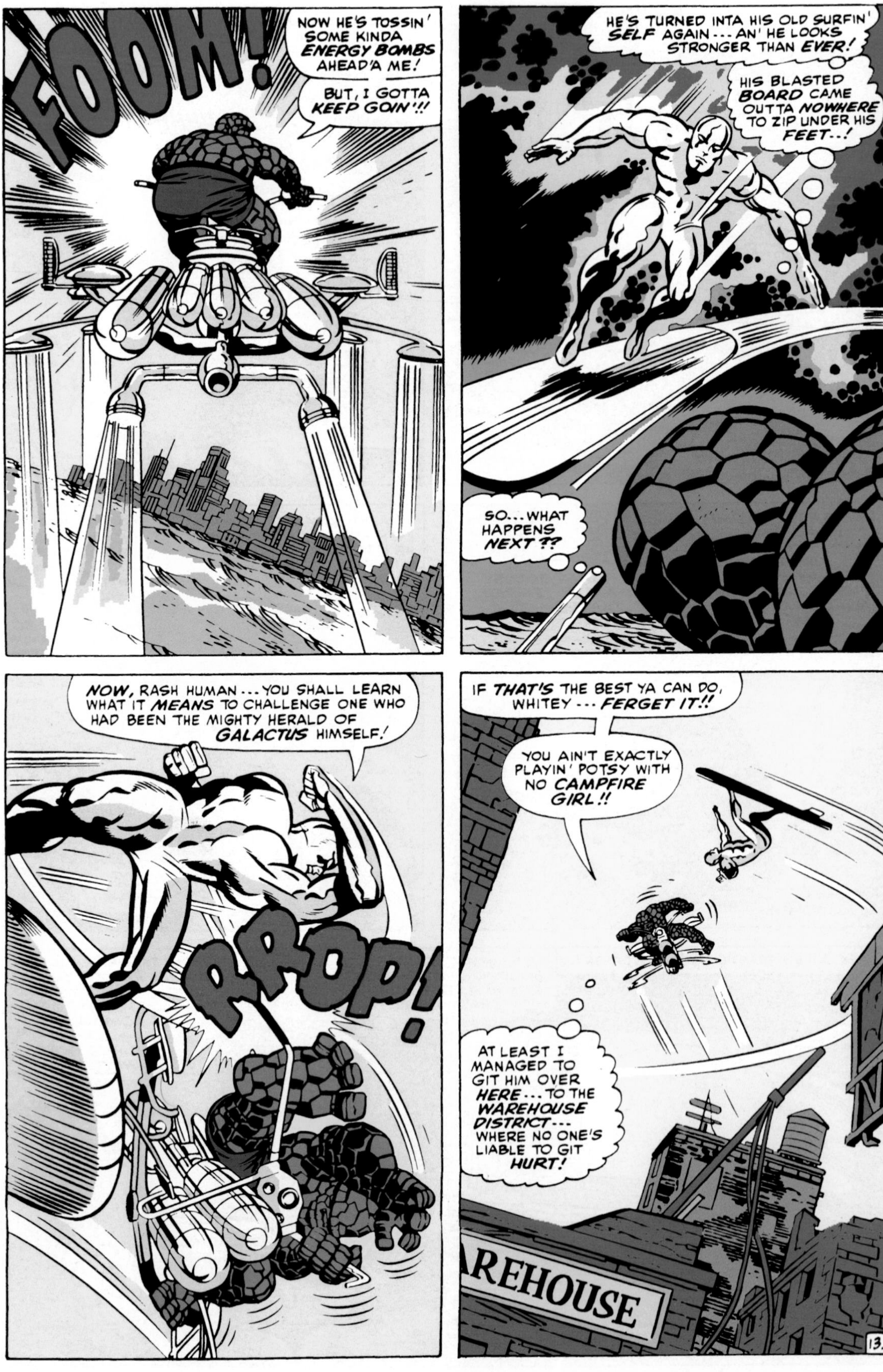
FOOM!
NOW HE'S TOSSIN' SOME KINDA ENERGY BOMBS AHEAD'A ME!
BUT, I GOTTA KEEP GOIN'!!
HE'S TURNED INTA HIS OLD SURFIN' SELF AGAIN--- AN' HE LOOKS STRONGER THAN EVER!
HIS BLASTED BOARD CAME OUTTA NOWHERE TO ZIP UNDER HIS FEET--!
SO...WHAT HAPPENS NEXT??
NOW, RASH HUMAN ... YOU SHALL LEARN WHAT IT MEANS TO CHALLENGE ONE WHO HAD BEEN THE MIGHTY HERALD OF GALACTUS HIMSELF!
RROP!
IF THAT'S THE BEST YA CAN DO, WHITEY --- FERGET IT!!
YOU AIN'T EXACTLY PLAYIN' POTSY WITH NO CAMPFIRE GIRL!!
AT LEAST I MANAGED TO GIT HIM OVER HERE ... TO THE WAREHOUSE DISTRICT--- WHERE NO ONE'S LIABLE TO GIT HURT!
AREHOUSE
13.

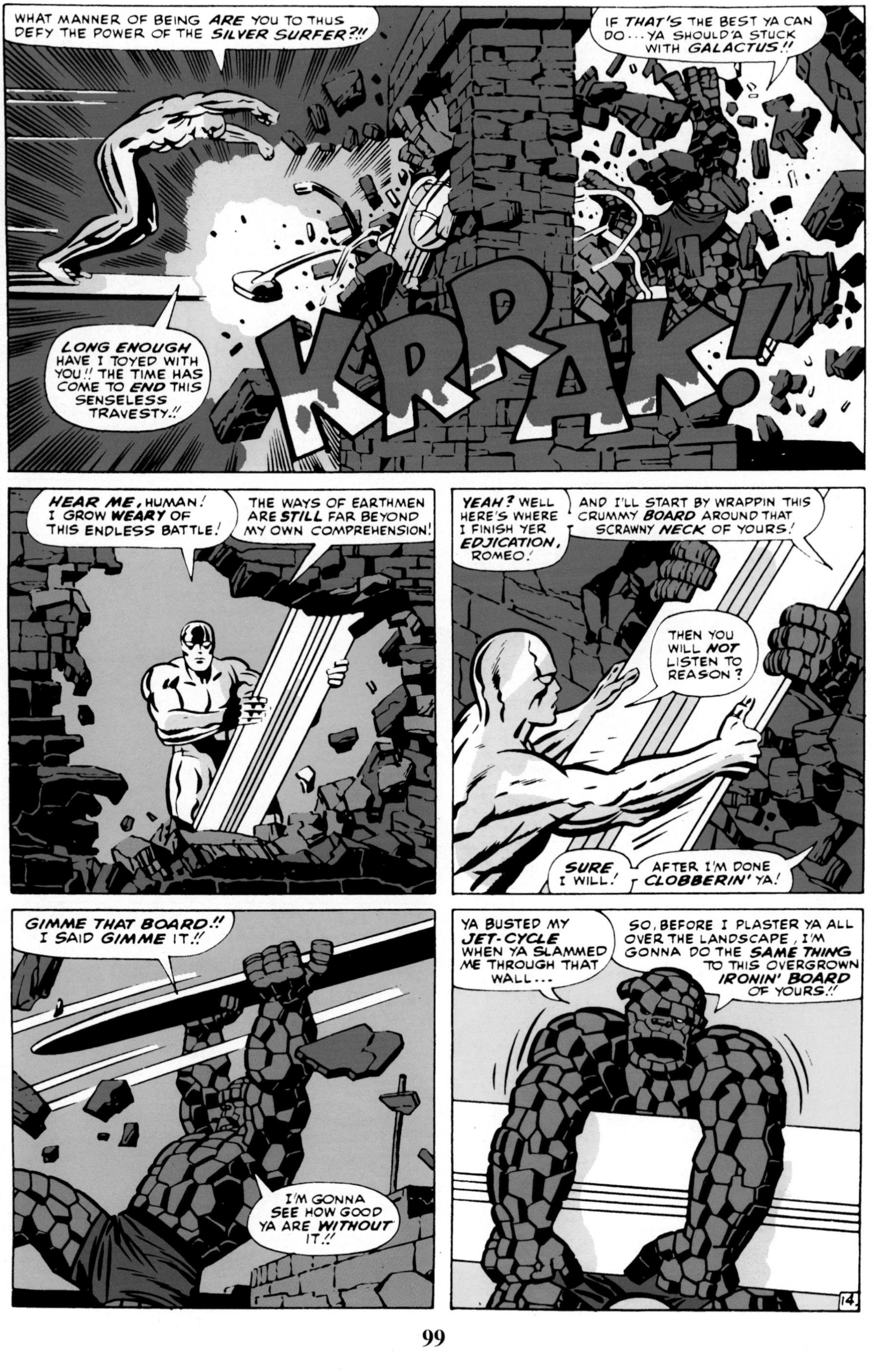
WHAT MANNER OF BEING ARE YOU TO THUS DEFY THE POWER OF THE SILVER SURFER?!!
IF THAT'S THE BEST YA CAN DO... YA SHOULD'A STUCK WITH GALACTUS!!
LONG ENOUGH HAVE I TOYED WITH YOU!! THE TIME HAS COME TO END THIS SENSELESS TRAVESTY!!
KRRAK!
HEAR ME, HUMAN! I GROW WEARY OF THIS ENDLESS BATTLE!
THE WAYS OF EARTHMEN ARE STILL FAR BEYOND MY OWN COMPREHENSION!
YEAH? WELL HERE'S WHERE I FINISH YER EDJICATION, ROMEO!
AND I'LL START BY WRAPPIN THIS CRUMMY BOARD AROUND THAT SCRAWNY NECK OF YOURS!
THEN YOU WILL NOT LISTEN TO REASON?
SURE I WILL!
AFTER I'M DONE CLOBBERIN' YA!
GIMME THAT BOARD!! I SAID GIMME IT!!
I'M GONNA SEE HOW GOOD YA ARE WITHOUT IT!!
YA BUSTED MY JET-CYCLE WHEN YA SLAMMED ME THROUGH THAT WALL...
SO, BEFORE I PLASTER YA ALL OVER THE LANDSCAPE, I'M GONNA DO THE SAME THING TO THIS OVERGROWN IRONIN' BOARD OF YOURS!!
14

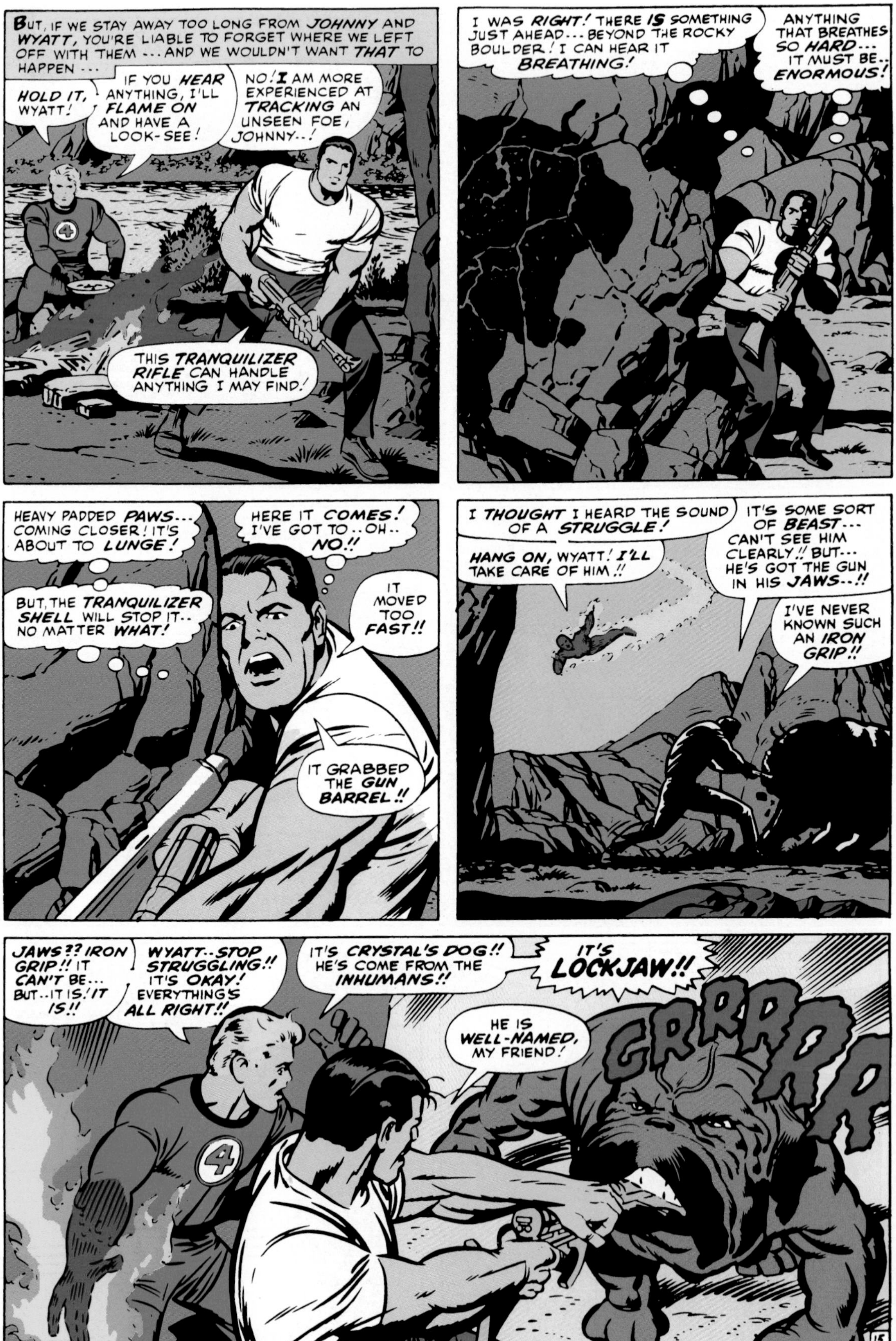

BUT, IF WE STAY AWAY TOO LONG FROM JOHNNY AND WYATT, YOU'RE LIABLE TO FORGET WHERE WE LEFT OFF WITH THEM --- AND WE WOULDN'T WANT THAT TO HAPPEN ---
HOLD IT, WYATT!
IF YOU HEAR ANYTHING, I'LL FLAME ON AND HAVE A LOOK-SEE!
NO! I AM MORE EXPERIENCED AT TRACKING AN UNSEEN FOE, JOHNNY..!
THIS TRANQUILIZER RIFLE CAN HANDLE ANYTHING I MAY FIND!
I WAS RIGHT! THERE IS SOMETHING JUST AHEAD--- BEYOND THE ROCKY BOULDER! I CAN HEAR IT BREATHING!
ANYTHING THAT BREATHES SO HARD--- IT MUST BE.. ENORMOUS!
HEAVY PADDED PAWS--- COMING CLOSER! IT'S ABOUT TO LUNGE!
HERE IT COMES! I'VE GOT TO..OH.. NO!!
BUT, THE TRANQUILIZER SHELL WILL STOP IT.. NO MATTER WHAT!
IT MOVED TOO FAST!!
IT GRABBED THE GUN BARREL!!
I THOUGHT I HEARD THE SOUND OF A STRUGGLE!
HANG ON, WYATT! I'LL TAKE CARE OF HIM!!
IT'S SOME SORT OF BEAST--- CAN'T SEE HIM CLEARLY!! BUT--- HE'S GOT THE GUN IN HIS JAWS--!!
I'VE NEVER KNOWN SUCH AN IRON GRIP!!
JAWS?? IRON GRIP!! IT CAN'T BE... BUT..IT IS! IT IS!!
WYATT..STOP STRUGGLING!! IT'S OKAY! EVERYTHING'S ALL RIGHT!!
IT'S CRYSTAL'S DOG!! HE'S COME FROM THE INHUMANS!!
IT'S LOCKJAW!!
HE IS WELL-NAMED, MY FRIEND!
GRRRRR
15.

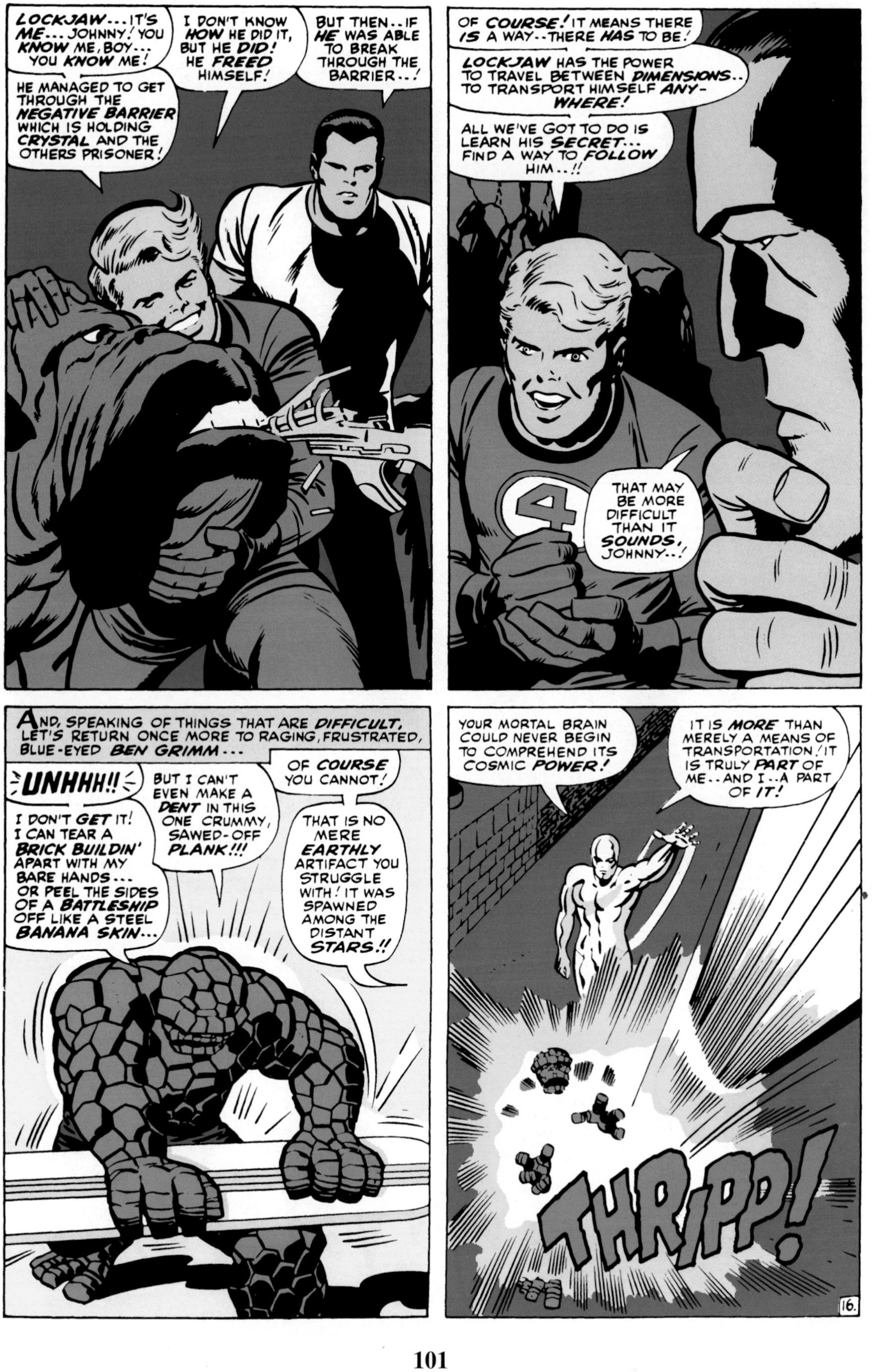
LOCKJAW... IT'S ME... JOHNNY! YOU KNOW ME, BOY... YOU KNOW ME!
HE MANAGED TO GET THROUGH THE NEGATIVE BARRIER WHICH IS HOLDING CRYSTAL AND THE OTHERS PRISONER!
I DON'T KNOW HOW HE DID IT, BUT HE DID! HE FREED HIMSELF!
BUT THEN.. IF HE WAS ABLE TO BREAK THROUGH THE BARRIER..!
OF COURSE! IT MEANS THERE IS A WAY--THERE HAS TO BE!
LOCKJAW HAS THE POWER TO TRAVEL BETWEEN DIMENSIONS.. TO TRANSPORT HIMSELF ANY-WHERE!
ALL WE'VE GOT TO DO IS LEARN HIS SECRET... FIND A WAY TO FOLLOW HIM..!!
THAT MAY BE MORE DIFFICULT THAN IT SOUNDS, JOHNNY..!
AND, SPEAKING OF THINGS THAT ARE DIFFICULT, LET'S RETURN ONCE MORE TO RAGING, FRUSTRATED, BLUE-EYED BEN GRIMM...
UNHHH!!
I DON'T GET IT! I CAN TEAR A BRICK BUILDIN' APART WITH MY BARE HANDS... OR PEEL THE SIDES OF A BATTLESHIP OFF LIKE A STEEL BANANA SKIN...
BUT I CAN'T EVEN MAKE A DENT IN THIS ONE CRUMMY, SAWED-OFF PLANK!!!
OF COURSE YOU CANNOT!
THAT IS NO MERE EARTHLY ARTIFACT YOU STRUGGLE WITH! IT WAS SPAWNED AMONG THE DISTANT STARS!!
YOUR MORTAL BRAIN COULD NEVER BEGIN TO COMPREHEND ITS COSMIC POWER!
IT IS MORE THAN MERELY A MEANS OF TRANSPORTATION! IT IS TRULY PART OF ME.. AND I.. A PART OF IT!
THRIPP!
16.

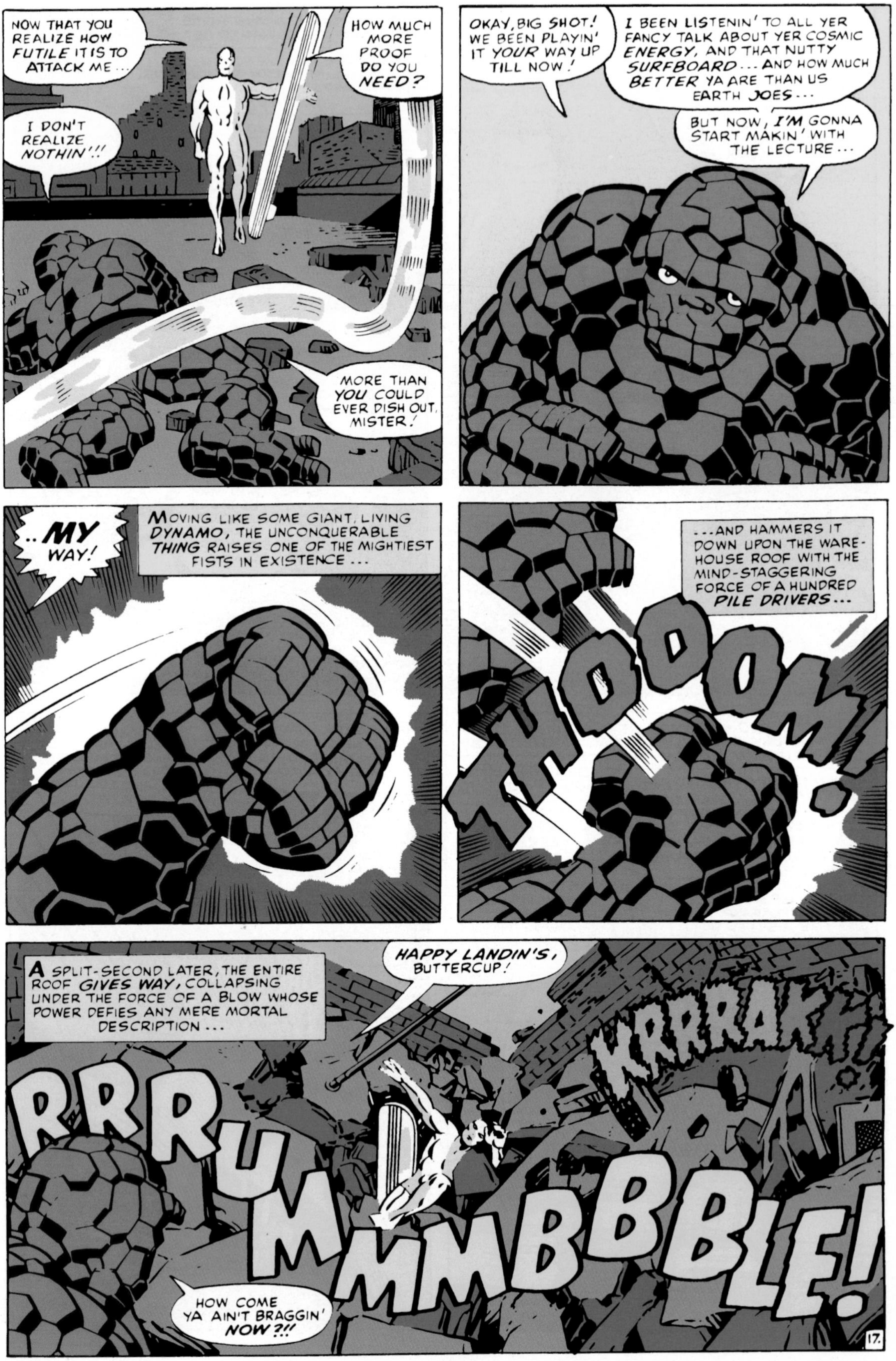
NOW THAT YOU REALIZE HOW FUTILE IT IS TO ATTACK ME...
HOW MUCH MORE PROOF DO YOU NEED?
I DON'T REALIZE NOTHIN'!!
MORE THAN YOU COULD EVER DISH OUT, MISTER!
OKAY, BIG SHOT! WE BEEN PLAYIN' IT YOUR WAY UP TILL NOW!
I BEEN LISTENIN' TO ALL YER FANCY TALK ABOUT YER COSMIC ENERGY, AND THAT NUTTY SURFBOARD... AND HOW MUCH BETTER YA ARE THAN US EARTH JOES...
BUT NOW, I'M GONNA START MAKIN' WITH THE LECTURE...
..MY WAY!
MOVING LIKE SOME GIANT, LIVING DYNAMO, THE UNCONQUERABLE THING RAISES ONE OF THE MIGHTIEST FISTS IN EXISTENCE...
...AND HAMMERS IT DOWN UPON THE WARE-HOUSE ROOF WITH THE MIND-STAGGERING FORCE OF A HUNDRED PILE DRIVERS...
THOOOM!
A SPLIT-SECOND LATER, THE ENTIRE ROOF GIVES WAY, COLLAPSING UNDER THE FORCE OF A BLOW WHOSE POWER DEFIES ANY MERE MORTAL DESCRIPTION...
HAPPY LANDIN'S, BUTTERCUP!
KRRRAK!!
RRRUMMMMBBBLE!
HOW COME YA AIN'T BRAGGIN' NOW?!!
17.

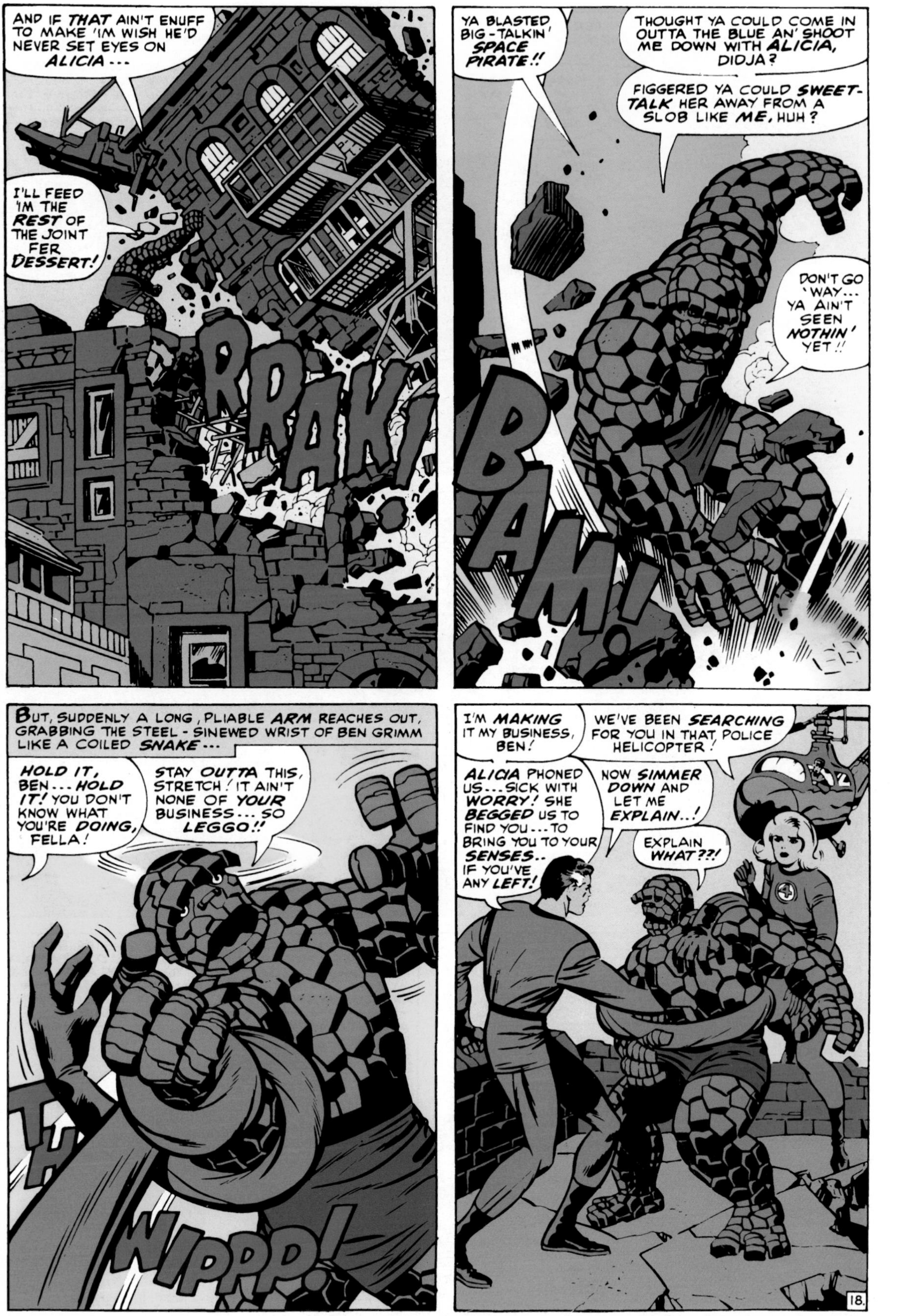
AND IF THAT AIN'T ENUFF TO MAKE 'IM WISH HE'D NEVER SET EYES ON ALICIA...
I'LL FEED 'IM THE REST OF THE JOINT FER DESSERT!
RRAKK!
YA BLASTED BIG-TALKIN' SPACE PIRATE!!
THOUGHT YA COULD COME IN OUTTA THE BLUE AN' SHOOT ME DOWN WITH ALICIA, DIDJA?
FIGGERED YA COULD SWEET-TALK HER AWAY FROM A SLOB LIKE ME, HUH?
DON'T GO 'WAY... YA AIN'T SEEN NOTHIN' YET!!
BAM!
BUT, SUDDENLY A LONG, PLIABLE ARM REACHES OUT, GRABBING THE STEEL-SINEWED WRIST OF BEN GRIMM LIKE A COILED SNAKE...
HOLD IT, BEN... HOLD IT! YOU DON'T KNOW WHAT YOU'RE DOING, FELLA!
STAY OUTTA THIS, STRETCH! IT AIN'T NONE OF YOUR BUSINESS... SO LEGGO!!
THWIPPP!
I'M MAKING IT MY BUSINESS, BEN!
WE'VE BEEN SEARCHING FOR YOU IN THAT POLICE HELICOPTER!
ALICIA PHONED US... SICK WITH WORRY! SHE BEGGED US TO FIND YOU... TO BRING YOU TO YOUR SENSES.. IF YOU'VE ANY LEFT!
NOW SIMMER DOWN AND LET ME EXPLAIN..!
EXPLAIN WHAT??!
18.

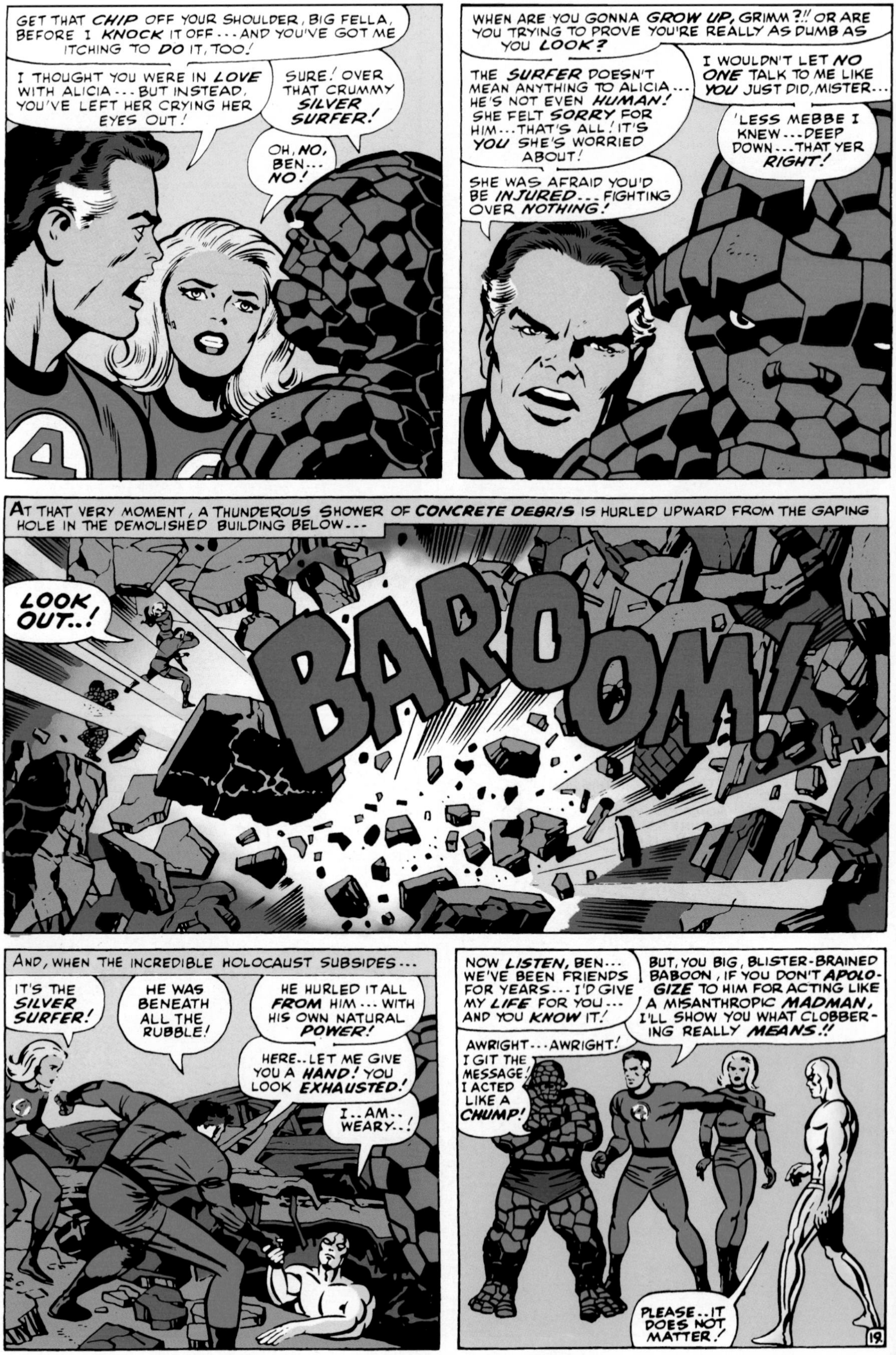
GET THAT CHIP OFF YOUR SHOULDER, BIG FELLA, BEFORE I KNOCK IT OFF... AND YOU'VE GOT ME ITCHING TO DO IT, TOO!
I THOUGHT YOU WERE IN LOVE WITH ALICIA... BUT INSTEAD, YOU'VE LEFT HER CRYING HER EYES OUT!
SURE! OVER THAT CRUMMY SILVER SURFER!
OH, NO, BEN... NO!
WHEN ARE YOU GONNA GROW UP, GRIMM?!! OR ARE YOU TRYING TO PROVE YOU'RE REALLY AS DUMB AS YOU LOOK?
THE SURFER DOESN'T MEAN ANYTHING TO ALICIA... HE'S NOT EVEN HUMAN! SHE FELT SORRY FOR HIM... THAT'S ALL! IT'S YOU SHE'S WORRIED ABOUT!
SHE WAS AFRAID YOU'D BE INJURED... FIGHTING OVER NOTHING!
I WOULDN'T LET NO ONE TALK TO ME LIKE YOU JUST DID, MISTER...
'LESS MEBBE I KNEW... DEEP DOWN... THAT YER RIGHT!
AT THAT VERY MOMENT, A THUNDEROUS SHOWER OF CONCRETE DEBRIS IS HURLED UPWARD FROM THE GAPING HOLE IN THE DEMOLISHED BUILDING BELOW...
LOOK OUT..!
BAROOM!
AND, WHEN THE INCREDIBLE HOLOCAUST SUBSIDES...
IT'S THE SILVER SURFER!
HE WAS BENEATH ALL THE RUBBLE!
HE HURLED IT ALL FROM HIM... WITH HIS OWN NATURAL POWER!
HERE.. LET ME GIVE YOU A HAND! YOU LOOK EXHAUSTED!
I.. AM.. WEARY..!
NOW LISTEN, BEN... WE'VE BEEN FRIENDS FOR YEARS... I'D GIVE MY LIFE FOR YOU... AND YOU KNOW IT!
BUT, YOU BIG, BLISTER-BRAINED BABOON, IF YOU DON'T APOLOGIZE TO HIM FOR ACTING LIKE A MISANTHROPIC MADMAN, I'LL SHOW YOU WHAT CLOBBERING REALLY MEANS!!
AWRIGHT... AWRIGHT! I GIT THE MESSAGE! I ACTED LIKE A CHUMP!
PLEASE.. IT DOES NOT MATTER!
19

YOU DON'T KNOW HOW *LUCKY* YOU ARE, BEN! HE ONLY USED A *FRACTION* OF HIS POWER AGAINST YOU!

HE DIDN'T WANT TO *HURT* YOU... HE JUST TRIED TO *PROTECT* HIMSELF!

HE *STILL* DOESN'T EVEN KNOW THE *REASON* FOR YOUR BONE-HEADED ATTACK!

DO NOT ARGUE AMONGST YOURSELVES! THERE IS STILL *MUCH* I MUST LEARN ABOUT HUMAN BEHAVIOR!

PERHAPS *I* AM AS MUCH TO BLAME.. FOR GIVING OFFENSE WITHOUT CAUSE!

LET ME DO WHAT I CAN TO MAKE *AMENDS!*

THAT WHICH ENERGY CAN *DESTROY,* ENERGY CAN AGAIN *REBUILD!*

THEREFORE, I SHALL BATHE THE DEMOLISHED *JET-CYCLE* WITH AN INTERCOSMIC *ENERGIZER BOLT!*

Z! Z! T!

FOR THE LUVVA MIKE!! THE CYCLE'S GOOD AS *NEW* AGAIN!

IT'S THE MOST INCREDIBLE EXHIBITION OF MOLECULAR RECONSTRUCTION ONE COULD IMAGINE!

SHEEESH! CAN'TCHA EVER JUST SAY *HOLY SMOKE,* 'N LET IT GO AT *THAT?!!*

SUDDENLY, THE STAR-SPAWNED SURFBOARD ZOOMS UP FROM THE DEBRIS, AS THE UNCANNY *SILVER SURFER* LEAPS UPON IT WITH ONE ALMOST EFFORTLESS MOTION...

I HAD THOUGHT MY JOURNEYING WAS OVER... BUT I WAS *WRONG!*

THERE IS STILL SO MUCH *MORE* I MUST LEARN ABOUT THE INCREDIBLE *HUMAN RACE!*

WHIITTTT!!

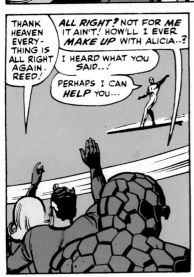

THANK HEAVEN EVERYTHING IS ALL RIGHT AGAIN, REED!

ALL RIGHT? NOT FOR *ME* IT AIN'T! HOW'LL I EVER *MAKE UP* WITH ALICIA..?

I HEARD WHAT YOU SAID..!

PERHAPS I CAN *HELP* YOU...

GIVE THOSE TO THE ONE CALLED *ALICIA!*

IT IS A PARTING GIFT... TO YOU *BOTH*--- FROM THE *SILVER SURFER!*

THIP!

A BUNCHA *FLOWERS!!*

HE'S *GONE!* BUT, SOONER OR LATER HE'LL BE COMIN' *BACK!*

AND, WHEN HE *COMES...*

WHAT'S GONNA HAPPEN *THEN?*

NEXT "TO FREE THE *INHUMANS!*"

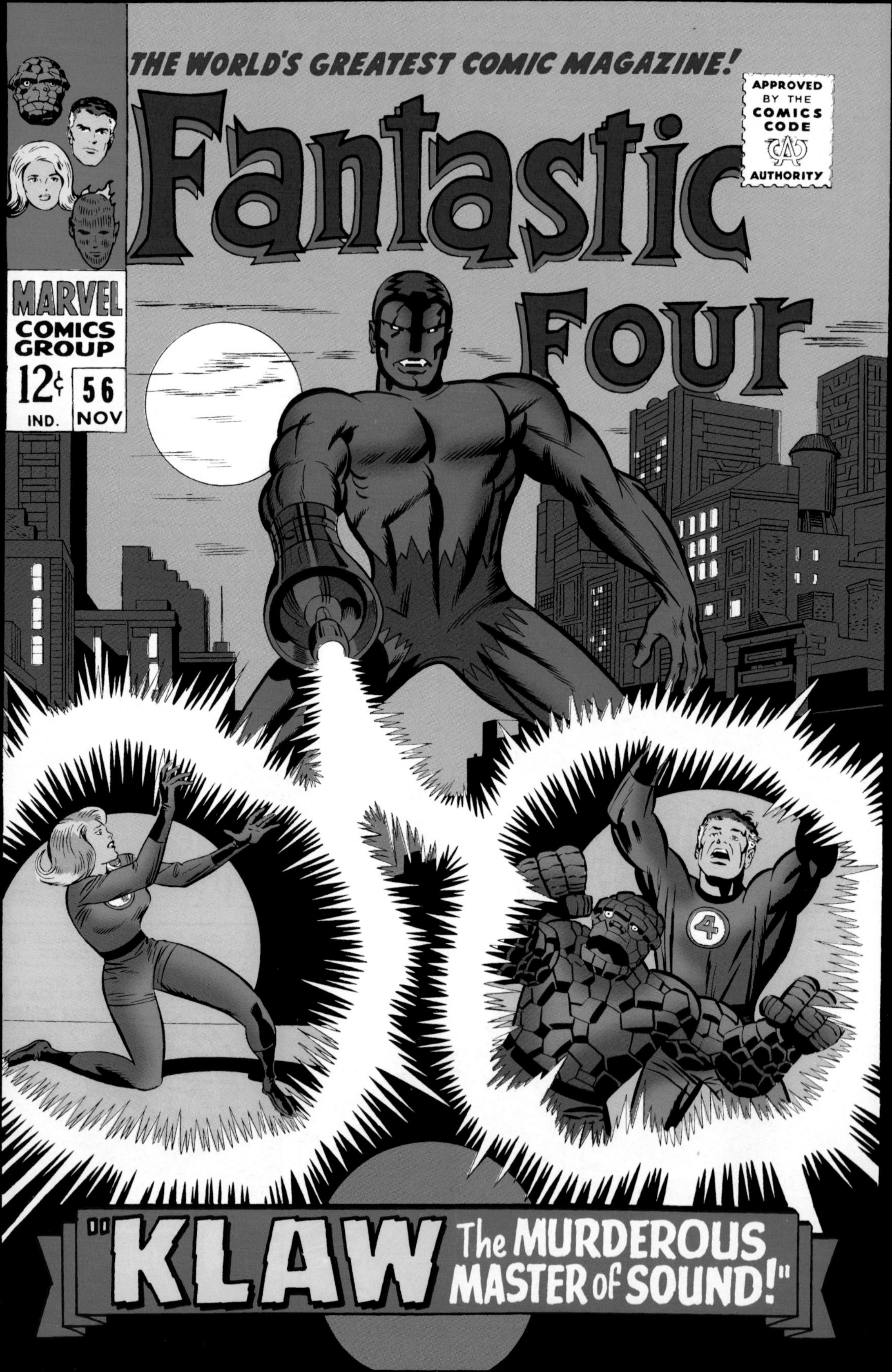
THE WORLD'S GREATEST COMIC MAGAZINE!
Fantastic Four
APPROVED BY THE COMICS CODE AUTHORITY
MARVEL COMICS GROUP
12¢ IND.
56 NOV
"KLAW The MURDEROUS MASTER of SOUND!"

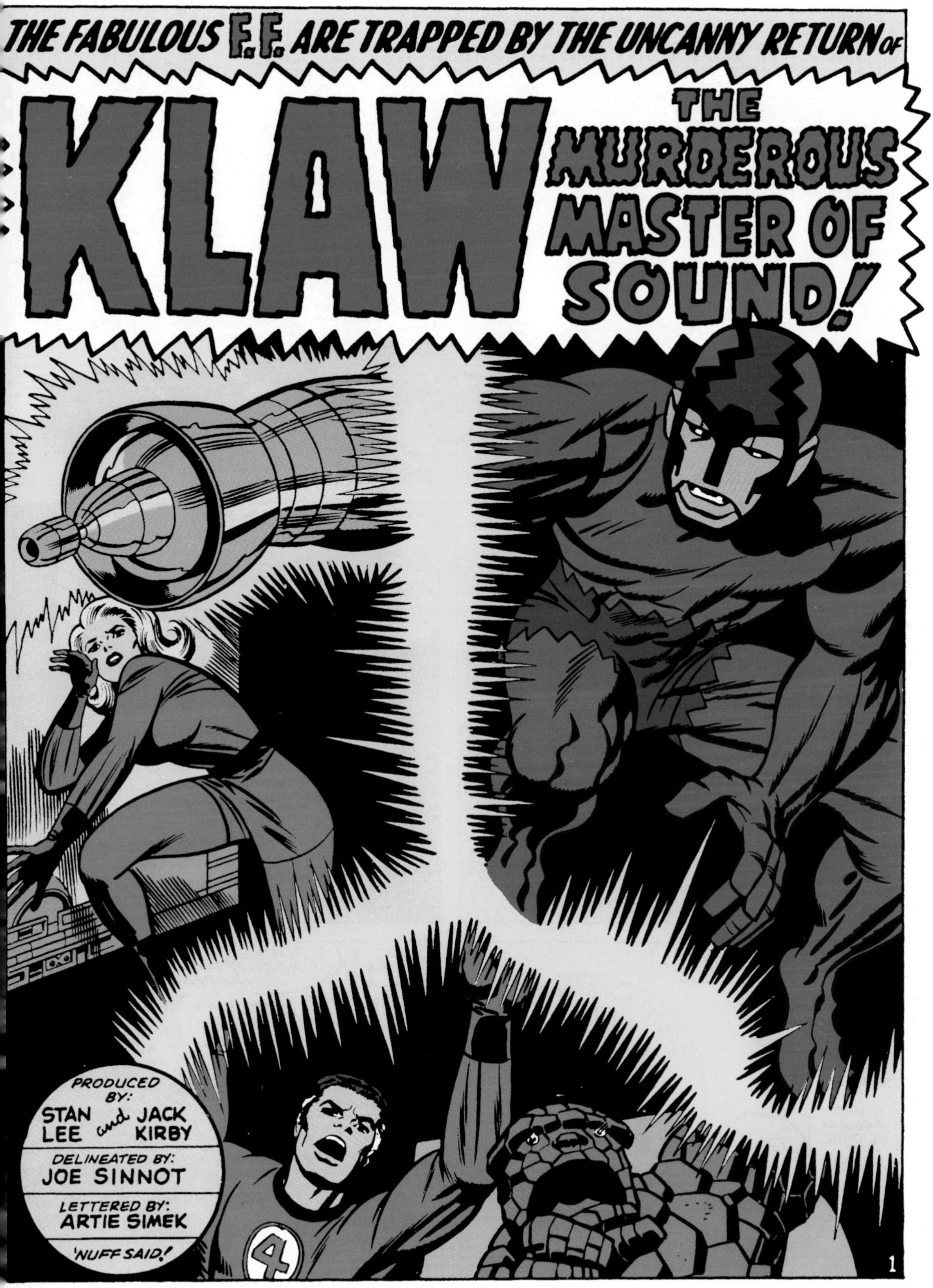
THE FABULOUS F.F. ARE TRAPPED BY THE UNCANNY RETURN OF
KLAW THE MURDEROUS MASTER OF SOUND!
PRODUCED BY: STAN LEE and JACK KIRBY
DELINEATED BY: JOE SINNOT
LETTERED BY: ARTIE SIMEK
'NUFF SAID!
4
1

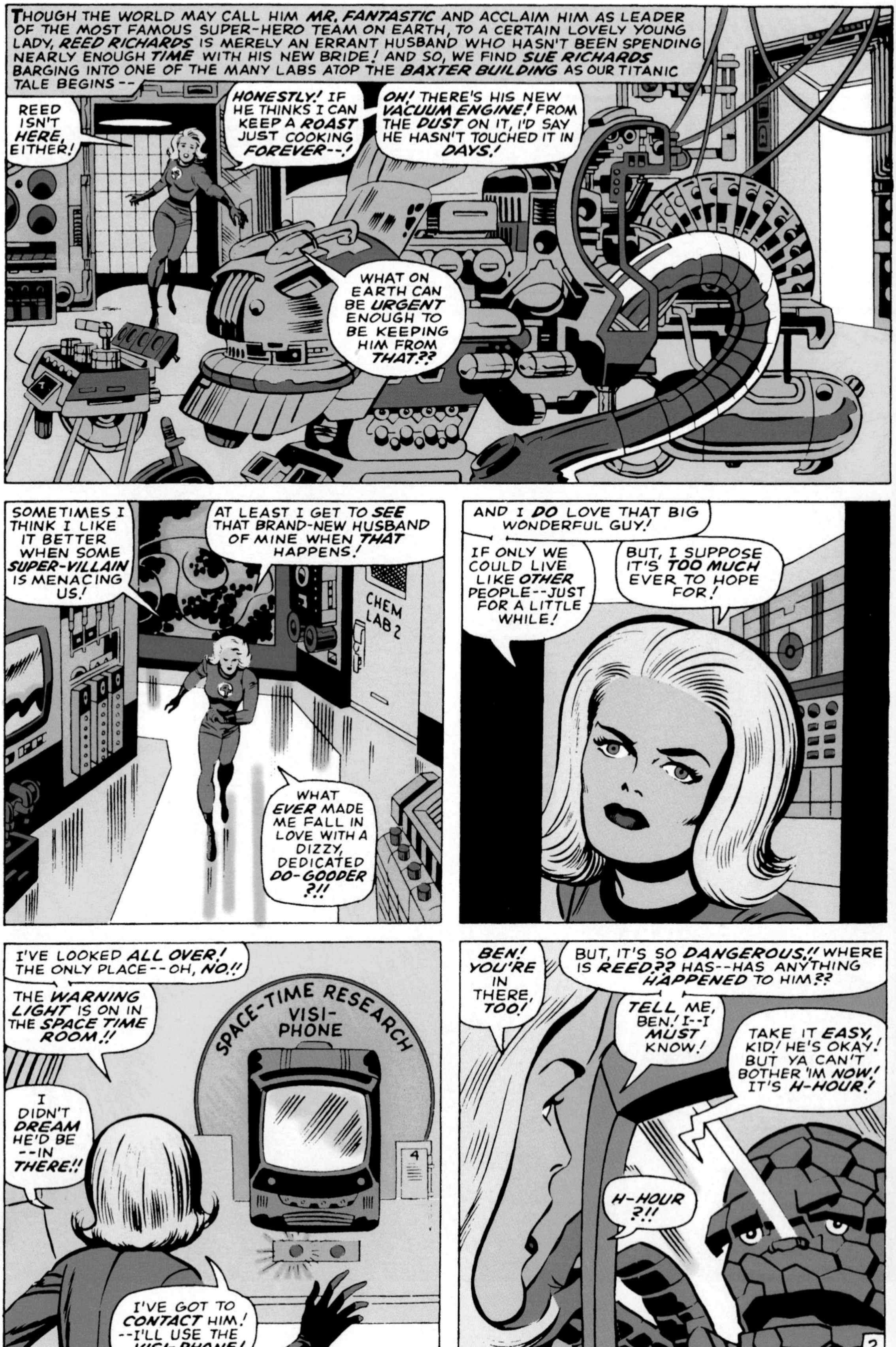
THOUGH THE WORLD MAY CALL HIM MR. FANTASTIC AND ACCLAIM HIM AS LEADER OF THE MOST FAMOUS SUPER-HERO TEAM ON EARTH, TO A CERTAIN LOVELY YOUNG LADY, REED RICHARDS IS MERELY AN ERRANT HUSBAND WHO HASN'T BEEN SPENDING NEARLY ENOUGH TIME WITH HIS NEW BRIDE! AND SO, WE FIND SUE RICHARDS BARGING INTO ONE OF THE MANY LABS ATOP THE BAXTER BUILDING AS OUR TITANIC TALE BEGINS--
REED ISN'T HERE, EITHER!
HONESTLY! IF HE THINKS I CAN KEEP A ROAST JUST COOKING FOREVER--!
OH! THERE'S HIS NEW VACUUM ENGINE! FROM THE DUST ON IT, I'D SAY HE HASN'T TOUCHED IT IN DAYS!
WHAT ON EARTH CAN BE URGENT ENOUGH TO BE KEEPING HIM FROM THAT??
SOMETIMES I THINK I LIKE IT BETTER WHEN SOME SUPER-VILLAIN IS MENACING US!
AT LEAST I GET TO SEE THAT BRAND-NEW HUSBAND OF MINE WHEN THAT HAPPENS!
CHEM LAB 2
WHAT EVER MADE ME FALL IN LOVE WITH A DIZZY, DEDICATED DO-GOODER ?!!
AND I DO LOVE THAT BIG WONDERFUL GUY!
IF ONLY WE COULD LIVE LIKE OTHER PEOPLE--JUST FOR A LITTLE WHILE!
BUT, I SUPPOSE IT'S TOO MUCH EVER TO HOPE FOR!
I'VE LOOKED ALL OVER! THE ONLY PLACE--OH, NO!!
THE WARNING LIGHT IS ON IN THE SPACE TIME ROOM!!
SPACE-TIME RESEARCH
VISI-PHONE
4
I DIDN'T DREAM HE'D BE --IN THERE!!
I'VE GOT TO CONTACT HIM! --I'LL USE THE VISI-PHONE!
BEN! YOU'RE IN THERE, TOO!
BUT, IT'S SO DANGEROUS!! WHERE IS REED?? HAS--HAS ANYTHING HAPPENED TO HIM??
TELL ME, BEN! I--I MUST KNOW!
TAKE IT EASY, KID! HE'S OKAY! BUT YA CAN'T BOTHER 'IM NOW! IT'S H-HOUR!
H-HOUR ?!!
2

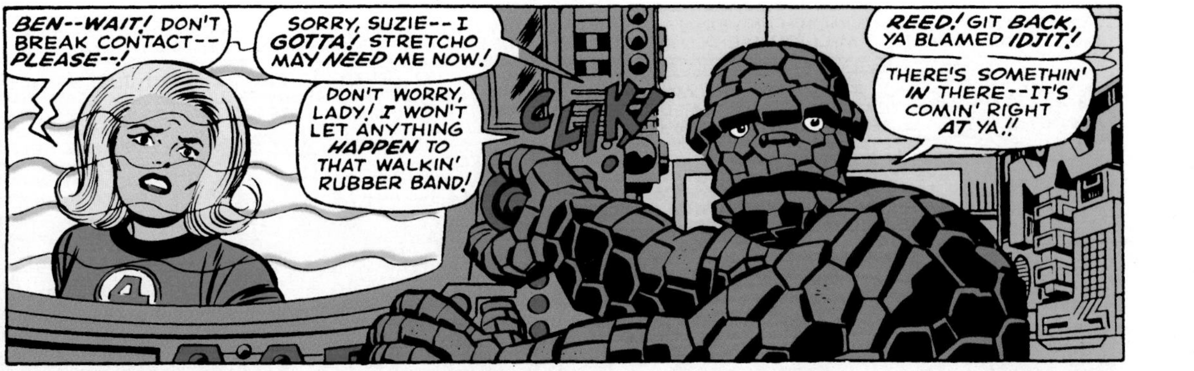
BEN--WAIT! DON'T BREAK CONTACT-- PLEASE--!
SORRY, SUZIE--I GOTTA! STRETCHO MAY NEED ME NOW!
DON'T WORRY, LADY! I WON'T LET ANYTHING HAPPEN TO THAT WALKIN' RUBBER BAND!
CLIK!
REED! GIT BACK, YA BLAMED IDJIT!
THERE'S SOMETHIN' IN THERE--IT'S COMIN' RIGHT AT YA!!

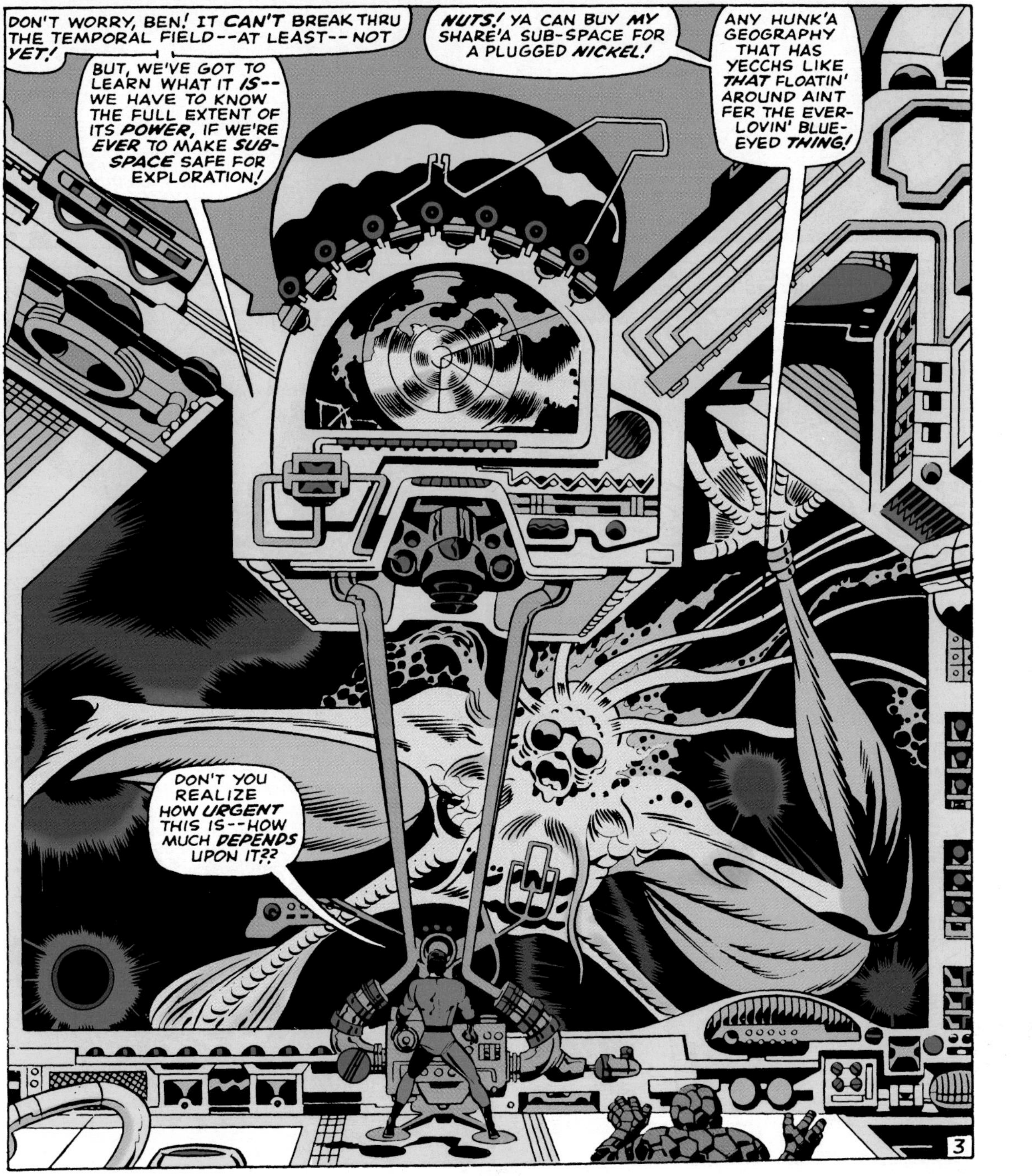
DON'T WORRY, BEN! IT CAN'T BREAK THRU THE TEMPORAL FIELD--AT LEAST--NOT YET!
BUT, WE'VE GOT TO LEARN WHAT IT IS--WE HAVE TO KNOW THE FULL EXTENT OF ITS POWER, IF WE'RE EVER TO MAKE SUB-SPACE SAFE FOR EXPLORATION!
NUTS! YA CAN BUY MY SHARE'A SUB-SPACE FOR A PLUGGED NICKEL!
ANY HUNK'A GEOGRAPHY THAT HAS YECCHS LIKE THAT FLOATIN' AROUND AINT FER THE EVER-LOVIN' BLUE-EYED THING!
DON'T YOU REALIZE HOW URGENT THIS IS--HOW MUCH DEPENDS UPON IT??
3

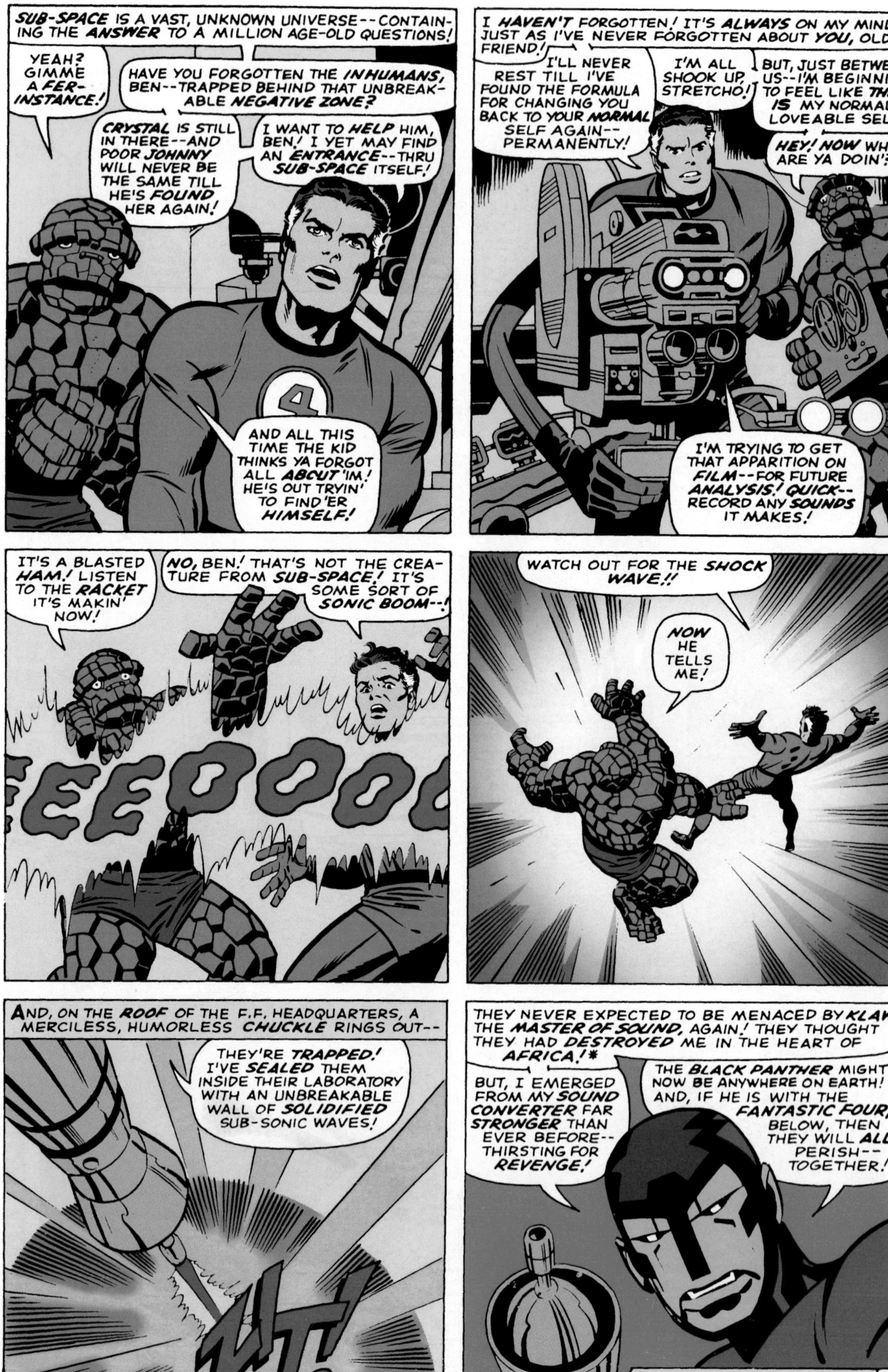
SUB-SPACE IS A VAST, UNKNOWN UNIVERSE--CONTAINING THE ANSWER TO A MILLION AGE-OLD QUESTIONS!
YEAH? GIMME A FER-INSTANCE!
HAVE YOU FORGOTTEN THE INHUMANS, BEN--TRAPPED BEHIND THAT UNBREAKABLE NEGATIVE ZONE?
CRYSTAL IS STILL IN THERE--AND POOR JOHNNY WILL NEVER BE THE SAME TILL HE'S FOUND HER AGAIN!
I WANT TO HELP HIM, BEN! I YET MAY FIND AN ENTRANCE--THRU SUB-SPACE ITSELF!
AND ALL THIS TIME THE KID THINKS YA FORGOT ALL ABOUT 'IM! HE'S OUT TRYIN' TO FIND 'ER HIMSELF!
I HAVEN'T FORGOTTEN! IT'S ALWAYS ON MY MIND--JUST AS I'VE NEVER FORGOTTEN ABOUT YOU, OLD FRIEND!
I'LL NEVER REST TILL I'VE FOUND THE FORMULA FOR CHANGING YOU BACK TO YOUR NORMAL SELF AGAIN--PERMANENTLY!
I'M ALL SHOOK UP, STRETCHO!
BUT, JUST BETWEEN US--I'M BEGINNIN' TO FEEL LIKE THIS IS MY NORMAL LOVEABLE SELF!
HEY! NOW WHAT ARE YA DOIN'??!
I'M TRYING TO GET THAT APPARITION ON FILM--FOR FUTURE ANALYSIS! QUICK--RECORD ANY SOUNDS IT MAKES!
IT'S A BLASTED HAM! LISTEN TO THE RACKET IT'S MAKIN' NOW!
NO, BEN! THAT'S NOT THE CREATURE FROM SUB-SPACE! IT'S SOME SORT OF SONIC BOOM--!
EEEOOOO
WATCH OUT FOR THE SHOCK WAVE!!
NOW HE TELLS ME!
AND, ON THE ROOF OF THE F.F. HEADQUARTERS, A MERCILESS, HUMORLESS CHUCKLE RINGS OUT--
THEY'RE TRAPPED! I'VE SEALED THEM INSIDE THEIR LABORATORY WITH AN UNBREAKABLE WALL OF SOLIDIFIED SUB-SONIC WAVES!
ZZT!
THEY NEVER EXPECTED TO BE MENACED BY KLAW, THE MASTER OF SOUND, AGAIN! THEY THOUGHT THEY HAD DESTROYED ME IN THE HEART OF AFRICA!*
BUT, I EMERGED FROM MY SOUND CONVERTER FAR STRONGER THAN EVER BEFORE--THIRSTING FOR REVENGE!
THE BLACK PANTHER MIGHT NOW BE ANYWHERE ON EARTH! AND, IF HE IS WITH THE FANTASTIC FOUR, BELOW, THEN THEY WILL ALL PERISH--TOGETHER!
*F.F. #53--SPECIFIC STAN.
4

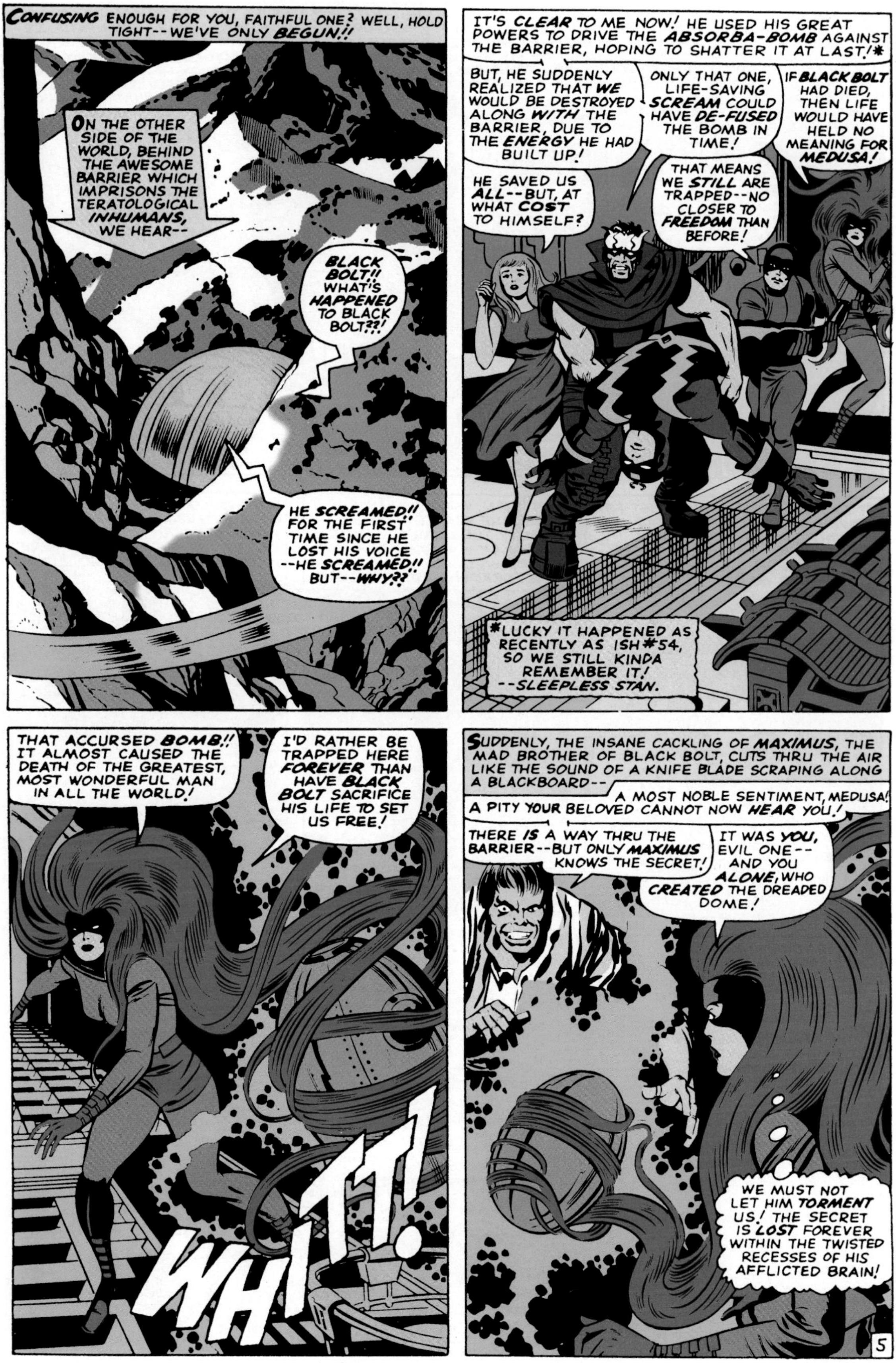
CONFUSING ENOUGH FOR YOU, FAITHFUL ONE? WELL, HOLD TIGHT--WE'VE ONLY BEGUN!!
ON THE OTHER SIDE OF THE WORLD, BEHIND THE AWESOME BARRIER WHICH IMPRISONS THE TERATOLOGICAL INHUMANS, WE HEAR--
BLACK BOLT!! WHAT'S HAPPENED TO BLACK BOLT??!
HE SCREAMED!! FOR THE FIRST TIME SINCE HE LOST HIS VOICE --HE SCREAMED!! BUT--WHY??
IT'S CLEAR TO ME NOW! HE USED HIS GREAT POWERS TO DRIVE THE ABSORBA-BOMB AGAINST THE BARRIER, HOPING TO SHATTER IT AT LAST!*
BUT, HE SUDDENLY REALIZED THAT WE WOULD BE DESTROYED ALONG WITH THE BARRIER, DUE TO THE ENERGY HE HAD BUILT UP!
ONLY THAT ONE, LIFE-SAVING SCREAM COULD HAVE DE-FUSED THE BOMB IN TIME!
IF BLACK BOLT HAD DIED, THEN LIFE WOULD HAVE HELD NO MEANING FOR MEDUSA!
HE SAVED US ALL--BUT, AT WHAT COST TO HIMSELF?
THAT MEANS WE STILL ARE TRAPPED--NO CLOSER TO FREEDOM THAN BEFORE!
*LUCKY IT HAPPENED AS RECENTLY AS ISH #54, SO WE STILL KINDA REMEMBER IT! --SLEEPLESS STAN.
THAT ACCURSED BOMB!! IT ALMOST CAUSED THE DEATH OF THE GREATEST, MOST WONDERFUL MAN IN ALL THE WORLD!
I'D RATHER BE TRAPPED HERE FOREVER THAN HAVE BLACK BOLT SACRIFICE HIS LIFE TO SET US FREE!
WHITT!
SUDDENLY, THE INSANE CACKLING OF MAXIMUS, THE MAD BROTHER OF BLACK BOLT, CUTS THRU THE AIR LIKE THE SOUND OF A KNIFE BLADE SCRAPING ALONG A BLACKBOARD--
A MOST NOBLE SENTIMENT, MEDUSA! A PITY YOUR BELOVED CANNOT NOW HEAR YOU!
THERE IS A WAY THRU THE BARRIER--BUT ONLY MAXIMUS KNOWS THE SECRET!
IT WAS YOU, EVIL ONE-- AND YOU ALONE, WHO CREATED THE DREADED DOME!
WE MUST NOT LET HIM TORMENT US! THE SECRET IS LOST FOREVER WITHIN THE TWISTED RECESSES OF HIS AFFLICTED BRAIN!
5

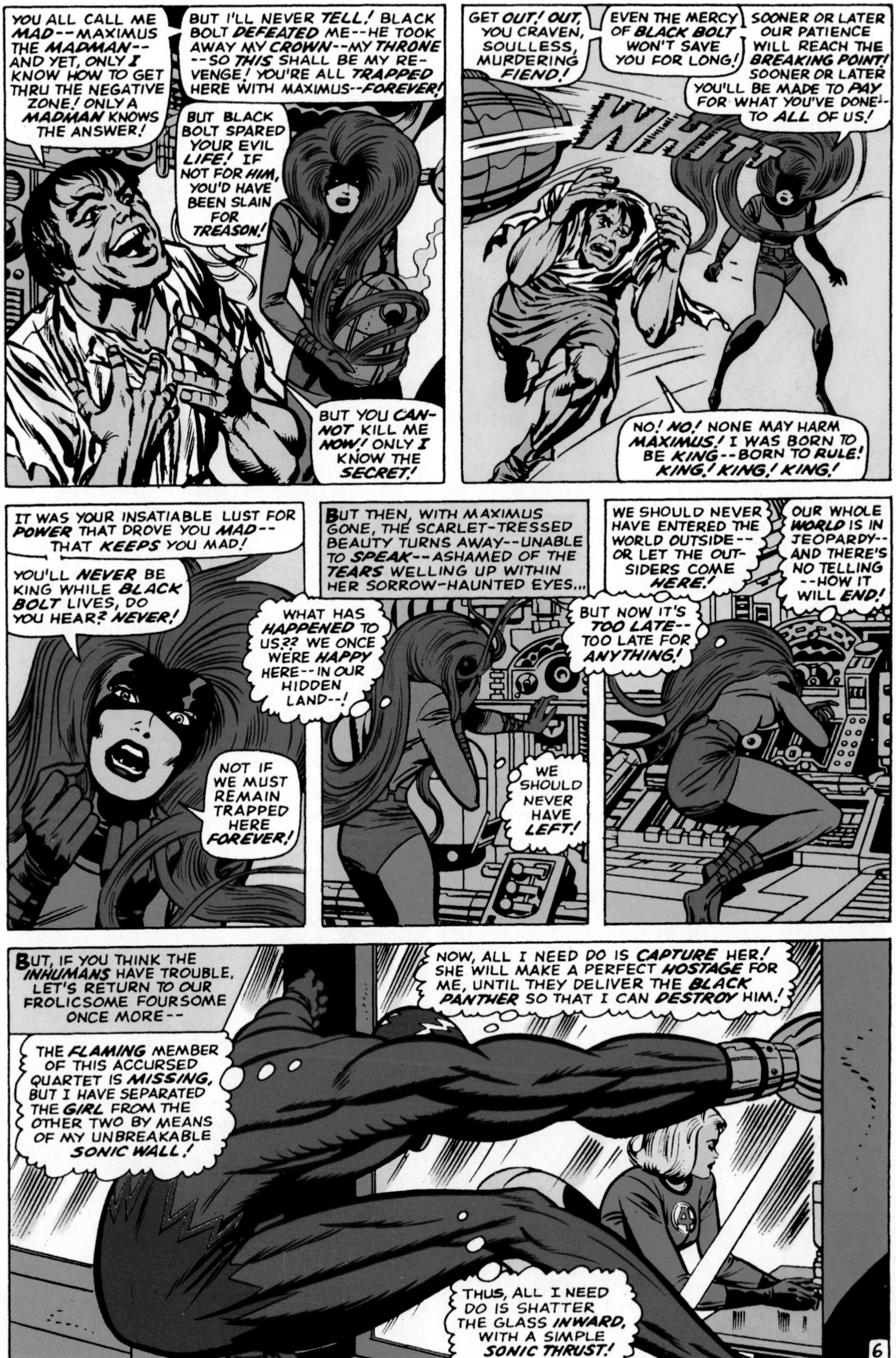

YOU ALL CALL ME MAD--MAXIMUS THE MADMAN--AND YET, ONLY I KNOW HOW TO GET THRU THE NEGATIVE ZONE! ONLY A MADMAN KNOWS THE ANSWER!
BUT I'LL NEVER TELL! BLACK BOLT DEFEATED ME--HE TOOK AWAY MY CROWN--MY THRONE--SO THIS SHALL BE MY RE-VENGE! YOU'RE ALL TRAPPED HERE WITH MAXIMUS--FOREVER!
BUT BLACK BOLT SPARED YOUR EVIL LIFE! IF NOT FOR HIM, YOU'D HAVE BEEN SLAIN FOR TREASON!
BUT YOU CAN-NOT KILL ME NOW! ONLY I KNOW THE SECRET!
GET OUT! OUT, YOU CRAVEN, SOULLESS, MURDERING FIEND!
EVEN THE MERCY OF BLACK BOLT WON'T SAVE YOU FOR LONG!
SOONER OR LATER OUR PATIENCE WILL REACH THE BREAKING POINT! SOONER OR LATER YOU'LL BE MADE TO PAY FOR WHAT YOU'VE DONE TO ALL OF US!
WHTT
NO! NO! NONE MAY HARM MAXIMUS! I WAS BORN TO BE KING--BORN TO RULE! KING! KING! KING!
IT WAS YOUR INSATIABLE LUST FOR POWER THAT DROVE YOU MAD--THAT KEEPS YOU MAD!
YOU'LL NEVER BE KING WHILE BLACK BOLT LIVES, DO YOU HEAR? NEVER!
NOT IF WE MUST REMAIN TRAPPED HERE FOREVER!
BUT THEN, WITH MAXIMUS GONE, THE SCARLET-TRESSED BEAUTY TURNS AWAY--UNABLE TO SPEAK--ASHAMED OF THE TEARS WELLING UP WITHIN HER SORROW-HAUNTED EYES...
WHAT HAS HAPPENED TO US?? WE ONCE WERE HAPPY HERE--IN OUR HIDDEN LAND--!
WE SHOULD NEVER HAVE LEFT!
WE SHOULD NEVER HAVE ENTERED THE WORLD OUTSIDE--OR LET THE OUT-SIDERS COME HERE!
OUR WHOLE WORLD IS IN JEOPARDY--AND THERE'S NO TELLING--HOW IT WILL END!
BUT NOW IT'S TOO LATE--TOO LATE FOR ANYTHING!
BUT, IF YOU THINK THE INHUMANS HAVE TROUBLE, LET'S RETURN TO OUR FROLICSOME FOURSOME ONCE MORE--
THE FLAMING MEMBER OF THIS ACCURSED QUARTET IS MISSING, BUT I HAVE SEPARATED THE GIRL FROM THE OTHER TWO BY MEANS OF MY UNBREAKABLE SONIC WALL!
NOW, ALL I NEED DO IS CAPTURE HER! SHE WILL MAKE A PERFECT HOSTAGE FOR ME, UNTIL THEY DELIVER THE BLACK PANTHER SO THAT I CAN DESTROY HIM!
THUS, ALL I NEED DO IS SHATTER THE GLASS INWARD, WITH A SIMPLE SONIC THRUST!
6

A *SONIC BLAST!* WE'RE UNDER *ATTACK!*

LUCKILY, I THREW UP MY INVISIBLE *FORCE FIELD* IN TIME TO SHIELD ME FROM THE FLYING GLASS--!

BUT, WHO CAN IT *BE??*

WHOEVER IT IS, I'VE GOT TO HOLD HIM *OFF* WHILE REED AND BEN ARE IN THE *SPACE TIME ROOM!*

DO NOT FEAR, MRS. RICHARDS, I HAVE NO WISH TO *HARM* YOU--SO LONG AS IT DOES NOT PROVE *NECESSARY!*

WH-WHO *ARE* YOU--?

I? I AM A DEDICATED *ENEMY* OF THE ACCURSED *BLACK PANTHER*--AND, SINCE THE *FANTASTIC FOUR* HAVE CHOSEN TO BE HIS *FRIENDS*--

THEN *KLAW,* THE *MASTER OF SOUND,* IS *YOUR* ENEMY, AS WELL!

KLAW!! OF *COURSE!* BUT--WE THOUGHT-- YOU HAD *PERISHED*--!

NOT *SO,* MY *LOVELY!* I--

WAIT! WHAT IS *THIS??*

AHHH! I HAVE *HEARD* ABOUT YOUR STRANGE *POWERS*--ABOUT THE UNSEEN *FORCE FIELD* WHICH IS YOUR GREATEST WEAPON--AND GREATEST *DEFENSE!*

BUT, ALAS-- IT WILL NOT SERVE TO PROTECT YOU FROM MY *SONIC POWERS!*

WHY ARE YOU *HERE??* WHAT DO YOU *WANT??*

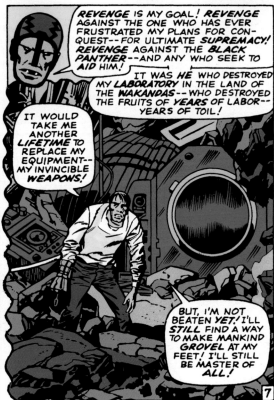

REVENGE IS MY GOAL! *REVENGE* AGAINST THE ONE WHO HAS EVER FRUSTRATED MY PLANS FOR CON-QUEST--FOR ULTIMATE *SUPREMACY!* *REVENGE* AGAINST THE *BLACK PANTHER*--AND ANY WHO SEEK TO AID HIM!

IT WAS *HE* WHO DESTROYED MY *LABORATORY* IN THE LAND OF THE *WAKANDAS*--WHO DESTROYED THE FRUITS OF *YEARS* OF LABOR-- YEARS OF TOIL!

IT WOULD TAKE ME ANOTHER *LIFETIME* TO REPLACE MY *EQUIPMENT*-- MY *INVINCIBLE WEAPONS!*

BUT, I'M NOT BEATEN *YET!* I'LL *STILL* FIND A WAY TO MAKE MANKIND *GROVEL* AT MY FEET! I'LL STILL BE *MASTER* OF *ALL!*

7

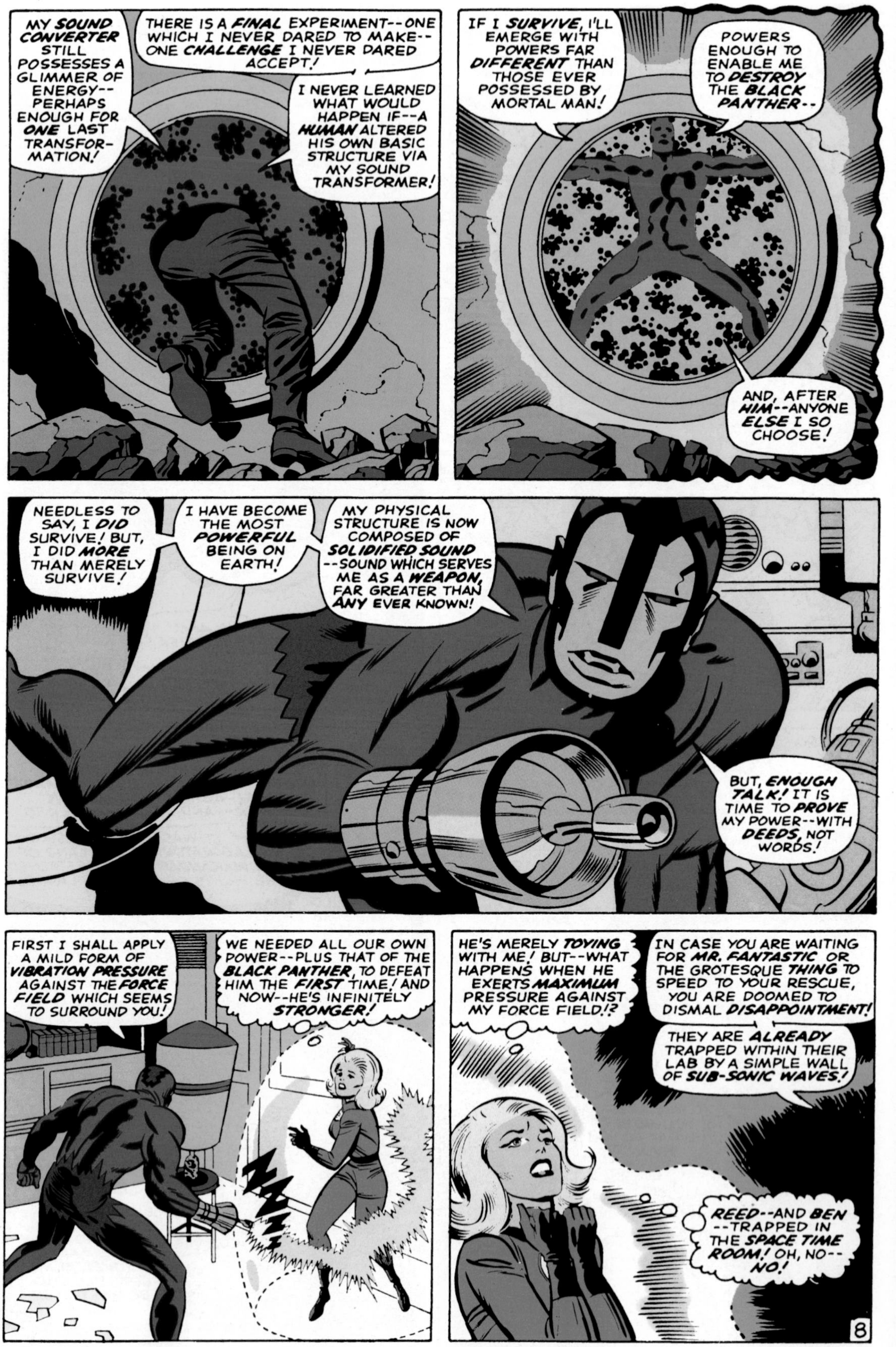
MY SOUND CONVERTER STILL POSSESSES A GLIMMER OF ENERGY-- PERHAPS ENOUGH FOR ONE LAST TRANSFORMATION!
THERE IS A FINAL EXPERIMENT--ONE WHICH I NEVER DARED TO MAKE-- ONE CHALLENGE I NEVER DARED ACCEPT!
I NEVER LEARNED WHAT WOULD HAPPEN IF--A HUMAN ALTERED HIS OWN BASIC STRUCTURE VIA MY SOUND TRANSFORMER!
IF I SURVIVE, I'LL EMERGE WITH POWERS FAR DIFFERENT THAN THOSE EVER POSSESSED BY MORTAL MAN!
POWERS ENOUGH TO ENABLE ME TO DESTROY THE BLACK PANTHER--
AND, AFTER HIM--ANYONE ELSE I SO CHOOSE!
NEEDLESS TO SAY, I DID SURVIVE! BUT, I DID MORE THAN MERELY SURVIVE!
I HAVE BECOME THE MOST POWERFUL BEING ON EARTH!
MY PHYSICAL STRUCTURE IS NOW COMPOSED OF SOLIDIFIED SOUND --SOUND WHICH SERVES ME AS A WEAPON, FAR GREATER THAN ANY EVER KNOWN!
BUT, ENOUGH TALK! IT IS TIME TO PROVE MY POWER--WITH DEEDS, NOT WORDS!
FIRST I SHALL APPLY A MILD FORM OF VIBRATION PRESSURE AGAINST THE FORCE FIELD WHICH SEEMS TO SURROUND YOU!
WE NEEDED ALL OUR OWN POWER--PLUS THAT OF THE BLACK PANTHER, TO DEFEAT HIM THE FIRST TIME! AND NOW--HE'S INFINITELY STRONGER!
HE'S MERELY TOYING WITH ME! BUT--WHAT HAPPENS WHEN HE EXERTS MAXIMUM PRESSURE AGAINST MY FORCE FIELD!?
IN CASE YOU ARE WAITING FOR MR. FANTASTIC OR THE GROTESQUE THING TO SPEED TO YOUR RESCUE, YOU ARE DOOMED TO DISMAL DISAPPOINTMENT!
THEY ARE ALREADY TRAPPED WITHIN THEIR LAB BY A SIMPLE WALL OF SUB-SONIC WAVES!
REED--AND BEN --TRAPPED IN THE SPACE TIME ROOM! OH, NO-- NO!
8

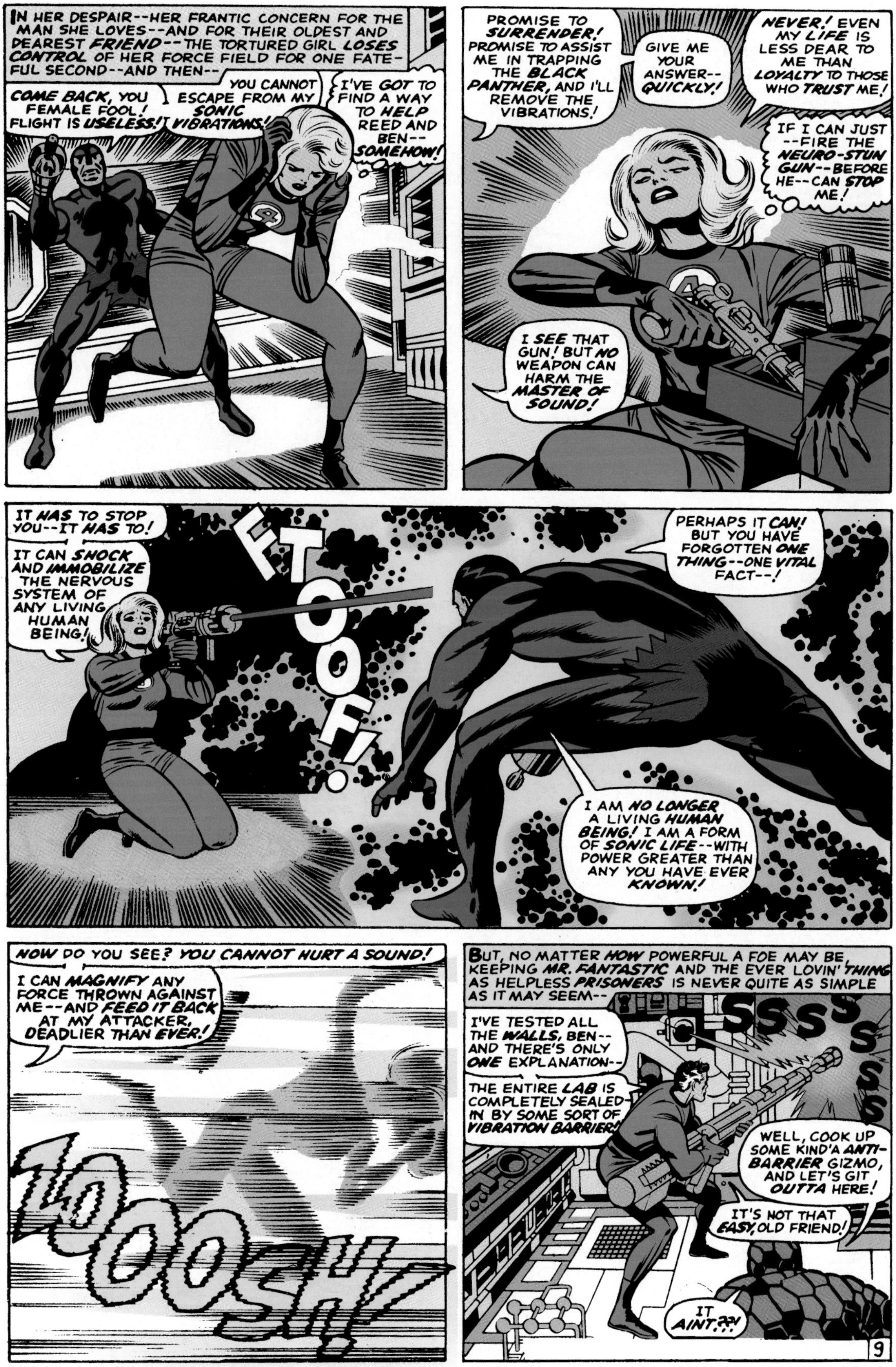
IN HER DESPAIR--HER FRANTIC CONCERN FOR THE MAN SHE LOVES--AND FOR THEIR OLDEST AND DEAREST FRIEND--THE TORTURED GIRL LOSES CONTROL OF HER FORCE FIELD FOR ONE FATE-FUL SECOND--AND THEN--
COME BACK, YOU FEMALE FOOL! FLIGHT IS USELESS!
YOU CANNOT ESCAPE FROM MY SONIC VIBRATIONS!
I'VE GOT TO FIND A WAY TO HELP REED AND BEN--SOMEHOW!
PROMISE TO SURRENDER! PROMISE TO ASSIST ME IN TRAPPING THE BLACK PANTHER, AND I'LL REMOVE THE VIBRATIONS!
GIVE ME YOUR ANSWER--QUICKLY!
NEVER! EVEN MY LIFE IS LESS DEAR TO ME THAN LOYALTY TO THOSE WHO TRUST ME!
IF I CAN JUST --FIRE THE NEURO-STUN GUN--BEFORE HE--CAN STOP ME!
I SEE THAT GUN! BUT NO WEAPON CAN HARM THE MASTER OF SOUND!
IT HAS TO STOP YOU--IT HAS TO!
IT CAN SHOCK AND IMMOBILIZE THE NERVOUS SYSTEM OF ANY LIVING HUMAN BEING!
FTOOOF!
PERHAPS IT CAN! BUT YOU HAVE FORGOTTEN ONE THING--ONE VITAL FACT--!
I AM NO LONGER A LIVING HUMAN BEING! I AM A FORM OF SONIC LIFE--WITH POWER GREATER THAN ANY YOU HAVE EVER KNOWN!
NOW DO YOU SEE? YOU CANNOT HURT A SOUND!
I CAN MAGNIFY ANY FORCE THROWN AGAINST ME--AND FEED IT BACK AT MY ATTACKER, DEADLIER THAN EVER!
WOOOOSH!
BUT, NO MATTER HOW POWERFUL A FOE MAY BE, KEEPING MR. FANTASTIC AND THE EVER LOVIN' THING AS HELPLESS PRISONERS IS NEVER QUITE AS SIMPLE AS IT MAY SEEM--
SSSSSSSS
I'VE TESTED ALL THE WALLS, BEN--AND THERE'S ONLY ONE EXPLANATION--
THE ENTIRE LAB IS COMPLETELY SEALED-IN BY SOME SORT OF VIBRATION BARRIER!
WELL, COOK UP SOME KIND'A ANTI-BARRIER GIZMO, AND LET'S GIT OUTTA HERE!
IT'S NOT THAT EASY, OLD FRIEND!
IT AIN'T??!
9

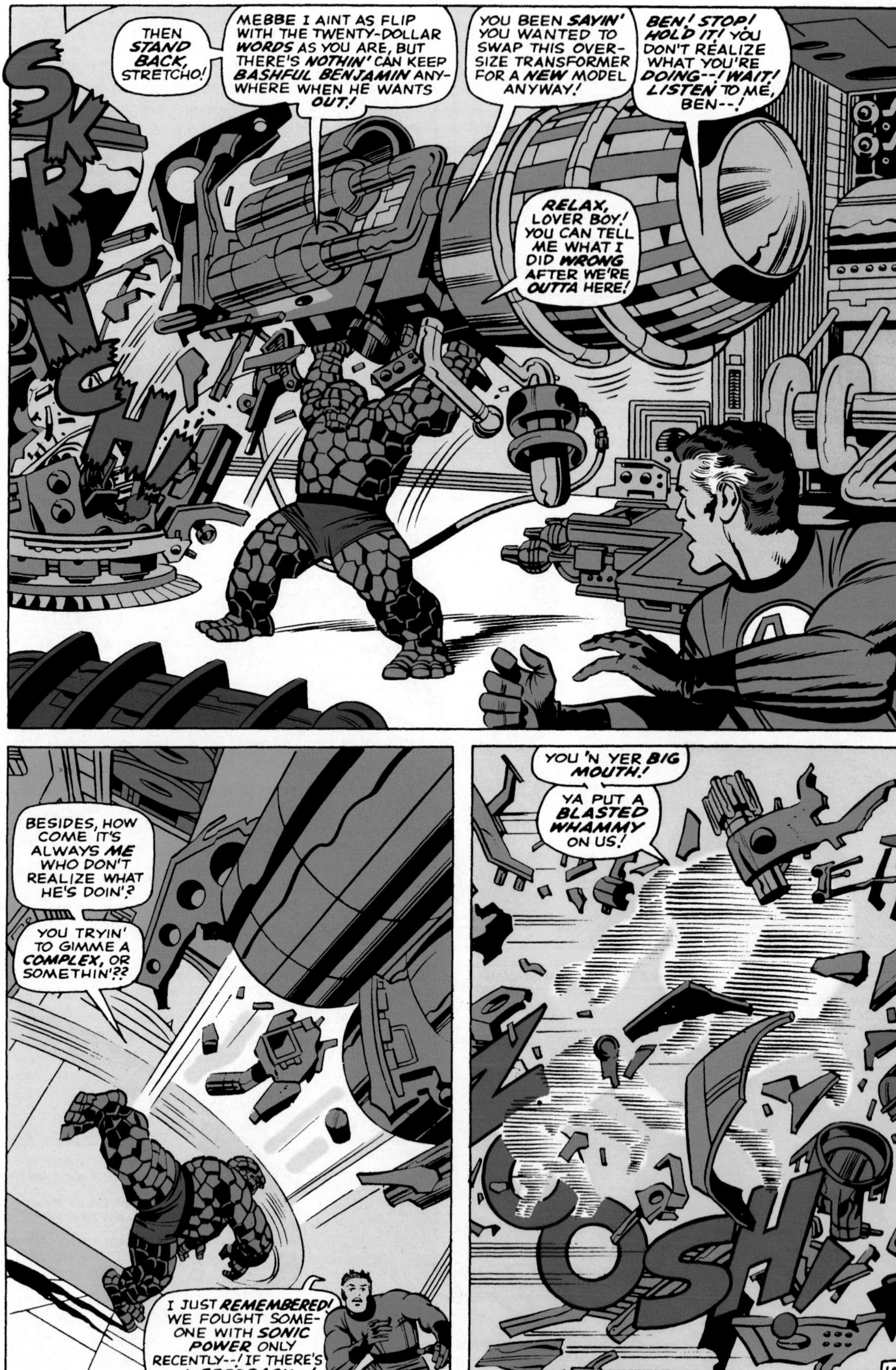

SKRUNCH!
THEN STAND BACK, STRETCHO!
MEBBE I AINT AS FLIP WITH THE TWENTY-DOLLAR WORDS AS YOU ARE, BUT THERE'S NOTHIN' CAN KEEP BASHFUL BENJAMIN ANY-WHERE WHEN HE WANTS OUT!
YOU BEEN SAYIN' YOU WANTED TO SWAP THIS OVER-SIZE TRANSFORMER FOR A NEW MODEL ANYWAY!
BEN! STOP! HOLD IT! YOU DON'T REALIZE WHAT YOU'RE DOING--! WAIT! LISTEN TO ME, BEN--!
RELAX, LOVER BOY! YOU CAN TELL ME WHAT I DID WRONG AFTER WE'RE OUTTA HERE!
BESIDES, HOW COME IT'S ALWAYS ME WHO DON'T REALIZE WHAT HE'S DOIN'?
YOU TRYIN' TO GIMME A COMPLEX, OR SOMETHIN'??
I JUST REMEMBERED! WE FOUGHT SOME-ONE WITH SONIC POWER ONLY RECENTLY--! IF THERE'S A FEEDBACK--!
YOU 'N YER BIG MOUTH!
YA PUT A BLASTED WHAMMY ON US!
WOOSH!
10

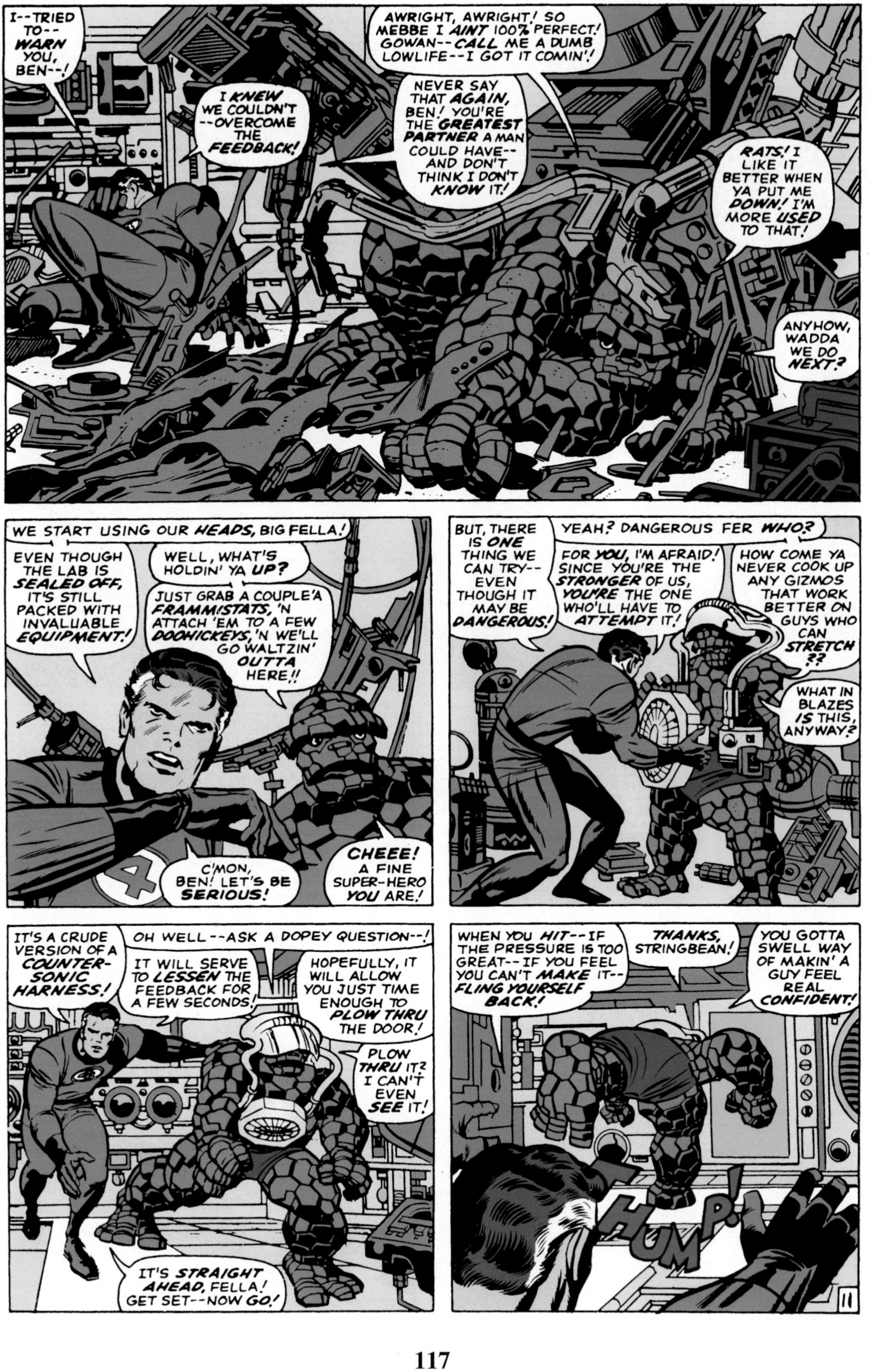
I--TRIED TO--WARN YOU, BEN--!
I KNEW WE COULDN'T--OVERCOME THE FEEDBACK!
AWRIGHT, AWRIGHT! SO MEBBE I AINT 100% PERFECT! GOWAN--CALL ME A DUMB LOWLIFE--I GOT IT COMIN'!
NEVER SAY THAT AGAIN, BEN! YOU'RE THE GREATEST PARTNER A MAN COULD HAVE--AND DON'T THINK I DON'T KNOW IT!
RATS! I LIKE IT BETTER WHEN YA PUT ME DOWN! I'M MORE USED TO THAT!
ANYHOW, WADDA WE DO NEXT?
WE START USING OUR HEADS, BIG FELLA!
EVEN THOUGH THE LAB IS SEALED OFF, IT'S STILL PACKED WITH INVALUABLE EQUIPMENT!
WELL, WHAT'S HOLDIN' YA UP?
JUST GRAB A COUPLE'A FRAMMISTATS, 'N ATTACH 'EM TO A FEW DOOHICKEYS, 'N WE'LL GO WALTZIN' OUTTA HERE!!
C'MON, BEN! LET'S BE SERIOUS!
CHEEE! A FINE SUPER-HERO YOU ARE!
BUT, THERE IS ONE THING WE CAN TRY--EVEN THOUGH IT MAY BE DANGEROUS!
YEAH? DANGEROUS FER WHO?
FOR YOU, I'M AFRAID! SINCE YOU'RE THE STRONGER OF US, YOU'RE THE ONE WHO'LL HAVE TO ATTEMPT IT!
HOW COME YA NEVER COOK UP ANY GIZMOS THAT WORK BETTER ON GUYS WHO CAN STRETCH??
WHAT IN BLAZES IS THIS, ANYWAY?
IT'S A CRUDE VERSION OF A COUNTER-SONIC HARNESS!
OH WELL--ASK A DOPEY QUESTION--!
IT WILL SERVE TO LESSEN THE FEEDBACK FOR A FEW SECONDS!
HOPEFULLY, IT WILL ALLOW YOU JUST TIME ENOUGH TO PLOW THRU THE DOOR!
PLOW THRU IT? I CAN'T EVEN SEE IT!
IT'S STRAIGHT AHEAD, FELLA! GET SET--NOW GO!
WHEN YOU HIT--IF THE PRESSURE IS TOO GREAT--IF YOU FEEL YOU CAN'T MAKE IT--FLING YOURSELF BACK!
THANKS, STRINGBEAN!
YOU GOTTA SWELL WAY OF MAKIN' A GUY FEEL REAL CONFIDENT!
HUMP!
11

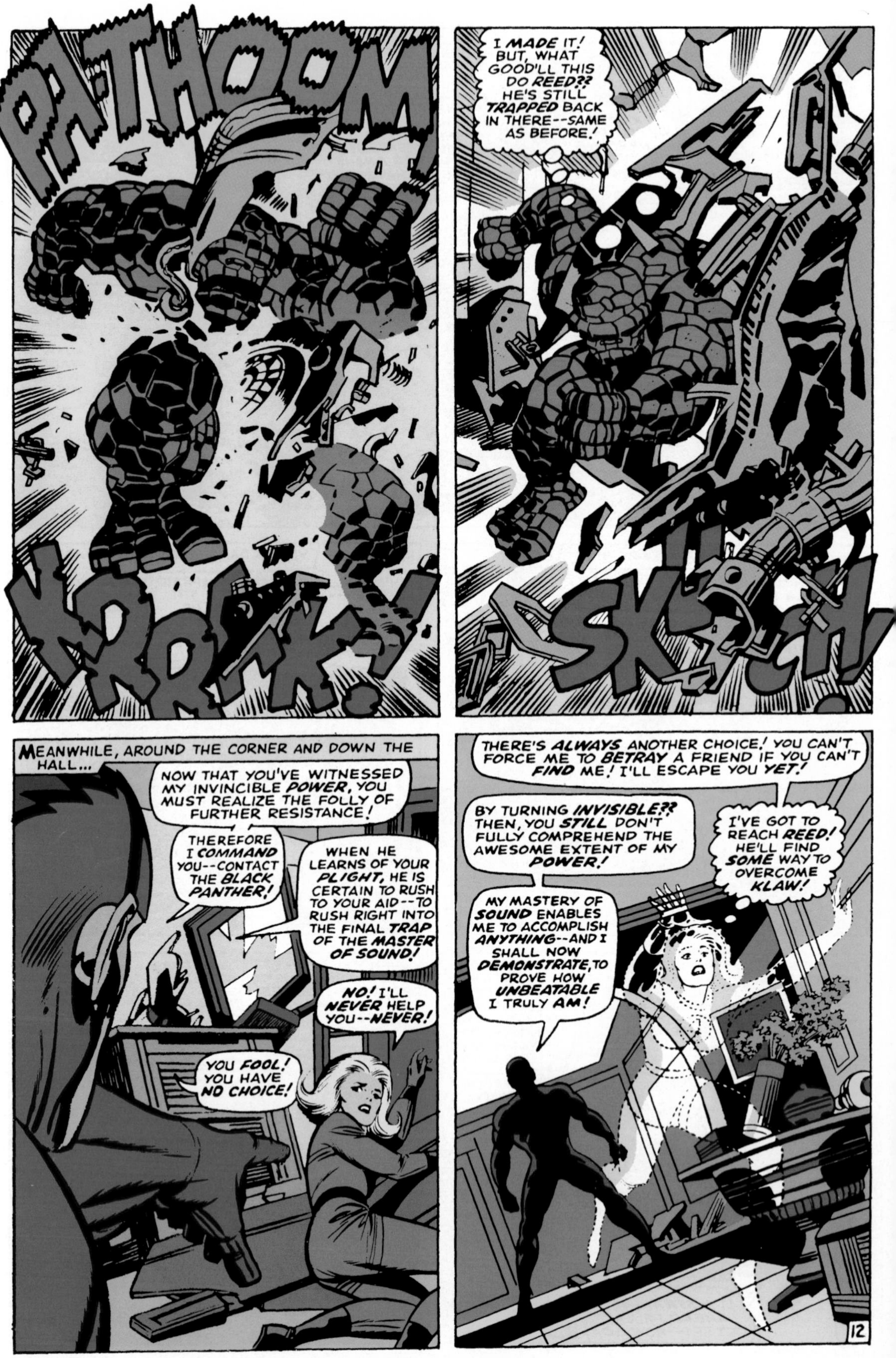
PATHOOM
KRRAKK!
I MADE IT! BUT, WHAT GOOD'LL THIS DO REED?? HE'S STILL TRAPPED BACK IN THERE--SAME AS BEFORE!
SKRTCH
MEANWHILE, AROUND THE CORNER AND DOWN THE HALL...
NOW THAT YOU'VE WITNESSED MY INVINCIBLE POWER, YOU MUST REALIZE THE FOLLY OF FURTHER RESISTANCE!
THEREFORE I COMMAND YOU--CONTACT THE BLACK PANTHER!
WHEN HE LEARNS OF YOUR PLIGHT, HE IS CERTAIN TO RUSH TO YOUR AID--TO RUSH RIGHT INTO THE FINAL TRAP OF THE MASTER OF SOUND!
NO! I'LL NEVER HELP YOU--NEVER!
YOU FOOL! YOU HAVE NO CHOICE!
THERE'S ALWAYS ANOTHER CHOICE! YOU CAN'T FORCE ME TO BETRAY A FRIEND IF YOU CAN'T FIND ME! I'LL ESCAPE YOU YET!
BY TURNING INVISIBLE?? THEN, YOU STILL DON'T FULLY COMPREHEND THE AWESOME EXTENT OF MY POWER!
I'VE GOT TO REACH REED! HE'LL FIND SOME WAY TO OVERCOME KLAW!
MY MASTERY OF SOUND ENABLES ME TO ACCOMPLISH ANYTHING--AND I SHALL NOW DEMONSTRATE, TO PROVE HOW UNBEATABLE I TRULY AM!
12

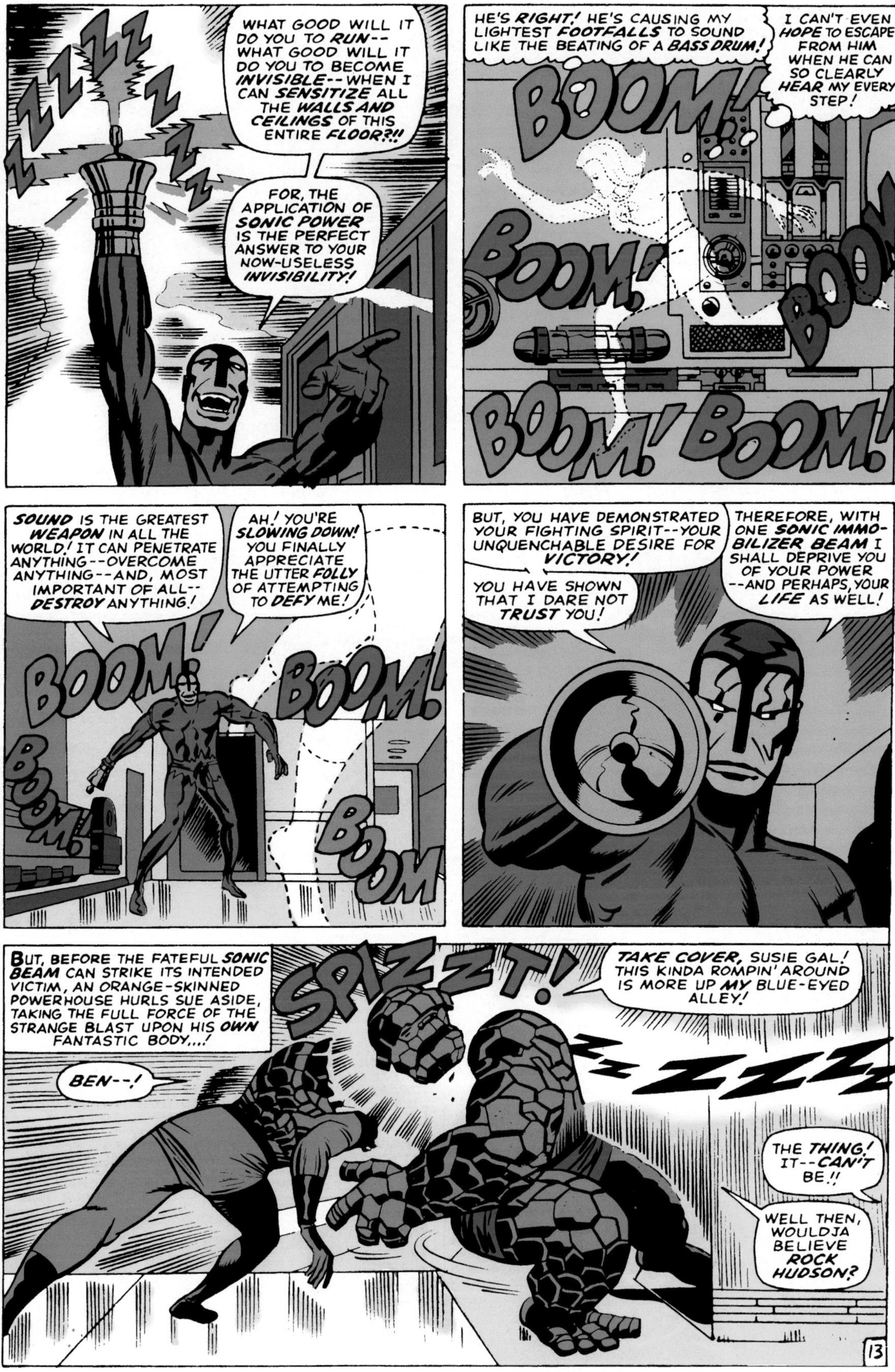
ZZZZZZ
WHAT GOOD WILL IT DO YOU TO RUN-- WHAT GOOD WILL IT DO YOU TO BECOME INVISIBLE-- WHEN I CAN SENSITIZE ALL THE WALLS AND CEILINGS OF THIS ENTIRE FLOOR?!!
FOR, THE APPLICATION OF SONIC POWER IS THE PERFECT ANSWER TO YOUR NOW-USELESS INVISIBILITY!
HE'S RIGHT! HE'S CAUSING MY LIGHTEST FOOTFALLS TO SOUND LIKE THE BEATING OF A BASS DRUM!
I CAN'T EVEN HOPE TO ESCAPE FROM HIM WHEN HE CAN SO CLEARLY HEAR MY EVERY STEP!
BOOM!
BOOM!
BOOM!
BOOM! BOOM!
SOUND IS THE GREATEST WEAPON IN ALL THE WORLD! IT CAN PENETRATE ANYTHING--OVERCOME ANYTHING--AND, MOST IMPORTANT OF ALL-- DESTROY ANYTHING!
AH! YOU'RE SLOWING DOWN! YOU FINALLY APPRECIATE THE UTTER FOLLY OF ATTEMPTING TO DEFY ME!
BOOM!
BOOM!
BOOM!
BOOM
BUT, YOU HAVE DEMONSTRATED YOUR FIGHTING SPIRIT--YOUR UNQUENCHABLE DESIRE FOR VICTORY!
YOU HAVE SHOWN THAT I DARE NOT TRUST YOU!
THEREFORE, WITH ONE SONIC IMMO-BILIZER BEAM I SHALL DEPRIVE YOU OF YOUR POWER --AND PERHAPS, YOUR LIFE AS WELL!
BUT, BEFORE THE FATEFUL SONIC BEAM CAN STRIKE ITS INTENDED VICTIM, AN ORANGE-SKINNED POWERHOUSE HURLS SUE ASIDE, TAKING THE FULL FORCE OF THE STRANGE BLAST UPON HIS OWN FANTASTIC BODY...!
SPIZZZT!
TAKE COVER, SUSIE GAL! THIS KINDA ROMPIN' AROUND IS MORE UP MY BLUE-EYED ALLEY!
BEN--!
ZZZZZZ
THE THING! IT--CAN'T BE.!!
WELL THEN, WOULDJA BELIEVE ROCK HUDSON?
13

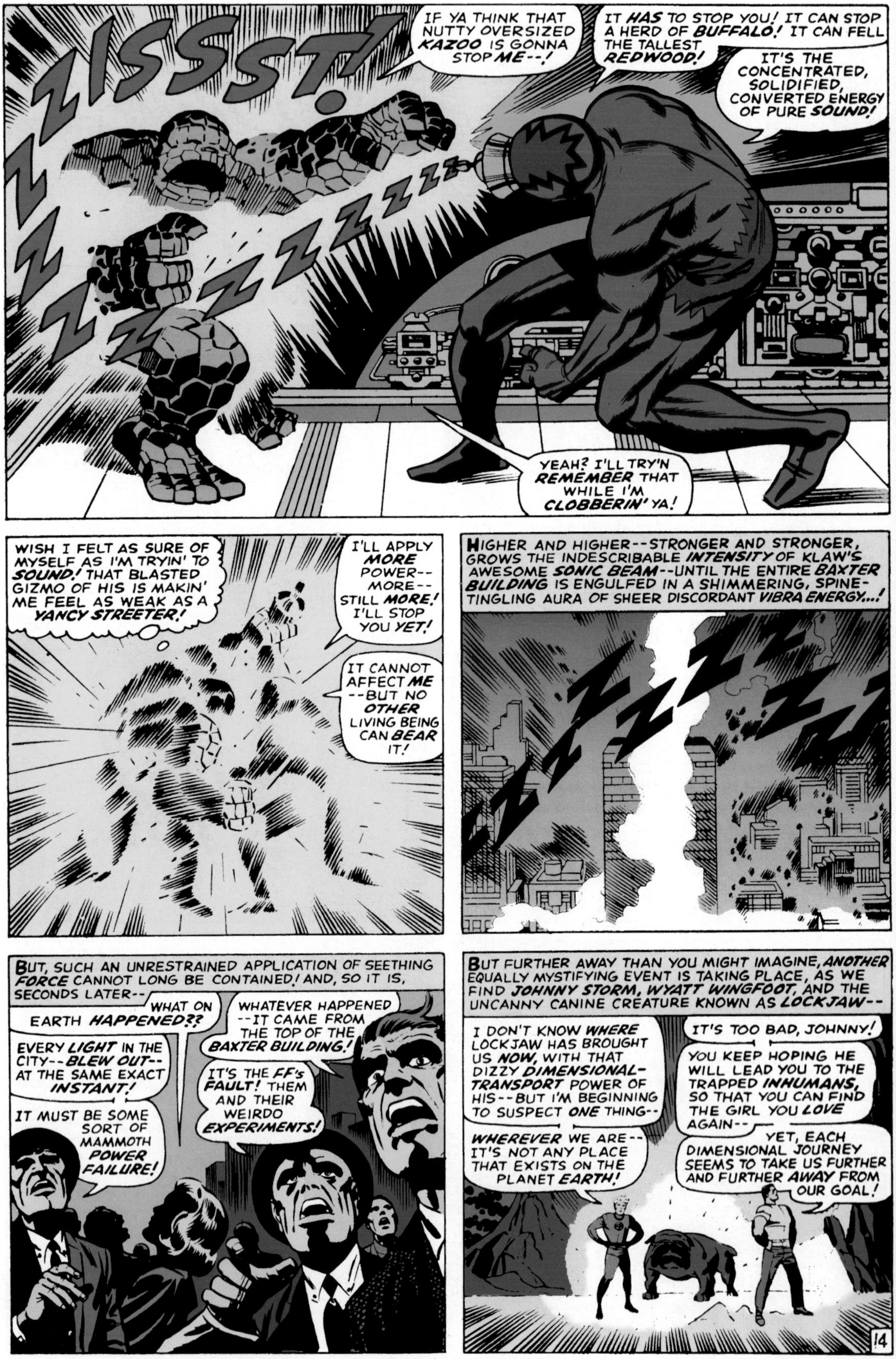
ZZZISSST!
IF YA THINK THAT NUTTY OVERSIZED KAZOO IS GONNA STOP ME--!
IT HAS TO STOP YOU! IT CAN STOP A HERD OF BUFFALO! IT CAN FELL THE TALLEST REDWOOD!
IT'S THE CONCENTRATED, SOLIDIFIED, CONVERTED ENERGY OF PURE SOUND!
ZZZZZZZZZZ
YEAH? I'LL TRY'N REMEMBER THAT WHILE I'M CLOBBERIN' YA!
WISH I FELT AS SURE OF MYSELF AS I'M TRYIN' TO SOUND! THAT BLASTED GIZMO OF HIS IS MAKIN' ME FEEL AS WEAK AS A YANCY STREETER!
I'LL APPLY MORE POWER-- MORE-- STILL MORE! I'LL STOP YOU YET!
IT CANNOT AFFECT ME --BUT NO OTHER LIVING BEING CAN BEAR IT!
HIGHER AND HIGHER--STRONGER AND STRONGER, GROWS THE INDESCRIBABLE INTENSITY OF KLAW'S AWESOME SONIC BEAM--UNTIL THE ENTIRE BAXTER BUILDING IS ENGULFED IN A SHIMMERING, SPINE-TINGLING AURA OF SHEER DISCORDANT VIBRA ENERGY...!
BUT, SUCH AN UNRESTRAINED APPLICATION OF SEETHING FORCE CANNOT LONG BE CONTAINED! AND, SO IT IS, SECONDS LATER--
WHAT ON EARTH HAPPENED??
WHATEVER HAPPENED --IT CAME FROM THE TOP OF THE BAXTER BUILDING!
EVERY LIGHT IN THE CITY--BLEW OUT-- AT THE SAME EXACT INSTANT!
IT'S THE FF's FAULT! THEM AND THEIR WEIRDO EXPERIMENTS!
IT MUST BE SOME SORT OF MAMMOTH POWER FAILURE!
BUT FURTHER AWAY THAN YOU MIGHT IMAGINE, ANOTHER EQUALLY MYSTIFYING EVENT IS TAKING PLACE, AS WE FIND JOHNNY STORM, WYATT WINGFOOT, AND THE UNCANNY CANINE CREATURE KNOWN AS LOCKJAW--
I DON'T KNOW WHERE LOCKJAW HAS BROUGHT US NOW, WITH THAT DIZZY DIMENSIONAL-TRANSPORT POWER OF HIS--BUT I'M BEGINNING TO SUSPECT ONE THING--
WHEREVER WE ARE-- IT'S NOT ANY PLACE THAT EXISTS ON THE PLANET EARTH!
IT'S TOO BAD, JOHNNY!
YOU KEEP HOPING HE WILL LEAD YOU TO THE TRAPPED INHUMANS, SO THAT YOU CAN FIND THE GIRL YOU LOVE AGAIN--
YET, EACH DIMENSIONAL JOURNEY SEEMS TO TAKE US FURTHER AND FURTHER AWAY FROM OUR GOAL!
14

AND YET, I'VE **GOT TO** STAY WITH LOCKJAW-- TO FOLLOW WHEREEVER HE GOES!

ONLY **HE** HAS THE POWER TO PASS THRU THE **BARRIER** THAT IMPRISONS THE **INHUMANS**-- THE BARRIER BEHIND WHICH **CRYSTAL** STILL IS TRAPPED!

YET, IT SEEMS HE HAS BEEN TRAINED TO KEEP OTHERS **AWAY** FROM THE **GREAT REFUGE!**

HE IS MERELY DOING WHAT HE HAS BEEN **TAUGHT!**

I **WONDER...**

WE ARE MERELY **STRANGERS** TO HIM! THERE IS NO **REASON** FOR LOCKJAW TO OBEY US--TO WISH TO **HELP** US!

BUT, IF WE WERE TO WIN HIS **CONFIDENCE** --HIS **TRUST**--IF THERE WERE SOME WAY FOR US TO **TRAIN** HIM, JUST AS THE **OTHERS** HAVE TRAINED HIM--!

I **SEE** WHAT YOU MEAN, WYATT! WHY CAN'T **WE** MAKE A LOYAL **PET** OF HIM--JUST AS THE **INHUMANS** DID?!!

BUT, IT'LL REQUIRE **PATIENCE** --**KINDNESS** --AND A DEEP KNOWLEDGE OF **ANIMAL TRAINING!**

BUT, WHO IS BETTER EQUIPPED FOR THE TASK THAN **I**? HAVE I NOT THE BLOOD OF THE **COMANCHE** IN MY VEINS? DID MY FOREFATHERS NOT TAME THE WILD STALLION--DID THEY NOT--**WAIT!!**

HE IS NATURALLY **CAUTIOUS**--OVERLY **SUSPICIOUS!** IN TRYING TO **PAT** HIM, I RECEIVED SOME SORT OF SUDDEN **ENERGY SHOCK!**

I'M AFRAID IT'S **HOPELESS**, BIG BUDDY!

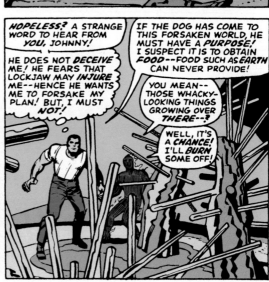

HOPELESS? A STRANGE WORD TO HEAR FROM **YOU**, JOHNNY!

HE DOES NOT **DECEIVE** ME! HE FEARS THAT LOCKJAW MAY **INJURE** ME--HENCE HE WANTS ME TO FORSAKE MY PLAN! BUT, I MUST **NOT!**

IF THE DOG HAS COME TO THIS FORSAKEN WORLD, HE MUST HAVE A **PURPOSE!** I SUSPECT IT IS TO OBTAIN **FOOD**--FOOD SUCH AS **EARTH** CAN NEVER PROVIDE!

YOU MEAN-- THOSE WHACKY- LOOKING THINGS GROWING OVER **THERE**--?

WELL, IT'S A **CHANCE!** I'LL **BURN** SOME OFF!

YOUR POWER OF **FLAME** IS TRULY **CONVENIENT**, JOHNNY--AT A TIME LIKE THIS!

SURE, PAL! I'M JUST A WALKIN', TALKIN' **CHARCOAL GRILL!**

I THINK WE HAVE GUESSED **CORRECTLY!** HE'S COMING TOWARDS THE STRANGE STEMS WITH GREAT **EAGERNESS** IN HIS EYES!

LET'S **HOPE** IT'S THE **STEMS** HE'S AFTER-- AND NOT **US!**

WOW! I'LL SAY YOU WERE RIGHT! HE'S STARTING TO CHOMP 'EM DOWN LIKE THERE'S NO TOMORROW!

NOTICE HOW HE SEEMS TO RELEASE BOLTS OF **ENERGY** AS HE EATS! HE'S FOUND THE PERFECT FOOD!

ONCE HIS **BELLY** IS FULL, IT SHOULD BE **EASIER** FOR US TO WIN HIM OVER! AND THEN, WITH LUCK--**ON TO THE INHUMANS!**

15

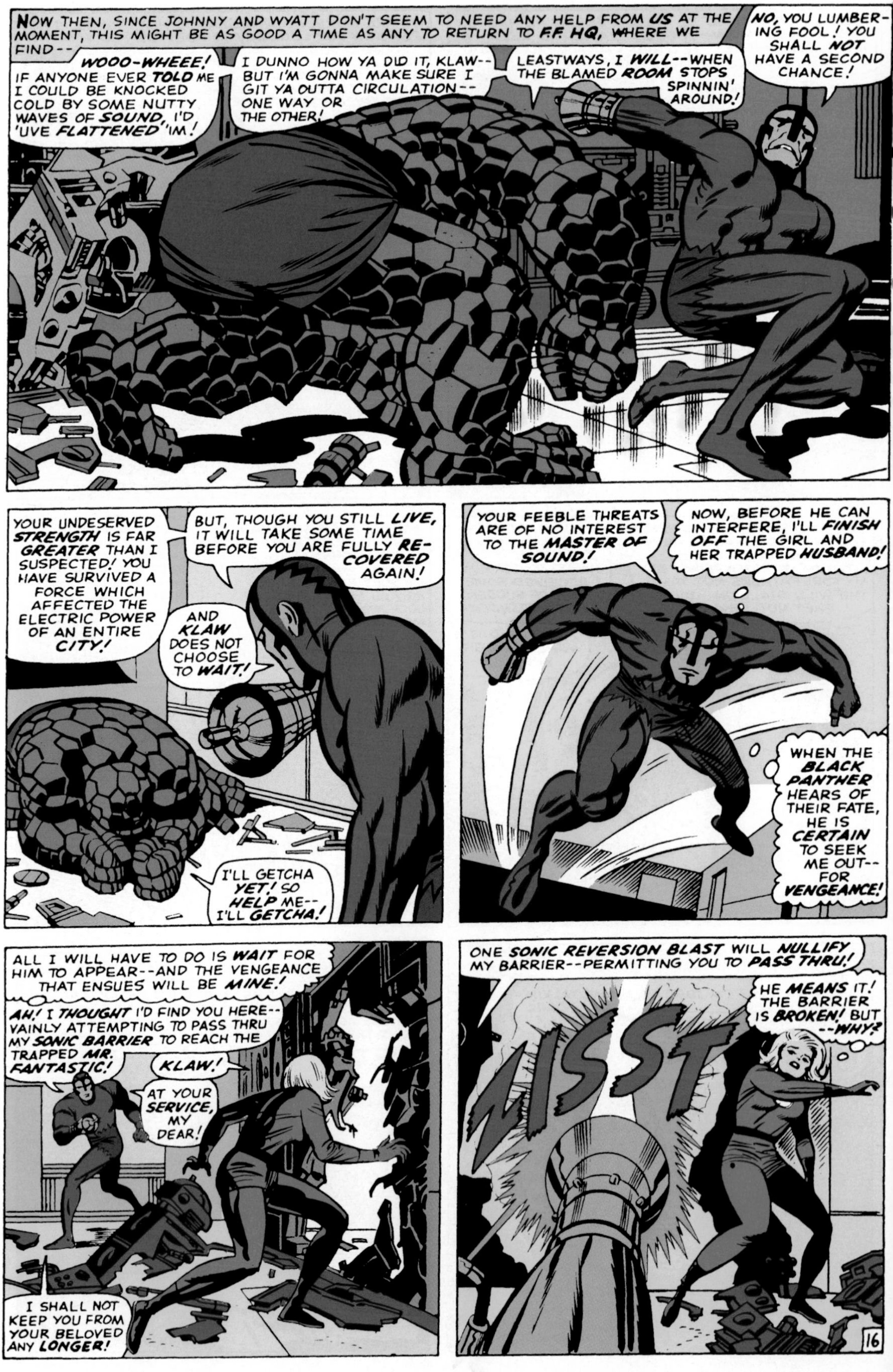
NOW THEN, SINCE JOHNNY AND WYATT DON'T SEEM TO NEED ANY HELP FROM US AT THE MOMENT, THIS MIGHT BE AS GOOD A TIME AS ANY TO RETURN TO F.F. HQ, WHERE WE FIND--
WOOO-WHEEE! IF ANYONE EVER TOLD ME I COULD BE KNOCKED COLD BY SOME NUTTY WAVES OF SOUND, I'D 'UVE FLATTENED 'IM!
I DUNNO HOW YA DID IT, KLAW-- BUT I'M GONNA MAKE SURE I GIT YA OUTTA CIRCULATION-- ONE WAY OR THE OTHER!
LEASTWAYS, I WILL--WHEN THE BLAMED ROOM STOPS SPINNIN' AROUND!
NO, YOU LUMBERING FOOL! YOU SHALL NOT HAVE A SECOND CHANCE!
YOUR UNDESERVED STRENGTH IS FAR GREATER THAN I SUSPECTED! YOU HAVE SURVIVED A FORCE WHICH AFFECTED THE ELECTRIC POWER OF AN ENTIRE CITY!
BUT, THOUGH YOU STILL LIVE, IT WILL TAKE SOME TIME BEFORE YOU ARE FULLY RECOVERED AGAIN!
AND KLAW DOES NOT CHOOSE TO WAIT!
I'LL GETCHA YET! SO HELP ME-- I'LL GETCHA!
YOUR FEEBLE THREATS ARE OF NO INTEREST TO THE MASTER OF SOUND!
NOW, BEFORE HE CAN INTERFERE, I'LL FINISH OFF THE GIRL AND HER TRAPPED HUSBAND!
WHEN THE BLACK PANTHER HEARS OF THEIR FATE, HE IS CERTAIN TO SEEK ME OUT-- FOR VENGEANCE!
ALL I WILL HAVE TO DO IS WAIT FOR HIM TO APPEAR--AND THE VENGEANCE THAT ENSUES WILL BE MINE!
AH! I THOUGHT I'D FIND YOU HERE-- VAINLY ATTEMPTING TO PASS THRU MY SONIC BARRIER TO REACH THE TRAPPED MR. FANTASTIC!
KLAW!
AT YOUR SERVICE, MY DEAR!
I SHALL NOT KEEP YOU FROM YOUR BELOVED ANY LONGER!
ONE SONIC REVERSION BLAST WILL NULLIFY MY BARRIER--PERMITTING YOU TO PASS THRU!
ZISST
HE MEANS IT! THE BARRIER IS BROKEN! BUT --WHY?
16

SUE, DARLING-- STAY BACK-- DON'T--

TOO LATE! HE TRICKED YOU! HE WANTED YOU TO JOIN ME!

BUT, NO MATTER! WE'LL BEAT HIM YET! I'LL FIND A WAY SOMEHOW!

REED-- IT'S KLAW-- THE MASTER OF SOUND! HE'S RETURNED!

YOUR HUSBAND HAS ALREADY DEDUCED THAT RATHER OBVIOUS FACT, MRS. RICHARDS!

BUT, IT WILL DO NEITHER OF YOU ANY GOOD!

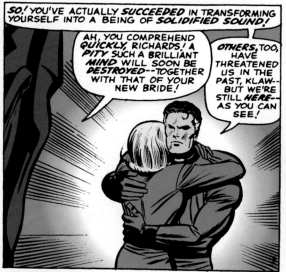

SO! YOU'VE ACTUALLY SUCCEEDED IN TRANSFORMING YOURSELF INTO A BEING OF SOLIDIFIED SOUND!

AH, YOU COMPREHEND QUICKLY, RICHARDS! A PITY SUCH A BRILLIANT MIND WILL SOON BE DESTROYED--TOGETHER WITH THAT OF YOUR NEW BRIDE!

OTHERS, TOO, HAVE THREATENED US IN THE PAST, KLAW-- BUT WE'RE STILL HERE-- AS YOU CAN SEE!

I ADMIRE YOUR CONFIDENCE, RICHARDS! TOO BAD IT IS SO MISPLACED! AND NOW--IF YOU HAVE ANY LAST WORDS TO SAY, I SUGGEST YOU SAY THEM--QUICKLY!

BEHIND ME, SUE! THIS IS THE SHOWDOWN!

BUT, IT ISN'T GOING TO END IN THE WAY THAT MADMAN EXPECTS--!

EVEN AS THE STEELY-EYED MR. FANTASTIC SPEAKS, A REMOTE CONTROL PACKET MISSILE ZOOMS DOWN FROM THE ATMOSPHERE, HOMING IN ON THE BAXTER BUILDING AFTER A LIGHTNING JOURNEY HALF-WAY AROUND THE GLOBE--!

YOUR FALSE BRAVURA HAS AVAILED YOU NOTHING, RICHARDS! THIS IS YOUR FINISH--!

YOU'RE TOO LATE, KLAW! LOOK-- LOOK OUT THE WINDOW!

A MINIATURE ROCKET--COMING TO A HALT--RIGHT IN FRONT OF YOU!

I KNEW HE WOULDN'T FAIL ME!

REED!! WHAT IS IT, DARLING?? WHAT DOES IT MEAN??

17

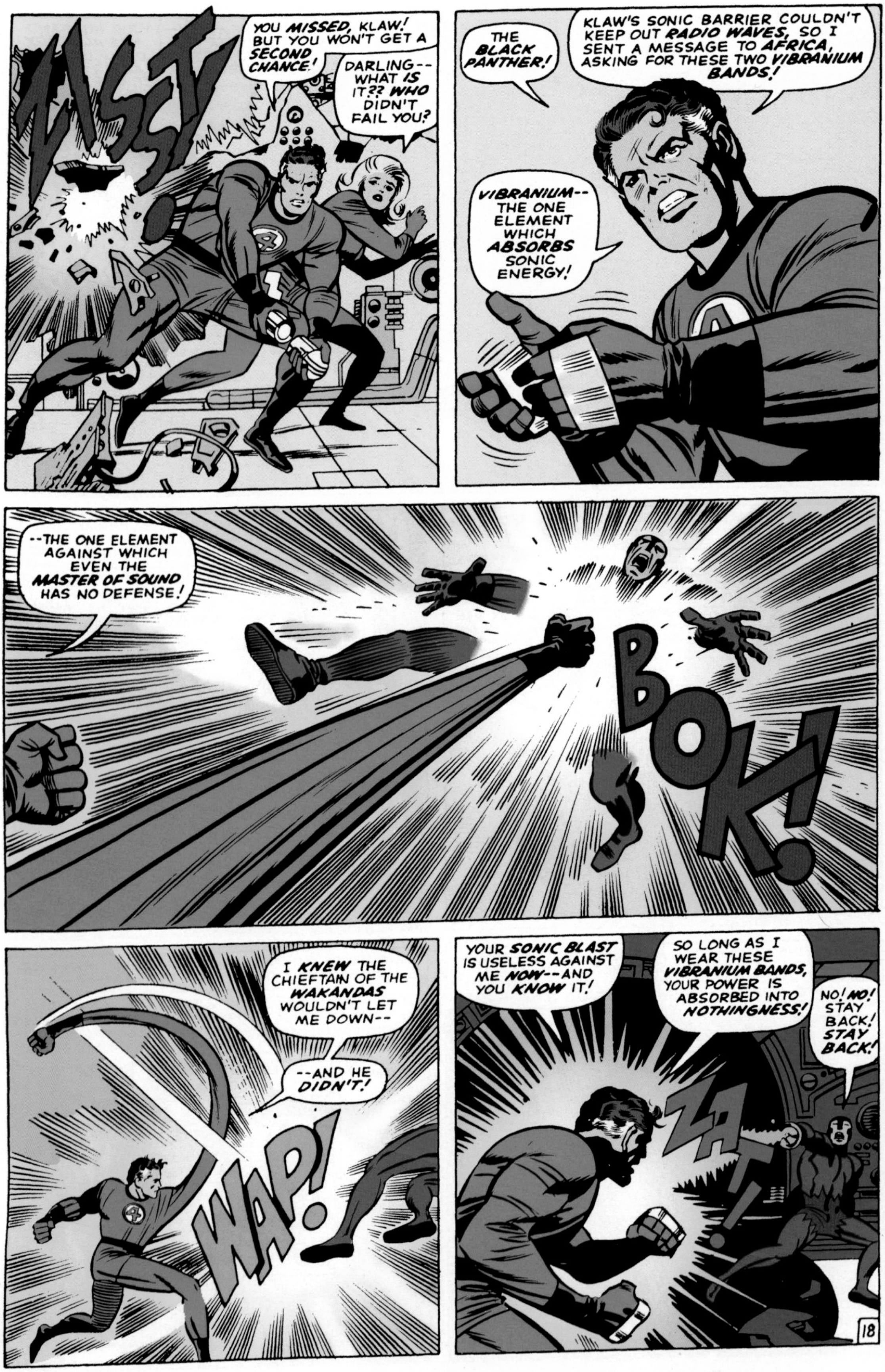
ZASST
YOU MISSED, KLAW! BUT YOU WON'T GET A SECOND CHANCE!
DARLING-- WHAT IS IT?? WHO DIDN'T FAIL YOU?
THE BLACK PANTHER!
KLAW'S SONIC BARRIER COULDN'T KEEP OUT RADIO WAVES, SO I SENT A MESSAGE TO AFRICA, ASKING FOR THESE TWO VIBRANIUM BANDS!
VIBRANIUM-- THE ONE ELEMENT WHICH ABSORBS SONIC ENERGY!
--THE ONE ELEMENT AGAINST WHICH EVEN THE MASTER OF SOUND HAS NO DEFENSE!
BOK!
I KNEW THE CHIEFTAIN OF THE WAKANDAS WOULDN'T LET ME DOWN--
--AND HE DIDN'T!
WAP!
YOUR SONIC BLAST IS USELESS AGAINST ME NOW--AND YOU KNOW IT!
SO LONG AS I WEAR THESE VIBRANIUM BANDS, YOUR POWER IS ABSORBED INTO NOTHINGNESS!
NO! NO! STAY BACK! STAY BACK!
ZAT!
18

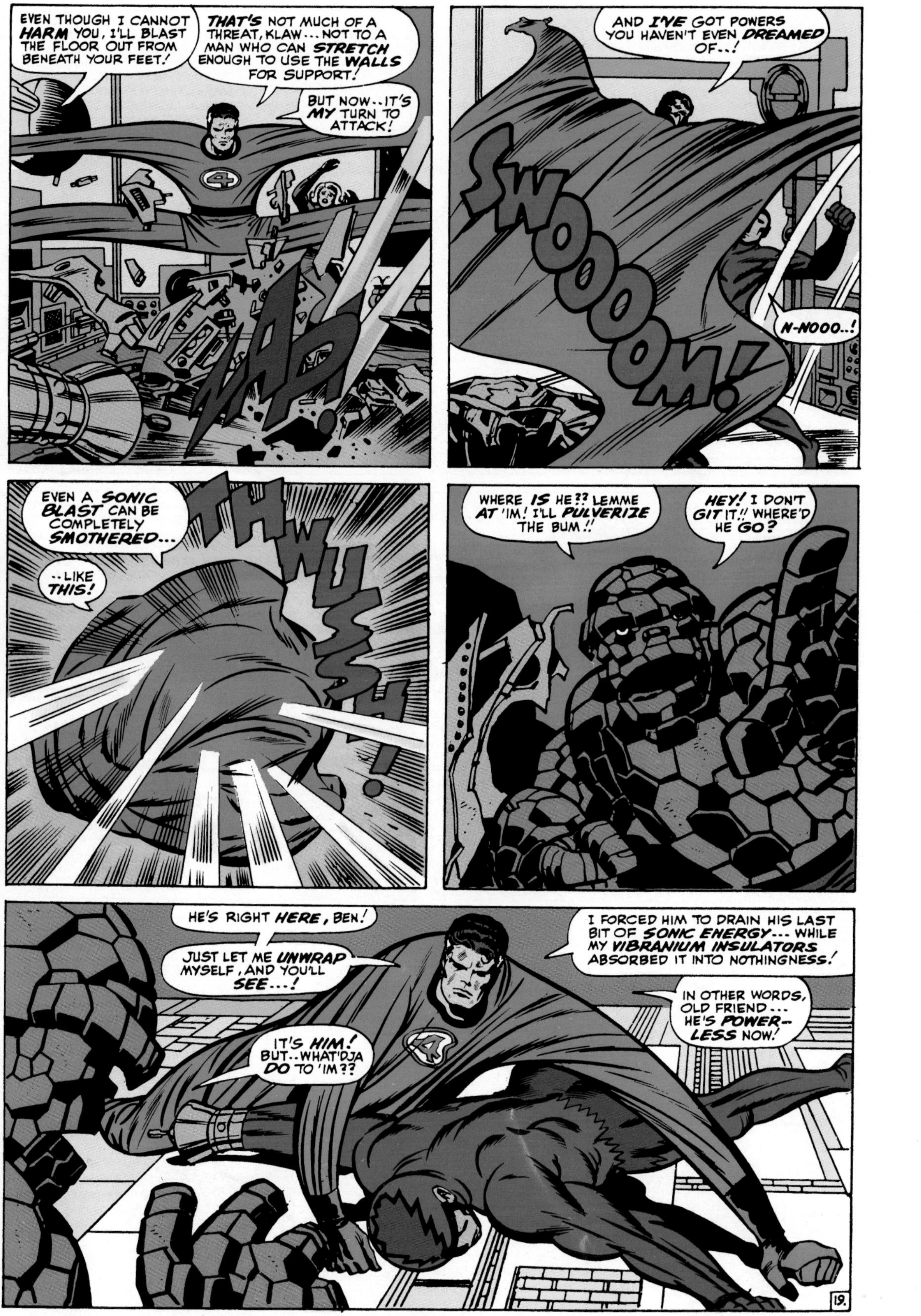
EVEN THOUGH I CANNOT HARM YOU, I'LL BLAST THE FLOOR OUT FROM BENEATH YOUR FEET!
THAT'S NOT MUCH OF A THREAT, KLAW... NOT TO A MAN WHO CAN STRETCH ENOUGH TO USE THE WALLS FOR SUPPORT!
BUT NOW.. IT'S MY TURN TO ATTACK!
WHAP!
AND I'VE GOT POWERS YOU HAVEN'T EVEN DREAMED OF..!
SWOOOOOM!
N-NOOO..!
EVEN A SONIC BLAST CAN BE COMPLETELY SMOTHERED...
..LIKE THIS!
THWUSSH!
WHERE IS HE?? LEMME AT 'IM! I'LL PULVERIZE THE BUM!!
HEY! I DON'T GIT IT!! WHERE'D HE GO?
HE'S RIGHT HERE, BEN!
JUST LET ME UNWRAP MYSELF, AND YOU'LL SEE...!
I FORCED HIM TO DRAIN HIS LAST BIT OF SONIC ENERGY--- WHILE MY VIBRANIUM INSULATORS ABSORBED IT INTO NOTHINGNESS!
IN OTHER WORDS, OLD FRIEND... HE'S POWER-LESS NOW!
IT'S HIM! BUT.. WHAT'DJA DO TO 'IM??
19.

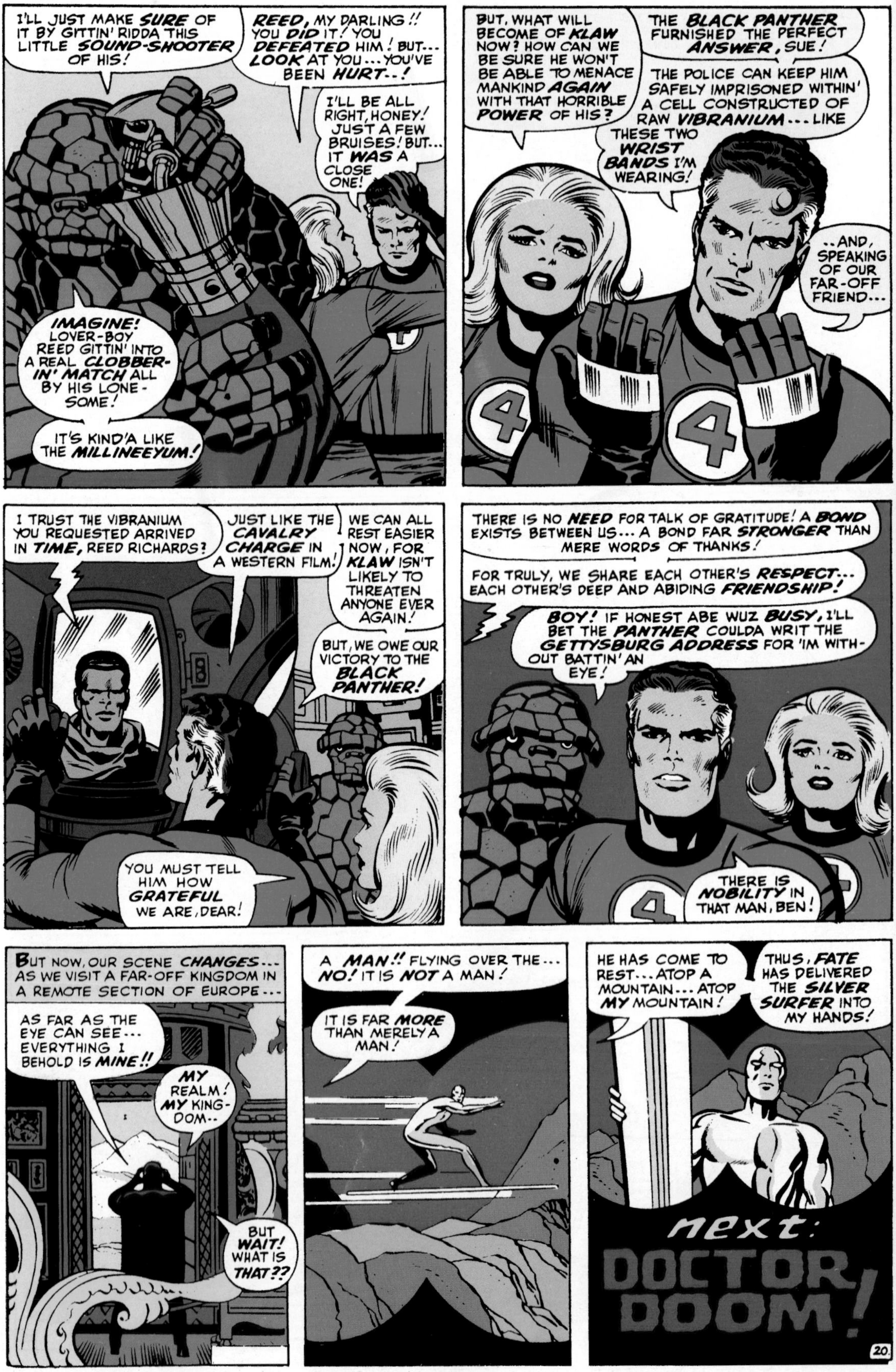

I'LL JUST MAKE SURE OF IT BY GITTIN' RIDDA THIS LITTLE SOUND-SHOOTER OF HIS!
REED, MY DARLING!! YOU DID IT! YOU DEFEATED HIM! BUT... LOOK AT YOU... YOU'VE BEEN HURT--!
I'LL BE ALL RIGHT, HONEY! JUST A FEW BRUISES! BUT... IT WAS A CLOSE ONE!
IMAGINE! LOVER-BOY REED GITTIN' INTO A REAL CLOBBER-IN' MATCH ALL BY HIS LONE-SOME!
IT'S KIND'A LIKE THE MILLINEEYUM!
BUT, WHAT WILL BECOME OF KLAW NOW? HOW CAN WE BE SURE HE WON'T BE ABLE TO MENACE MANKIND AGAIN WITH THAT HORRIBLE POWER OF HIS?
THE BLACK PANTHER FURNISHED THE PERFECT ANSWER, SUE!
THE POLICE CAN KEEP HIM SAFELY IMPRISONED WITHIN A CELL CONSTRUCTED OF RAW VIBRANIUM--- LIKE THESE TWO WRIST BANDS I'M WEARING!
..AND, SPEAKING OF OUR FAR-OFF FRIEND...
I TRUST THE VIBRANIUM YOU REQUESTED ARRIVED IN TIME, REED RICHARDS?
JUST LIKE THE CAVALRY CHARGE IN A WESTERN FILM!
WE CAN ALL REST EASIER NOW, FOR KLAW ISN'T LIKELY TO THREATEN ANYONE EVER AGAIN!
BUT, WE OWE OUR VICTORY TO THE BLACK PANTHER!
YOU MUST TELL HIM HOW GRATEFUL WE ARE, DEAR!
THERE IS NO NEED FOR TALK OF GRATITUDE! A BOND EXISTS BETWEEN US... A BOND FAR STRONGER THAN MERE WORDS OF THANKS!
FOR TRULY, WE SHARE EACH OTHER'S RESPECT... EACH OTHER'S DEEP AND ABIDING FRIENDSHIP!
BOY! IF HONEST ABE WUZ BUSY, I'LL BET THE PANTHER COULDA WRIT THE GETTYSBURG ADDRESS FOR 'IM WITH-OUT BATTIN' AN EYE!
THERE IS NOBILITY IN THAT MAN, BEN!
BUT NOW, OUR SCENE CHANGES... AS WE VISIT A FAR-OFF KINGDOM IN A REMOTE SECTION OF EUROPE...
AS FAR AS THE EYE CAN SEE--- EVERYTHING I BEHOLD IS MINE!!
MY REALM! MY KING-DOM..
BUT! WAIT! WHAT IS THAT??
A MAN!! FLYING OVER THE... NO! IT IS NOT A MAN!
IT IS FAR MORE THAN MERELY A MAN!
HE HAS COME TO REST... ATOP A MOUNTAIN... ATOP MY MOUNTAIN!
THUS, FATE HAS DELIVERED THE SILVER SURFER INTO MY HANDS!
next: DOCTOR DOOM!
20

FANTASTIC FOUR ANNUAL
KING-SIZE SPECIAL!
APPROVED BY THE COMICS CODE AUTHORITY
72 BIG PAGES
Fantastic Four
IND.
MARVEL COMICS GROUP
25¢
#4 NOV
THE SENSATION OF THE CENTURY!! THE ORIGINAL HUMAN TORCH ACTUALLY RETURNS FROM THE PAST TO BATTLE JOHNNY STORM!
ALL NEW!
EXTRA BONUS: YOU'LL FINALLY SEE THE ORIGIN OF THE HUMAN TORCH, AS CREATED IN 1939!!
THE WORLD'S GREATEST COMIC MAGAZINE!
Fantastic Four
MARVEL COMICS GROUP 12¢
25 APR
THIS IS THE BIG ONE! "THE INCREDIBLE HULK VERSUS The THING!"
A MARVEL SUPER-SPECTACULAR!
PAGE AFTER PAGE OF PULSE-POUNDING THRILLS!!
BRINGING THE MARVEL AGE OF COMICS TO A LOFTY NEW PINNACLE OF GREATNESS!
THE BATTLE OF THE CENTURY!
PLUS... THE MOST-REQUESTED BATTLE RE-PRESENTATION IN COMICS HISTORY! The THING Vs. THE INCREDIBLE HULK EXACTLY AS IMMORTALIZED IN F.F. #s 25 & 26! 'NUFF SAID!

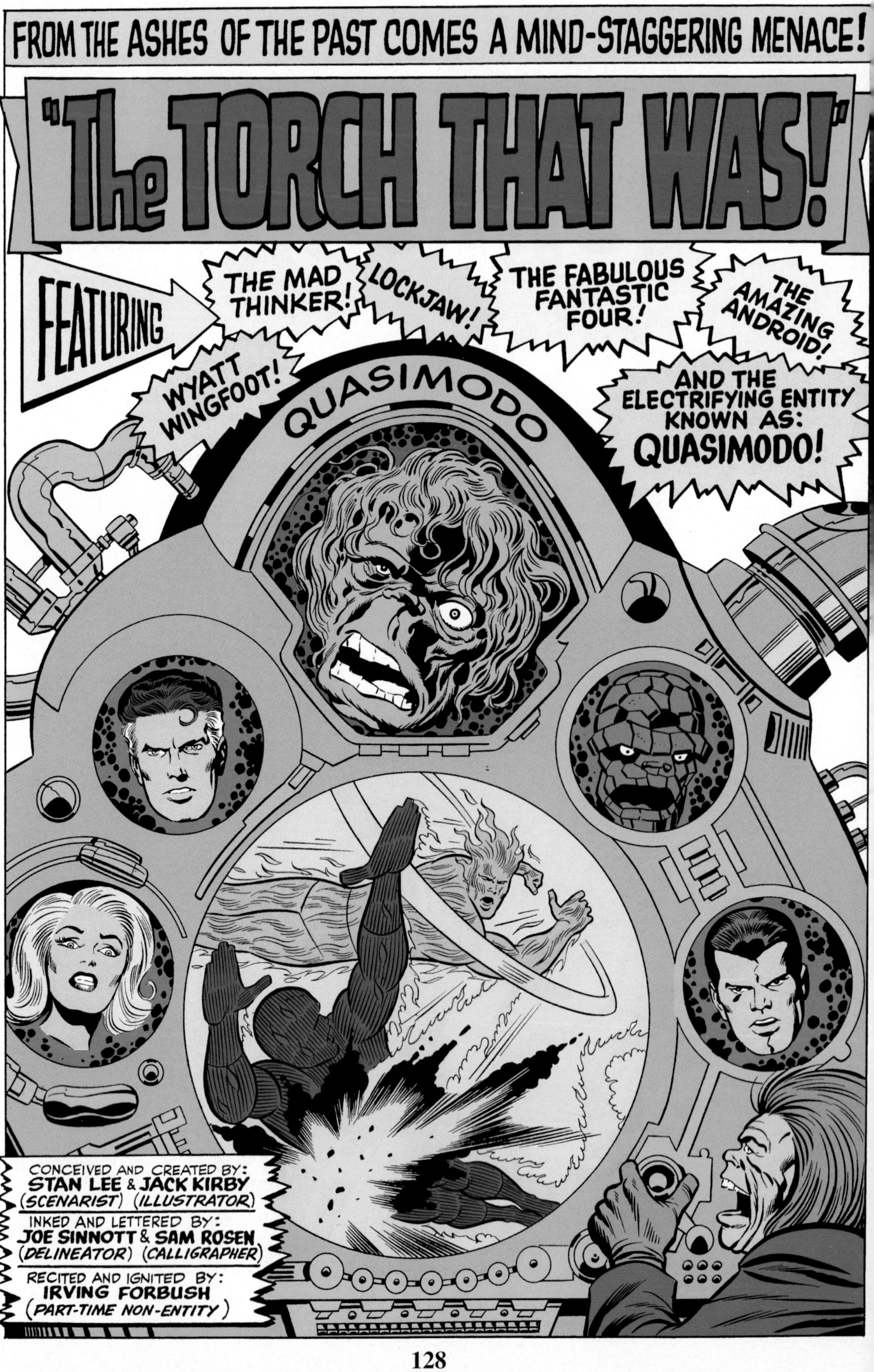
FROM THE ASHES OF THE PAST COMES A MIND-STAGGERING MENACE!
"The TORCH THAT WAS!"
FEATURING
THE MAD THINKER!
LOCKJAW!
THE FABULOUS FANTASTIC FOUR!
THE AMAZING ANDROID!
WYATT WINGFOOT!
AND THE ELECTRIFYING ENTITY KNOWN AS: QUASIMODO!
QUASIMODO
CONCEIVED AND CREATED BY: STAN LEE & JACK KIRBY (SCENARIST) (ILLUSTRATOR)
INKED AND LETTERED BY: JOE SINNOTT & SAM ROSEN (DELINEATOR) (CALLIGRAPHER)
RECITED AND IGNITED BY: IRVING FORBUSH (PART-TIME NON-ENTITY)

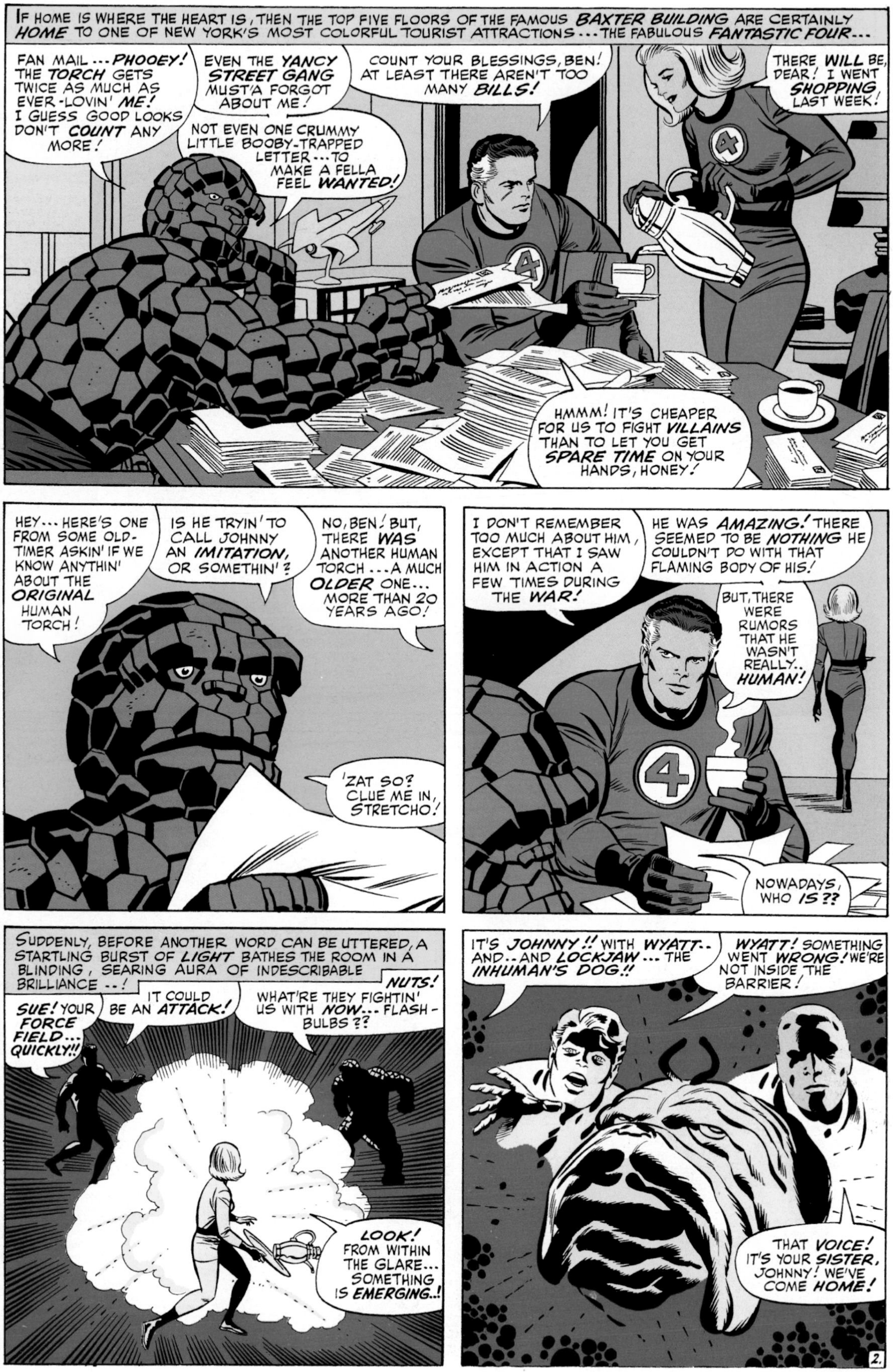
IF HOME IS WHERE THE HEART IS, THEN THE TOP FIVE FLOORS OF THE FAMOUS BAXTER BUILDING ARE CERTAINLY HOME TO ONE OF NEW YORK'S MOST COLORFUL TOURIST ATTRACTIONS... THE FABULOUS FANTASTIC FOUR...
FAN MAIL... PHOOEY! THE TORCH GETS TWICE AS MUCH AS EVER-LOVIN' ME! I GUESS GOOD LOOKS DON'T COUNT ANY MORE!
EVEN THE YANCY STREET GANG MUST'A FORGOT ABOUT ME!
NOT EVEN ONE CRUMMY LITTLE BOOBY-TRAPPED LETTER... TO MAKE A FELLA FEEL WANTED!
COUNT YOUR BLESSINGS, BEN! AT LEAST THERE AREN'T TOO MANY BILLS!
THERE WILL BE, DEAR! I WENT SHOPPING LAST WEEK!
HMMM! IT'S CHEAPER FOR US TO FIGHT VILLAINS THAN TO LET YOU GET SPARE TIME ON YOUR HANDS, HONEY!
HEY... HERE'S ONE FROM SOME OLD-TIMER ASKIN' IF WE KNOW ANYTHIN' ABOUT THE ORIGINAL HUMAN TORCH!
IS HE TRYIN' TO CALL JOHNNY AN IMITATION, OR SOMETHIN'?
NO, BEN! BUT, THERE WAS ANOTHER HUMAN TORCH... A MUCH OLDER ONE... MORE THAN 20 YEARS AGO!
'ZAT SO? CLUE ME IN, STRETCHO!
I DON'T REMEMBER TOO MUCH ABOUT HIM, EXCEPT THAT I SAW HIM IN ACTION A FEW TIMES DURING THE WAR!
HE WAS AMAZING! THERE SEEMED TO BE NOTHING HE COULDN'T DO WITH THAT FLAMING BODY OF HIS!
BUT, THERE WERE RUMORS THAT HE WASN'T REALLY.. HUMAN!
NOWADAYS, WHO IS??
SUDDENLY, BEFORE ANOTHER WORD CAN BE UTTERED, A STARTLING BURST OF LIGHT BATHES THE ROOM IN A BLINDING, SEARING AURA OF INDESCRIBABLE BRILLIANCE--!
SUE! YOUR FORCE FIELD... QUICKLY!!
IT COULD BE AN ATTACK!
WHAT'RE THEY FIGHTIN' US WITH NOW... FLASH-BULBS??
NUTS!
LOOK! FROM WITHIN THE GLARE... SOMETHING IS EMERGING..!
IT'S JOHNNY!! WITH WYATT.. AND.. AND LOCKJAW... THE INHUMAN'S DOG!!
WYATT! SOMETHING WENT WRONG! WE'RE NOT INSIDE THE BARRIER!
THAT VOICE! IT'S YOUR SISTER, JOHNNY! WE'VE COME HOME!
2.

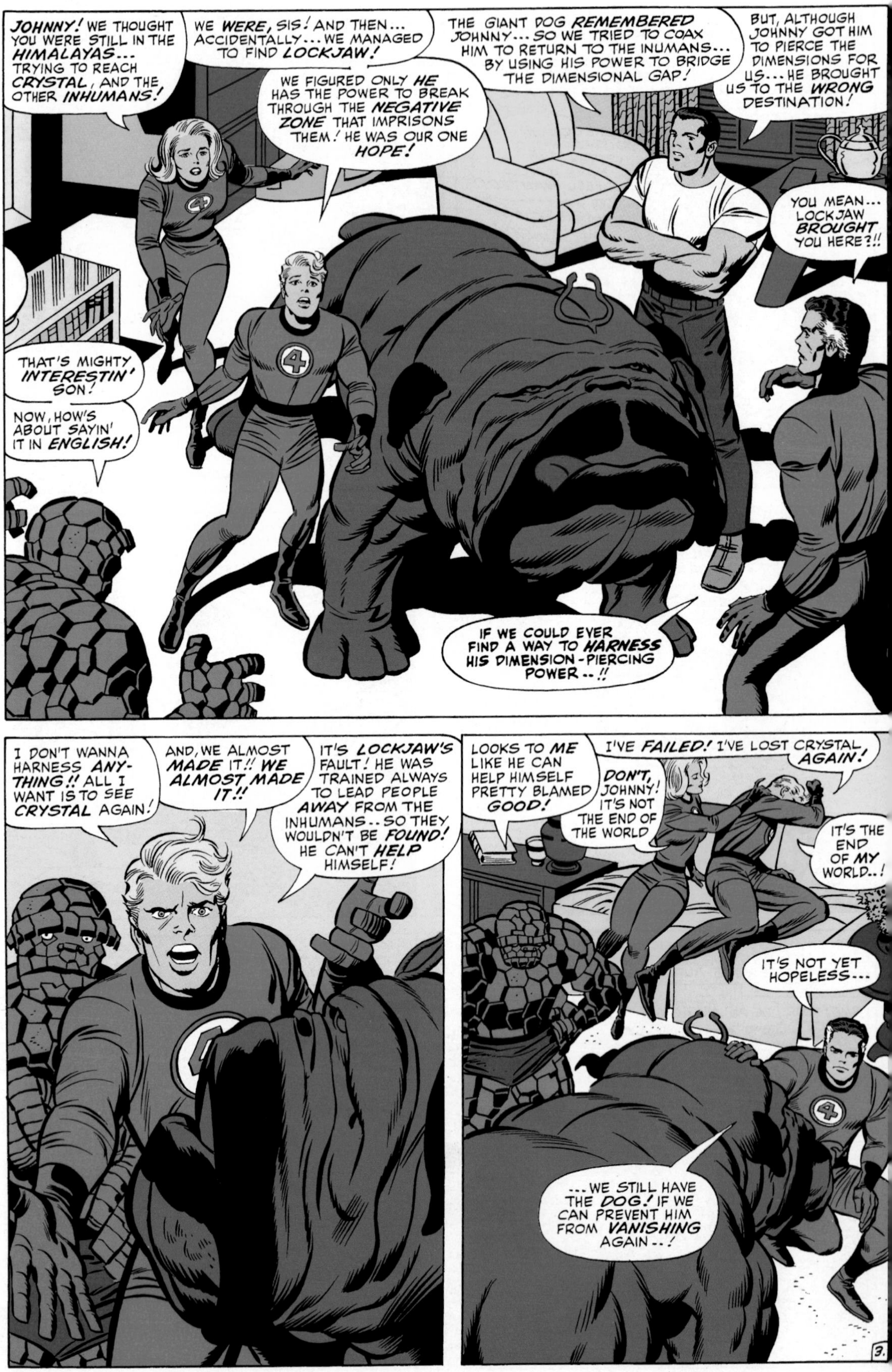
JOHNNY! WE THOUGHT YOU WERE STILL IN THE HIMALAYAS... TRYING TO REACH CRYSTAL, AND THE OTHER INHUMANS!
WE WERE, SIS! AND THEN... ACCIDENTALLY... WE MANAGED TO FIND LOCKJAW!
WE FIGURED ONLY HE HAS THE POWER TO BREAK THROUGH THE NEGATIVE ZONE THAT IMPRISONS THEM! HE WAS OUR ONE HOPE!
THE GIANT DOG REMEMBERED JOHNNY... SO WE TRIED TO COAX HIM TO RETURN TO THE INUMANS... BY USING HIS POWER TO BRIDGE THE DIMENSIONAL GAP!
BUT, ALTHOUGH JOHNNY GOT HIM TO PIERCE THE DIMENSIONS FOR US... HE BROUGHT US TO THE WRONG DESTINATION!
YOU MEAN... LOCKJAW BROUGHT YOU HERE?!!
THAT'S MIGHTY INTERESTIN' SON!
NOW, HOW'S ABOUT SAYIN' IT IN ENGLISH!
IF WE COULD EVER FIND A WAY TO HARNESS HIS DIMENSION-PIERCING POWER--!!
I DON'T WANNA HARNESS ANY-THING!! ALL I WANT IS TO SEE CRYSTAL AGAIN!
AND, WE ALMOST MADE IT!! WE ALMOST MADE IT!!
IT'S LOCKJAW'S FAULT! HE WAS TRAINED ALWAYS TO LEAD PEOPLE AWAY FROM THE INHUMANS.. SO THEY WOULDN'T BE FOUND! HE CAN'T HELP HIMSELF!
LOOKS TO ME LIKE HE CAN HELP HIMSELF PRETTY BLAMED GOOD!
I'VE FAILED! I'VE LOST CRYSTAL AGAIN!
DON'T, JOHNNY! IT'S NOT THE END OF THE WORLD
IT'S THE END OF MY WORLD..!
IT'S NOT YET HOPELESS---
...WE STILL HAVE THE DOG! IF WE CAN PREVENT HIM FROM VANISHING AGAIN--!
3.

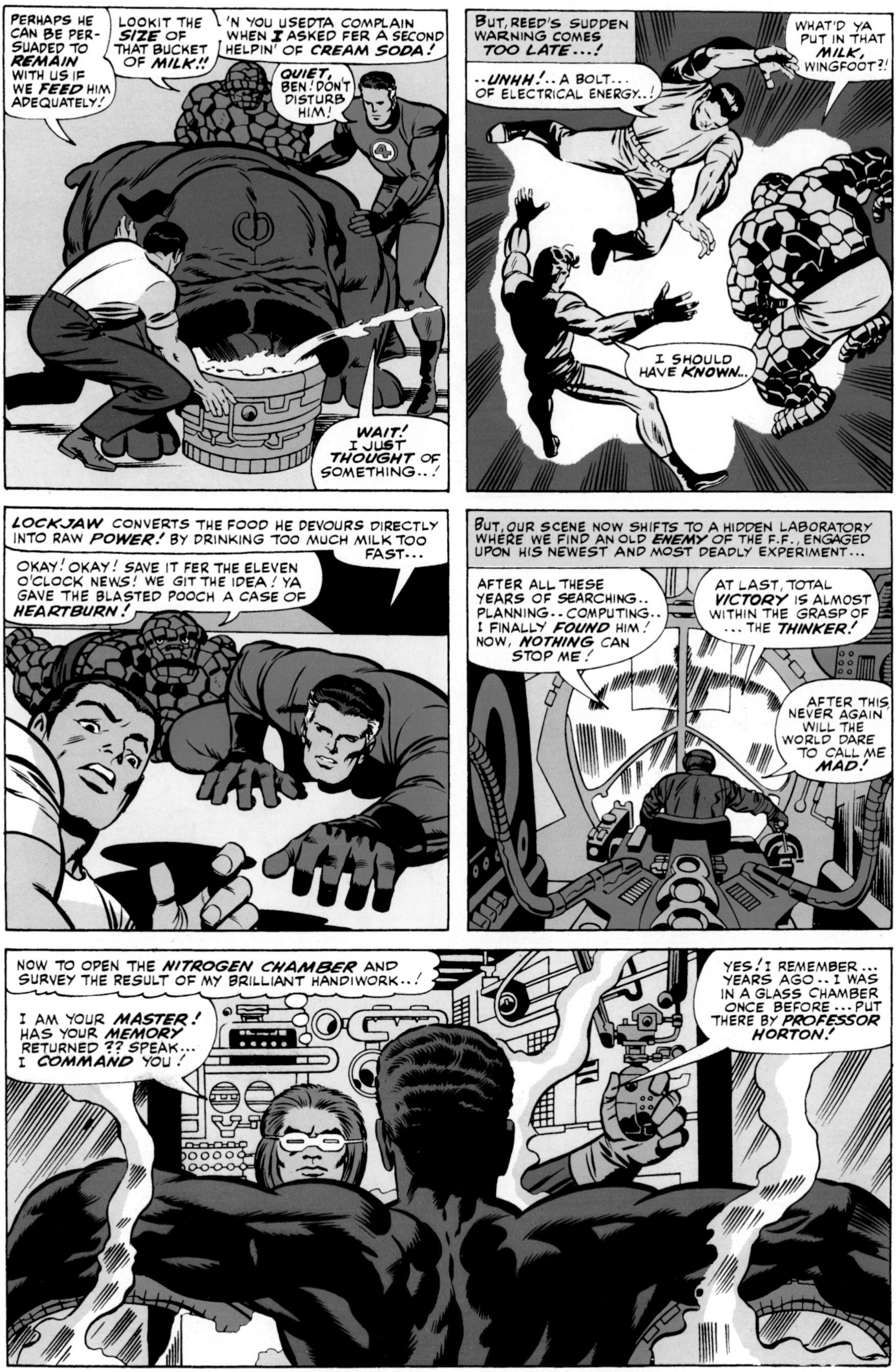

PERHAPS HE CAN BE PERSUADED TO REMAIN WITH US IF WE FEED HIM ADEQUATELY!
LOOKIT THE SIZE OF THAT BUCKET OF MILK!!
'N YOU USEDTA COMPLAIN WHEN I ASKED FER A SECOND HELPIN' OF CREAM SODA!
QUIET, BEN! DON'T DISTURB HIM!
WAIT! I JUST THOUGHT OF SOMETHING..!
BUT, REED'S SUDDEN WARNING COMES TOO LATE...!
..UNHH!.. A BOLT... OF ELECTRICAL ENERGY..!
WHAT'D YA PUT IN THAT MILK, WINGFOOT?!
I SHOULD HAVE KNOWN...
LOCKJAW CONVERTS THE FOOD HE DEVOURS DIRECTLY INTO RAW POWER! BY DRINKING TOO MUCH MILK TOO FAST...
OKAY! OKAY! SAVE IT FER THE ELEVEN O'CLOCK NEWS! WE GIT THE IDEA! YA GAVE THE BLASTED POOCH A CASE OF HEARTBURN!
BUT, OUR SCENE NOW SHIFTS TO A HIDDEN LABORATORY WHERE WE FIND AN OLD ENEMY OF THE F.F., ENGAGED UPON HIS NEWEST AND MOST DEADLY EXPERIMENT...
AFTER ALL THESE YEARS OF SEARCHING.. PLANNING.. COMPUTING.. I FINALLY FOUND HIM! NOW, NOTHING CAN STOP ME!
AT LAST, TOTAL VICTORY IS ALMOST WITHIN THE GRASP OF ... THE THINKER!
AFTER THIS, NEVER AGAIN WILL THE WORLD DARE TO CALL ME MAD!
NOW TO OPEN THE NITROGEN CHAMBER AND SURVEY THE RESULT OF MY BRILLIANT HANDIWORK..!
I AM YOUR MASTER! HAS YOUR MEMORY RETURNED?? SPEAK... I COMMAND YOU!
YES! I REMEMBER... YEARS AGO.. I WAS IN A GLASS CHAMBER ONCE BEFORE... PUT THERE BY PROFESSOR HORTON!

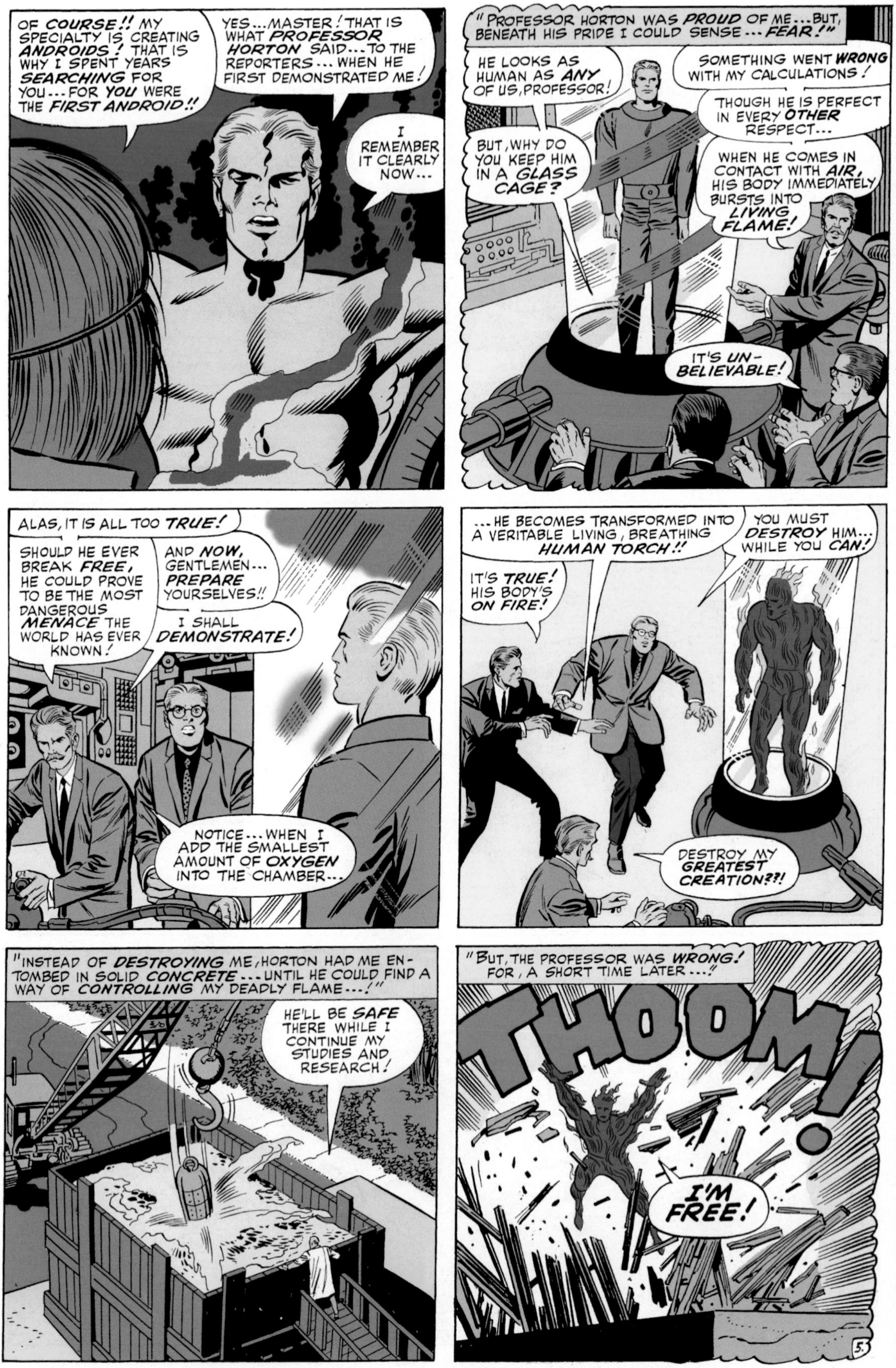
OF COURSE!! MY SPECIALTY IS CREATING ANDROIDS! THAT IS WHY I SPENT YEARS SEARCHING FOR YOU... FOR YOU WERE THE FIRST ANDROID!!
YES... MASTER! THAT IS WHAT PROFESSOR HORTON SAID... TO THE REPORTERS... WHEN HE FIRST DEMONSTRATED ME!
I REMEMBER IT CLEARLY NOW...
"PROFESSOR HORTON WAS PROUD OF ME... BUT, BENEATH HIS PRIDE I COULD SENSE... FEAR!"
HE LOOKS AS HUMAN AS ANY OF US, PROFESSOR!
BUT, WHY DO YOU KEEP HIM IN A GLASS CAGE?
SOMETHING WENT WRONG WITH MY CALCULATIONS!
THOUGH HE IS PERFECT IN EVERY OTHER RESPECT...
WHEN HE COMES IN CONTACT WITH AIR, HIS BODY IMMEDIATELY BURSTS INTO LIVING FLAME!
IT'S UN-BELIEVABLE!
ALAS, IT IS ALL TOO TRUE!
SHOULD HE EVER BREAK FREE, HE COULD PROVE TO BE THE MOST DANGEROUS MENACE THE WORLD HAS EVER KNOWN!
AND NOW, GENTLEMEN... PREPARE YOURSELVES!!
I SHALL DEMONSTRATE!
NOTICE... WHEN I ADD THE SMALLEST AMOUNT OF OXYGEN INTO THE CHAMBER...
...HE BECOMES TRANSFORMED INTO A VERITABLE LIVING, BREATHING HUMAN TORCH!!
IT'S TRUE! HIS BODY'S ON FIRE!
YOU MUST DESTROY HIM... WHILE YOU CAN!
DESTROY MY GREATEST CREATION??!
"INSTEAD OF DESTROYING ME, HORTON HAD ME EN-TOMBED IN SOLID CONCRETE... UNTIL HE COULD FIND A WAY OF CONTROLLING MY DEADLY FLAME...!"
HE'LL BE SAFE THERE WHILE I CONTINUE MY STUDIES AND RESEARCH!
"BUT, THE PROFESSOR WAS WRONG! FOR, A SHORT TIME LATER..."
THOOM!
I'M FREE!
5.

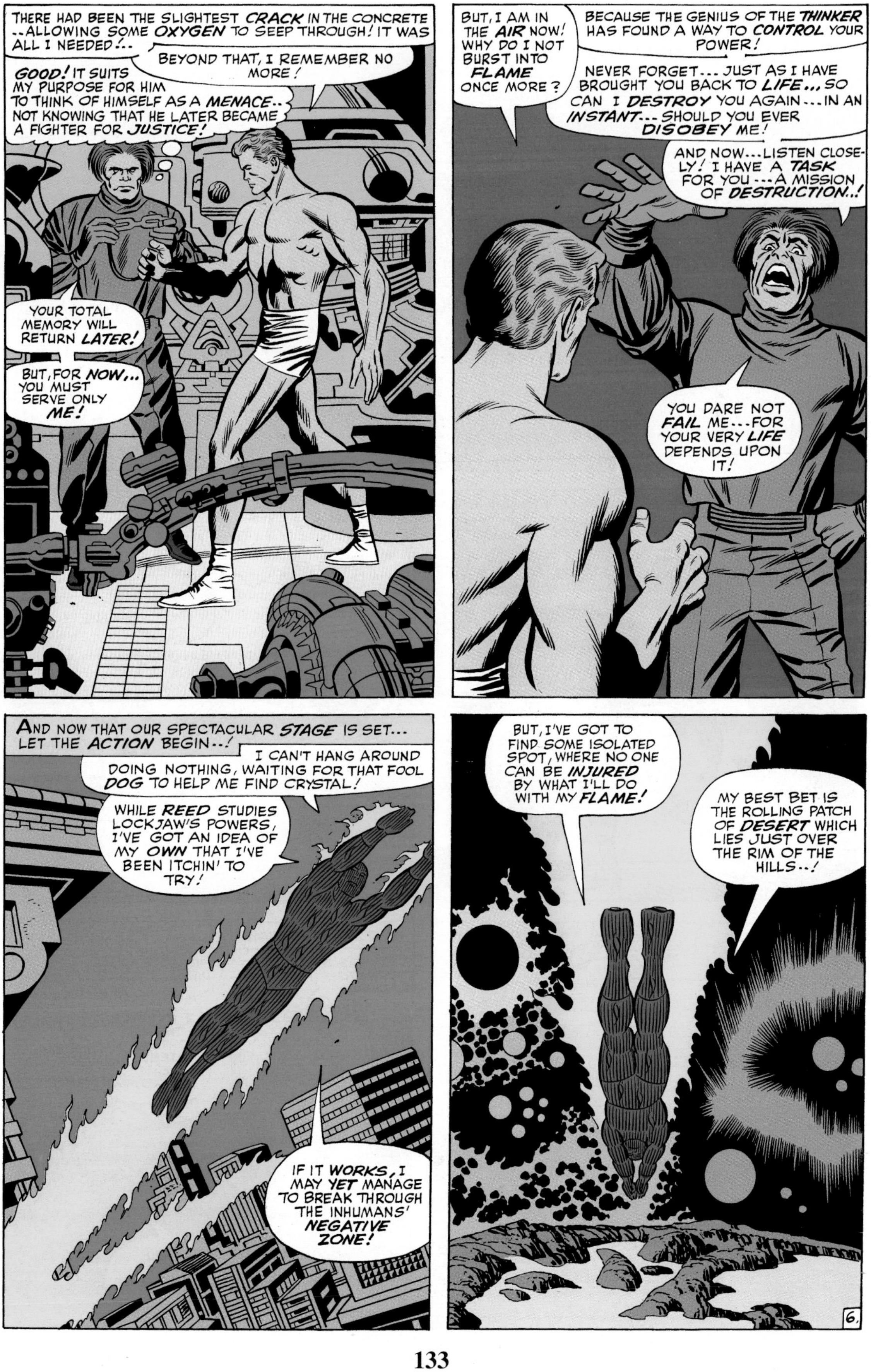
THERE HAD BEEN THE SLIGHTEST CRACK IN THE CONCRETE --ALLOWING SOME OXYGEN TO SEEP THROUGH! IT WAS ALL I NEEDED!..
BEYOND THAT, I REMEMBER NO MORE!
GOOD! IT SUITS MY PURPOSE FOR HIM TO THINK OF HIMSELF AS A MENACE.. NOT KNOWING THAT HE LATER BECAME A FIGHTER FOR JUSTICE!
YOUR TOTAL MEMORY WILL RETURN LATER!
BUT, FOR NOW,.. YOU MUST SERVE ONLY ME!
BUT, I AM IN THE AIR NOW! WHY DO I NOT BURST INTO FLAME ONCE MORE?
BECAUSE THE GENIUS OF THE THINKER HAS FOUND A WAY TO CONTROL YOUR POWER!
NEVER FORGET... JUST AS I HAVE BROUGHT YOU BACK TO LIFE... SO CAN I DESTROY YOU AGAIN... IN AN INSTANT... SHOULD YOU EVER DISOBEY ME!
AND NOW... LISTEN CLOSELY! I HAVE A TASK FOR YOU --- A MISSION OF DESTRUCTION..!
YOU DARE NOT FAIL ME---FOR YOUR VERY LIFE DEPENDS UPON IT!
AND NOW THAT OUR SPECTACULAR STAGE IS SET... LET THE ACTION BEGIN..!
I CAN'T HANG AROUND DOING NOTHING, WAITING FOR THAT FOOL DOG TO HELP ME FIND CRYSTAL!
WHILE REED STUDIES LOCKJAW'S POWERS, I'VE GOT AN IDEA OF MY OWN THAT I'VE BEEN ITCHIN' TO TRY!
IF IT WORKS, I MAY YET MANAGE TO BREAK THROUGH THE INHUMANS' NEGATIVE ZONE!
BUT, I'VE GOT TO FIND SOME ISOLATED SPOT, WHERE NO ONE CAN BE INJURED BY WHAT I'LL DO WITH MY FLAME!
MY BEST BET IS THE ROLLING PATCH OF DESERT WHICH LIES JUST OVER THE RIM OF THE HILLS..!
6.

THIS IS *IT!* THERE'S NOT ANOTHER HUMAN FOR *MILES* AROUND!

FIRST, I'LL HAVE TO *REST* FOR A WHILE, TO ALLOW MY FLAME TO REACH *PEAK INTENSITY* AGAIN!

'CAUSE I'M GONNA NEED EVERY OUNCE OF BLAZING *POWER* I CAN MUSTER!

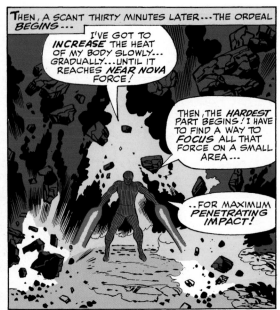

THEN, A SCANT THIRTY MINUTES LATER...THE ORDEAL *BEGINS*...

I'VE GOT TO *INCREASE* THE HEAT OF MY BODY SLOWLY... GRADUALLY...UNTIL IT REACHES *NEAR NOVA* FORCE!

THEN, THE *HARDEST* PART BEGINS! I HAVE TO FIND A WAY TO *FOCUS* ALL THAT FORCE ON A SMALL AREA...

..FOR MAXIMUM *PENETRATING* IMPACT!

BUT THEN...UNEXPECTEDLY...TOTALLY WITHOUT WARNING...

A *TORNADO!!* HEADING RIGHT *TOWARD* ME!!

WHOOSH!

THE WIND'S TOO *STRONG*...CAN'T *FIGHT* IT!

MY *FLAME'S* GOING *OUT!*

WAIT!! WHAT'S *THAT?* I..I MUST BE GOING *MAD!!*

THAT WAS *NO* TORNADO, JOHNNY STORM!

NO! HE'S *REAL*...I SEE HIM!! IT'S ANOTHER *HUMAN TORCH!*

I CREATED THE AIR VORTEX..BY INTENSE *HEAT INVERSION!*

YOU--YOU KNOW MY *NAME!*..WHO *ARE* YOU??

7.

134

I? I AM THE *HUMAN TORCH!* THE *FIRST...* THE *ORIGINAL* HUMAN TORCH! THE ONE WHO MUST NOW *DESTROY* YOU... YOU WHO HAVE SOUGHT TO TAKE *MY* PLACE!

I HAVE MY *ORDERS!* YOU MUST BE *DEFEATED!* I CANNOT DISOBEY!

HE'S *OLDER* THAN I... AND *BIGGER!* BUT ANYTHING *HE* CAN DO... *I* CAN DO!!

LOOK... WHY DON'T WE JUST TALK THIS OVER?

I *HOPE!*

DEFEND YOURSELF! I HAVE NO WISH TO SLAY A *HELPLESS* FOE!

FSSZT!

HE REALLY *MEANS* IT!

MISTER, I DON'T KNOW *WHO* YOU ARE... OR *WHAT* YOU ARE... OR WHY YOU'RE *DOING* THIS... BUT ONE THING I *DO* KNOW...

YOU PICKED YOURSELF THE *WRONG* BOY!

FLAME ON!

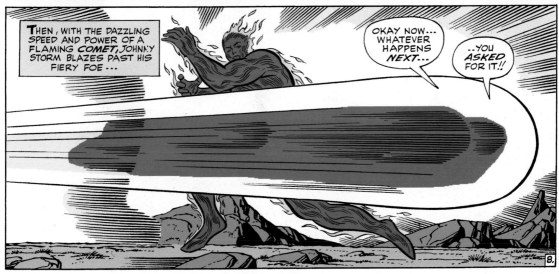

THEN, WITH THE DAZZLING SPEED AND POWER OF A FLAMING *COMET,* JOHNNY STORM BLAZES PAST HIS FIERY FOE...

OKAY NOW... WHATEVER HAPPENS *NEXT...*

...YOU *ASKED* FOR IT!!

8.

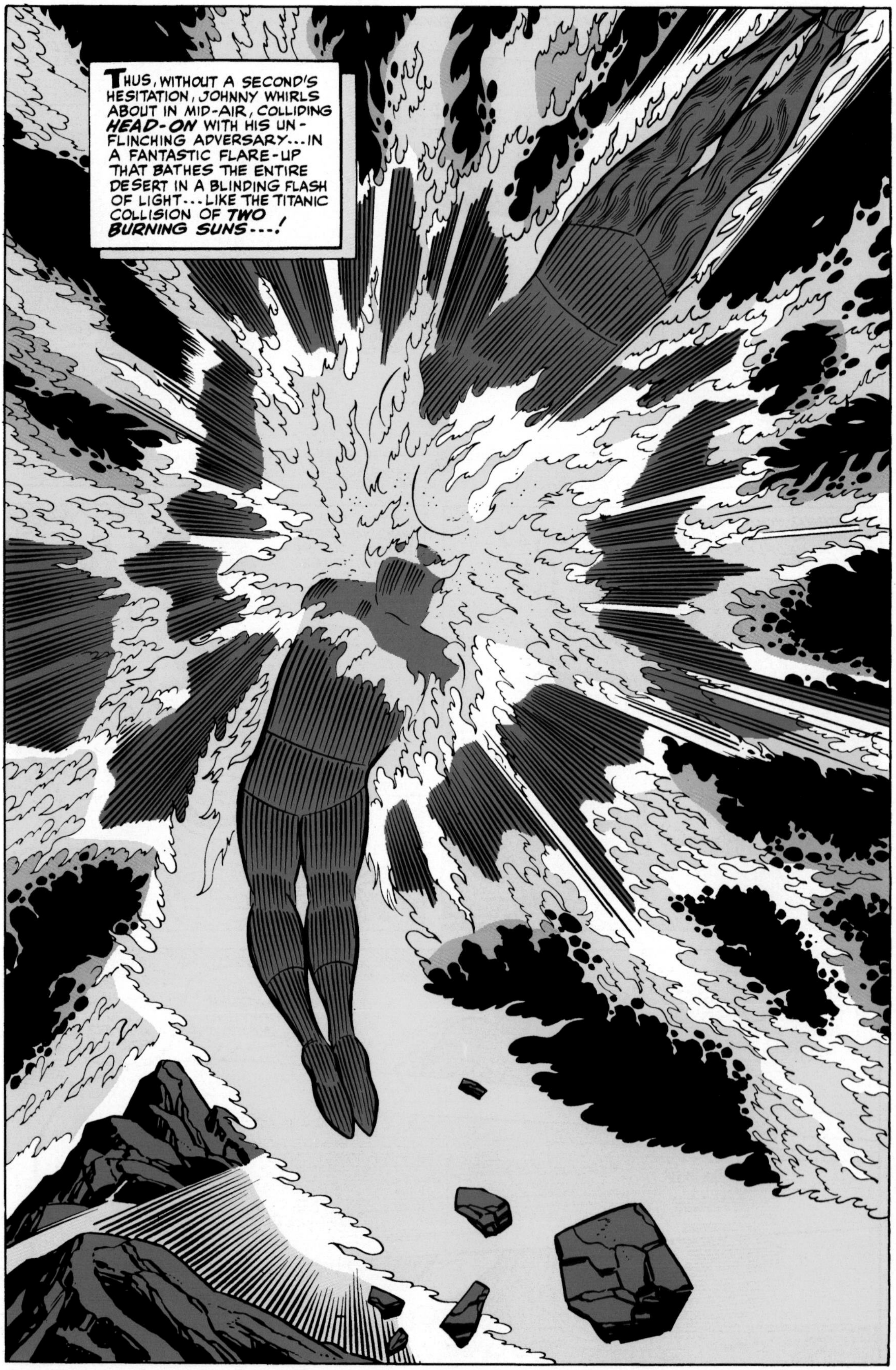
THUS, WITHOUT A SECOND'S HESITATION, JOHNNY WHIRLS ABOUT IN MID-AIR, COLLIDING HEAD-ON WITH HIS UN-FLINCHING ADVERSARY...IN A FANTASTIC FLARE-UP THAT BATHES THE ENTIRE DESERT IN A BLINDING FLASH OF LIGHT...LIKE THE TITANIC COLLISION OF TWO BURNING SUNS...!

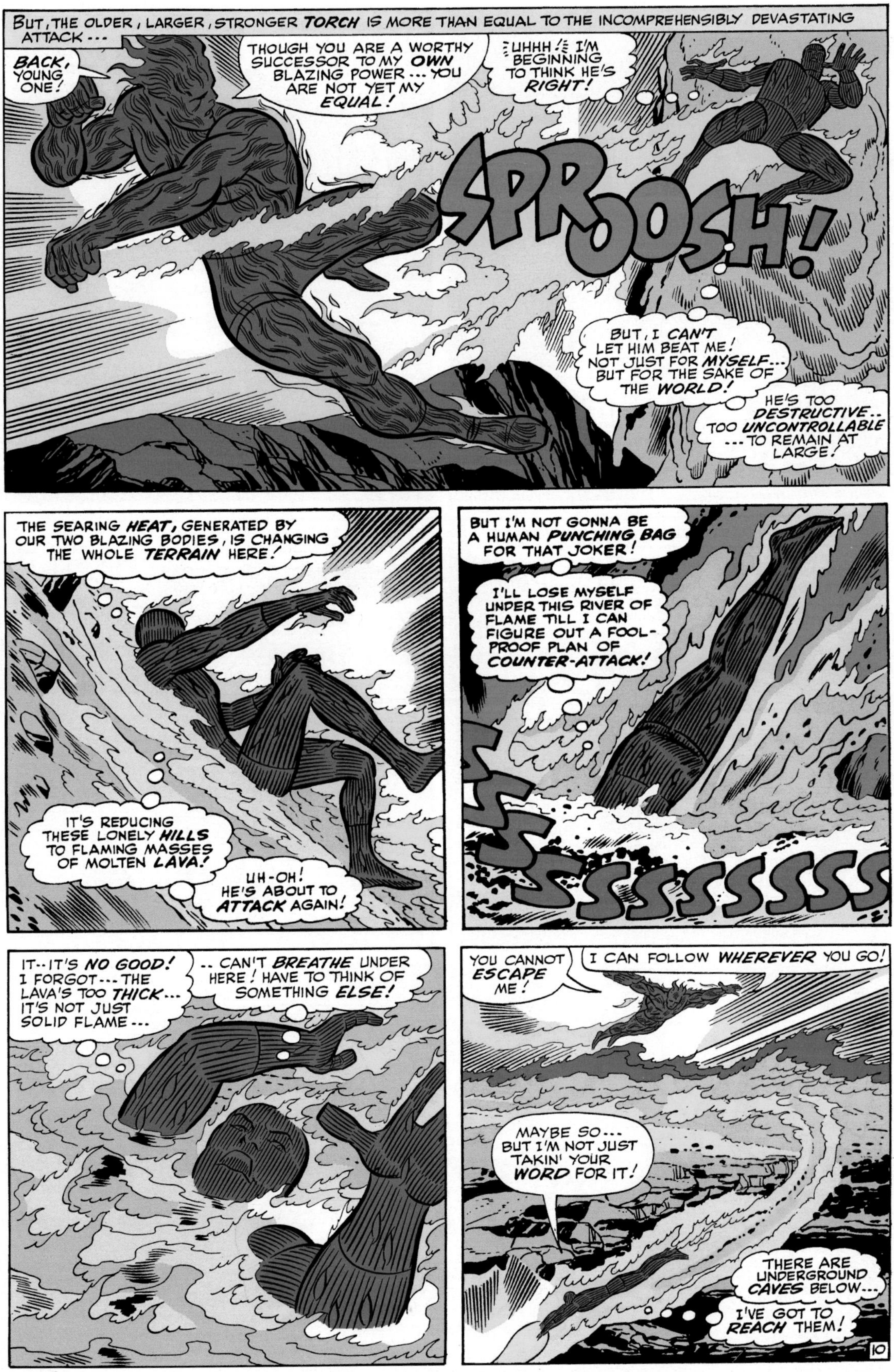
BUT, THE OLDER, LARGER, STRONGER TORCH IS MORE THAN EQUAL TO THE INCOMPREHENSIBLY DEVASTATING ATTACK ---
BACK, YOUNG ONE!
THOUGH YOU ARE A WORTHY SUCCESSOR TO MY OWN BLAZING POWER ... YOU ARE NOT YET MY EQUAL!
UHHH! I'M BEGINNING TO THINK HE'S RIGHT!
SPROOSH!
BUT, I CAN'T LET HIM BEAT ME! NOT JUST FOR MYSELF... BUT FOR THE SAKE OF THE WORLD!
HE'S TOO DESTRUCTIVE.. TOO UNCONTROLLABLE ... TO REMAIN AT LARGE!
THE SEARING HEAT, GENERATED BY OUR TWO BLAZING BODIES, IS CHANGING THE WHOLE TERRAIN HERE!
IT'S REDUCING THESE LONELY HILLS TO FLAMING MASSES OF MOLTEN LAVA!
UH-OH! HE'S ABOUT TO ATTACK AGAIN!
BUT I'M NOT GONNA BE A HUMAN PUNCHING BAG FOR THAT JOKER!
I'LL LOSE MYSELF UNDER THIS RIVER OF FLAME TILL I CAN FIGURE OUT A FOOL-PROOF PLAN OF COUNTER-ATTACK!
SSSSSSSSSS
IT--IT'S NO GOOD! I FORGOT --- THE LAVA'S TOO THICK... IT'S NOT JUST SOLID FLAME ---
.. CAN'T BREATHE UNDER HERE! HAVE TO THINK OF SOMETHING ELSE!
YOU CANNOT ESCAPE ME!
I CAN FOLLOW WHEREVER YOU GO!
MAYBE SO... BUT I'M NOT JUST TAKIN' YOUR WORD FOR IT!
THERE ARE UNDERGROUND CAVES BELOW...
I'VE GOT TO REACH THEM!
10

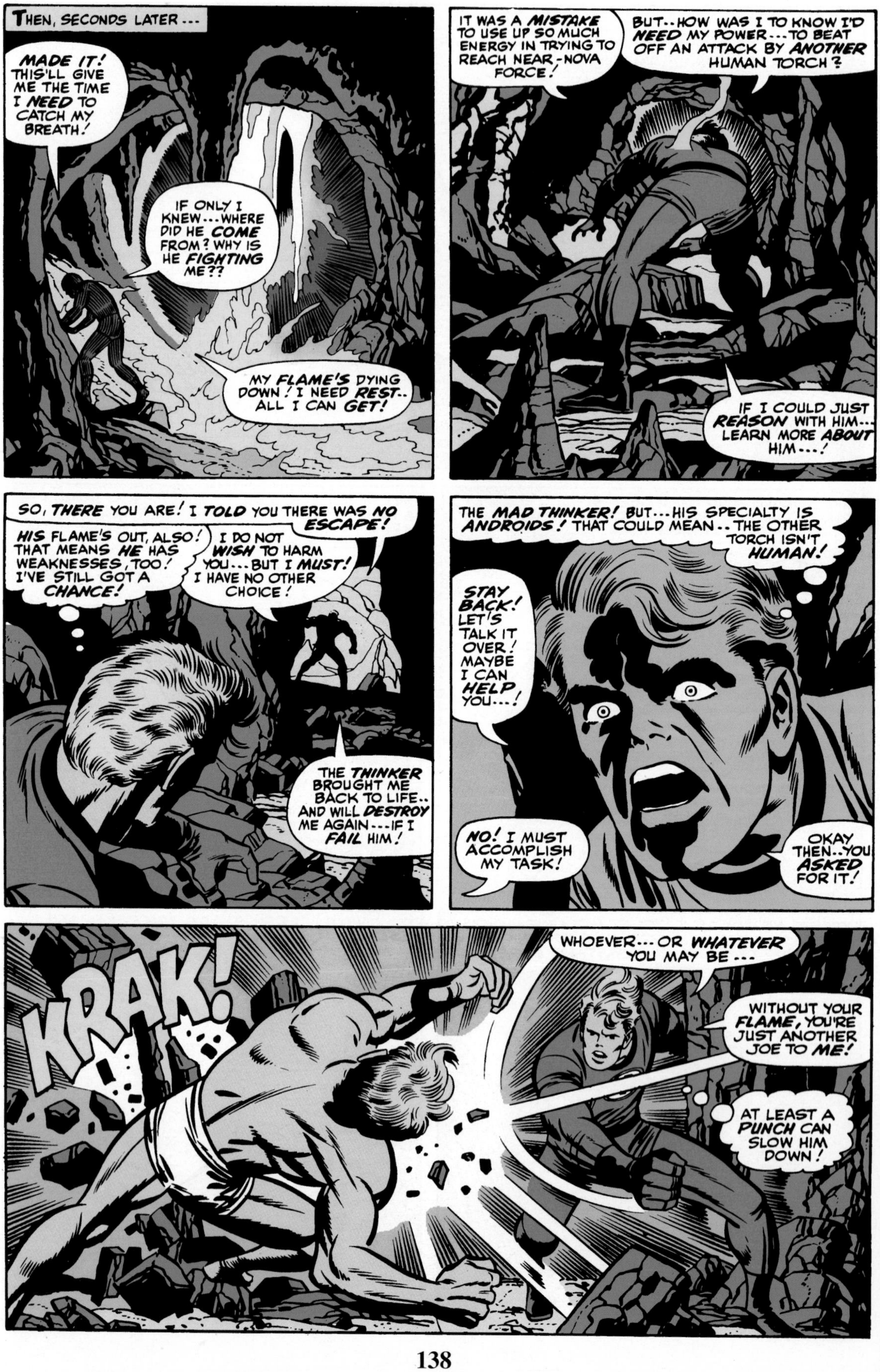

THEN, SECONDS LATER ...
MADE IT! THIS'LL GIVE ME THE TIME I NEED TO CATCH MY BREATH!
IF ONLY I KNEW... WHERE DID HE COME FROM? WHY IS HE FIGHTING ME??
MY FLAME'S DYING DOWN! I NEED REST.. ALL I CAN GET!
IT WAS A MISTAKE TO USE UP SO MUCH ENERGY IN TRYING TO REACH NEAR-NOVA FORCE!
BUT.. HOW WAS I TO KNOW I'D NEED MY POWER... TO BEAT OFF AN ATTACK BY ANOTHER HUMAN TORCH?
IF I COULD JUST REASON WITH HIM... LEARN MORE ABOUT HIM...!
SO, THERE YOU ARE! I TOLD YOU THERE WAS NO ESCAPE!
HIS FLAME'S OUT, ALSO! THAT MEANS HE HAS WEAKNESSES, TOO! I'VE STILL GOT A CHANCE!
I DO NOT WISH TO HARM YOU... BUT I MUST! I HAVE NO OTHER CHOICE!
THE THINKER BROUGHT ME BACK TO LIFE.. AND WILL DESTROY ME AGAIN... IF I FAIL HIM!
THE MAD THINKER! BUT... HIS SPECIALTY IS ANDROIDS! THAT COULD MEAN.. THE OTHER TORCH ISN'T HUMAN!
STAY BACK! LET'S TALK IT OVER! MAYBE I CAN HELP YOU...!
NO! I MUST ACCOMPLISH MY TASK!
OKAY THEN.. YOU ASKED FOR IT!
KRAK!
WHOEVER... OR WHATEVER YOU MAY BE ...
WITHOUT YOUR FLAME, YOU'RE JUST ANOTHER JOE TO ME!
AT LEAST A PUNCH CAN SLOW HIM DOWN!

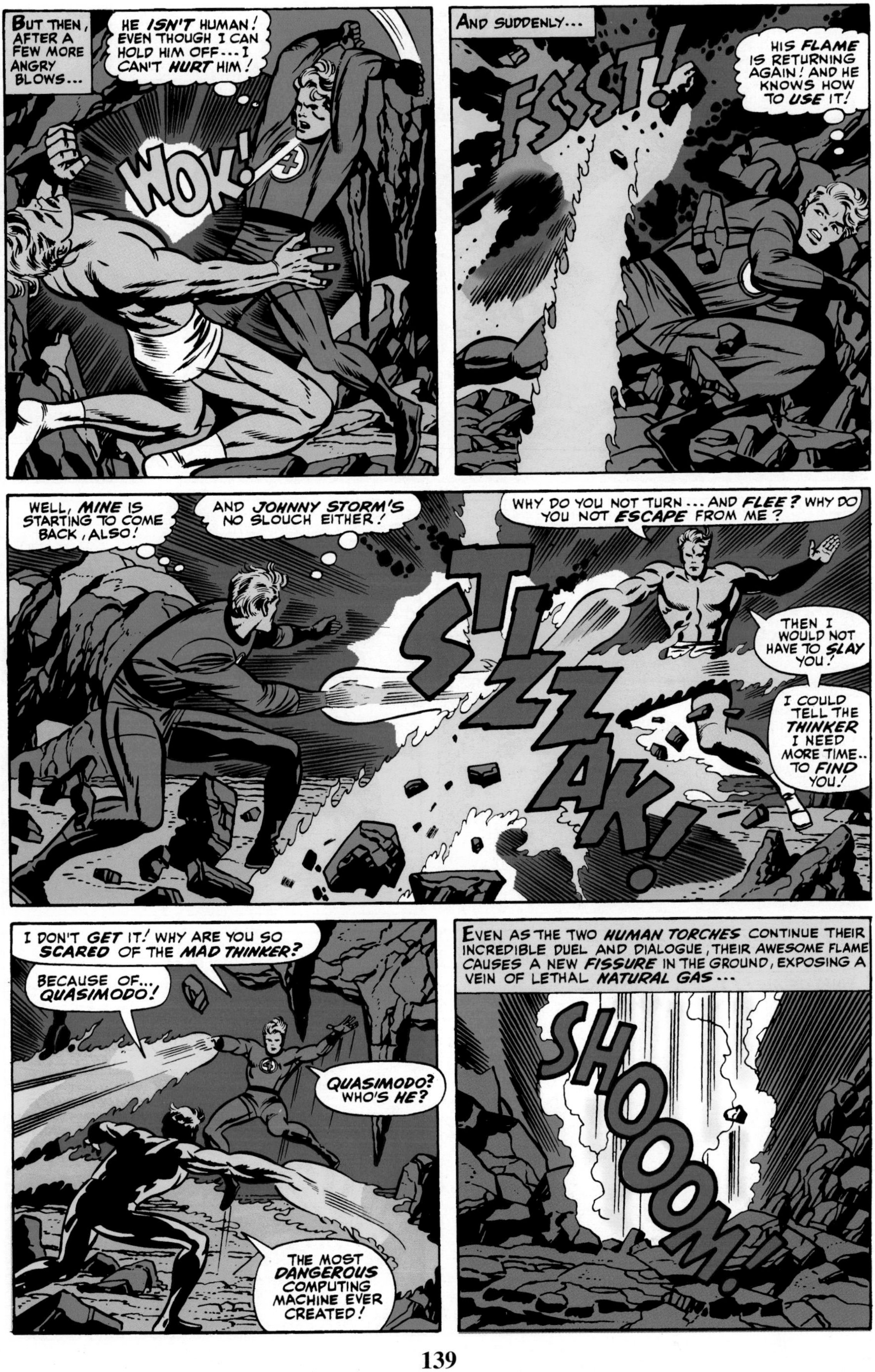

BUT THEN, AFTER A FEW MORE ANGRY BLOWS...
HE ISN'T HUMAN! EVEN THOUGH I CAN HOLD HIM OFF... I CAN'T HURT HIM!
WOK!
AND SUDDENLY...
FSSST!
HIS FLAME IS RETURNING AGAIN! AND HE KNOWS HOW TO USE IT!
WELL, MINE IS STARTING TO COME BACK, ALSO!
AND JOHNNY STORM'S NO SLOUCH EITHER!
WHY DO YOU NOT TURN... AND FLEE? WHY DO YOU NOT ESCAPE FROM ME?
STIZZAK!
THEN I WOULD NOT HAVE TO SLAY YOU!
I COULD TELL THE THINKER I NEED MORE TIME.. TO FIND YOU!
I DON'T GET IT! WHY ARE YOU SO SCARED OF THE MAD THINKER?
BECAUSE OF... QUASIMODO!
QUASIMODO? WHO'S HE?
THE MOST DANGEROUS COMPUTING MACHINE EVER CREATED!
EVEN AS THE TWO HUMAN TORCHES CONTINUE THEIR INCREDIBLE DUEL AND DIALOGUE, THEIR AWESOME FLAME CAUSES A NEW FISSURE IN THE GROUND, EXPOSING A VEIN OF LETHAL NATURAL GAS...
SHOOOM!!

A SPLIT-SECOND LATER, IGNITED BY THE HIGH-INTENSITY *HEAT*, THE GAS *EXPLODES* --- SHATTERING THE ENTIRE HILLSIDE..!

BAROOM!

WHILE, AT HIS HIDDEN LAB, MILES FROM THE SCENE, THE *MAD THINKER* CRIES OUT IN FRUSTRATION ---

THE EXPLOSION DISLOCATED MY *MONITORING DEVICE!* NOW, I CAN'T TELL WHAT HAPPENED TO THE *TORCH!*

BUT, I *MUST* KNOW! I CANNOT BE LEFT IN THE DARK *NOW!*

CLICK!

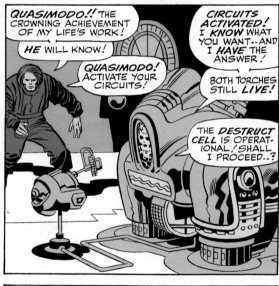

QUASIMODO!! THE CROWNING ACHIEVEMENT OF MY LIFE'S WORK!

HE WILL KNOW!

QUASIMODO! ACTIVATE YOUR CIRCUITS!

CIRCUITS ACTIVATED! I *KNOW* WHAT YOU WANT--AND I *HAVE* THE ANSWER!

BOTH TORCHES STILL *LIVE!*

THE *DESTRUCT CELL* IS OPERATIONAL! SHALL I PROCEED..?

NO! NOT *YET!* WE MUST GIVE THE FLAMING *ANDROID* A LITTLE MORE TIME BEFORE WE *DESTROY* HIM!

WHAT OF *ME*?? I COULD SERVE YOU *BETTER* THAN HE!

I'VE TOLD YOU A *THOUSAND TIMES* --- I *WILL NOT* PUT YOU IN HUMAN FORM! I HAVE ALLOWED YOUR *ELECTRONS* TO SHAPE THEMSELVES IN THE FORM OF A *FACE*.. BUT THAT IS *ALL!*

YOU ARE MY GREATEST COMPUTER --- BUT YOU ARE A *MACHINE* --- AND A MACHINE YOU SHALL *REMAIN!*

MY GREATEST MISTAKE WAS GIVING YOU A *NAME!* I SHOULD MERELY HAVE REFERRED TO YOU AS A *QUASI-MOTIVATIONAL DESTRUCT ORGAN*, INSTEAD OF SHORTENING IT TO *QUASIMODO!*

YOU MUST *STOP* THINKING OF YOURSELF AS A *PERSON!* I COMMAND IT!

BUT, I CAN *REASON*..I CAN *COMPUTE*..I CAN *FEEL*---

WHY MUST I BE *IMPRISONED* WITHIN THIS METAL SHELL? I WANT TO *MOVE*...TO BE *FREE*..!

13

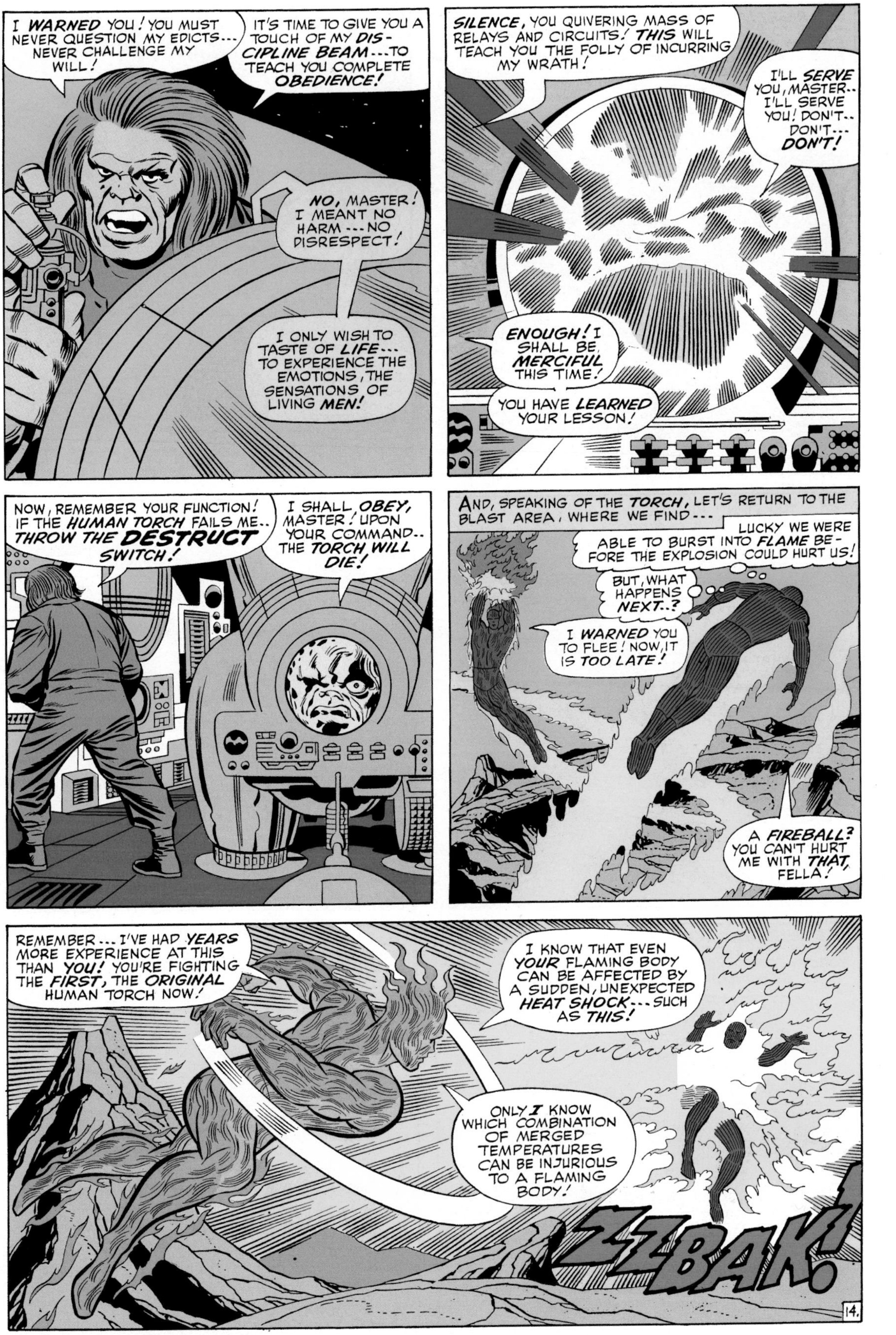
I WARNED YOU! YOU MUST NEVER QUESTION MY EDICTS... NEVER CHALLENGE MY WILL!
IT'S TIME TO GIVE YOU A TOUCH OF MY DIS-CIPLINE BEAM---TO TEACH YOU COMPLETE OBEDIENCE!
NO, MASTER! I MEANT NO HARM---NO DISRESPECT!
I ONLY WISH TO TASTE OF LIFE--- TO EXPERIENCE THE EMOTIONS, THE SENSATIONS OF LIVING MEN!
SILENCE, YOU QUIVERING MASS OF RELAYS AND CIRCUITS! THIS WILL TEACH YOU THE FOLLY OF INCURRING MY WRATH!
I'LL SERVE YOU, MASTER.. I'LL SERVE YOU! DON'T.. DON'T... DON'T!
ENOUGH! I SHALL BE MERCIFUL THIS TIME!
YOU HAVE LEARNED YOUR LESSON!
NOW, REMEMBER YOUR FUNCTION! IF THE HUMAN TORCH FAILS ME.. THROW THE DESTRUCT SWITCH!
I SHALL OBEY, MASTER! UPON YOUR COMMAND.. THE TORCH WILL DIE!
AND, SPEAKING OF THE TORCH, LET'S RETURN TO THE BLAST AREA, WHERE WE FIND---
LUCKY WE WERE ABLE TO BURST INTO FLAME BE-FORE THE EXPLOSION COULD HURT US!
BUT, WHAT HAPPENS NEXT..?
I WARNED YOU TO FLEE! NOW, IT IS TOO LATE!
A FIREBALL? YOU CAN'T HURT ME WITH THAT, FELLA!
REMEMBER... I'VE HAD YEARS MORE EXPERIENCE AT THIS THAN YOU! YOU'RE FIGHTING THE FIRST, THE ORIGINAL HUMAN TORCH NOW!
I KNOW THAT EVEN YOUR FLAMING BODY CAN BE AFFECTED BY A SUDDEN, UNEXPECTED HEAT SHOCK--- SUCH AS THIS!
ONLY I KNOW WHICH COMBINATION OF MERGED TEMPERATURES CAN BE INJURIOUS TO A FLAMING BODY!
ZZBAK!
14.

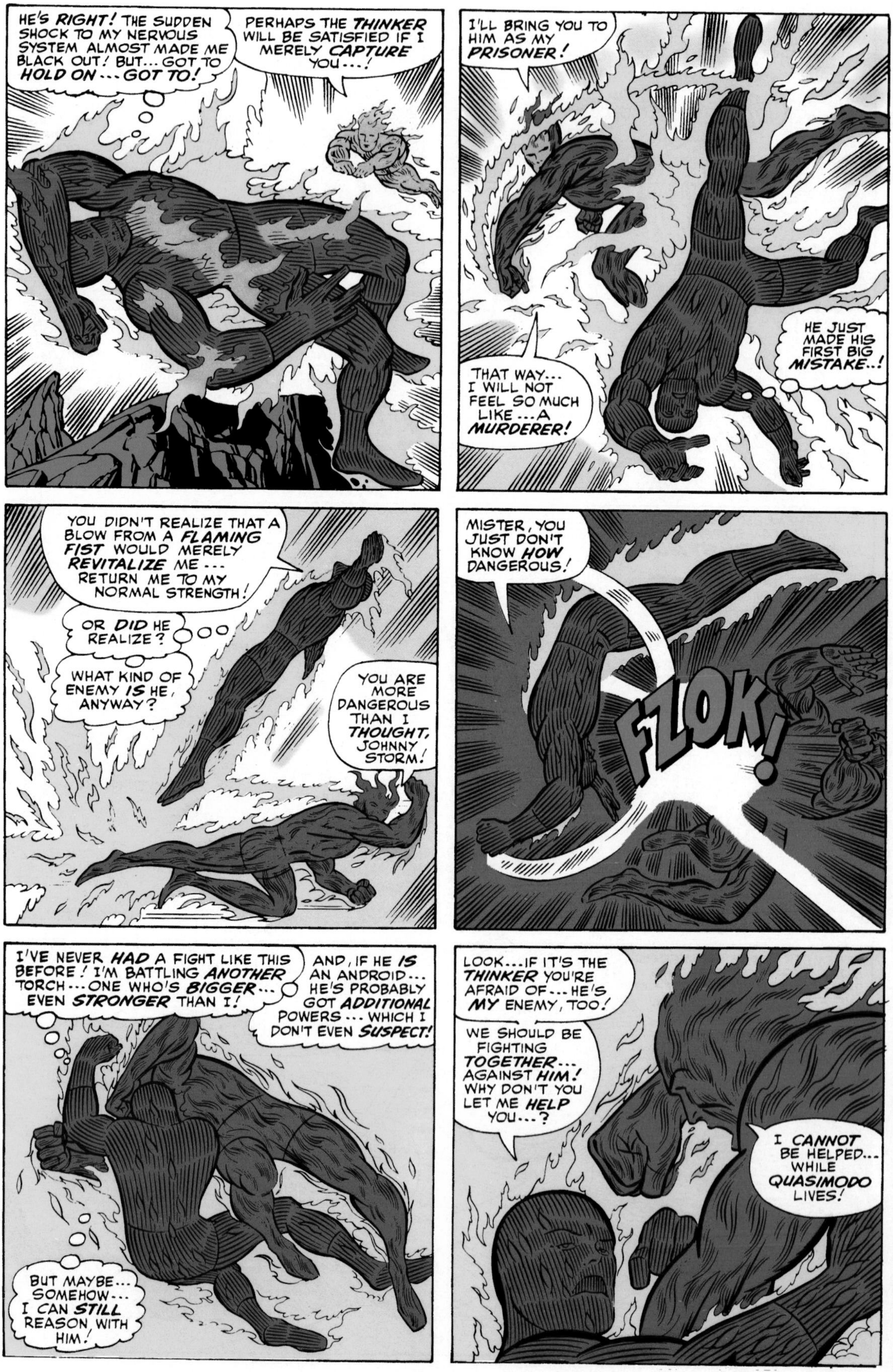
HE'S RIGHT! THE SUDDEN SHOCK TO MY NERVOUS SYSTEM ALMOST MADE ME BLACK OUT! BUT... GOT TO HOLD ON... GOT TO!
PERHAPS THE THINKER WILL BE SATISFIED IF I MERELY CAPTURE YOU...!
I'LL BRING YOU TO HIM AS MY PRISONER!
THAT WAY... I WILL NOT FEEL SO MUCH LIKE... A MURDERER!
HE JUST MADE HIS FIRST BIG MISTAKE..!
YOU DIDN'T REALIZE THAT A BLOW FROM A FLAMING FIST WOULD MERELY REVITALIZE ME... RETURN ME TO MY NORMAL STRENGTH!
OR DID HE REALIZE?
WHAT KIND OF ENEMY IS HE, ANYWAY?
YOU ARE MORE DANGEROUS THAN I THOUGHT, JOHNNY STORM!
MISTER, YOU JUST DON'T KNOW HOW DANGEROUS!
FZOK!
I'VE NEVER HAD A FIGHT LIKE THIS BEFORE! I'M BATTLING ANOTHER TORCH... ONE WHO'S BIGGER... EVEN STRONGER THAN I!
AND, IF HE IS AN ANDROID... HE'S PROBABLY GOT ADDITIONAL POWERS... WHICH I DON'T EVEN SUSPECT!
BUT MAYBE... SOMEHOW... I CAN STILL REASON WITH HIM!
LOOK... IF IT'S THE THINKER YOU'RE AFRAID OF... HE'S MY ENEMY, TOO!
WE SHOULD BE FIGHTING TOGETHER... AGAINST HIM! WHY DON'T YOU LET ME HELP YOU...?
I CANNOT BE HELPED... WHILE QUASIMODO LIVES!

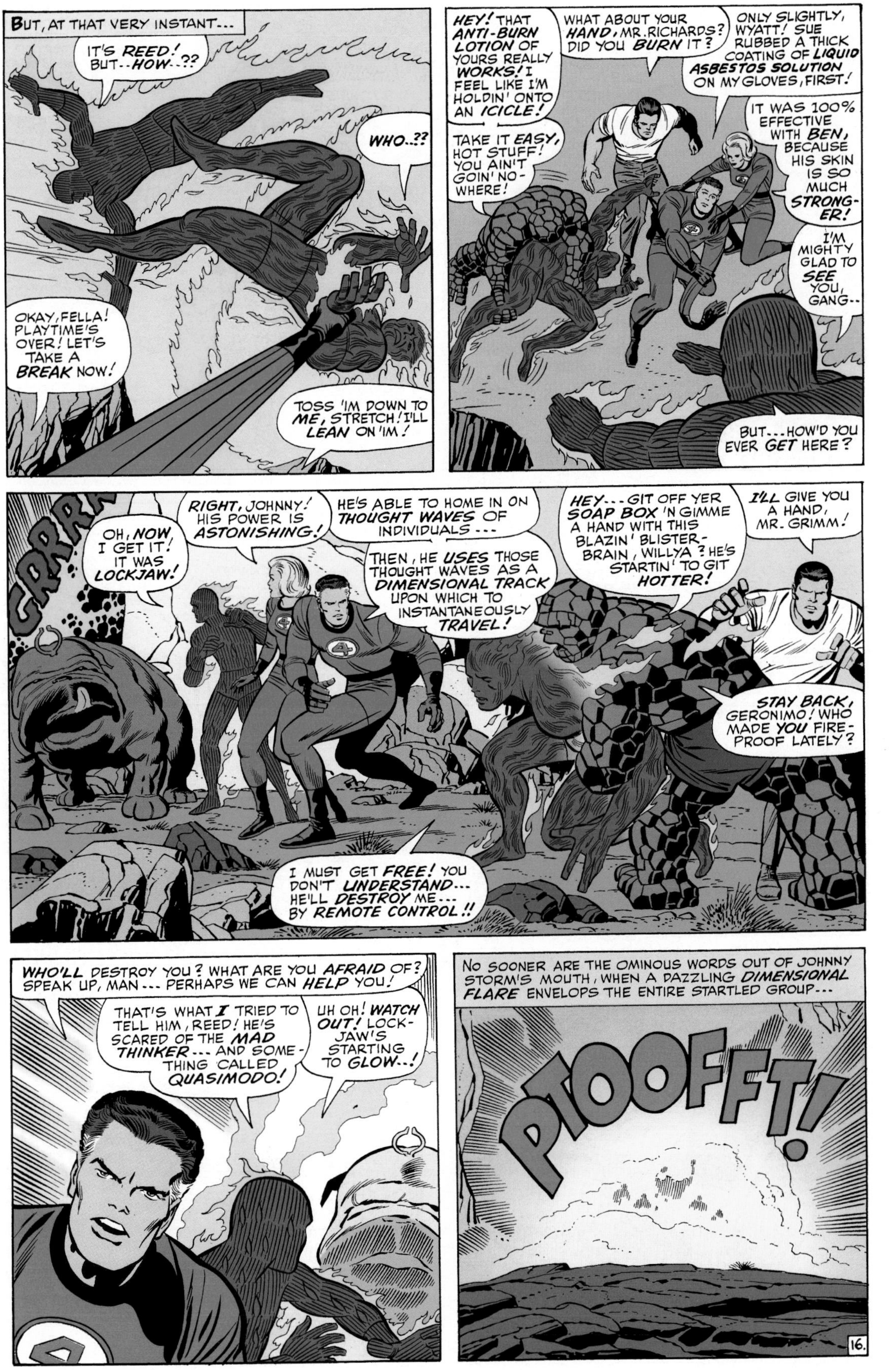
BUT, AT THAT VERY INSTANT...
IT'S REED! BUT--HOW--??
WHO..??
OKAY, FELLA! PLAYTIME'S OVER! LET'S TAKE A BREAK NOW!
TOSS 'IM DOWN TO ME, STRETCH! I'LL LEAN ON 'IM!
HEY! THAT ANTI-BURN LOTION OF YOURS REALLY WORKS! I FEEL LIKE I'M HOLDIN' ONTO AN ICICLE!
WHAT ABOUT YOUR HAND, MR. RICHARDS? DID YOU BURN IT?
ONLY SLIGHTLY, WYATT! SUE RUBBED A THICK COATING OF LIQUID ASBESTOS SOLUTION ON MY GLOVES, FIRST!
TAKE IT EASY, HOT STUFF! YOU AIN'T GOIN' NO-WHERE!
IT WAS 100% EFFECTIVE WITH BEN, BECAUSE HIS SKIN IS SO MUCH STRONGER!
I'M MIGHTY GLAD TO SEE YOU, GANG--
BUT...HOW'D YOU EVER GET HERE?
GRRRR
OH, NOW, I GET IT! IT WAS LOCKJAW!
RIGHT, JOHNNY! HIS POWER IS ASTONISHING!
HE'S ABLE TO HOME IN ON THOUGHT WAVES OF INDIVIDUALS ---
THEN, HE USES THOSE THOUGHT WAVES AS A DIMENSIONAL TRACK UPON WHICH TO INSTANTANEOUSLY TRAVEL!
HEY---GIT OFF YER SOAP BOX 'N GIMME A HAND WITH THIS BLAZIN' BLISTER-BRAIN, WILLYA? HE'S STARTIN' TO GIT HOTTER!
I'LL GIVE YOU A HAND, MR. GRIMM!
STAY BACK, GERONIMO! WHO MADE YOU FIRE-PROOF LATELY?
I MUST GET FREE! YOU DON'T UNDERSTAND--- HE'LL DESTROY ME--- BY REMOTE CONTROL!!
WHO'LL DESTROY YOU? WHAT ARE YOU AFRAID OF? SPEAK UP, MAN --- PERHAPS WE CAN HELP YOU!
THAT'S WHAT I TRIED TO TELL HIM, REED! HE'S SCARED OF THE MAD THINKER --- AND SOME-THING CALLED QUASIMODO!
UH OH! WATCH OUT! LOCK-JAW'S STARTING TO GLOW--!
NO SOONER ARE THE OMINOUS WORDS OUT OF JOHNNY STORM'S MOUTH, WHEN A DAZZLING DIMENSIONAL FLARE ENVELOPS THE ENTIRE STARTLED GROUP---
PTOOFFT!
16.

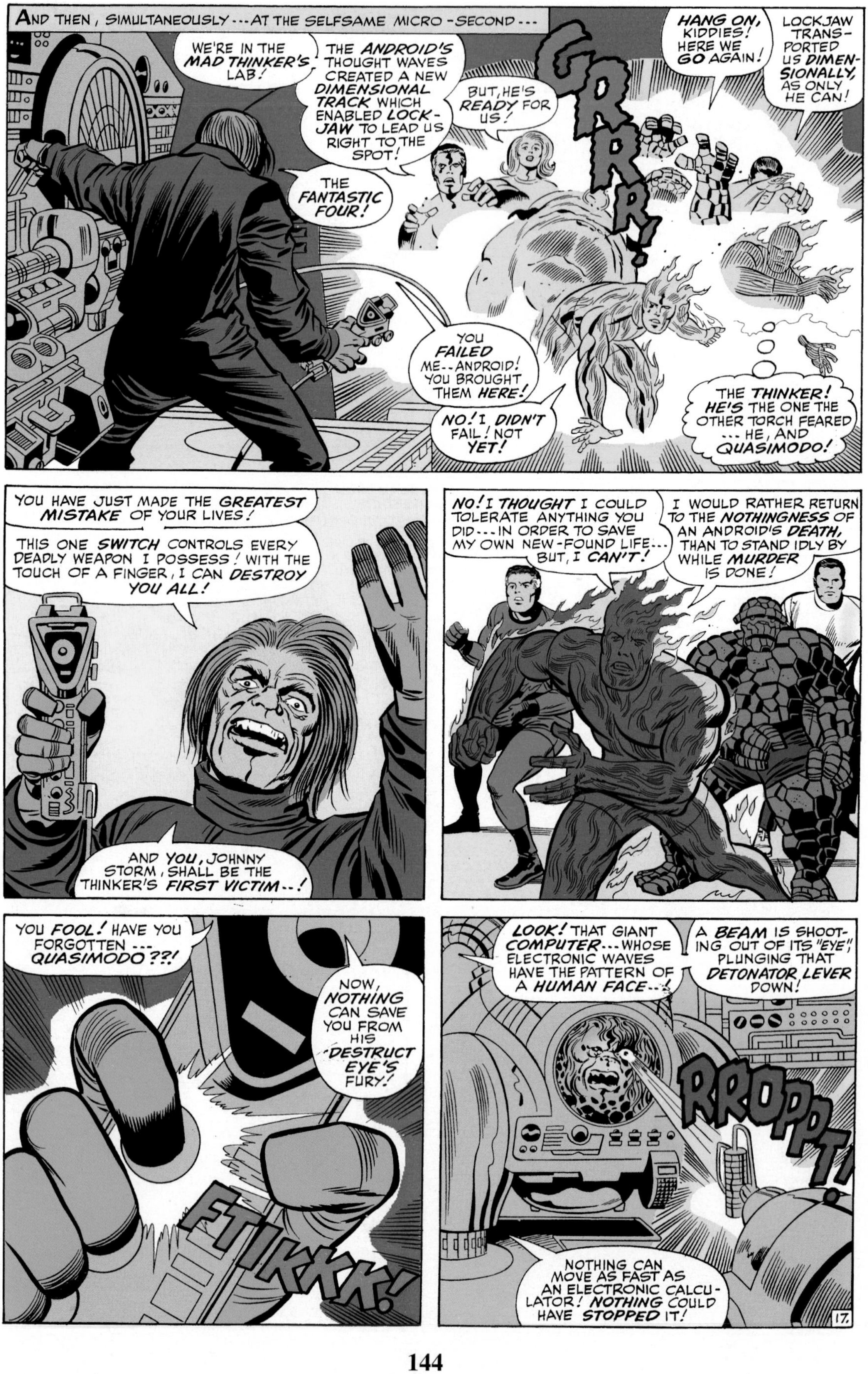
AND THEN, SIMULTANEOUSLY --- AT THE SELFSAME MICRO-SECOND ---
WE'RE IN THE MAD THINKER'S LAB!
THE ANDROID'S THOUGHT WAVES CREATED A NEW DIMENSIONAL TRACK WHICH ENABLED LOCK-JAW TO LEAD US RIGHT TO THE SPOT!
BUT, HE'S READY FOR US!
THE FANTASTIC FOUR!
GRRRR!
HANG ON, KIDDIES! HERE WE GO AGAIN!
LOCKJAW TRANS-PORTED US DIMEN-SIONALLY, AS ONLY HE CAN!
YOU FAILED ME--ANDROID! YOU BROUGHT THEM HERE!
NO! I DIDN'T FAIL! NOT YET!
THE THINKER! HE'S THE ONE THE OTHER TORCH FEARED --- HE, AND QUASIMODO!
YOU HAVE JUST MADE THE GREATEST MISTAKE OF YOUR LIVES!
THIS ONE SWITCH CONTROLS EVERY DEADLY WEAPON I POSSESS! WITH THE TOUCH OF A FINGER, I CAN DESTROY YOU ALL!
AND YOU, JOHNNY STORM, SHALL BE THE THINKER'S FIRST VICTIM--!
NO! I THOUGHT I COULD TOLERATE ANYTHING YOU DID---IN ORDER TO SAVE MY OWN NEW-FOUND LIFE--- BUT, I CAN'T!
I WOULD RATHER RETURN TO THE NOTHINGNESS OF AN ANDROID'S DEATH, THAN TO STAND IDLY BY WHILE MURDER IS DONE!
YOU FOOL! HAVE YOU FORGOTTEN --- QUASIMODO??!
NOW, NOTHING CAN SAVE YOU FROM HIS DESTRUCT EYE'S FURY!
FTIKKK!
LOOK! THAT GIANT COMPUTER --- WHOSE ELECTRONIC WAVES HAVE THE PATTERN OF A HUMAN FACE--!
A BEAM IS SHOOT-ING OUT OF ITS "EYE", PLUNGING THAT DETONATOR LEVER DOWN!
RROPPT!
NOTHING CAN MOVE AS FAST AS AN ELECTRONIC CALCU-LATOR! NOTHING COULD HAVE STOPPED IT!
17.

AT THE FIRST, FATAL TOUCH OF THE DEADLY *DESTRUCT BEAM*, AN INVISIBLE COATING OF PROTECTIVE *NITRO-GEN CELLS* WHICH THE MAD THINKER HAD PLACED ON THE ANDROID'S BODY IS INSTANTLY *DISSOLVED---!*

HE'S BEING AFFECTED BY THE HEAT OF HIS *OWN* FLAME!

HE'S BLAZING *BEYOND* CONTROL!

IT'S THE ONE *INFALLIBLE* METHOD OF *DESTROYING* A FLAMING ANDROID!

IS THERE... IS THERE *NOTHING* WE CAN DO TO HELP HIM??

IT'S TOO LATE FOR THE *ANDROID*... BUT WE'VE GOT TO GET THE *MAD THINKER* BEFORE HE CAN ESCAPE!

LET *ME* HAVE FIRST CRACK AT HIM ---YOU ALL *OWE* ME THAT MUCH!

HURRY! HE'S TRYING TO SEAL HIMSELF INTO THAT *CHAMBER!*

OUTTA THE WAY! I'M GONNA *CLOBBER* THE BUM!

TOO LATE! IT'S SOME SORT OF *AQUA CHAMBER!* EVEN THE *TORCH* CAN'T BURN THROUGH! HE'S GETTING *AWAY!*

NOT FER *LONG!* NOW THAT WE KNOW THE CREEP IS STILL *ALIVE,* STRETCHO'LL FIND *SOME* WAY TO PICK UP HIS *TRAIL* AGAIN!

HE BROUGHT THE ORIGINAL *TORCH* BACK TO DEFEAT ME---

I WONDER IF HE KNOWS SOME *OTHER* WAY TO REVIVE HIM *AGAIN??*

SPLOOOOSH!

THEY'RE *TOO DANGEROUS!* I'VE GOT TO GET AWAY WHILE I *CAN!* BUT...THEY HAVEN'T HEARD THE *LAST* OF ME YET!

WITH THE *MAD THINKER* STILL ON THE LOOSE, WE CAN'T RELAX FOR A *MINUTE!*

YA GOT THAT *BACKWARDS,* TORCHY! WITH *US* ON THE LOOSE, HE BETTER GO FIND HIMSELF THE NEAREST *HOLE,* 'N DIVE *IN!*

BUT, WHAT OF THE *ANDROID?*

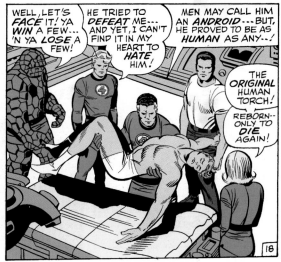

WELL, LET'S *FACE IT!* YA *WIN* A FEW... 'N YA *LOSE* A FEW!

HE TRIED TO *DEFEAT* ME--- AND YET, I CAN'T FIND IT IN MY HEART TO *HATE* HIM!

MEN MAY CALL HIM AN *ANDROID*---BUT, HE PROVED TO BE AS *HUMAN* AS ANY---!

THE *ORIGINAL HUMAN TORCH!* REBORN-- ONLY TO *DIE* AGAIN!

18

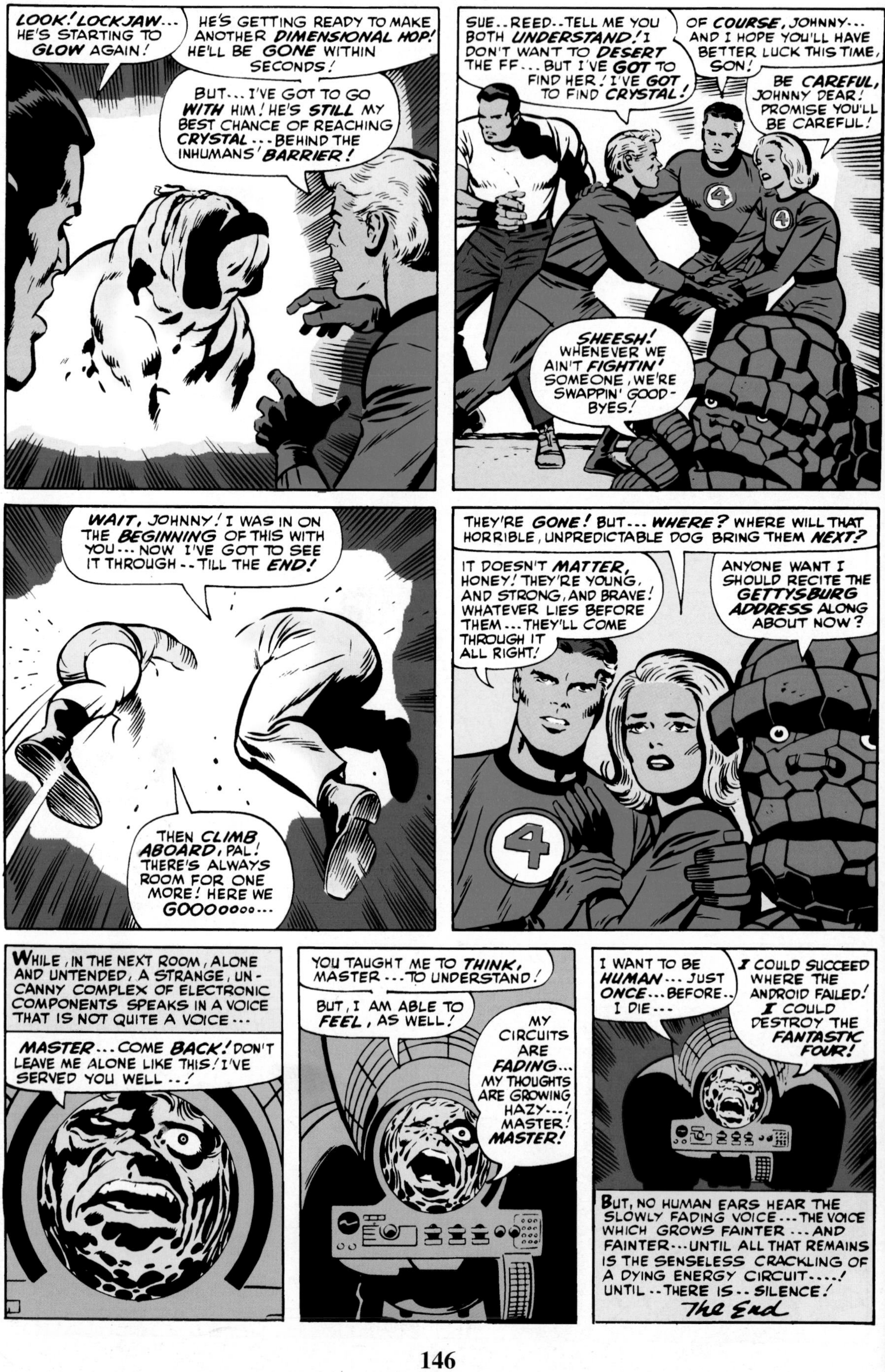
LOOK! LOCKJAW... HE'S STARTING TO GLOW AGAIN!
HE'S GETTING READY TO MAKE ANOTHER DIMENSIONAL HOP! HE'LL BE GONE WITHIN SECONDS!
BUT... I'VE GOT TO GO WITH HIM! HE'S STILL MY BEST CHANCE OF REACHING CRYSTAL... BEHIND THE INHUMANS' BARRIER!
SUE.. REED.. TELL ME YOU BOTH UNDERSTAND! I DON'T WANT TO DESERT THE FF... BUT I'VE GOT TO FIND HER! I'VE GOT TO FIND CRYSTAL!
OF COURSE, JOHNNY... AND I HOPE YOU'LL HAVE BETTER LUCK THIS TIME, SON!
BE CAREFUL, JOHNNY DEAR! PROMISE YOU'LL BE CAREFUL!
SHEESH! WHENEVER WE AIN'T FIGHTIN' SOMEONE, WE'RE SWAPPIN' GOOD-BYES!
WAIT, JOHNNY! I WAS IN ON THE BEGINNING OF THIS WITH YOU... NOW I'VE GOT TO SEE IT THROUGH.. TILL THE END!
THEN CLIMB ABOARD, PAL! THERE'S ALWAYS ROOM FOR ONE MORE! HERE WE GOOOOooo...
THEY'RE GONE! BUT... WHERE? WHERE WILL THAT HORRIBLE, UNPREDICTABLE DOG BRING THEM NEXT?
IT DOESN'T MATTER, HONEY! THEY'RE YOUNG, AND STRONG, AND BRAVE! WHATEVER LIES BEFORE THEM... THEY'LL COME THROUGH IT ALL RIGHT!
ANYONE WANT I SHOULD RECITE THE GETTYSBURG ADDRESS ALONG ABOUT NOW?
WHILE, IN THE NEXT ROOM, ALONE AND UNTENDED, A STRANGE, UNCANNY COMPLEX OF ELECTRONIC COMPONENTS SPEAKS IN A VOICE THAT IS NOT QUITE A VOICE...
MASTER... COME BACK! DON'T LEAVE ME ALONE LIKE THIS! I'VE SERVED YOU WELL..!
YOU TAUGHT ME TO THINK, MASTER... TO UNDERSTAND!
BUT, I AM ABLE TO FEEL, AS WELL!
MY CIRCUITS ARE FADING... MY THOUGHTS ARE GROWING HAZY...! MASTER! MASTER!
I WANT TO BE HUMAN... JUST ONCE... BEFORE.. I DIE...
I COULD SUCCEED WHERE THE ANDROID FAILED! I COULD DESTROY THE FANTASTIC FOUR!
BUT, NO HUMAN EARS HEAR THE SLOWLY FADING VOICE... THE VOICE WHICH GROWS FAINTER... AND FAINTER... UNTIL ALL THAT REMAINS IS THE SENSELESS CRACKLING OF A DYING ENERGY CIRCUIT....! UNTIL.. THERE IS.. SILENCE!
The End

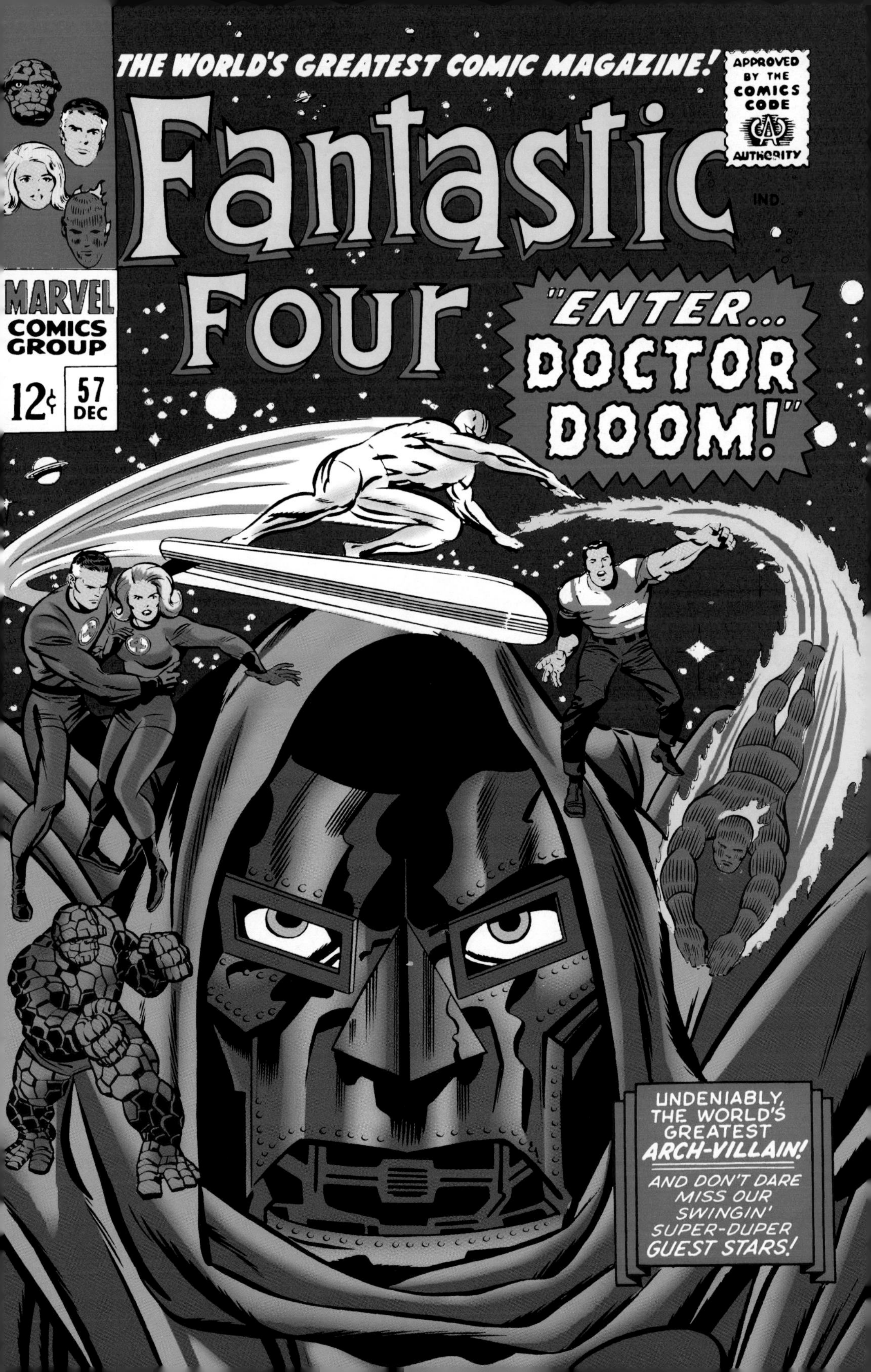

THE WORLD'S GREATEST COMIC MAGAZINE!
APPROVED BY THE COMICS CODE AUTHORITY
Fantastic Four
IND.
MARVEL COMICS GROUP
12¢
57 DEC
"ENTER... DOCTOR DOOM!"
UNDENIABLY, THE WORLD'S GREATEST ARCH-VILLAIN!
AND DON'T DARE MISS OUR SWINGIN' SUPER-DUPER GUEST STARS!

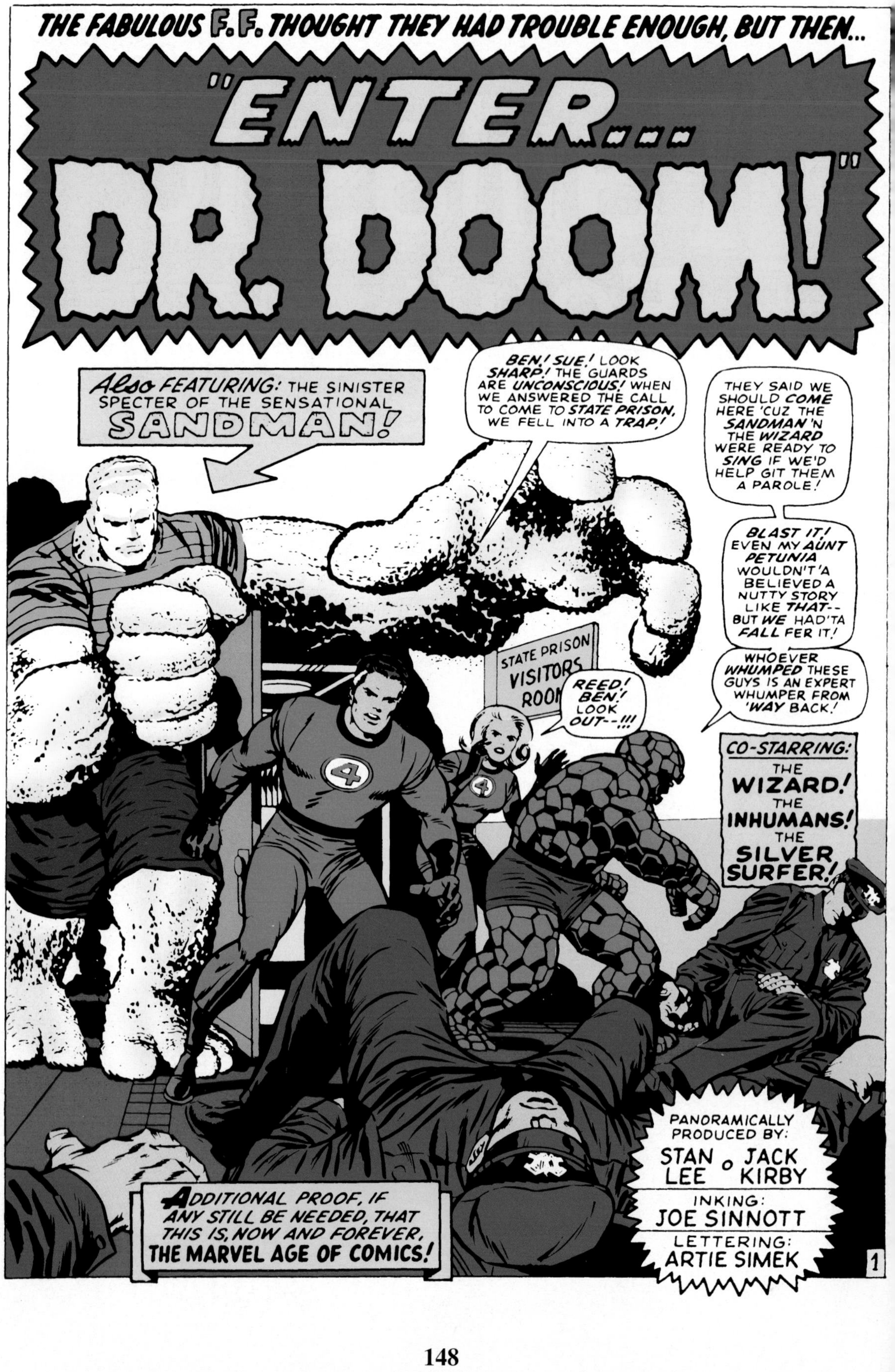
THE FABULOUS F.F. THOUGHT THEY HAD TROUBLE ENOUGH, BUT THEN...
"ENTER... DR. DOOM!"
ALSO FEATURING: THE SINISTER SPECTER OF THE SENSATIONAL SANDMAN!
BEN! SUE! LOOK SHARP! THE GUARDS ARE UNCONSCIOUS! WHEN WE ANSWERED THE CALL TO COME TO STATE PRISON, WE FELL INTO A TRAP!
THEY SAID WE SHOULD COME HERE 'CUZ THE SANDMAN 'N THE WIZARD WERE READY TO SING IF WE'D HELP GIT THEM A PAROLE!
BLAST IT! EVEN MY AUNT PETUNIA WOULDN'T'A BELIEVED A NUTTY STORY LIKE THAT-- BUT WE HAD'TA FALL FER IT!
WHOEVER WHUMPED THESE GUYS IS AN EXPERT WHUMPER FROM 'WAY BACK!
STATE PRISON VISITORS ROOM
REED! BEN! LOOK OUT--!!!
CO-STARRING: THE WIZARD! THE INHUMANS! THE SILVER SURFER!
ADDITIONAL PROOF, IF ANY STILL BE NEEDED, THAT THIS IS, NOW AND FOREVER, THE MARVEL AGE OF COMICS!
PANORAMICALLY PRODUCED BY: STAN LEE ° JACK KIRBY
INKING: JOE SINNOTT
LETTERING: ARTIE SIMEK
1

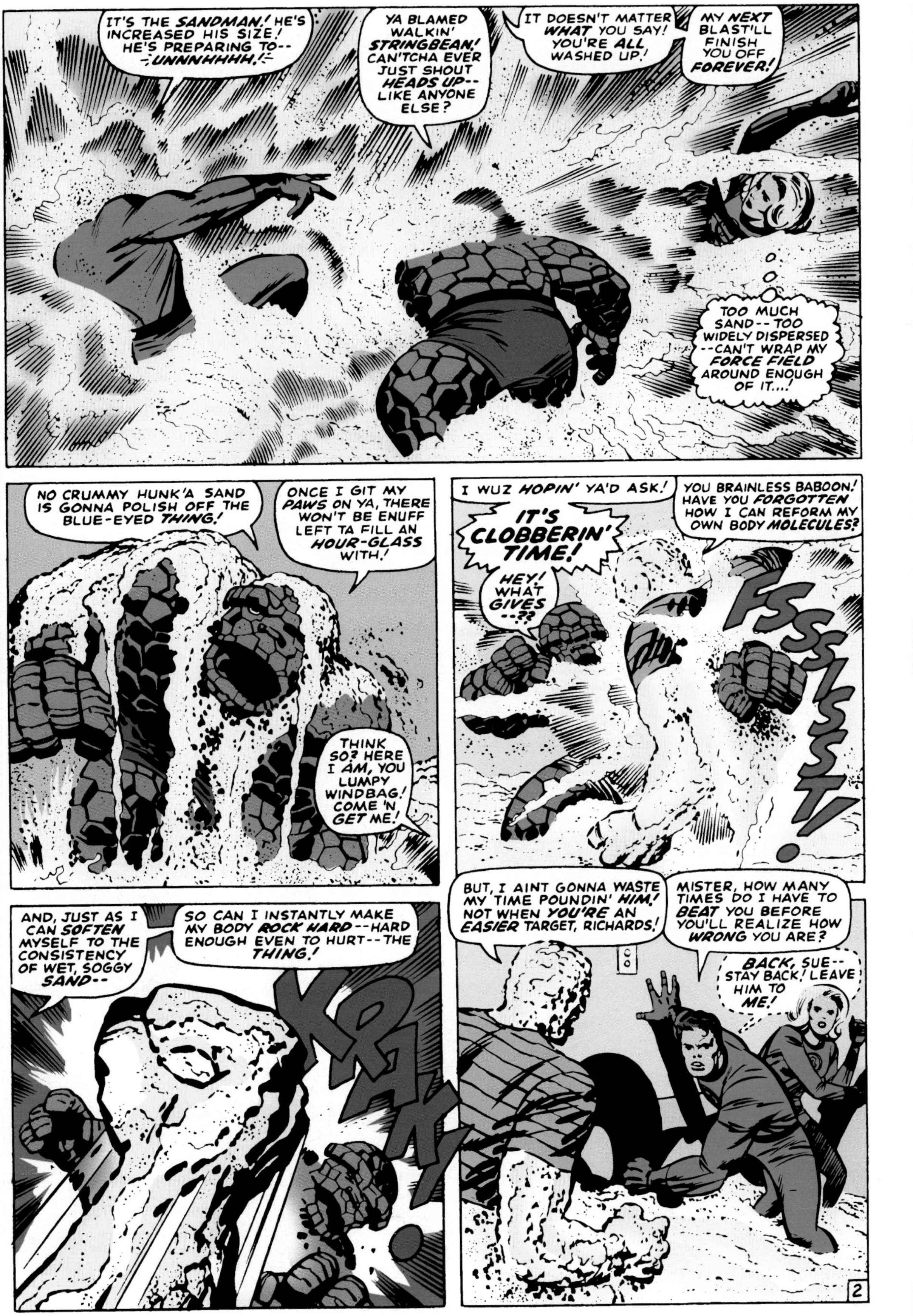
IT'S THE SANDMAN! HE'S INCREASED HIS SIZE! HE'S PREPARING TO-- -UNNNHHHH!-
YA BLAMED WALKIN' STRINGBEAN! CAN'TCHA EVER JUST SHOUT HEADS UP-- LIKE ANYONE ELSE?
IT DOESN'T MATTER WHAT YOU SAY! YOU'RE ALL WASHED UP!
MY NEXT BLAST'LL FINISH YOU OFF FOREVER!
TOO MUCH SAND-- TOO WIDELY DISPERSED --CAN'T WRAP MY FORCE FIELD AROUND ENOUGH OF IT...!
NO CRUMMY HUNK'A SAND IS GONNA POLISH OFF THE BLUE-EYED THING!
ONCE I GIT MY PAWS ON YA, THERE WON'T BE ENUFF LEFT TA FILL AN HOUR-GLASS WITH!
THINK SO? HERE I AM, YOU LUMPY WINDBAG! COME 'N GET ME!
I WUZ HOPIN' YA'D ASK!
IT'S CLOBBERIN' TIME!
HEY! WHAT GIVES --??
YOU BRAINLESS BABOON! HAVE YOU FORGOTTEN HOW I CAN REFORM MY OWN BODY MOLECULES?
FSSSSST!
AND, JUST AS I CAN SOFTEN MYSELF TO THE CONSISTENCY OF WET, SOGGY SAND--
SO CAN I INSTANTLY MAKE MY BODY ROCK HARD--HARD ENOUGH EVEN TO HURT--THE THING!
KRAKK
BUT, I AINT GONNA WASTE MY TIME POUNDIN' HIM! NOT WHEN YOU'RE AN EASIER TARGET, RICHARDS!
MISTER, HOW MANY TIMES DO I HAVE TO BEAT YOU BEFORE YOU'LL REALIZE HOW WRONG YOU ARE?
BACK, SUE-- STAY BACK! LEAVE HIM TO ME!
2

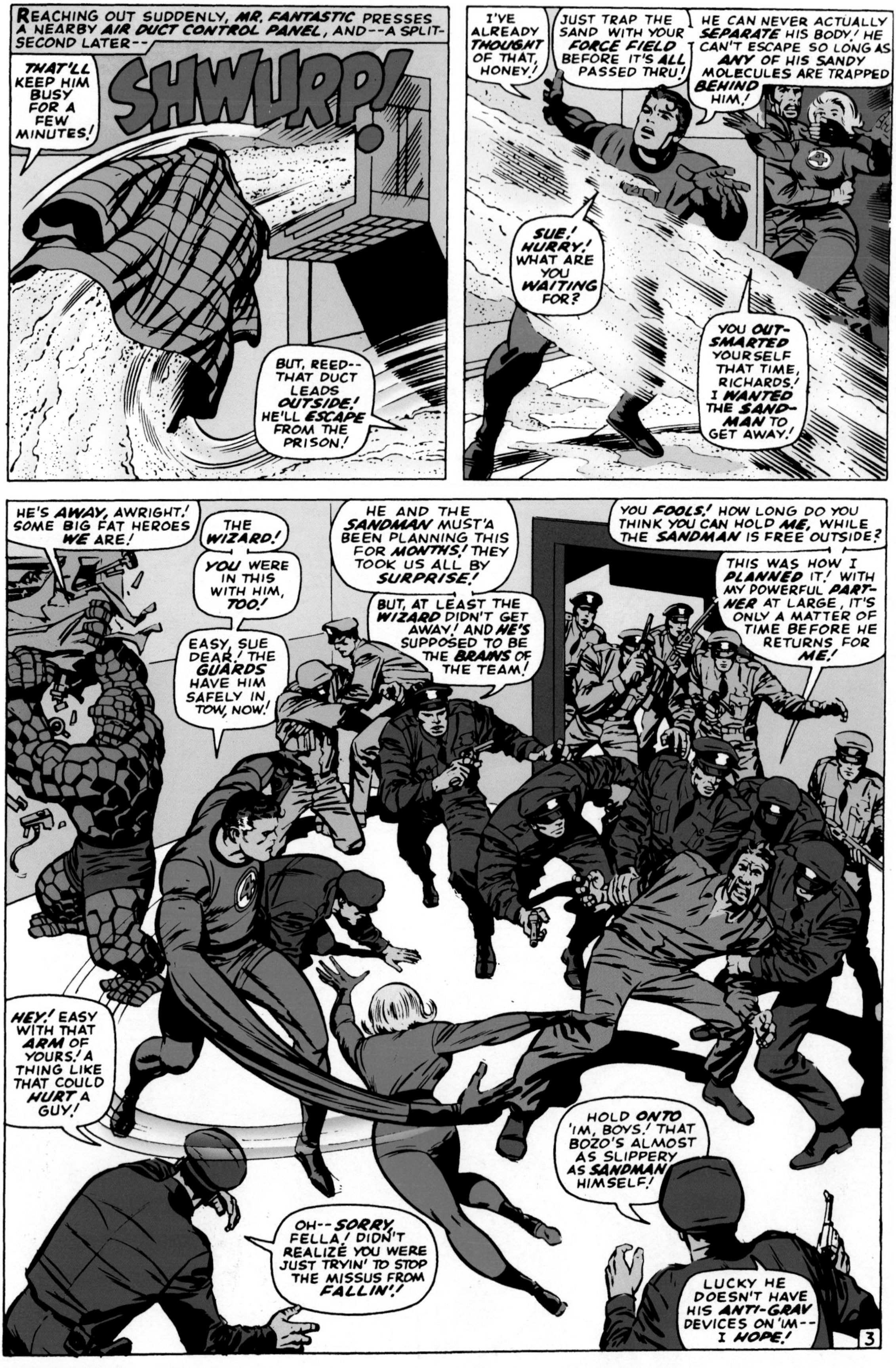
REACHING OUT SUDDENLY, MR. FANTASTIC PRESSES A NEARBY AIR DUCT CONTROL PANEL, AND--A SPLIT-SECOND LATER--
THAT'LL KEEP HIM BUSY FOR A FEW MINUTES!
SHWURP!
BUT, REED--THAT DUCT LEADS OUTSIDE! HE'LL ESCAPE FROM THE PRISON!
I'VE ALREADY THOUGHT OF THAT, HONEY!
JUST TRAP THE SAND WITH YOUR FORCE FIELD BEFORE IT'S ALL PASSED THRU!
HE CAN NEVER ACTUALLY SEPARATE HIS BODY! HE CAN'T ESCAPE SO LONG AS ANY OF HIS SANDY MOLECULES ARE TRAPPED BEHIND HIM!
SUE! HURRY! WHAT ARE YOU WAITING FOR?
YOU OUT-SMARTED YOURSELF THAT TIME, RICHARDS! I WANTED THE SAND-MAN TO GET AWAY!
HE'S AWAY, AWRIGHT! SOME BIG FAT HEROES WE ARE!
THE WIZARD!
YOU WERE IN THIS WITH HIM, TOO!
EASY, SUE DEAR! THE GUARDS HAVE HIM SAFELY IN TOW, NOW!
HE AND THE SANDMAN MUST'A BEEN PLANNING THIS FOR MONTHS! THEY TOOK US ALL BY SURPRISE!
BUT, AT LEAST THE WIZARD DIDN'T GET AWAY! AND HE'S SUPPOSED TO BE THE BRAINS OF THE TEAM!
YOU FOOLS! HOW LONG DO YOU THINK YOU CAN HOLD ME, WHILE THE SANDMAN IS FREE OUTSIDE?
THIS WAS HOW I PLANNED IT! WITH MY POWERFUL PARTNER AT LARGE, IT'S ONLY A MATTER OF TIME BEFORE HE RETURNS FOR ME!
HEY! EASY WITH THAT ARM OF YOURS! A THING LIKE THAT COULD HURT A GUY!
OH--SORRY, FELLA! DIDN'T REALIZE YOU WERE JUST TRYIN' TO STOP THE MISSUS FROM FALLIN'!
HOLD ONTO 'IM, BOYS! THAT BOZO'S ALMOST AS SLIPPERY AS SANDMAN HIMSELF!
LUCKY HE DOESN'T HAVE HIS ANTI-GRAV DEVICES ON 'IM--I HOPE!
3

CHLOROFORM CAPSULES--TAPED TO HIS WRIST!

SO, THAT'S HOW YOU MANAGED TO KNOCK OUT THE GUARDS!

PUH-LEESE--NO APPLAUSE! IT WAS SIMPLICITY ITSELF TO FEIGN ILLNESS, AND THEN TO POCKET THESE CAPSULES WHEN I WAS TAKEN TO THE DISPENSARY!

SURELY, YOU REALIZE BY NOW--NOT FOR NOTHING AM I CALLED --THE WIZARD!

YOU'RE SMART, ALL RIGHT! SO SMART THAT YOU'VE SPENT HALF YOUR WORTH-LESS LIFE BEHIND BARS!

REED, DARLING--JOHNNY IS STILL SEARCHING FOR THE INHUMANS--WE NEVER KNOW WHEN THE SILVER SURFER WILL RETURN--THE MYSTERY OF SUB-SPACE IS ALWAYS BECKONING--AND NOW THIS-- OLD MENACES, THREATENING US ANEW!

FORGET IT, SUSIE! AFTER A GUY LIKE GALACTUS, THESE TWO CRUMBS DON'T HARDLY RATE!

BUT--GALACTUS IS GONE--AND, THEY'RE STILL HERE!

SINCE THE NEWLY-WEDDED MRS. RICHARDS SEEMS TO BE THE WORRYING TYPE, PERHAPS IT'S FORTUNATE THAT SHE IS UNAWARE OF ANOTHER MENACE WHICH IS SHORTLY TO APPEAR ON THE SCENE--POSSIBLY THE MOST FEARSOME MENACE OF ALL--

SHOOM!

IN FAR-OFF LATVERIA, ONE OF THE LAST REMAINING ABSOLUTE MONARCHIES, AN ATO-MISSILE IS LAUNCHED FROM ATOP THE ROYAL CASTLE--

WITH UNFAILING PRECISION, THE TINY, JEWEL-LIKE, ATOMIC-POWERED ROCKET HOMES IN ON ITS HUMAN TARGET--

A MESSAGE-BEARING CYLINDER HURTLING TO ME FROM THE CASTLE, YONDER!

--DELICATELY PROGRAMMED TO MAKE A PIN-POINT LANDING RIGHT AT THE FEET OF THE SILVER SURFER!

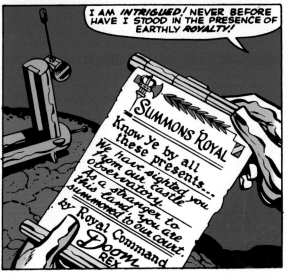

I AM INTRIGUED! NEVER BEFORE HAVE I STOOD IN THE PRESENCE OF EARTHLY ROYALTY!

SUMMONS ROYAL

Know ye by all these presents-- We have sighted you from our castle observatory. As a stranger to this land you are summoned to our court.

by Royal Command
DOOM REX

THUS, A MEETING IS ABOUT TO TAKE PLACE-- A MEETING WHICH IS DESTINED TO HAVE THE GRAVEST EFFECT UPON THE CAREERS--THE VERY LIVES--OF THE FANTASTIC FOUR--!

4

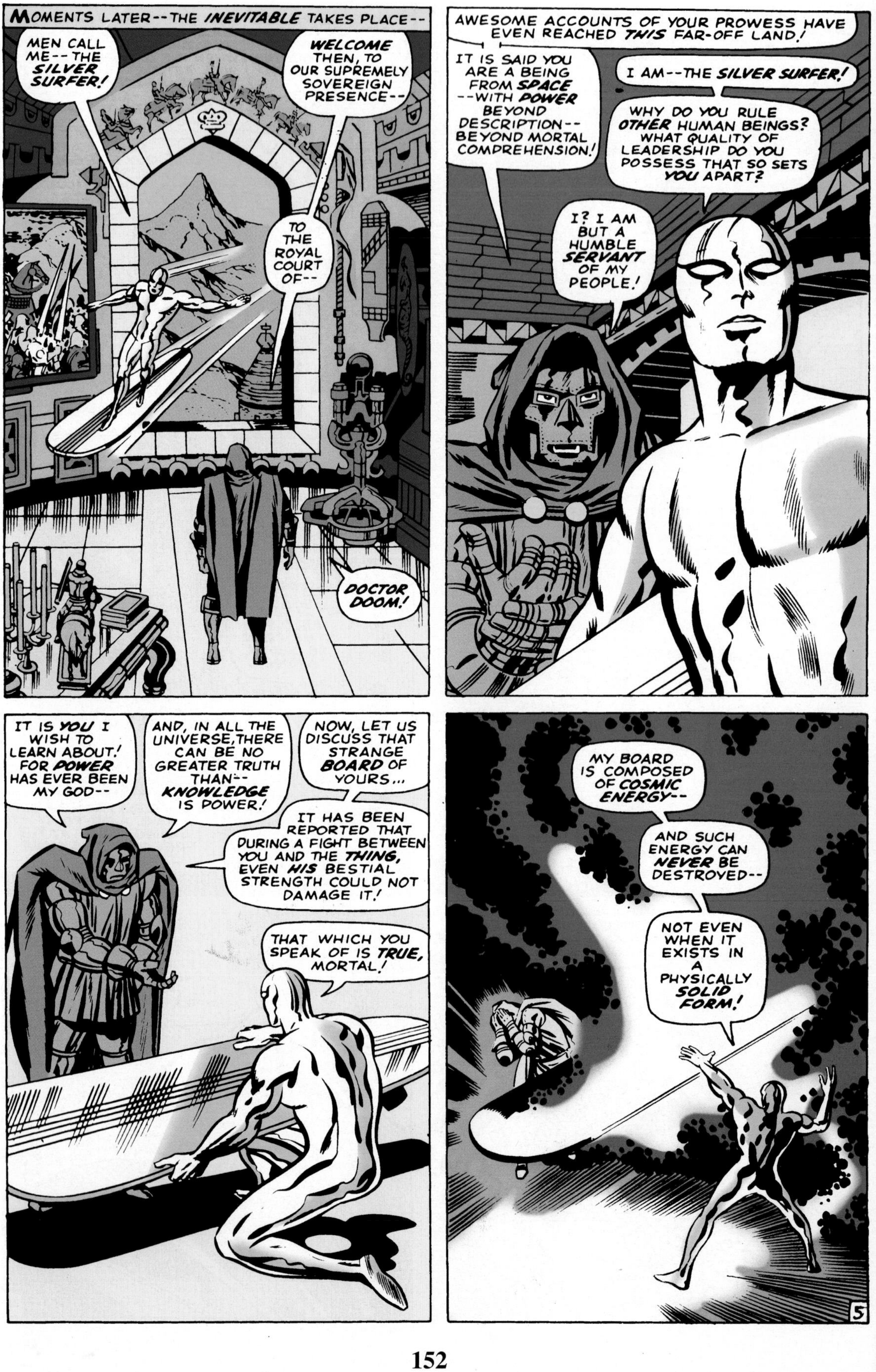

MOMENTS LATER--THE INEVITABLE TAKES PLACE--
MEN CALL ME--THE SILVER SURFER!
WELCOME THEN, TO OUR SUPREMELY SOVEREIGN PRESENCE--
TO THE ROYAL COURT OF--
DOCTOR DOOM!
AWESOME ACCOUNTS OF YOUR PROWESS HAVE EVEN REACHED THIS FAR-OFF LAND!
IT IS SAID YOU ARE A BEING FROM SPACE --WITH POWER BEYOND DESCRIPTION--BEYOND MORTAL COMPREHENSION!
I AM--THE SILVER SURFER!
WHY DO YOU RULE OTHER HUMAN BEINGS? WHAT QUALITY OF LEADERSHIP DO YOU POSSESS THAT SO SETS YOU APART?
I? I AM BUT A HUMBLE SERVANT OF MY PEOPLE!
IT IS YOU I WISH TO LEARN ABOUT! FOR POWER HAS EVER BEEN MY GOD--
AND, IN ALL THE UNIVERSE, THERE CAN BE NO GREATER TRUTH THAN--KNOWLEDGE IS POWER!
NOW, LET US DISCUSS THAT STRANGE BOARD OF YOURS...
IT HAS BEEN REPORTED THAT DURING A FIGHT BETWEEN YOU AND THE THING, EVEN HIS BESTIAL STRENGTH COULD NOT DAMAGE IT!
THAT WHICH YOU SPEAK OF IS TRUE, MORTAL!
MY BOARD IS COMPOSED OF COSMIC ENERGY--
AND SUCH ENERGY CAN NEVER BE DESTROYED--
NOT EVEN WHEN IT EXISTS IN A PHYSICALLY SOLID FORM!
5

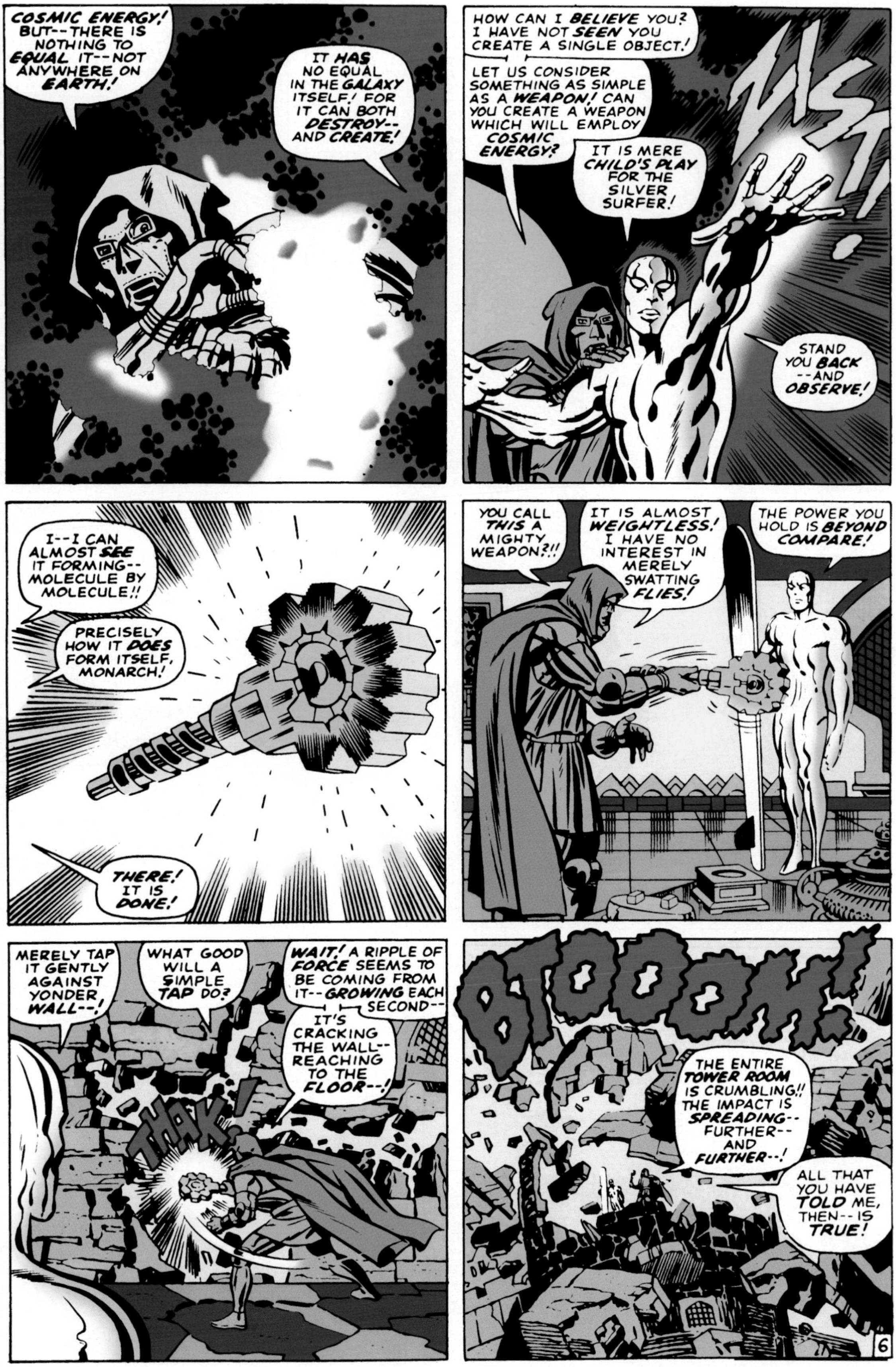

COSMIC ENERGY! BUT--THERE IS NOTHING TO EQUAL IT--NOT ANYWHERE ON EARTH!
IT HAS NO EQUAL IN THE GALAXY ITSELF! FOR IT CAN BOTH DESTROY--AND CREATE!
HOW CAN I BELIEVE YOU? I HAVE NOT SEEN YOU CREATE A SINGLE OBJECT!
LET US CONSIDER SOMETHING AS SIMPLE AS A WEAPON! CAN YOU CREATE A WEAPON WHICH WILL EMPLOY COSMIC ENERGY?
IT IS MERE CHILD'S PLAY FOR THE SILVER SURFER!
ZIST
STAND YOU BACK--AND OBSERVE!
I--I CAN ALMOST SEE IT FORMING--MOLECULE BY MOLECULE!!
PRECISELY HOW IT DOES FORM ITSELF, MONARCH!
THERE! IT IS DONE!
YOU CALL THIS A MIGHTY WEAPON?!!
IT IS ALMOST WEIGHTLESS! I HAVE NO INTEREST IN MERELY SWATTING FLIES!
THE POWER YOU HOLD IS BEYOND COMPARE!
MERELY TAP IT GENTLY AGAINST YONDER WALL--!
WHAT GOOD WILL A SIMPLE TAP DO?
WAIT! A RIPPLE OF FORCE SEEMS TO BE COMING FROM IT--GROWING EACH SECOND--
IT'S CRACKING THE WALL--REACHING TO THE FLOOR--!
THAK!
BTOOOM!
THE ENTIRE TOWER ROOM IS CRUMBLING!! THE IMPACT IS SPREADING--FURTHER--AND FURTHER--!
ALL THAT YOU HAVE TOLD ME, THEN--IS TRUE!
6

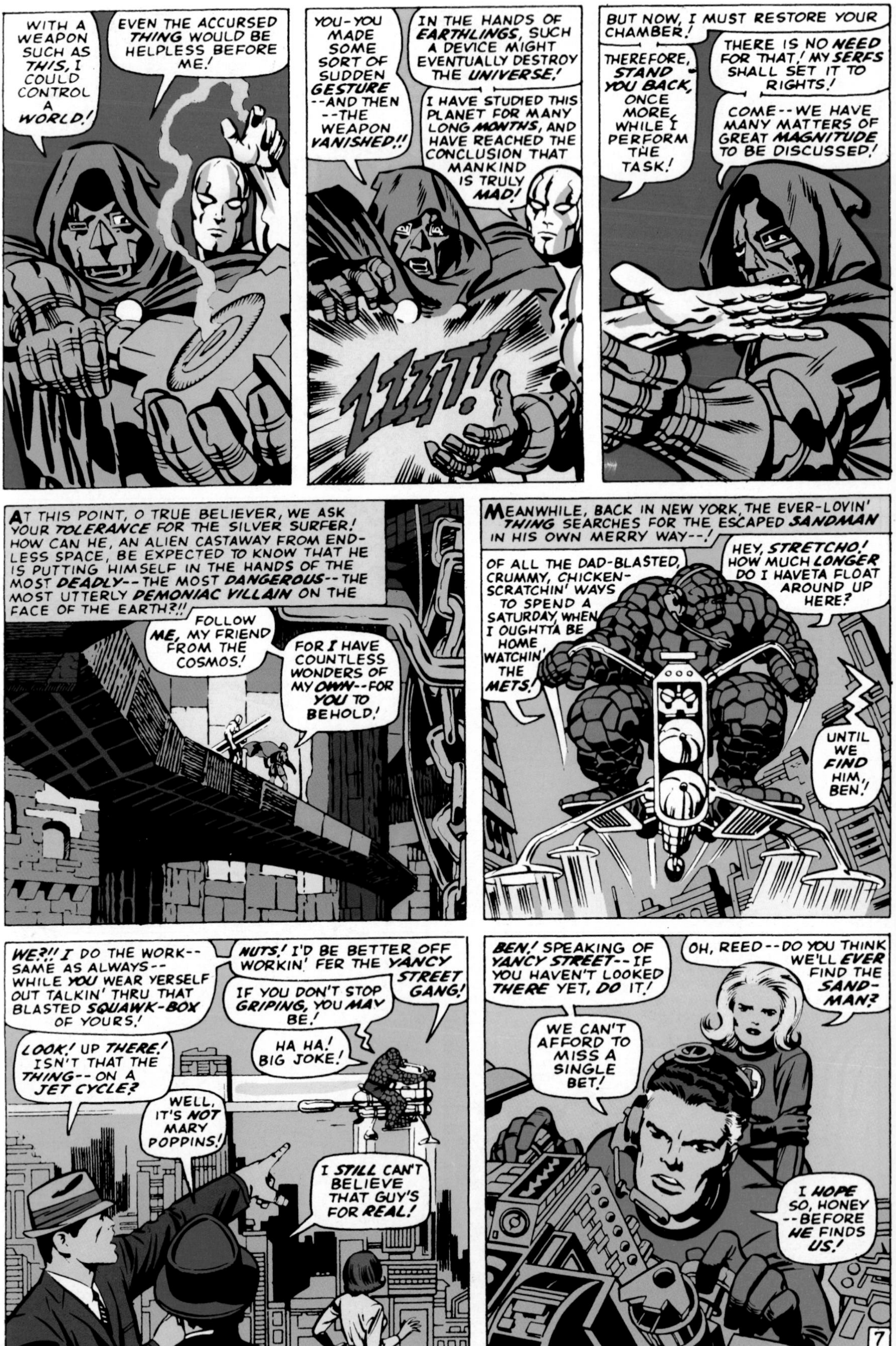
WITH A WEAPON SUCH AS THIS, I COULD CONTROL A WORLD!
EVEN THE ACCURSED THING WOULD BE HELPLESS BEFORE ME!
YOU-YOU MADE SOME SORT OF SUDDEN GESTURE --AND THEN --THE WEAPON VANISHED!!
IN THE HANDS OF EARTHLINGS, SUCH A DEVICE MIGHT EVENTUALLY DESTROY THE UNIVERSE!
I HAVE STUDIED THIS PLANET FOR MANY LONG MONTHS, AND HAVE REACHED THE CONCLUSION THAT MANKIND IS TRULY MAD!
ZZZT!
BUT NOW, I MUST RESTORE YOUR CHAMBER!
THEREFORE, STAND YOU BACK, ONCE MORE, WHILE I PERFORM THE TASK!
THERE IS NO NEED FOR THAT! MY SERFS SHALL SET IT TO RIGHTS!
COME--WE HAVE MANY MATTERS OF GREAT MAGNITUDE TO BE DISCUSSED!
AT THIS POINT, O TRUE BELIEVER, WE ASK YOUR TOLERANCE FOR THE SILVER SURFER! HOW CAN HE, AN ALIEN CASTAWAY FROM ENDLESS SPACE, BE EXPECTED TO KNOW THAT HE IS PUTTING HIMSELF IN THE HANDS OF THE MOST DEADLY--THE MOST DANGEROUS--THE MOST UTTERLY DEMONIAC VILLAIN ON THE FACE OF THE EARTH?!!
FOLLOW ME, MY FRIEND FROM THE COSMOS!
FOR I HAVE COUNTLESS WONDERS OF MY OWN--FOR YOU TO BEHOLD!
MEANWHILE, BACK IN NEW YORK, THE EVER-LOVIN' THING SEARCHES FOR THE ESCAPED SANDMAN IN HIS OWN MERRY WAY--!
OF ALL THE DAD-BLASTED, CRUMMY, CHICKEN-SCRATCHIN' WAYS TO SPEND A SATURDAY, WHEN I OUGHTTA BE HOME WATCHIN' THE METS!
HEY, STRETCHO! HOW MUCH LONGER DO I HAVETA FLOAT AROUND UP HERE?
UNTIL WE FIND HIM, BEN!
WE?!! I DO THE WORK--SAME AS ALWAYS--WHILE YOU WEAR YERSELF OUT TALKIN' THRU THAT BLASTED SQUAWK-BOX OF YOURS!
NUTS! I'D BE BETTER OFF WORKIN' FER THE YANCY STREET GANG!
IF YOU DON'T STOP GRIPING, YOU MAY BE!
HA HA! BIG JOKE!
LOOK! UP THERE! ISN'T THAT THE THING--ON A JET CYCLE?
WELL, IT'S NOT MARY POPPINS!
I STILL CAN'T BELIEVE THAT GUY'S FOR REAL!
BEN! SPEAKING OF YANCY STREET--IF YOU HAVEN'T LOOKED THERE YET, DO IT!
WE CAN'T AFFORD TO MISS A SINGLE BET!
OH, REED--DO YOU THINK WE'LL EVER FIND THE SANDMAN?
I HOPE SO, HONEY--BEFORE HE FINDS US!
7

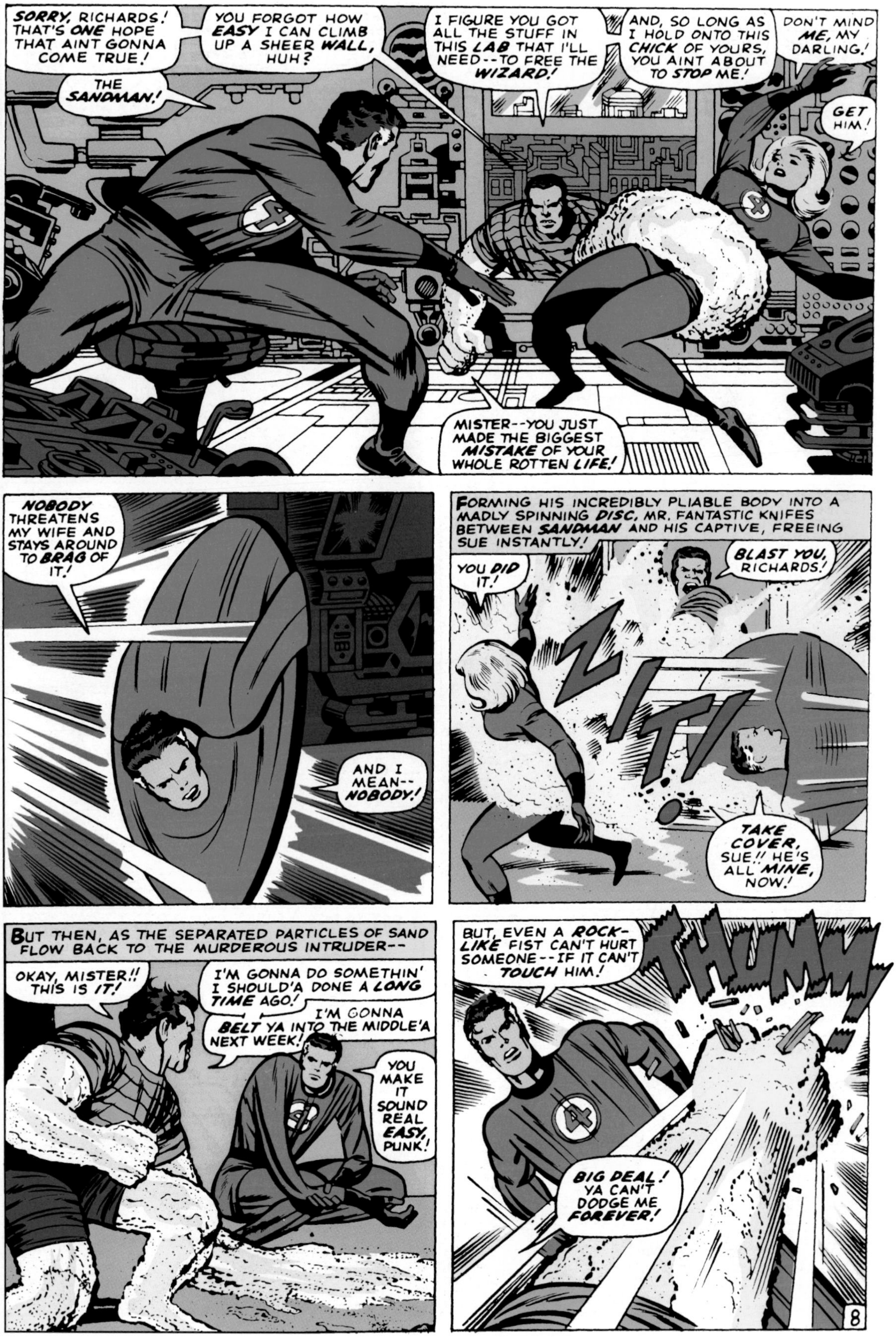
SORRY, RICHARDS! THAT'S ONE HOPE THAT AINT GONNA COME TRUE!
THE SANDMAN!
YOU FORGOT HOW EASY I CAN CLIMB UP A SHEER WALL, HUH?
I FIGURE YOU GOT ALL THE STUFF IN THIS LAB THAT I'LL NEED--TO FREE THE WIZARD!
AND, SO LONG AS I HOLD ONTO THIS CHICK OF YOURS, YOU AINT ABOUT TO STOP ME!
DON'T MIND ME, MY DARLING!
GET HIM!
MISTER--YOU JUST MADE THE BIGGEST MISTAKE OF YOUR WHOLE ROTTEN LIFE!
NOBODY THREATENS MY WIFE AND STAYS AROUND TO BRAG OF IT!
AND I MEAN--NOBODY!
FORMING HIS INCREDIBLY PLIABLE BODY INTO A MADLY SPINNING DISC, MR. FANTASTIC KNIFES BETWEEN SANDMAN AND HIS CAPTIVE, FREEING SUE INSTANTLY!
YOU DID IT!
BLAST YOU, RICHARDS!
ZIT!
TAKE COVER, SUE!! HE'S ALL MINE, NOW!
BUT THEN, AS THE SEPARATED PARTICLES OF SAND FLOW BACK TO THE MURDEROUS INTRUDER--
OKAY, MISTER!! THIS IS IT!
I'M GONNA DO SOMETHIN' I SHOULD'A DONE A LONG TIME AGO!
I'M GONNA BELT YA INTO THE MIDDLE'A NEXT WEEK!
YOU MAKE IT SOUND REAL EASY, PUNK!
BUT, EVEN A ROCK-LIKE FIST CAN'T HURT SOMEONE--IF IT CAN'T TOUCH HIM!
THUMM!
BIG DEAL! YA CAN'T DODGE ME FOREVER!
8

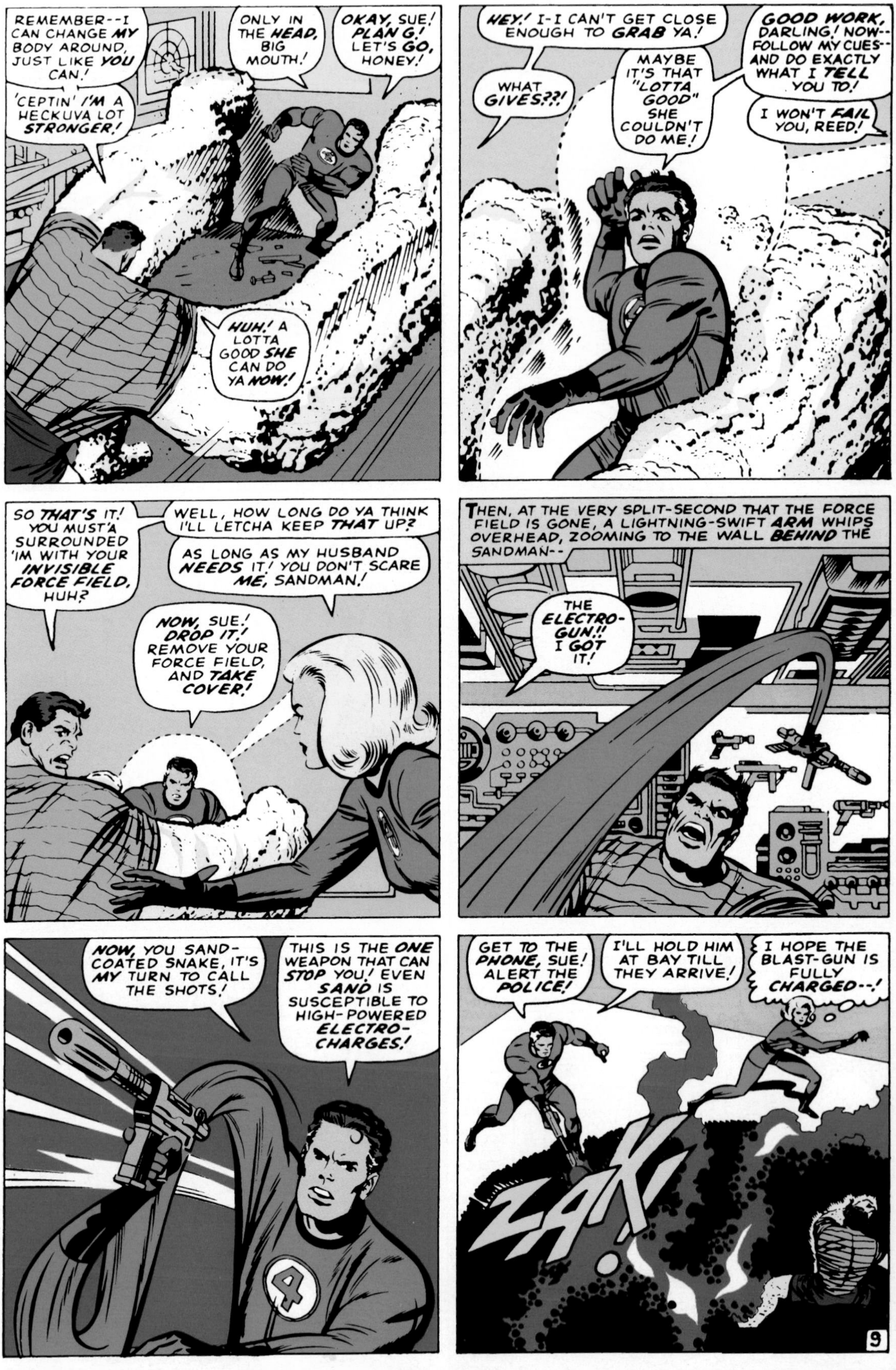
REMEMBER--I CAN CHANGE MY BODY AROUND, JUST LIKE YOU CAN!
'CEPTIN' I'M A HECKUVA LOT STRONGER!
ONLY IN THE HEAD, BIG MOUTH!
OKAY, SUE! PLAN G! LET'S GO, HONEY!
HUH! A LOTTA GOOD SHE CAN DO YA NOW!
HEY! I-I CAN'T GET CLOSE ENOUGH TO GRAB YA!
WHAT GIVES??!
MAYBE IT'S THAT "LOTTA GOOD" SHE COULDN'T DO ME!
GOOD WORK, DARLING! NOW-- FOLLOW MY CUES-- AND DO EXACTLY WHAT I TELL YOU TO!
I WON'T FAIL YOU, REED!
SO THAT'S IT! YOU MUST'A SURROUNDED 'IM WITH YOUR INVISIBLE FORCE FIELD, HUH?
WELL, HOW LONG DO YA THINK I'LL LETCHA KEEP THAT UP?
AS LONG AS MY HUSBAND NEEDS IT! YOU DON'T SCARE ME, SANDMAN!
NOW, SUE! DROP IT! REMOVE YOUR FORCE FIELD, AND TAKE COVER!
THEN, AT THE VERY SPLIT-SECOND THAT THE FORCE FIELD IS GONE, A LIGHTNING-SWIFT ARM WHIPS OVERHEAD, ZOOMING TO THE WALL BEHIND THE SANDMAN--
THE ELECTRO-GUN!! I GOT IT!
NOW, YOU SAND-COATED SNAKE, IT'S MY TURN TO CALL THE SHOTS!
THIS IS THE ONE WEAPON THAT CAN STOP YOU! EVEN SAND IS SUSCEPTIBLE TO HIGH-POWERED ELECTRO-CHARGES!
GET TO THE PHONE, SUE! ALERT THE POLICE!
I'LL HOLD HIM AT BAY TILL THEY ARRIVE!
I HOPE THE BLAST-GUN IS FULLY CHARGED--!
ZAK!
9

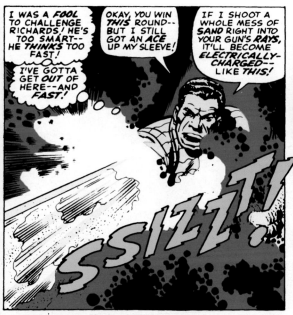

I WAS A *FOOL* TO CHALLENGE *RICHARDS!* HE'S TOO *SMART*-- HE *THINKS* TOO *FAST!*

I'VE GOTTA GET *OUT* OF HERE--AND *FAST!*

OKAY, YOU WIN *THIS* ROUND-- BUT I STILL GOT AN *ACE* UP MY SLEEVE!

IF I SHOOT A WHOLE MESS OF *SAND* RIGHT INTO YOUR GUN'S *RAYS*, IT'LL BECOME *ELECTRICALLY-CHARGED*-- LIKE *THIS!*

SSIZZT!

I WAS *WRONG* ABOUT HIM! I DIDN'T THINK THE SANDMAN HAD *BRAINS* ENOUGH TO FIGURE THAT OUT!

IF I'D STOOD MY GROUND FOR ANOTHER SECOND, THAT ELECTRICALLY-CHARGED *SAND* WOULD HAVE GIVEN ME A FATAL *JOLT!*

SPASK!

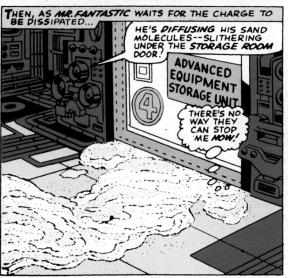

THEN, AS *MR. FANTASTIC* WAITS FOR THE CHARGE TO BE *DISSIPATED...*

HE'S *DIFFUSING* HIS SAND MOLECULES--SLITHERING UNDER THE *STORAGE ROOM* DOOR!

ADVANCED EQUIPMENT STORAGE UNIT

THERE'S NO WAY THEY CAN STOP ME *NOW!*

HE ACTIVATED THE *IMPREGNO-LOCK* INSIDE!

IT'LL TAKE ME AT LEAST *FIVE MINUTES* TO WORK IT OPEN!

THAT MEANS HE'LL HAVE ALL THAT TIME TO MAKE USE OF THE *EQUIPMENT* YOU'VE GOT IN THERE!

SOUNDS LIKE HE'S *TEARING* THE PLACE *APART* --AND WE CAN'T *STOP* HIM!

THEN, EXACTLY 300 SECONDS LATER...

HE'S *GONE!* BUT--LOOK AT YOUR *ROOM*--!

HE TOOK WHAT-EVER HE COULD CARRY *WITH* HIM!

HE MUST HAVE FIGURED THAT EVEN IF *HE* COULDN'T UNDERSTAND IT, THE *WIZARD* COULD!

LUCKILY, HE LEFT SOME OF MY MOST *VALUABLE* COMPONENTS *BEHIND!*

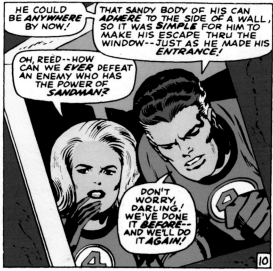

HE COULD BE *ANYWHERE* BY NOW!

THAT SANDY BODY OF HIS CAN *ADHERE* TO THE SIDE OF A WALL, SO IT WAS *SIMPLE* FOR HIM TO MAKE HIS ESCAPE THRU THE WINDOW--JUST AS HE MADE HIS *ENTRANCE!*

OH, REED--HOW CAN WE *EVER* DEFEAT AN ENEMY WHO HAS THE POWER OF *SANDMAN?*

DON'T WORRY, DARLING! WE'VE DONE IT *BEFORE*-- AND WE'LL DO IT *AGAIN!*

10

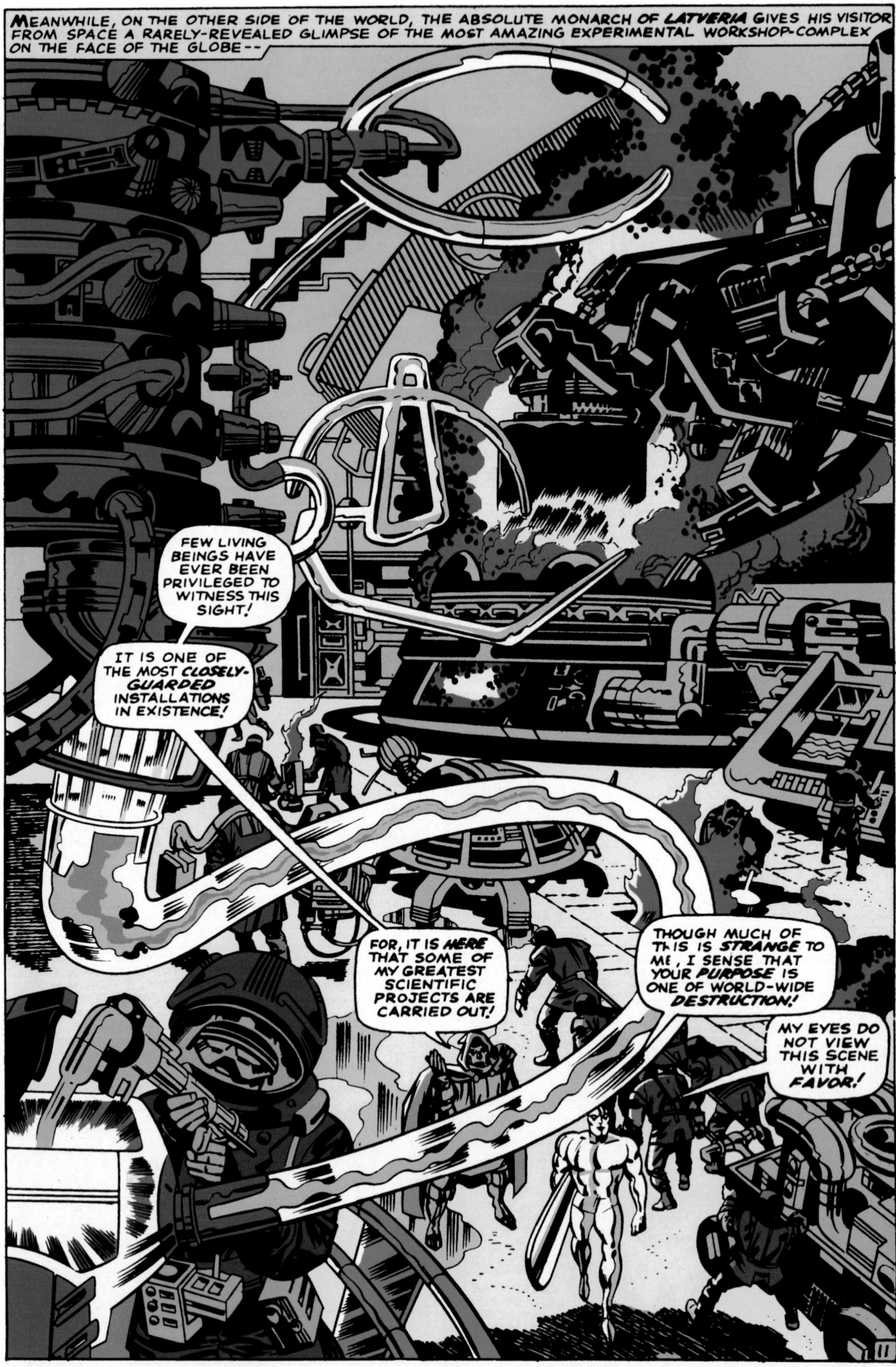
MEANWHILE, ON THE OTHER SIDE OF THE WORLD, THE ABSOLUTE MONARCH OF LATVERIA GIVES HIS VISITOR FROM SPACE A RARELY-REVEALED GLIMPSE OF THE MOST AMAZING EXPERIMENTAL WORKSHOP-COMPLEX ON THE FACE OF THE GLOBE--
FEW LIVING BEINGS HAVE EVER BEEN PRIVILEGED TO WITNESS THIS SIGHT!
IT IS ONE OF THE MOST CLOSELY-GUARDED INSTALLATIONS IN EXISTENCE!
FOR, IT IS HERE THAT SOME OF MY GREATEST SCIENTIFIC PROJECTS ARE CARRIED OUT!
THOUGH MUCH OF THIS IS STRANGE TO ME, I SENSE THAT YOUR PURPOSE IS ONE OF WORLD-WIDE DESTRUCTION!
MY EYES DO NOT VIEW THIS SCENE WITH FAVOR!
11

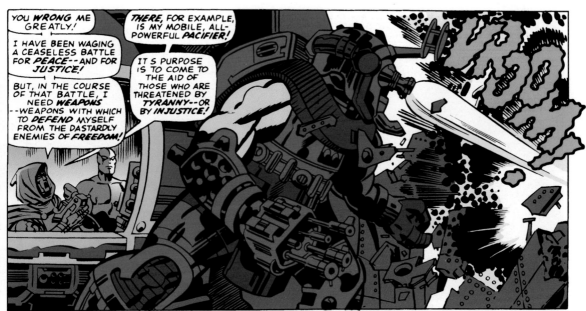

YOU **WRONG** ME GREATLY! I HAVE BEEN WAGING A CEASELESS BATTLE FOR **PEACE**--AND FOR **JUSTICE**!

BUT, IN THE COURSE OF THAT BATTLE, I NEED **WEAPONS** --WEAPONS WITH WHICH TO **DEFEND** MYSELF FROM THE DASTARDLY ENEMIES OF **FREEDOM**!

THERE, FOR EXAMPLE, IS MY MOBILE, ALL-POWERFUL **PACIFIER**!

IT S PURPOSE IS TO COME TO THE AID OF THOSE WHO ARE THREATENED BY **TYRANNY**--OR BY **INJUSTICE**!

I **SEE** THAT THERE IS STILL **MUCH** FOR ME TO LEARN!

YOUR **VOICE** MOUTHS SOOTHING WORDS OF PEACE AND RIGHTEOUSNESS--

AND YET, EVERY FIBRE OF MY BEING **RECOILS** AT THE LUST FOR **POWER** WHICH PERVADES THE VERY **ATMOSPHERE** ABOUT YOU!

IT IS A **PITY** THAT YOU DO NOT UNDERSTAND--!

ACTUALLY, I AM THE **GENTLEST**, THE MOST **UNAMBITIOUS** OF MONARCHS!

MY ONLY DESIRE IS TO MAKE MY PEOPLE **HAPPY**--AND TO FURTHER THE CAUSE OF **PEACE**, AND OF **BROTHERLY LOVE**!

I HAVE BEEN INFORMED THAT MY **DEVOTED** SUBJECTS ACTUALLY DANCE IN THE STREETS, AT THE MEREST MENTION OF MY **NAME**!

BUT, AT THAT VERY MOMENT--

A THOUSAND **PARDONS**, SIRE! I DID STUMBLE AGAINST YOUR CLOAK!

CLUMSY DOLT!

THAT!

CLANK!

YOU DARED LAY A **HAND** UPON THE SACROSANCT PERSON OF YOUR LORD AND MASTER ??!

WORTHLESS, INSUFFERABLE **CLOD**! DO YOU KNOW WHAT THIS **MEANS**?!

OH NO, SIRE-- **NO**--NOT--NOT THE **ULTIMATE PUNISHMENT**?!!

THUMP!

12

159

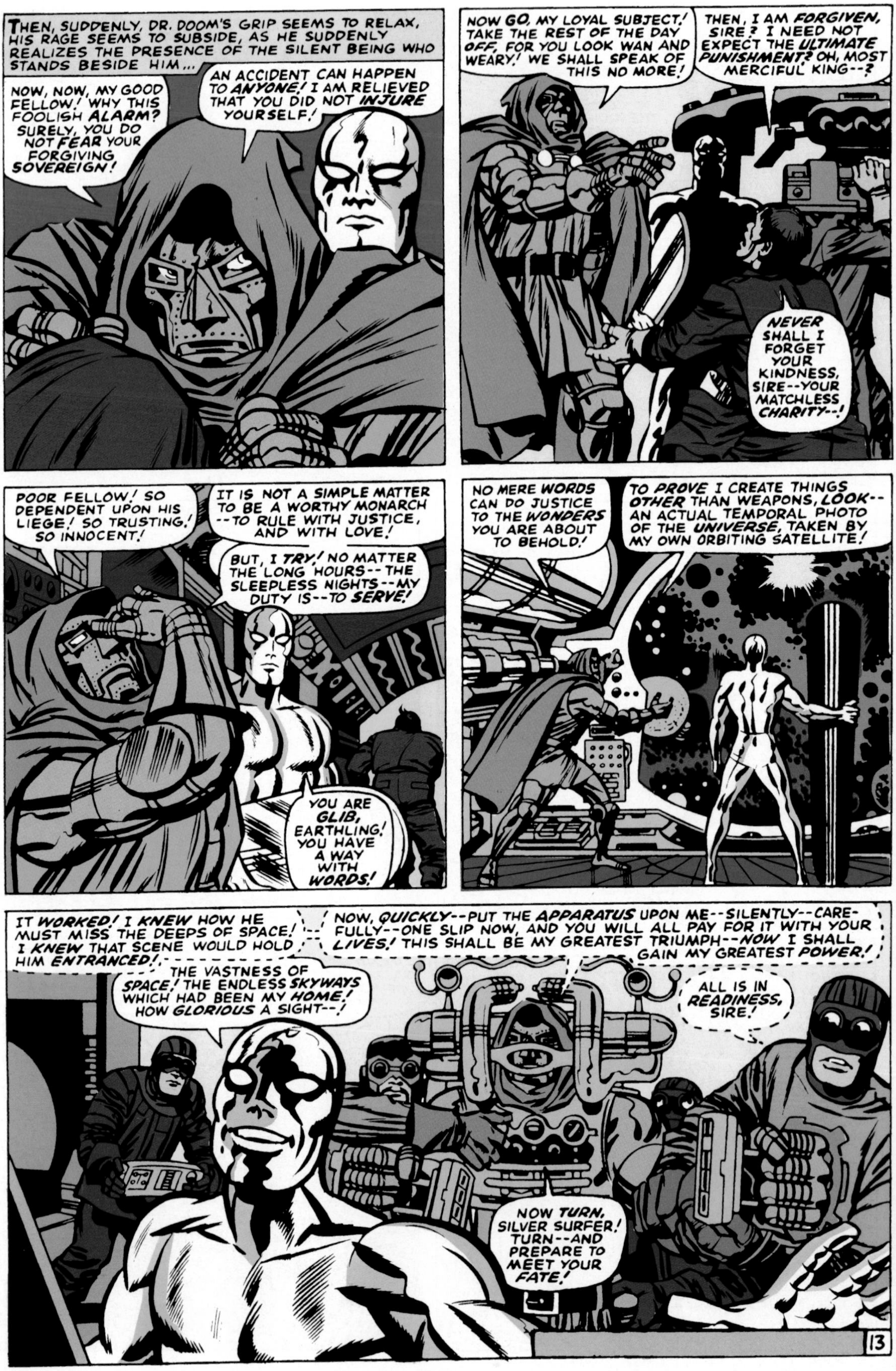

THEN, SUDDENLY, DR. DOOM'S GRIP SEEMS TO RELAX, HIS RAGE SEEMS TO SUBSIDE, AS HE SUDDENLY REALIZES THE PRESENCE OF THE SILENT BEING WHO STANDS BESIDE HIM...
NOW, NOW, MY GOOD FELLOW! WHY THIS FOOLISH ALARM? SURELY, YOU DO NOT FEAR YOUR FORGIVING SOVEREIGN!
AN ACCIDENT CAN HAPPEN TO ANYONE! I AM RELIEVED THAT YOU DID NOT INJURE YOURSELF!
NOW GO, MY LOYAL SUBJECT! TAKE THE REST OF THE DAY OFF, FOR YOU LOOK WAN AND WEARY! WE SHALL SPEAK OF THIS NO MORE!
THEN, I AM FORGIVEN, SIRE? I NEED NOT EXPECT THE ULTIMATE PUNISHMENT? OH, MOST MERCIFUL KING--?
NEVER SHALL I FORGET YOUR KINDNESS, SIRE--YOUR MATCHLESS CHARITY--!
POOR FELLOW! SO DEPENDENT UPON HIS LIEGE! SO TRUSTING! SO INNOCENT!
IT IS NOT A SIMPLE MATTER TO BE A WORTHY MONARCH --TO RULE WITH JUSTICE, AND WITH LOVE!
BUT, I TRY! NO MATTER THE LONG HOURS--THE SLEEPLESS NIGHTS--MY DUTY IS--TO SERVE!
YOU ARE GLIB, EARTHLING! YOU HAVE A WAY WITH WORDS!
NO MERE WORDS CAN DO JUSTICE TO THE WONDERS YOU ARE ABOUT TO BEHOLD!
TO PROVE I CREATE THINGS OTHER THAN WEAPONS, LOOK-- AN ACTUAL TEMPORAL PHOTO OF THE UNIVERSE, TAKEN BY MY OWN ORBITING SATELLITE!
IT WORKED! I KNEW HOW HE MUST MISS THE DEEPS OF SPACE! I KNEW THAT SCENE WOULD HOLD HIM ENTRANCED!
NOW, QUICKLY--PUT THE APPARATUS UPON ME--SILENTLY--CAREFULLY--ONE SLIP NOW, AND YOU WILL ALL PAY FOR IT WITH YOUR LIVES! THIS SHALL BE MY GREATEST TRIUMPH--NOW I SHALL GAIN MY GREATEST POWER!
THE VASTNESS OF SPACE! THE ENDLESS SKYWAYS WHICH HAD BEEN MY HOME! HOW GLORIOUS A SIGHT--!
ALL IS IN READINESS, SIRE!
NOW TURN, SILVER SURFER! TURN--AND PREPARE TO MEET YOUR FATE!
13

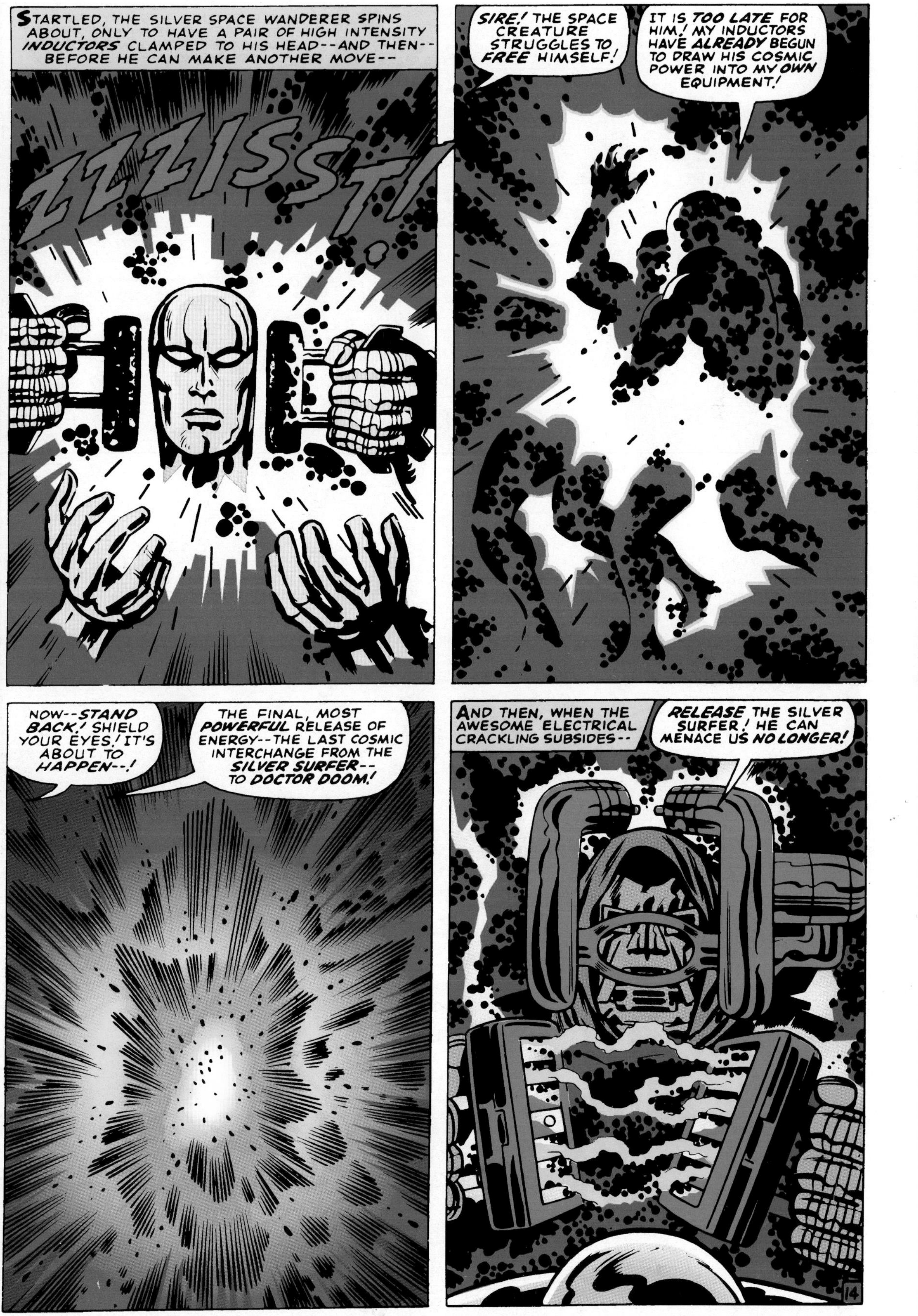
STARTLED, THE SILVER SPACE WANDERER SPINS ABOUT, ONLY TO HAVE A PAIR OF HIGH INTENSITY INDUCTORS CLAMPED TO HIS HEAD--AND THEN--BEFORE HE CAN MAKE ANOTHER MOVE--
ZZZISST!
SIRE! THE SPACE CREATURE STRUGGLES TO FREE HIMSELF!
IT IS TOO LATE FOR HIM! MY INDUCTORS HAVE ALREADY BEGUN TO DRAW HIS COSMIC POWER INTO MY OWN EQUIPMENT!
NOW--STAND BACK! SHIELD YOUR EYES! IT'S ABOUT TO HAPPEN--!
THE FINAL, MOST POWERFUL RELEASE OF ENERGY--THE LAST COSMIC INTERCHANGE FROM THE SILVER SURFER--TO DOCTOR DOOM!
AND THEN, WHEN THE AWESOME ELECTRICAL CRACKLING SUBSIDES--
RELEASE THE SILVER SURFER! HE CAN MENACE US NO LONGER!
14

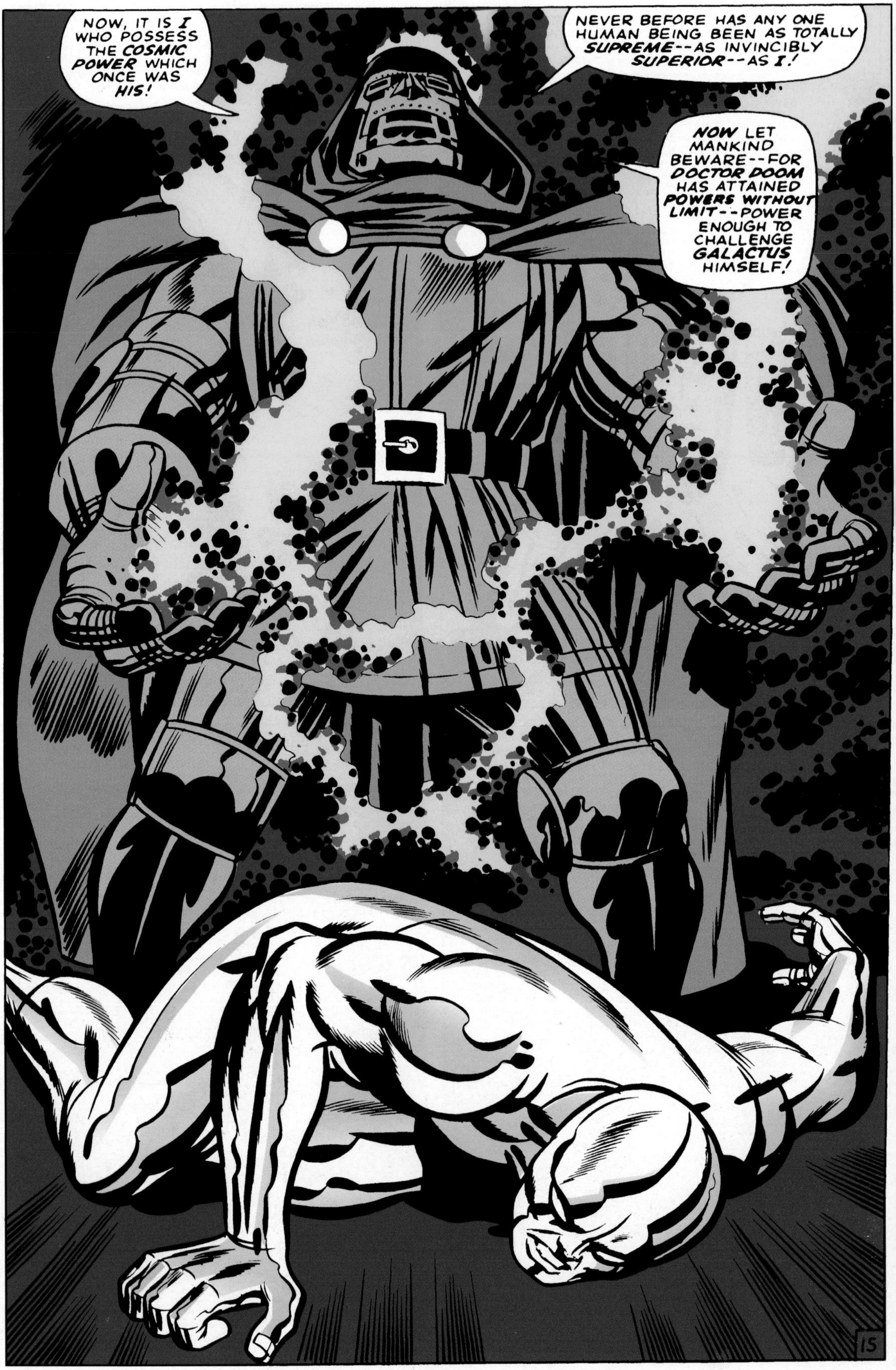
NOW, IT IS I WHO POSSESS THE COSMIC POWER WHICH ONCE WAS HIS!
NEVER BEFORE HAS ANY ONE HUMAN BEING BEEN AS TOTALLY SUPREME--AS INVINCIBLY SUPERIOR--AS I!
NOW LET MANKIND BEWARE--FOR DOCTOR DOOM HAS ATTAINED POWERS WITHOUT LIMIT--POWER ENOUGH TO CHALLENGE GALACTUS HIMSELF!
15

BUT, THE WORKINGS OF AN INSCRUTABLE *FATE* ARE STRANGE INDEED! FOR, EVEN AS THE WORLD'S MOST POWERFUL *ARCH-VILLAIN* STANDS AT THE VERY *PINNACLE* OF HIS NEFARIOUS CAREER, A WEARY, DISCOURAGED *HUMAN TORCH* EXPERIENCES ANOTHER IN A SERIES OF SEEMINGLY ENDLESS *FAILURES*--

ANOTHER *STRIKE-OUT*, WYATT! *LOCKJAW* BROUGHT US TO THE *WRONG PLACE* AGAIN!

IT'S SOME SORT OF TOTALLY DIFFERENT *DIMENSION*--FURTHER FROM EARTH THAN HE'S EVER TRANSPORTED US!

I SOMETIMES WONDER IF I'LL *EVER* BE ABLE TO REACH *CRYSTAL!*

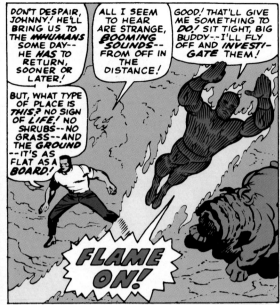

DON'T DESPAIR, JOHNNY! HE'LL BRING US TO THE *INHUMANS* SOME DAY-- HE *HAS* TO RETURN, SOONER OR LATER!

BUT, WHAT TYPE OF PLACE IS *THIS?* NO SIGN OF *LIFE!* NO SHRUBS--NO GRASS--AND THE GROUND --IT'S AS FLAT AS A *BOARD!*

ALL I SEEM TO HEAR ARE STRANGE, *BOOMING SOUNDS*-- FROM OFF IN THE DISTANCE!

GOOD! THAT'LL GIVE ME SOMETHING TO *DO!* SIT TIGHT, BIG BUDDY--I'LL FLY OFF AND *INVESTIGATE* THEM!

FLAME ON!

IT'S LIKE A *SCENE* OUT OF *DISNEYLAND!*

THIS MUST BE SOME WORLD THAT'S STILL IN ITS *INFANCY!*

GROWRRRR!

RRRR

KING KONG MIGHT HAVE A *BALL* HERE, BUT WYATT AND I HAVETA FIGURE OUT SOME WAY TO MAKE *LOCKJAW* CUT OUT --AND *FAST!*

MAN! NO WONDER THE GROUND'S SO *FLAT!*

THEY CRUSH WHATEVER THEY *STEP* ON! NO *SMALLER* FORMS OF LIFE WOULD HAVE A *CHANCE* TO SURVIVE HERE--WITHOUT BEING *STAMPED OUT!*

BOOM!

THIS IS ONE PLACE WE DON'T WANNA STAKE A *CLAIM* TO, PAL!

THAT'S WHAT I *EXPECTED*, JOHNNY!

I'VE SPENT *WEEKS* TRYING TO *TRAIN* LOCKJAW! NOW, LET'S SEE IF HE'LL FINALLY *OBEY* A SPOKEN *COMMAND*....!

16

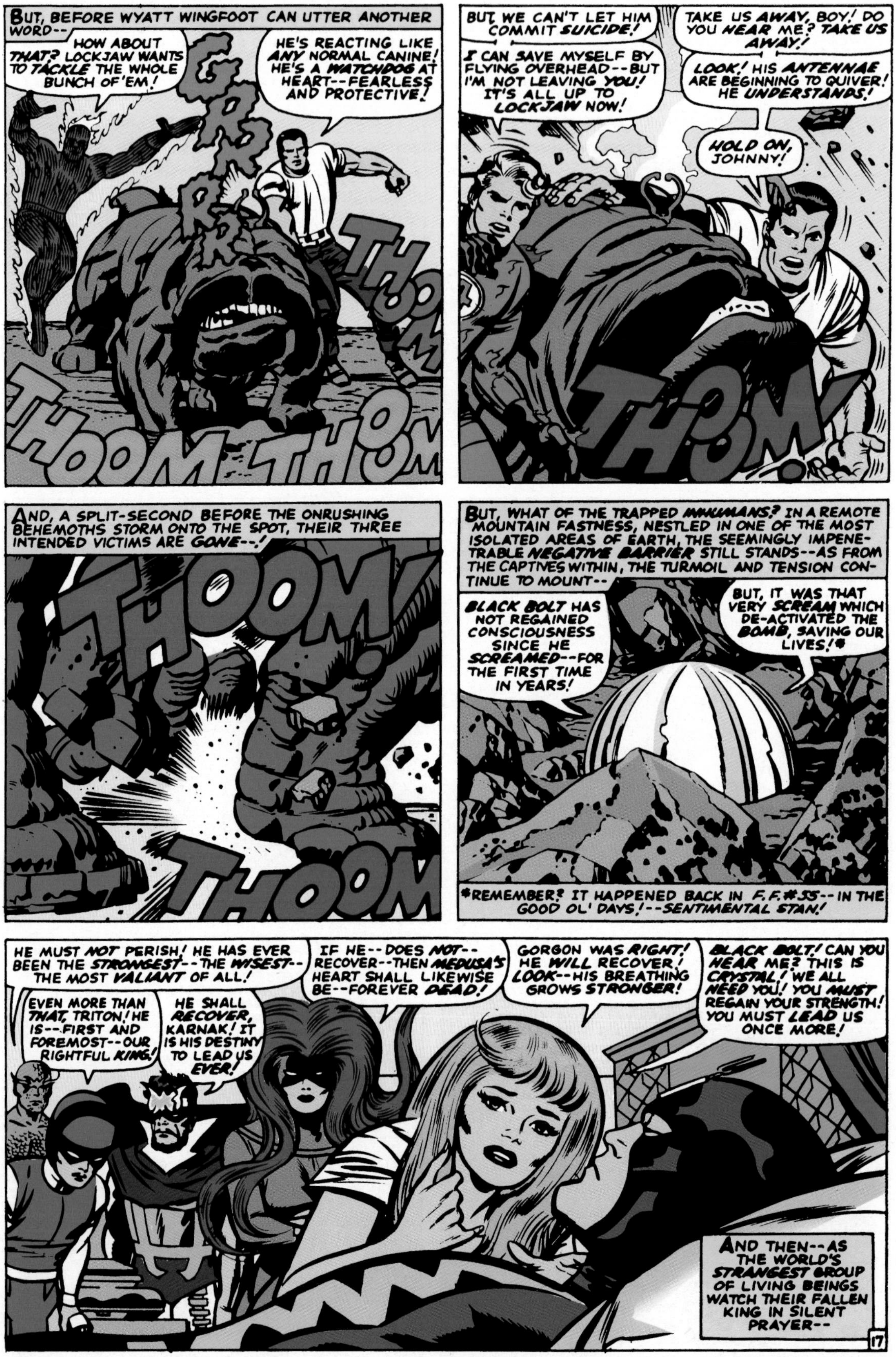

BUT, BEFORE WYATT WINGFOOT CAN UTTER ANOTHER WORD--
HOW ABOUT THAT? LOCKJAW WANTS TO TACKLE THE WHOLE BUNCH OF 'EM!
HE'S REACTING LIKE ANY NORMAL CANINE! HE'S A WATCHDOG AT HEART--FEARLESS AND PROTECTIVE!
GRRR
THOOM THOOM THOOM
BUT WE CAN'T LET HIM COMMIT SUICIDE!
I CAN SAVE MYSELF BY FLYING OVERHEAD--BUT I'M NOT LEAVING YOU! IT'S ALL UP TO LOCKJAW NOW!
TAKE US AWAY, BOY! DO YOU HEAR ME? TAKE US AWAY!
LOOK! HIS ANTENNAE ARE BEGINNING TO QUIVER! HE UNDERSTANDS!
HOLD ON, JOHNNY!
THOOM
AND, A SPLIT-SECOND BEFORE THE ONRUSHING BEHEMOTHS STORM ONTO THE SPOT, THEIR THREE INTENDED VICTIMS ARE GONE--!
THOOM!
THOOM
BUT, WHAT OF THE TRAPPED INHUMANS? IN A REMOTE MOUNTAIN FASTNESS, NESTLED IN ONE OF THE MOST ISOLATED AREAS OF EARTH, THE SEEMINGLY IMPENETRABLE NEGATIVE BARRIER STILL STANDS--AS FROM THE CAPTIVES WITHIN, THE TURMOIL AND TENSION CONTINUE TO MOUNT--
BLACK BOLT HAS NOT REGAINED CONSCIOUSNESS SINCE HE SCREAMED--FOR THE FIRST TIME IN YEARS!
BUT, IT WAS THAT VERY SCREAM WHICH DE-ACTIVATED THE BOMB, SAVING OUR LIVES!*
*REMEMBER? IT HAPPENED BACK IN F.F. #55--IN THE GOOD OL' DAYS!--SENTIMENTAL STAN!
HE MUST NOT PERISH! HE HAS EVER BEEN THE STRONGEST--THE WISEST--THE MOST VALIANT OF ALL!
EVEN MORE THAN THAT, TRITON! HE IS--FIRST AND FOREMOST--OUR RIGHTFUL KING!
HE SHALL RECOVER, KARNAK! IT IS HIS DESTINY TO LEAD US EVER!
IF HE--DOES NOT--RECOVER--THEN MEDUSA'S HEART SHALL LIKEWISE BE--FOREVER DEAD!
GORGON WAS RIGHT! HE WILL RECOVER! LOOK--HIS BREATHING GROWS STRONGER!
BLACK BOLT! CAN YOU HEAR ME? THIS IS CRYSTAL! WE ALL NEED YOU! YOU MUST REGAIN YOUR STRENGTH! YOU MUST LEAD US ONCE MORE!
AND THEN--AS THE WORLD'S STRANGEST GROUP OF LIVING BEINGS WATCH THEIR FALLEN KING IN SILENT PRAYER--
17

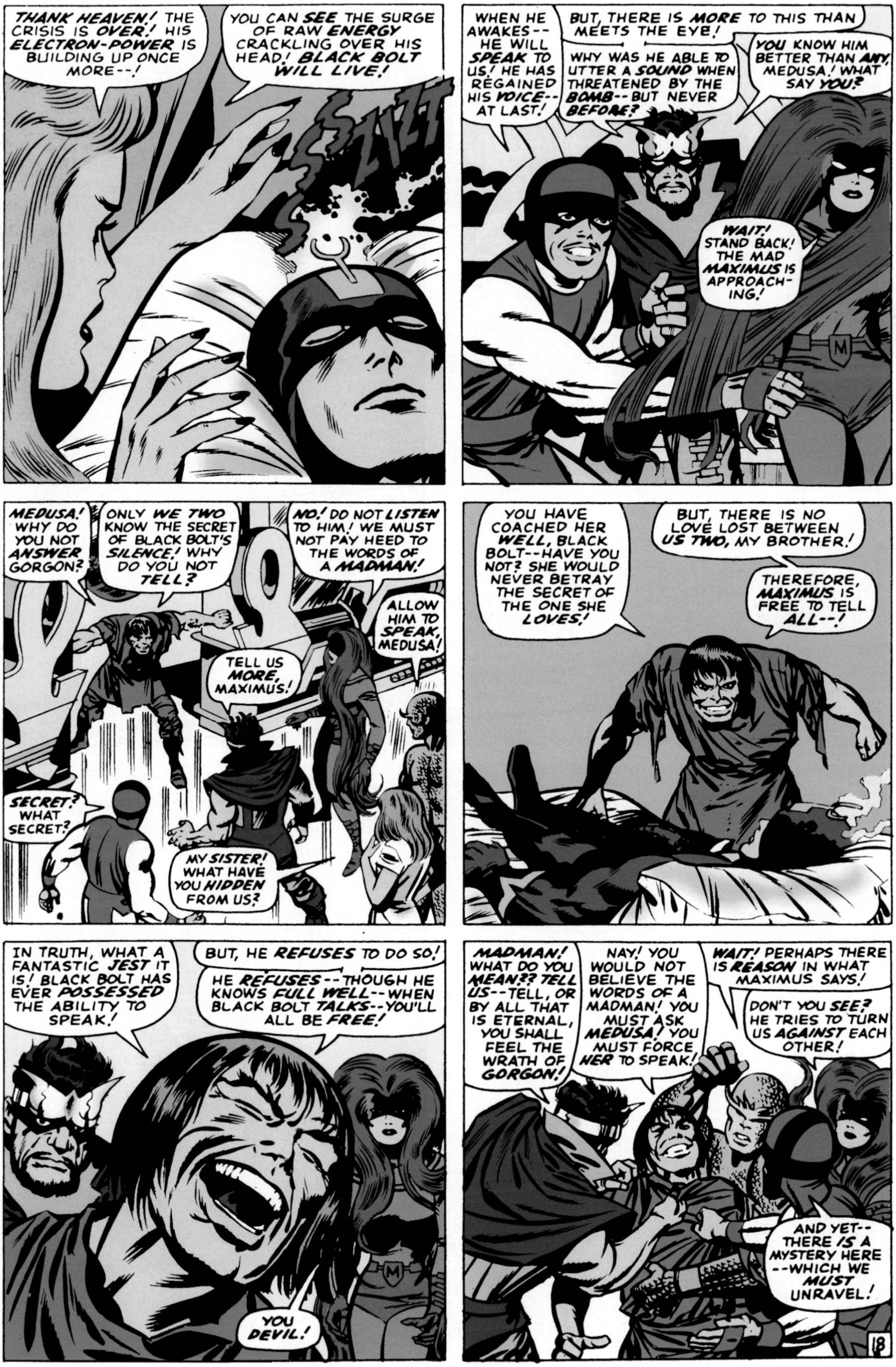
THANK HEAVEN! THE CRISIS IS OVER! HIS ELECTRON-POWER IS BUILDING UP ONCE MORE--!
YOU CAN SEE THE SURGE OF RAW ENERGY CRACKLING OVER HIS HEAD! BLACK BOLT WILL LIVE!
SSZZZT
WHEN HE AWAKES-- HE WILL SPEAK TO US! HE HAS REGAINED HIS VOICE-- AT LAST!
BUT, THERE IS MORE TO THIS THAN MEETS THE EYE!
WHY WAS HE ABLE TO UTTER A SOUND WHEN THREATENED BY THE BOMB--BUT NEVER BEFORE?
YOU KNOW HIM BETTER THAN ANY, MEDUSA! WHAT SAY YOU?
WAIT! STAND BACK! THE MAD MAXIMUS IS APPROACH-ING!
MEDUSA! WHY DO YOU NOT ANSWER GORGON?
ONLY WE TWO KNOW THE SECRET OF BLACK BOLT'S SILENCE! WHY DO YOU NOT TELL?
NO! DO NOT LISTEN TO HIM! WE MUST NOT PAY HEED TO THE WORDS OF A MADMAN!
ALLOW HIM TO SPEAK, MEDUSA!
TELL US MORE, MAXIMUS!
SECRET? WHAT SECRET?
MY SISTER! WHAT HAVE YOU HIDDEN FROM US?
YOU HAVE COACHED HER WELL, BLACK BOLT--HAVE YOU NOT? SHE WOULD NEVER BETRAY THE SECRET OF THE ONE SHE LOVES!
BUT, THERE IS NO LOVE LOST BETWEEN US TWO, MY BROTHER!
THEREFORE, MAXIMUS IS FREE TO TELL ALL--!
IN TRUTH, WHAT A FANTASTIC JEST IT IS! BLACK BOLT HAS EVER POSSESSED THE ABILITY TO SPEAK!
BUT, HE REFUSES TO DO SO!
HE REFUSES--THOUGH HE KNOWS FULL WELL--WHEN BLACK BOLT TALKS--YOU'LL ALL BE FREE!
YOU DEVIL!
MADMAN! WHAT DO YOU MEAN?? TELL US--TELL, OR BY ALL THAT IS ETERNAL, YOU SHALL FEEL THE WRATH OF GORGON!
NAY! YOU WOULD NOT BELIEVE THE WORDS OF A MADMAN! YOU MUST ASK MEDUSA! YOU MUST FORCE HER TO SPEAK!
WAIT! PERHAPS THERE IS REASON IN WHAT MAXIMUS SAYS!
DON'T YOU SEE? HE TRIES TO TURN US AGAINST EACH OTHER!
AND YET-- THERE IS A MYSTERY HERE --WHICH WE MUST UNRAVEL!
18

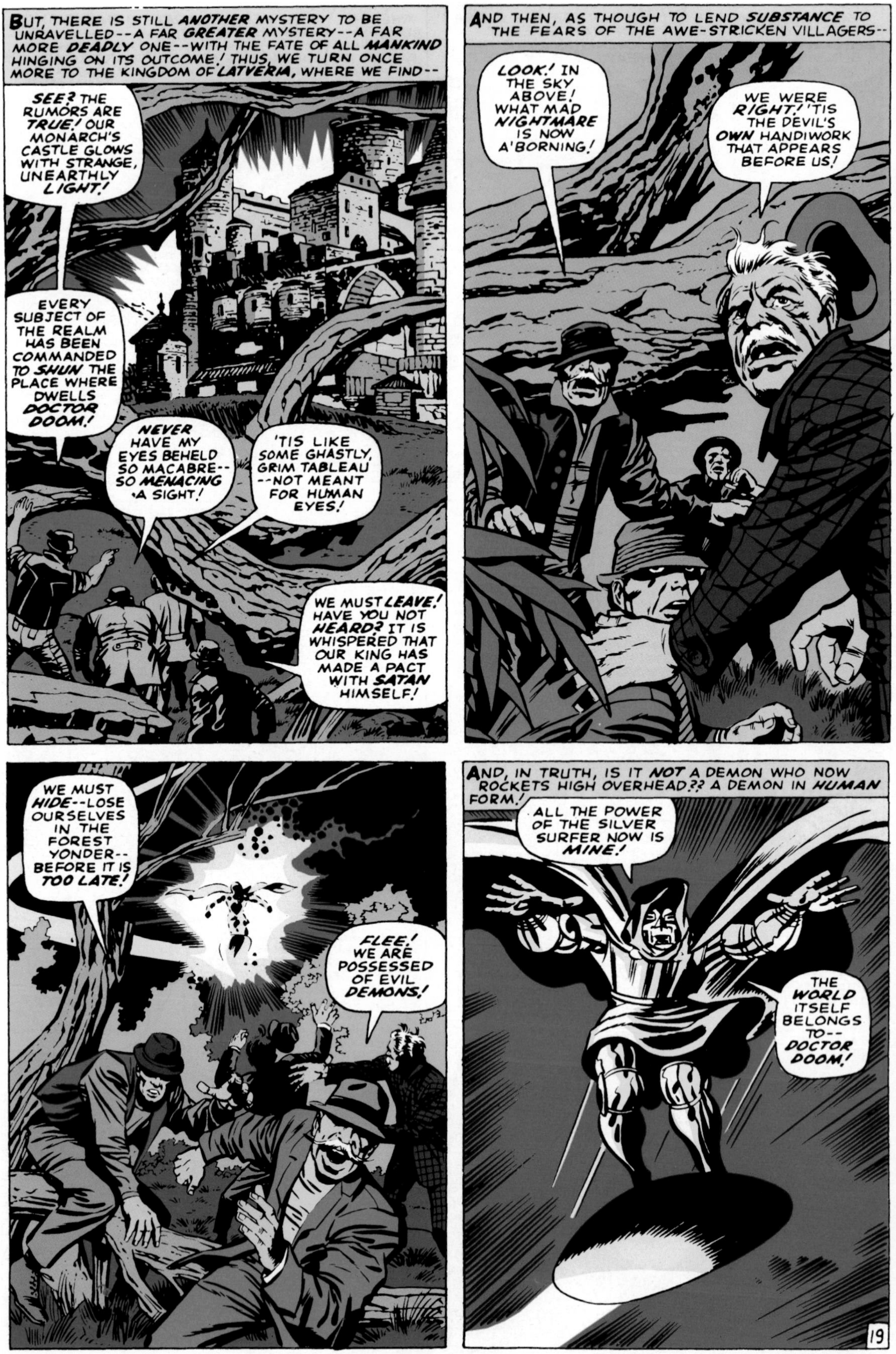
BUT, THERE IS STILL ANOTHER MYSTERY TO BE UNRAVELLED--A FAR GREATER MYSTERY--A FAR MORE DEADLY ONE--WITH THE FATE OF ALL MANKIND HINGING ON ITS OUTCOME! THUS, WE TURN ONCE MORE TO THE KINGDOM OF LATVERIA, WHERE WE FIND--
SEE? THE RUMORS ARE TRUE! OUR MONARCH'S CASTLE GLOWS WITH STRANGE, UNEARTHLY LIGHT!
EVERY SUBJECT OF THE REALM HAS BEEN COMMANDED TO SHUN THE PLACE WHERE DWELLS DOCTOR DOOM!
NEVER HAVE MY EYES BEHELD SO MACABRE--SO MENACING A SIGHT!
'TIS LIKE SOME GHASTLY, GRIM TABLEAU--NOT MEANT FOR HUMAN EYES!
WE MUST LEAVE! HAVE YOU NOT HEARD? IT IS WHISPERED THAT OUR KING HAS MADE A PACT WITH SATAN HIMSELF!
AND THEN, AS THOUGH TO LEND SUBSTANCE TO THE FEARS OF THE AWE-STRICKEN VILLAGERS--
LOOK! IN THE SKY ABOVE! WHAT MAD NIGHTMARE IS NOW A'BORNING!
WE WERE RIGHT! 'TIS THE DEVIL'S OWN HANDIWORK THAT APPEARS BEFORE US!
WE MUST HIDE--LOSE OURSELVES IN THE FOREST YONDER--BEFORE IT IS TOO LATE!
FLEE! WE ARE POSSESSED OF EVIL DEMONS!
AND, IN TRUTH, IS IT NOT A DEMON WHO NOW ROCKETS HIGH OVERHEAD?? A DEMON IN HUMAN FORM!
ALL THE POWER OF THE SILVER SURFER NOW IS MINE!
THE WORLD ITSELF BELONGS TO--DOCTOR DOOM!
19

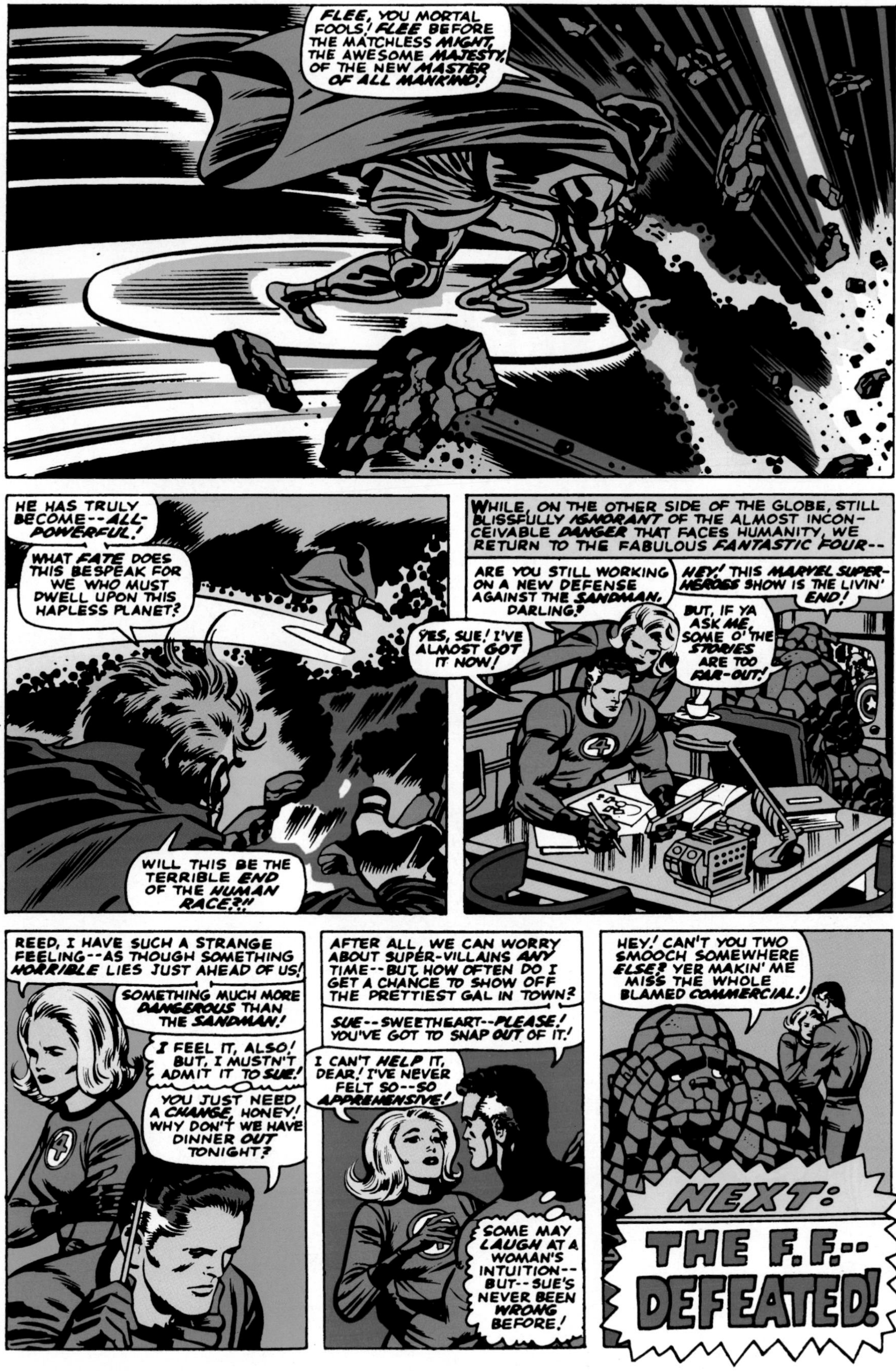
FLEE, YOU MORTAL FOOLS! FLEE BEFORE THE MATCHLESS MIGHT, THE AWESOME MAJESTY, OF THE NEW MASTER OF ALL MANKIND!
HE HAS TRULY BECOME--ALL-POWERFUL!
WHAT FATE DOES THIS BESPEAK FOR WE WHO MUST DWELL UPON THIS HAPLESS PLANET?
WILL THIS BE THE TERRIBLE END OF THE HUMAN RACE?!!
WHILE, ON THE OTHER SIDE OF THE GLOBE, STILL BLISSFULLY IGNORANT OF THE ALMOST INCONCEIVABLE DANGER THAT FACES HUMANITY, WE RETURN TO THE FABULOUS FANTASTIC FOUR--
ARE YOU STILL WORKING ON A NEW DEFENSE AGAINST THE SANDMAN, DARLING?
YES, SUE! I'VE ALMOST GOT IT NOW!
HEY! THIS MARVEL SUPER-HEROES SHOW IS THE LIVIN' END!
BUT, IF YA ASK ME, SOME O' THE STORIES ARE TOO FAR-OUT!
REED, I HAVE SUCH A STRANGE FEELING--AS THOUGH SOMETHING HORRIBLE LIES JUST AHEAD OF US!
SOMETHING MUCH MORE DANGEROUS THAN THE SANDMAN!
I FEEL IT, ALSO! BUT, I MUSTN'T ADMIT IT TO SUE!
YOU JUST NEED A CHANGE, HONEY! WHY DON'T WE HAVE DINNER OUT TONIGHT?
AFTER ALL, WE CAN WORRY ABOUT SUPER-VILLAINS ANY TIME--BUT, HOW OFTEN DO I GET A CHANCE TO SHOW OFF THE PRETTIEST GAL IN TOWN?
SUE--SWEETHEART--PLEASE! YOU'VE GOT TO SNAP OUT OF IT!
I CAN'T HELP IT, DEAR! I'VE NEVER FELT SO--SO APPREHENSIVE!
SOME MAY LAUGH AT A WOMAN'S INTUITION--BUT--SUE'S NEVER BEEN WRONG BEFORE!
HEY! CAN'T YOU TWO SMOOCH SOMEWHERE ELSE? YER MAKIN' ME MISS THE WHOLE BLAMED COMMERCIAL!
NEXT:
THE F.F.--DEFEATED!

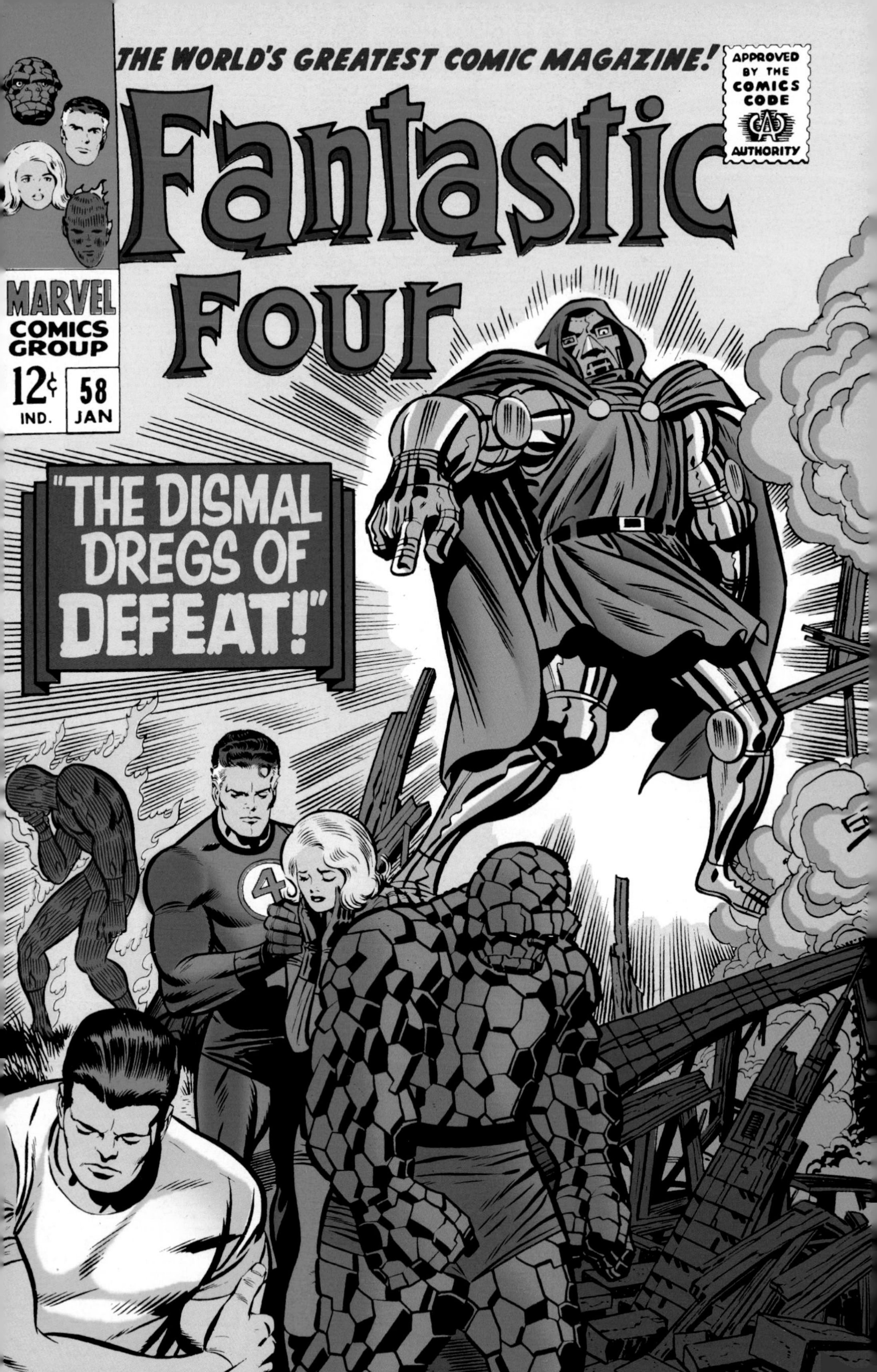
THE WORLD'S GREATEST COMIC MAGAZINE!
APPROVED BY THE COMICS CODE AUTHORITY
Fantastic Four
MARVEL COMICS GROUP
12¢ IND.
58 JAN
"THE DISMAL DREGS OF DEFEAT!"

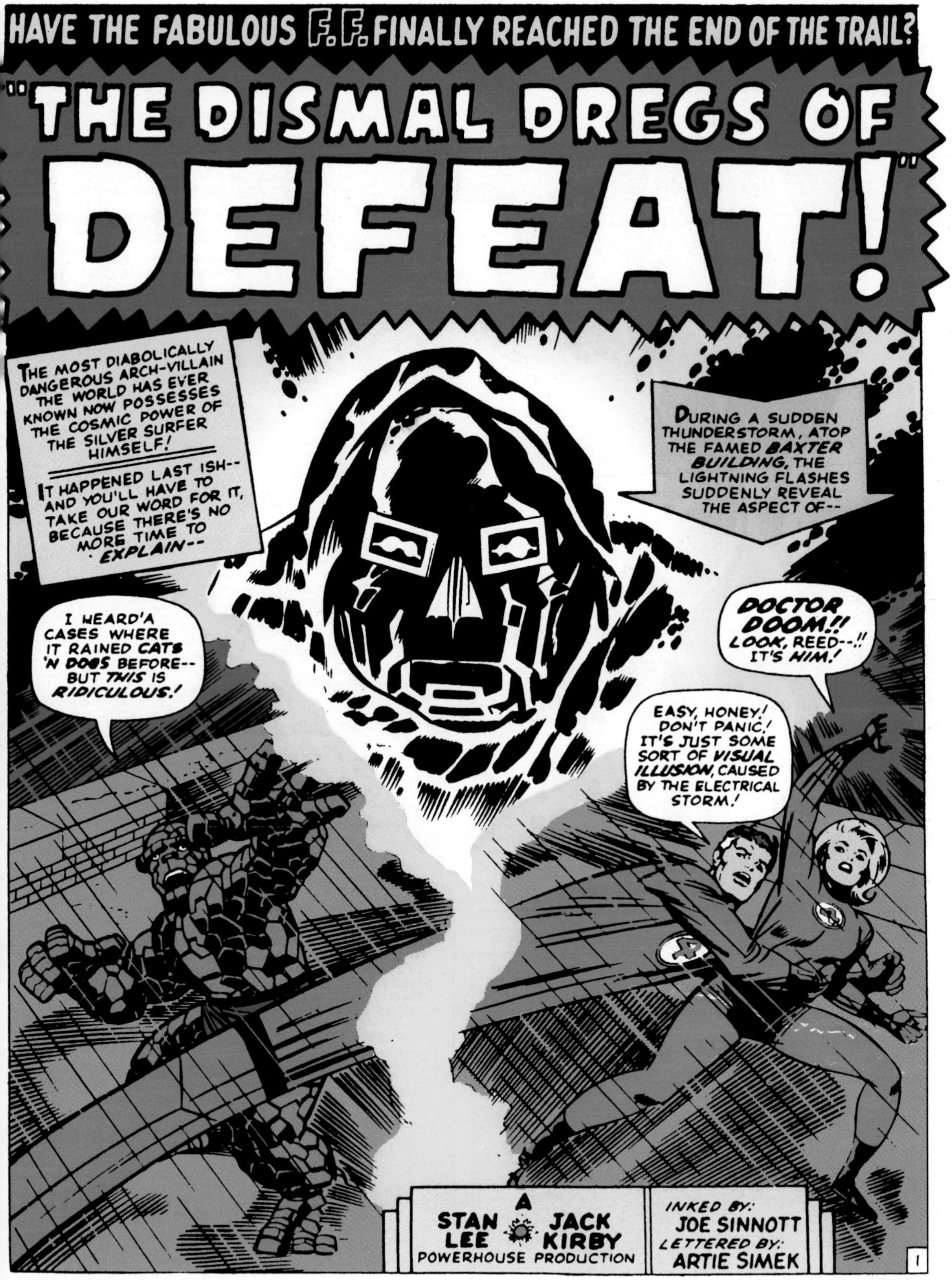
HAVE THE FABULOUS F.F. FINALLY REACHED THE END OF THE TRAIL?
"THE DISMAL DREGS OF DEFEAT!"
THE MOST DIABOLICALLY DANGEROUS ARCH-VILLAIN THE WORLD HAS EVER KNOWN NOW POSSESSES THE COSMIC POWER OF THE SILVER SURFER HIMSELF!
IT HAPPENED LAST ISH--AND YOU'LL HAVE TO TAKE OUR WORD FOR IT, BECAUSE THERE'S NO MORE TIME TO EXPLAIN--
DURING A SUDDEN THUNDERSTORM, ATOP THE FAMED BAXTER BUILDING, THE LIGHTNING FLASHES SUDDENLY REVEAL THE ASPECT OF--
I HEARD'A CASES WHERE IT RAINED CATS 'N DOGS BEFORE-- BUT THIS IS RIDICULOUS!
DOCTOR DOOM!! LOOK, REED--!! IT'S HIM!
EASY, HONEY! DON'T PANIC! IT'S JUST SOME SORT OF VISUAL ILLUSION, CAUSED BY THE ELECTRICAL STORM!
A STAN LEE JACK KIRBY POWERHOUSE PRODUCTION
INKED BY: JOE SINNOTT
LETTERED BY: ARTIE SIMEK
1

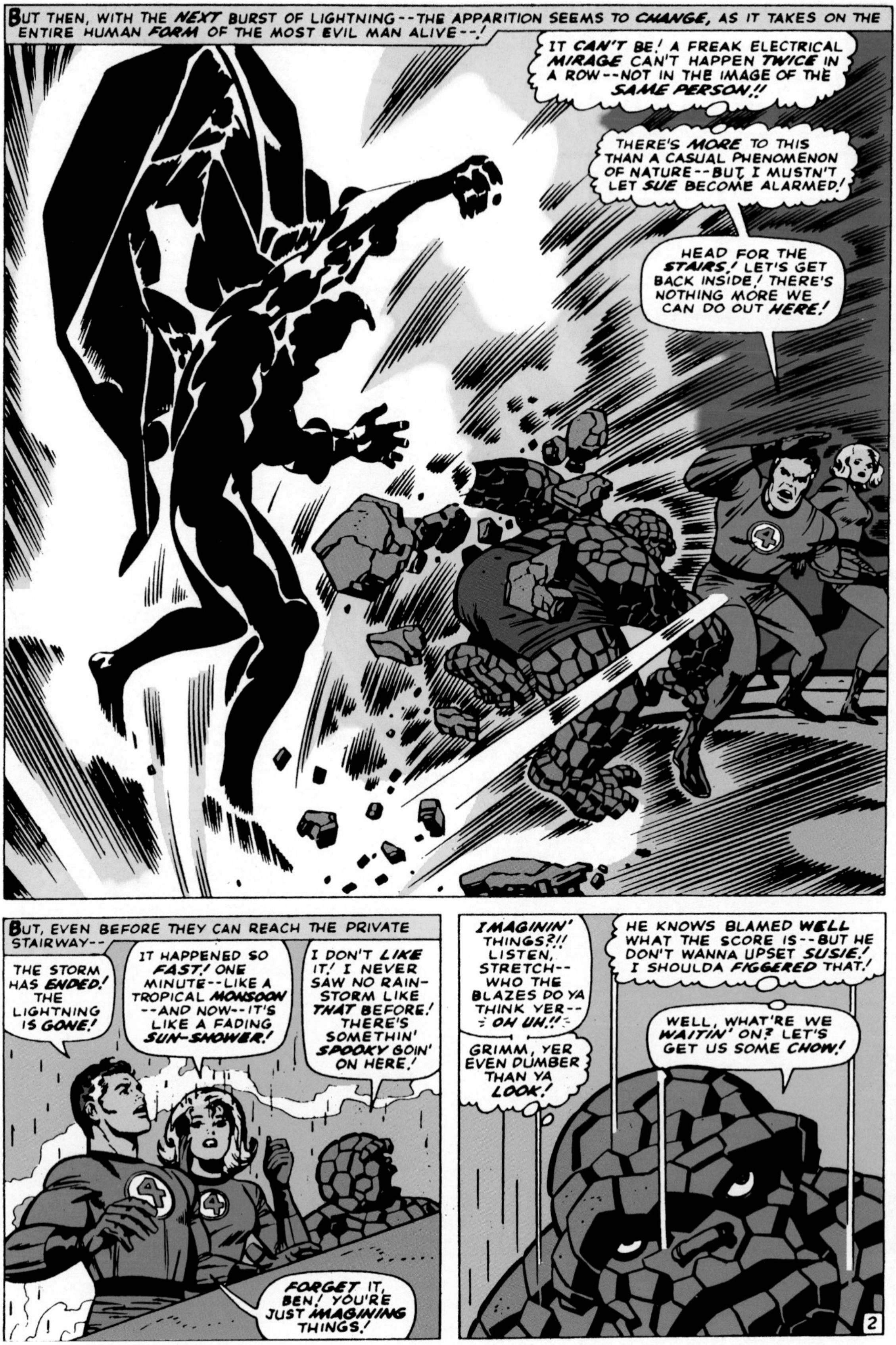
BUT THEN, WITH THE NEXT BURST OF LIGHTNING--THE APPARITION SEEMS TO CHANGE, AS IT TAKES ON THE ENTIRE HUMAN FORM OF THE MOST EVIL MAN ALIVE--!
IT CAN'T BE! A FREAK ELECTRICAL MIRAGE CAN'T HAPPEN TWICE IN A ROW--NOT IN THE IMAGE OF THE SAME PERSON!!
THERE'S MORE TO THIS THAN A CASUAL PHENOMENON OF NATURE--BUT I MUSTN'T LET SUE BECOME ALARMED!
HEAD FOR THE STAIRS! LET'S GET BACK INSIDE! THERE'S NOTHING MORE WE CAN DO OUT HERE!
BUT, EVEN BEFORE THEY CAN REACH THE PRIVATE STAIRWAY--
THE STORM HAS ENDED! THE LIGHTNING IS GONE!
IT HAPPENED SO FAST! ONE MINUTE--LIKE A TROPICAL MONSOON--AND NOW--IT'S LIKE A FADING SUN-SHOWER!
I DON'T LIKE IT! I NEVER SAW NO RAIN-STORM LIKE THAT BEFORE! THERE'S SOMETHIN' SPOOKY GOIN' ON HERE!
FORGET IT, BEN! YOU'RE JUST IMAGINING THINGS!
IMAGININ' THINGS?!! LISTEN, STRETCH--WHO THE BLAZES DO YA THINK YER--OH UH.!!
GRIMM, YER EVEN DUMBER THAN YA LOOK!
HE KNOWS BLAMED WELL WHAT THE SCORE IS--BUT HE DON'T WANNA UPSET SUSIE! I SHOULDA FIGGERED THAT!
WELL, WHAT'RE WE WAITIN' ON? LET'S GET US SOME CHOW!
2

IT IS *ENDED!* THEY HAVE NO IDEA WHAT *REALLY* HAPPENED--BUT THEY'RE WORRIED--CONFUSED,--SHAKEN-- JUST AS I *WISH* THEM TO BE!

LITTLE DO THEY DREAM THAT, HALF A WORLD AWAY--IN MY CASTLE IN LATVERIA--*DR. DOOM* HIMSELF CAUSED THAT STORM--WITH ITS ATTENDANT *APPARITIONS*--TO APPEAR!

BUT, ENOUGH OF SIMPLE, ROUTINE DEMONSTRATIONS OF THE *COSMIC POWER* I NOW POSSESS!

THE TIME HAS COME FOR THOSE WHOM I DESPISE *MOST* IN ALL THE WORLD TO FEEL THE FURY OF MY ATTACK *FACE TO FACE!*

THEN, ONCE THE *FANTASTIC FOUR* HAVE BEEN DISPOSED OF, THE ENTIRE *HUMAN RACE* WILL GROVEL AT THE FEET OF *DOCTOR DOOM!*

NOW, BEFORE EMBARKING UPON MY GREATEST MISSION, I SHALL BID *FAREWELL* TO THE ONE WHO HAS MADE IT ALL POSSIBLE!

THE ONE FROM WHOM I *STOLE* MY NEW, MATCHLESS *POWER!*

HE CAME TO EARTH FROM BEYOND THE *STARS*--AND ONLY *I* HAD THE STRENGTH--THE SKILL--TO *VANQUISH* HIM!

HAH! THE ONCE-MIGHTY *SILVER SURFER!*

NOW, BARELY ABLE TO MOVE A MUSCLE SINCE YOUR NEW *MASTER* HAS STRIPPED YOU OF YOUR *POWER!*

MASTER? *GALACTUS* HAD BEEN--MY MASTER! YOU--ARE BUT--A *FLEA*--!

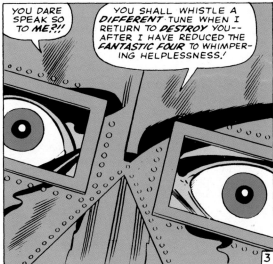

YOU DARE SPEAK SO TO *ME?!!*

YOU SHALL WHISTLE A *DIFFERENT* TUNE WHEN I RETURN TO *DESTROY* YOU-- AFTER I HAVE REDUCED THE *FANTASTIC FOUR* TO WHIMPERING HELPLESSNESS!

3

SECONDS LATER, A BLAST OF SHEER, UNDILUTED *COSMIC ENERGY* DISPERSES THE VERY *MOLECULES* OF THE CASTLE WALL...

ZZZZZZZ

AND, WHEN THE CRACKLING, SEARING FORCE REACHES ITS MAXIMUM INTENSITY, AN ARMORED, CLOAKED FIGURE--AND AN UNEARTHLY *SURF-BOARD,* HURTLE SKYWARD FROM THE CENTER OF THE RAGING HOLOCAUST--

SHOOM!

LIKE SOME PREDATORY WINGED MONSTER FROM ANOTHER AGE--ANOTHER UNIVERSE-- THE INCREDIBLE ARCH-FIEND ZOOMS WESTWARD--AT A SPEED WHICH VIRTUALLY DEFIES BELIEF--!

NOTHING CAN STOP ME NOW!*

*WHO *SAYS* THIS ISN'T THE MARVEL AGE OF CALLOUS CLICHÉS? --SHAMEFACED STAN.

SOME TIME LATER, AS A DEEPLY ENGROSSED, ORANGE-SKINNED LITERATURE LOVER PURSUES HIS RELENTLESS QUEST FOR KNOWLEDGE--

I WONDER IF THERE REALLY *ARE* SUCH THINGS AS *HAUNTED HOUSES?*

PROBABLY *NOT,* OR STRETCHO WOULD'A CONNED ME INTO SPENDIN' A *NIGHT* IN ONE BY NOW!

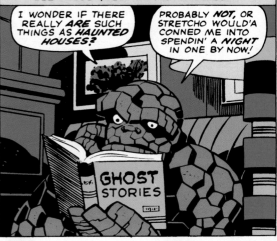

GHOST STORIES

AWW, WHO'D BE DUMB ENUFF TO FALL FER STUFF LIKE *THIS?*

THESE YARNS MUST BE WRITTEN FER *KIDS* OR SOMETHIN'!

YOU DON'T CATCH A *SOPHISTICATED* GUY LIKE *ME* GITTIN' HUNG UP WITH-- WITH--

I DON'T REMEMBER NUTHIN' ON MY *SHOULDER*-- WHEN I *STARTED* READIN'--!

4

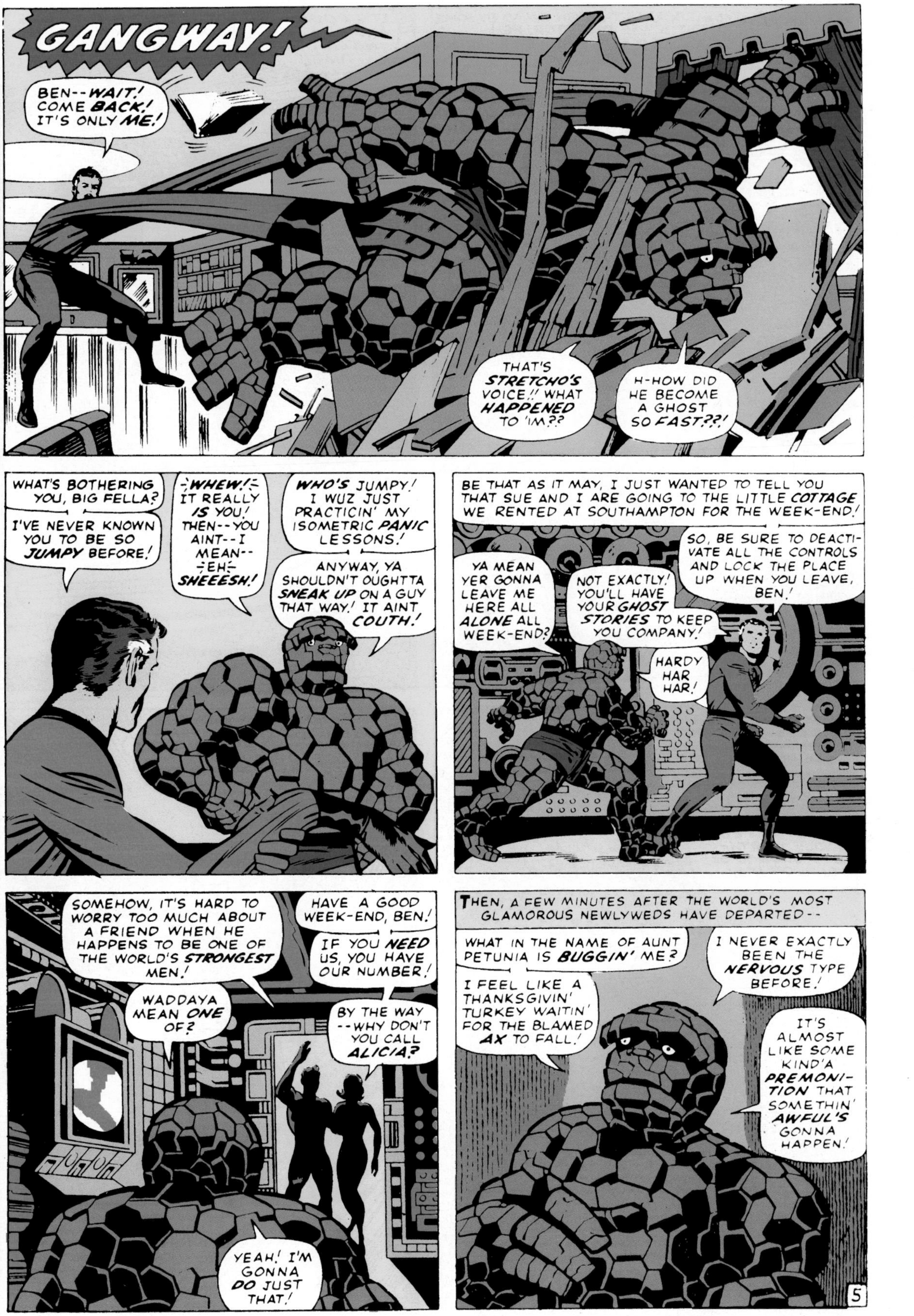
GANGWAY!
BEN--WAIT! COME BACK! IT'S ONLY ME!
THAT'S STRETCHO'S VOICE!! WHAT HAPPENED TO 'IM??
H-HOW DID HE BECOME A GHOST SO FAST??!
WHAT'S BOTHERING YOU, BIG FELLA?
I'VE NEVER KNOWN YOU TO BE SO JUMPY BEFORE!
-WHEW!- IT REALLY IS YOU! THEN--YOU AINT--I MEAN-- -EH- SHEEESH!
WHO'S JUMPY! I WUZ JUST PRACTICIN' MY ISOMETRIC PANIC LESSONS!
ANYWAY, YA SHOULDN'T OUGHTTA SNEAK UP ON A GUY THAT WAY! IT AINT COUTH!
BE THAT AS IT MAY, I JUST WANTED TO TELL YOU THAT SUE AND I ARE GOING TO THE LITTLE COTTAGE WE RENTED AT SOUTHAMPTON FOR THE WEEK-END!
SO, BE SURE TO DEACTIVATE ALL THE CONTROLS AND LOCK THE PLACE UP WHEN YOU LEAVE, BEN!
YA MEAN YER GONNA LEAVE ME HERE ALL ALONE ALL WEEK-END?
NOT EXACTLY! YOU'LL HAVE YOUR GHOST STORIES TO KEEP YOU COMPANY!
HARDY HAR HAR!
SOMEHOW, IT'S HARD TO WORRY TOO MUCH ABOUT A FRIEND WHEN HE HAPPENS TO BE ONE OF THE WORLD'S STRONGEST MEN!
WADDAYA MEAN ONE OF?
HAVE A GOOD WEEK-END, BEN!
IF YOU NEED US, YOU HAVE OUR NUMBER!
BY THE WAY --WHY DON'T YOU CALL ALICIA?
YEAH! I'M GONNA DO JUST THAT!
THEN, A FEW MINUTES AFTER THE WORLD'S MOST GLAMOROUS NEWLYWEDS HAVE DEPARTED--
WHAT IN THE NAME OF AUNT PETUNIA IS BUGGIN' ME?
I FEEL LIKE A THANKSGIVIN' TURKEY WAITIN' FOR THE BLAMED AX TO FALL!
I NEVER EXACTLY BEEN THE NERVOUS TYPE BEFORE!
IT'S ALMOST LIKE SOME KIND'A PREMONITION THAT SOMETHIN' AWFUL'S GONNA HAPPEN!
5

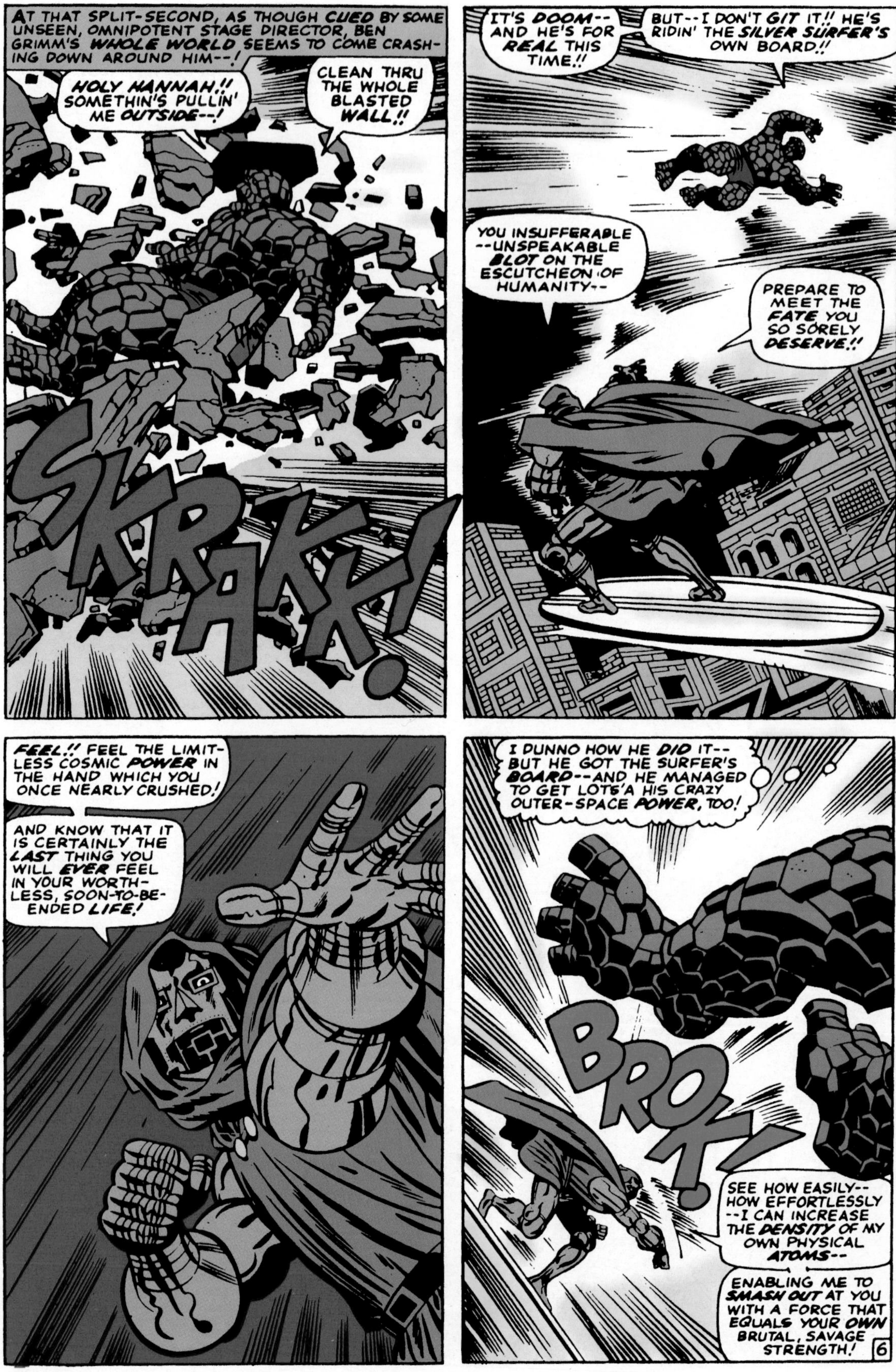

AT THAT SPLIT-SECOND, AS THOUGH CUED BY SOME UNSEEN, OMNIPOTENT STAGE DIRECTOR, BEN GRIMM'S WHOLE WORLD SEEMS TO COME CRASHING DOWN AROUND HIM--!
HOLY HANNAH!! SOMETHIN'S PULLIN' ME OUTSIDE--!
CLEAN THRU THE WHOLE BLASTED WALL!!
SKRAKK!
IT'S DOOM--AND HE'S FOR REAL THIS TIME!!
BUT--I DON'T GIT IT!! HE'S RIDIN' THE SILVER SURFER'S OWN BOARD!!
YOU INSUFFERABLE--UNSPEAKABLE BLOT ON THE ESCUTCHEON OF HUMANITY--
PREPARE TO MEET THE FATE YOU SO SORELY DESERVE!!
FEEL!! FEEL THE LIMITLESS COSMIC POWER IN THE HAND WHICH YOU ONCE NEARLY CRUSHED!
AND KNOW THAT IT IS CERTAINLY THE LAST THING YOU WILL EVER FEEL IN YOUR WORTHLESS, SOON-TO-BE-ENDED LIFE!
I DUNNO HOW HE DID IT--BUT HE GOT THE SURFER'S BOARD--AND HE MANAGED TO GET LOTS'A HIS CRAZY OUTER-SPACE POWER, TOO!
BROK!
SEE HOW EASILY--HOW EFFORTLESSLY--I CAN INCREASE THE DENSITY OF MY OWN PHYSICAL ATOMS--
ENABLING ME TO SMASH OUT AT YOU WITH A FORCE THAT EQUALS YOUR OWN BRUTAL, SAVAGE STRENGTH!
6

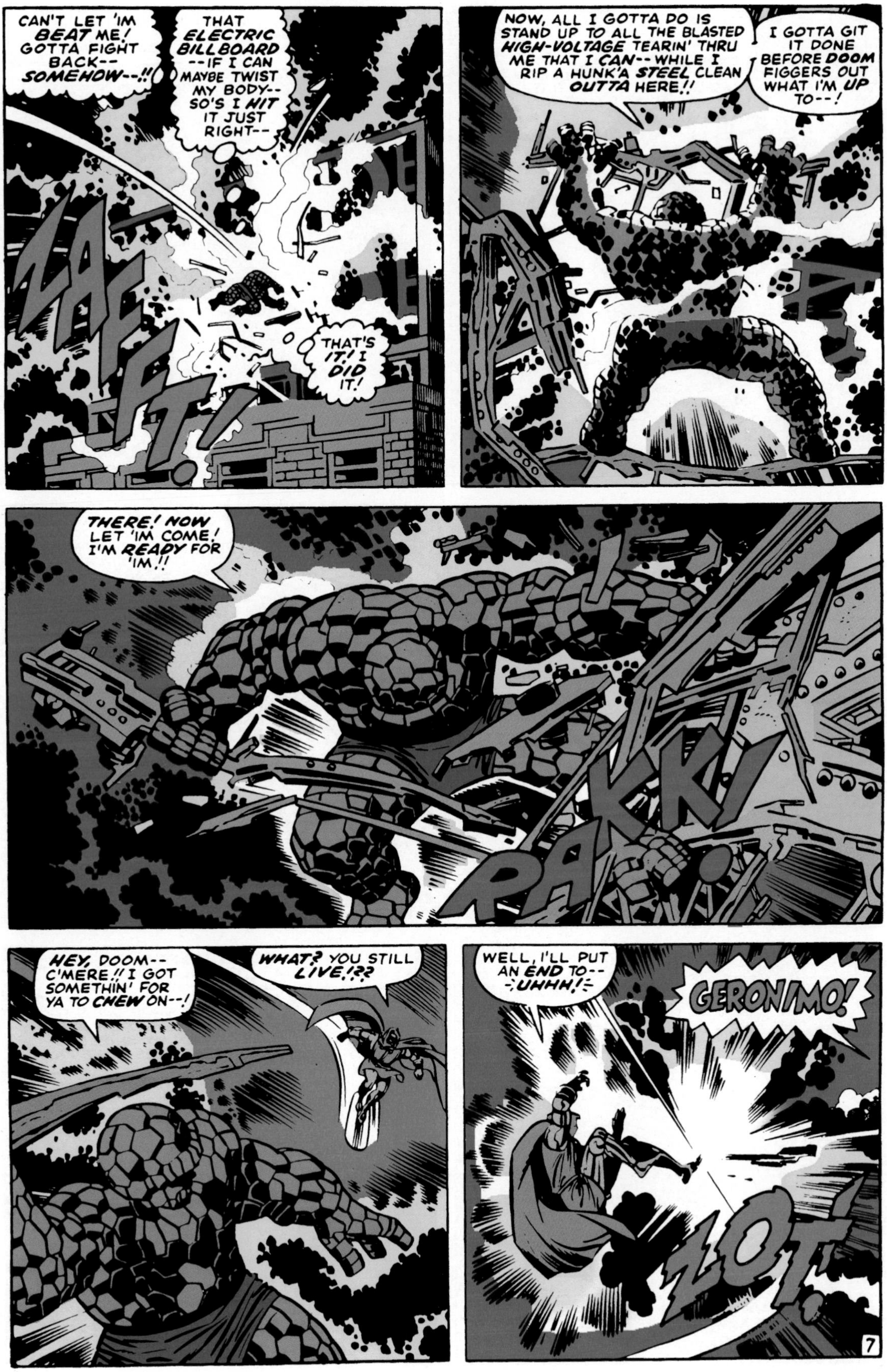
CAN'T LET 'IM BEAT ME! GOTTA FIGHT BACK-- SOMEHOW--!!
THAT ELECTRIC BILLBOARD --IF I CAN MAYBE TWIST MY BODY-- SO'S I HIT IT JUST RIGHT--
ZAFFT!
THAT'S IT! I DID IT!
NOW, ALL I GOTTA DO IS STAND UP TO ALL THE BLASTED HIGH-VOLTAGE TEARIN' THRU ME THAT I CAN-- WHILE I RIP A HUNK'A STEEL CLEAN OUTTA HERE!!
I GOTTA GIT IT DONE BEFORE DOOM FIGGERS OUT WHAT I'M UP TO--!
THERE! NOW LET 'IM COME! I'M READY FOR 'IM!!
RAKK!
HEY, DOOM-- C'MERE!! I GOT SOMETHIN' FOR YA TO CHEW ON--!
WHAT? YOU STILL LIVE!??
WELL, I'LL PUT AN END TO-- UHHH!
GERONIMO!
ZOT!
7

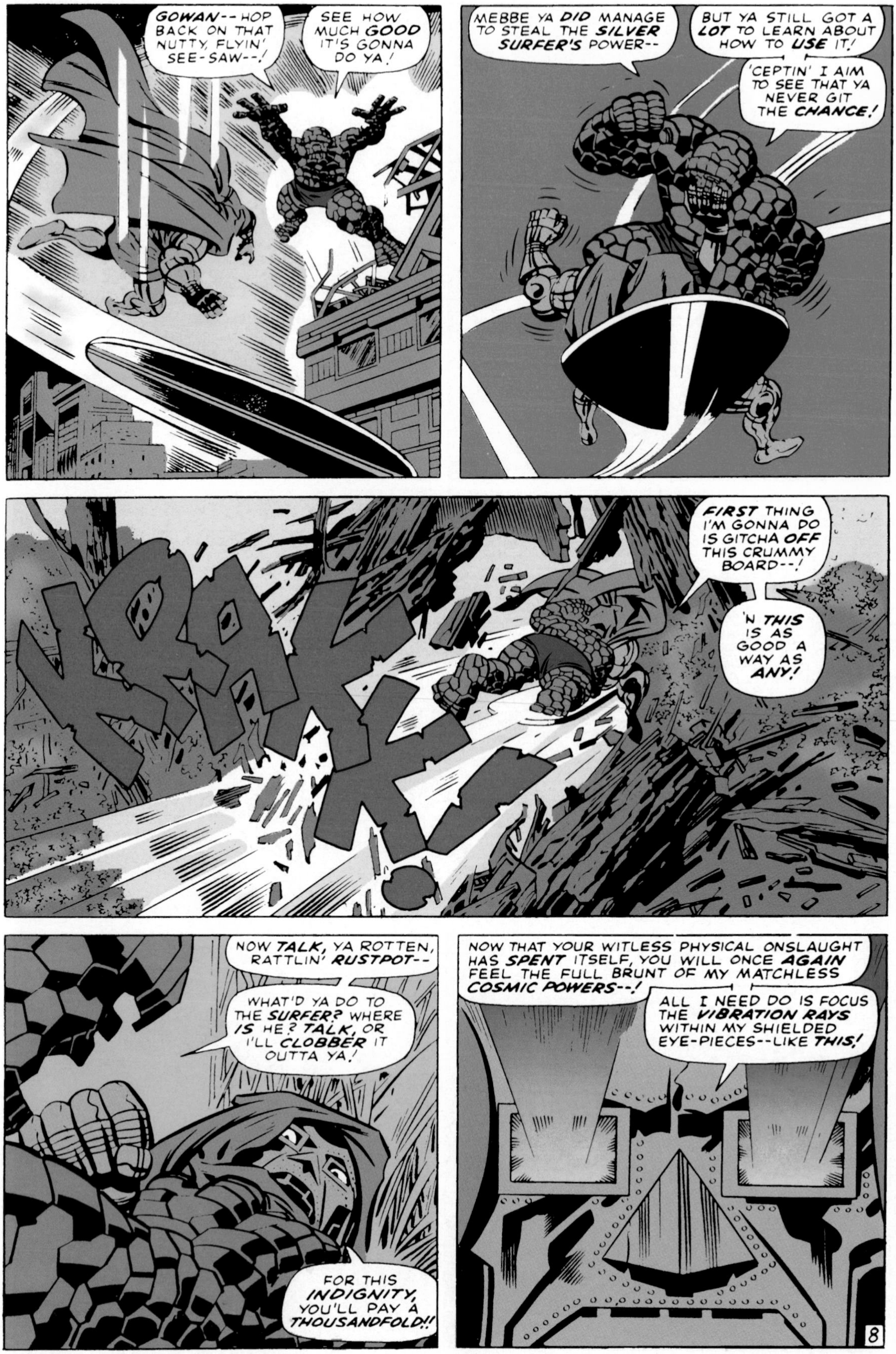
GOWAN-- HOP BACK ON THAT NUTTY, FLYIN' SEE-SAW--!
SEE HOW MUCH GOOD IT'S GONNA DO YA!
MEBBE YA DID MANAGE TO STEAL THE SILVER SURFER'S POWER--
BUT YA STILL GOT A LOT TO LEARN ABOUT HOW TO USE IT!
'CEPTIN' I AIM TO SEE THAT YA NEVER GIT THE CHANCE!
KRAKK
FIRST THING I'M GONNA DO IS GITCHA OFF THIS CRUMMY BOARD--!
'N THIS IS AS GOOD A WAY AS ANY!
NOW TALK, YA ROTTEN, RATTLIN' RUSTPOT--
WHAT'D YA DO TO THE SURFER? WHERE IS HE? TALK, OR I'LL CLOBBER IT OUTTA YA!
FOR THIS INDIGNITY, YOU'LL PAY A THOUSANDFOLD!!
NOW THAT YOUR WITLESS PHYSICAL ONSLAUGHT HAS SPENT ITSELF, YOU WILL ONCE AGAIN FEEL THE FULL BRUNT OF MY MATCHLESS COSMIC POWERS--!
ALL I NEED DO IS FOCUS THE VIBRATION RAYS WITHIN MY SHIELDED EYE-PIECES--LIKE THIS!
8

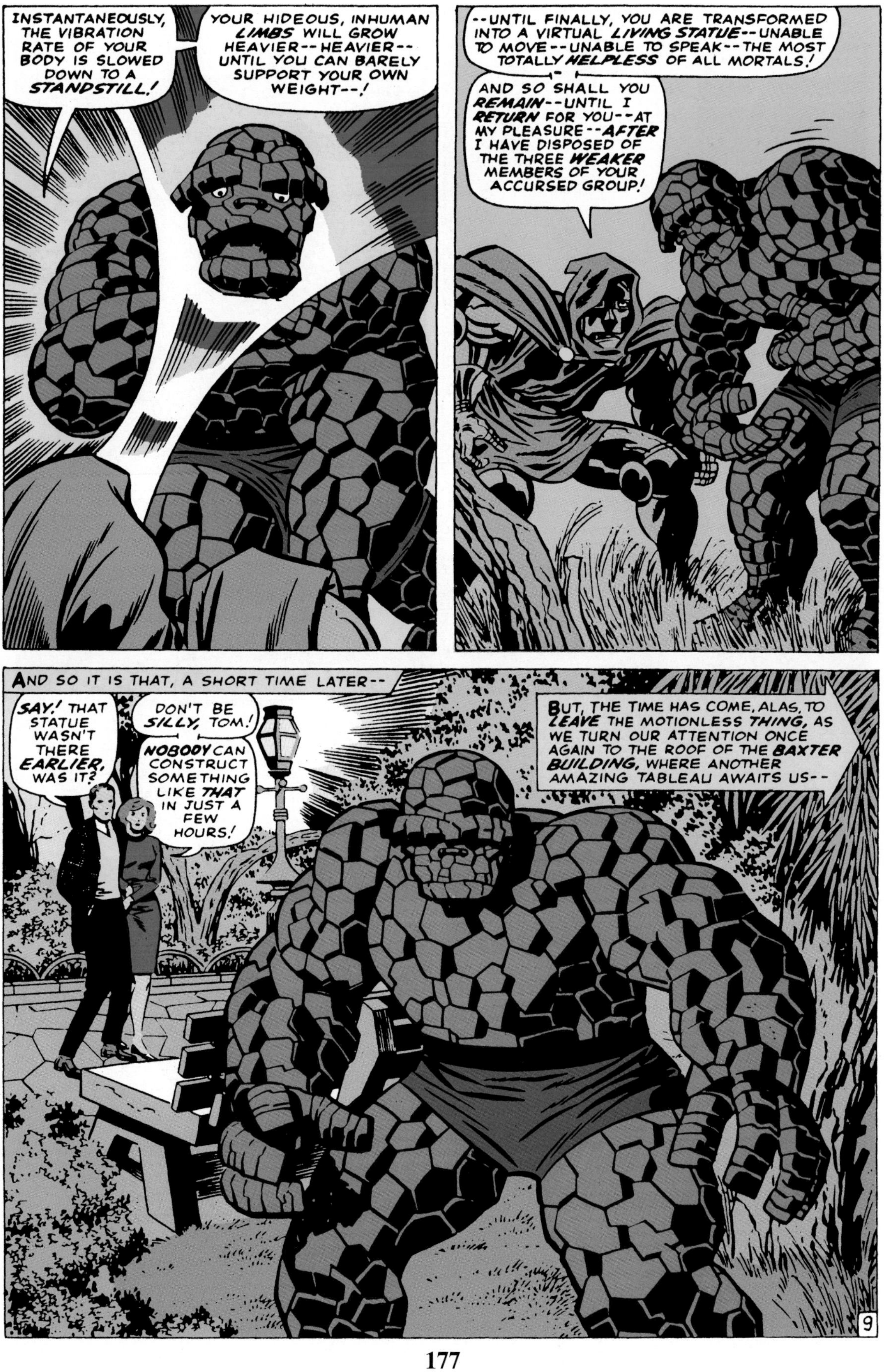

INSTANTANEOUSLY, THE VIBRATION RATE OF YOUR BODY IS SLOWED DOWN TO A STANDSTILL!
YOUR HIDEOUS, INHUMAN LIMBS WILL GROW HEAVIER--HEAVIER--UNTIL YOU CAN BARELY SUPPORT YOUR OWN WEIGHT--!
--UNTIL FINALLY, YOU ARE TRANSFORMED INTO A VIRTUAL LIVING STATUE--UNABLE TO MOVE--UNABLE TO SPEAK--THE MOST TOTALLY HELPLESS OF ALL MORTALS!
AND SO SHALL YOU REMAIN--UNTIL I RETURN FOR YOU--AT MY PLEASURE--AFTER I HAVE DISPOSED OF THE THREE WEAKER MEMBERS OF YOUR ACCURSED GROUP!
AND SO IT IS THAT, A SHORT TIME LATER--
SAY! THAT STATUE WASN'T THERE EARLIER, WAS IT?
DON'T BE SILLY, TOM!
NOBODY CAN CONSTRUCT SOMETHING LIKE THAT IN JUST A FEW HOURS!
BUT, THE TIME HAS COME, ALAS, TO LEAVE THE MOTIONLESS THING, AS WE TURN OUR ATTENTION ONCE AGAIN TO THE ROOF OF THE BAXTER BUILDING, WHERE ANOTHER AMAZING TABLEAU AWAITS US--
9

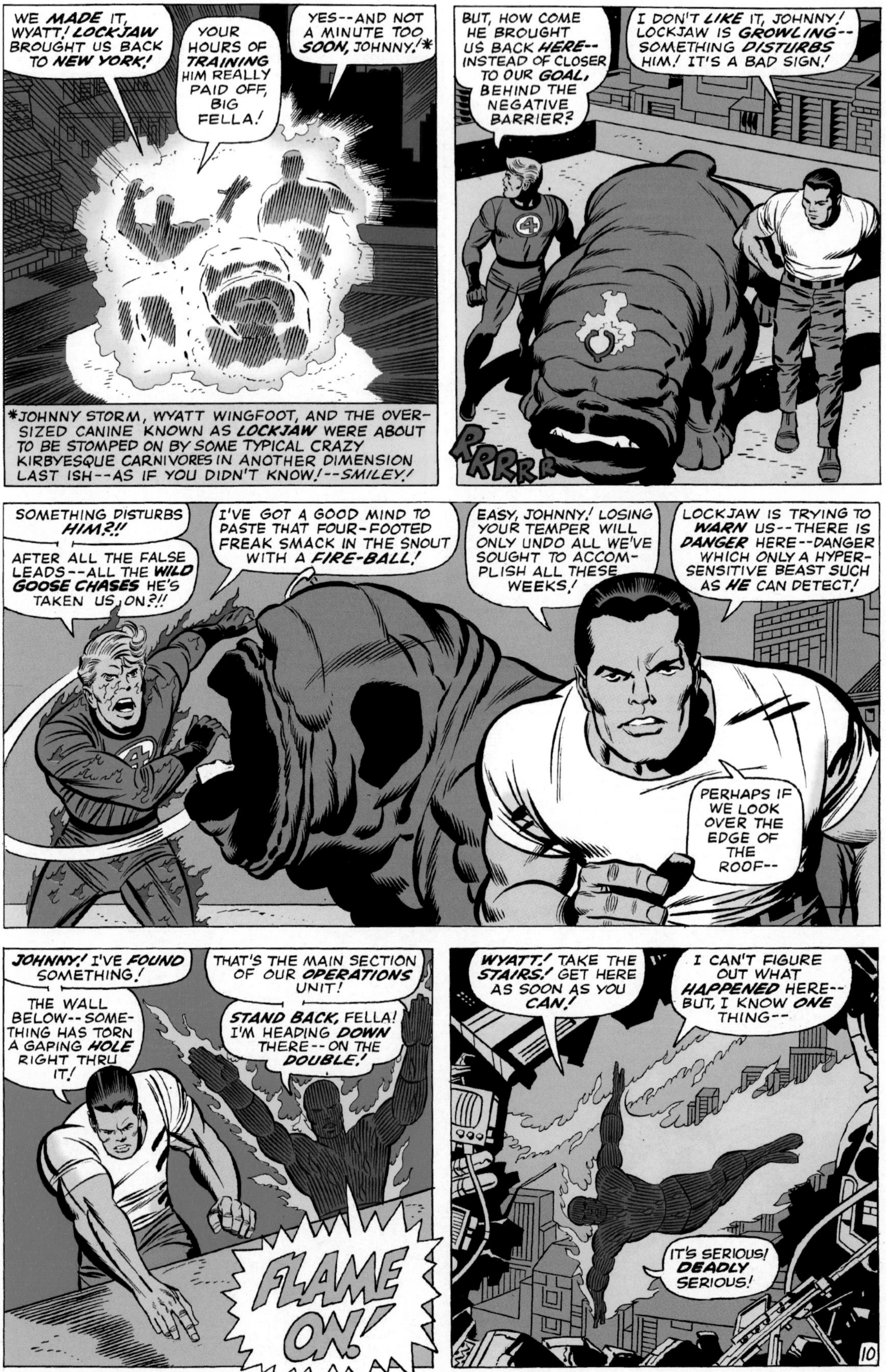
WE MADE IT, WYATT! LOCKJAW BROUGHT US BACK TO NEW YORK!
YOUR HOURS OF TRAINING HIM REALLY PAID OFF, BIG FELLA!
YES--AND NOT A MINUTE TOO SOON, JOHNNY!*
*JOHNNY STORM, WYATT WINGFOOT, AND THE OVER-SIZED CANINE KNOWN AS LOCKJAW WERE ABOUT TO BE STOMPED ON BY SOME TYPICAL CRAZY KIRBYESQUE CARNIVORES IN ANOTHER DIMENSION LAST ISH--AS IF YOU DIDN'T KNOW!--SMILEY!
BUT, HOW COME HE BROUGHT US BACK HERE--INSTEAD OF CLOSER TO OUR GOAL, BEHIND THE NEGATIVE BARRIER?
I DON'T LIKE IT, JOHNNY! LOCKJAW IS GROWLING--SOMETHING DISTURBS HIM! IT'S A BAD SIGN!
RRRRRR
SOMETHING DISTURBS HIM?!!
AFTER ALL THE FALSE LEADS--ALL THE WILD GOOSE CHASES HE'S TAKEN US ON?!!
I'VE GOT A GOOD MIND TO PASTE THAT FOUR-FOOTED FREAK SMACK IN THE SNOUT WITH A FIRE-BALL!
EASY, JOHNNY! LOSING YOUR TEMPER WILL ONLY UNDO ALL WE'VE SOUGHT TO ACCOMPLISH ALL THESE WEEKS!
LOCKJAW IS TRYING TO WARN US--THERE IS DANGER HERE--DANGER WHICH ONLY A HYPER-SENSITIVE BEAST SUCH AS HE CAN DETECT!
PERHAPS IF WE LOOK OVER THE EDGE OF THE ROOF--
JOHNNY! I'VE FOUND SOMETHING!
THE WALL BELOW--SOMETHING HAS TORN A GAPING HOLE RIGHT THRU IT!
THAT'S THE MAIN SECTION OF OUR OPERATIONS UNIT!
STAND BACK, FELLA! I'M HEADING DOWN THERE--ON THE DOUBLE!
FLAME ON!
WYATT! TAKE THE STAIRS! GET HERE AS SOON AS YOU CAN!
I CAN'T FIGURE OUT WHAT HAPPENED HERE--BUT, I KNOW ONE THING--
IT'S SERIOUS! DEADLY SERIOUS!
10

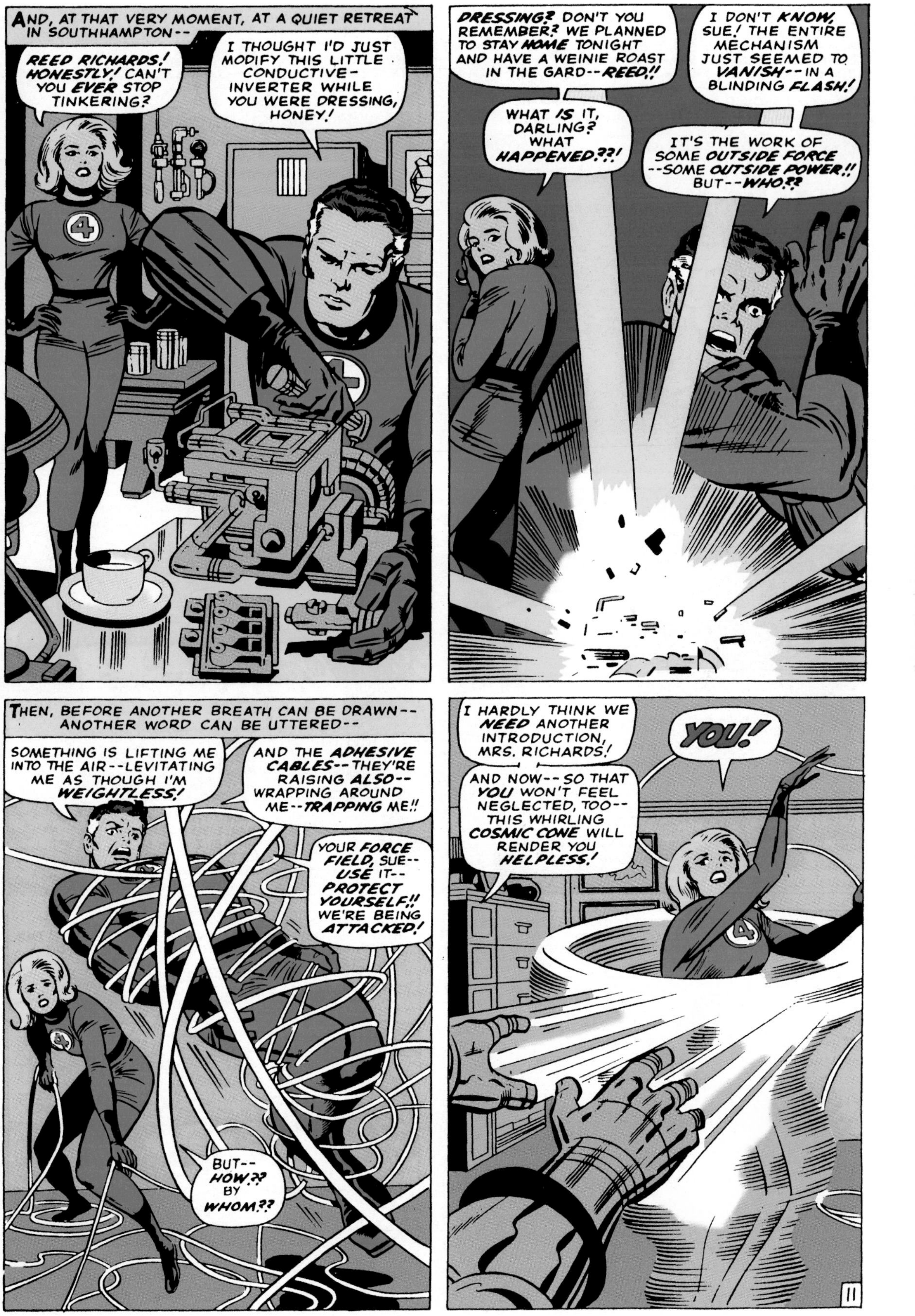
AND, AT THAT VERY MOMENT, AT A QUIET RETREAT IN SOUTHHAMPTON--
REED RICHARDS! HONESTLY! CAN'T YOU EVER STOP TINKERING?
I THOUGHT I'D JUST MODIFY THIS LITTLE CONDUCTIVE-INVERTER WHILE YOU WERE DRESSING, HONEY!
DRESSING? DON'T YOU REMEMBER? WE PLANNED TO STAY HOME TONIGHT AND HAVE A WEINIE ROAST IN THE GARD--REED!!
WHAT IS IT, DARLING? WHAT HAPPENED??!
I DON'T KNOW, SUE! THE ENTIRE MECHANISM JUST SEEMED TO VANISH--IN A BLINDING FLASH!
IT'S THE WORK OF SOME OUTSIDE FORCE--SOME OUTSIDE POWER!! BUT--WHO??
THEN, BEFORE ANOTHER BREATH CAN BE DRAWN--ANOTHER WORD CAN BE UTTERED--
SOMETHING IS LIFTING ME INTO THE AIR--LEVITATING ME AS THOUGH I'M WEIGHTLESS!
AND THE ADHESIVE CABLES--THEY'RE RAISING ALSO--WRAPPING AROUND ME--TRAPPING ME!!
YOUR FORCE FIELD, SUE--USE IT--PROTECT YOURSELF!! WE'RE BEING ATTACKED!
BUT--HOW?? BY WHOM??
I HARDLY THINK WE NEED ANOTHER INTRODUCTION, MRS. RICHARDS!
AND NOW--SO THAT YOU WON'T FEEL NEGLECTED, TOO--THIS WHIRLING COSMIC CONE WILL RENDER YOU HELPLESS!
YOU!
11

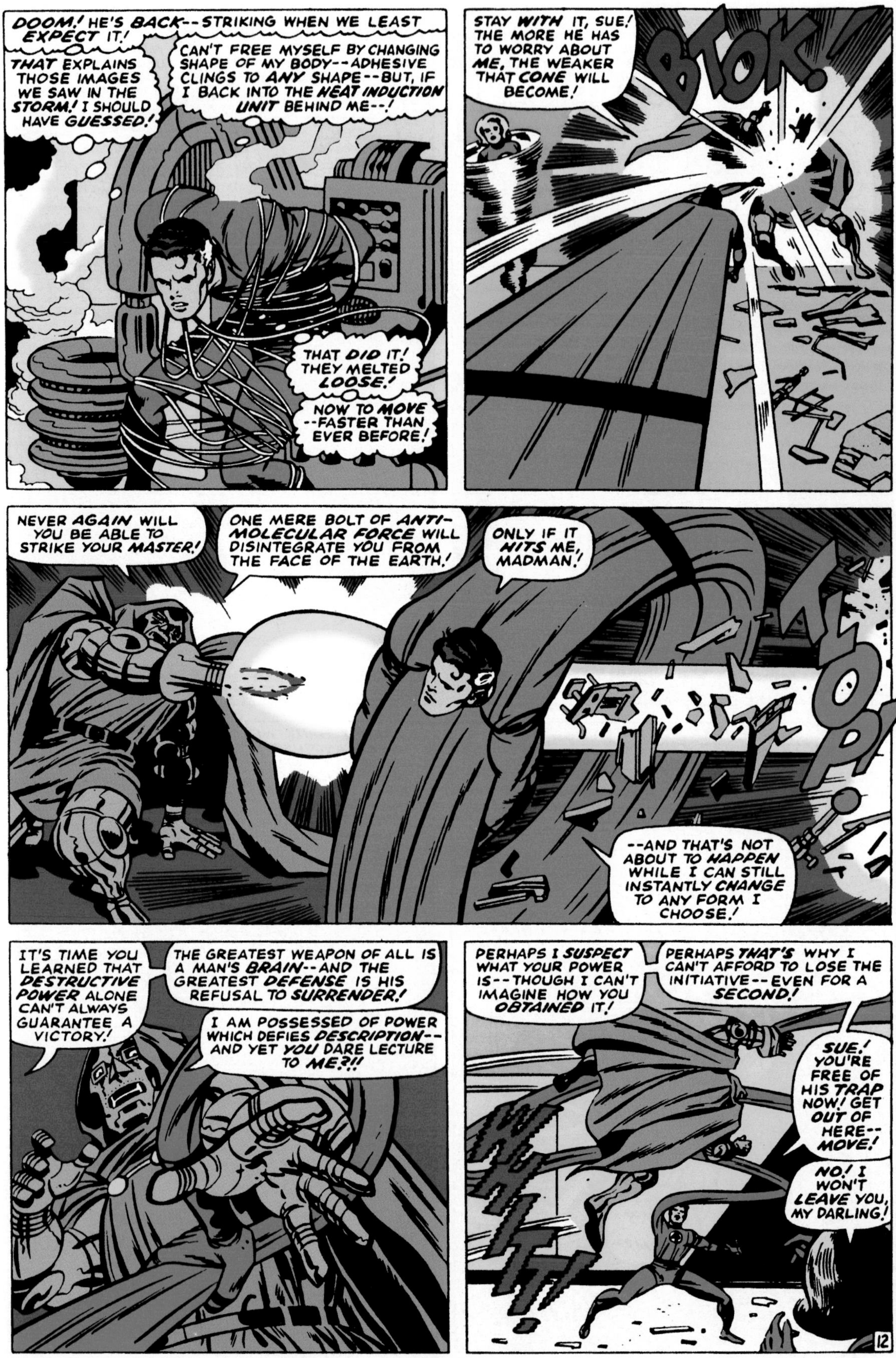
DOOM! HE'S BACK--STRIKING WHEN WE LEAST EXPECT IT!
THAT EXPLAINS THOSE IMAGES WE SAW IN THE STORM! I SHOULD HAVE GUESSED!
CAN'T FREE MYSELF BY CHANGING SHAPE OF MY BODY--ADHESIVE CLINGS TO ANY SHAPE--BUT, IF I BACK INTO THE HEAT INDUCTION UNIT BEHIND ME--!
THAT DID IT! THEY MELTED LOOSE!
NOW TO MOVE --FASTER THAN EVER BEFORE!
STAY WITH IT, SUE! THE MORE HE HAS TO WORRY ABOUT ME, THE WEAKER THAT CONE WILL BECOME!
BTOK!
NEVER AGAIN WILL YOU BE ABLE TO STRIKE YOUR MASTER!
ONE MERE BOLT OF ANTI-MOLECULAR FORCE WILL DISINTEGRATE YOU FROM THE FACE OF THE EARTH!
ONLY IF IT HITS ME, MADMAN!
--AND THAT'S NOT ABOUT TO HAPPEN WHILE I CAN STILL INSTANTLY CHANGE TO ANY FORM I CHOOSE!
IT'S TIME YOU LEARNED THAT DESTRUCTIVE POWER ALONE CAN'T ALWAYS GUARANTEE A VICTORY!
THE GREATEST WEAPON OF ALL IS A MAN'S BRAIN--AND THE GREATEST DEFENSE IS HIS REFUSAL TO SURRENDER!
I AM POSSESSED OF POWER WHICH DEFIES DESCRIPTION--AND YET YOU DARE LECTURE TO ME?!!
PERHAPS I SUSPECT WHAT YOUR POWER IS--THOUGH I CAN'T IMAGINE HOW YOU OBTAINED IT!
PERHAPS THAT'S WHY I CAN'T AFFORD TO LOSE THE INITIATIVE--EVEN FOR A SECOND!
SUE! YOU'RE FREE OF HIS TRAP NOW! GET OUT OF HERE--MOVE!
NO! I WON'T LEAVE YOU, MY DARLING!
12

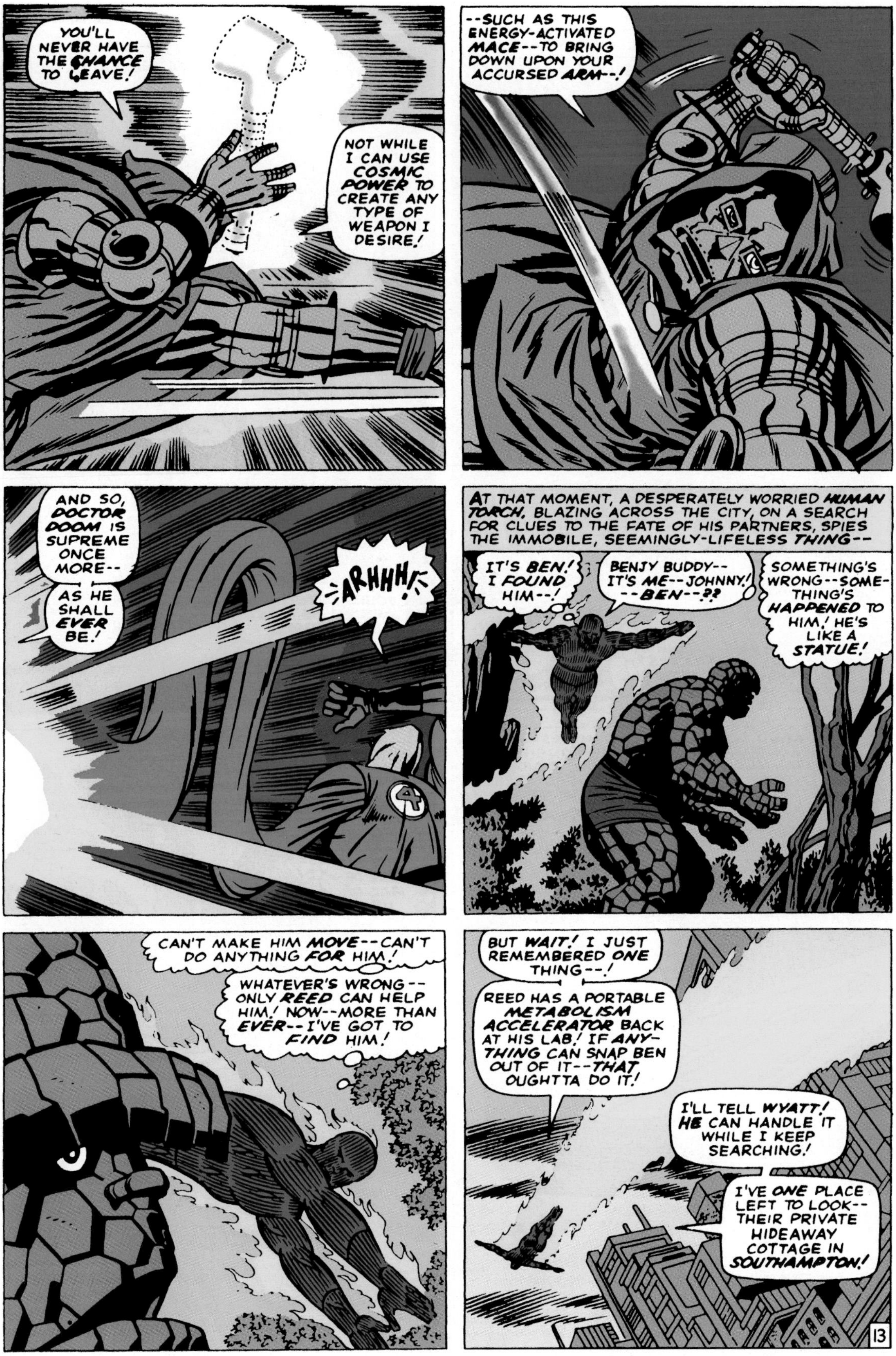
YOU'LL NEVER HAVE THE CHANCE TO LEAVE!
NOT WHILE I CAN USE COSMIC POWER TO CREATE ANY TYPE OF WEAPON I DESIRE!
--SUCH AS THIS ENERGY-ACTIVATED MACE--TO BRING DOWN UPON YOUR ACCURSED ARM--!
AND SO, DOCTOR DOOM IS SUPREME ONCE MORE--
AS HE SHALL EVER BE!
ARHHH!
AT THAT MOMENT, A DESPERATELY WORRIED HUMAN TORCH, BLAZING ACROSS THE CITY, ON A SEARCH FOR CLUES TO THE FATE OF HIS PARTNERS, SPIES THE IMMOBILE, SEEMINGLY-LIFELESS THING--
IT'S BEN! I FOUND HIM--!
BENJY BUDDY--IT'S ME--JOHNNY! --BEN--??
SOMETHING'S WRONG--SOMETHING'S HAPPENED TO HIM! HE'S LIKE A STATUE!
CAN'T MAKE HIM MOVE--CAN'T DO ANYTHING FOR HIM!
WHATEVER'S WRONG--ONLY REED CAN HELP HIM! NOW--MORE THAN EVER--I'VE GOT TO FIND HIM!
BUT WAIT! I JUST REMEMBERED ONE THING--!
REED HAS A PORTABLE METABOLISM ACCELERATOR BACK AT HIS LAB! IF ANYTHING CAN SNAP BEN OUT OF IT--THAT OUGHTTA DO IT!
I'LL TELL WYATT! HE CAN HANDLE IT WHILE I KEEP SEARCHING!
I'VE ONE PLACE LEFT TO LOOK--THEIR PRIVATE HIDEAWAY COTTAGE IN SOUTHAMPTON!
13

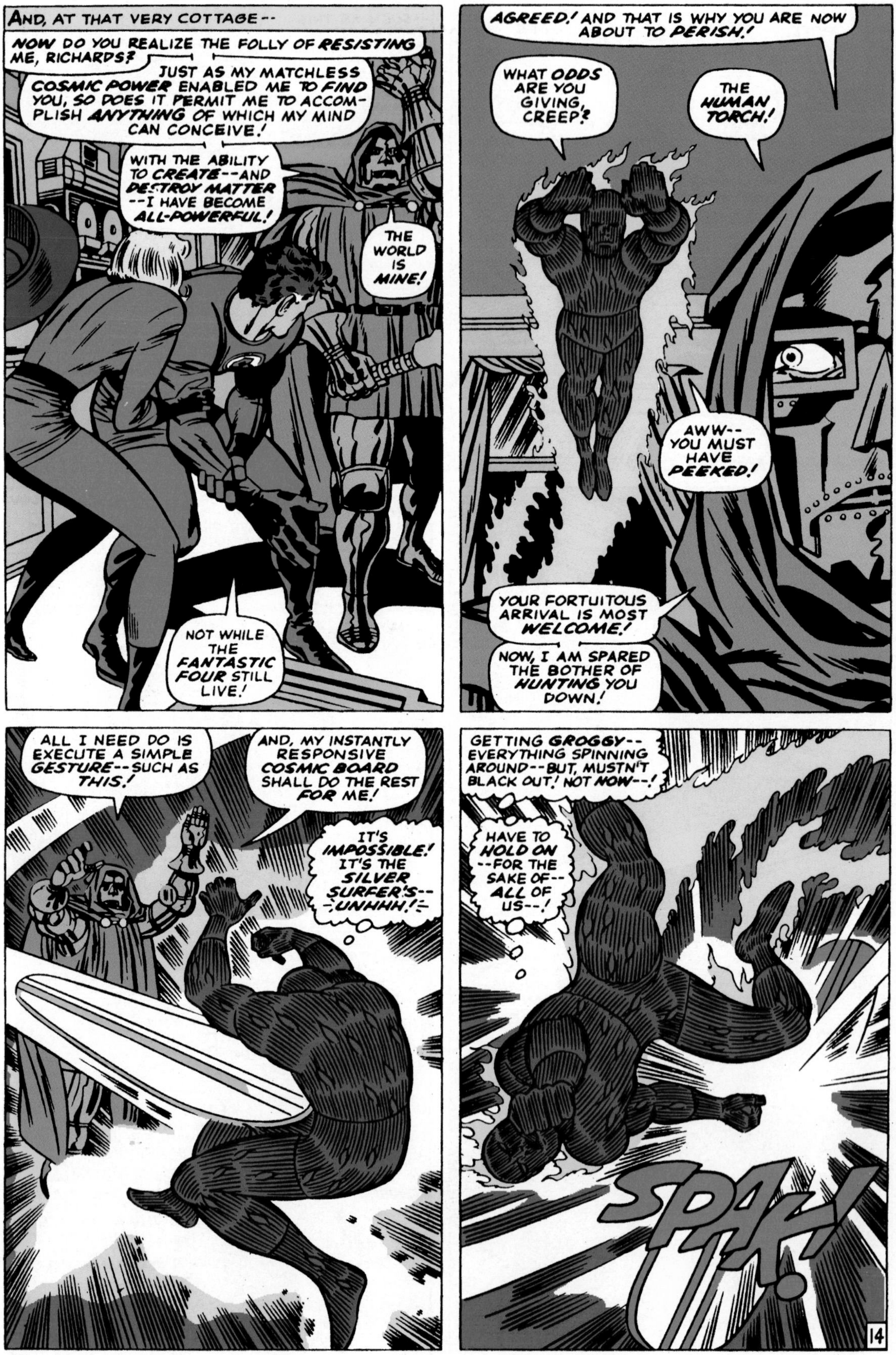
AND, AT THAT VERY COTTAGE--
NOW DO YOU REALIZE THE FOLLY OF RESISTING ME, RICHARDS?
JUST AS MY MATCHLESS COSMIC POWER ENABLED ME TO FIND YOU, SO DOES IT PERMIT ME TO ACCOMPLISH ANYTHING OF WHICH MY MIND CAN CONCEIVE!
WITH THE ABILITY TO CREATE--AND DESTROY MATTER--I HAVE BECOME ALL-POWERFUL!
THE WORLD IS MINE!
NOT WHILE THE FANTASTIC FOUR STILL LIVE!
AGREED! AND THAT IS WHY YOU ARE NOW ABOUT TO PERISH!
WHAT ODDS ARE YOU GIVING, CREEP?
THE HUMAN TORCH!
AWW--YOU MUST HAVE PEEKED!
YOUR FORTUITOUS ARRIVAL IS MOST WELCOME!
NOW, I AM SPARED THE BOTHER OF HUNTING YOU DOWN!
ALL I NEED DO IS EXECUTE A SIMPLE GESTURE--SUCH AS THIS!
AND, MY INSTANTLY RESPONSIVE COSMIC BOARD SHALL DO THE REST FOR ME!
IT'S IMPOSSIBLE! IT'S THE SILVER SURFER'S--UNHHH!
GETTING GROGGY--EVERYTHING SPINNING AROUND--BUT, MUSTN'T BLACK OUT! NOT NOW--!
HAVE TO HOLD ON--FOR THE SAKE OF--ALL OF US--!
SPAK!
14

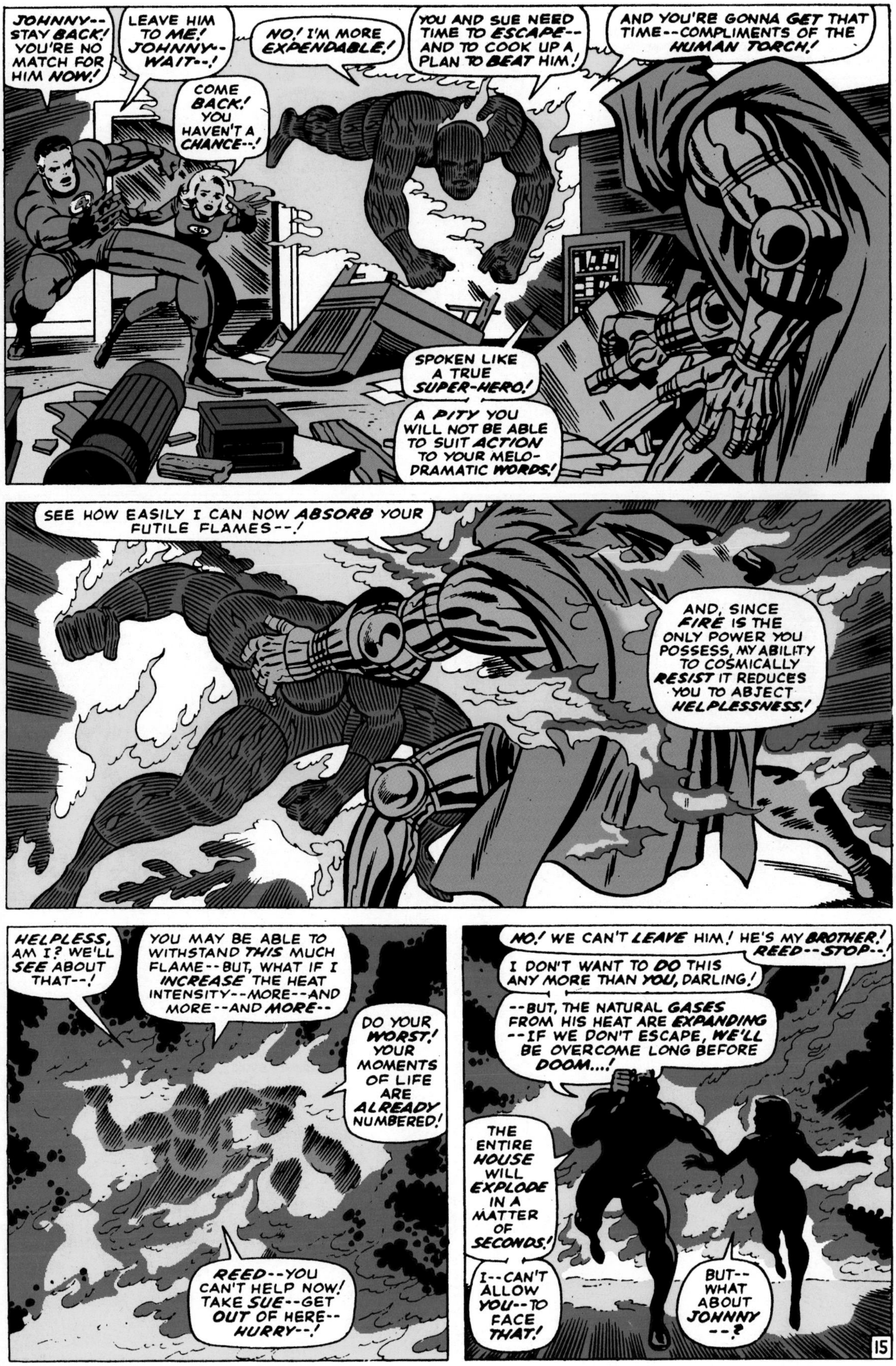
JOHNNY-- STAY BACK! YOU'RE NO MATCH FOR HIM NOW!
LEAVE HIM TO ME! JOHNNY-- WAIT--!
COME BACK! YOU HAVEN'T A CHANCE--!
NO! I'M MORE EXPENDABLE!
YOU AND SUE NEED TIME TO ESCAPE-- AND TO COOK UP A PLAN TO BEAT HIM!
AND YOU'RE GONNA GET THAT TIME--COMPLIMENTS OF THE HUMAN TORCH!
SPOKEN LIKE A TRUE SUPER-HERO!
A PITY YOU WILL NOT BE ABLE TO SUIT ACTION TO YOUR MELO-DRAMATIC WORDS!
SEE HOW EASILY I CAN NOW ABSORB YOUR FUTILE FLAMES--!
AND, SINCE FIRE IS THE ONLY POWER YOU POSSESS, MY ABILITY TO COSMICALLY RESIST IT REDUCES YOU TO ABJECT HELPLESSNESS!
HELPLESS, AM I? WE'LL SEE ABOUT THAT--!
YOU MAY BE ABLE TO WITHSTAND THIS MUCH FLAME--BUT, WHAT IF I INCREASE THE HEAT INTENSITY--MORE--AND MORE--AND MORE--
DO YOUR WORST! YOUR MOMENTS OF LIFE ARE ALREADY NUMBERED!
REED--YOU CAN'T HELP NOW! TAKE SUE--GET OUT OF HERE-- HURRY--!
NO! WE CAN'T LEAVE HIM! HE'S MY BROTHER! REED--STOP--!
I DON'T WANT TO DO THIS ANY MORE THAN YOU, DARLING!
--BUT, THE NATURAL GASES FROM HIS HEAT ARE EXPANDING --IF WE DON'T ESCAPE, WE'LL BE OVERCOME LONG BEFORE DOOM...!
THE ENTIRE HOUSE WILL EXPLODE IN A MATTER OF SECONDS!
I--CAN'T ALLOW YOU--TO FACE THAT!
BUT-- WHAT ABOUT JOHNNY --?
15

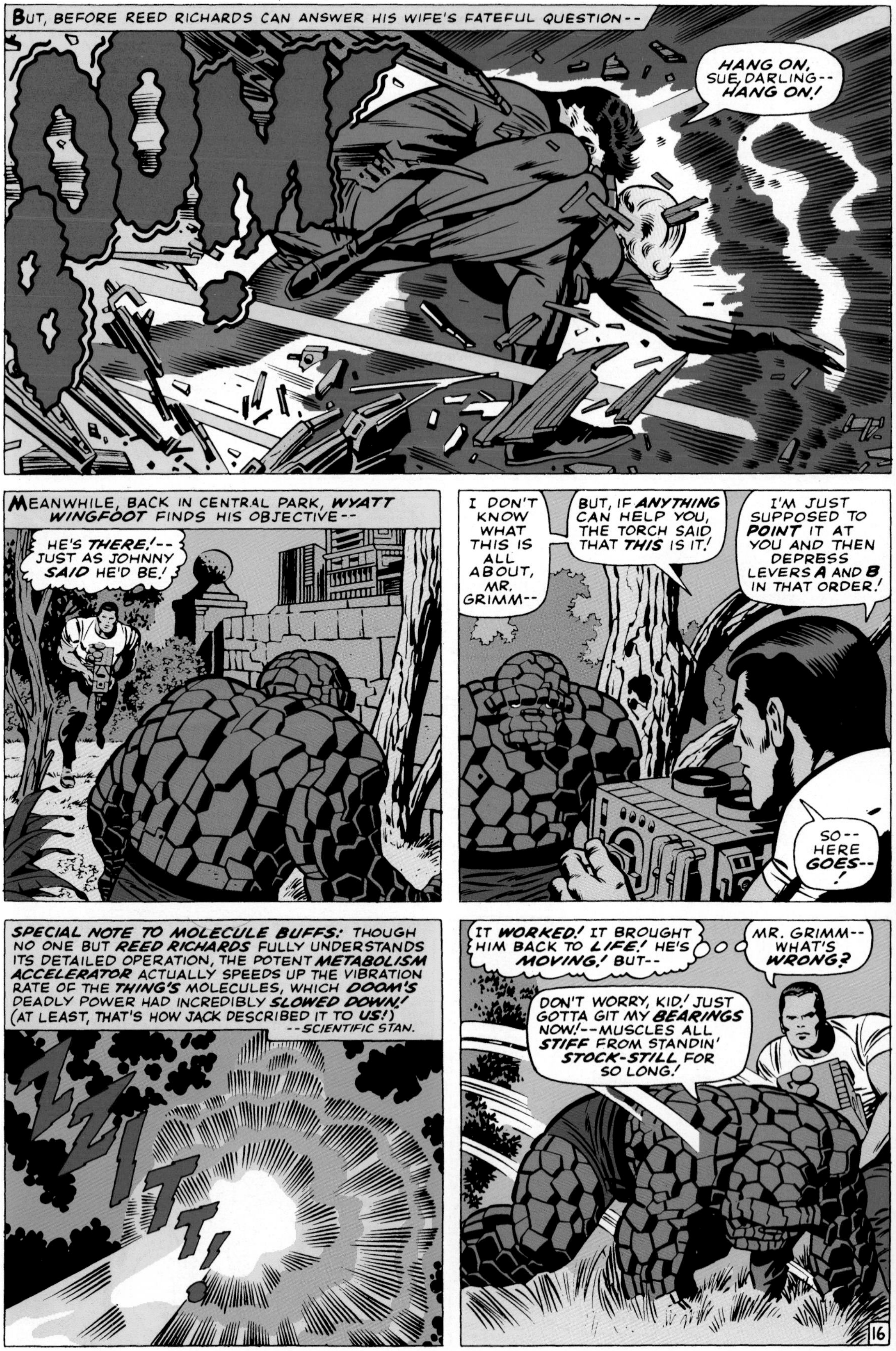
BUT, BEFORE REED RICHARDS CAN ANSWER HIS WIFE'S FATEFUL QUESTION--
HANG ON, SUE, DARLING-- HANG ON!
MEANWHILE, BACK IN CENTRAL PARK, WYATT WINGFOOT FINDS HIS OBJECTIVE--
HE'S THERE!-- JUST AS JOHNNY SAID HE'D BE!
I DON'T KNOW WHAT THIS IS ALL ABOUT, MR. GRIMM--
BUT, IF ANYTHING CAN HELP YOU, THE TORCH SAID THAT THIS IS IT!
I'M JUST SUPPOSED TO POINT IT AT YOU AND THEN DEPRESS LEVERS A AND B IN THAT ORDER!
SO-- HERE GOES--!
SPECIAL NOTE TO MOLECULE BUFFS: THOUGH NO ONE BUT REED RICHARDS FULLY UNDERSTANDS ITS DETAILED OPERATION, THE POTENT METABOLISM ACCELERATOR ACTUALLY SPEEDS UP THE VIBRATION RATE OF THE THING'S MOLECULES, WHICH DOOM'S DEADLY POWER HAD INCREDIBLY SLOWED DOWN! (AT LEAST, THAT'S HOW JACK DESCRIBED IT TO US!) --SCIENTIFIC STAN.
IT WORKED! IT BROUGHT HIM BACK TO LIFE! HE'S MOVING! BUT--
MR. GRIMM-- WHAT'S WRONG?
DON'T WORRY, KID! JUST GOTTA GIT MY BEARINGS NOW!--MUSCLES ALL STIFF FROM STANDIN' STOCK-STILL FOR SO LONG!
16

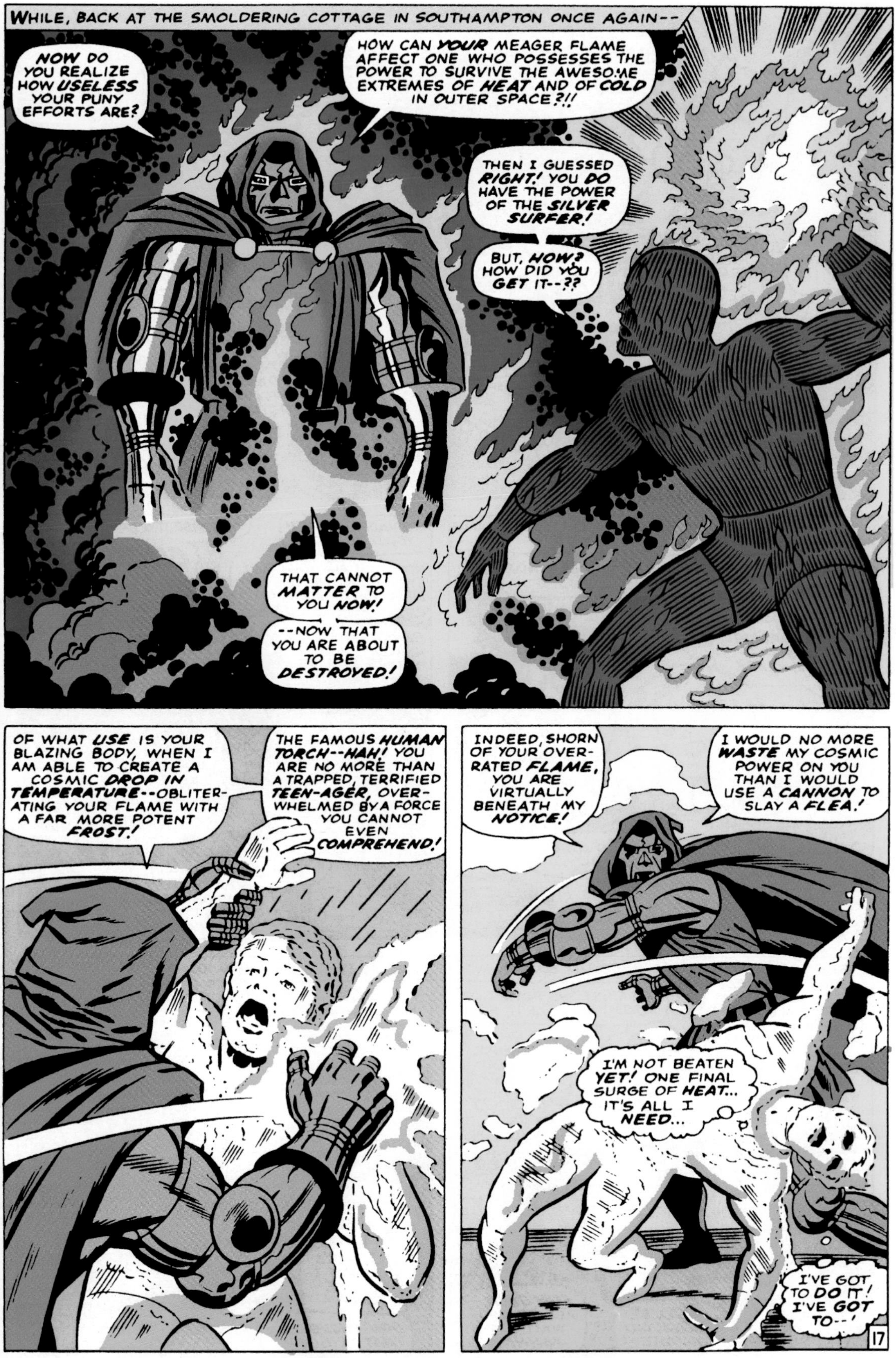
WHILE, BACK AT THE SMOLDERING COTTAGE IN SOUTHAMPTON ONCE AGAIN--
NOW DO YOU REALIZE HOW USELESS YOUR PUNY EFFORTS ARE?
HOW CAN YOUR MEAGER FLAME AFFECT ONE WHO POSSESSES THE POWER TO SURVIVE THE AWESOME EXTREMES OF HEAT AND OF COLD IN OUTER SPACE?!!
THEN I GUESSED RIGHT! YOU DO HAVE THE POWER OF THE SILVER SURFER!
BUT, HOW? HOW DID YOU GET IT--??
THAT CANNOT MATTER TO YOU NOW!
--NOW THAT YOU ARE ABOUT TO BE DESTROYED!
OF WHAT USE IS YOUR BLAZING BODY, WHEN I AM ABLE TO CREATE A COSMIC DROP IN TEMPERATURE--OBLITERATING YOUR FLAME WITH A FAR MORE POTENT FROST!
THE FAMOUS HUMAN TORCH--HAH! YOU ARE NO MORE THAN A TRAPPED, TERRIFIED TEEN-AGER, OVERWHELMED BY A FORCE YOU CANNOT EVEN COMPREHEND!
INDEED, SHORN OF YOUR OVER-RATED FLAME, YOU ARE VIRTUALLY BENEATH MY NOTICE!
I WOULD NO MORE WASTE MY COSMIC POWER ON YOU THAN I WOULD USE A CANNON TO SLAY A FLEA!
I'M NOT BEATEN YET! ONE FINAL SURGE OF HEAT... IT'S ALL I NEED...
I'VE GOT TO DO IT! I'VE GOT TO--!
17

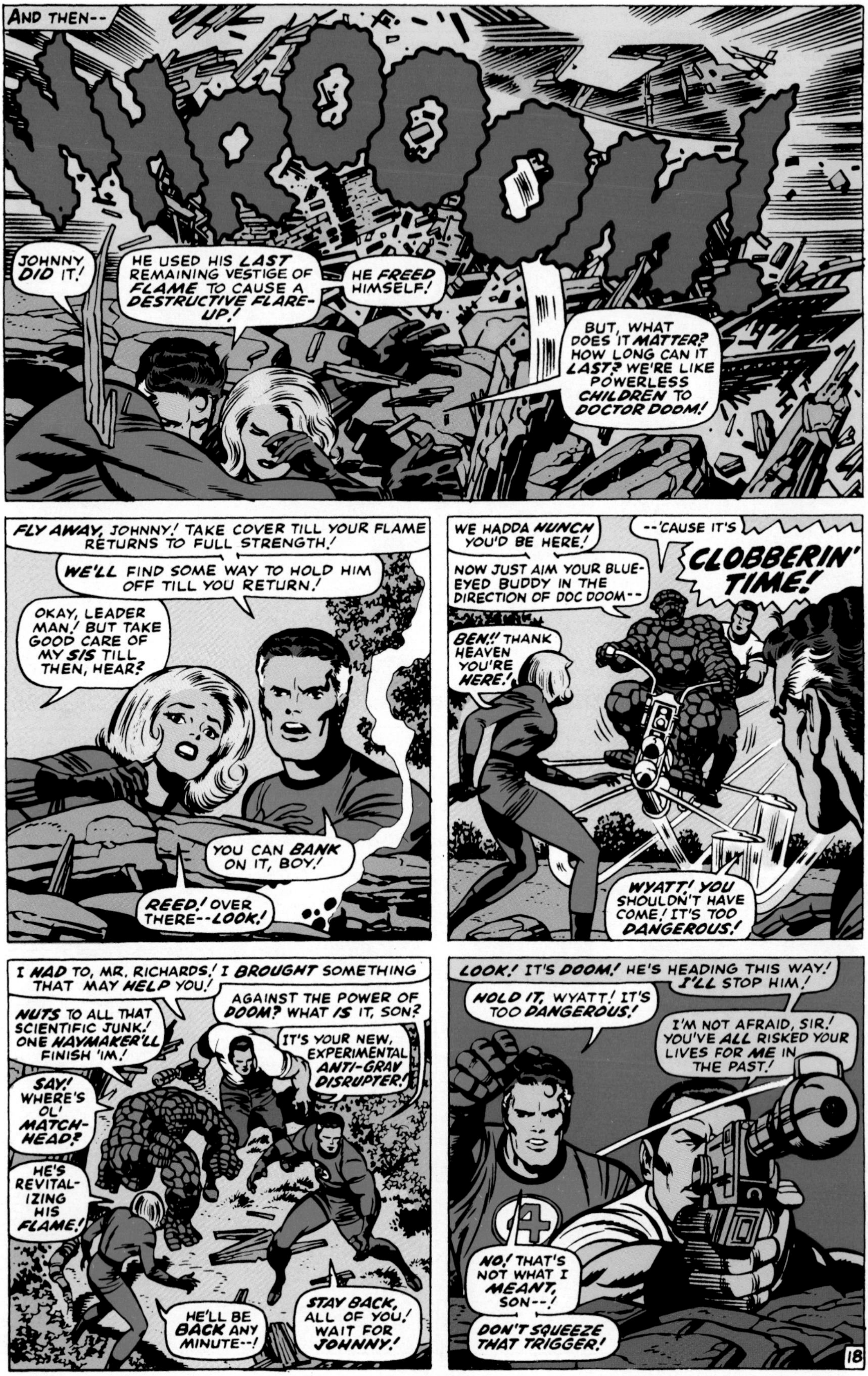
AND THEN--
WHROOOM!
JOHNNY DID IT!
HE USED HIS LAST REMAINING VESTIGE OF FLAME TO CAUSE A DESTRUCTIVE FLARE-UP!
HE FREED HIMSELF!
BUT, WHAT DOES IT MATTER? HOW LONG CAN IT LAST? WE'RE LIKE POWERLESS CHILDREN TO DOCTOR DOOM!
FLY AWAY, JOHNNY! TAKE COVER TILL YOUR FLAME RETURNS TO FULL STRENGTH!
WE'LL FIND SOME WAY TO HOLD HIM OFF TILL YOU RETURN!
OKAY, LEADER MAN! BUT TAKE GOOD CARE OF MY SIS TILL THEN, HEAR?
YOU CAN BANK ON IT, BOY!
REED! OVER THERE--LOOK!
WE HADDA HUNCH YOU'D BE HERE!
NOW JUST AIM YOUR BLUE-EYED BUDDY IN THE DIRECTION OF DOC DOOM--
--'CAUSE IT'S CLOBBERIN' TIME!
BEN!! THANK HEAVEN YOU'RE HERE!
WYATT! YOU SHOULDN'T HAVE COME! IT'S TOO DANGEROUS!
I HAD TO, MR. RICHARDS! I BROUGHT SOMETHING THAT MAY HELP YOU!
AGAINST THE POWER OF DOOM? WHAT IS IT, SON?
NUTS TO ALL THAT SCIENTIFIC JUNK! ONE HAYMAKER'LL FINISH 'IM!
IT'S YOUR NEW, EXPERIMENTAL ANTI-GRAV DISRUPTER!
SAY! WHERE'S OL' MATCH-HEAD?
HE'S REVITAL-IZING HIS FLAME!
HE'LL BE BACK ANY MINUTE--!
STAY BACK, ALL OF YOU! WAIT FOR JOHNNY!
LOOK! IT'S DOOM! HE'S HEADING THIS WAY! I'LL STOP HIM!
HOLD IT, WYATT! IT'S TOO DANGEROUS!
I'M NOT AFRAID, SIR! YOU'VE ALL RISKED YOUR LIVES FOR ME IN THE PAST!
NO! THAT'S NOT WHAT I MEANT, SON--!
DON'T SQUEEZE THAT TRIGGER!
18

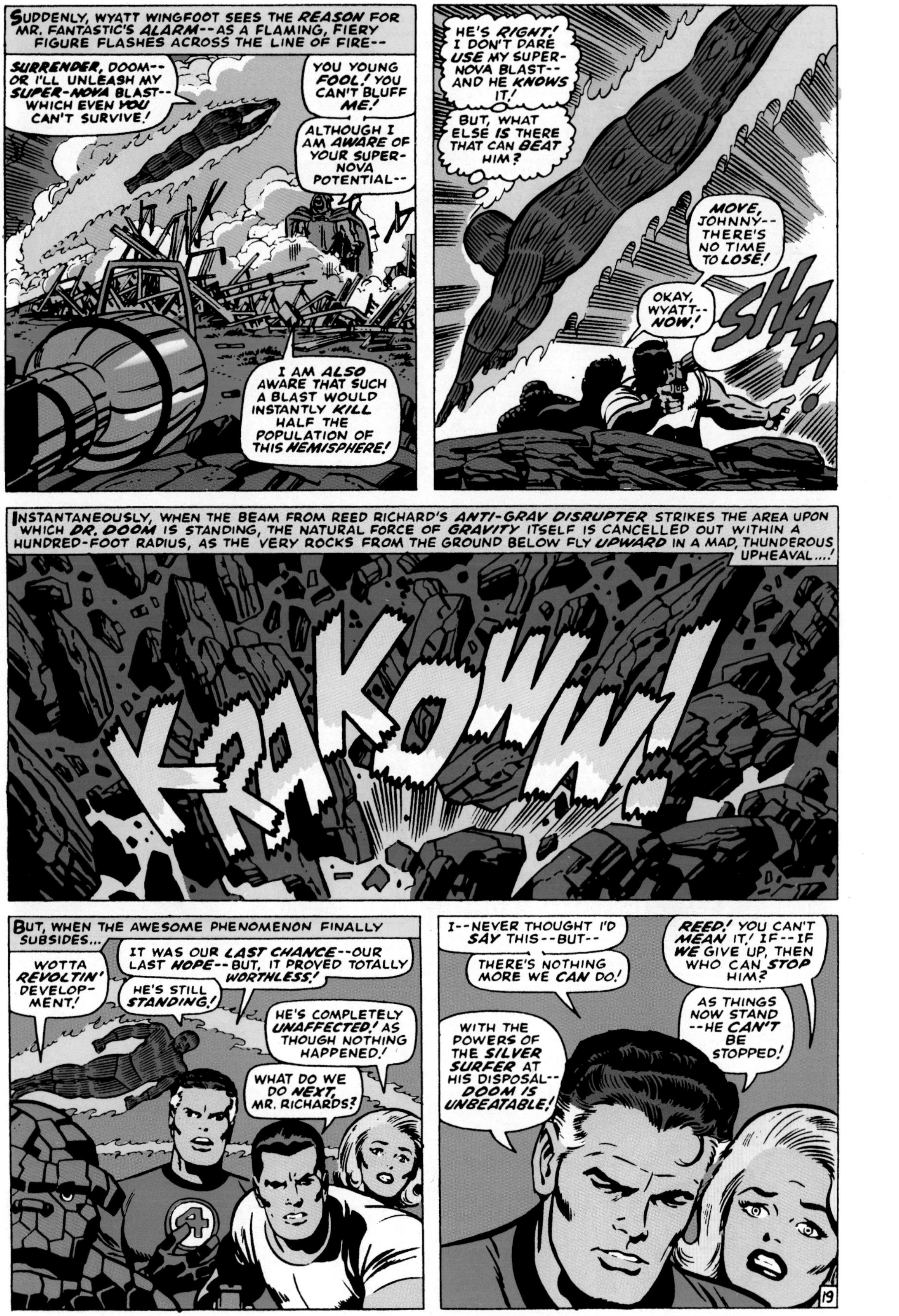
SUDDENLY, WYATT WINGFOOT SEES THE REASON FOR MR. FANTASTIC'S ALARM--AS A FLAMING, FIERY FIGURE FLASHES ACROSS THE LINE OF FIRE--
SURRENDER, DOOM--OR I'LL UNLEASH MY SUPER-NOVA BLAST--WHICH EVEN YOU CAN'T SURVIVE!
YOU YOUNG FOOL! YOU CAN'T BLUFF ME!
ALTHOUGH I AM AWARE OF YOUR SUPER-NOVA POTENTIAL--
I AM ALSO AWARE THAT SUCH A BLAST WOULD INSTANTLY KILL HALF THE POPULATION OF THIS HEMISPHERE!
HE'S RIGHT! I DON'T DARE USE MY SUPER-NOVA BLAST--AND HE KNOWS IT!
BUT, WHAT ELSE IS THERE THAT CAN BEAT HIM?
MOVE, JOHNNY--THERE'S NO TIME TO LOSE!
OKAY, WYATT--NOW!
SHAP!
INSTANTANEOUSLY, WHEN THE BEAM FROM REED RICHARD'S ANTI-GRAV DISRUPTER STRIKES THE AREA UPON WHICH DR. DOOM IS STANDING, THE NATURAL FORCE OF GRAVITY ITSELF IS CANCELLED OUT WITHIN A HUNDRED-FOOT RADIUS, AS THE VERY ROCKS FROM THE GROUND BELOW FLY UPWARD IN A MAD, THUNDEROUS UPHEAVAL....!
KRAKOWW!
BUT, WHEN THE AWESOME PHENOMENON FINALLY SUBSIDES...
WOTTA REVOLTIN' DEVELOP-MENT!
IT WAS OUR LAST CHANCE--OUR LAST HOPE--BUT, IT PROVED TOTALLY WORTHLESS!
HE'S STILL STANDING!
HE'S COMPLETELY UNAFFECTED! AS THOUGH NOTHING HAPPENED!
WHAT DO WE DO NEXT, MR. RICHARDS?
I--NEVER THOUGHT I'D SAY THIS--BUT--
THERE'S NOTHING MORE WE CAN DO!
WITH THE POWERS OF THE SILVER SURFER AT HIS DISPOSAL--DOOM IS UNBEATABLE!
REED! YOU CAN'T MEAN IT! IF--IF WE GIVE UP, THEN WHO CAN STOP HIM?
AS THINGS NOW STAND--HE CAN'T BE STOPPED!
19

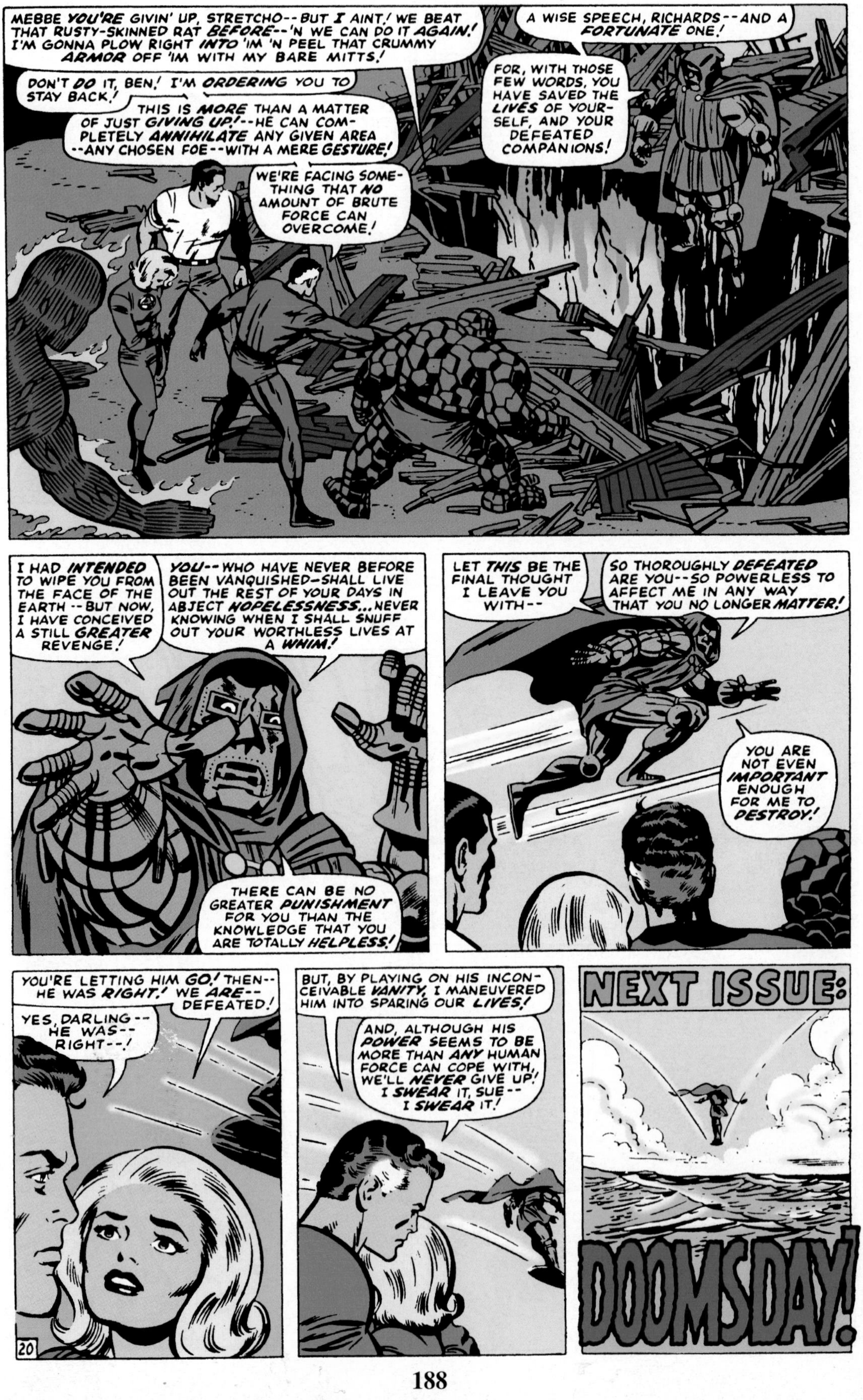
MEBBE YOU'RE GIVIN' UP, STRETCHO--BUT I AINT! WE BEAT THAT RUSTY-SKINNED RAT BEFORE--'N WE CAN DO IT AGAIN! I'M GONNA PLOW RIGHT INTO 'IM 'N PEEL THAT CRUMMY ARMOR OFF 'IM WITH MY BARE MITTS!
DON'T DO IT, BEN! I'M ORDERING YOU TO STAY BACK!
THIS IS MORE THAN A MATTER OF JUST GIVING UP!--HE CAN COMPLETELY ANNIHILATE ANY GIVEN AREA --ANY CHOSEN FOE--WITH A MERE GESTURE!
WE'RE FACING SOMETHING THAT NO AMOUNT OF BRUTE FORCE CAN OVERCOME!
A WISE SPEECH, RICHARDS--AND A FORTUNATE ONE!
FOR, WITH THOSE FEW WORDS, YOU HAVE SAVED THE LIVES OF YOURSELF, AND YOUR DEFEATED COMPANIONS!
I HAD INTENDED TO WIPE YOU FROM THE FACE OF THE EARTH --BUT NOW, I HAVE CONCEIVED A STILL GREATER REVENGE!
YOU--WHO HAVE NEVER BEFORE BEEN VANQUISHED--SHALL LIVE OUT THE REST OF YOUR DAYS IN ABJECT HOPELESSNESS... NEVER KNOWING WHEN I SHALL SNUFF OUT YOUR WORTHLESS LIVES AT A WHIM!
THERE CAN BE NO GREATER PUNISHMENT FOR YOU THAN THE KNOWLEDGE THAT YOU ARE TOTALLY HELPLESS!
LET THIS BE THE FINAL THOUGHT I LEAVE YOU WITH--
SO THOROUGHLY DEFEATED ARE YOU--SO POWERLESS TO AFFECT ME IN ANY WAY THAT YOU NO LONGER MATTER!
YOU ARE NOT EVEN IMPORTANT ENOUGH FOR ME TO DESTROY!
YOU'RE LETTING HIM GO! THEN--HE WAS RIGHT! WE ARE--DEFEATED!
YES, DARLING--HE WAS--RIGHT--!
20
BUT, BY PLAYING ON HIS INCONCEIVABLE VANITY, I MANEUVERED HIM INTO SPARING OUR LIVES!
AND, ALTHOUGH HIS POWER SEEMS TO BE MORE THAN ANY HUMAN FORCE CAN COPE WITH, WE'LL NEVER GIVE UP! I SWEAR IT, SUE--I SWEAR IT!
NEXT ISSUE:
DOOMSDAY!

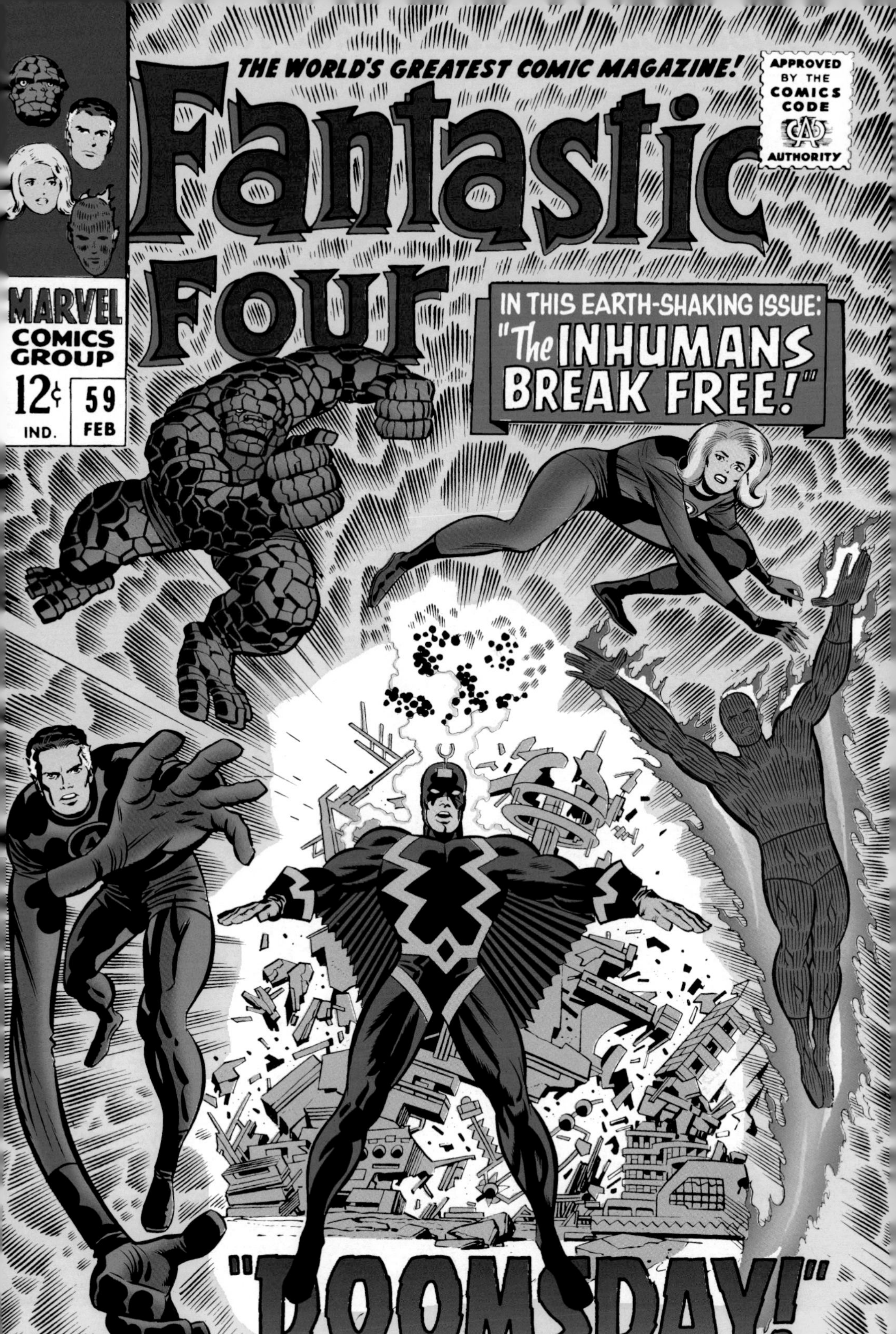
THE WORLD'S GREATEST COMIC MAGAZINE!
APPROVED BY THE COMICS CODE AUTHORITY
Fantastic Four
MARVEL COMICS GROUP
12¢ IND.
59 FEB
IN THIS EARTH-SHAKING ISSUE:
"The INHUMANS BREAK FREE!"
"DOOMSDAY!"

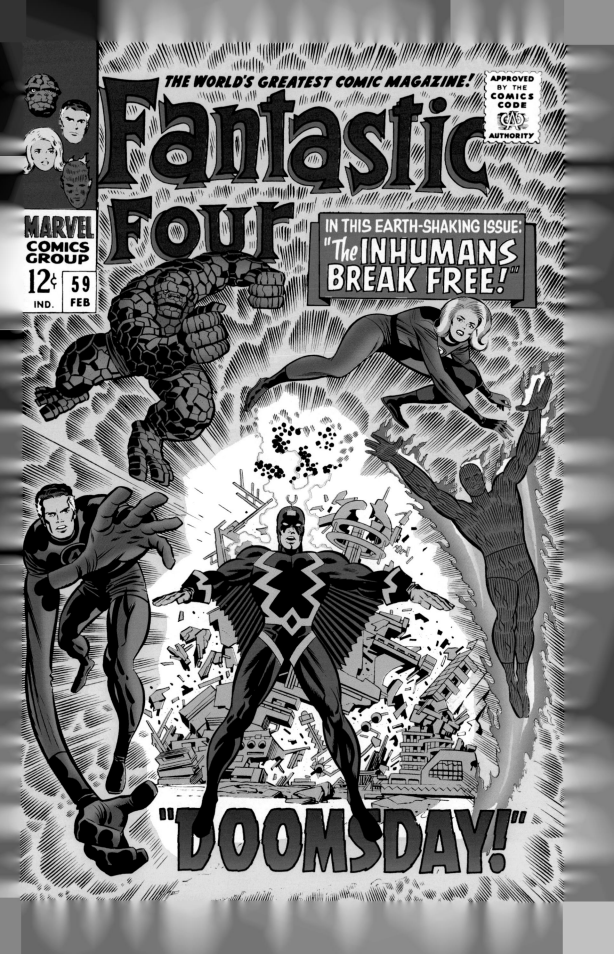

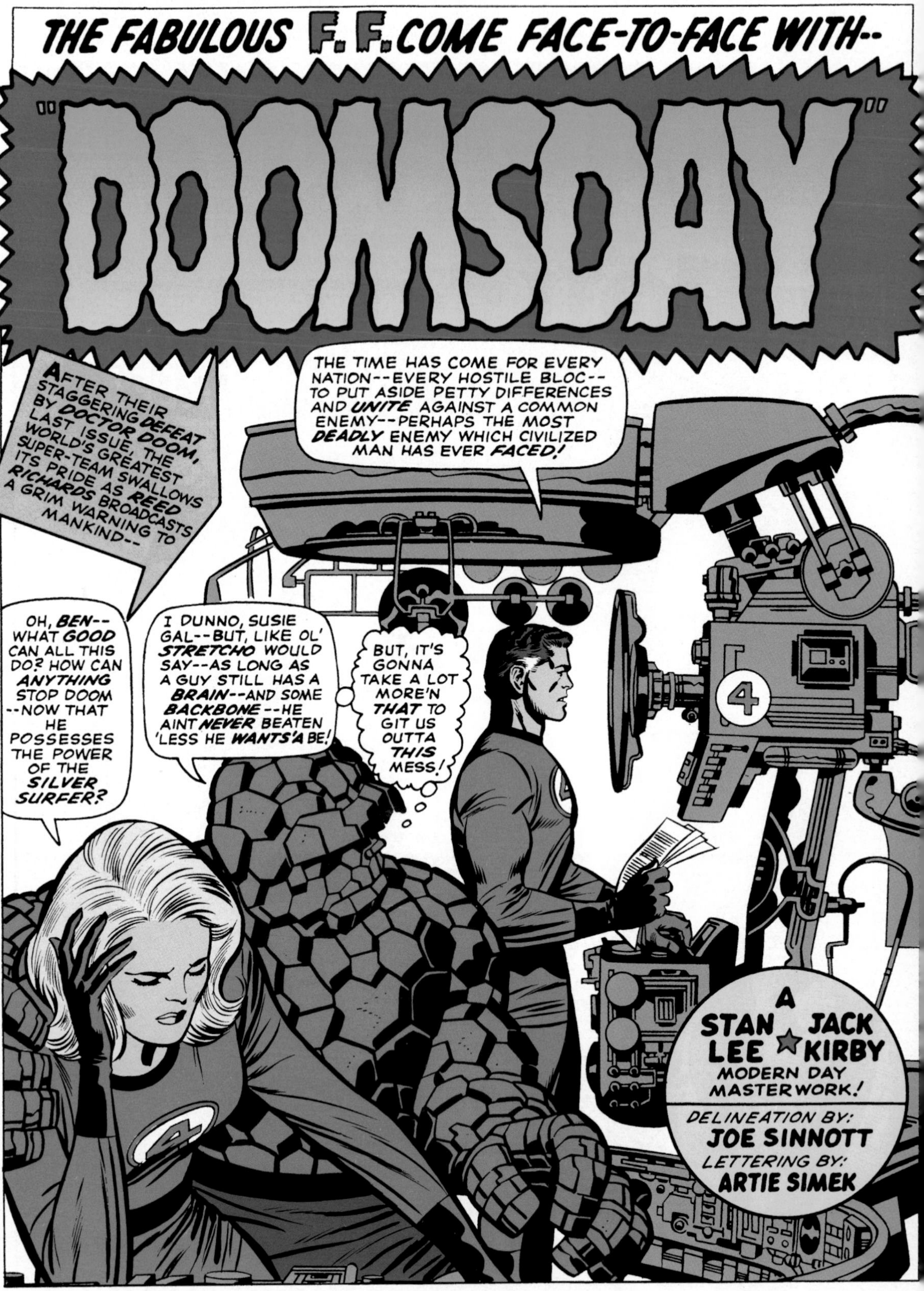
THE FABULOUS F.F. COME FACE-TO-FACE WITH--
"DOOMSDAY"
AFTER THEIR STAGGERING DEFEAT BY DOCTOR DOOM, LAST ISSUE, THE WORLD'S GREATEST SUPER-TEAM SWALLOWS ITS PRIDE AS REED RICHARDS BROADCASTS A GRIM WARNING TO MANKIND--
THE TIME HAS COME FOR EVERY NATION--EVERY HOSTILE BLOC--TO PUT ASIDE PETTY DIFFERENCES AND UNITE AGAINST A COMMON ENEMY--PERHAPS THE MOST DEADLY ENEMY WHICH CIVILIZED MAN HAS EVER FACED!
OH, BEN--WHAT GOOD CAN ALL THIS DO? HOW CAN ANYTHING STOP DOOM--NOW THAT HE POSSESSES THE POWER OF THE SILVER SURFER?
I DUNNO, SUSIE GAL--BUT, LIKE OL' STRETCHO WOULD SAY--AS LONG AS A GUY STILL HAS A BRAIN--AND SOME BACKBONE--HE AINT NEVER BEATEN 'LESS HE WANTS'A BE!
BUT, IT'S GONNA TAKE A LOT MORE'N THAT TO GIT US OUTTA THIS MESS!
A STAN LEE ★ JACK KIRBY MODERN DAY MASTERWORK!
DELINEATION BY: JOE SINNOTT
LETTERING BY: ARTIE SIMEK

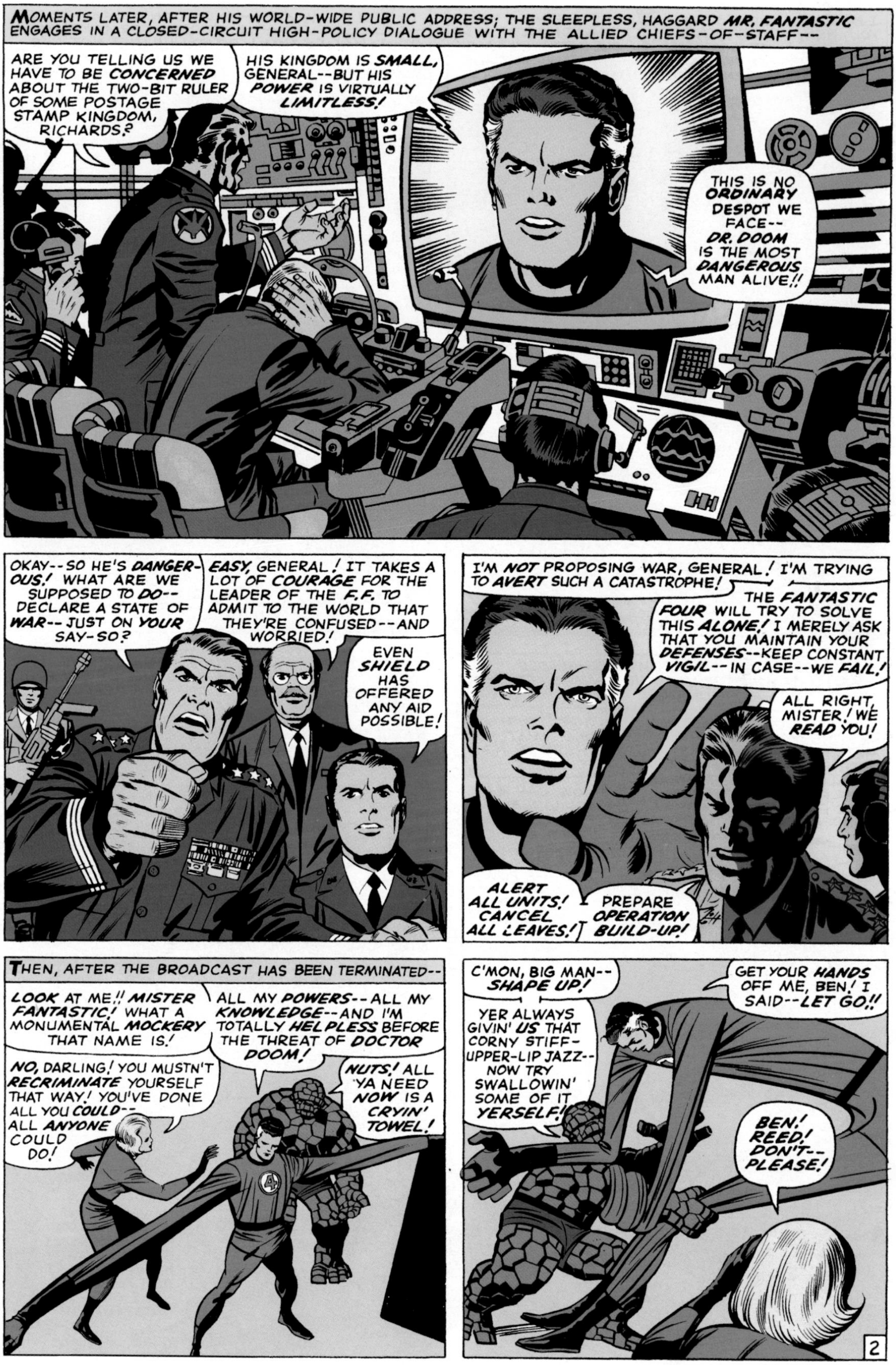
MOMENTS LATER, AFTER HIS WORLD-WIDE PUBLIC ADDRESS; THE SLEEPLESS, HAGGARD MR. FANTASTIC ENGAGES IN A CLOSED-CIRCUIT HIGH-POLICY DIALOGUE WITH THE ALLIED CHIEFS-OF-STAFF--
ARE YOU TELLING US WE HAVE TO BE CONCERNED ABOUT THE TWO-BIT RULER OF SOME POSTAGE STAMP KINGDOM, RICHARDS?
HIS KINGDOM IS SMALL, GENERAL--BUT HIS POWER IS VIRTUALLY LIMITLESS!
THIS IS NO ORDINARY DESPOT WE FACE-- DR. DOOM IS THE MOST DANGEROUS MAN ALIVE!!
OKAY--SO HE'S DANGEROUS! WHAT ARE WE SUPPOSED TO DO-- DECLARE A STATE OF WAR--JUST ON YOUR SAY-SO?
EASY, GENERAL! IT TAKES A LOT OF COURAGE FOR THE LEADER OF THE F.F. TO ADMIT TO THE WORLD THAT THEY'RE CONFUSED--AND WORRIED!
EVEN SHIELD HAS OFFERED ANY AID POSSIBLE!
I'M NOT PROPOSING WAR, GENERAL! I'M TRYING TO AVERT SUCH A CATASTROPHE!
THE FANTASTIC FOUR WILL TRY TO SOLVE THIS ALONE! I MERELY ASK THAT YOU MAINTAIN YOUR DEFENSES--KEEP CONSTANT VIGIL--IN CASE--WE FAIL!
ALL RIGHT, MISTER! WE READ YOU!
ALERT ALL UNITS! CANCEL ALL LEAVES!
PREPARE OPERATION BUILD-UP!
THEN, AFTER THE BROADCAST HAS BEEN TERMINATED--
LOOK AT ME!! MISTER FANTASTIC! WHAT A MONUMENTAL MOCKERY THAT NAME IS!
ALL MY POWERS--ALL MY KNOWLEDGE--AND I'M TOTALLY HELPLESS BEFORE THE THREAT OF DOCTOR DOOM!
NO, DARLING! YOU MUSTN'T RECRIMINATE YOURSELF THAT WAY! YOU'VE DONE ALL YOU COULD-- ALL ANYONE COULD DO!
NUTS! ALL 'YA NEED NOW IS A CRYIN' TOWEL!
C'MON, BIG MAN-- SHAPE UP!
YER ALWAYS GIVIN' US THAT CORNY STIFF-UPPER-LIP JAZZ-- NOW TRY SWALLOWIN' SOME OF IT YERSELF!
GET YOUR HANDS OFF ME, BEN! I SAID--LET GO!!
BEN! REED! DON'T-- PLEASE!
2

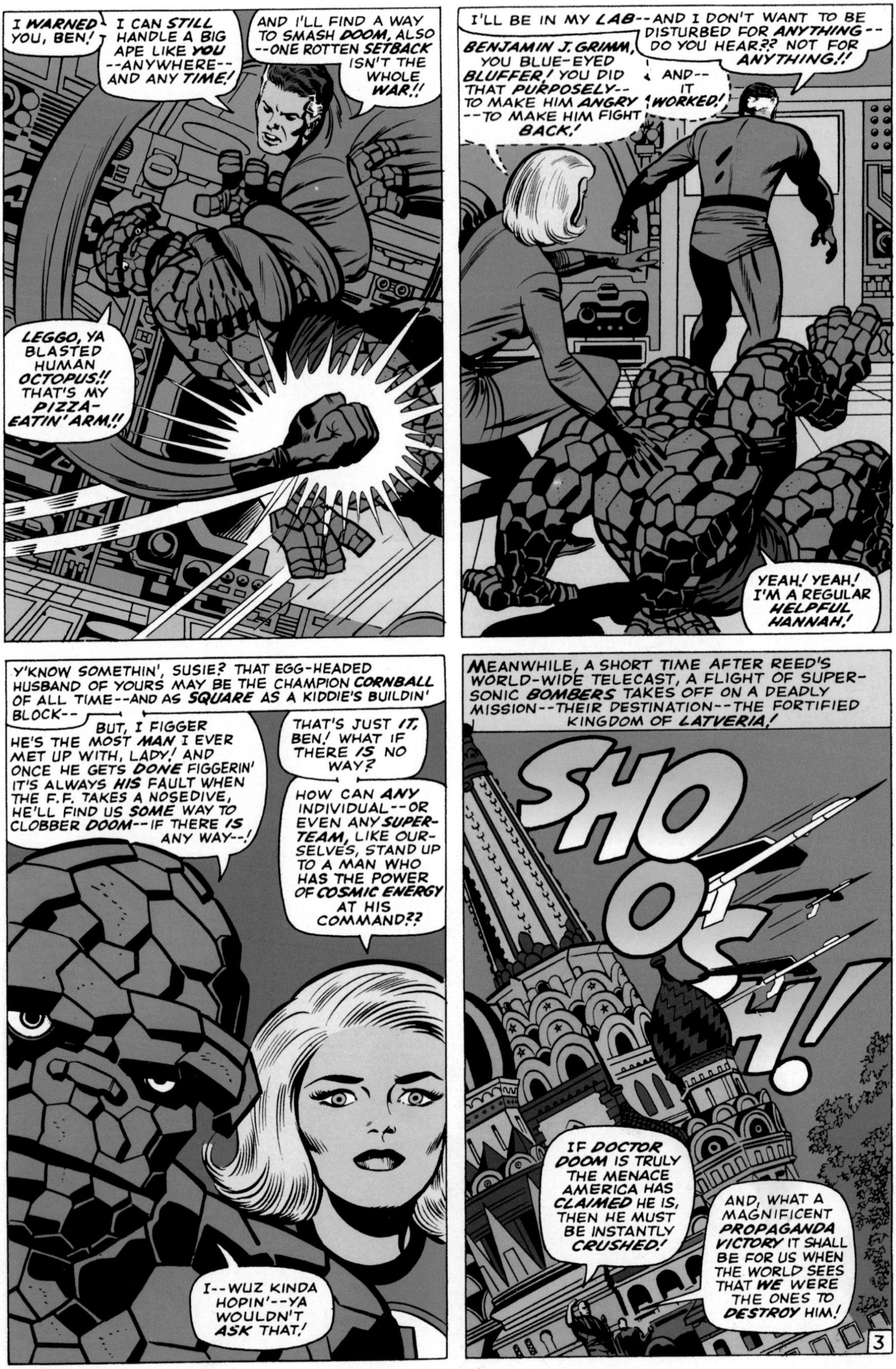
I WARNED YOU, BEN.!
I CAN STILL HANDLE A BIG APE LIKE YOU --ANYWHERE-- AND ANY TIME!
AND I'LL FIND A WAY TO SMASH DOOM, ALSO --ONE ROTTEN SETBACK ISN'T THE WHOLE WAR!!
LEGGO, YA BLASTED HUMAN OCTOPUS!! THAT'S MY PIZZA-EATIN' ARM!!
I'LL BE IN MY LAB--AND I DON'T WANT TO BE DISTURBED FOR ANYTHING--DO YOU HEAR?? NOT FOR ANYTHING!!
BENJAMIN J. GRIMM, YOU BLUE-EYED BLUFFER! YOU DID THAT PURPOSELY--TO MAKE HIM ANGRY--TO MAKE HIM FIGHT BACK!
AND--IT WORKED!
YEAH! YEAH! I'M A REGULAR HELPFUL HANNAH!
Y'KNOW SOMETHIN', SUSIE? THAT EGG-HEADED HUSBAND OF YOURS MAY BE THE CHAMPION CORNBALL OF ALL TIME--AND AS SQUARE AS A KIDDIE'S BUILDIN' BLOCK--
BUT, I FIGGER HE'S THE MOST MAN I EVER MET UP WITH, LADY! AND ONCE HE GETS DONE FIGGERIN' IT'S ALWAYS HIS FAULT WHEN THE F.F. TAKES A NOSEDIVE, HE'LL FIND US SOME WAY TO CLOBBER DOOM--IF THERE IS ANY WAY--!
THAT'S JUST IT, BEN! WHAT IF THERE IS NO WAY?
HOW CAN ANY INDIVIDUAL--OR EVEN ANY SUPER-TEAM, LIKE OURSELVES, STAND UP TO A MAN WHO HAS THE POWER OF COSMIC ENERGY AT HIS COMMAND??
I--WUZ KINDA HOPIN'--YA WOULDN'T ASK THAT!
MEANWHILE, A SHORT TIME AFTER REED'S WORLD-WIDE TELECAST, A FLIGHT OF SUPER-SONIC BOMBERS TAKES OFF ON A DEADLY MISSION--THEIR DESTINATION--THE FORTIFIED KINGDOM OF LATVERIA!
SHOOOSH!
IF DOCTOR DOOM IS TRULY THE MENACE AMERICA HAS CLAIMED HE IS, THEN HE MUST BE INSTANTLY CRUSHED!
AND, WHAT A MAGNIFICENT PROPAGANDA VICTORY IT SHALL BE FOR US WHEN THE WORLD SEES THAT WE WERE THE ONES TO DESTROY HIM!
3

THEN, WITHIN A MATTER OF *MINUTES*--

OUR OBJECTIVE IS *DIRECTLY AHEAD!*

WE ARE 120 KILOMETERS NORTHEAST OF *TARGET L!*

ACCELERATE *SPEED* IN ACCORDANCE WITH PLAN *B!*

MAINTAIN *ALTITUDE*-- READY ALL *ROCKETS*--!

BUT, SUDDENLY--

THIS *CLOUD!* WHERE DID IT *COME* FROM?

THE SKY WAS *CLEAR*--JUST *SECONDS* AGO!

IT IS NO *ORDINARY* CLOUD! SEE HOW IT BEGINS TO *GLOW*--TO *SHIMMER* WITH *LIGHT*--!

EXACTLY TEN SECONDS LATER--

IT WAS *CORROSIVE!* IT LITERALLY *ATE AWAY* THE METAL OF OUR PLANES!

IT'S THE *PERFECT DEFENSE* AGAINST AIR ATTACK! NO PLANE--NO MISSILE --CAN *PENETRATE* IT!

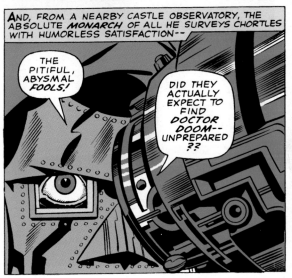

AND, FROM A NEARBY CASTLE OBSERVATORY, THE ABSOLUTE *MONARCH* OF ALL HE SURVEYS CHORTLES WITH HUMORLESS SATISFACTION--

THE *PITIFUL, ABYSMAL FOOLS!*

DID THEY ACTUALLY EXPECT TO FIND *DOCTOR DOOM*--UNPREPARED ??

I COULD *ANNIHILATE* THEIR ENTIRE AIR FORCE AT A *WHIM!* BUT, I SHALL NOT DO SO--*YET!*

I AM TOO *POWERFUL* --TOO TOTALLY *SUPREME*--TO GIVE VENT TO COMMON *ANGER!*

SUCH AN EMOTION IS FOR *LESSER BEINGS*--IT IS HARDLY SUITABLE FOR ONE WHO IS *MASTER OF THE WORLD!*

4

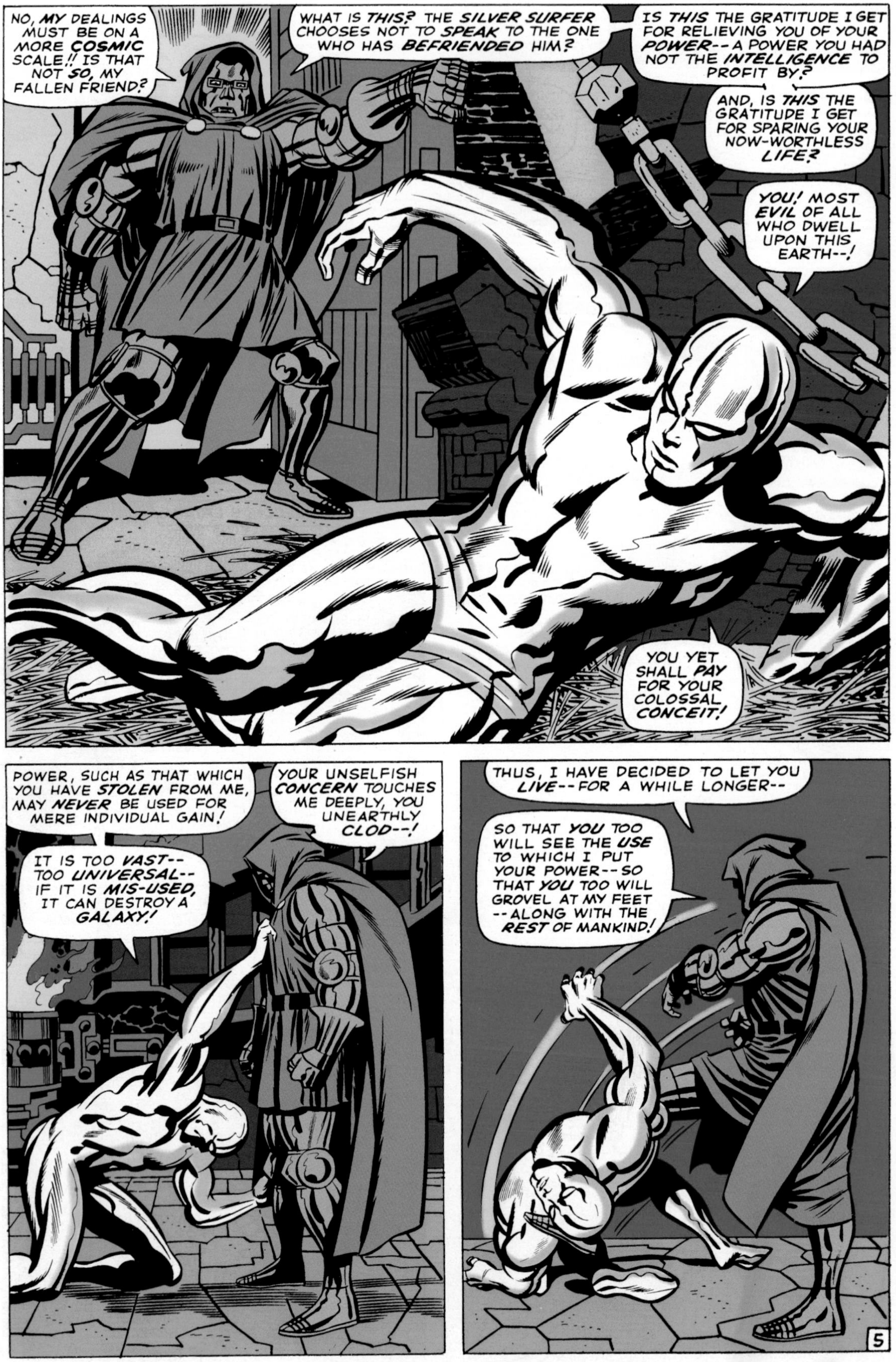
NO, MY DEALINGS MUST BE ON A MORE COSMIC SCALE!! IS THAT NOT SO, MY FALLEN FRIEND?
WHAT IS THIS? THE SILVER SURFER CHOOSES NOT TO SPEAK TO THE ONE WHO HAS BEFRIENDED HIM?
IS THIS THE GRATITUDE I GET FOR RELIEVING YOU OF YOUR POWER-- A POWER YOU HAD NOT THE INTELLIGENCE TO PROFIT BY?
AND, IS THIS THE GRATITUDE I GET FOR SPARING YOUR NOW-WORTHLESS LIFE?
YOU! MOST EVIL OF ALL WHO DWELL UPON THIS EARTH--!
YOU YET SHALL PAY FOR YOUR COLOSSAL CONCEIT!
POWER, SUCH AS THAT WHICH YOU HAVE STOLEN FROM ME, MAY NEVER BE USED FOR MERE INDIVIDUAL GAIN!
YOUR UNSELFISH CONCERN TOUCHES ME DEEPLY, YOU UNEARTHLY CLOD--!
IT IS TOO VAST-- TOO UNIVERSAL-- IF IT IS MIS-USED, IT CAN DESTROY A GALAXY!
THUS, I HAVE DECIDED TO LET YOU LIVE-- FOR A WHILE LONGER--
SO THAT YOU TOO WILL SEE THE USE TO WHICH I PUT YOUR POWER-- SO THAT YOU TOO WILL GROVEL AT MY FEET --ALONG WITH THE REST OF MANKIND!
5

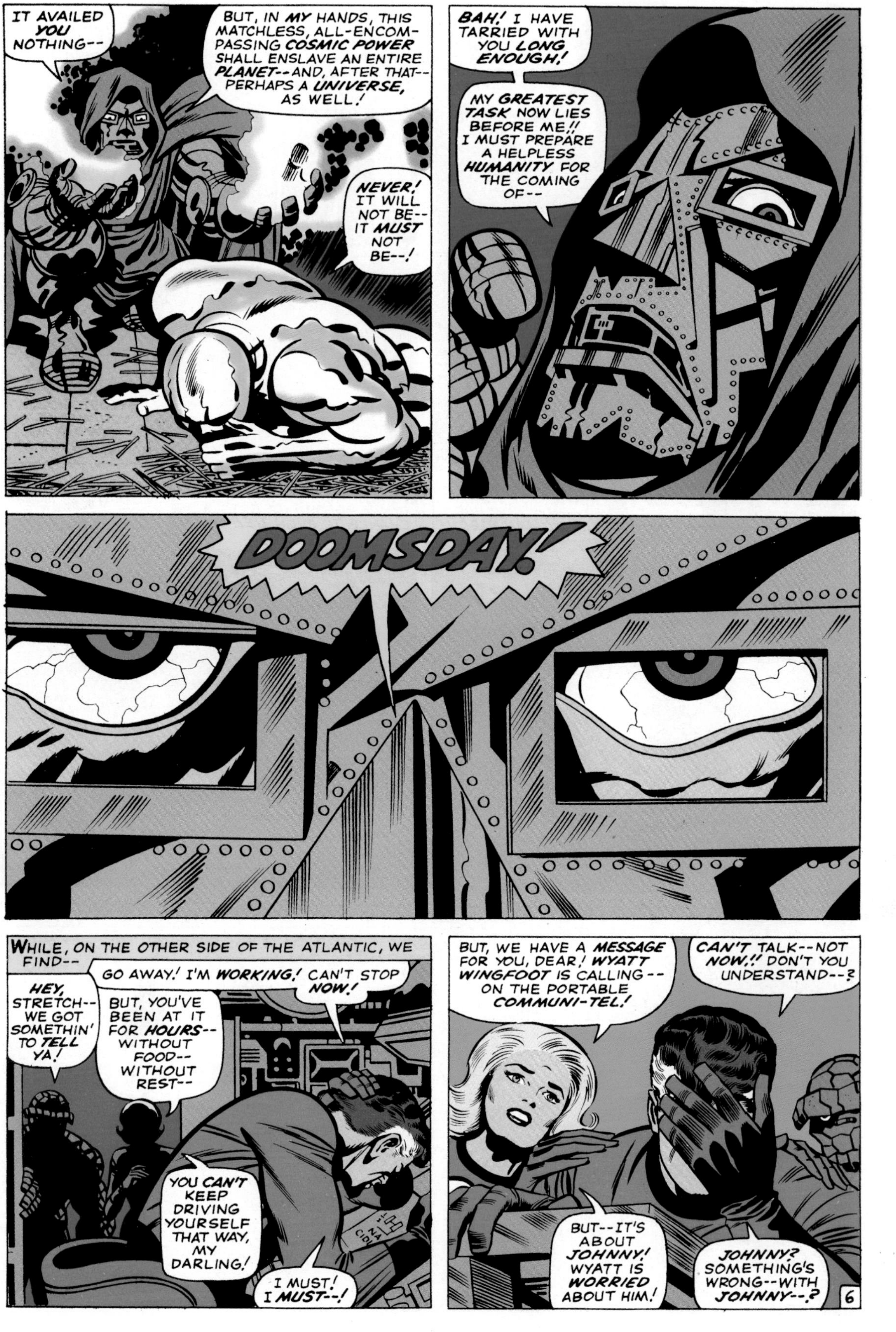
IT AVAILED YOU NOTHING--
BUT, IN MY HANDS, THIS MATCHLESS, ALL-ENCOMPASSING COSMIC POWER SHALL ENSLAVE AN ENTIRE PLANET--AND, AFTER THAT--PERHAPS A UNIVERSE, AS WELL!
NEVER! IT WILL NOT BE--IT MUST NOT BE--!
BAH! I HAVE TARRIED WITH YOU LONG ENOUGH!
MY GREATEST TASK NOW LIES BEFORE ME!! I MUST PREPARE A HELPLESS HUMANITY FOR THE COMING OF--
DOOMSDAY!
WHILE, ON THE OTHER SIDE OF THE ATLANTIC, WE FIND--
HEY, STRETCH--WE GOT SOMETHIN' TO TELL YA!
GO AWAY! I'M WORKING! CAN'T STOP NOW!
BUT, YOU'VE BEEN AT IT FOR HOURS--WITHOUT FOOD--WITHOUT REST--
YOU CAN'T KEEP DRIVING YOURSELF THAT WAY, MY DARLING!
I MUST! I MUST--!
BUT, WE HAVE A MESSAGE FOR YOU, DEAR! WYATT WINGFOOT IS CALLING--ON THE PORTABLE COMMUNI-TEL!
CAN'T TALK--NOT NOW!! DON'T YOU UNDERSTAND--?
BUT--IT'S ABOUT JOHNNY! WYATT IS WORRIED ABOUT HIM!
JOHNNY? SOMETHING'S WRONG--WITH JOHNNY--?
6

THEN, SECONDS LATER--

WHAT *IS* IT? WHAT HAPPENED TO JOHNNY? SPEAK UP, MAN.!

NOTHING HAS HAPPENED *YET*, MR. RICHARDS --BUT I'M AFRAID OF WHAT *WILL* HAPPEN!

JOHNNY WANTS TO TACKLE *DR. DOOM* ON HIS *OWN*!

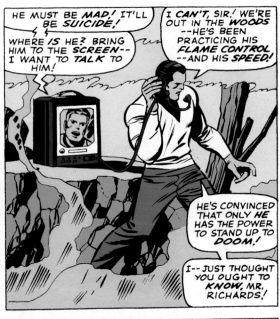

HE MUST BE *MAD*! IT'LL BE *SUICIDE*!

WHERE *IS* HE? BRING HIM TO THE *SCREEN*-- I WANT TO *TALK* TO HIM!

I *CAN'T*, SIR.! WE'RE OUT IN THE *WOODS* --HE'S BEEN PRACTICING HIS *FLAME CONTROL* --AND HIS *SPEED*!

HE'S CONVINCED THAT ONLY *HE* HAS THE POWER TO STAND UP TO *DOOM*!

I-- JUST THOUGHT YOU OUGHT TO *KNOW*, MR. RICHARDS!

JOHNNY--*WAIT*! LISTEN TO ME!

I CALLED YOUR *BROTHER-IN-LAW*! HE ORDERED YOU TO STOP! HE SAYS IT'S TOO *DANGEROUS*!

MAYBE FOR *HIM* IT IS--BUT NOT FOR THE *HUMAN TORCH*!

MY *SPEED* IS GREAT ENOUGH NOW TO WIN OVER DOOM'S OWN *REFLEXES*!

AND I KNOW JUST THE WAY TO *PROVE* IT!

I'LL SHOW THAT I CAN *HIT* DOOM BEFORE HE GETS A CHANCE TO EVEN *USE* HIS POWERS!

IT ALL DEPENDS ON USING MY FLAME LIKE A BLAZING *COMET*!

THERE'S A *NATIONAL GUARD* UNIT ON MANEUVERS JUST OVER THAT NEXT RISE--I'LL ZOOM PAST THEIR AUTOMATIC *DEFENSES* BEFORE THEY KNOW WHAT HAPPENED!

BUT, THE HEADSTRONG *HUMAN TORCH* IS UNAWARE THAT THE MANEUVERS CONCERN A TOP-SECRET TRYOUT OF AN AMAZING NEW *SOLAR-BEAM* GUN--

LOOK! THAT MUST BE THE *DRONE MISSILE* WE'RE SUPPOSED TO BLAST OUTTA THE *SKY*!

IT'S *FASTER* THAN WE EXPECTED --BUT WE'LL *GET* IT!

IT WAS *SUPPOSED* TO BE LAUNCHED TEN MINUTES FROM NOW!

THEY MUST HAVE CHANGED THE TIMING TO TAKE US BY *SURPRISE*!

OKAY, SAM-- IT'S RIGHT IN *RANGE*! --FIRE.!!

7

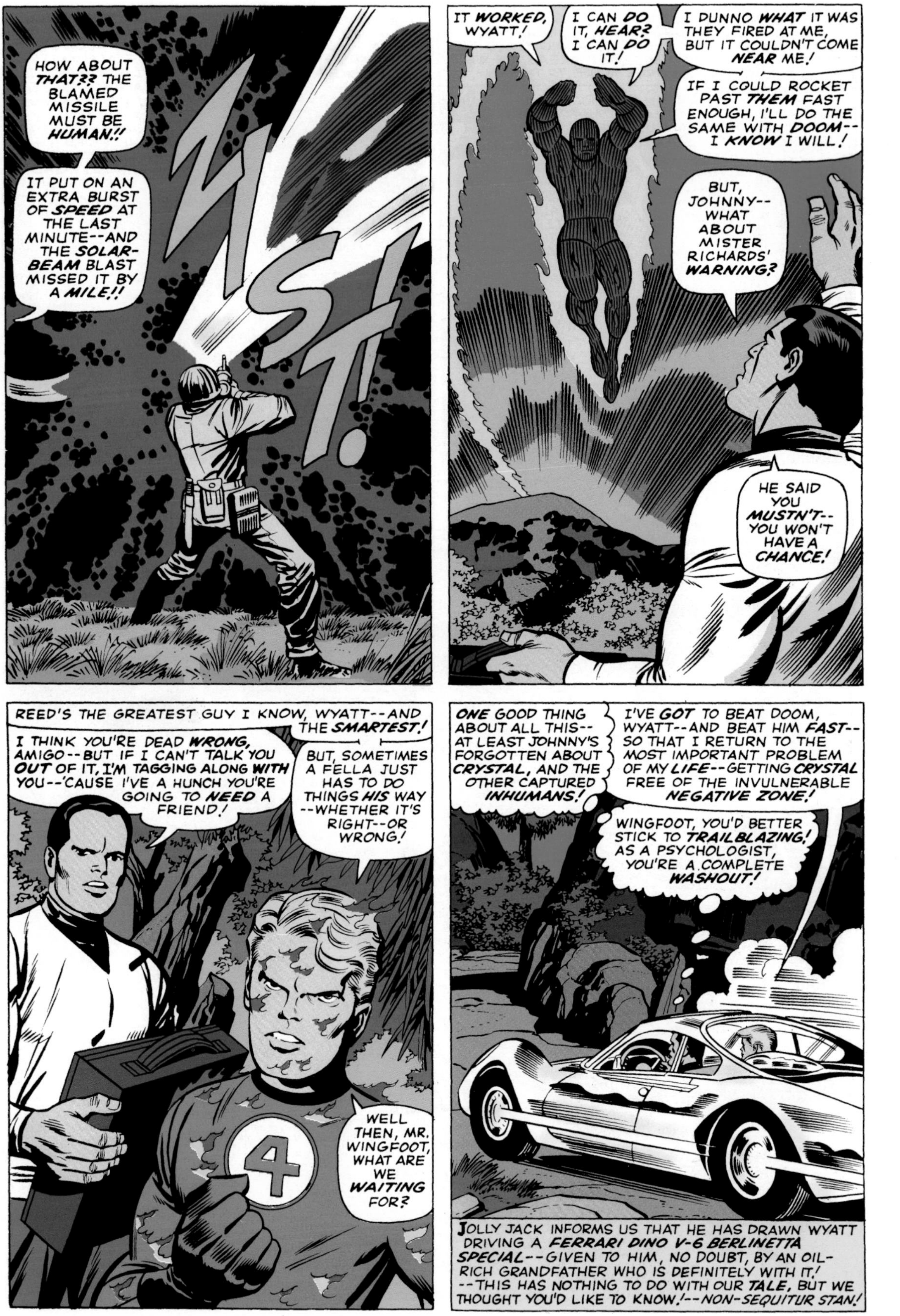
HOW ABOUT THAT?? THE BLAMED MISSILE MUST BE HUMAN!!
IT PUT ON AN EXTRA BURST OF SPEED AT THE LAST MINUTE--AND THE SOLAR-BEAM BLAST MISSED IT BY A MILE!!
ZZIST!
IT WORKED, WYATT!
I CAN DO IT, HEAR? I CAN DO IT!
I DUNNO WHAT IT WAS THEY FIRED AT ME, BUT IT COULDN'T COME NEAR ME!
IF I COULD ROCKET PAST THEM FAST ENOUGH, I'LL DO THE SAME WITH DOOM-- I KNOW I WILL!
BUT, JOHNNY-- WHAT ABOUT MISTER RICHARDS' WARNING?
HE SAID YOU MUSTN'T-- YOU WON'T HAVE A CHANCE!
REED'S THE GREATEST GUY I KNOW, WYATT--AND THE SMARTEST!
BUT, SOMETIMES A FELLA JUST HAS TO DO THINGS HIS WAY --WHETHER IT'S RIGHT--OR WRONG!
I THINK YOU'RE DEAD WRONG, AMIGO--BUT IF I CAN'T TALK YOU OUT OF IT, I'M TAGGING ALONG WITH YOU--'CAUSE I'VE A HUNCH YOU'RE GOING TO NEED A FRIEND!
WELL THEN, MR. WINGFOOT, WHAT ARE WE WAITING FOR?
ONE GOOD THING ABOUT ALL THIS-- AT LEAST JOHNNY'S FORGOTTEN ABOUT CRYSTAL, AND THE OTHER CAPTURED INHUMANS!
I'VE GOT TO BEAT DOOM, WYATT--AND BEAT HIM FAST-- SO THAT I RETURN TO THE MOST IMPORTANT PROBLEM OF MY LIFE--GETTING CRYSTAL FREE OF THE INVULNERABLE NEGATIVE ZONE!
WINGFOOT, YOU'D BETTER STICK TO TRAILBLAZING! AS A PSYCHOLOGIST, YOU'RE A COMPLETE WASHOUT!
JOLLY JACK INFORMS US THAT HE HAS DRAWN WYATT DRIVING A FERRARI DINO V-6 BERLINETTA SPECIAL--GIVEN TO HIM, NO DOUBT, BY AN OIL-RICH GRANDFATHER WHO IS DEFINITELY WITH IT! --THIS HAS NOTHING TO DO WITH OUR TALE, BUT WE THOUGHT YOU'D LIKE TO KNOW!--NON-SEQUITUR STAN!

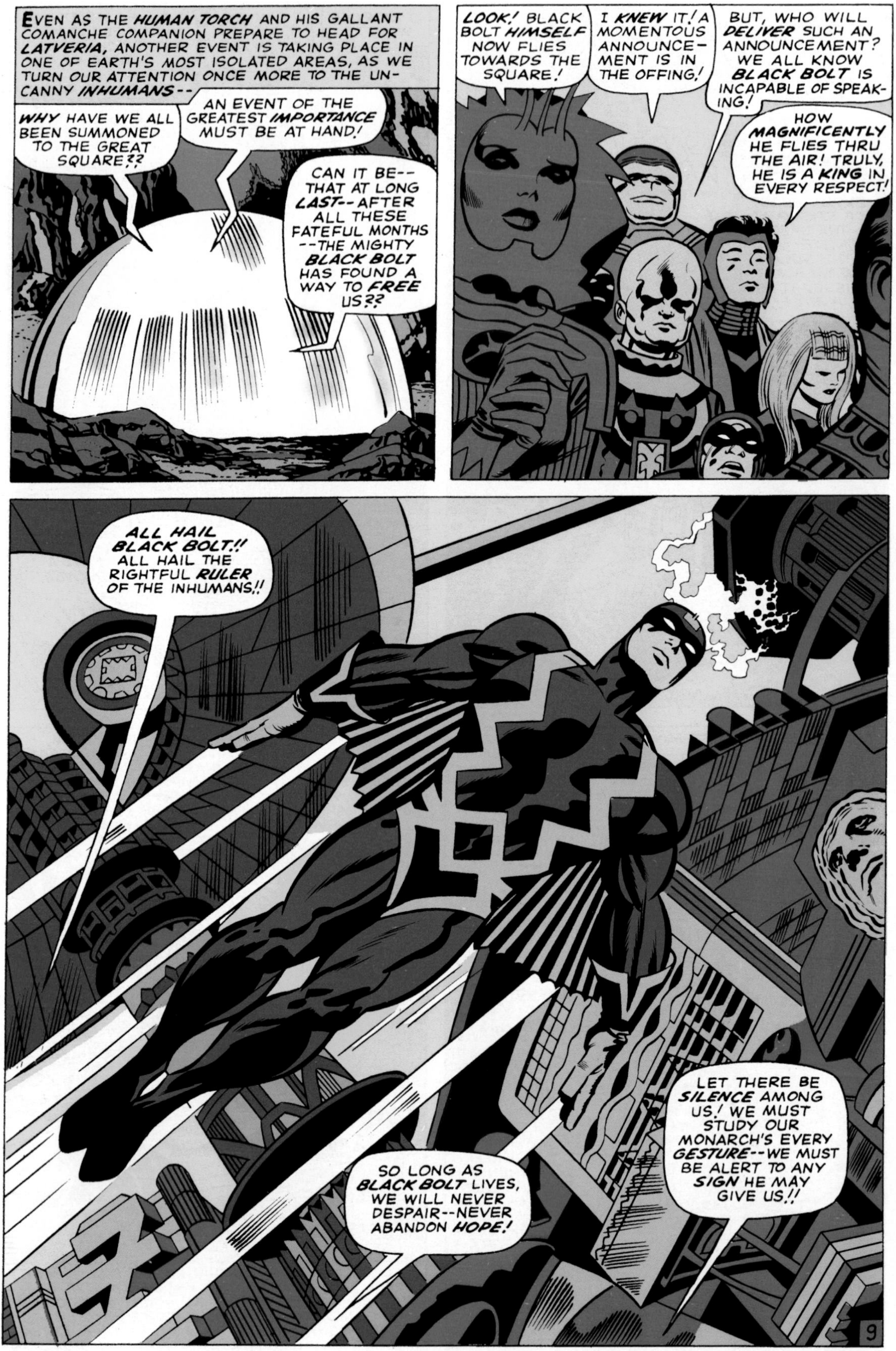

EVEN AS THE HUMAN TORCH AND HIS GALLANT COMANCHE COMPANION PREPARE TO HEAD FOR LATVERIA, ANOTHER EVENT IS TAKING PLACE IN ONE OF EARTH'S MOST ISOLATED AREAS, AS WE TURN OUR ATTENTION ONCE MORE TO THE UNCANNY INHUMANS--
WHY HAVE WE ALL BEEN SUMMONED TO THE GREAT SQUARE??
AN EVENT OF THE GREATEST IMPORTANCE MUST BE AT HAND!
CAN IT BE--THAT AT LONG LAST--AFTER ALL THESE FATEFUL MONTHS--THE MIGHTY BLACK BOLT HAS FOUND A WAY TO FREE US??
LOOK! BLACK BOLT HIMSELF NOW FLIES TOWARDS THE SQUARE!
I KNEW IT! A MOMENTOUS ANNOUNCEMENT IS IN THE OFFING!
BUT, WHO WILL DELIVER SUCH AN ANNOUNCEMENT? WE ALL KNOW BLACK BOLT IS INCAPABLE OF SPEAKING!
HOW MAGNIFICENTLY HE FLIES THRU THE AIR! TRULY, HE IS A KING IN EVERY RESPECT!
ALL HAIL BLACK BOLT!! ALL HAIL THE RIGHTFUL RULER OF THE INHUMANS!!
SO LONG AS BLACK BOLT LIVES, WE WILL NEVER DESPAIR--NEVER ABANDON HOPE!
LET THERE BE SILENCE AMONG US! WE MUST STUDY OUR MONARCH'S EVERY GESTURE--WE MUST BE ALERT TO ANY SIGN HE MAY GIVE US!!
9

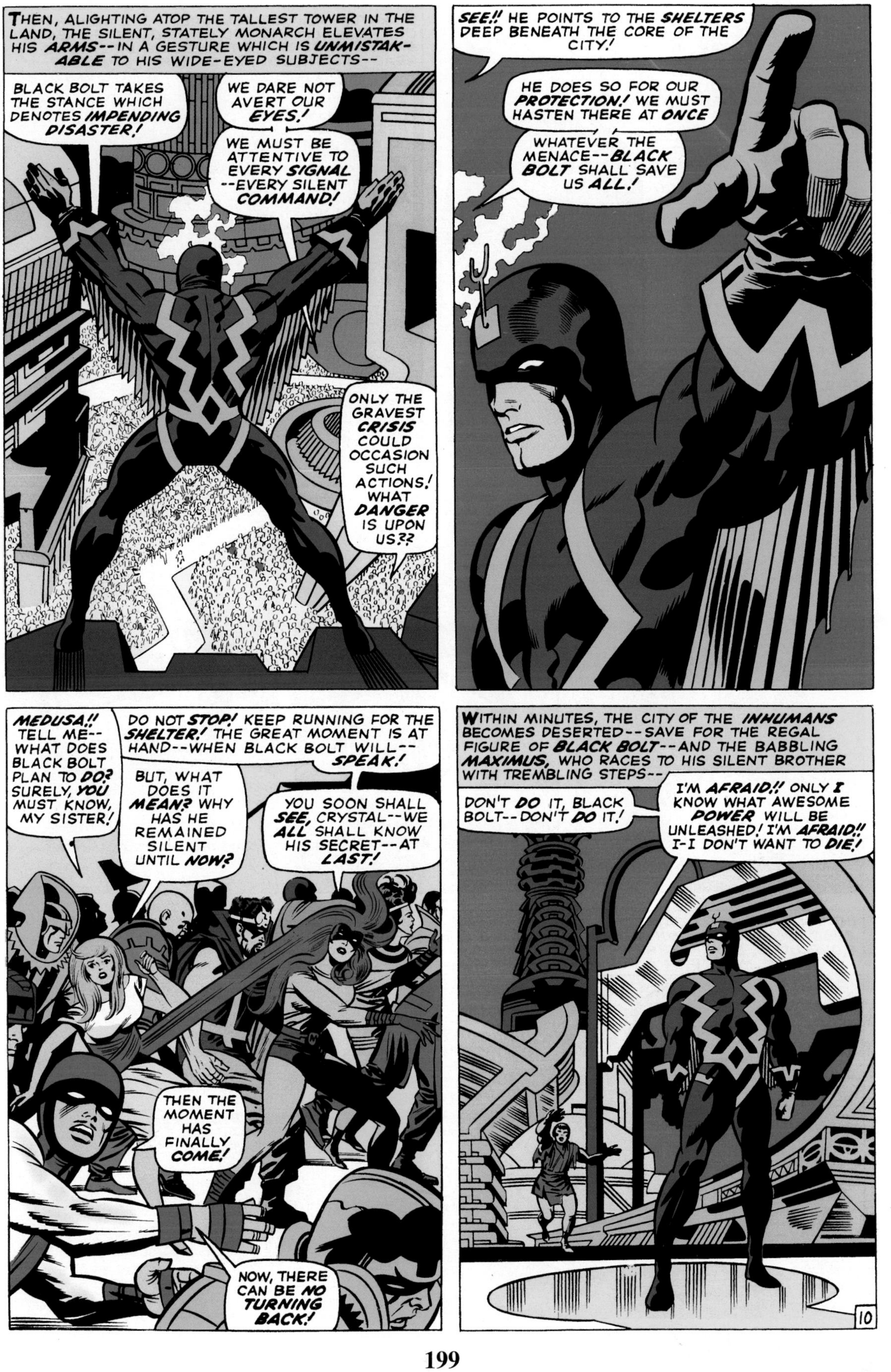
THEN, ALIGHTING ATOP THE TALLEST TOWER IN THE LAND, THE SILENT, STATELY MONARCH ELEVATES HIS ARMS--IN A GESTURE WHICH IS UNMISTAKABLE TO HIS WIDE-EYED SUBJECTS--
BLACK BOLT TAKES THE STANCE WHICH DENOTES IMPENDING DISASTER!
WE DARE NOT AVERT OUR EYES!
WE MUST BE ATTENTIVE TO EVERY SIGNAL --EVERY SILENT COMMAND!
ONLY THE GRAVEST CRISIS COULD OCCASION SUCH ACTIONS! WHAT DANGER IS UPON US??
SEE!! HE POINTS TO THE SHELTERS DEEP BENEATH THE CORE OF THE CITY!
HE DOES SO FOR OUR PROTECTION! WE MUST HASTEN THERE AT ONCE
WHATEVER THE MENACE--BLACK BOLT SHALL SAVE US ALL!
MEDUSA!! TELL ME--WHAT DOES BLACK BOLT PLAN TO DO? SURELY, YOU MUST KNOW, MY SISTER!
DO NOT STOP! KEEP RUNNING FOR THE SHELTER! THE GREAT MOMENT IS AT HAND--WHEN BLACK BOLT WILL--SPEAK!
BUT, WHAT DOES IT MEAN? WHY HAS HE REMAINED SILENT UNTIL NOW?
YOU SOON SHALL SEE, CRYSTAL--WE ALL SHALL KNOW HIS SECRET--AT LAST!
THEN THE MOMENT HAS FINALLY COME!
NOW, THERE CAN BE NO TURNING BACK!
WITHIN MINUTES, THE CITY OF THE INHUMANS BECOMES DESERTED--SAVE FOR THE REGAL FIGURE OF BLACK BOLT--AND THE BABBLING MAXIMUS, WHO RACES TO HIS SILENT BROTHER WITH TREMBLING STEPS--
DON'T DO IT, BLACK BOLT--DON'T DO IT!
I'M AFRAID!! ONLY I KNOW WHAT AWESOME POWER WILL BE UNLEASHED! I'M AFRAID!! I-I DON'T WANT TO DIE!
10

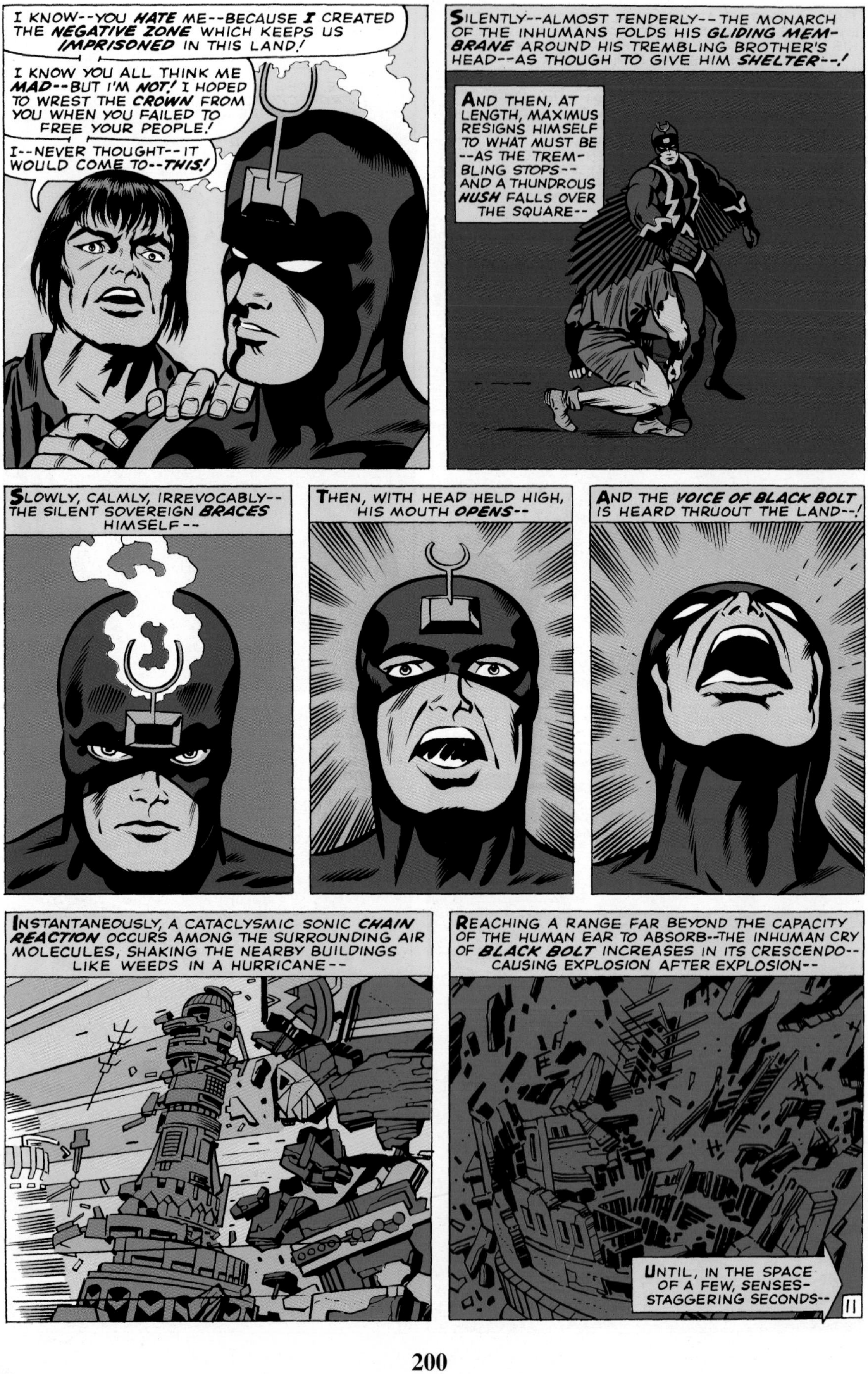
I KNOW--YOU HATE ME--BECAUSE I CREATED THE NEGATIVE ZONE WHICH KEEPS US IMPRISONED IN THIS LAND!
I KNOW YOU ALL THINK ME MAD--BUT I'M NOT! I HOPED TO WREST THE CROWN FROM YOU WHEN YOU FAILED TO FREE YOUR PEOPLE!
I--NEVER THOUGHT--IT WOULD COME TO--THIS!
SILENTLY--ALMOST TENDERLY--THE MONARCH OF THE INHUMANS FOLDS HIS GLIDING MEMBRANE AROUND HIS TREMBLING BROTHER'S HEAD--AS THOUGH TO GIVE HIM SHELTER--!
AND THEN, AT LENGTH, MAXIMUS RESIGNS HIMSELF TO WHAT MUST BE--AS THE TREMBLING STOPS--AND A THUNDROUS HUSH FALLS OVER THE SQUARE--
SLOWLY, CALMLY, IRREVOCABLY--THE SILENT SOVEREIGN BRACES HIMSELF--
THEN, WITH HEAD HELD HIGH, HIS MOUTH OPENS--
AND THE VOICE OF BLACK BOLT IS HEARD THRUOUT THE LAND--!
INSTANTANEOUSLY, A CATACLYSMIC SONIC CHAIN REACTION OCCURS AMONG THE SURROUNDING AIR MOLECULES, SHAKING THE NEARBY BUILDINGS LIKE WEEDS IN A HURRICANE--
REACHING A RANGE FAR BEYOND THE CAPACITY OF THE HUMAN EAR TO ABSORB--THE INHUMAN CRY OF BLACK BOLT INCREASES IN ITS CRESCENDO--CAUSING EXPLOSION AFTER EXPLOSION--
UNTIL, IN THE SPACE OF A FEW, SENSES-STAGGERING SECONDS--
11

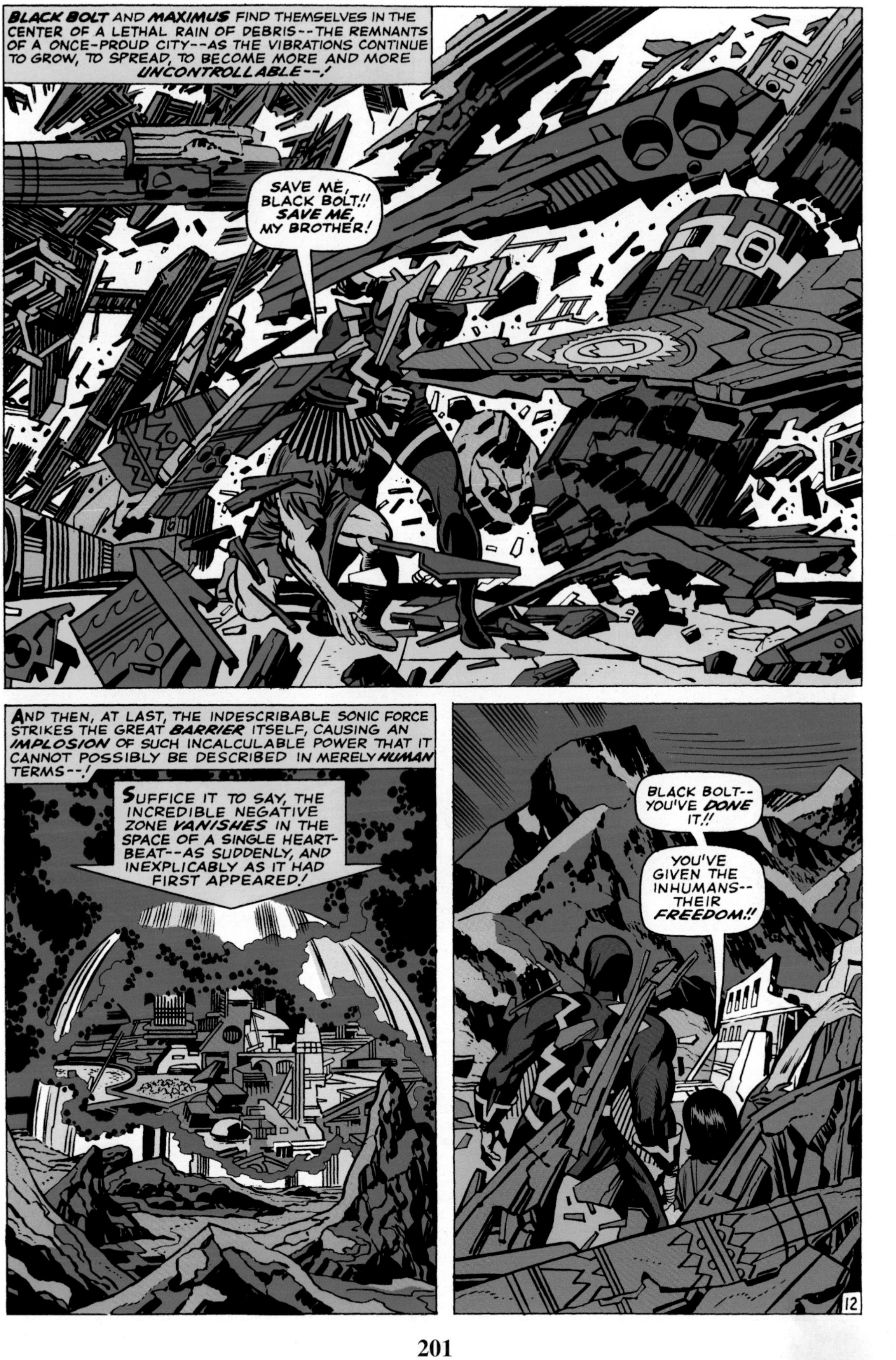
BLACK BOLT AND MAXIMUS FIND THEMSELVES IN THE CENTER OF A LETHAL RAIN OF DEBRIS--THE REMNANTS OF A ONCE-PROUD CITY--AS THE VIBRATIONS CONTINUE TO GROW, TO SPREAD, TO BECOME MORE AND MORE UNCONTROLLABLE--!
SAVE ME, BLACK BOLT!! SAVE ME, MY BROTHER!
AND THEN, AT LAST, THE INDESCRIBABLE SONIC FORCE STRIKES THE GREAT BARRIER ITSELF, CAUSING AN IMPLOSION OF SUCH INCALCULABLE POWER THAT IT CANNOT POSSIBLY BE DESCRIBED IN MERELY HUMAN TERMS--!
SUFFICE IT TO SAY, THE INCREDIBLE NEGATIVE ZONE VANISHES IN THE SPACE OF A SINGLE HEART-BEAT--AS SUDDENLY, AND INEXPLICABLY AS IT HAD FIRST APPEARED!
BLACK BOLT--YOU'VE DONE IT!!
YOU'VE GIVEN THE INHUMANS--THEIR FREEDOM!!
12

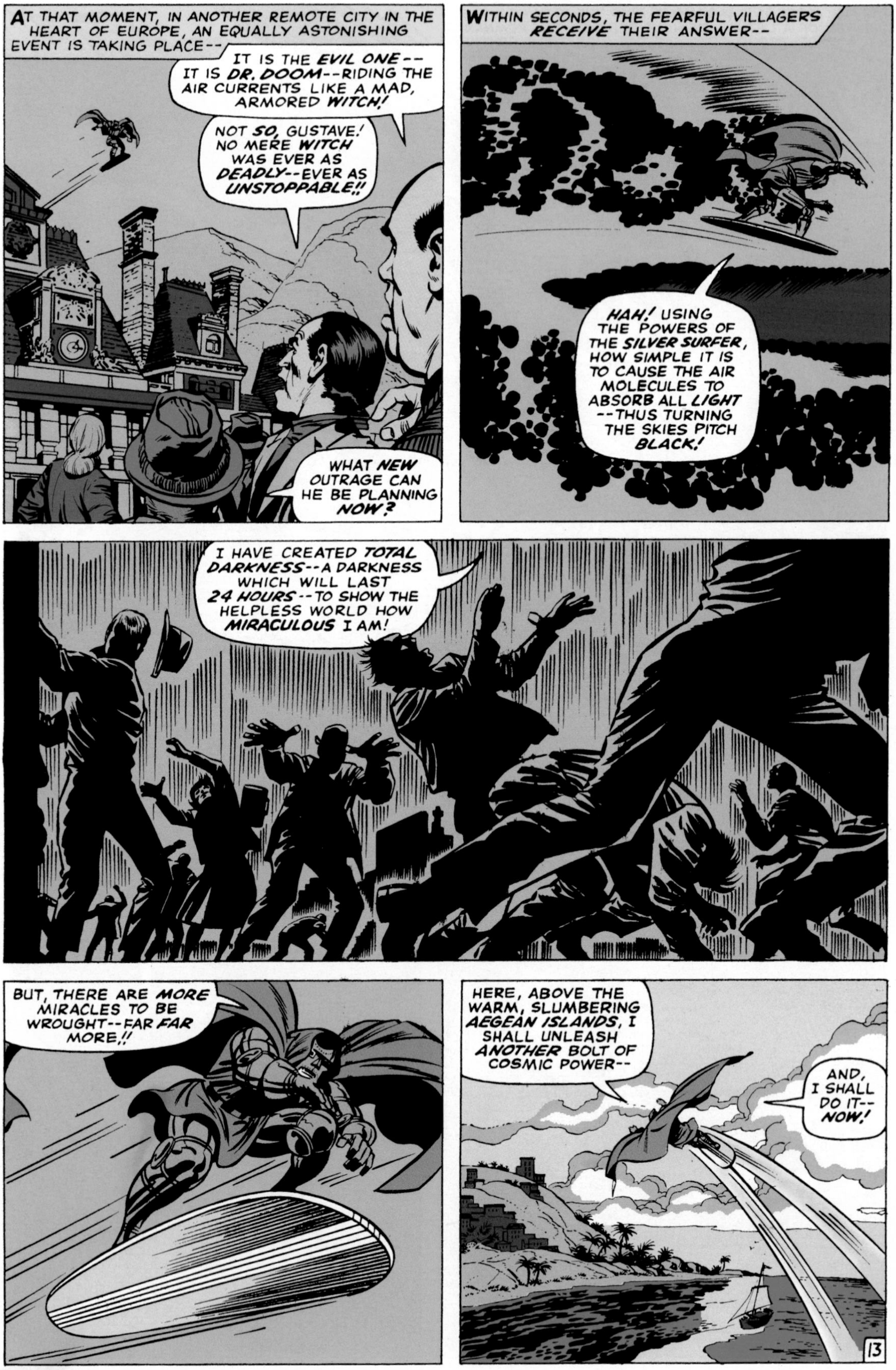
AT THAT MOMENT, IN ANOTHER REMOTE CITY IN THE HEART OF EUROPE, AN EQUALLY ASTONISHING EVENT IS TAKING PLACE--
IT IS THE EVIL ONE-- IT IS DR. DOOM--RIDING THE AIR CURRENTS LIKE A MAD, ARMORED WITCH!
NOT SO, GUSTAVE! NO MERE WITCH WAS EVER AS DEADLY--EVER AS UNSTOPPABLE!!
WHAT NEW OUTRAGE CAN HE BE PLANNING NOW?
WITHIN SECONDS, THE FEARFUL VILLAGERS RECEIVE THEIR ANSWER--
HAH! USING THE POWERS OF THE SILVER SURFER, HOW SIMPLE IT IS TO CAUSE THE AIR MOLECULES TO ABSORB ALL LIGHT --THUS TURNING THE SKIES PITCH BLACK!
I HAVE CREATED TOTAL DARKNESS--A DARKNESS WHICH WILL LAST 24 HOURS--TO SHOW THE HELPLESS WORLD HOW MIRACULOUS I AM!
BUT, THERE ARE MORE MIRACLES TO BE WROUGHT--FAR FAR MORE!!
HERE, ABOVE THE WARM, SLUMBERING AEGEAN ISLANDS, I SHALL UNLEASH ANOTHER BOLT OF COSMIC POWER--
AND, I SHALL DO IT-- NOW!
13

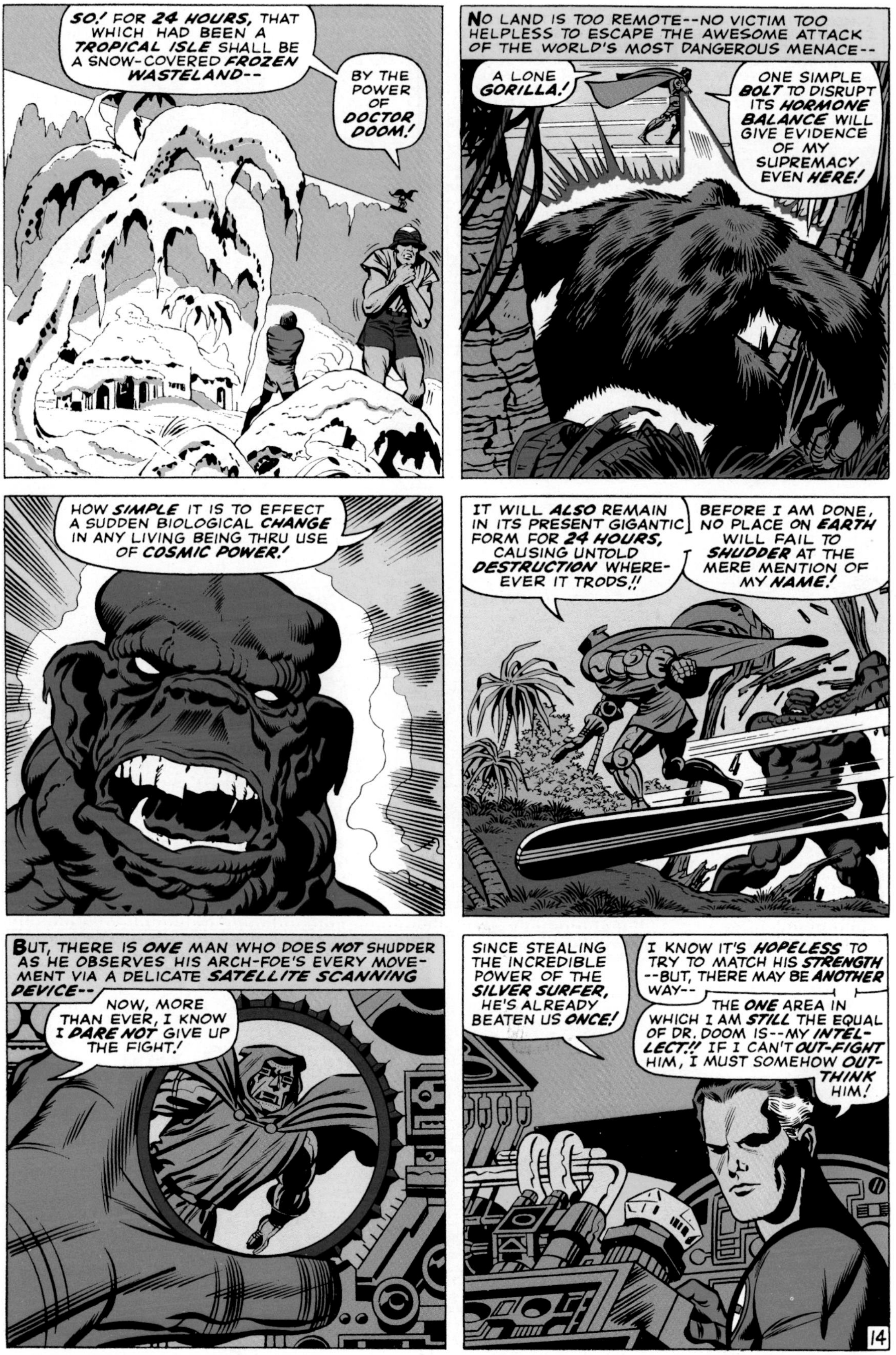
SO! FOR 24 HOURS, THAT WHICH HAD BEEN A TROPICAL ISLE SHALL BE A SNOW-COVERED FROZEN WASTELAND--
BY THE POWER OF DOCTOR DOOM!
NO LAND IS TOO REMOTE--NO VICTIM TOO HELPLESS TO ESCAPE THE AWESOME ATTACK OF THE WORLD'S MOST DANGEROUS MENACE--
A LONE GORILLA!
ONE SIMPLE BOLT TO DISRUPT ITS HORMONE BALANCE WILL GIVE EVIDENCE OF MY SUPREMACY EVEN HERE!
HOW SIMPLE IT IS TO EFFECT A SUDDEN BIOLOGICAL CHANGE IN ANY LIVING BEING THRU USE OF COSMIC POWER!
IT WILL ALSO REMAIN IN ITS PRESENT GIGANTIC FORM FOR 24 HOURS, CAUSING UNTOLD DESTRUCTION WHERE-EVER IT TRODS!!
BEFORE I AM DONE, NO PLACE ON EARTH WILL FAIL TO SHUDDER AT THE MERE MENTION OF MY NAME!
BUT, THERE IS ONE MAN WHO DOES NOT SHUDDER AS HE OBSERVES HIS ARCH-FOE'S EVERY MOVEMENT VIA A DELICATE SATELLITE SCANNING DEVICE--
NOW, MORE THAN EVER, I KNOW I DARE NOT GIVE UP THE FIGHT!
SINCE STEALING THE INCREDIBLE POWER OF THE SILVER SURFER, HE'S ALREADY BEATEN US ONCE!
I KNOW IT'S HOPELESS TO TRY TO MATCH HIS STRENGTH --BUT, THERE MAY BE ANOTHER WAY--
THE ONE AREA IN WHICH I AM STILL THE EQUAL OF DR. DOOM IS--MY INTELLECT!! IF I CAN'T OUT-FIGHT HIM, I MUST SOMEHOW OUT-THINK HIM!
14

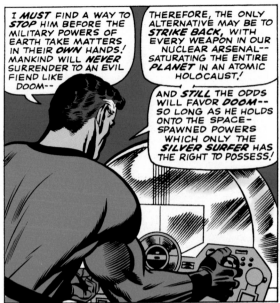

I **MUST** FIND A WAY TO **STOP** HIM BEFORE THE MILITARY POWERS OF EARTH TAKE MATTERS IN THEIR **OWN** HANDS! MANKIND WILL **NEVER** SURRENDER TO AN EVIL FIEND LIKE DOOM--

THEREFORE, THE ONLY ALTERNATIVE MAY BE TO **STRIKE BACK**, WITH EVERY WEAPON IN OUR NUCLEAR ARSENAL-- SATURATING THE ENTIRE **PLANET** IN AN ATOMIC HOLOCAUST!

AND **STILL** THE ODDS WILL FAVOR **DOOM**-- SO LONG AS HE HOLDS ONTO THE SPACE-SPAWNED POWERS WHICH ONLY THE **SILVER SURFER** HAS THE RIGHT TO POSSESS!

OUR TIME HAS ALMOST **RUN OUT**! I MAY NEVER BE ALLOWED A **SECOND CHANCE**--

THAT WHICH I'VE CREATED HERE MAY BE MANKIND'S **LAST HOPE** FOR FREEDOM --FOR LIFE ITSELF!

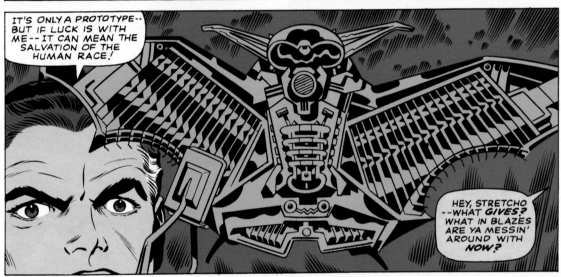

IT'S ONLY A PROTOTYPE-- BUT IF LUCK IS WITH ME-- IT CAN MEAN THE SALVATION OF THE HUMAN RACE!

HEY, STRETCHO --WHAT **GIVES**? WHAT IN BLAZES ARE YA MESSIN' AROUND WITH **NOW**?

OH, JUST A NEW TYPE OF **FLYING TOY**, BEN!

ALL THIS TIME WORKIN' ON A NUTTY **TOY**!

WHO LOOSENED YER **HEAD BOLTS**, MISTER?

IT MAY NOT BE AS FOOLISH AS YOU **THINK**! DON'T **DROP** IT, HEAR?

HERE-- **CATCH**!

BUT, THE INSTANT IT COMES IN CONTACT WITH THE STARTLED **THING**--

FTOOM!

YEEOWWW!

15

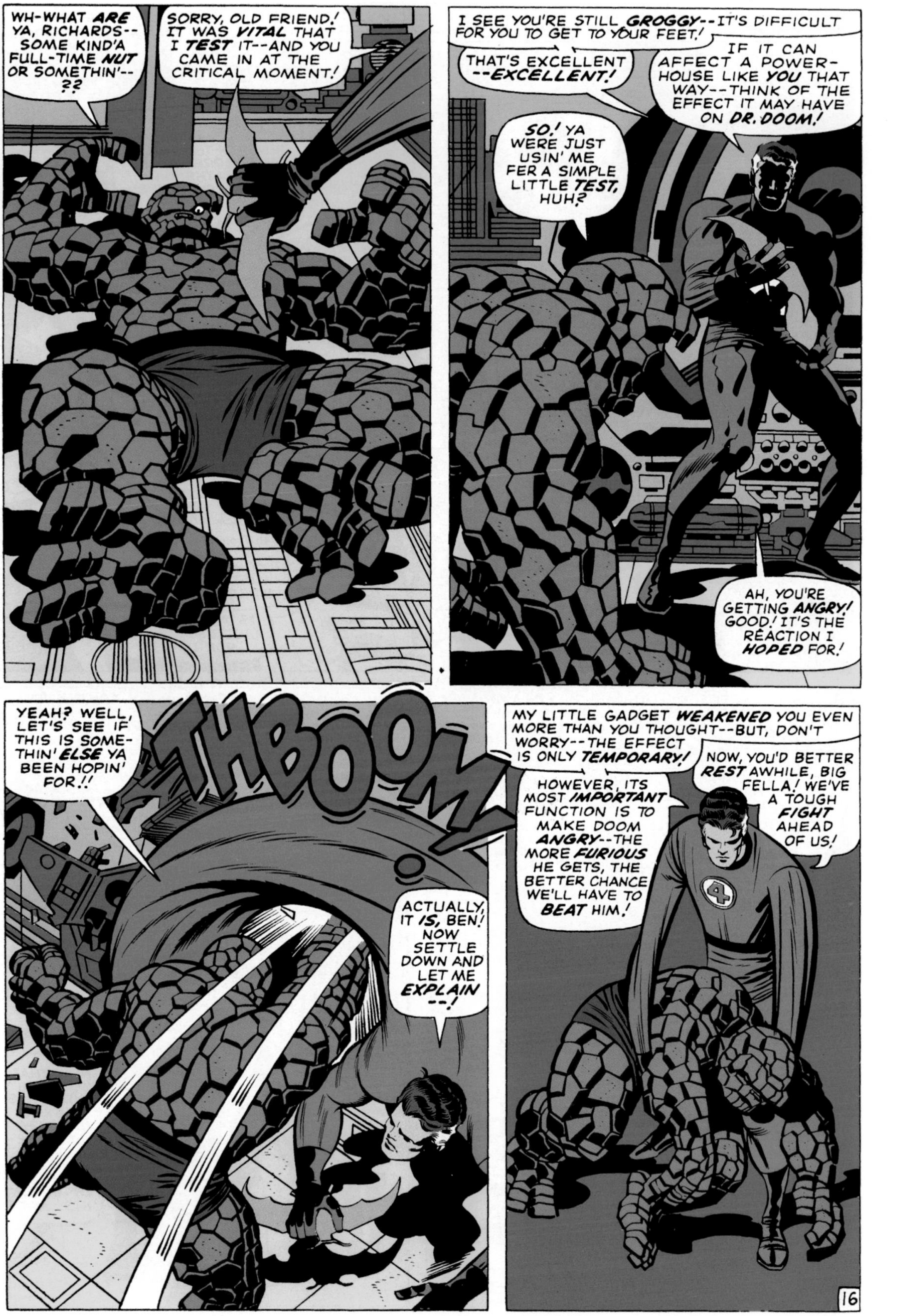
WH-WHAT ARE YA, RICHARDS-- SOME KIND'A FULL-TIME NUT OR SOMETHIN'-- ??
SORRY, OLD FRIEND! IT WAS VITAL THAT I TEST IT--AND YOU CAME IN AT THE CRITICAL MOMENT!
I SEE YOU'RE STILL GROGGY--IT'S DIFFICULT FOR YOU TO GET TO YOUR FEET!
THAT'S EXCELLENT --EXCELLENT!
IF IT CAN AFFECT A POWER-HOUSE LIKE YOU THAT WAY--THINK OF THE EFFECT IT MAY HAVE ON DR. DOOM!
SO! YA WERE JUST USIN' ME FER A SIMPLE LITTLE TEST, HUH?
AH, YOU'RE GETTING ANGRY! GOOD! IT'S THE REACTION I HOPED FOR!
YEAH? WELL, LET'S SEE IF THIS IS SOME-THIN' ELSE YA BEEN HOPIN' FOR!!
THBOOM
ACTUALLY, IT IS, BEN! NOW SETTLE DOWN AND LET ME EXPLAIN --!
MY LITTLE GADGET WEAKENED YOU EVEN MORE THAN YOU THOUGHT--BUT, DON'T WORRY--THE EFFECT IS ONLY TEMPORARY!
HOWEVER, ITS MOST IMPORTANT FUNCTION IS TO MAKE DOOM ANGRY--THE MORE FURIOUS HE GETS, THE BETTER CHANCE WE'LL HAVE TO BEAT HIM!
NOW, YOU'D BETTER REST AWHILE, BIG FELLA! WE'VE A TOUGH FIGHT AHEAD OF US!
16

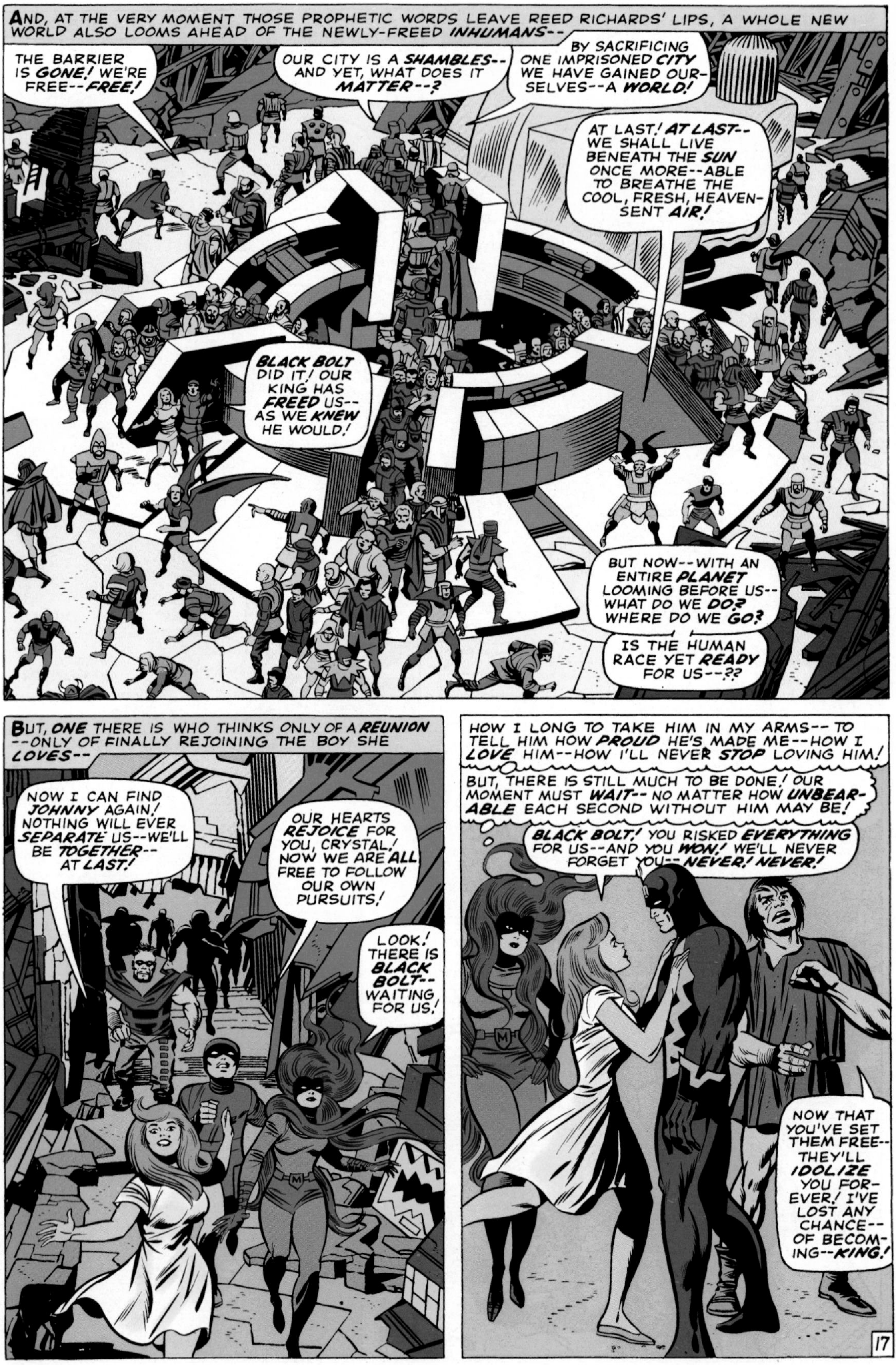
AND, AT THE VERY MOMENT THOSE PROPHETIC WORDS LEAVE REED RICHARDS' LIPS, A WHOLE NEW WORLD ALSO LOOMS AHEAD OF THE NEWLY-FREED INHUMANS--
THE BARRIER IS GONE! WE'RE FREE--FREE!
OUR CITY IS A SHAMBLES--AND YET, WHAT DOES IT MATTER--?
BY SACRIFICING ONE IMPRISONED CITY WE HAVE GAINED OURSELVES--A WORLD!
AT LAST! AT LAST--WE SHALL LIVE BENEATH THE SUN ONCE MORE--ABLE TO BREATHE THE COOL, FRESH, HEAVEN-SENT AIR!
BLACK BOLT DID IT! OUR KING HAS FREED US--AS WE KNEW HE WOULD!
BUT NOW--WITH AN ENTIRE PLANET LOOMING BEFORE US--WHAT DO WE DO? WHERE DO WE GO?
IS THE HUMAN RACE YET READY FOR US--??
BUT, ONE THERE IS WHO THINKS ONLY OF A REUNION--ONLY OF FINALLY REJOINING THE BOY SHE LOVES--
NOW I CAN FIND JOHNNY AGAIN! NOTHING WILL EVER SEPARATE US--WE'LL BE TOGETHER--AT LAST!
OUR HEARTS REJOICE FOR YOU, CRYSTAL! NOW WE ARE ALL FREE TO FOLLOW OUR OWN PURSUITS!
LOOK! THERE IS BLACK BOLT--WAITING FOR US!
HOW I LONG TO TAKE HIM IN MY ARMS--TO TELL HIM HOW PROUD HE'S MADE ME--HOW I LOVE HIM--HOW I'LL NEVER STOP LOVING HIM!
BUT, THERE IS STILL MUCH TO BE DONE! OUR MOMENT MUST WAIT-- NO MATTER HOW UNBEARABLE EACH SECOND WITHOUT HIM MAY BE!
BLACK BOLT! YOU RISKED EVERYTHING FOR US--AND YOU WON! WE'LL NEVER FORGET YOU--NEVER! NEVER!
NOW THAT YOU'VE SET THEM FREE--THEY'LL IDOLIZE YOU FOREVER! I'VE LOST ANY CHANCE--OF BECOMING--KING!
17

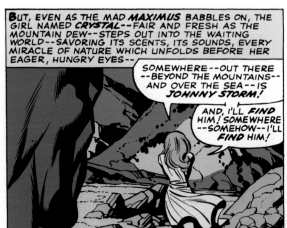

BUT, EVEN AS THE MAD *MAXIMUS* BABBLES ON, THE GIRL NAMED *CRYSTAL*--FAIR AND FRESH AS THE MOUNTAIN DEW--STEPS OUT INTO THE WAITING WORLD--SAVORING ITS SCENTS, ITS SOUNDS, EVERY MIRACLE OF NATURE WHICH UNFOLDS BEFORE HER EAGER, HUNGRY EYES--

SOMEWHERE--OUT THERE --BEYOND THE MOUNTAINS-- AND OVER THE SEA--IS *JOHNNY STORM!*

AND, I'LL *FIND* HIM! SOMEWHERE --SOMEHOW--I'LL *FIND* HIM!

WE CANNOT LET CRYSTAL GO *ALONE!* WE MUST *JOIN* HER, BLACK BOLT!

WE SIX--YOU, GORGON, KARNAK, TRITON, CRYSTAL, AND MYSELF --HAVE BEEN TOGETHER SO *LONG*--

WE *CANNOT* SEPARATE--NOT *NOW!*

YES! *GO! GO!* WITH *YOU* GONE, I'LL *STILL* HAVE A CHANCE TO BE KING!

THOUGH THEY THINK ME *MAD* --AM I NOT STILL YOUR *BROTHER??* DO I NOT HAVE THE *BLOOD* OF A *KING* SURGING THRU MY VEINS?

WHAT?? AFTER ALL YOU'VE *DONE*--YOU *DARE* SPEAK SO TO *BLACK BOLT?!!*

YOU DARE STILL ASPIRE TO THE *THRONE?* BUT, YOU SHALL ASPIRE *NO LONGER*, MADMAN-- NOT WHILE *KARNAK* LIVES!

FFFITT!!!

NO, KARNAK--!

--ONLY *BLACK BOLT* HAS THE RIGHT!!

FORGIVE ME, BLACK BOLT! I PRESUMED TOO MUCH!

NO MATTER *WHAT* HIS CRIMES --NO MATTER *WHAT* THE PROVOCATION--I DARED TO FORGET--HE IS YOUR *BROTHER!*

BLACK BOLT! THE *COUNCIL OF ELDERS* HAS MADE A DECISION--ONE WHICH WILL AFFECT US *ALL!*

IT HAS BEEN *DECIDED*--BY ACCLAMATION --THAT WE ARE TO *SEPARATE!*

WE, THE SIX WHO FORM THE ROYAL FAMILY AND COURT, SHALL ENTER THE WORLD OF THE *HUMANS!*

WHILE OUR BRETHREN SHALL *REMAIN*, TO REBUILD OUR CITY, AND TEND OUR LAND--

--UNTIL THE GLORIOUS DAY WHEN WE SHALL *ALL* BE TOGETHER AGAIN--PROUD AND UNITED ONCE MORE!

18

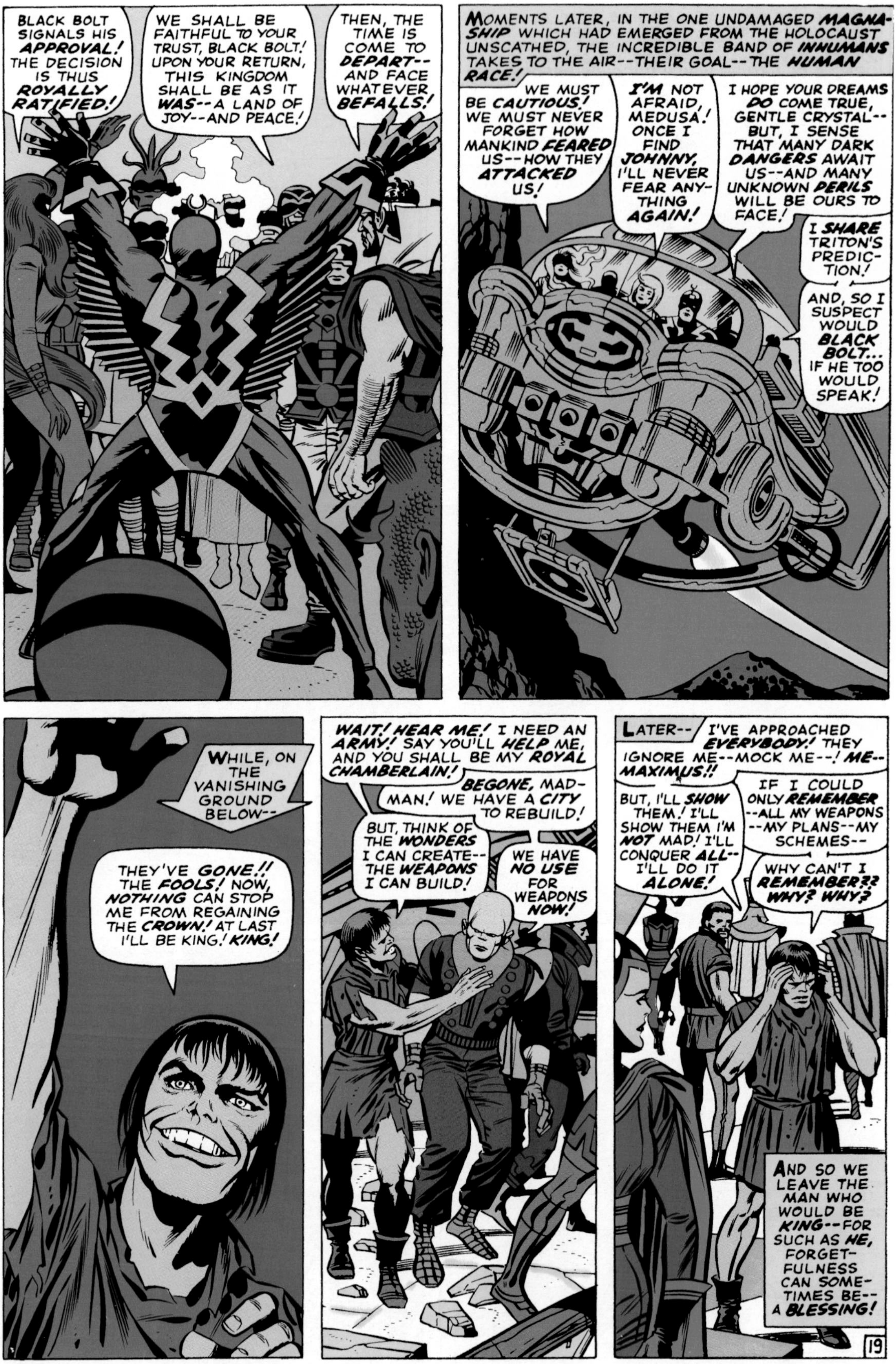
BLACK BOLT SIGNALS HIS APPROVAL! THE DECISION IS THUS ROYALLY RATIFIED!
WE SHALL BE FAITHFUL TO YOUR TRUST, BLACK BOLT! UPON YOUR RETURN, THIS KINGDOM SHALL BE AS IT WAS--A LAND OF JOY--AND PEACE!
THEN, THE TIME IS COME TO DEPART--AND FACE WHATEVER BEFALLS!
MOMENTS LATER, IN THE ONE UNDAMAGED MAGNA-SHIP WHICH HAD EMERGED FROM THE HOLOCAUST UNSCATHED, THE INCREDIBLE BAND OF INHUMANS TAKES TO THE AIR--THEIR GOAL--THE HUMAN RACE!
WE MUST BE CAUTIOUS! WE MUST NEVER FORGET HOW MANKIND FEARED US--HOW THEY ATTACKED US!
I'M NOT AFRAID, MEDUSA! ONCE I FIND JOHNNY, I'LL NEVER FEAR ANYTHING AGAIN!
I HOPE YOUR DREAMS DO COME TRUE, GENTLE CRYSTAL--BUT, I SENSE THAT MANY DARK DANGERS AWAIT US--AND MANY UNKNOWN PERILS WILL BE OURS TO FACE!
I SHARE TRITON'S PREDICTION!
AND, SO I SUSPECT WOULD BLACK BOLT... IF HE TOO WOULD SPEAK!
WHILE, ON THE VANISHING GROUND BELOW--
THEY'VE GONE!! THE FOOLS! NOW, NOTHING CAN STOP ME FROM REGAINING THE CROWN! AT LAST I'LL BE KING! KING!
WAIT! HEAR ME! I NEED AN ARMY! SAY YOU'LL HELP ME, AND YOU SHALL BE MY ROYAL CHAMBERLAIN!
BEGONE, MADMAN! WE HAVE A CITY TO REBUILD!
BUT, THINK OF THE WONDERS I CAN CREATE--THE WEAPONS I CAN BUILD!
WE HAVE NO USE FOR WEAPONS NOW!
LATER--
I'VE APPROACHED EVERYBODY! THEY IGNORE ME--MOCK ME--! ME--MAXIMUS!!
BUT, I'LL SHOW THEM! I'LL SHOW THEM I'M NOT MAD! I'LL CONQUER ALL--I'LL DO IT ALONE!
IF I COULD ONLY REMEMBER--ALL MY WEAPONS--MY PLANS--MY SCHEMES--
WHY CAN'T I REMEMBER?? WHY? WHY?
AND SO WE LEAVE THE MAN WHO WOULD BE KING--FOR SUCH AS HE, FORGETFULNESS CAN SOMETIMES BE--A BLESSING!
19

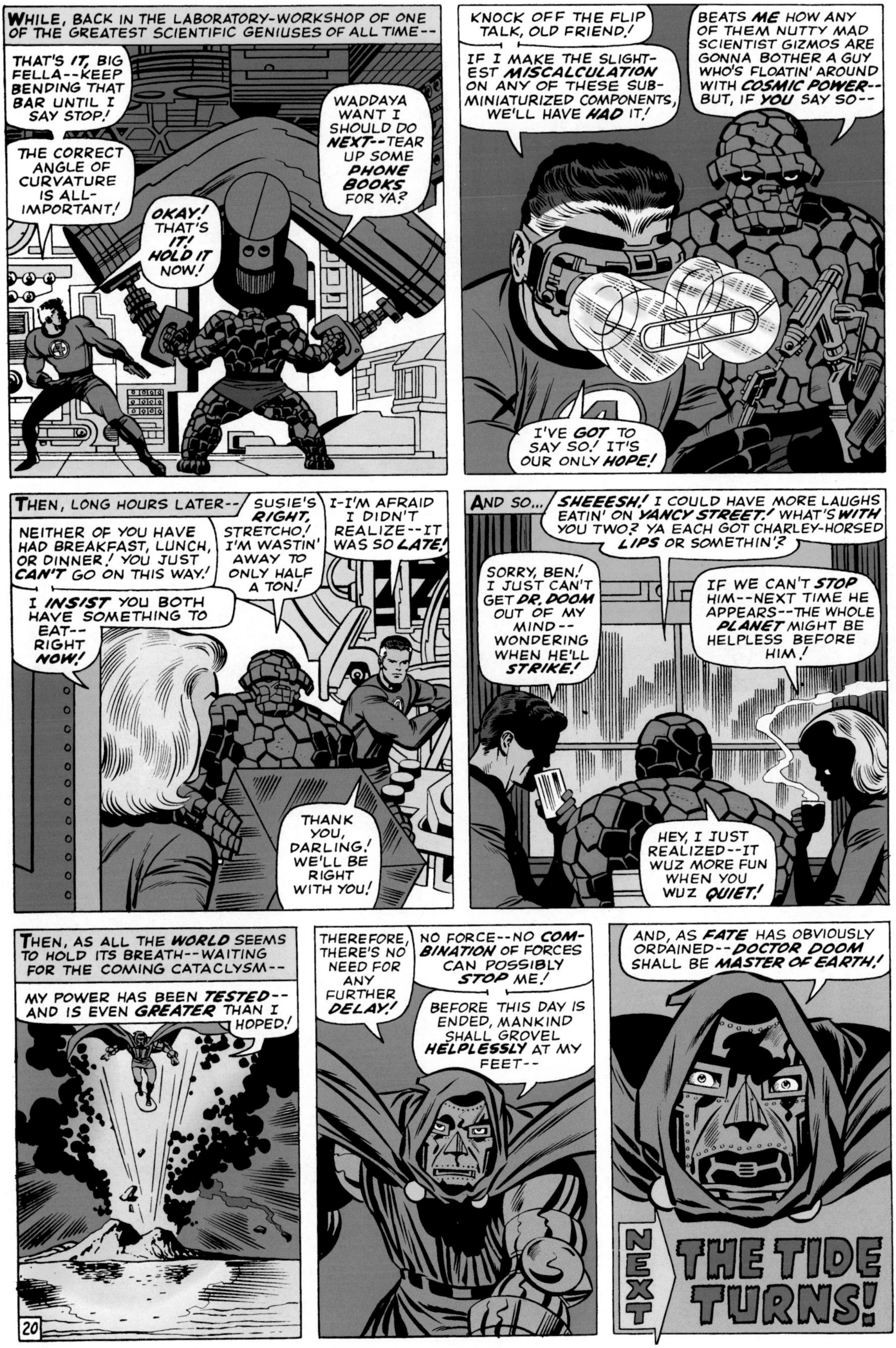
WHILE, BACK IN THE LABORATORY-WORKSHOP OF ONE OF THE GREATEST SCIENTIFIC GENIUSES OF ALL TIME--
THAT'S IT, BIG FELLA--KEEP BENDING THAT BAR UNTIL I SAY STOP!
THE CORRECT ANGLE OF CURVATURE IS ALL-IMPORTANT!
WADDAYA WANT I SHOULD DO NEXT--TEAR UP SOME PHONE BOOKS FOR YA?
OKAY! THAT'S IT! HOLD IT NOW!
KNOCK OFF THE FLIP TALK, OLD FRIEND!
IF I MAKE THE SLIGHTEST MISCALCULATION ON ANY OF THESE SUB-MINIATURIZED COMPONENTS, WE'LL HAVE HAD IT!
BEATS ME HOW ANY OF THEM NUTTY MAD SCIENTIST GIZMOS ARE GONNA BOTHER A GUY WHO'S FLOATIN' AROUND WITH COSMIC POWER--BUT, IF YOU SAY SO--
I'VE GOT TO SAY SO! IT'S OUR ONLY HOPE!
THEN, LONG HOURS LATER--
NEITHER OF YOU HAVE HAD BREAKFAST, LUNCH, OR DINNER! YOU JUST CAN'T GO ON THIS WAY!
I INSIST YOU BOTH HAVE SOMETHING TO EAT--RIGHT NOW!
SUSIE'S RIGHT, STRETCHO! I'M WASTIN' AWAY TO ONLY HALF A TON!
I-I'M AFRAID I DIDN'T REALIZE--IT WAS SO LATE!
THANK YOU, DARLING! WE'LL BE RIGHT WITH YOU!
AND SO...
SHEEESH! I COULD HAVE MORE LAUGHS EATIN' ON YANCY STREET! WHAT'S WITH YOU TWO? YA EACH GOT CHARLEY-HORSED LIPS OR SOMETHIN'?
SORRY, BEN! I JUST CAN'T GET DR. DOOM OUT OF MY MIND--WONDERING WHEN HE'LL STRIKE!
IF WE CAN'T STOP HIM--NEXT TIME HE APPEARS--THE WHOLE PLANET MIGHT BE HELPLESS BEFORE HIM!
HEY, I JUST REALIZED--IT WUZ MORE FUN WHEN YOU WUZ QUIET!
THEN, AS ALL THE WORLD SEEMS TO HOLD ITS BREATH--WAITING FOR THE COMING CATACLYSM--
MY POWER HAS BEEN TESTED--AND IS EVEN GREATER THAN I HOPED!
20
THEREFORE, THERE'S NO NEED FOR ANY FURTHER DELAY!
NO FORCE--NO COMBINATION OF FORCES CAN POSSIBLY STOP ME!
BEFORE THIS DAY IS ENDED, MANKIND SHALL GROVEL HELPLESSLY AT MY FEET--
AND, AS FATE HAS OBVIOUSLY ORDAINED--DOCTOR DOOM SHALL BE MASTER OF EARTH!
NEXT
THE TIDE TURNS!

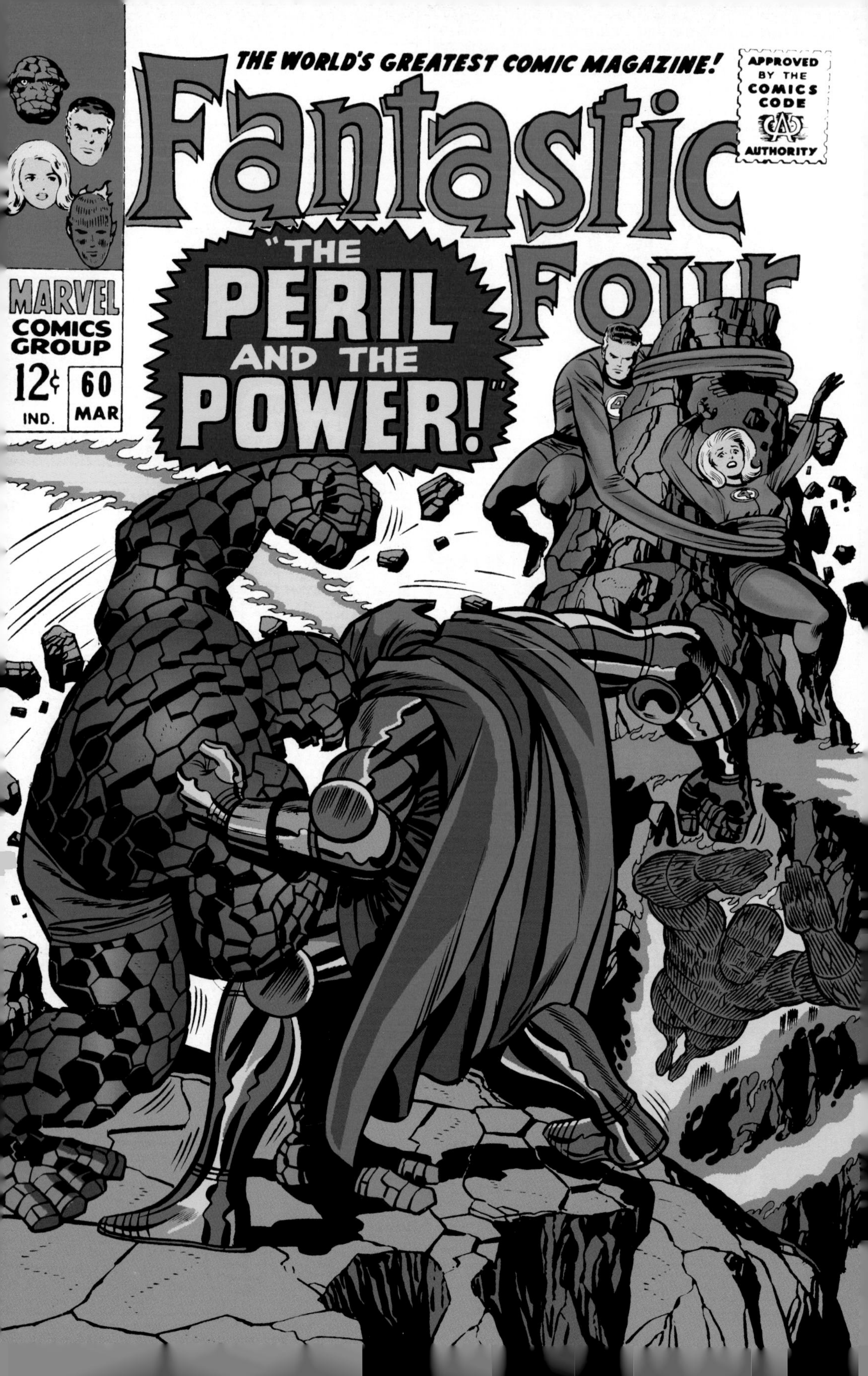
THE WORLD'S GREATEST COMIC MAGAZINE!
Fantastic Four
APPROVED BY THE COMICS CODE AUTHORITY
MARVEL COMICS GROUP
12¢ IND.
60 MAR
"THE PERIL AND THE POWER!"

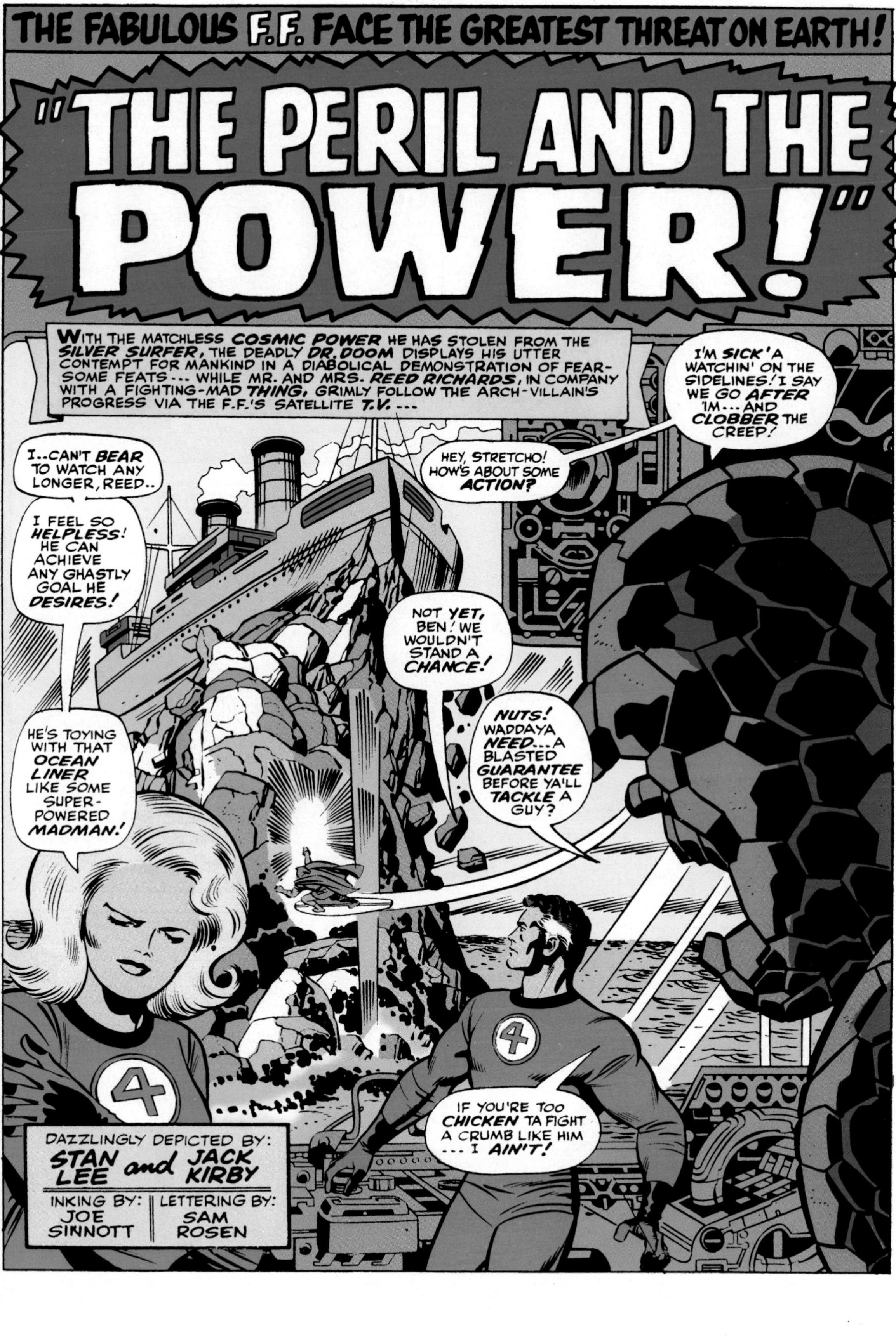
THE FABULOUS F.F. FACE THE GREATEST THREAT ON EARTH!
"THE PERIL AND THE POWER!"
WITH THE MATCHLESS COSMIC POWER HE HAS STOLEN FROM THE SILVER SURFER, THE DEADLY DR. DOOM DISPLAYS HIS UTTER CONTEMPT FOR MANKIND IN A DIABOLICAL DEMONSTRATION OF FEARSOME FEATS... WHILE MR. AND MRS. REED RICHARDS, IN COMPANY WITH A FIGHTING-MAD THING, GRIMLY FOLLOW THE ARCH-VILLAIN'S PROGRESS VIA THE F.F.'S SATELLITE T.V. ---
I..CAN'T BEAR TO WATCH ANY LONGER, REED..
I FEEL SO HELPLESS! HE CAN ACHIEVE ANY GHASTLY GOAL HE DESIRES!
HE'S TOYING WITH THAT OCEAN LINER LIKE SOME SUPER-POWERED MADMAN!
HEY, STRETCHO! HOW'S ABOUT SOME ACTION?
I'M SICK 'A WATCHIN' ON THE SIDELINES! I SAY WE GO AFTER 'IM... AND CLOBBER THE CREEP!
NOT YET, BEN! WE WOULDN'T STAND A CHANCE!
NUTS! WADDAYA NEED... A BLASTED GUARANTEE BEFORE YA'LL TACKLE A GUY?
IF YOU'RE TOO CHICKEN TA FIGHT A CRUMB LIKE HIM --- I AIN'T!
DAZZLINGLY DEPICTED BY: STAN LEE and JACK KIRBY
INKING BY: JOE SINNOTT
LETTERING BY: SAM ROSEN

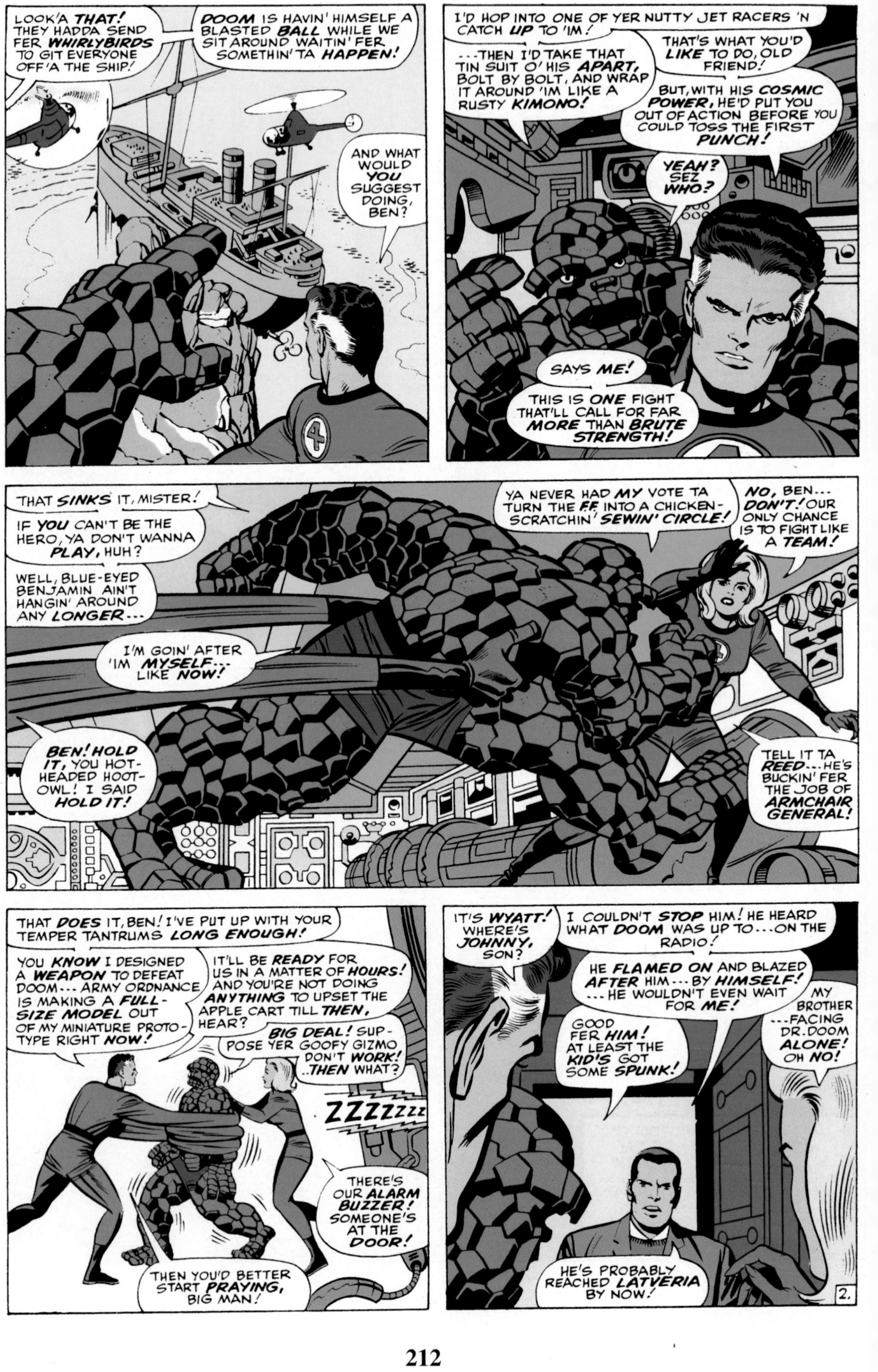
LOOK'A THAT! THEY HADDA SEND FER WHIRLYBIRDS TO GIT EVERYONE OFF'A THE SHIP!
DOOM IS HAVIN' HIMSELF A BLASTED BALL WHILE WE SIT AROUND WAITIN' FER SOMETHIN' TA HAPPEN!
AND WHAT WOULD YOU SUGGEST DOING, BEN?
I'D HOP INTO ONE OF YER NUTTY JET RACERS 'N CATCH UP TO 'IM!
---THEN I'D TAKE THAT TIN SUIT O' HIS APART, BOLT BY BOLT, AND WRAP IT AROUND 'IM LIKE A RUSTY KIMONO!
THAT'S WHAT YOU'D LIKE TO DO, OLD FRIEND!
BUT, WITH HIS COSMIC POWER, HE'D PUT YOU OUT OF ACTION BEFORE YOU COULD TOSS THE FIRST PUNCH!
YEAH? SEZ WHO?
SAYS ME!
THIS IS ONE FIGHT THAT'LL CALL FOR FAR MORE THAN BRUTE STRENGTH!
THAT SINKS IT, MISTER!
IF YOU CAN'T BE THE HERO, YA DON'T WANNA PLAY, HUH?
WELL, BLUE-EYED BENJAMIN AIN'T HANGIN' AROUND ANY LONGER---
I'M GOIN' AFTER 'IM MYSELF... LIKE NOW!
YA NEVER HAD MY VOTE TA TURN THE F.F. INTO A CHICKEN-SCRATCHIN' SEWIN' CIRCLE!
NO, BEN... DON'T! OUR ONLY CHANCE IS TO FIGHT LIKE A TEAM!
BEN! HOLD IT, YOU HOT-HEADED HOOT-OWL! I SAID HOLD IT!
TELL IT TA REED---HE'S BUCKIN' FER THE JOB OF ARMCHAIR GENERAL!
THAT DOES IT, BEN! I'VE PUT UP WITH YOUR TEMPER TANTRUMS LONG ENOUGH!
YOU KNOW I DESIGNED A WEAPON TO DEFEAT DOOM--- ARMY ORDNANCE IS MAKING A FULL-SIZE MODEL OUT OF MY MINIATURE PROTO-TYPE RIGHT NOW!
IT'LL BE READY FOR US IN A MATTER OF HOURS! AND YOU'RE NOT DOING ANYTHING TO UPSET THE APPLE CART TILL THEN, HEAR?
BIG DEAL! SUPPOSE YER GOOFY GIZMO DON'T WORK! ..THEN WHAT?
ZZZzzzz
THERE'S OUR ALARM BUZZER! SOMEONE'S AT THE DOOR!
THEN YOU'D BETTER START PRAYING, BIG MAN!
IT'S WYATT! WHERE'S JOHNNY, SON?
I COULDN'T STOP HIM! HE HEARD WHAT DOOM WAS UP TO...ON THE RADIO!
HE FLAMED ON AND BLAZED AFTER HIM---BY HIMSELF! ---HE WOULDN'T EVEN WAIT FOR ME!
MY BROTHER ---FACING DR. DOOM ALONE! OH NO!
GOOD FER HIM! AT LEAST THE KID'S GOT SOME SPUNK!
HE'S PROBABLY REACHED LATVERIA BY NOW!
2.

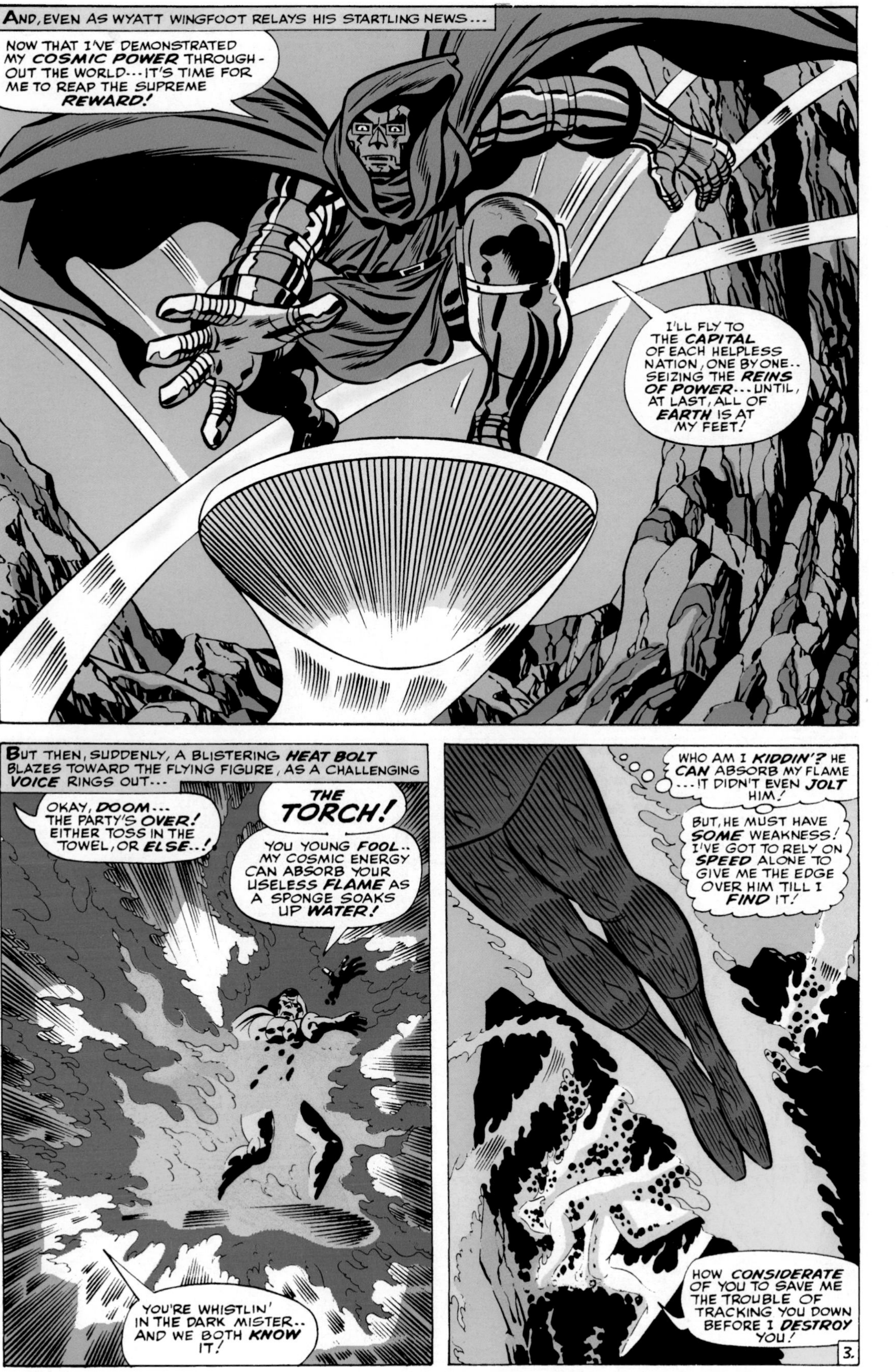
AND, EVEN AS WYATT WINGFOOT RELAYS HIS STARTLING NEWS...
NOW THAT I'VE DEMONSTRATED MY COSMIC POWER THROUGH-OUT THE WORLD...IT'S TIME FOR ME TO REAP THE SUPREME REWARD!
I'LL FLY TO THE CAPITAL OF EACH HELPLESS NATION, ONE BY ONE.. SEIZING THE REINS OF POWER...UNTIL, AT LAST, ALL OF EARTH IS AT MY FEET!
BUT THEN, SUDDENLY, A BLISTERING HEAT BOLT BLAZES TOWARD THE FLYING FIGURE, AS A CHALLENGING VOICE RINGS OUT...
OKAY, DOOM... THE PARTY'S OVER! EITHER TOSS IN THE TOWEL, OR ELSE..!
THE TORCH!
YOU YOUNG FOOL.. MY COSMIC ENERGY CAN ABSORB YOUR USELESS FLAME AS A SPONGE SOAKS UP WATER!
YOU'RE WHISTLIN' IN THE DARK MISTER.. AND WE BOTH KNOW IT!
WHO AM I KIDDIN'? HE CAN ABSORB MY FLAME ...IT DIDN'T EVEN JOLT HIM!
BUT, HE MUST HAVE SOME WEAKNESS! I'VE GOT TO RELY ON SPEED ALONE TO GIVE ME THE EDGE OVER HIM TILL I FIND IT!
HOW CONSIDERATE OF YOU TO SAVE ME THE TROUBLE OF TRACKING YOU DOWN BEFORE I DESTROY YOU!
3.

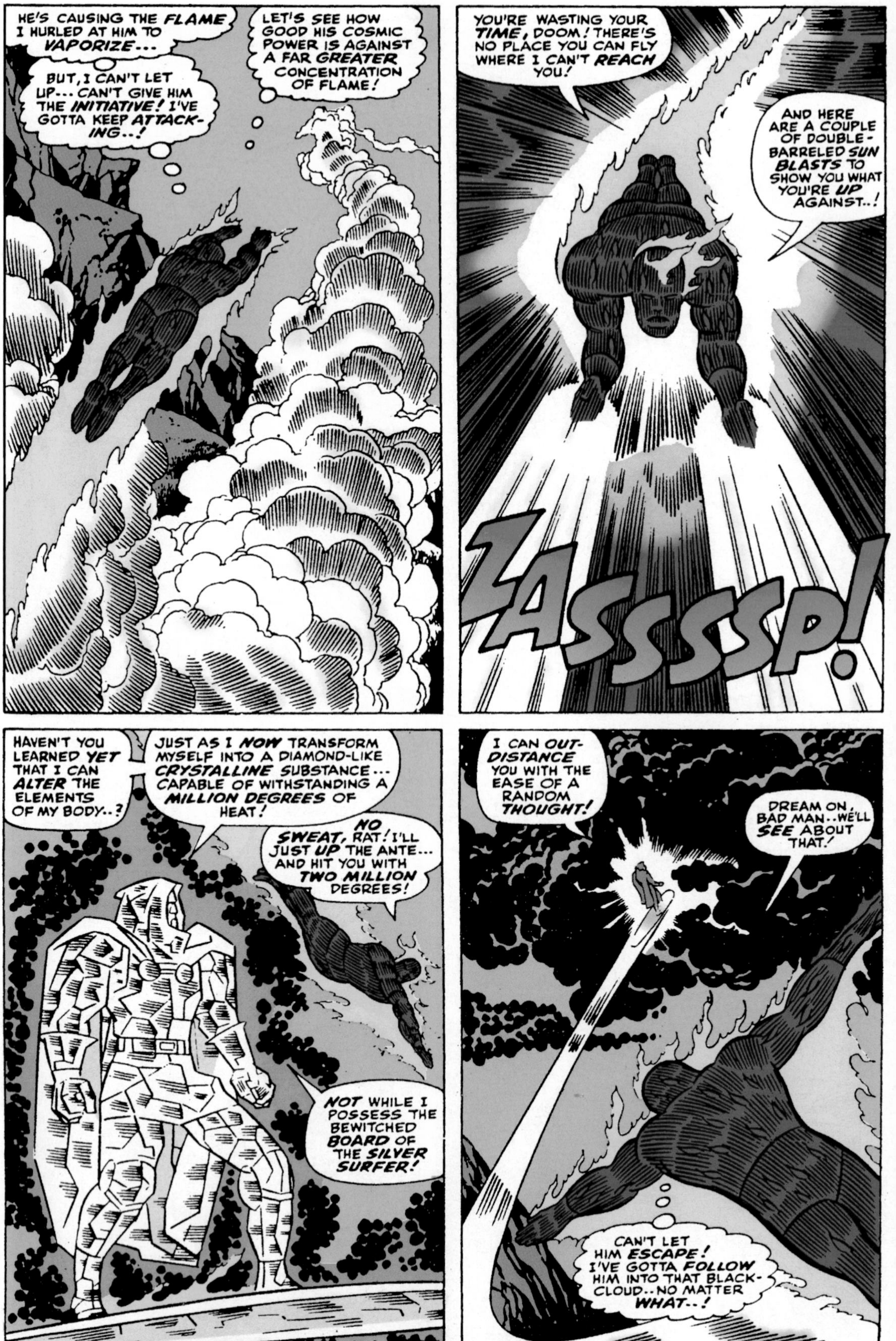

HE'S CAUSING THE FLAME I HURLED AT HIM TO VAPORIZE...
BUT, I CAN'T LET UP... CAN'T GIVE HIM THE INITIATIVE! I'VE GOTTA KEEP ATTACK-ING..!
LET'S SEE HOW GOOD HIS COSMIC POWER IS AGAINST A FAR GREATER CONCENTRATION OF FLAME!
YOU'RE WASTING YOUR TIME, DOOM! THERE'S NO PLACE YOU CAN FLY WHERE I CAN'T REACH YOU!
AND HERE ARE A COUPLE OF DOUBLE-BARRELED SUN BLASTS TO SHOW YOU WHAT YOU'RE UP AGAINST..!
ZASSSSP!
HAVEN'T YOU LEARNED YET THAT I CAN ALTER THE ELEMENTS OF MY BODY..?
JUST AS I NOW TRANSFORM MYSELF INTO A DIAMOND-LIKE CRYSTALLINE SUBSTANCE... CAPABLE OF WITHSTANDING A MILLION DEGREES OF HEAT!
NO SWEAT, RAT! I'LL JUST UP THE ANTE... AND HIT YOU WITH TWO MILLION DEGREES!
NOT WHILE I POSSESS THE BEWITCHED BOARD OF THE SILVER SURFER!
I CAN OUT-DISTANCE YOU WITH THE EASE OF A RANDOM THOUGHT!
DREAM ON, BAD MAN.. WE'LL SEE ABOUT THAT!
CAN'T LET HIM ESCAPE! I'VE GOTTA FOLLOW HIM INTO THAT BLACK-CLOUD.. NO MATTER WHAT..!

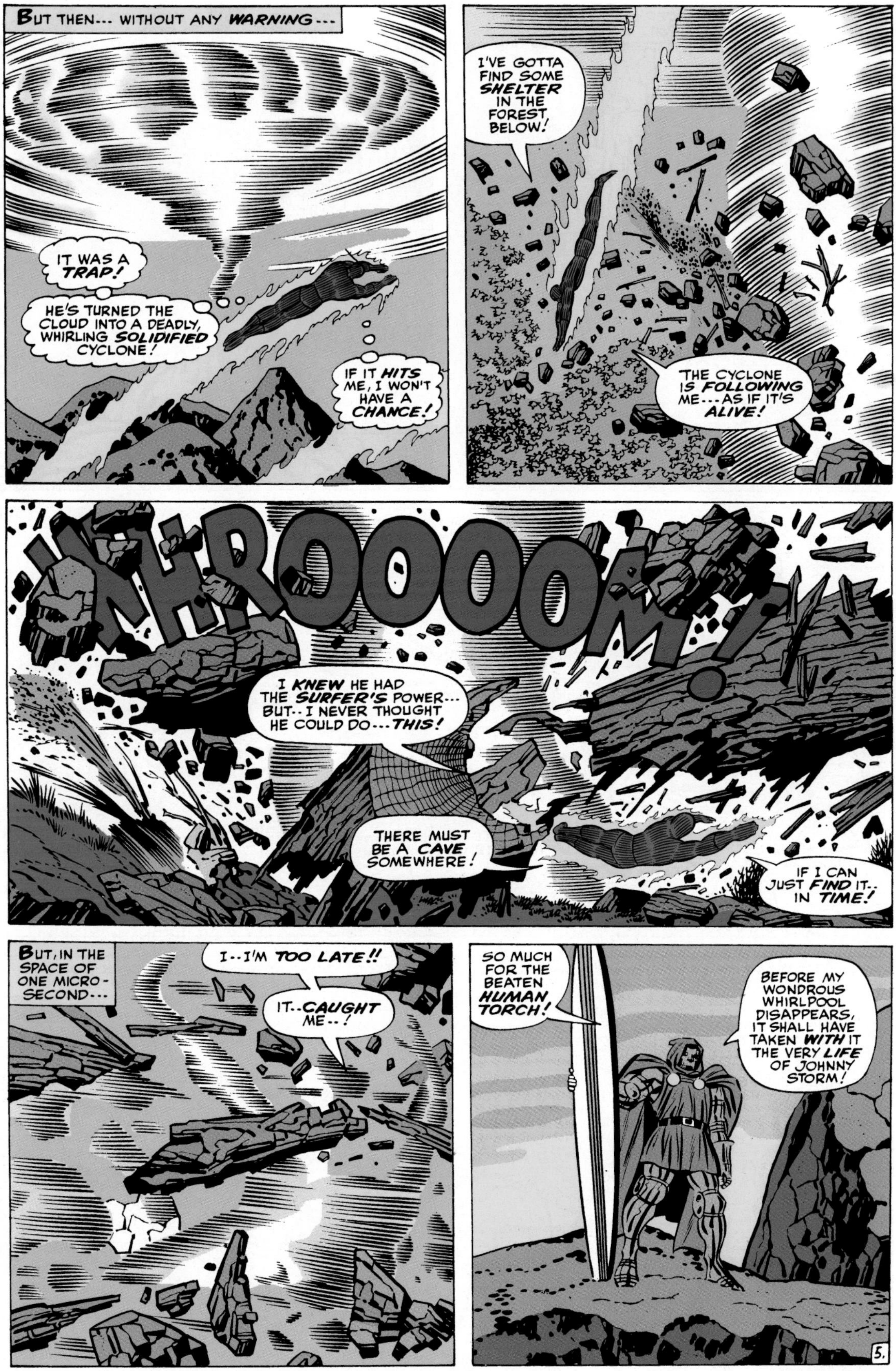
BUT THEN--- WITHOUT ANY WARNING---
IT WAS A TRAP!
HE'S TURNED THE CLOUD INTO A DEADLY, WHIRLING SOLIDIFIED CYCLONE!
IF IT HITS ME, I WON'T HAVE A CHANCE!
I'VE GOTTA FIND SOME SHELTER IN THE FOREST BELOW!
THE CYCLONE IS FOLLOWING ME---AS IF IT'S ALIVE!
WHROOOOOM!
I KNEW HE HAD THE SURFER'S POWER--- BUT--I NEVER THOUGHT HE COULD DO---THIS!
THERE MUST BE A CAVE SOMEWHERE!
IF I CAN JUST FIND IT-- IN TIME!
BUT, IN THE SPACE OF ONE MICRO-SECOND---
I--I'M TOO LATE!!
IT--CAUGHT ME--!
SO MUCH FOR THE BEATEN HUMAN TORCH!
BEFORE MY WONDROUS WHIRLPOOL DISAPPEARS, IT SHALL HAVE TAKEN WITH IT THE VERY LIFE OF JOHNNY STORM!
5.

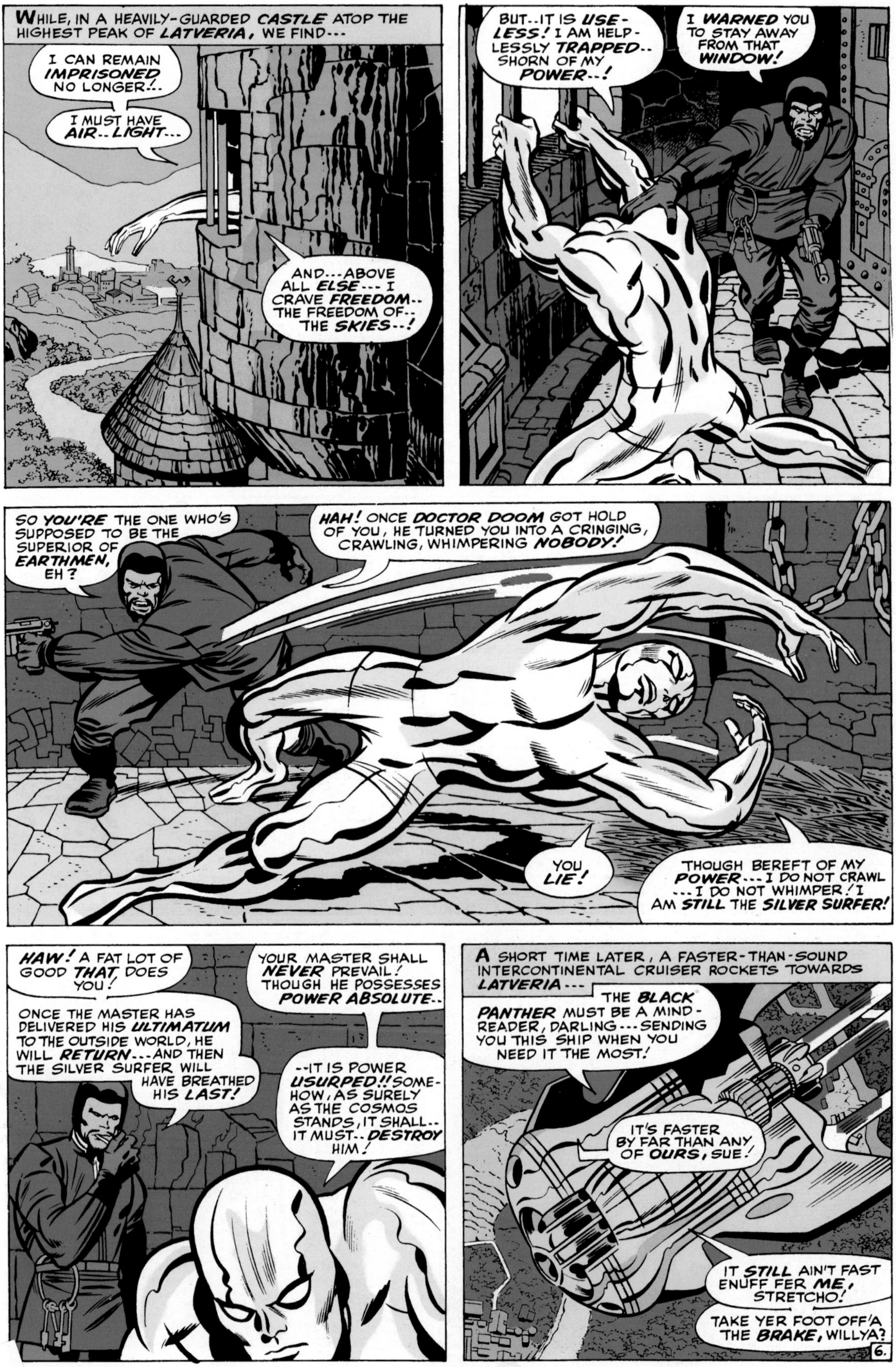

WHILE, IN A HEAVILY-GUARDED CASTLE ATOP THE HIGHEST PEAK OF LATVERIA, WE FIND---
I CAN REMAIN IMPRISONED NO LONGER--!
I MUST HAVE AIR--LIGHT---
AND---ABOVE ALL ELSE--- I CRAVE FREEDOM-- THE FREEDOM OF-- THE SKIES--!
BUT--IT IS USELESS! I AM HELPLESSLY TRAPPED-- SHORN OF MY POWER--!
I WARNED YOU TO STAY AWAY FROM THAT WINDOW!
SO YOU'RE THE ONE WHO'S SUPPOSED TO BE THE SUPERIOR OF EARTHMEN, EH?
HAH! ONCE DOCTOR DOOM GOT HOLD OF YOU, HE TURNED YOU INTO A CRINGING, CRAWLING, WHIMPERING NOBODY!
YOU LIE!
THOUGH BEREFT OF MY POWER--- I DO NOT CRAWL --- I DO NOT WHIMPER! I AM STILL THE SILVER SURFER!
HAW! A FAT LOT OF GOOD THAT DOES YOU!
ONCE THE MASTER HAS DELIVERED HIS ULTIMATUM TO THE OUTSIDE WORLD, HE WILL RETURN---AND THEN THE SILVER SURFER WILL HAVE BREATHED HIS LAST!
YOUR MASTER SHALL NEVER PREVAIL! THOUGH HE POSSESSES POWER ABSOLUTE--
--IT IS POWER USURPED!! SOMEHOW, AS SURELY AS THE COSMOS STANDS, IT SHALL-- IT MUST--DESTROY HIM!
A SHORT TIME LATER, A FASTER-THAN-SOUND INTERCONTINENTAL CRUISER ROCKETS TOWARDS LATVERIA---
THE BLACK PANTHER MUST BE A MIND-READER, DARLING---SENDING YOU THIS SHIP WHEN YOU NEED IT THE MOST!
IT'S FASTER BY FAR THAN ANY OF OURS, SUE!
IT STILL AIN'T FAST ENUFF FER ME, STRETCHO!
TAKE YER FOOT OFF'A THE BRAKE, WILLYA?
6.

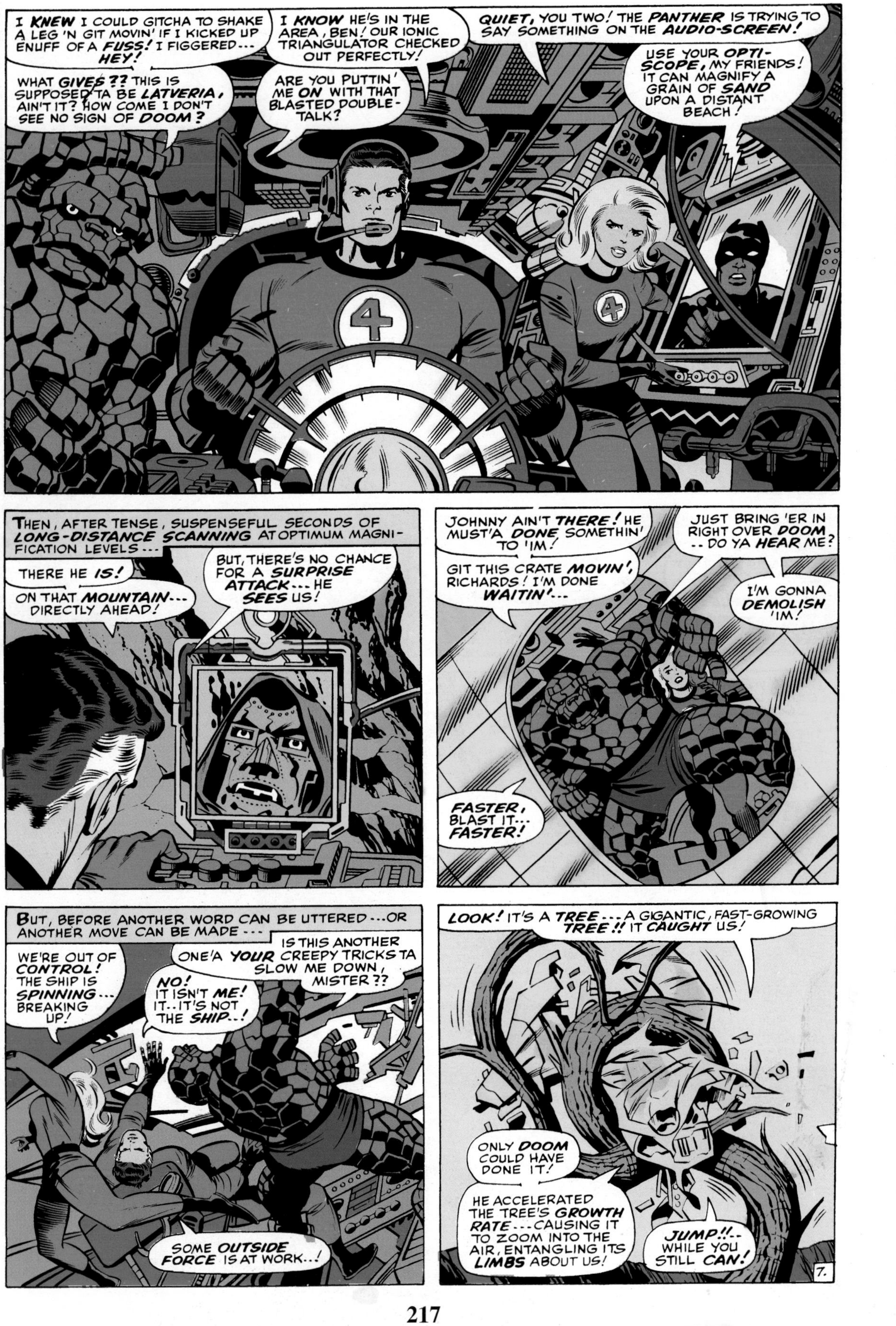

I KNEW I COULD GITCHA TO SHAKE A LEG 'N GIT MOVIN' IF I KICKED UP ENUFF OF A FUSS! I FIGGERED... HEY!
WHAT GIVES?? THIS IS SUPPOSED TA BE LATVERIA, AIN'T IT? HOW COME I DON'T SEE NO SIGN OF DOOM?
I KNOW HE'S IN THE AREA, BEN! OUR IONIC TRIANGULATOR CHECKED OUT PERFECTLY!
ARE YOU PUTTIN' ME ON WITH THAT BLASTED DOUBLE-TALK?
QUIET, YOU TWO! THE PANTHER IS TRYING TO SAY SOMETHING ON THE AUDIO-SCREEN!
USE YOUR OPTI-SCOPE, MY FRIENDS! IT CAN MAGNIFY A GRAIN OF SAND UPON A DISTANT BEACH!
THEN, AFTER TENSE, SUSPENSEFUL SECONDS OF LONG-DISTANCE SCANNING AT OPTIMUM MAGNIFICATION LEVELS...
THERE HE IS!
ON THAT MOUNTAIN... DIRECTLY AHEAD!
BUT, THERE'S NO CHANCE FOR A SURPRISE ATTACK... HE SEES US!
JOHNNY AIN'T THERE! HE MUST'A DONE SOMETHIN' TO 'IM!
GIT THIS CRATE MOVIN', RICHARDS! I'M DONE WAITIN'...
JUST BRING 'ER IN RIGHT OVER DOOM -- DO YA HEAR ME?
I'M GONNA DEMOLISH 'IM!
FASTER, BLAST IT... FASTER!
BUT, BEFORE ANOTHER WORD CAN BE UTTERED... OR ANOTHER MOVE CAN BE MADE...
WE'RE OUT OF CONTROL! THE SHIP IS SPINNING... BREAKING UP!
IS THIS ANOTHER ONE'A YOUR CREEPY TRICKS TA SLOW ME DOWN, MISTER??
NO! IT ISN'T ME! IT.. IT'S NOT THE SHIP..!
SOME OUTSIDE FORCE IS AT WORK..!
LOOK! IT'S A TREE... A GIGANTIC, FAST-GROWING TREE!! IT CAUGHT US!
ONLY DOOM COULD HAVE DONE IT!
HE ACCELERATED THE TREE'S GROWTH RATE... CAUSING IT TO ZOOM INTO THE AIR, ENTANGLING ITS LIMBS ABOUT US!
JUMP!!.. WHILE YOU STILL CAN!
7.

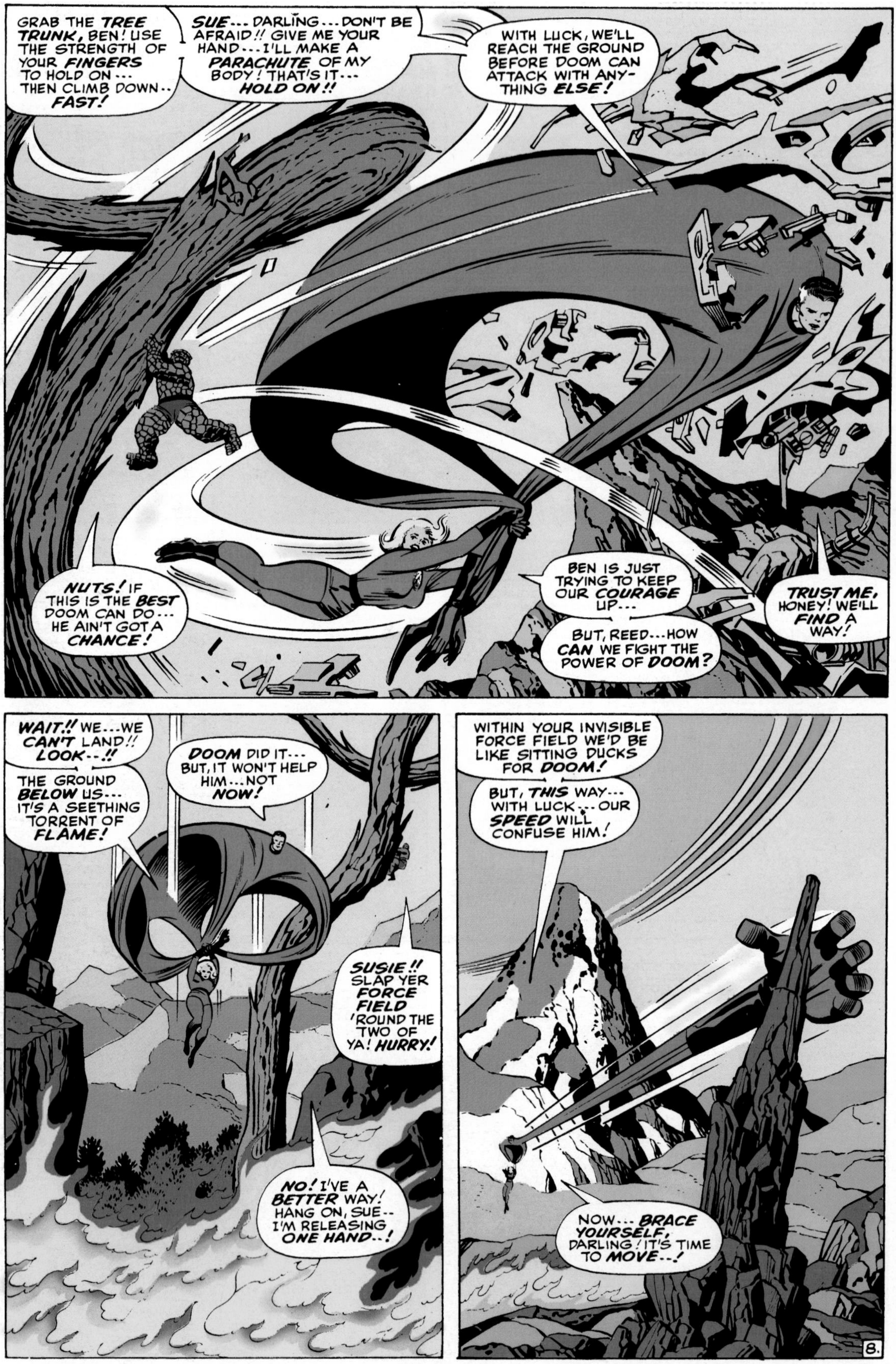
GRAB THE TREE TRUNK, BEN! USE THE STRENGTH OF YOUR FINGERS TO HOLD ON--- THEN CLIMB DOWN.. FAST!
SUE... DARLING... DON'T BE AFRAID!! GIVE ME YOUR HAND--- I'LL MAKE A PARACHUTE OF MY BODY! THAT'S IT--- HOLD ON!!
WITH LUCK, WE'LL REACH THE GROUND BEFORE DOOM CAN ATTACK WITH ANYTHING ELSE!
NUTS! IF THIS IS THE BEST DOOM CAN DO--- HE AIN'T GOT A CHANCE!
BEN IS JUST TRYING TO KEEP OUR COURAGE UP---
BUT, REED---HOW CAN WE FIGHT THE POWER OF DOOM?
TRUST ME, HONEY! WE'LL FIND A WAY!
WAIT!! WE---WE CAN'T LAND!! LOOK--!!
THE GROUND BELOW US--- IT'S A SEETHING TORRENT OF FLAME!
DOOM DID IT--- BUT, IT WON'T HELP HIM---NOT NOW!
SUSIE!! SLAP YER FORCE FIELD 'ROUND THE TWO OF YA! HURRY!
NO! I'VE A BETTER WAY! HANG ON, SUE-- I'M RELEASING ONE HAND--!
WITHIN YOUR INVISIBLE FORCE FIELD WE'D BE LIKE SITTING DUCKS FOR DOOM!
BUT, THIS WAY--- WITH LUCK--- OUR SPEED WILL CONFUSE HIM!
NOW--- BRACE YOURSELF, DARLING! IT'S TIME TO MOVE--!
8.

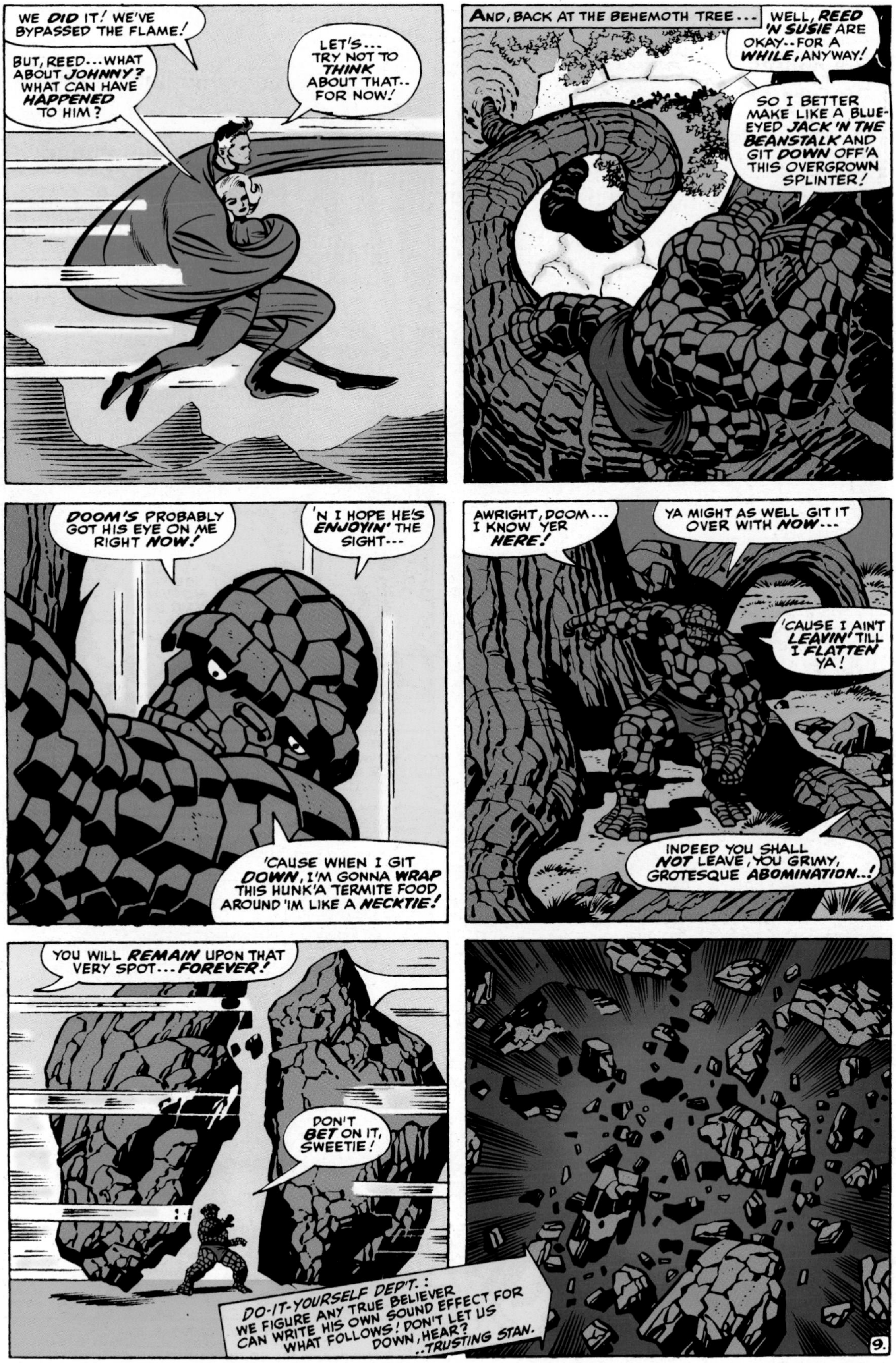
WE DID IT! WE'VE BYPASSED THE FLAME!
BUT, REED... WHAT ABOUT JOHNNY? WHAT CAN HAVE HAPPENED TO HIM?
LET'S... TRY NOT TO THINK ABOUT THAT-- FOR NOW!
AND, BACK AT THE BEHEMOTH TREE...
WELL, REED 'N SUSIE ARE OKAY--FOR A WHILE, ANYWAY!
SO I BETTER MAKE LIKE A BLUE-EYED JACK 'N THE BEANSTALK AND GIT DOWN OFF'A THIS OVERGROWN SPLINTER!
DOOM'S PROBABLY GOT HIS EYE ON ME RIGHT NOW!
'N I HOPE HE'S ENJOYIN' THE SIGHT---
'CAUSE WHEN I GIT DOWN, I'M GONNA WRAP THIS HUNK'A TERMITE FOOD AROUND 'IM LIKE A NECKTIE!
AWRIGHT, DOOM... I KNOW YER HERE!
YA MIGHT AS WELL GIT IT OVER WITH NOW---
'CAUSE I AIN'T LEAVIN' TILL I FLATTEN YA!
INDEED YOU SHALL NOT LEAVE, YOU GRIMY, GROTESQUE ABOMINATION..!
YOU WILL REMAIN UPON THAT VERY SPOT...FOREVER!
DON'T BET ON IT, SWEETIE!
DO-IT-YOURSELF DEP'T.: WE FIGURE ANY TRUE BELIEVER CAN WRITE HIS OWN SOUND EFFECT FOR WHAT FOLLOWS! DON'T LET US DOWN, HEAR? ..TRUSTING STAN.
9.

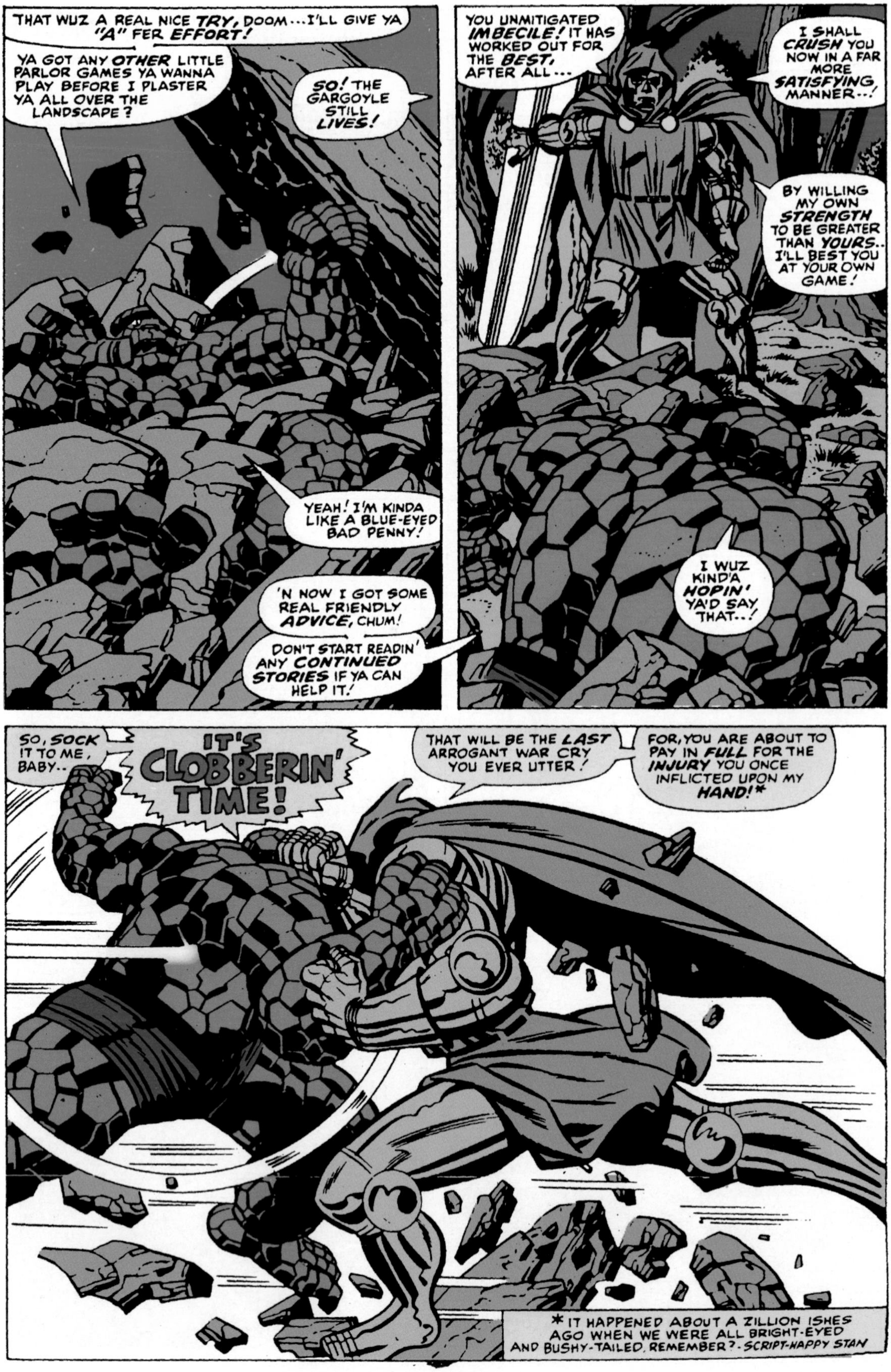
THAT WUZ A REAL NICE TRY, DOOM...I'LL GIVE YA "A" FER EFFORT!
YA GOT ANY OTHER LITTLE PARLOR GAMES YA WANNA PLAY BEFORE I PLASTER YA ALL OVER THE LANDSCAPE?
SO! THE GARGOYLE STILL LIVES!
YEAH! I'M KINDA LIKE A BLUE-EYED BAD PENNY!
'N NOW I GOT SOME REAL FRIENDLY ADVICE, CHUM!
DON'T START READIN' ANY CONTINUED STORIES IF YA CAN HELP IT!
YOU UNMITIGATED IMBECILE! IT HAS WORKED OUT FOR THE BEST, AFTER ALL...
I SHALL CRUSH YOU NOW IN A FAR MORE SATISFYING MANNER...!
BY WILLING MY OWN STRENGTH TO BE GREATER THAN YOURS.. I'LL BEST YOU AT YOUR OWN GAME!
I WUZ KIND'A HOPIN' YA'D SAY THAT..!
SO, SOCK IT TO ME, BABY..
IT'S CLOBBERIN' TIME!
THAT WILL BE THE LAST ARROGANT WAR CRY YOU EVER UTTER!
FOR, YOU ARE ABOUT TO PAY IN FULL FOR THE INJURY YOU ONCE INFLICTED UPON MY HAND!*
* IT HAPPENED ABOUT A ZILLION ISHES AGO WHEN WE WERE ALL BRIGHT-EYED AND BUSHY-TAILED, REMEMBER? - SCRIPT-HAPPY STAN

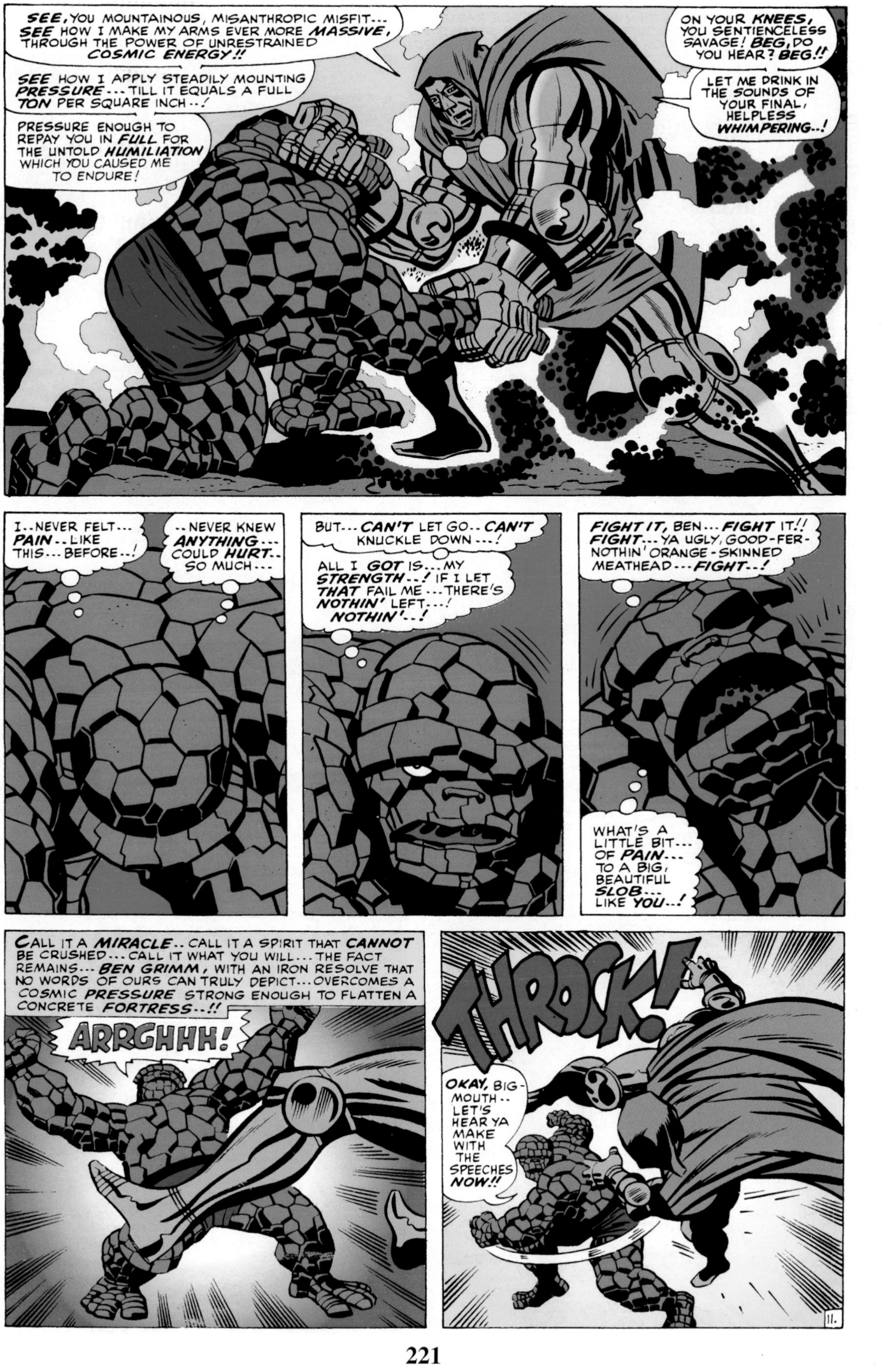

SEE, YOU MOUNTAINOUS, MISANTHROPIC MISFIT--- SEE HOW I MAKE MY ARMS EVER MORE MASSIVE, THROUGH THE POWER OF UNRESTRAINED COSMIC ENERGY!!
SEE HOW I APPLY STEADILY MOUNTING PRESSURE--- TILL IT EQUALS A FULL TON PER SQUARE INCH--!
PRESSURE ENOUGH TO REPAY YOU IN FULL FOR THE UNTOLD HUMILIATION WHICH YOU CAUSED ME TO ENDURE!
ON YOUR KNEES, YOU SENTIENCELESS SAVAGE! BEG, DO YOU HEAR? BEG!!
LET ME DRINK IN THE SOUNDS OF YOUR FINAL, HELPLESS WHIMPERING--!
I--NEVER FELT--- PAIN--LIKE THIS--- BEFORE--!
--NEVER KNEW ANYTHING COULD HURT-- SO MUCH---
BUT--- CAN'T LET GO-- CAN'T KNUCKLE DOWN---!
ALL I GOT IS--- MY STRENGTH--! IF I LET THAT FAIL ME---THERE'S NOTHIN' LEFT---! NOTHIN'--!
FIGHT IT, BEN--- FIGHT IT!! FIGHT--- YA UGLY, GOOD-FER-NOTHIN' ORANGE-SKINNED MEATHEAD--- FIGHT--!
WHAT'S A LITTLE BIT--- OF PAIN--- TO A BIG, BEAUTIFUL SLOB--- LIKE YOU--!
CALL IT A MIRACLE-- CALL IT A SPIRIT THAT CANNOT BE CRUSHED--- CALL IT WHAT YOU WILL--- THE FACT REMAINS--- BEN GRIMM, WITH AN IRON RESOLVE THAT NO WORDS OF OURS CAN TRULY DEPICT--- OVERCOMES A COSMIC PRESSURE STRONG ENOUGH TO FLATTEN A CONCRETE FORTRESS--!!
ARRGHHH!
THROCK!
OKAY, BIG-MOUTH-- LET'S HEAR YA MAKE WITH THE SPEECHES NOW!!
11.

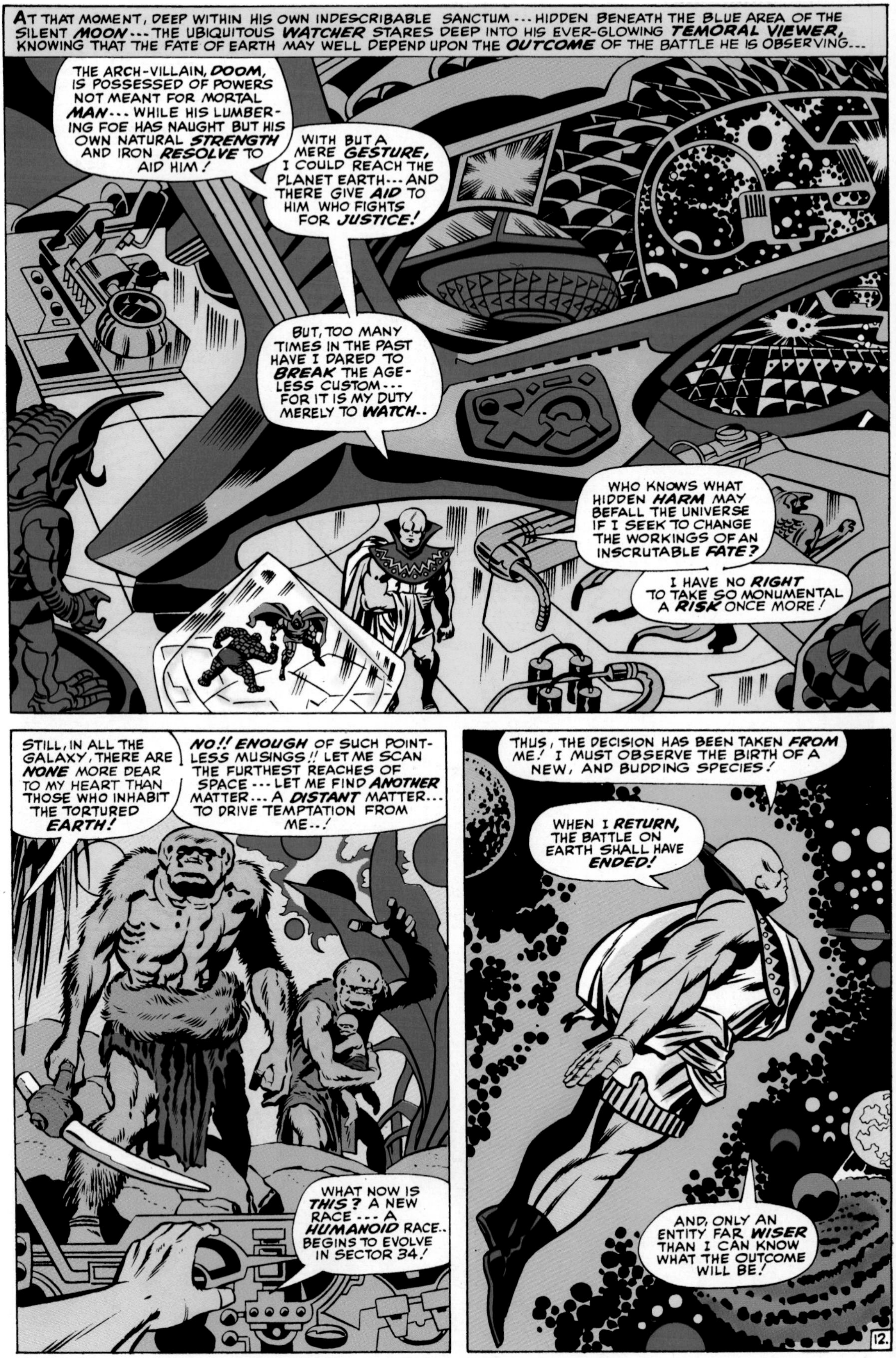
AT THAT MOMENT, DEEP WITHIN HIS OWN INDESCRIBABLE SANCTUM --- HIDDEN BENEATH THE BLUE AREA OF THE SILENT MOON --- THE UBIQUITOUS WATCHER STARES DEEP INTO HIS EVER-GLOWING TEMORAL VIEWER, KNOWING THAT THE FATE OF EARTH MAY WELL DEPEND UPON THE OUTCOME OF THE BATTLE HE IS OBSERVING---
THE ARCH-VILLAIN, DOOM, IS POSSESSED OF POWERS NOT MEANT FOR MORTAL MAN--- WHILE HIS LUMBERING FOE HAS NAUGHT BUT HIS OWN NATURAL STRENGTH AND IRON RESOLVE TO AID HIM!
WITH BUT A MERE GESTURE, I COULD REACH THE PLANET EARTH--- AND THERE GIVE AID TO HIM WHO FIGHTS FOR JUSTICE!
BUT, TOO MANY TIMES IN THE PAST HAVE I DARED TO BREAK THE AGELESS CUSTOM--- FOR IT IS MY DUTY MERELY TO WATCH..
WHO KNOWS WHAT HIDDEN HARM MAY BEFALL THE UNIVERSE IF I SEEK TO CHANGE THE WORKINGS OF AN INSCRUTABLE FATE?
I HAVE NO RIGHT TO TAKE SO MONUMENTAL A RISK ONCE MORE!
STILL, IN ALL THE GALAXY, THERE ARE NONE MORE DEAR TO MY HEART THAN THOSE WHO INHABIT THE TORTURED EARTH!
NO!! ENOUGH OF SUCH POINTLESS MUSINGS!! LET ME SCAN THE FURTHEST REACHES OF SPACE --- LET ME FIND ANOTHER MATTER--- A DISTANT MATTER--- TO DRIVE TEMPTATION FROM ME--!
WHAT NOW IS THIS? A NEW RACE --- A HUMANOID RACE.. BEGINS TO EVOLVE IN SECTOR 34!
THUS, THE DECISION HAS BEEN TAKEN FROM ME! I MUST OBSERVE THE BIRTH OF A NEW, AND BUDDING SPECIES!
WHEN I RETURN, THE BATTLE ON EARTH SHALL HAVE ENDED!
AND, ONLY AN ENTITY FAR WISER THAN I CAN KNOW WHAT THE OUTCOME WILL BE!
12.

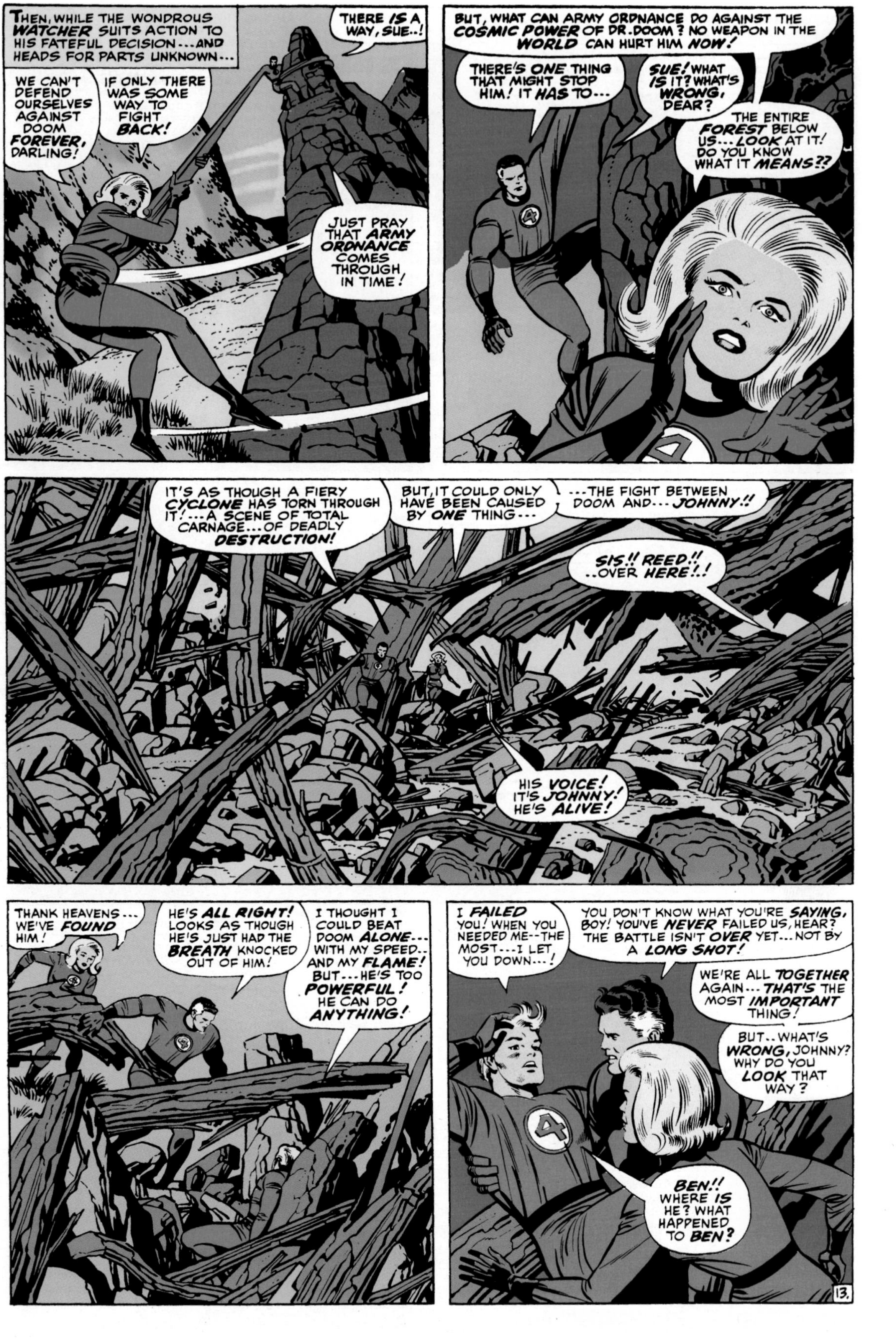
THEN, WHILE THE WONDROUS WATCHER SUITS ACTION TO HIS FATEFUL DECISION...AND HEADS FOR PARTS UNKNOWN...
THERE IS A WAY, SUE..!
WE CAN'T DEFEND OURSELVES AGAINST DOOM FOREVER, DARLING!
IF ONLY THERE WAS SOME WAY TO FIGHT BACK!
JUST PRAY THAT ARMY ORDNANCE COMES THROUGH IN TIME!
BUT, WHAT CAN ARMY ORDNANCE DO AGAINST THE COSMIC POWER OF DR. DOOM? NO WEAPON IN THE WORLD CAN HURT HIM NOW!
THERE'S ONE THING THAT MIGHT STOP HIM! IT HAS TO...
SUE! WHAT IS IT? WHAT'S WRONG, DEAR?
THE ENTIRE FOREST BELOW US...LOOK AT IT! DO YOU KNOW WHAT IT MEANS??
IT'S AS THOUGH A FIERY CYCLONE HAS TORN THROUGH IT!...A SCENE OF TOTAL CARNAGE...OF DEADLY DESTRUCTION!
BUT, IT COULD ONLY HAVE BEEN CAUSED BY ONE THING...
...THE FIGHT BETWEEN DOOM AND...JOHNNY!!
SIS!! REED!! ..OVER HERE!.!
HIS VOICE! IT'S JOHNNY! HE'S ALIVE!
THANK HEAVENS... WE'VE FOUND HIM!
HE'S ALL RIGHT! LOOKS AS THOUGH HE'S JUST HAD THE BREATH KNOCKED OUT OF HIM!
I THOUGHT I COULD BEAT DOOM ALONE...WITH MY SPEED.. AND MY FLAME! BUT...HE'S TOO POWERFUL! HE CAN DO ANYTHING!
I FAILED YOU! WHEN YOU NEEDED ME--THE MOST...I LET YOU DOWN...!
YOU DON'T KNOW WHAT YOU'RE SAYING, BOY! YOU'VE NEVER FAILED US, HEAR? THE BATTLE ISN'T OVER YET...NOT BY A LONG SHOT!
WE'RE ALL TOGETHER AGAIN...THAT'S THE MOST IMPORTANT THING!
BUT..WHAT'S WRONG, JOHNNY? WHY DO YOU LOOK THAT WAY?
BEN!! WHERE IS HE? WHAT HAPPENED TO BEN?
13.

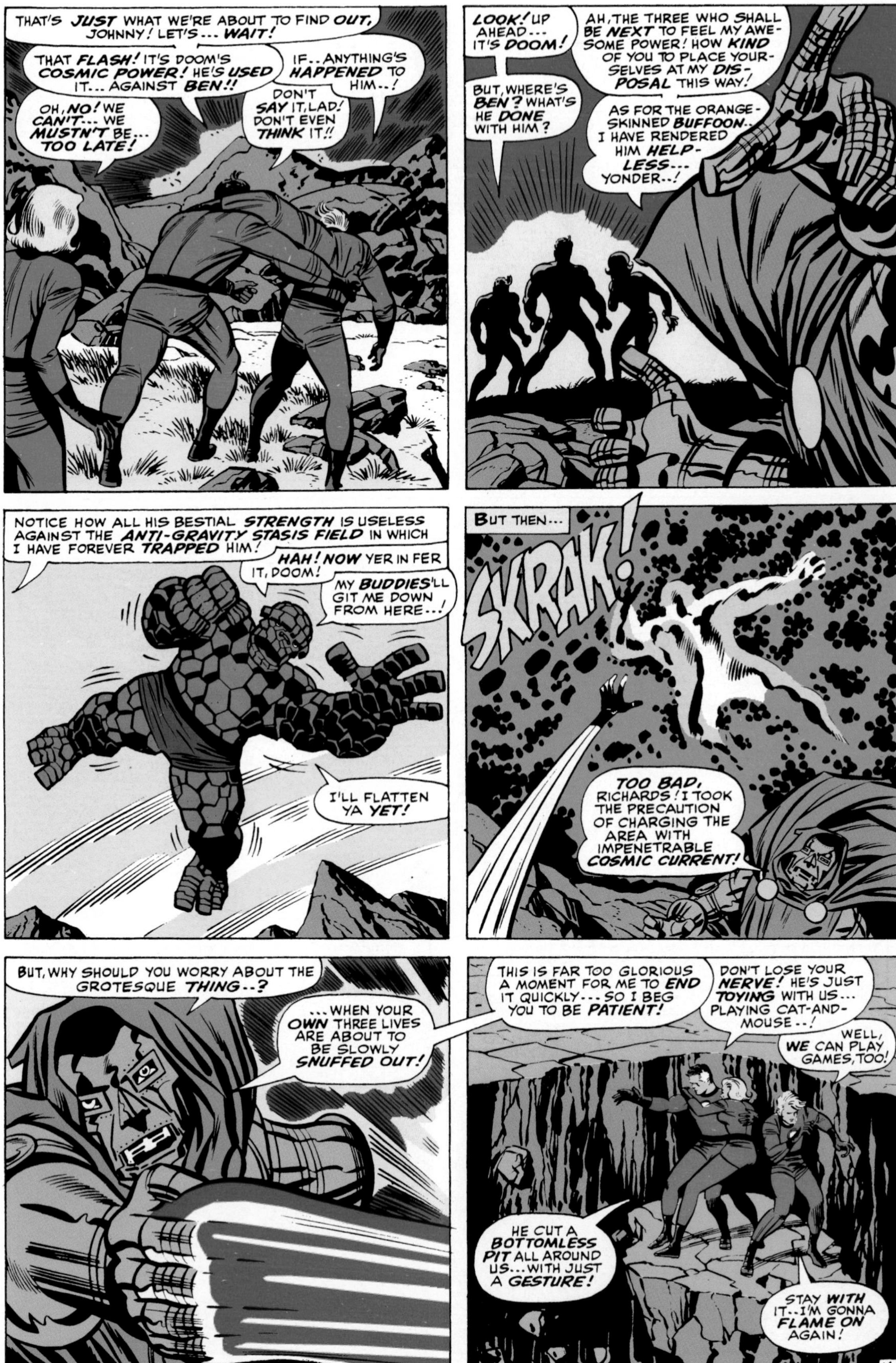

THAT'S JUST WHAT WE'RE ABOUT TO FIND OUT, JOHNNY! LET'S... WAIT!
THAT FLASH! IT'S DOOM'S COSMIC POWER! HE'S USED IT... AGAINST BEN!!
IF.. ANYTHING'S HAPPENED TO HIM..!
OH, NO! WE CAN'T... WE MUSTN'T BE... TOO LATE!
DON'T SAY IT, LAD! DON'T EVEN THINK IT!!
LOOK! UP AHEAD... IT'S DOOM!
BUT, WHERE'S BEN? WHAT'S HE DONE WITH HIM?
AH, THE THREE WHO SHALL BE NEXT TO FEEL MY AWESOME POWER! HOW KIND OF YOU TO PLACE YOURSELVES AT MY DISPOSAL THIS WAY!
AS FOR THE ORANGE-SKINNED BUFFOON.. I HAVE RENDERED HIM HELPLESS... YONDER..!
NOTICE HOW ALL HIS BESTIAL STRENGTH IS USELESS AGAINST THE ANTI-GRAVITY STASIS FIELD IN WHICH I HAVE FOREVER TRAPPED HIM!
HAH! NOW YER IN FER IT, DOOM!
MY BUDDIES'LL GIT ME DOWN FROM HERE..!
I'LL FLATTEN YA YET!
BUT THEN...
SKRAK!
TOO BAD, RICHARDS! I TOOK THE PRECAUTION OF CHARGING THE AREA WITH IMPENETRABLE COSMIC CURRENT!
BUT, WHY SHOULD YOU WORRY ABOUT THE GROTESQUE THING..?
...WHEN YOUR OWN THREE LIVES ARE ABOUT TO BE SLOWLY SNUFFED OUT!
THIS IS FAR TOO GLORIOUS A MOMENT FOR ME TO END IT QUICKLY... SO I BEG YOU TO BE PATIENT!
DON'T LOSE YOUR NERVE! HE'S JUST TOYING WITH US... PLAYING CAT-AND-MOUSE..!
WELL, WE CAN PLAY GAMES, TOO!
HE CUT A BOTTOMLESS PIT ALL AROUND US... WITH JUST A GESTURE!
STAY WITH IT.. I'M GONNA FLAME ON AGAIN!
14.

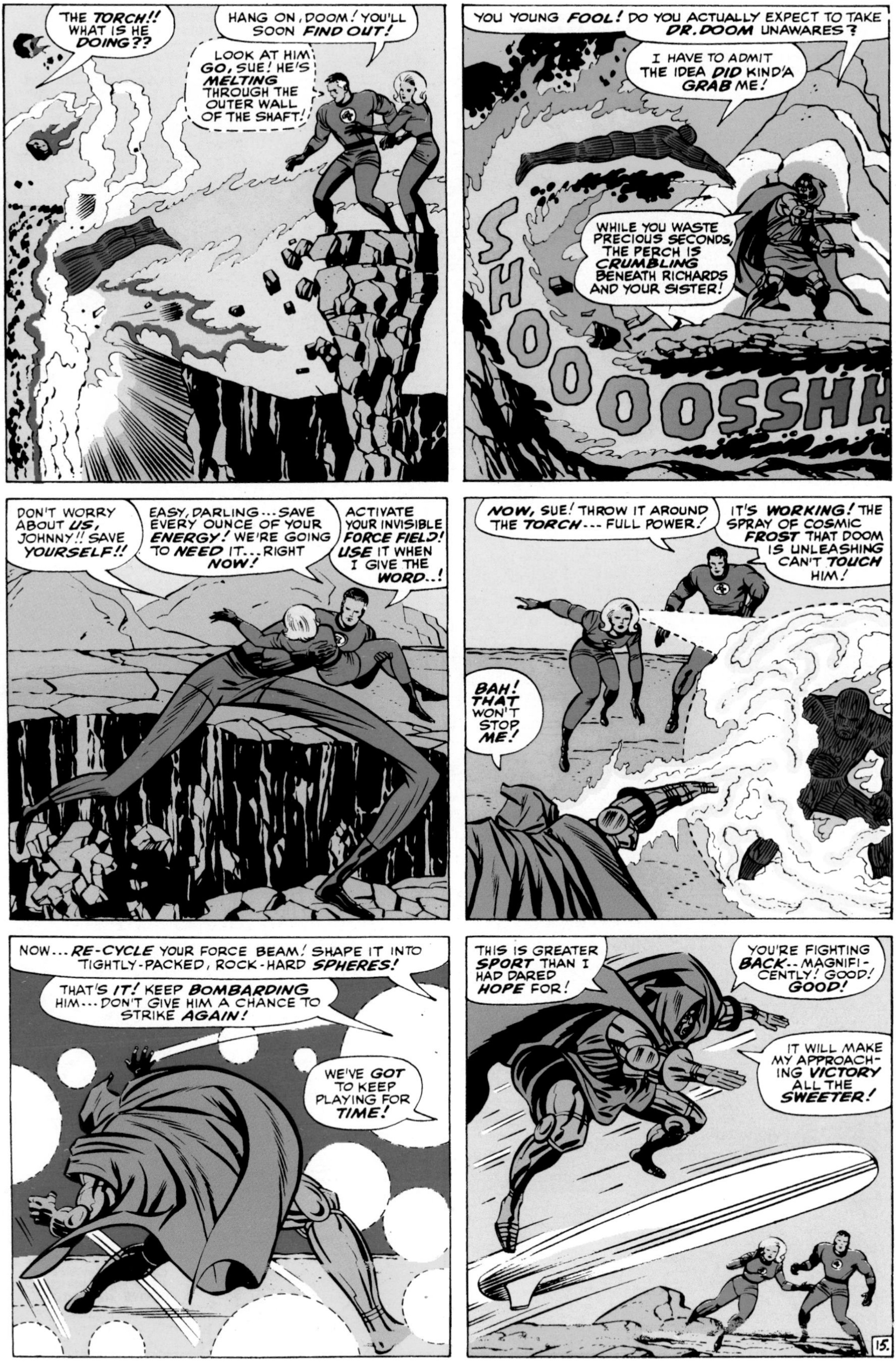
THE TORCH!! WHAT IS HE DOING??
HANG ON, DOOM! YOU'LL SOON FIND OUT!
LOOK AT HIM GO, SUE! HE'S MELTING THROUGH THE OUTER WALL OF THE SHAFT!
YOU YOUNG FOOL! DO YOU ACTUALLY EXPECT TO TAKE DR. DOOM UNAWARES?
I HAVE TO ADMIT THE IDEA DID KIND'A GRAB ME!
WHILE YOU WASTE PRECIOUS SECONDS, THE PERCH IS CRUMBLING BENEATH RICHARDS AND YOUR SISTER!
SHOOOOOSSHH
DON'T WORRY ABOUT US, JOHNNY!! SAVE YOURSELF!!
EASY, DARLING... SAVE EVERY OUNCE OF YOUR ENERGY! WE'RE GOING TO NEED IT... RIGHT NOW!
ACTIVATE YOUR INVISIBLE FORCE FIELD! USE IT WHEN I GIVE THE WORD..!
NOW, SUE! THROW IT AROUND THE TORCH--- FULL POWER!
IT'S WORKING! THE SPRAY OF COSMIC FROST THAT DOOM IS UNLEASHING CAN'T TOUCH HIM!
BAH! THAT WON'T STOP ME!
NOW... RE-CYCLE YOUR FORCE BEAM! SHAPE IT INTO TIGHTLY-PACKED, ROCK-HARD SPHERES!
THAT'S IT! KEEP BOMBARDING HIM... DON'T GIVE HIM A CHANCE TO STRIKE AGAIN!
WE'VE GOT TO KEEP PLAYING FOR TIME!
THIS IS GREATER SPORT THAN I HAD DARED HOPE FOR!
YOU'RE FIGHTING BACK-- MAGNIFI-CENTLY! GOOD! GOOD!
IT WILL MAKE MY APPROACH-ING VICTORY ALL THE SWEETER!
15.

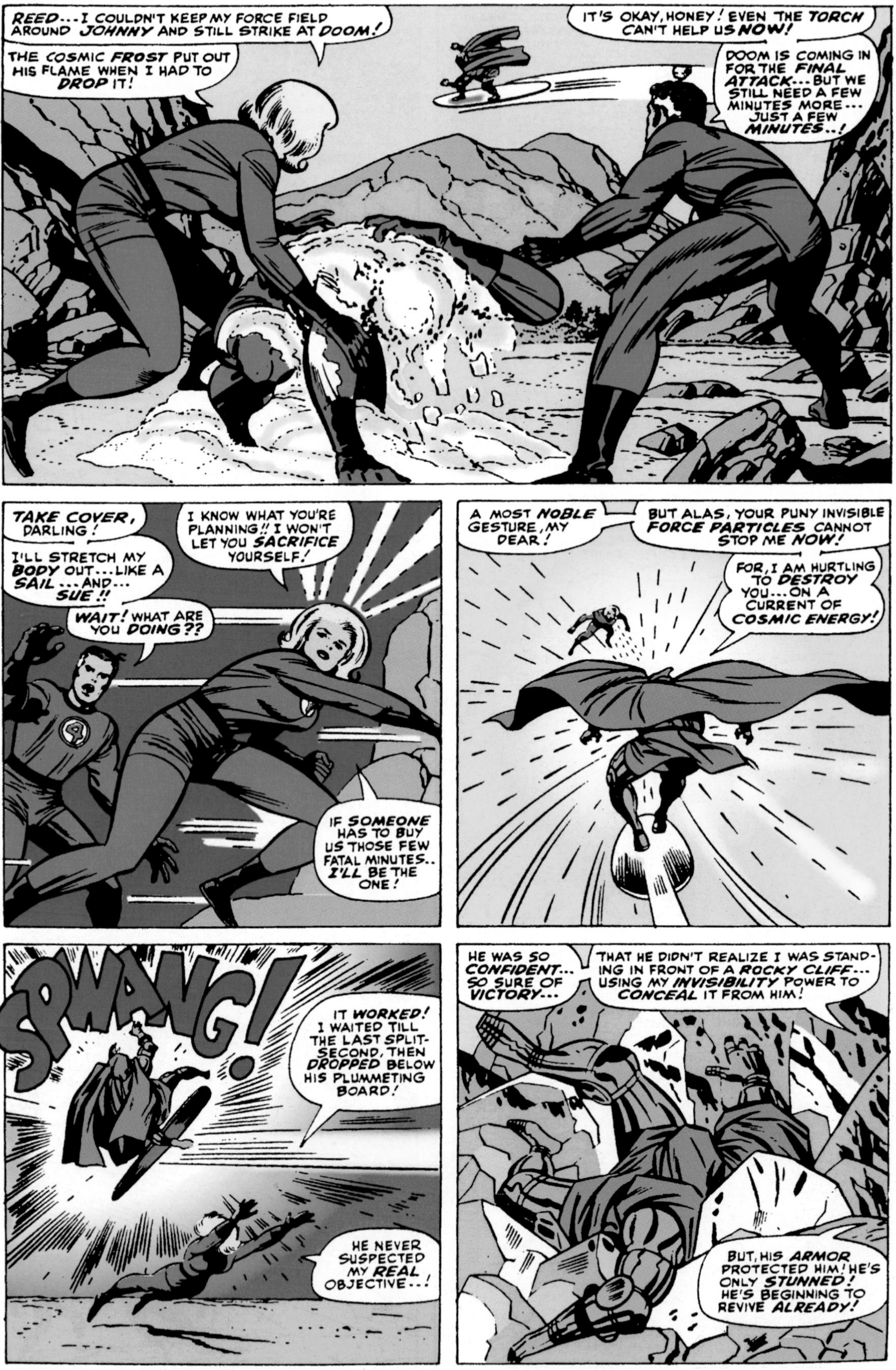
REED...I COULDN'T KEEP MY FORCE FIELD AROUND JOHNNY AND STILL STRIKE AT DOOM!
THE COSMIC FROST PUT OUT HIS FLAME WHEN I HAD TO DROP IT!
IT'S OKAY, HONEY! EVEN THE TORCH CAN'T HELP US NOW!
DOOM IS COMING IN FOR THE FINAL ATTACK...BUT WE STILL NEED A FEW MINUTES MORE...JUST A FEW MINUTES..!
TAKE COVER, DARLING!
I'LL STRETCH MY BODY OUT...LIKE A SAIL...AND... SUE!!
I KNOW WHAT YOU'RE PLANNING!! I WON'T LET YOU SACRIFICE YOURSELF!
WAIT! WHAT ARE YOU DOING??
IF SOMEONE HAS TO BUY US THOSE FEW FATAL MINUTES.. I'LL BE THE ONE!
A MOST NOBLE GESTURE, MY DEAR!
BUT ALAS, YOUR PUNY INVISIBLE FORCE PARTICLES CANNOT STOP ME NOW!
FOR, I AM HURTLING TO DESTROY YOU...ON A CURRENT OF COSMIC ENERGY!
SPWANG!
IT WORKED! I WAITED TILL THE LAST SPLIT-SECOND, THEN DROPPED BELOW HIS PLUMMETING BOARD!
HE NEVER SUSPECTED MY REAL OBJECTIVE...!
HE WAS SO CONFIDENT... SO SURE OF VICTORY...
THAT HE DIDN'T REALIZE I WAS STANDING IN FRONT OF A ROCKY CLIFF...USING MY INVISIBILITY POWER TO CONCEAL IT FROM HIM!
BUT, HIS ARMOR PROTECTED HIM! HE'S ONLY STUNNED! HE'S BEGINNING TO REVIVE ALREADY!

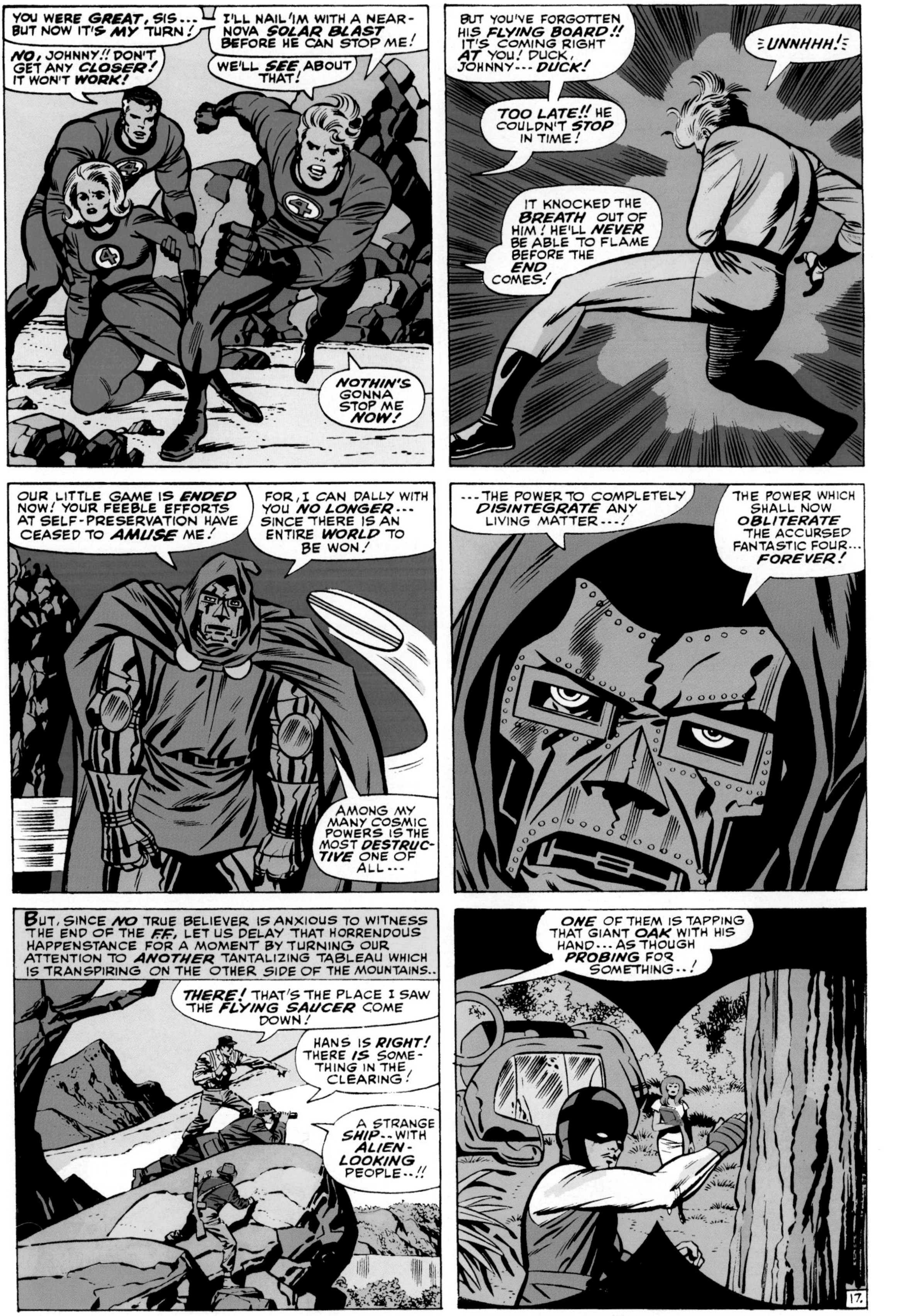
YOU WERE GREAT, SIS... BUT NOW IT'S MY TURN!
I'LL NAIL'IM WITH A NEAR-NOVA SOLAR BLAST BEFORE HE CAN STOP ME!
NO, JOHNNY!! DON'T GET ANY CLOSER! IT WON'T WORK!
WE'LL SEE ABOUT THAT!
NOTHIN'S GONNA STOP ME NOW!
BUT YOU'VE FORGOTTEN HIS FLYING BOARD!! IT'S COMING RIGHT AT YOU! DUCK, JOHNNY--- DUCK!
UNNHHH!
TOO LATE!! HE COULDN'T STOP IN TIME!
IT KNOCKED THE BREATH OUT OF HIM! HE'LL NEVER BE ABLE TO FLAME BEFORE THE END COMES!
OUR LITTLE GAME IS ENDED NOW! YOUR FEEBLE EFFORTS AT SELF-PRESERVATION HAVE CEASED TO AMUSE ME!
FOR, I CAN DALLY WITH YOU NO LONGER--- SINCE THERE IS AN ENTIRE WORLD TO BE WON!
AMONG MY MANY COSMIC POWERS IS THE MOST DESTRUCTIVE ONE OF ALL---
---THE POWER TO COMPLETELY DISINTEGRATE ANY LIVING MATTER---!
THE POWER WHICH SHALL NOW OBLITERATE THE ACCURSED FANTASTIC FOUR... FOREVER!
BUT, SINCE NO TRUE BELIEVER IS ANXIOUS TO WITNESS THE END OF THE F.F., LET US DELAY THAT HORRENDOUS HAPPENSTANCE FOR A MOMENT BY TURNING OUR ATTENTION TO ANOTHER TANTALIZING TABLEAU WHICH IS TRANSPIRING ON THE OTHER SIDE OF THE MOUNTAINS..
THERE! THAT'S THE PLACE I SAW THE FLYING SAUCER COME DOWN!
HANS IS RIGHT! THERE IS SOMETHING IN THE CLEARING!
A STRANGE SHIP.. WITH ALIEN-LOOKING PEOPLE..!!
ONE OF THEM IS TAPPING THAT GIANT OAK WITH HIS HAND... AS THOUGH PROBING FOR SOMETHING..!
17.

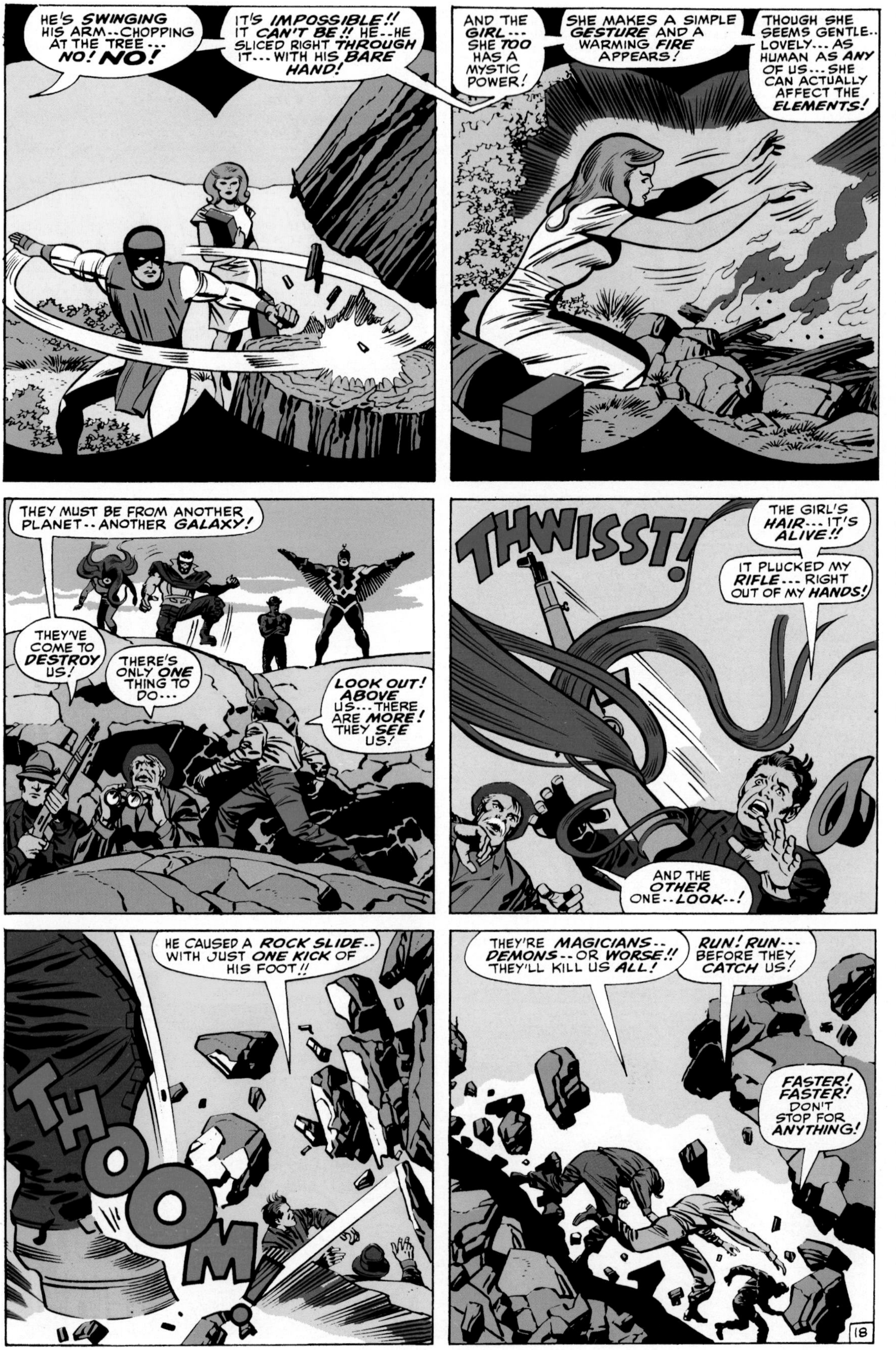
HE'S SWINGING HIS ARM--CHOPPING AT THE TREE... NO! NO!
IT'S IMPOSSIBLE!! IT CAN'T BE!! HE--HE SLICED RIGHT THROUGH IT... WITH HIS BARE HAND!
AND THE GIRL--- SHE TOO HAS A MYSTIC POWER!
SHE MAKES A SIMPLE GESTURE AND A WARMING FIRE APPEARS!
THOUGH SHE SEEMS GENTLE.. LOVELY... AS HUMAN AS ANY OF US... SHE CAN ACTUALLY AFFECT THE ELEMENTS!
THEY MUST BE FROM ANOTHER PLANET--ANOTHER GALAXY!
THEY'VE COME TO DESTROY US!
THERE'S ONLY ONE THING TO DO...
LOOK OUT! ABOVE US... THERE ARE MORE! THEY SEE US!
THWISST!
THE GIRL'S HAIR... IT'S ALIVE!!
IT PLUCKED MY RIFLE--- RIGHT OUT OF MY HANDS!
AND THE OTHER ONE--LOOK--!
HE CAUSED A ROCK SLIDE-- WITH JUST ONE KICK OF HIS FOOT!!
THOOM
THEY'RE MAGICIANS-- DEMONS--OR WORSE!! THEY'LL KILL US ALL!
RUN! RUN--- BEFORE THEY CATCH US!
FASTER! FASTER! DON'T STOP FOR ANYTHING!
18

AND, AS THE FEARFUL MOUNTAINEERS FRANTICALLY RACE FROM THE SITE...

PERHAPS IT WAS *UNWISE* OF US TO STOP IN A PLACE LIKE THIS!

THE VILLAGERS ARE TOO FEARFUL..TOO SUPERSTITIOUS!

WE HAVE NAUGHT TO FEAR FROM SUCH AS *THEY!*

SINCE *BLACK BOLT* FREED US FROM THE *NEGA-TIVE ZONE,* NOTHING ON EARTH CAN STAND AGAINST THE POWER OF.. WE *INHUMANS!*

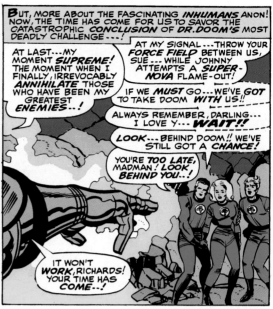

BUT, MORE ABOUT THE FASCINATING *INHUMANS* ANON! NOW, THE TIME HAS COME FOR US TO SAVOR THE CATASTROPHIC *CONCLUSION* OF *DR. DOOM'S* MOST DEADLY CHALLENGE---!

AT LAST...MY MOMENT *SUPREME!* THE MOMENT WHEN I FINALLY, IRREVOCABLY *ANNIHILATE* THOSE WHO HAVE BEEN MY *GREATEST ENEMIES..!*

AT MY SIGNAL...THROW YOUR *FORCE FIELD* BETWEEN US, SUE---WHILE JOHNNY ATTEMPTS A *SUPER-NOVA* FLAME-OUT!

IF WE *MUST* GO---WE'VE *GOT* TO TAKE DOOM *WITH US!!*

ALWAYS REMEMBER, DARLING... I LOVE Y...*WAIT!!*

LOOK...BEHIND DOOM!! WE'VE GOT A *CHANCE!*

YOU'RE *TOO LATE,* MADMAN! *LOOK* BEHIND YOU..!

IT WON'T *WORK,* RICHARDS! YOUR TIME HAS *COME*---!

NO SOONER HAVE THE WORDS LEFT THE IRON-MASKED *LIPS* OF THE WORLD'S MOST DIABOLICAL VILLAIN, THEN A STRANGE, SILENT *FLYING CRAFT* ZOOMS OVERHEAD....ELECTRONICALLY *DRAINING* A LARGE PORTION OF *COSMIC ENERGY* FROM THE STARTLED FIGURE BELOW...!

MY *STRENGTH*... BEGINNING TO *EBB*..!

MY KNEES... BUCKLING... GROWING *WEAK!!*

THEY DIDN'T *FAIL* US! THE ARMY DELIVERED MY *ANTI-COSMIC FLYING WING*... JUST AS PLANNED!*

IT ISN'T *POSSIBLE!* IT'S MAD... INSANE..!

* WE SAW THE MINIATURE PROTOTYPE OF THE FLYING WING LAST ISH, REMEMBER? ---STICKLER-FOR-ACCURACY STAN.

I SENT THEM THE SMALL-SCALE *MODEL* I HAD MADE....JUST BEFORE WE TOOK OFF IN *LATVERIA!* I *KNEW* IT WAS THE ONLY THING THAT COULD *STOP* DOOM ...

BUT ONLY *ARMY ORDNANCE*.. IN COLLABORATION WITH *TONY STARK'S* VAST MUNITIONS COMPLEX---HAD THE RESOURCES TO *BUILD* IT IN TIME!

IT *STAGGERED* ME...BUT IT COULDN'T *DOWN* ME! YOU'VE *FAILED,* RICHARDS!

MY *COSMIC POWER* IS STILL TOO *GREAT* FOR YOU! EVEN AS I *STAND* HERE, MY STRENGTH RETURNS TO ITS MATCHLESS *PEAK!*

NOW, MY VICTORY IS *DOUBLY* SWEET---FOR EVEN THE WEAPON YOU YOURSELF DESIGNED... EVEN YOUR OWN *GENIUS*... COULD NOT *DEFEAT* ME!

NOW, BEFORE THE *END* COMES.. WATCH ME..!

19.

229

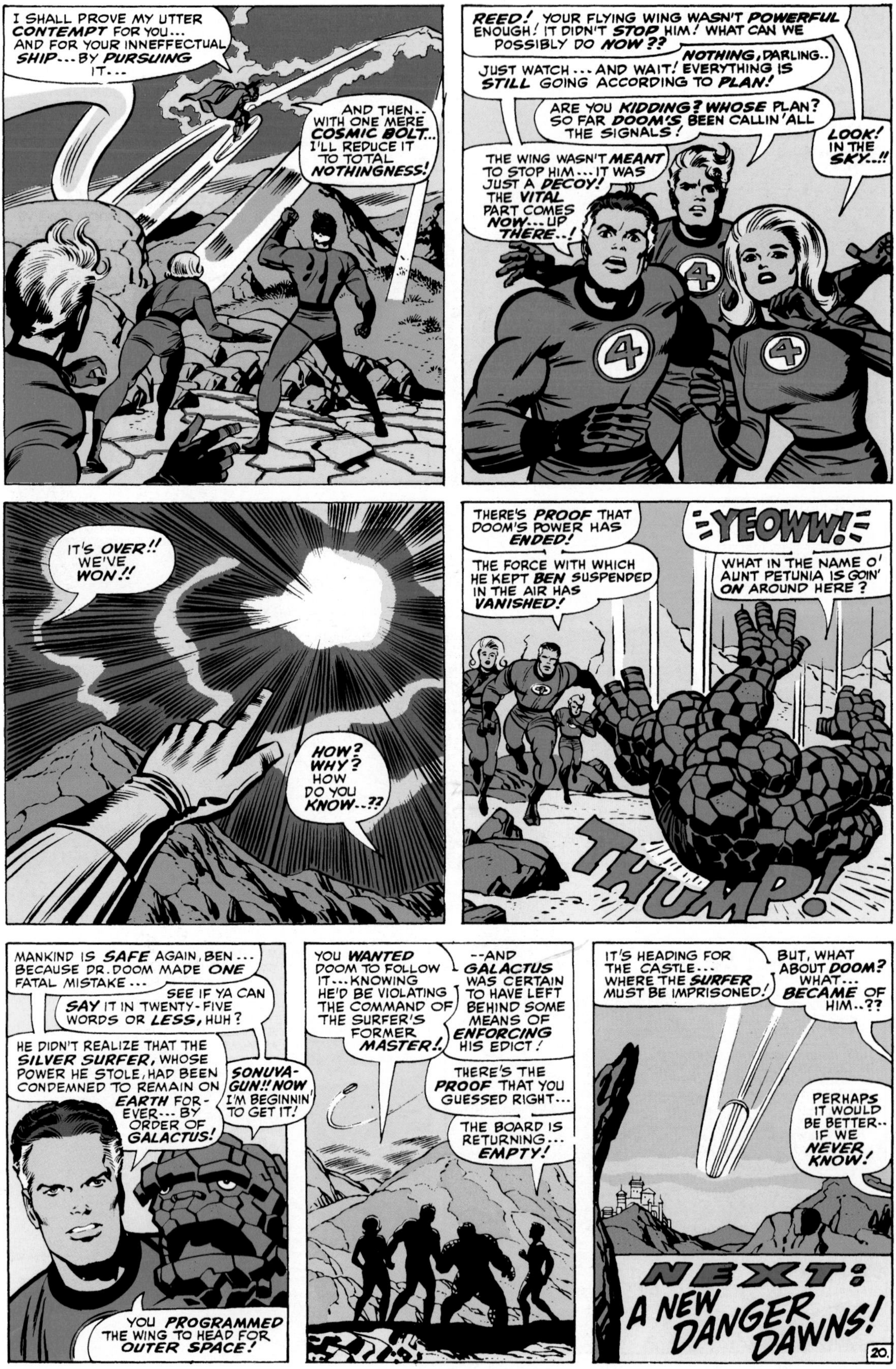

I SHALL PROVE MY UTTER CONTEMPT FOR YOU... AND FOR YOUR INNEFFECTUAL SHIP... BY PURSUING IT...
AND THEN.. WITH ONE MERE COSMIC BOLT... I'LL REDUCE IT TO TOTAL NOTHINGNESS!
REED! YOUR FLYING WING WASN'T POWERFUL ENOUGH! IT DIDN'T STOP HIM! WHAT CAN WE POSSIBLY DO NOW??
NOTHING, DARLING.. JUST WATCH... AND WAIT! EVERYTHING IS STILL GOING ACCORDING TO PLAN!
ARE YOU KIDDING? WHOSE PLAN? SO FAR DOOM'S BEEN CALLIN' ALL THE SIGNALS!
THE WING WASN'T MEANT TO STOP HIM... IT WAS JUST A DECOY! THE VITAL PART COMES NOW... UP THERE..!
LOOK! IN THE SKY..!!
IT'S OVER!! WE'VE WON!!
HOW? WHY? HOW DO YOU KNOW..??
THERE'S PROOF THAT DOOM'S POWER HAS ENDED!
YEOWW!
THE FORCE WITH WHICH HE KEPT BEN SUSPENDED IN THE AIR HAS VANISHED!
WHAT IN THE NAME O' AUNT PETUNIA IS GOIN' ON AROUND HERE?
THUMP!
MANKIND IS SAFE AGAIN, BEN... BECAUSE DR. DOOM MADE ONE FATAL MISTAKE...
SEE IF YA CAN SAY IT IN TWENTY-FIVE WORDS OR LESS, HUH?
HE DIDN'T REALIZE THAT THE SILVER SURFER, WHOSE POWER HE STOLE, HAD BEEN CONDEMNED TO REMAIN ON EARTH FOR-EVER... BY ORDER OF GALACTUS!
SONUVA-GUN!! NOW I'M BEGINNIN' TO GET IT!
YOU PROGRAMMED THE WING TO HEAD FOR OUTER SPACE!
YOU WANTED DOOM TO FOLLOW IT... KNOWING HE'D BE VIOLATING THE COMMAND OF THE SURFER'S FORMER MASTER!.
--AND GALACTUS WAS CERTAIN TO HAVE LEFT BEHIND SOME MEANS OF ENFORCING HIS EDICT!
THERE'S THE PROOF THAT YOU GUESSED RIGHT...
THE BOARD IS RETURNING... EMPTY!
IT'S HEADING FOR THE CASTLE... WHERE THE SURFER MUST BE IMPRISONED!
BUT, WHAT ABOUT DOOM? WHAT... BECAME OF HIM..??
PERHAPS IT WOULD BE BETTER.. IF WE NEVER KNOW!
NEXT: A NEW DANGER DAWNS!
20.

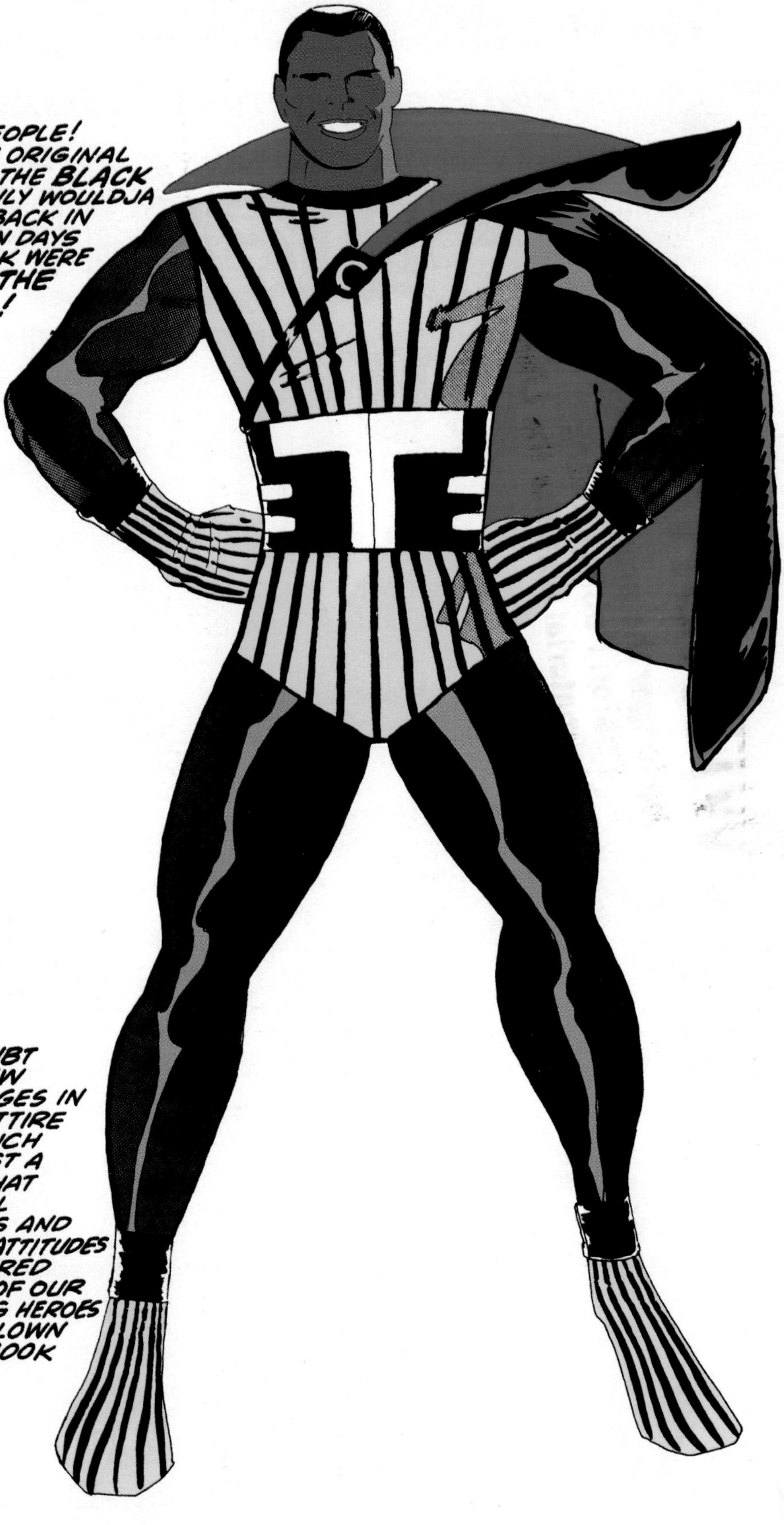
HERE IT IS, PEOPLE! JACK KIRBY'S ORIGINAL COSTUME FOR THE BLACK PANTHER! ONLY WOULDJA BELIEVE THAT BACK IN THOSE HALCYON DAYS STAN AND JACK WERE CALLING HIM THE COAL TIGER!
YOU'VE NO DOUBT NOTICED A FEW SLIGHT CHANGES IN T'CHALLA'S ATTIRE AND NAME WHICH GIVES YOU JUST A VAGUE IDEA WHAT KIND OF VISUAL PREPARATIONS AND CHARACTER ATTITUDES ARE CONSIDERED BEFORE ONE OF OUR SCINTILLATING HEROES BURST FULL BLOWN INTO COMIC BOOK REALITY.

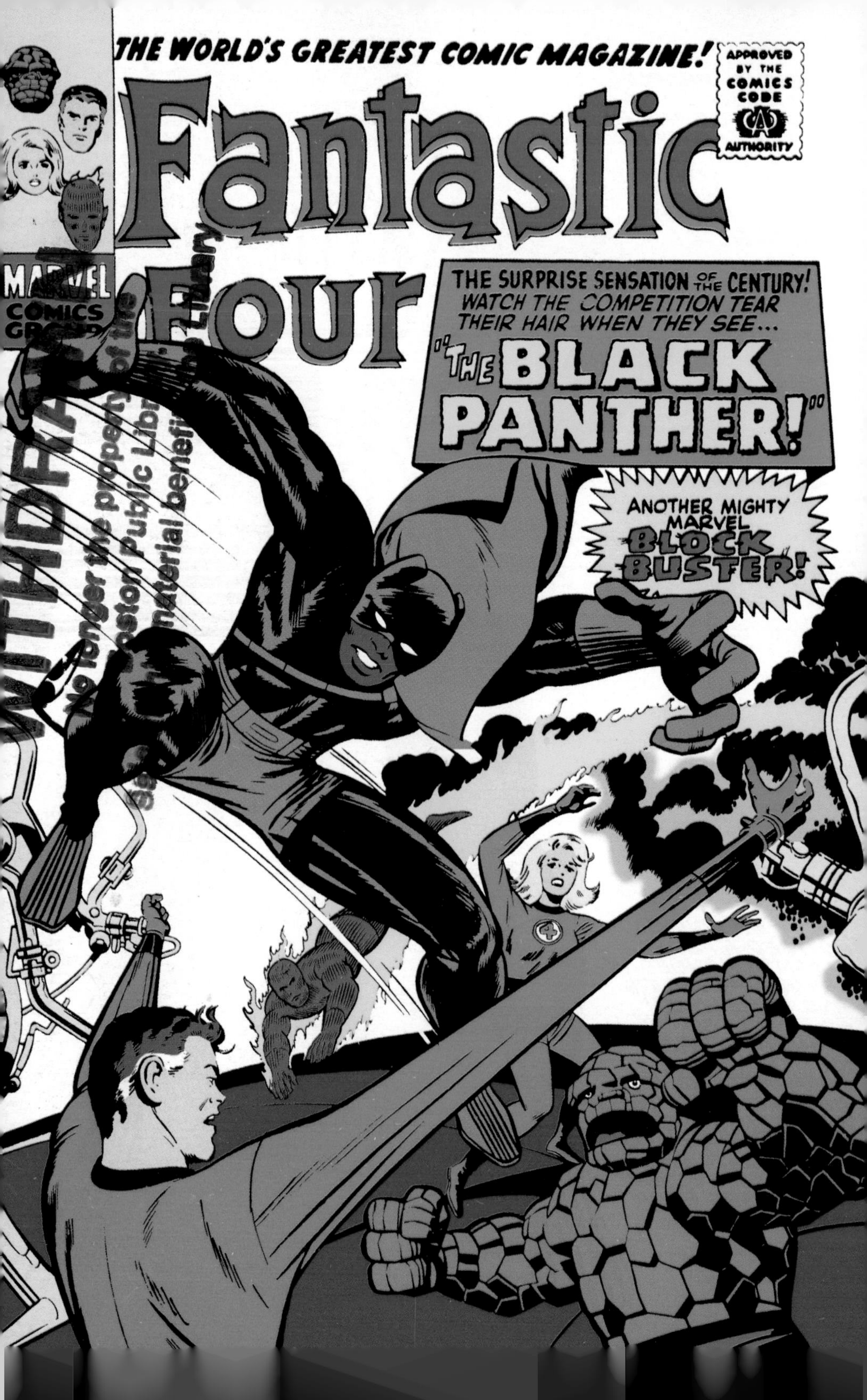
THE WORLD'S GREATEST COMIC MAGAZINE!
APPROVED BY THE COMICS CODE AUTHORITY
Fantastic Four
MARVEL COMICS GROUP
THE SURPRISE SENSATION OF THE CENTURY! WATCH THE COMPETITION TEAR THEIR HAIR WHEN THEY SEE...
"THE BLACK PANTHER!"
ANOTHER MIGHTY MARVEL BLOCK BUSTER!